Less managing. More teaching. Greater learning.

 INSTRUCTORS...

Would you like your **students** to show up for class **more prepared**?
(Let's face it, class is much more fun if everyone is engaged and prepared...)

Want an **easy way to assign** homework online and track student **progress**?
(Less time grading means more time teaching...)

Want an **instant view** of student or class performance relative to learning objectives? *(No more wondering if students understand...)*

Need to **collect data and generate reports** required for administration or accreditation? *(Say goodbye to manually tracking student learning outcomes...)*

Want to **record and post your lectures** for students to view online?

 With **McGraw-Hill's *Connect*® Plus Accounting,**

INSTRUCTORS GET:

- Simple **assignment management**, allowing you to spend more time teaching.

- **Auto-graded** assignments, quizzes, and tests.

- **Detailed Visual Reporting** where student and section results can be viewed and analyzed.

- Sophisticated **online testing** capability.

- A **filtering and reporting** function that allows you to easily assign and report on materials that are correlated to accreditation standards, learning outcomes, and Bloom's taxonomy.

- An easy-to-use **lecture capture** tool.

- The option to **upload course documents** for student access.

Want an online, **searchable version** of your textbook?

Wish your textbook could be **available online** while you're doing your assignments?

 ### *Connect® Plus Accounting* eBook

If you choose to use *Connect® Plus Accounting*, you have an affordable and searchable online version of your book integrated with your other online tools.

Connect® Plus Accounting eBook offers features like:

- Topic search
- Direct links from assignments
- Adjustable text size
- Jump to page number
- Print by section

 Want to get more **value** from your textbook purchase?

Think learning accounting should be a bit more **interesting**?

 ### Check out the STUDENT RESOURCES section under the *Connect®* Library tab.

Here you'll find a wealth of resources designed to help you achieve your goals in the course. You'll find things like **quizzes, PowerPoints, and Internet activities** to help you study. Every student has different needs, so explore the STUDENT RESOURCES to find the materials best suited to you.

Financial Accounting: Making the Connection

McGraw-Hill Irwin

FINANCIAL ACCOUNTING: MAKING THE CONNECTION

Published by McGraw-Hill/Irwin, a business unit of The McGraw-Hill Companies, Inc., 1221 Avenue of the Americas, New York, NY, 10020. Copyright © 2013 by The McGraw-Hill Companies, Inc. All rights reserved. Printed in the United States of America. No part of this publication may be reproduced or distributed in any form or by any means, or stored in a database or retrieval system, without the prior written consent of The McGraw-Hill Companies, Inc., including, but not limited to, in any network or other electronic storage or transmission, or broadcast for distance learning.

Some ancillaries, including electronic and print components, may not be available to customers outside the United States.

This book is printed on acid-free paper.

1 2 3 4 5 6 7 8 9 0 RJE/RJE 1 0 9 8 7 6 5 4 3 2

ISBN 978-0-07-786226-8
MHID 0-07-786226-0

Vice president and editor-in-chief: *Brent Gordon*
Publisher: *Tim Vertovec*
Senior sponsoring editor: *Dana L. Woo*
Director of development: *Ann Torbert*
Managing development editor: *Christina A. Sanders*
Vice president and director of marketing: *Robin J. Zwettler*
Marketing director: *Brad Parkins*
Senior marketing manager: *Kathleen Klehr*
Vice president of editing, design, and production: *Sesha Bolisetty*
Lead project manager: *Pat Frederickson*
Senior buyer: *Michael R. McCormick*
Cover and interior designer: *Laurie Entringer*
Senior photo research coordinator: *Jeremy Cheshareck*
Media project managers: *Rachel Townsend and Ron Nelms*
Typeface: *10/12.5 New Aster LT Std*
Compositor: *Laserwords Private Limited*
Printer: *R. R. Donnelley*

Library of Congress Cataloging-in-Publication Data
Spiceland, J. David, 1949–
    Financial accounting : making the connection / J. David Spiceland, Wayne Thomas, Don Herrmann.
      p. cm.
    Includes index.
    ISBN-13: 978-0-07-786226-8 (alk. paper)
    ISBN-10: 0-07-786226-0 (alk. paper)
    1. Accounting. I. Thomas, Wayne, 1969– II. Herrmann, Don. III. Title.
  HF5636.S772 2013
  657—dc23

                                                                                    2011044283

www.mhhe.com

Financial Accounting: Making the Connection

J. DAVID SPICELAND
University of Memphis

WAYNE THOMAS
University of Oklahoma

DON HERRMANN
Oklahoma State University

McGraw-Hill Irwin

Dedicated to:

David's wife Charlene, daughters Denise and Jessica, and three sons Michael David, Michael, and David

Wayne's wife Julee, daughter Olivia, and three sons Jake, Eli, and Luke

Don's wife Mary, daughter Rachel, and three sons David, Nathan, and Micah

About the Authors

DAVID SPICELAND

David Spiceland is professor of accounting at the University of Memphis, where he teaches intermediate accounting and other financial accounting courses at the undergraduate and master's levels. He received his BS degree in finance from the University of Tennessee, his MBA from Southern Illinois University, and his PhD in accounting from the University of Arkansas.

Professor Spiceland's primary research interests are in earnings management and educational research. He has published articles in a variety of journals including *The Accounting Review, Accounting and Business Research, Journal of Financial Research,* and *Journal of Accounting Education.* David has received university and college awards and recognition for his teaching, research, and technological innovations in the classroom. David is lead author of McGraw-Hill's best-selling *Intermediate Accounting* text.

David is the Memphis Tigers' No. 1 basketball fan. He enjoys playing basketball, is a former all-state linebacker, and an avid fisherman. Cooking is a passion for David, who served as sous chef for Paula Deen at a Mid-South Fair cooking demonstration.

WAYNE THOMAS

Wayne Thomas is the John T. Steed Chair in Accounting at the University of Oklahoma, where he teaches introductory financial accounting to nearly 600 students per year. He received his bachelor's degree in accounting from Southwestern Oklahoma State University, and his master's and PhD in accounting from Oklahoma State University.

Professor Thomas's primary research interests are in markets-based accounting research, financial disclosures, financial statement analysis, and international accounting issues. He currently serves as an editor of *The Accounting Review* and has published articles in a variety of journals including *The Accounting Review, Journal of Accounting and Economics, Journal of Accounting Research, Review of Accounting Studies,* and *Contemporary Accounting Research.* He has won several research awards, including the American Accounting Association's Competitive Manuscript Award. Professor Thomas has won teaching awards at the university, college, and departmental levels, and has received the Outstanding Educator Award from the Oklahoma Society of CPAs.

Wayne enjoys playing sports (basketball, tennis, golf, and ping pong), solving crossword puzzles, and coaching little league sports. He has participated in several adventure races, like you'll read about in the Great Adventures continuing problem at the end of each chapter.

DON HERRMANN

Don Herrmann is the Deloitte Professor of Accounting at Oklahoma State University, where he teaches financial accounting, intermediate accounting, and a doctoral-level course in financial accounting research. He received his bachelor's degree in business from John Brown University, his master's degree in accounting from Kansas State University, and his PhD in accounting from Oklahoma State University.

Professor Herrmann's research interests are in earnings forecasts, segment reporting, financial statement analysis, and international accounting issues. He is past president of the American Accounting Association International Section and has served on the editorial and review board of the top research journal in the field of accounting, *The Accounting Review.* He has published articles in a variety of journals including *The Accounting Review, Journal of Accounting Research, Accounting Horizons, Journal of Business, Finance, and Accounting,* and the *Journal of Accounting and Public Policy.* Don Herrmann and Wayne Thomas often work together, having co-authored over 15 research articles. Professor Herrmann has received many teaching awards at the department, college, and university levels, including Professor of the Year in the University Greek System.

Don, like his co-authors, is a big sports fan. He played tennis on scholarship in college and enjoys playing soccer, basketball, running, biking, and swimming. He also coaches soccer, basketball, and little league baseball in his home town.

> You have created a text that is likely to become **the gold standard of Intro texts.**—Christian Wurst, *Temple University*

> **This is an excellent book and I love the writing style.** I would describe the text as well-written with excellent examples that truly describes how accounting information is used to make better business decisions.—Mark Judd, *University of San Diego*

> **If you like Spiceland's intermediate text, you will be thrilled with the financial accounting principles text.** It is written in the same conversational style, addresses topics directly and clearly, and the illustrations are terrific too.—Nancy L. Snow, *University of Toledo*

> This is a wonderful and innovative book that covers the basics and really makes a serious effort to bring accounting alive.—S.A. Marino, *SUNY/Westchester Community College*

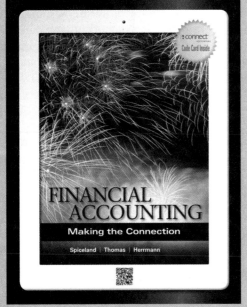

Have you experienced those moments in your course when students became fully engaged? When the "Aha!" revelations are bursting like fireworks? David Spiceland, Wayne Thomas, and Don Herrmann have developed a unique textbook based on over 50 collective years of experience in the classroom. Building on the tremendous success of the authors' previous works, they've brought together best practices like highlighting Common Mistakes, offering frequent Let's Review exercises, integrating the course with a running Continuing Problem, demonstrating the relevance of the course to nonmajors with a Career Corner, and communicating it all in a student-friendly conversational writing style.

Financial Accounting: Making the Connection also provides study materials and explanations through short tutorial videos and practice activities that can be accessed via smartphones or tablets by scanning the Quick Response (QR) codes in the margin. All the text's brief exercises, exercises, and problems are housed soley in McGraw-Hill *Connect*® *Accounting*, where students can submit their homework online and receive immediate feedback on their assignments. *Connect Accounting* also allows students to reinforce concepts by connecting them with additional study and practice resources such as Interactive Presentations, Guided Example videos, LearnSmart modules, and Self-Quiz and Study. As the old adage goes, "practice makes perfect;" *Financial Accounting: Marking the Connection* provides students the tools to: Learn, Practice, and Succeed.

WITH FIVE DISTINGUISHING FEATURES

1 Conversational Writing Style The authors took special care to write a textbook that fosters a friendly dialogue between the text and each individual student. The tone of the presentation is intentionally conversational—creating the impression of *speaking with* the student, as opposed to *teaching to* the student.

> The authors **successfully employ humor and a conversational writing style** in developing scenarios, examples and explanations which remain in the reader's mind and make these oftentimes complicated subjects understandable.—Dennis L. Kovach, *Community College of Allegheny County*

> It offers a very readable presentation, with easy-to-follow pedagogy. The writing is clear and crisp—**it is not boring.**—Al Hartgraves, *Emory University*

2 Innovative Pedagogy Reviewers enthusiastically embraced the innovative pedagogy used throughout the book, including **Common Mistake** boxes that help students avoid common pitfalls of beginning students and **Flip Side** problems and scenarios that show students the two sides of various accounting transactions.

3 Real-World Focus Students learn best when they see how concepts are applied in the real world. For that reason, real-world examples from companies, such as **Dell** and **Apple**, are used extensively and routinely to enhance the presentation. The real-world focus adds realism to discussions and serves as the foundation for exercises, problems, and cases.

> **This text has a logical layout and incorporates tools** to keep the student's attention. It makes the student think about the impact on the financials based upon the different principles and estimates selected.
> —Victor Stanton, *University of California–Berkeley*

4 Decision Maker's Perspective Each chapter includes one or more distinctive **Decision Maker's Perspective** sections, which offer insights into how the information discussed in the chapters affects decisions made by investors, creditors, managers, and others. Each chapter also contains **Decision Points** highlighting specific decisions in the chapter that can be made using financial accounting information.

5 A Strong Supplements Package The **authors write all of the major supplements** for *Financial Accounting*, including the Testbank, Solutions Manual, and the Instructor's Manual. *Connect Accounting* provides a rich array of online materials for various types of learners with LearnSmart, Interactive Presentations, Guided Examples, and the Self-Quiz and Study. Quick Response codes in the margin allow students to access additional study materials and explanations directly through their smartphones while they are on the go. With narrated PowerPoints and online quizzing, Spiceland's *Financial Accounting: Making the Connection* provides the cutting-edge technology demanded by today's accounting instructors and students.

McGraw-Hill *Connect*® *Accounting*

LESS MANAGING. MORE TEACHING. GREATER LEARNING.

McGraw-Hill *Connect Accounting* is an online assignment and assessment solution that connects students with the tools and resources they'll need to achieve success.

McGraw-Hill *Connect Accounting* helps prepare students for their future by enabling faster learning, more efficient studying, and higher retention of knowledge.

Connect Accounting offers a number of powerful tools and features to make managing assignments easier, so faculty can spend more time teaching. With *Connect Accounting,* students can engage with their coursework anytime and anywhere, making the learning process more accessible and efficient. *Connect Accounting* offers you the features described below.

SIMPLE ASSIGNMENT MANAGEMENT

With *Connect Accounting,* creating assignments is easier than ever, so you can spend more time teaching and less time managing. The assignment management function enables you to:

- Create and deliver assignments easily with selectable end-of-chapter questions and testbank items.
- Streamline lesson planning, student progress reporting, and assignment grading to make classroom management more efficient than ever.
- Assign algorithmic brief exercises, exercises, or problems so each student has a different problem to work on.

SMART GRADING

When it comes to studying, time is precious. *Connect Accounting* helps students learn more efficiently by providing feedback and practice material when they need it, where they need it. When it comes to teaching, your time also is precious. The grading function enables you to:

- Have assignments scored automatically, giving students immediate feedback on their work and side-by-side comparisons with correct answers.
- Access and review each response; manually change grades, or leave comments for students to review.
- Reinforce classroom concepts with practice tests and instant quizzes.

MAKE THE CONNECTION

LEARNSMART

Students can make the best use of their study time, with the LearnSmart adaptive self-study technology within *Connect Accounting*. LearnSmart provides a seamless combination of practice, assessment, and remediation for every concept in the textbook. LearnSmart's intelligent software adapts to each student by supplying questions on a new concept when he or she is ready to learn it. With LearnSmart, students will spend less time on topics they understand and practice more on those they have yet to master.

NARRATED GUIDED EXAMPLES

The Guided Examples in *Connect Accounting* provide a step-by-step walk-through of an exercise similar to one which the student is working. These short presentations provide reinforcement when students need it most.

INTERACTIVE PRESENTATIONS

The interactive presentations provide engaging narratives of key chapter concepts in an interactive online format. The presentations are tied specifically to *Financial Accounting: Making the Connection*. They follow the structure of the text and are organized to match the Learning Objectives within each chapter. While the interactive presentations are not meant to replace the textbook in this course, they provide additional explanation and enhancement of material from the text chapter, allowing students to learn, study, and practice with instant feedback at their own pace.

SELF-QUIZ AND STUDY

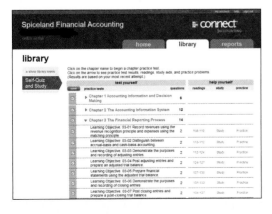

The Self-Quiz and Study (SQS) connects students to the learning resources they need to succeed in the course. For each chapter, students can take a practice quiz and immediately see how well they performed. A study plan then recommends specific readings from the text, supplemental study material, and practice exercises that will improve understanding and mastery of each Learning Objective.

ACCOMMODATE A VARIETY OF LEARNING STYLES

INSTRUCTOR LIBRARY

The *Connect Accounting* Instructor Library is your repository for additional resources to improve student engagement in and out of class. You can select and use any asset that enhances your lecture. The *Connect Accounting* Instructor Library includes:
- *eBook*
- *PowerPoint® slides*
- *Online quizzes*

STUDENT PROGRESS TRACKING

Connect Accounting keeps instructors informed about how each student, section, and class is performing, allowing for more productive use of lecture and office hours. The progress-tracking function enables you to:
- View scored work immediately and track individual or group performance with assignment and grade reports.
- Access an instant view of student or class performance relative to learning objectives.
- Collect data and generate reports required by many accreditation organizations, such as AACSB and AICPA.

MCGRAW-HILL *CONNECT® PLUS*

McGraw-Hill reinvents the textbook learning experience for the modern student with *Connect Plus*. A seamless integration of an eBook and *Connect Accounting, Connect Plus* provides all of the *Connect Accounting* features plus the following:
- An integrated eBook, allowing for anytime, anywhere access to the textbook.
- Dynamic links between the problems or questions you assign to your students and the location in the eBook where that problem or question is covered.
- A powerful search function to pinpoint and connect key concepts in a snap.

In short, *Connect Accounting* offers you and your students powerful tools and features that optimize your time and energies, enabling you to focus on course content, teaching, and student learning. *Connect Accounting* also offers a wealth of content resources for both instructors and students. This state-of-the-art, thoroughly tested system supports you in preparing students for the world that awaits.

For more information about Connect, go to **connect.mcgraw-hill.com,** or contact your local McGraw-Hill sales representative.

UNIQUE PEDAGOGICAL ELEMENTS

Common Mistakes made by financial accounting students are highlighted throughout each of the chapters. With greater awareness of the pitfalls the average student will find in a first accounting class, students can avoid making the same mistakes and gain a deeper understanding of the chapter material.

> Easy to read, love the Key Points and Common Mistakes—these sound like me talking to my students and are exactly the points I make in class! Really!
>
> —Christa Morgan, *Georgia Perimeter College*

Accounting is not a number-crunching desk job. Many business professionals call accounting the "language of business"; a solid understanding of accounting can lead to a wide variety of job opportunities. The **Career Corner** boxes highlight the exciting career opportunities in accounting and the important role that accountants play. These boxes also discuss how nonaccountants use accounting information in their business functions.

Because of the widespread adoption of international financial reporting standards issued by the **International Accounting Standards Board (IASB)**, differences between international standards and U.S. GAAP are highlighted throughout the text in **International Financial Reporting Standards** boxes.

The **Key Points** provide quick synopses of the critical pieces of information presented throughout each chapter.

Similarly, students will be acquainted with ethical implications of topics under discussion by the inclusion of short **Ethical Dilemma** boxes. The need to discuss ethics in accounting has become evident in light of recent accounting scandals.

A financial transaction always involves two parties—the **Flip Side** feature demonstrates how various transactions are viewed by each participant. Including the "flip side" of a transaction—in context—enhances the student's understanding of both the initial and the related transaction. Selected homework in the end-of-chapter materials also includes the Flip Side transactions for students to reinforce their understanding of this concept.

Let's Review

Each chapter contains one or more **Let's Review** sections that test students' comprehension of key concepts. These short review exercises, with solutions, are intended to reinforce the students' understanding of specific chapter material and allow them to apply concepts and procedures learned in the chapter prior to attempting their homework assignment.

Use your web-enabled, camera smartphone or tablet to scan the Quick Response (QR) codes you see throughout the book to access Guided tutorial videos and practice activities.

Getting started with QR codes is easy:

1. Use your smartphone to download any two-demensional or QR-enabled barcode reader from your provider's marketplace.
2. Focus your smartphone's camera on any code in the book.
3. From the list that appears, select the tutorial you'd like to see.

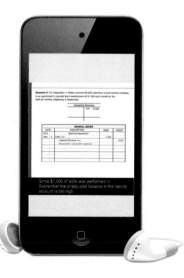

PRACTICE MAKES PERFECT

■ LO1

1. Accounts receivable are best described as:
   a. Liabilities of the company that represent the amount owed to suppliers.
   b. Amounts that have previously been received from customers.
   c. Assets of the company representing the amount owed by customers.
   d. Amounts that have previously been paid to suppliers.

■ LO2

2. On March 17, Fox Lumber sells materials to Whitney Construction for $12,0(
   terms 2/10, n/30. Whitney pays for the materials on March 23. What amount
   would Fox record as revenue on March 17?
   a. $12,400.
   b. $11,760.
   c. $12,000.
   d. $12,240.

■ LO2

3. Refer to the information in the previous question. What is the amount of net
   revenues (sales minus sales discounts) as of March 23?
   a. $0.
   b. $11,760

Self-Study Questions consist of 10 multiple-choice questions in each chapter. Answers appear at the end of the respective chapters. Students also are directed to the course website, where these same questions are available in the form of self-grading online quizzes with a more detailed analysis of correct and incorrect answers.

Review Questions are provided for the major concepts in each chapter, providing students with an opportunity to review key parts of the chapter and answer evocative questions about what they have learned.

REVIEW QUESTIONS

■ LO1

1. When recording a credit sale, what account do we debit? Describe account is reported in the financial statements.

■ LO1

2. What is the difference between a trade receivable and a nontrade re

■ LO2

3. Explain the difference between a trade discount and a sales discoun sales discounts reported in the income statement?

■ LO2

4. Briefly explain the accounting treatment for sales returns and allow are these accounts reported in the income statement?

■ LO2

5. Revenue can be earned at one point or over a period. Provide an exa

■ LO3

6. Explain the correct way companies should account for uncollectibl receivable (bad debts).

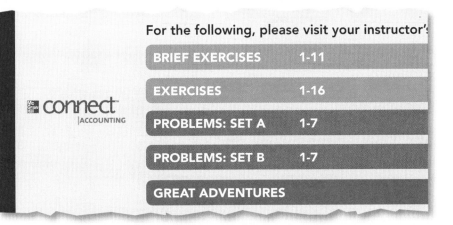

For the following, please visit your instructor'

BRIEF EXERCISES	1-11
EXERCISES	1-16
PROBLEMS: SET A	1-7
PROBLEMS: SET B	1-7
GREAT ADVENTURES	

All Brief Exercises, Exercises, and Problem Set A and B are housed solely in *Connect Accounting*. Access your homework assignments online anytime and receive immediate feedback.

Brief Exercises address single concepts from a single perspective.

Exercises typically add one or more additional dimensions to the same topics covered with Brief Exercises. An additional set of Exercises can be found on the book's website.

Exercise 1-2 Identify account classifications and business activities [LO2]
Falcon Incorporated has the following transactions with Wildcat Corporation.

Transactions	Falcon's Related Account
1. Falcon purchases common stock of Wildcat.	Investment
2. Falcon borrows from Wildcat by signing a note.	Notes payable
3. Wildcat pays dividends to Falcon.	Dividend revenue
4. Falcon provides services to Wildcat.	Service revenue
5. Falcon pays interest to Wildcat on borrowing.	Interest expense

Required:
For each transaction, indicate whether Falcon would classify the related account as an asset, liability, stockholders' equity to be reported in the balance sheet, revenue or expense to be reported in the income statement, dividend to be reported in the statement of stockholders' equity and the type of activity as financing, investing, or operating.

Transactions	Account	Activity
1. Falcon purchases common stock of Wildcat.	Asset	Investing
2. Falcon borrows from Wildcat by signing a note.	Liability	Financing
3. Wildcat pays dividends to Falcon.	Dividend	Operating
4. Falcon provides services to Wildcat.	(Click to select)	(Click to select)
5. Falcon pays interest to Wildcat on borrowing.	(Click to select)	(Click to select)

(Click to select) Stockholders' equity / Expense / Dividend / Asset / Liability / Revenue

contact MH Publishing   check my work   eBook Lin

Problems typically address multiple concepts from the chapter or multiple levels of analytical perspective within the given scenarios. Where feasible, problems are built around real companies and business situations.

Problem 1-3A Prepare financial statements [LO3]
Longhorn Corporation provides low-cost food delivery services to senior citizens. At the end of the year, the company reports the following amounts:

Cash	$ 1,300	Service revenue	$62,700
Equipment	24,000	Cost of goods sold (food expense)	52,400
Accounts payable	3,400	Buildings	30,000
Delivery expense	1,600	Supplies	2,400
Salaries expense	4,500	Salaries payable	900

In addition, the company had common stock of $30,000 at the beginning of the year and issued an additional $3,000 during the year. The company also had retained earnings of $16,200 at the beginning of the year.

Required:
Prepare the following for Longhorn Corporation.

(a) Income statement. (Input all amounts as positive values. Omit the "$" sign in your response.)

LONGHORN CORPORATION
Income Statement

Service revenue	$	62,700
Expenses:		
Salaries	$ 4,500	
Cost of goods sold	52,400	
(Click to select)		

(Click to select) Delivery / Cash / Salaries / Service revenue / Cost of goods sold

Each chapter provides twin sets of problems to offer instructors flexibility in presentation and assignment. The material in **Problem Set A** is similar in format to the material in **Problem Set B**, and each set reinforces the other. An additional set of Problems can be found on the book's website.

Problem 1-3B Prepare financial statements [LO3]
Gator Investments provides financial services related to investment selections, retirement planning, and general insurance needs. For the current year, the company reports the following amounts:

Advertising expense	$ 32,500	Service revenues	$122,600
Buildings	140,000	Interest expense	2,500
Salaries expense	64,100	Utilities expense	14,500
Accounts payable	5,400	Equipment	22,000
Cash	4,500	Notes payable	25,000

In addition, the company had common stock of $100,000 at the beginning of the year and issued an additional $10,000 during the year. The company also had retained earnings of $21,300 at the beginning of the year and paid dividends of $4,200.

Required:
Prepare the following for Gator Investments.

(a) Income statement. (Input all amounts as positive values. Omit the "$" sign in your response.)

GATOR INVESTMENTS
Income Statement

Service revenue	$	122,600
Expenses:		
Advertising	$ 32,500	
Salaries	64,100	
Utilities	14,500	
(Click to select)		

(Click to select) Interest / Service revenue / Advertising / Utilities / Salaries

CHALLENGE YOUR STUDENTS TO SEE AN ADDITIONAL PERSPECTIVE

The Additional Perspectives section, located in Appendix F at the end of the book, offers the most distinctive variety of case material available in financial accounting textbooks. Cases and activities are designed to allow students to apply the knowledge and skills they've learned in provocative, real, or realistic situations. Students are placed in the role of decision maker, presented with a set of information, and asked to draw conclusions that test their understanding of the issues discussed in the chapters. Each chapter offers an engaging mix of activities and opportunities to perform real-world financial accounting analysis:

ADDITIONAL PERSPECTIVES

Great Adventures

(This is a continuation of the Great Adventures problem from earlier chapters.)

AP8–1 Great Adventures is a defendant in litigation involving a biking accident during one of its adventure races. The front tire on one of the bikes came off during the race, resulting in serious injury to the rider. However, Great Adventures can document that each bike was carefully inspected prior to the race. It may have been that the rider loosened the wheel during the race and then forgot to tighten the quick-release mechanism.

Continuing Problem

QB

Required:

For each of the following scenarios, determine the appropriate way to report the situation. Explain your reasoning and record any necessary entry.
1. The likelihood of a payment occurring is probable, and the estimated amount is $120,000.
2. The likelihood of a payment occurring is probable, and the amount is estimated to be in the range of $100,000 to $150,000.
3. The likelihood of a payment occurring is reasonably possible, and the estimated amount is $120,000.

Continuing Problem—The story of Great Adventures progresses from chapter to chapter, encompassing the accounting issues of each new chapter as the story unfolds. This problem allows students to see how each chapter's topics can be integrated into the operations of a single company; this problem is also available in McGraw-Hill *Connect*.

American Eagle Outfitters, Inc.

AP5–2 Financial information for **American Eagle** is presented in Appendix A at the end of the book.

Financial Analysis

Required:
1. Determine whether the trend in net sales has been increasing or decreasing for the past three years.
2. Where is accounts receivable reported? Explain why using net sales to calculate the receivables turnover ratio might not be a good indicator of a company's ability to efficiently manage receivables for a retail company like American Eagle, which typically sells
3. Does Americ
sheet? If so, I

Financial Analysis: American Eagle Outfitters, Inc.—Students are asked to gather information from the annual report of American Eagle, located in Appendix A.

The Buckle, Inc.

AP5–3 Financial information for **The Buckle** is presented in Appendix B at the end of the book.

Financial Analysis

Buckle

Required:
1. Determine whether the trend in net sales has been increasing or decreasing for the past three years.
2. Where is accounts receivable reported? Explain why using net sales to calculate the receivables turnover ratio might not be a good indicator of a company's ability to efficiently manage receivables for a retail company like The Buckle, which typically sells clothing for cash.
3. Does The Buckle report an allowance for uncollectible accounts in the balance sheet? If so, how much is reported for the most recent year?

Financial Analysis: The Buckle, Inc.—Students are asked to gather information from the annual report of The Buckle, located in Appendix B.

American Eagle Outfitters, Inc., vs. The Buckle, Inc.

AP5–4 Financial information for **American Eagle** is presented in Appendix A at the end of the book, and financial information for **The Buckle** is presented in Appendix B at the end of the book.

Comparative Analysis

Buckle

Required:
Try to estimate each company's ratio of total current receivables to total current assets. Do you see problems with either company's management of receivables?

Comparative Analysis—In addition to separately analyzing the financial information of American Eagle and The Buckle, students are asked to compare financial information between the two companies.

Ethics—Encourage consideration of ethical issues as they pertain to accounting decisions, including the outcome of those decisions on various stakeholders.

Ethics

AP4–5 Between his freshman and sophomore years of college, Jack takes a job as ticket collector at a local movie theatre. Moviegoers purchase a ticket from a separate employee outside the theatre and then enter through a single set of doors. Jack takes half their ticket, and they proceed to the movie of their choice.

Besides trying to earn enough money for college the next year, Jack loves to watch movies. One of the perks of working for the movie theatre is that all employees are allowed to watch one free movie per day. However, in the employee handbook it states that friends and family of employees are not allowed to watch free movies. In addition, employees must pay full price for all concession items.

Soon after starting work at the theatre, Jack notices that most other employees regularly bring their friends and family to the movie without purchasing a ticket. When Jack stops them at the door to ask for their ticket, they say, "Jack, no one really follows that policy. Just be cool and let us in. You can do the same." Jack even notices that upper management does not follow the policy of no family and friends watching free movies. Furthermore, employees commonly bring their own cups to get free soft drinks and their own containers to eat free popcorn.

Jack considers whether he should also start bringing friends and family and enjoying the free popcorn and beverages. He reasons, "Why should I be the only one following

Internet Research—Allow students to develop and practice research skills by requiring them to locate and extract relevant information from available resource material such as financial reports or official standards on the Internet, perhaps identifying the appropriate resources to support a decision.

Internet Research

AP4–6 Financial accounting information can often be found at financial websites. These websites are useful for collecting information about a company's stock price, analysts' forecasts, dividend history, historical financial accounting information, and much more. One such site is Yahoo! Finance (*finance.yahoo.com*).

Required:

1. Visit Yahoo! Finance and get a stock quote for **Google**. To do this, type "GOOG" in the "Get Quotes" box. Under "Financials" click on the "Cash Flow" link. Calculate Google's free cash flows for the three most recent years.
2. Calculate **IBM's** free cash flows in the same way by typing "IBM" in the "Get Quotes" box.

Written Communication—Provide the opportunity not only to apply analysis and judgment skills but also to express information or persuade by means of a writing assignment.

Written Communication

AP4–7 Consider the following independent situations:

1. John Smith is the petty-cash custodian. John approves all requests for payment out of the $200 fund, which is replenished at the end of each month. At the end of each month, John submits a list of all accounts and amounts to be charged, and a check is written to him for the total amount. John is the only person ever to tally the fund.
2. All of the company's cash disbursements are made by check. Each check must be

Earnings Management—Provide challenging earnings management situations in which students analyze the implications of their accounting decisions on a company's earnings.

Earnings Management

AP7–8 Edward L. Vincent is CFO of Energy Resources, Inc. The company specializes in the exploration and development of natural gas. It's near year-end, and Edward is feeling terrific. Natural gas prices have risen throughout the year, and Energy Resources is set to report record-breaking performance that will greatly exceed analysts' expectations. However, during an executive meeting this morning, management agreed to "tone down" profits due to concerns that reporting excess profits could encourage additional government regulations in the industry, hindering future profitability.

Edward decides to adjust the estimated service life of development equipment from

This book has the **largest quantity of exercises and problems of any text that I've reviewed.** I think it is very important for students to work incrementally on some of the more difficult concepts. I usually don't have such an impressive quantity from which to select.—Kathleen M. Metcalf, *Muscatine Community College*

AUTHOR-WRITTEN SUPPLEMENTS TO ENSURE QUALITY AND CONSISTENCY

> The textbook is well organized and **noticeably written by individuals who have an excellent understanding of accounting,** the accounting profession, and the issues confronting the accounting profession. A large number of supplements for students and instructors are available, including high-tech supplements.—Richard A. Moellenberndt, *Washburn University*

INSTRUCTOR'S RESOURCE MANUAL

This manual provides for each chapter: (a) a chapter overview; (b) a comprehensive lecture outline; (c) a variety of suggested class activities (real world, ethics, annual report, professional development activities including research, analysis, communication and judgment, and others); and (d) an assignment chart indicating topic, learning objective, and estimated completion time for every question, exercise, problem, and case.

SOLUTIONS MANUAL

The Solutions Manual includes detailed solutions for every question, exercise, problem, and case in the text.

TESTBANK

Written by the authors, this comprehensive Testbank contains over 1,800 problems and true/false, matching, multiple-choice, problems, and essay questions.

AUDIO-NARRATED SLIDES

The Audio-Narrated Slides include an accompanying audio lecture with notes and are available on the Online Learning Center (OLC). Separate sets of PowerPoints are available for instructors and students.

ONLINE LEARNING CENTER (OLC)

Our OLC requires no building or maintenance on your part, and is ready to go the moment you and your students type in the URL. As your students study, they can access the OLC website for such benefits as:

- Self-grading quizzes
- Student PowerPoint Tutorials
- Alternate exercises and problems
- Check figures
- Excel templates
- QuickBooks templates

Additional Resources for Your Students

ALTERNATE EXERCISES AND PROBLEMS

This manual is available on the OLC. It includes exercises and problems for each chapter in the text.

EXCEL TEMPLATES

Selected end-of-chapter exercises and problems can be solved using these Microsoft Excel templates, located on the OLC.

QUICKBOOKS TEMPLATES

QuickBooks Templates are available for selected problems in the end-of-chapter material for *Financial Accounting: Making the Connection.* As the premier accounting software in use today, students will get a head start on learning how accounting is done in the real world!

THE TECHNOLOGY INSTRUCTORS NEED

HOW CAN TEXT-RELATED WEB RESOURCES ENRICH MY COURSE?

McGraw-Hill Higher Education and Blackboard have teamed up.
What does this mean for you?

The Best of
Both Worlds

1. **Your life, simplified.** Now you and your students can access McGraw-Hill *Connect* and *Create*™ right from within your Blackboard course—all with one single sign-on. Say goodbye to the days of logging in to multiple applications.

2. **Deep integration of content and tools.** Not only do you get single sign-on with *Connect* and *Create*, you also get deep integration of McGraw-Hill content and content engines right in Blackboard. Whether you're choosing a book for your course or building *Connect* assignments, all the tools you need are right where you want them—inside Blackboard.

3. **Seamless Gradebooks.** Are you tired of keeping multiple gradebooks and manually synchronizing grades into Blackboard? We thought so. When a student completes an integrated *Connect* assignment, the grade for that assignment automatically (and instantly) feeds your Blackboard grade center.

4. **A solution for everyone.** Whether your institution is already using Blackboard or you just want to try Blackboard on your own, we have a solution for you. McGraw-Hill and Blackboard can now offer you easy access to industry-leading technology and content, whether your campus hosts it or we do. Be sure to ask your local McGraw-Hill representative for details.

ALEKS®

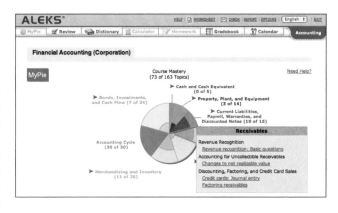

Available online in partnership with McGraw-Hill/Irwin, ALEKS is a unique program that uses artificial intelligence and adaptive questioning to precisely assess a student's knowledge in accounting and provide personalized instruction on the exact topics the student is most ready to learn. ALEKS targets gaps in student skills and enables students to master course content quickly and easily within an environment tailored to each student's level of preparedness. By providing comprehensive explanations, practice, and feedback, ALEKS dramatically improves student performance and retention.

The ALEKS Instructor Module offers powerful, assignment-driven features and extensive content flexibility to simplify course management so instructors can spend less time with administrative tasks and more time directing student learning. The complimentary Instructor Module provides a course calendar, customizable gradebook, automatically-graded assignments, textbook integration, and dynamic reports to monitor student and class progress.

To learn more about ALEKS, visit **www.aleks.com/highered/business**.

ALEKS is a registered trademark of ALEKS Corporation.

ASSURANCE OF LEARNING READY

Many educational institutions today are focused on the notion of *assurance of learning,* an important element of some accreditation standards. *Financial Accounting: Making the Connection* is designed specifically to support your assurance of learning initiatives with a simple, yet powerful solution.

Each Testbank question for *Financial Accounting* maps to a specific chapter learning objective listed in the text. You can use our Testbank software, EZ Test Online, or *Connect Accounting* to easily query for learning objectives that directly relate to the learning objectives for your course. You can then use the reporting features of EZ Test to aggregate student results in similar fashion, making the collection and presentation of assurance of learning data simple and easy.

AACSB STATEMENT

The McGraw-Hill Companies is a proud corporate member of AACSB International. Understanding the importance and value of AACSB accreditation, *Financial Accounting* recognizes the curricula guidelines detailed in the AACSB standards for business accreditation by connecting selected questions in the text and the Testbank to the six general knowledge and skill guidelines in the AACSB standards.

The statements contained in *Financial Accounting* are provided only as a guide for the users of this textbook. The AACSB leaves content coverage and assessment within the purview of individual schools, the mission of the school, and the faculty. While *Financial Accounting* and the teaching package make no claim of any specific AACSB qualification or evaluation, we have within *Financial Accounting* labeled selected questions according to the six general knowledge and skills areas.

Try a New e-Book Option!

COURSESMART

CourseSmart is a new way to find and buy eTextbooks. At CourseSmart you can save up to 50 percent off the cost of a printed textbook, reduce your impact on the environment, and gain access to powerful Web tools for learning. CourseSmart has the largest selection of eTextbooks available anywhere, offering thousands of the most commonly adopted textbooks from a wide variety of higher education publishers. CourseSmart eTextbooks are available in one standard online reader with full text search, notes and highlighting, and e-mail tools for sharing notes between classmates.

MCGRAW-HILL/IRWIN CUSTOMER EXPERIENCE CONTACT INFORMATION

At McGraw-Hill/Irwin, we understand that getting the most from new technology can be challenging. That's why our services don't stop after you purchase our product. You can e-mail our Product Specialists 24 hours a day, get product training online, or search our knowledge bank of Frequently Asked Questions on our support website. For all Customer Support call **(800) 331-5094,** or visit **www.mhhe.com/support**. One of our Technical Support Analysts will be able to assist you in a timely fashion.

The version of *Financial Accounting: Making the Connection* you are reading would not be the same book without the valuable suggestions, keen insights, and constructive criticisms of the list of reviewers below. Each professor listed here contributed in substantive ways to the organization of chapters, coverage of topics, and selective use of pedagogy. We are grateful to them for taking the time to read each chapter and offer their insights:

Dawn Addington, *Central New Mexico Community College*
Peter Aghimien, *Indiana University –South Bend*
James J. Aitken, *Central Michigan University*
Fouad Alnajjar, *Baker College*
Janice Ammons, *Quinnipiac University*
Craig Bain, *Northern Arizona University*
Kashi Balachandran, *New York University*
Patricia C. Bancroft, *Bridgewater State College*
Randall P. Bandura, *Frostburg State University*
Lisa Banks, *Mott Community College*
Joyce Barden, *DeVry University*
Cheryl Bartlett, *Central New Mexico Community College*
Mohammad S. Bazaz, *Oakland University*
Stephen Benner, *Eastern Illinois University*
Amy Bentley, *Tallahassee Community College*
Larry Bergin, *Winona State University*
Brenda Bindschatel, *Green River Community College–Auburn*
Cynthia Birk, *University of Nevada–Reno*
Eddy Birrer, *Gonzaga University*
Sandra Bitenc, *University of Texas at Arlington*
Claude Black, *Seattle Central Community College*
David Bojarsky, *California State University –Long Beach*
Charlie Bokemeier, *Michigan State University*
Jack Borke, *University of Wisconsin –Platteville*
Lisa N. Bostick, *The University of Tampa*
Amy Bourne, *Oregon State University*
Benoit Boyer, *Sacred Heart University*
Jerold K. Braun, *Daytona State College*
Linnae Bryant, *Chicago State University*
R. Eugene Bryson, *University of Alabama –Huntsville*
Georgia Buckles, *Manchester Community College*
Charles I. Bunn, *Wake Tech Community College*
Sandra Byrd, *Missouri State University*
Scott Cairns, *Shippensburg University of PA*
Ernest Carraway, *North Carolina State University*
Bruce Cassel, *Dutchess Community College*
Valrie Chambers, *Texas A&M University*
Betty Chavis, *California State University –Fullerton*

Al Chen, *North Carolina State University –Raleigh*
Alan Cherry, *Loyola Marymount University*
Bea Chiang, *The College of New Jersey*
Cal Christian, *East Carolina University*
Leslie Cohen, *University of Arizona*
Jackie Conrecode, *Florida Gulf Coast University*
Debora Constable, *Georgia Perimeter College*
Pat Cook, *Manchester Community College*
Betty Cossitt, *University of Nevada–Reno*
Meg Costello Lambert, *Oakland Community College*
Samantha Cox, *Wake Tech Community College*
Leonard Cronin, *Rochester Community & Technical College*
Jim Crowther, *Kirkwood Community College*
Karl Dahlberg, *Rutgers University*
Dori Danko, *Grand Valley State University*
Kreag Danvers, *Clarion University of PA*
Alan Davis, *Community College of Philadelphia*
Harold Davis, *Southeastern Louisiana University*
Mark DeFond, *University of Southern California*
Guenther DerManelian, *Johnson & Wales University*
Patricia Derrick, *Salisbury University*
Rosemond Desir, *Colorado State University*
Carlton Donchess, *Bridgewater State College*
Alex Dontoh, *New York University*
Jamie Doran, *Muhlenberg College*
Lisa Dutchik, *Kirkwood Community College*
Carol Dutton, *South Florida Community College*
Cynthia Eakin, *University of the Pacific*
Susan Eldridge, *University of Nebraska –Omaha*
Sheri Erickson, *Minnesota State University –Moorhead*
Harlan Etheridge, *University of Louisiana –Lafayette*
Janice Fergusson, *University of South Carolina*
Linda Flaming, *Monmouth University*
Amy Ford, *Western Illinois University*
Brenda Fowler, *Alamance Community College*
Martha Lou Fowler, *Missouri Western State University*
Tom Fuhrmann, *Missouri Western State University*
Harlan Fuller, *Illinois State University*
Ed Furticella, *Purdue University*
Mohamed Gaber, *SUNY Plattsburgh*
John Gardner, *University of Wisconsin –Lacrosse*
Daniel Gibbons, *Waubonsee Community College*
Lisa Gillespie, *Loyola University*
Ruth Goran, *Northeastern Illinois University*
Sherry Gordon, *Palomar College*

Janet Grange, *Chicago State University*
Tony Greig, *Purdue University*
Sanjay Gupta, *Valdosta State University*
Geoffrey Gurka, *Mesa State College*
Jeffry Haber, *Iona College*
Ronald Halsac, *Community College of Allegheny County*
Heidi Hansel, *Kirkwood Community College*
Sheldon Hanson, *Chippewa Valley Technical College*
Coby Harmon, *University of California–Santa Barbara*
Erskine Hawkins, *Georgia Perimeter College*
Daniel He, *Monmouth University*
Haihong He, *California State University –Los Angeles*
Kevin Hee, *San Diego State University*
Joshua Herbold, *University of Montana*
Joyce Hicks, *Saint Mary's College*
Dan Hinchliffe, *University of North Carolina –Asheville*
Frank Hodge, *University of Washington*
Anthony Holder, *Case Western Reserve University*
Mary Hollars, *Vincennes University*
Linda Holmes, *University of Wisconsin –Whitewater*
Sharon Hoover-Dice, *Clinton Community College*
Steven Hornik, *University of Central Florida*
Kathy Hsiao Yu Hsu, *University of Louisiana –Lafayette*
Marsha Huber, *Otterbein College*
Peggy Ann Hughes, *Montclair State University*
Laura Ilcisin, *University of Nebraska at Omaha*
Paula Irwin, *Muhlenberg College*
Norma Jacobs, *Austin Community College*
Marianne James, *California State University –Los Angeles*
Raymond Johnson, *Guilford College*
Shondra Johnson, *Bradley University*
Rita Jones, *Columbus State University*
Mark Judd, *University of San Diego*
David Juriga, *Saint Louis Community College–Forest Park*
Robert Kachur, *Richard Stockton College of New Jersey*
Elliot Kamlet, *Binghamton University*
Lara Kessler, *Grand Valley State University*
Tim Kizirian, *California State University –Chico*
Janice Klimek, *University of Central Missouri*
Christine Kloezeman, *Glendale Community College*
Stephen A. Kolenda, *Hartwick College*
Emil Koren, *Saint Leo University*
Dennis Kovach, *Community College of Allegheny County*
Joan Lacher, *Nassau Community College*

Steven J. LaFave, *Augsburg College*
Sheldon Langsam, *Western Michigan University*
Cathy Larson, *Middlesex Community College*
Douglas A. Larson, *Salem State College*
Laurie Larson-Gardner, *Valencia Community College*
Michael D. Lawrence, *Portland Community College*
Suzanne Lay, *Mesa State College*
Chuo-Hsuan Lee, *SUNY Plattsburgh*
Deborah Lee, *Northeastern State University*
Christy Lefevers-Land, *Catawba Valley Community College*
Pamela Legner, *College of DuPage*
Stacy LeJeune, *Nicholls State University*
Elliott Levy, *Bentley College*
Xu Li, *University of Texas at Dallas*
Beixin Lin, *Montclair State University*
Joseph Lipari, *Montclair State University*
Joseph Lupino, *Saint Mary's College of California*
Anna Lusher, *Slippery Rock University of PA*
Kirk Lynch, *Sandhills Community College*
Nancy Lynch, *West Virginia University*
Mostafa Maksy, *Northeastern Illinois University*
Sal Marino, *Westchester Community College*
Angie Martin, *Tarrant County College*
James Martin, *Washburn University*
Peter Martino, *Johnson & Wales University*
Christian Mastilak, *Xavier University*
Josephine Mathias, *Mercer County Community College*
Betsy Mayes, *University of North Carolina –Asheville*
Lynn Mazzola, *Nassau Community College*
Maureen McBeth, *College of DuPage*
Florence McGovern, *Bergen Community College*
Chris McNamara, *Finger Lakes Community College*
Sara Melendy, *Gonzaga University*
Terri Meta, *Seminole Community College*
Kathleen M. Metcalf, *Muscatine Community College*
Jean Meyer, *Loyola University*
Pam Meyer, *University of Louisiana–Lafayette*
James Miller, *Gannon University*
Julie Miller, *Chippewa Valley Technical College*
Claudette Milligan, *Trident Technical College*
Tim Mills, *Eastern Illinois University*
Laurel Bond Mitchell, *University of Redlands*
Laura Mizaur, *Creighton University*
Richard A. Moellenberndt, *Washburn University*
Kathy Moffeit, *West Georgia University*
J. Lowell Mooney, *Georgia Southern University*
Tommy Moores, *University of Nevada–Las Vegas*
Michelle Moshier, *University at Albany*
Gerald Motl, *Xavier University*

Lisa Murawa, *Mott Community College*
Volkan Muslu, *University of Texas at Dallas*
Al Nagy, *John Carroll University*
Presha Neidermeyer, *West Virginia University*
Micki Nickla, *Ivy Tech Community College of Indiana*
Tracie Nobles, *Austin Community College*
Hossein Noorian, *Wentworth Institute of Technology*
Ron O'Brien, *Fayetteville Tech Community College*
Dan O'Brien, *North Central Technical College*
Kanalis Ockree, *Washburn University*
Karen Osterheld, *Bentley College*
Don Pagach, *North Carolina State University –Raleigh*
Janet Papiernik, *Indiana University/Purdue University–Ft Wayne*
Glenn Pate, *Palm Beach Community College*
Keith F. Patterson, *Brigham Young University*
Richard J. Pettit, *Mountain View College*
Jan Pitera, *Broome Community College*
John Plouffe, *California State University –Los Angeles*
Linda Poulson, *Elon University*
Matthew Probst, *Ivy Tech Community College of Indiana*
Atul Rai, *Wichita State University*
Richard Rand, *Tennessee Tech University*
David Randolph, *Xavier University*
July Ratley, *Shasta College*
Donald J. Raux, *Siena College*
Aaron Reeves, *Saint Louis Community College–Forest Park*
Patrick Reihing, *Nassau Community College*
Raymond Reisig, *Pace University*
Gayle Richardson, *Bakersfield College*
Laura Rickett, *Kent State University*
Sharon Robinson, *Frostburg State University*
Joanne Rockness, *University of North Carolina–Wilmington*
Carol Rogers, *Central New Mexico Community College*
Richard Roscher, *University of North Carolina–Wilmington*
Mark Ross, *Western Kentucky University*
John A. Rude, *Bloomsburg University of PA*
Robert Russ, *Northern Kentucky University*
Huldah A. Ryan, *Iona College*
Angela Sandberg, *Jacksonville State University*
Amy Santos, *State College of Florida*
Gary Schader, *Kean University*
Linda Schain, *Hofstra University*
Megan Schaupp, *West Virginia University*
Arnold Schneider, *Georgia Institute of Technology*
Steve Sefcik, *University of Washington*
Joann Segovia, *Minnesota State University –Moorhead*
Ann E. Selk, *University of Wisconsin–Green Bay*

Michael Serif, *Dowling College*
Randall Serrett, *University of Houston –Downtown*
Suzanne Sevalstad, *University of Nevada*
Kathy Sevigny, *Bridgewater State College*
Geeta Shankar, *University of Dayton*
Robbie Sheffy, *Tarrant County College*
Lori Simonsen, *University of Nebraska at Omaha*
Mike Slaubaugh, *Indiana University/Purdue University–Ft Wayne*
Erik Slayter, *California Polytechnic University*
G. Phillip Smilanick, *Truckee Meadows Community College*
Becky L. Smith, *York College of PA*
Sondra Smith, *West Georgia University*
Warren Smock, *Ivy Tech Community College of Indiana*
Mary Speth, *Sandhills Community College*
Barbara Squires, *Corning Community College*
Victor Stanton, *University of California, Berkeley*
Maureen Stefanini, *Worcester State College*
Ron Stone, *California State University –Northridge*
Arlene Strawn, *Tallahassee Community College*
Edith Strickland, *Tallahassee Community College*
Ron Strittmater, *North Hennepin Community College*
John Surdick, *Xavier University*
Jan Sweeney, *Bernard M. Baruch College*
Paulette Tandy, *University of Nevada–Las Vegas*
Linda Tarrago, *Hillsborough Community College*
Peter Theuri, *Northern Kentucky University*
Amanda Thompson, *Marshall University*
Lisa Thornton Buehler, *Truckee Meadows Community College*
Paula Tigerman, *Black Hawk College*
Theresa Tiggeman, *University of the Incarnate Word*
Melanie Torborg, *Minnesota School of Business*
Yvette Travis, *Bishop State Community College*
Nancy Uddin, *Monmouth University*
Karen Varnell, *Tarleton State University*
Stacy R. Wade, *Western Kentucky University*
Elisabeth Peltier Wagner, *Bernard M. Baruch College*
Mary Jeanne Walsh, *La Salle University*
Li Wang, *University of Akron*
Larry Watkins, *Northern Arizona University*
Olga Dupuis Watts, *McNeese State University*
Andrea Weickgenannt, *Northern Kentucky University*
Kristin Wentzel, *La Salle University*
Cathy West, *University of Massachusetts –Amherst*
Cheryl Westen, *Western Illinois University*

Allen Wright, *Hillsborough Community College*
Lorraine Wright, *North Carolina State University–Raleigh*
Christian Wurst, *Temple University*
Kathryn Yarbrough, *Appalachian State University*
Gregory C. Yost, *University of West Florida*
Thomas M. Young, *Lone Star College*
Marjorie Yuschak, *Sacred Heart University*
Emmanuel Zur, *Bernard M. Baruch College*
Robert Zwicker, *Pace University*
James J. Aitken, *Central Michigan University*
Christie P. Anderson, *Whitworth University*
Marjorie Ashton, *Truckee Meadows Community College*
Steven Ault, *Montana State University –Bozeman*
Tim Baker, *California State University–Fresno*
Joyce Barden, *Devry University–Phoenix*
Deborah F. Beard, *Southeast Missouri State University*
Judy Benish, *Fox Valley Tech College*
Joseph Berlinski, *Prairie State College*
Eddy Birrer, *Gonzaga University*
Jack Borke, *University of Wisconsin –Platteville*
Lisa N. Bostick, *The University of Tampa*
Bruce Bradford, *Fairfield University*
Thomas Brady, *University of Dayton*
Linda Bressler, *University of Houston –Downtown*
Madeline Brogan, *North Harris College*
Carol Brown, *Oregon State University*
Helen Brubeck, *San Jose State University*
R. Eugene Bryson, *University of Alabama –Huntsville*
Charles I. Bunn, *Wake Tech Community College*
Ron Burrows, *University of Dayton*
Thane Butt, *Champlain College*
Sandra Byrd, *Missouri State University*
Kay C. Carnes, *Gonzaga University*
Bea Bih-Horng Chiang, *The College of New Jersey*
Cal Christian, *East Carolina University*
John Coulter, *Western New England College*
Sue Cullers, *Tarleton State University*
Kreag Danvers, *Clarion University of PA*
Peggy Dejong, *Kirkwood Community College*
Laura Delaune, *Louisiana State University –Baton Rouge*
Shannon Donovan, *Bridgewater State College*
Allan Drebin, *Northwestern University*
Ahmed Ebrahim, *State University of NY–New Paltz*
Thomas Finnegan, *University of Illinois –Champaign*
Linda Flaming, *Monmouth University*
Martha Lou Fowler, *Missouri Western State University*

Tom Fuhrmann, *Missouri Western State University*
Mohamed Gaber, *State University of New York –Plattsburgh*
Rena Galloway, *State Fair Community College*
Margaret Garnsey, *Siena College*
David L. Gilbertson, *Western Washington University*
Lisa Gillespie, *Loyola University–Chicago*
Ruth Goran, *Northeastern Illinois University*
Jeffry Haber, *Iona College–New Rochelle*
Heidi Hansel, *Kirkwood Community College*
Sheldon Hanson, *Chippewa Valley Tech College*
Al Hartgraves, *Emory University*
Bob Hartman, *University of Iowa–Iowa City*
K.D. Hatheway-Dial, *University of Idaho*
John Hathorn, *Metro State College of Denver*
Byron K. Henry, *Howard University*
Joshua Herbold, *University of Montana*
Margaret Hicks, *Howard University*
Mary Hollars, *Vincennes University*
Sharon Hoover-Dice, *Clinton Community College*
Steven Hornik, *University of Central Florida*
Marsha Huber, *Otterbein College*
David Hurtt, *Baylor University*
Laura Ilcisin, *University of Nebraska–Omaha*
Paula Irwin, *Muhlenberg College*
Marianne James, *California State University –Los Angeles*
Raymond Johnson, *Guilford College*
Melissa Jordan, *College of DuPage*
David Juriga, *St. Louis Community College –Forest Park*
Dennis L. Kovach, *Community College of Allegheny County*
Steven J. LaFave, *Augsburg College*
Phillip D. Landers, *Pennsylvania College of Technology*
Douglas A. Larson, *Salem State College*
Laurie Larson-Gardner, *Valencia Community College East*
Daniel Law, *Gonzaga University*
Suzanne Lay, *Mesa State College*
Christy Lefevers-Land, *Catawba Valley Community College*
Joseph Lipari, *Montclair State University*
Chao-Shin Liu, *University of Notre Dame*
Mostafa Maksy, *Northeastern Illinois University*
S. A. Marino, *SUNY/Westchester Community College*
Dawn Massey, *Fairfield University*
Joyce Matthews, *Central New Mexico Community College*
Mark McCarthy, *East Carolina University*
Robert W. McGee, *Barry University*
Chris McNamara, *Finger Lakes Community College*

Kathleen M. Metcalf, *Muscatine Community College*
Herbert L. Meyer, *Scott Community College –Davenport*
Jean Meyer, *Loyola University*
Pam Meyer, *University of Louisiana–Lafayette*
Laurel Bond Mitchell, *University of Redlands*
Richard A. Moellenberndt, *Washburn University*
Dennis P. Moore, *Worcester State College*
Tommy Moores, *University of Nevada –Las Vegas*
Ron O'Brien, *Fayetteville Tech Community College*
George Pate, *Robeson Community College*
Keith Patterson, *Brigham Young University –Idaho*
Susanna Pendergast, *Western Illinois University*
Jan Pitera, *Broome Community College*
John Plouffe, *California State University –Los Angeles*
Alan Ransom, *Cypress College*
Laura Rickett, *Kent State University*
John A. Rude, *Bloomsburg University of PA*
Amy Santos, *Manatee Community College –Bradenton*
Dick Schroeder, *University of North Carolina –Charlotte*
Ann E. Selk, *University of Wisconsin –Green Bay*
Seleshi Sisaye, *Duquesne University*
Rodney Smith, *California State University –Long Beach*
Nancy L. Snow, *University of Toledo*
Victor Stanton, *University of California –Berkeley*
Gracelyn Stuart, *Palm Beach Community College*
John J. Surdick, *Xavier University*
G. A. Swanson, *Tennessee Tech University*
Aida Sy, *University of Bridgeport*
Christine Tan, *Baruch College*
Steve Teeter, *Utah Valley State College*
Peter Theuri, *Northern Kentucky University*
Ada Till, *Prairie View A&M University*
Michael Tyler, *Barry University*
Joan Van Hise, *Fairfield University*
Marcia R. Veit, *University of Central Florida*
Stacy R. Wade, *Western Kentucky University*
Susan Wessels, *Meredith College*
Peter Woodlock, *Youngstown State University*
Gregg S. Woodruff, *Western Illinois University*
Christian Wurst, *Temple University –Philadelphia*
Thomas M. Young, *Tomball College*
Benny Zachry, *Nicholls State University*
Lin Zheng, *Georgia College and State University*
Robert Zwicker, *Pace University*

ASSURANCE OF ACCURACY

Dear Colleague,

As textbook authors, and more importantly, as instructors of financial accounting, we recognize the great importance placed on accuracy—not only in the book you are now holding, but in the supplements as well. With this in mind, we have taken the following steps to ensure that *Financial Accounting: Making the Connection* is error-free:

1. We received detailed feedback from over 330 instructor reviews, starting with first draft manuscript through the final draft submitted to the publisher. Each review contributed in significant ways to the accuracy of the content.
2. We personally class-tested the manuscript with our students before it was published.
3. Each of us wrote, reviewed, and carefully checked all of the assignment material.
4. A developmental writer went through each sentence to ensure that our language was as clear as possible.
5. Multiple accuracy checkers reviewed each chapter and its accompanying assignment material—once when the final manuscript was submitted to the publisher, and again when our final formatted pages were completed.
6. A copyeditor checked the grammar of the final manuscript.
7. A proofreader reviewed each page to ensure no errors remained.
8. Our Solutions Manual and Testbank were created by the authors and reviewed by multiple independent accuracy checkers.

Given the steps taken above, we have the utmost confidence that you and your students will have a great experience using *Financial Accounting: Making the Connection.*

Sincerely,

David Spiceland   **Wayne Thomas**   **Don Herrmann**

ACKNOWLEDGMENTS

Many talented people contributed to the creation of this, "connected," edition, and we would like to thank them for their valuable contributions. Ilene Persoff of Long Island University/C. W. Post Campus did a wonderful job accuracy checking our second edition manuscript. Mark McCarthy of East Carolina University contributed a helpful accuracy check of the page proofs; we thank him for his speedy and insightful comments. Carol Yacht and Jack Terry contributed the QuickBooks templates and Excel templates (respectively) that accompany the end-of-chapter material. We appreciate the very helpful Lori Cody from The Buckle, Inc., and Elizabeth Rush from American Eagle Outfitters, Inc., for helping us get permission to use their companies' annual reports in the appendices.

We appreciate the excellent *Connect* accuracy checking work completed by Mark McCarthy, East Carolina University; Angela Sandberg, Jacksonville State University; Janice Fergusson, University of South Carolina; and all of the staff at ANSR Source. Janice Fergusson at the University of South Carolina did an excellent job accuracy checking our Testbank. The authors also wish to thank David Bojarsky for his contributions to the Self-Quiz and Study feature in Connect.

We also appreciate the expert attention given to this project by the staff at McGraw-Hill/Irwin, especially; Tim Vertovec, Publisher; Dana Woo, Senior Sponsoring Editor; Ann Torbert, Director of Development; Kathleen Klehr, Senior Marketing Manager; Christina Sanders, Managing Development Editor; Pat Plumb, Director of Digital Content; Pat Frederickson, Lead Project Manager; Rachel Townsend, Allison Souter, and Ron Nelms, Media Product Managers; Xin Lin, Digital Product Manager; Laurie Entringer, Designer; and Michael McCormick, Buyer.

Contents in Brief

Contents

9 CHAPTER
Long-Term Liabilities 284

10 CHAPTER
Stockholders' Equity 318

11 CHAPTER
Statement of Cash Flows 354

12 CHAPTER
Financial Statement Analysis 390

Financial Accounting:
Making the Connection

Accounting Information and Decision Making

AFTER STUDYING THIS CHAPTER, YOU SHOULD BE ABLE TO:

- ■ **LO1** Describe the two primary functions of financial accounting.
- ■ **LO2** Identify the three fundamental business activities that financial accounting measures.
- ■ **LO3** Discuss how financial accounting information is communicated through financial statements.
- ■ **LO4** Describe the role that financial accounting plays in the efficient distribution of society's resources.
- ■ **LO5** Explain the term generally accepted accounting principles (GAAP) and describe the role of GAAP in financial accounting.
- ■ **LO6** Identify career opportunities in accounting.

Appendix

- ■ **LO7** Explain the nature of the conceptual framework used to develop generally accepted accounting principles.

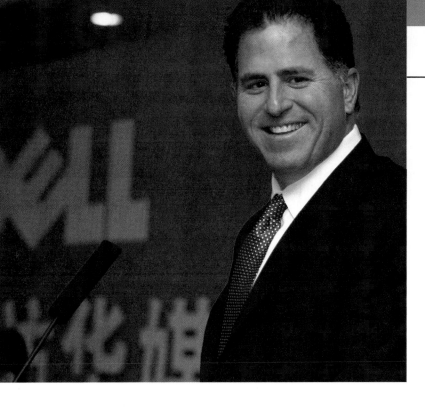

DELL INCORPORATED: **COMPUTING THE SUCCESS OF AN ENTREPRENEUR**

Feature Story

Michael was not your average college student. Since age 12, when he started his first business venture selling stamps, he realized that if you have a good idea, work hard, and treat customers with special care, you can make money—and sometimes, a lot of money. After a series of small, successful business ventures through high school, at age 19 Michael came up with his next business idea. In 1984, with an initial investment of only $1,000, he started a company that custom-built personal computers for sale directly to customers. The company enjoyed immediate success. In 1988, the company offered for sale to the public 3,500,000 shares of stock for $8.50 per share and changed its name to **Dell Incorporated**.

By the age of 26, Michael Dell had become the youngest CEO of a company ever included on the prestigious **Fortune** 500 list. Better yet, Dell's stock enjoyed greater growth than any other stock during the 1990s. By December 31, 1999, each share had increased in value nearly 60,000%. If you had invested just $1,000 in Dell at its initial public offering in 1988, your investment would have increased to nearly $600,000 by the end of 1999!

What if instead of investing $1,000 in Dell in 1988, you had invested $1,000 in **Polaroid Corporation**, most famous for its instant-film cameras? You would have watched your $1,000 shrink to $0 by 2001, when the company declared bankruptcy.

How do investors decide where to invest their money? Thousands of stocks are available in the United States, and thousands more on stock exchanges around the world. How do investors separate the successful companies from the unsuccessful companies?

The key source of information investors use to identify successful and unsuccessful companies is financial accounting—the subject of this book. As you read through the chapters, you'll begin to understand the information that financial accounting provides to investors making business decisions. And as the contrast between Dell and Polaroid demonstrates, the payoffs for understanding (or failing to understand) the financial position of a company can be quite large.

PART A

ACCOUNTING AS A MEASUREMENT/ COMMUNICATION PROCESS

Welcome to accounting. A common misconception about this course is that it is a math class, much like college algebra, calculus, or business statistics. You will soon see that this is *not* a math class. Don't say to yourself, "I'm not good at math so I probably won't be good at accounting." Though it's true that we use numbers heavily throughout each chapter, accounting is far more than adding, subtracting, and solving for unknown variables. So, what exactly is accounting? We'll take a close look at this next.

Defining Accounting

■ **LO1**
Describe the two primary functions of financial accounting.

Accounting is "the language of business." More precisely, accounting is a system of maintaining records of a company's operations and communicating that information to decision makers. Perhaps the earliest use of such systematic recordkeeping dates back thousands of years to ancient Mesopotamia (present-day Iraq), where records were kept of delivered agricultural products. Using accounting to maintain a record of multiple transactions allowed for better exchange among individuals and aided in the development of more complex societies.[1] In this class, you'll learn how to read, interpret, and communicate using the language of business.

Today, many millions of people every day must make informed decisions about companies. While investors and creditors (lenders) are the primary users of financial accounting information, there are many others. Illustration 1–1 identifies some of those people and examples of decisions they make about the companies.

ILLUSTRATION 1–1

Decisions People Make About Companies

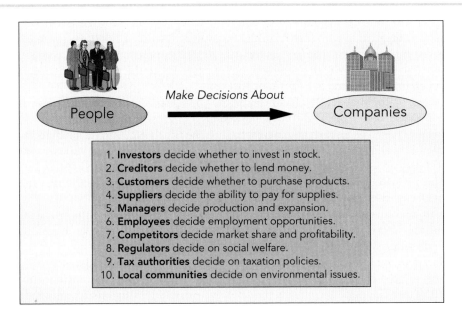

People   Make Decisions About   Companies

1. **Investors** decide whether to invest in stock.
2. **Creditors** decide whether to lend money.
3. **Customers** decide whether to purchase products.
4. **Suppliers** decide the ability to pay for supplies.
5. **Managers** decide production and expansion.
6. **Employees** decide employment opportunities.
7. **Competitors** decide market share and profitability.
8. **Regulators** decide on social welfare.
9. **Tax authorities** decide on taxation policies.
10. **Local communities** decide on environmental issues.

People and organizations need useful information in order to make good decisions. This is where accounting plays a key role. As Illustration 1–2 shows, **the functions of accounting are to *measure* the activities of the company and *communicate* those measurements to people.**

We classify accounting into two broad categories: managerial accounting and financial accounting. **Managerial accounting** deals with the methods accountants use to provide information to an organization's *internal* users—that is, its own managers. These are the subjects of another course.

---

[1]S. Basu and G. Waymire. 2006. Recordkeeping and Human Evolution. *Accounting Horizons* 20(3): 201–229.

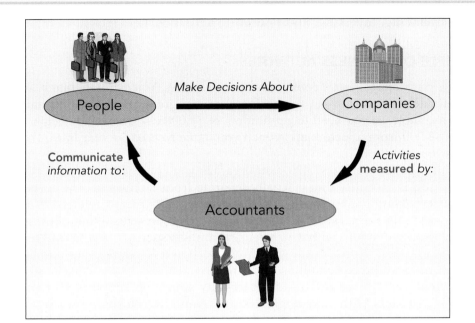

ILLUSTRATION 1–2
Functions of
Accounting

In this class, we focus on financial accounting. The two primary functions of financial accounting are to measure business activities of a company and to communicate those measurements to *external* parties for decision-making purposes. The two primary external users of financial accounting information (users outside the firm) are investors and creditors. **Investors** make decisions related to buying and selling the company's stock (shares of ownership): Is the company profitable? Will the company's stock increase in value? **Creditors** make decisions related to lending money to the company: Will the company be able to repay its debt when it comes due? Will it be able to pay interest in the meantime?

spiceland.mhhe.com/c1

User's Guide For learning objectives throughout the book, you will see boxed sections, like this one, titled *Key Point*. These boxed items will highlight the central focus of the learning objectives.

KEY POINT

The functions of financial accounting are to measure business activities of a company and to communicate information about those activities to investors and creditors and other outside users for decision-making purposes.

Business Activities to Measure

The first of financial accounting's functions is to measure business activities. A business engages in three fundamental activities—financing, investing, and operating.

- Financing activities are transactions involving external sources of funding. There are two basic sources of this external funding—the owners of the company who invest their own funds in the business, and creditors who lend money to the company. With this financing, the company engages in investing activities.
- Investing activities include the purchase and sale of (1) long-term resources such as land, buildings, equipment, and machinery and (2) any resources not directly related to a company's normal operations. Once these investments are in place, the company has the resources needed to run the business and can perform operating activities.
- Operating activities include transactions that relate to the primary operations of the company, such as providing products and services to customers and the associated costs of doing so, like utilities, taxes, advertising, wages, rent, and maintenance.

■ **LO2**
Identify the three fundamental business activities that financial accounting measures.

The first role of financial accounting is to measure (or keep a record of) a company's financing, investing, and operating activities. Let's look at an example.

EXAMPLE OF BUSINESS ACTIVITIES

Suppose you want to start a computer-repair business. You estimate that it will cost approximately $10,000 to get the business up and going. However, you have only $1,000 available, so you need to get funding of $9,000 elsewhere. You begin by borrowing $2,000 from a local bank, which you agree to repay a year later. Thus, the bank is your creditor.

To raise the remaining $7,000, you organize your business as a corporation. A corporation is an entity that is legally separate from its owners. The corporation raises external funding by selling shares of ownership (typically referred to as common stock) in the corporation. Each share of stock represents a unit of ownership. Many of the corporations with which you are familiar, such as **Coca-Cola, American Eagle, Apple Inc., Ford Motor Co., Microsoft,** and **Starbucks** have millions of stockholders and therefore millions of owners.

For your computer-repair business, let's say you issue 800 shares of common stock for $10 each. With your original $1,000, you buy 100 shares of stock, giving you one-eighth ownership in the corporation (your 100 shares ÷ 800 shares total). Other investors purchase the remaining 700 shares, giving them seven-eighths ownership in the company.

In this example, the *financing* activities of the company are cash inflows of $2,000 from creditors and $8,000 from investors.

Creditors (local bank)	$ 2,000	} Financing
Investors (you and others)	8,000	
	$10,000	

With this financing of $10,000, your company purchases a truck costing $6,000 and equipment costing $3,000. With these resources in place, you are ready to begin operations. You start by purchasing advertising in the local newspaper for $200 and paying for the first month's office rent of $800.

You've now engaged in the second and third types of business activities: Your *investing* activities include the purchase of the truck and equipment; they involve the purchase of long-term resources. Advertising and office rent are examples of *operating* activities; they are more directly related to normal operations.

Truck	$ 6,000	} Investing
Equipment	3,000	
Advertising	200	} Operating
Office rent	800	
	$10,000	

HOW TO MEASURE BUSINESS ACTIVITIES

How should accountants measure these business activities? In other words, what information would a company's investors and creditors be interested in knowing to make informed decisions about your computer-repair business? **Ultimately, investors and creditors want to know about the company's resources and their claims to those resources.** Accounting uses some conventional categories to describe such resources and claims.

Assets, liabilities, and stockholders' equity. We measure resources owned by a company as assets. Recall that with the start-up funds of $10,000, your computer-repair business bought a truck ($6,000) and equipment ($3,000). You will measure the $9,000 as assets. Other assets typical of most businesses include such items as cash, inventories, supplies, and buildings. Cash is a resource used to make purchases; inventories represent resources used to make product sales to customers; supplies include resources used to perform basic business functions; and buildings are resources used by employees as a location from which to operate a company.

As discussed earlier, two parties claim the resources of the company—creditors and investors. Amounts owed to creditors are liabilities. The computer-repair business has a liability of $2,000 to a local bank. Other examples of liabilities are amounts owed to suppliers, workers, utility companies, and governments (in the form of taxes). Liabilities must be paid by a specified date.

Investors, or owners, claim any resources of the company not owed to creditors. You can see this relationship in home ownership: Your house (an asset) is worth $300,000. The bank that helped finance its purchase holds a $200,000 mortgage (a liability). Your *equity* in the house is $100,000. For a corporation, we refer to owners' claims to resources as stockholders' equity, since stockholders are the owners of the corporation.

We express the relationship among the three measurement categories in what is called the basic accounting equation, depicted in Illustration 1–3. It shows that a company's resources equal creditors' and owners' claims to those resources.

User's Guide Pay close attention to the accounting categories we define here. These may be new terms for you. We promise that very soon they will be second nature to you.

Assets	=	Liabilities (creditors' claims)	+	Stockholders' Equity (owners' claims)
(resources)		(claims to resources)		

ILLUSTRATION 1–3

The Basic Accounting Equation

Another way to think about this relationship is to replace the parenthetical descriptions under each of the three parts of the equation:

Assets	=	Liabilities	+	Stockholders' Equity
(company owns)		(company owes)		(difference)

Also, as with any equation, we can move the components (by following mathematical rules you learned in high school). For example, to isolate stockholders' equity, we can subtract liabilities from both sides of the equal sign.

Assets	–	Liabilities	=	Stockholders' Equity
(company owns)		(company owes)		(difference)

Thus, the computer-repair business has assets of $9,000 but liabilities of $2,000. How much equity do stockholders have? They have $9,000 − $2,000, or $7,000.

The accounting equation illustrates a fundamental model of business valuation. The value of a company to its owners equals total resources of the company minus amounts owed to creditors. Creditors expect to receive only resources equal to the amount owed them. Stockholders, on the other hand, can claim all resources in excess of the amount owed to creditors.

Revenues, expenses, and dividends.   Of course, all businesses intend to increase the amount of their resources through their operations and eventually to own more than they owe. We broadly define such increases as profits. (Later, we'll define profits a bit more narrowly.) Because stockholders claim all resources in excess of amounts owed to creditors, profits of the company, which add to total resources, are claimed solely by stockholders, the owners of the company.

We calculate a company's profits by comparing its revenues and expenses. Revenues are the amounts earned from selling products or services to customers. For example, when your computer-repair business provides services to a customer, it earns revenues. When **McDonald's** sells you a burger, fries, and drink, McDonald's earns revenue.

However, as you've probably heard, "It takes money to make money." To operate your computer-repair business, for example, you purchased advertising ($200) and paid the first month's rent ($800). We record these amounts as expenses. Expenses are the costs of providing products and services. You'll record expenses of $1,000 for your computer-repair business.

When McDonald's sells you a Big Mac, it incurs expenses for two all-beef patties, special sauce, lettuce, cheese, pickles, onions, and a sesame-seed bun. McDonald's also pays the person who took your order, the cook behind the partition, and the person who cleans up after you're gone. Then there's the cost of having and maintaining the building, TV ads, expenses of the corporate headquarters, utilities, equipment maintenance, income taxes, interest on debt, and many, many more.

Common Terms Other common names for net income include *earnings* and *profit*.

We measure the difference between revenues and expenses as net income. All businesses want revenues to be greater than expenses, producing a positive net income. However, if expenses exceed revenues, as happens from time to time, the difference between them is a negative amount—a **net loss**. You'll notice the use of the term *net* to describe a company's profitability. In business, the term *net* is used often to describe the difference between two amounts. Here, we measure revenues *net* of (or minus) expenses to calculate the net income or net loss.

Illustration 1–4 reports McDonald's revenues, expenses, and net income from its operations around the world.

ILLUSTRATION 1–4

Revenue and Expenses for McDonald's Corporation, as of 2009

($ in millions)	Revenues	–	Expenses	=	Net Income
United States	$7,943.8	–	$4,712.1	=	$3,231.7
Europe	9,273.8	–	6,685.7	=	2,588.1
Asia/Pacific, Middle East, Africa	4,337.0	–	3,347.5	=	989.5

spiceland.mhhe.com/c2

Notice that McDonald's generates only about one-third of its revenues in the United States, but almost half its net income comes from the United States. This means that McDonald's is able to make more profit per dollar of revenue in the United States than anywhere else in the world.

If the corporation has positive net income, it typically will distribute to its owners, the stockholders, some of those profits. It does so by making cash payments to its stockholders (usually every three months), in payments called dividends. McDonald's, for example, has paid a dividend to stockholders every three months for over 30 years. In 2009, McDonald's paid dividends of $2.05 per share. If you owned 100 shares of McDonald's stock, you would have received $205.00 from McDonald's in cash. Unlike creditors, who lend money to the company in expectation of being repaid, stockholders are not guaranteed regular cash payments from the firm.

Match the term with the appropriate definition.

1. _____ Assets
2. _____ Liabilities
3. _____ Stockholders' equity
4. _____ Dividends
5. _____ Revenues
6. _____ Expenses

A. Costs of selling products or services.
B. Amounts earned from sales of products or services.
C. Amounts owed.
D. Distributions to stockholders.
E. Owners' claims to resources.
F. Resources owned.

Let's Review

User's Guide Let's Review exercises break each chapter into manageable review modules to enhance your learning.

Suggested Homework:
BE1-4;
E1-2, E1-3;
P1-2A&B

Solution:

1. F; 2. C; 3. E; 4. D; 5. B; 6. A

In summary, the measurement role of accounting is to create a record of the financing, investing, and operating activities of the company. To make this possible, the firm must maintain an accurate record of its assets, liabilities, stockholders' equity, revenues, expenses, and dividends. Be sure you understand the meaning of these items. We will refer to them throughout this book. Illustration 1–5 summarizes the business activities and the categories that measure them.

	Activities Related to:	Measurement Category
Financing Activities	• Borrowing • Stockholders' investment • Distributions to stockholders	• Liabilities • Stockholders' equity • Dividends
Investing Activities	• Resources owned by the company	• Assets
Operating Activities	• Sales to customers • Costs of selling to customers	• Revenues • Expenses

ILLUSTRATION 1–5

Business Activities and Their Measurement

KEY POINT

Financing activities include transactions with creditors and owners. Investing activities generally include the purchase or disposal of productive assets. Operating activities relate to earning revenues and incurring expenses.

As you learn to measure business activities, you will often find it helpful to consider both sides of the transaction: When someone pays cash, someone else receives cash; when someone borrows money, another lends money. Likewise, an expense for one company can be a revenue for another company; one company's asset can be another company's liability. Throughout this book, you will find discussions of the "flip side" of certain transactions, indicated by the icon you see here in the margin. In addition, certain homework problems, also marked by the icon, will ask you specifically to address the "flip side" in your computations. (See page 91 for the first such example.)

Flip Side

FORMS OF BUSINESS ORGANIZATION

The computer-repair business introduced earlier was organized as a corporation. Other common business forms include sole proprietorships and partnerships. A **sole proprietorship** is a business owned by one person, whereas a **partnership** is a business owned by two or more persons. If you had decided to start the computer-repair business without outside investors, you could have formed a sole proprietorship. Or, you and a friend could have formed a partnership.

To decide on a form of business organization, you need to understand their advantages and disadvantages. The major *advantage* of the corporate form of business is the limited liability of the corporation's stockholders. **Limited liability** means the stockholders are not held personally responsible for the financial obligations of the corporation. If the business fails, stockholders can lose no more than the investment they already made by purchasing stock. In other words, stockholders are not obligated to pay the corporation's remaining debts out of their own pockets. In contrast, if a sole proprietorship or partnership is unable to pay its legal obligations to creditors, the owner(s) may be forced to surrender personal assets, such as homes, cars, computers, and furniture to satisfy those debts.

The *disadvantage* of the corporate form of business is the higher tax burden on the owners. Generally, the corporate income tax rate is greater than the individual income tax rate. Moreover, a corporation's income is taxed twice—first when the company earns it and pays corporate income taxes on it, and then again when stockholders pay personal income taxes on amounts the firm distributes to them as dividends. This is called *double taxation.* Any income of a sole proprietorship or a partnership is taxed only once, and at the personal income tax rate.

Because most of the largest companies in the United States are corporations, in this book we will primarily focus on accounting from a corporation's perspective. Focusing on corporations also highlights the importance of financial accounting—to measure and communicate activities of a company when owners (shareholders) are typically separated from management of the company. (A more detailed discussion of the advantages and disadvantages of a corporation can be found in Chapter 10.)

Communicating through Financial Statements

■ **LO3**
Discuss how financial accounting information is communicated through financial statements.

We've discussed that different business activities produce assets, liabilities, stockholders' equity, dividends, revenues, and expenses, and that the first important role of financial accounting is to record the relevant transactions of a company. Its second vital role is to communicate these business activities to those outside the company. The primary means of communicating business activities is through financial statements. Financial statements are periodic reports published by the company for the purpose of providing information to external users. We have four primary financial statements:

1. Income statement
2. Statement of stockholders' equity
3. Balance sheet
4. Statement of cash flows

These financial statements give investors and creditors the key information they need when making decisions about a company: Should I buy the company's stock? Should I lend money to the company? Is management efficiently operating the company? Without these financial statements, it would be difficult for those outside the company to see what's going on inside.

Let's go through a simple set of financial statements to see what they look like. We'll start with the income statement of a simple, fictitious company. Actual companies' financial statements often report items you haven't yet encountered. However, because actual companies' financial information will be useful in helping you understand certain accounting topics, we'll sample them often throughout the book.

THE INCOME STATEMENT

The income statement is a financial statement that reports the company's revenues and expenses over an interval of time. It shows whether the company was able to generate enough revenue to cover the expenses of running the business. If revenues exceed expenses, then the company reports *net income:*

$$\textbf{Revenues} - \textbf{Expenses} = \textbf{Net income}$$

If expenses exceed revenues, then the company reports a *net loss.*

Now, let's look at our fictitious company. On January 1 Eagle Golf Academy begins operations by offering lessons to junior golfers. The lessons include a variety of skills intended to develop players for a top university golf program and perhaps even one day playing on the PGA Tour. For the first month of operations, Eagle Golf Academy reports its income statement as shown in Illustration 1–6.

Common Terms Other common names for the income statement include *statement of operations* and *statement of income.*

EAGLE GOLF ACADEMY
Income Statement
For the month ended January 31

Revenues:	
Service revenue	$6,360
Expenses:	
Salaries expense	3,100
Rent expense	500
Supplies expense	800
Interest expense	100
Utilities expense	960
Other expenses	400
Total expenses	5,860
Net income	$ 500

ILLUSTRATION 1–6

Income Statement for Eagle Golf Academy

Notice the heading of the income statement: It includes the company's name, the title of the financial statement, and the time period covered by the financial statement. The three major captions in the income statement include **revenues** and **expenses,** discussed earlier, and the difference between them—**net income.**

We can determine from the income statement that for the month of January Eagle Golf Academy earns revenues of $6,360. This means that Eagle provides golf training and bills customers for a total of $6,360. Total expenses associated with generating those revenues, including salaries, rent, supplies, and other items listed here, are $5,860. These are typical costs that we might expect of any company. The income statement shows that revenues *exceed* expenses ($6,360 is greater than $5,860), and thus the academy is able to report net income of $500.

The fact that Eagle reports a positive net income is, in some sense, a signal of the company's success. The company is able to charge its customers a price higher than the costs of running the business. Do you assume most companies sell their products and services for a profit? It's not as easy as you might think. In recent years, **American Airlines, OfficeMax, Eastman Kodak, Ford Motor Co., Goodyear Tire and Rubber, ConocoPhillips, CBS, U.S. Cellular, Gateway, Sirius Satellite Radio, Sprint PCS, Blockbuster**, and hundreds of others have reported net losses.

KEY POINT

The income statement compares revenues and expenses for the current period to assess the company's ability to earn a profit from running its operations.

Decision Point

User's Guide *Decision Points* in each chapter highlight specific decisions related to chapter topics that can be made using financial accounting information.

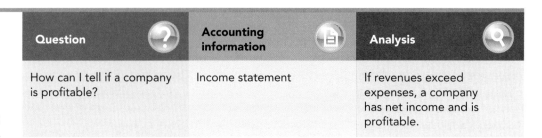

Question ?	Accounting information	Analysis
How can I tell if a company is profitable?	Income statement	If revenues exceed expenses, a company has net income and is profitable.

THE STATEMENT OF STOCKHOLDERS' EQUITY

The statement of stockholders' equity is a financial statement that summarizes the changes in stockholders' equity over an interval of time. The reporting period coincides with the time period covered by the income statement.

Stockholders' equity has two primary components—common stock and retained earnings. Recall that common stock represents amounts invested by stockholders (the owners of the corporation) when they purchase shares of stock. Common stock is an *external* source of stockholders' equity.

Retained earnings, on the other hand, is an *internal* source of stockholders' equity. Retained earnings represents the cumulative amount of net income, earned over the life of the company, that has *not* been distributed to stockholders as dividends. Since all profits of the company are owned by stockholders, any net income in excess of dividends paid to stockholders represents stockholders' equity retained in the business. Thus, both common stock and retained earnings make up total stockholders' equity. This concept is shown in Illustration 1–7.

Common Terms
Another common name for retained earnings is *profits reinvested in the business.*

ILLUSTRATION 1–7

Components of Stockholders' Equity

You will notice that some financial statements have parentheses around some amounts. As you will learn as you study this book, accounting convention uses parentheses to highlight negative amounts (such as the subtraction of dividends here) or to show cash outflows (which we will point out later).

Suppose Eagle obtains financing in January by issuing common stock for $25,000. This transaction will distribute shares of common stock to investors in return for the company's receiving cash of $25,000. Let's say that at the end of January, Eagle pays dividends of $200 to stockholders. Illustration 1–8 (next page) shows the statement of stockholders' equity for Eagle Golf Academy.

When the company begins operations on January 1, the balances of common stock and retained earnings are **$0**. Once the company issues common stock, its balance increases to **$25,000**. The balance of retained earnings always increases by the amount of net income less any dividends paid to stockholders—here, $500 − $200 = $300. **The name *retained earnings* is descriptive. The balance of retained earnings represents the amount of "earnings retained" (not paid out in the form of dividends) over the life of the company.**

EAGLE GOLF ACADEMY Statement of Stockholders' Equity For the month ended January 31			
	Common Stock	Retained Earnings	Total Stockholders' Equity
Beginning balance (Jan. 1)	$ -0-	$ -0-	$ -0-
Issuance of common stock	25,000		25,000
Add: **Net income for January**		500	500
Less: Dividends		(200)	(200)
Ending balance (Jan. 31)	$25,000	$300	$25,300

ILLUSTRATION 1–8

Statement of Stockholders' Equity for Eagle Golf Academy

Retained earnings includes net income less dividends. Note that the items shown here in blue come from the income statement.

COMMON MISTAKE

Dividends represent the payment of cash but are not considered an expense in running the business. Students sometimes mistakenly include the amount of dividends as an expense in the income statement, rather than as a distribution of net income in the statement of stockholders' equity.

User's Guide Throughout each chapter, you will see sections titled *Common Mistake.* Information in these boxes will help you avoid common mistakes on exams, quizzes, and homework.

By adding common stock and the retained earnings of $300, we calculate the balance of total stockholders' equity at January 31 to be **$25,300**. In accounting terms, this amount represents the value of the firm to its owners, the stockholders. The company creates value *externally* through investment by owners (common stock) and *internally* by generating and retaining profits (retained earnings).

KEY POINT

The statement of stockholders' equity reports information related to changes in common stock and retained earnings each period. The change in retained earnings equals net income less dividends for the period.

Question	Accounting information	Analysis	
Was the change in company value (stockholders' equity) the result of external or internal sources?	Statement of stockholders' equity	When a company sells common stock, company value increases due to external sources (stockholders). When a company has profits during the year in excess of dividends paid, company value increases due to internal sources (company operations).	**Decision Point**

THE BALANCE SHEET

The balance sheet is a financial statement that presents the financial position of the company on a particular date. The financial position of a company is summarized by the basic accounting equation (see Illustration 1–3): **Assets = Liabilities + Stockholders' Equity.** As discussed earlier, this equation provides a fundamental model of business valuation. Assets are the resources owned by the company, and liabilities are amounts owed to creditors. Stockholders have equity in the company to the extent that assets exceed liabilities. Creditors also need to understand the balance sheet; it's the company's assets that will be used to pay liabilities (the amounts due creditors) as they become due.

Illustration 1–9 shows the balance sheet of Eagle Golf Academy. The first thing to notice is the time period included in the heading. Recall that the income statement and statement of stockholders' equity both show activity over an *interval of time*. The balance sheet, in contrast, reports assets, liabilities, and stockholders' equity at a *point in time*. For example, Eagle's income statement shows revenue and expense activity occurring *from* January 1 to January 31; its balance sheet shows assets, liabilities, and stockholders' equity of the company *on* January 31.

> The income statement is like a video (shows events over time), whereas a balance sheet is like a photograph (shows events at a point in time).

ILLUSTRATION 1–9
Balance Sheet for Eagle Golf Academy

Total assets must equal total liabilities and stockholders' equity.

We show the stockholders' equity items in purple here, to indicate they came from the statement of stockholders' equity (Illustration 1–8).

EAGLE GOLF ACADEMY
Balance Sheet
January 31

Assets		Liabilities	
Cash	$ 6,200	Accounts payable	$ 2,300
Accounts receivable	2,700	Salaries payable	300
Supplies	1,500	Interest payable	100
Equipment, net	23,600	Utilities payable	960
Other assets	5,500	Notes payable	10,000
		Other liabilities	540
		Total liabilities	14,200
		Stockholders' Equity	
		Common stock	25,000
		Retained earnings	300
		Total stockholders' equity	**25,300**
Total assets	$39,500	Total liabilities and stockholders' equity	$39,500

Common Terms
Another common name for the balance sheet is *statement of financial position*.

For Eagle Golf Academy on January 31, total assets equal $39,500 and include some of the typical resources owned by most businesses, such as cash, supplies, and equipment. You'll learn about many other assets as you go through this book. Total liabilities equal $14,200 and include amounts owed to regular vendors (accounts payable), as well as amounts owed for other items such as employee salaries, interest, and utilities. As you'll begin to learn, many liabilities are referred to as "payables" to signify amounts that must be paid.

The difference between assets and liabilities of **$25,300** represents stockholders' equity. Total stockholders' equity includes the amount of common stock plus the amount of retained earnings from the statement of stockholders' equity. Notice that the amounts listed in the balance sheet show that the accounting equation balances:

Assets	=	Liabilities	+	Stockholders' Equity
(resources)		(creditors' claims)		(owners' claims)
$39,500	=	$14,200	+	$25,300

KEY POINT

The balance sheet demonstrates that the company's resources (assets) equal creditors' claims (liabilities) plus owners' claims (stockholders' equity) to those resources.

Decision Point

Question	Accounting information	Analysis
What are creditors' claims and owners' claims to the company's resources?	Balance sheet	The amount of total liabilities equals creditors' claims to the company's resources. The extent to which total assets exceed total liabilities represents owners' claims.

THE STATEMENT OF CASH FLOWS

The statement of cash flows is a financial statement that measures activities involving cash receipts and cash payments over an interval of time. We can classify all cash transactions into three categories that correspond to the three fundamental business activities—operating, investing, and financing—we discussed earlier in the chapter:

- **Operating cash flows** include cash receipts and cash payments for transactions involving revenues and expenses.
- **Investing cash flows** generally include cash transactions for the purchase and sale of investments and productive long-term assets. Long-term assets are resources owned by a company that are thought to provide benefits for more than one year.
- **Financing cash flows** include cash transactions with lenders, such as borrowing money and repaying debt, and with stockholders, such as issuing stock and paying dividends.

Decision Maker's Perspective

The statement of cash flows can be an important source of information to investors and creditors. For example, investors use the relationship between net income (revenues minus expenses) and operating cash flows (cash flows from revenue and expense activities) to forecast a company's future profitability. Creditors compare operating cash flows and investing cash flows to assess a company's ability to repay debt. Financing activities provide information to investors and creditors about the mix of external financing of the company. ●

User's Guide Decision Maker's Perspective sections discuss the usefulness of accounting information to decision makers such as investors, creditors, and company managers.

Illustration 1–10 (next page) provides the statement of cash flows for Eagle Golf Academy. Notice that the three sections in the statement of cash flows show the types of inflows and outflows of cash during the period. Inflows are shown as positive amounts; outflows are shown in parentheses to indicate negative cash flows. The final line in each section shows, in the right-most column, the difference between inflows and outflows as *net cash flow* for that type of activity.

 KEY POINT

The statement of cash flows reports cash transactions from operating, investing, and financing activities.

ILLUSTRATION 1–10

Statement of Cash Flows for Eagle Golf Academy

EAGLE GOLF ACADEMY Statement of Cash Flows For the month ended January 31		
Cash Flows from Operating Activities		
Cash inflows:		
From customers	$ 4,200	
Cash outflows:		
For salaries	(2,800)	
For rent	(6,000)	
Net cash flows from operating activities		($4,600)
Cash Flows from Investing Activities		
Purchase equipment	(24,000)	
Net cash flows from investing activities		(24,000)
Cash Flows from Financing Activities		
Issue common stock	25,000	
Borrow from bank	10,000	
Pay dividends	(200)	
Net cash flows from financing activities		34,800
Net increase in cash		6,200
Cash at the beginning of the month		-0-
Cash at the end of the month		$6,200

Remember, amounts in parentheses indicate outflows of cash, consistent with accounting convention.

The total of the net cash flows from operating, investing, and financing activities equals the *net change in cash* during the period. For Eagle, that net change in cash for January was an increase of **$6,200**. To this change, we add the beginning balance of cash. Because this is the first month of operations for Eagle, cash at the beginning of the month is zero. Thus, the ending balance of cash is the same as that reported in the balance sheet in Illustration 1–9. This reconciliation of the beginning and ending cash balances emphasizes that the statement of cash flows explains *why* the cash reported in the balance sheet changed.

THE LINKS AMONG FINANCIAL STATEMENTS

The four financial statements are linked, because events that are reported in one financial statement often affect amounts reported in another. Many times, a single business transaction, such as receiving cash from a customer when providing services, will affect more than one of the financial statements. Providing services to a customer, for example, results in revenues recorded in the income statement, which are used to calculate net income. Net income, in turn, is reported in the calculation of retained earnings in the statement of stockholders' equity. Then, the ending balance of retained earnings is reported in the balance sheet. **Thus, any transaction that affects the income statement ultimately affects the balance sheet through the balance of retained earnings.** The cash received from customers will be reported as part of the ending cash balance in the balance sheet and as part of operating cash flows in the statement of cash flows.

Illustration 1–11 shows the links among the financial statements of Eagle Golf Academy in Illustrations 1–6, 1–8, 1–9, and 1–10. Link (1) shows that net income from the income statement is reported in the statement of stockholders' equity as part of the calculation of retained earnings. Link (2) shows that after we calculate the balance of retained earnings, the amount of total stockholders' equity can be reported in the balance sheet. Finally, link (3) demonstrates that the balance of cash in the balance sheet equals the amount of cash reported in the statement of cash flows.

ILLUSTRATION 1–11
Relationship between Financial Statements

[1] Notice that the amount of net income on the income statement reappears in the statement of stockholders' equity.

[2] Notice that the ending balance in the statement of stockholders' equity reappears in the balance sheet.

[3] Notice that the amount of cash in the balance sheet reappears as the ending cash balance in the statement of cash flows.

 KEY POINT

All transactions that affect revenues or expenses reported in the income statement ultimately affect the balance sheet through the balance in retained earnings.

spiceland.mhhe.com/c3

OTHER INFORMATION REPORTED TO OUTSIDERS

Financial statements provide a summary of the most important financial accounting information. Two other sources of information provide important detail: (1) management's discussion and analysis and (2) note disclosures to the financial statements. Publicly traded firms are required to report both of these items in their annual reports, along with the financial statements we've discussed.

The **management discussion and analysis** (MD&A) section typically includes management's views on significant events, trends, and uncertainties pertaining to the company's operations and resources. **Note disclosures** offer additional information either to explain the information presented in the financial statements or to provide information not included in the financial statements. For example, companies are required to report total revenues in the income statement, but they also often report revenues itemized by geographic region in a note disclosure. We'll discuss these items throughout the book.

Let's Review

spiceland.mhhe.com/t1

Test your understanding of what you've read so far. The Computer Shop repairs laptops, desktops, and mainframe computers. On December 31, 2012, the company reports the following year-end amounts:

Assets:	Cash	$10,000	Revenues:	Service	$65,000
	Supplies	8,000			
	Equipment, net	26,000			
			Expenses:	Rent	6,000
Liabilities:	Accounts payable	4,000		Supplies	14,000
	Notes payable	10,000		Salaries	40,000

Additional information:

a. The balance of retained earnings at the beginning of the year is $7,000.

b. The company pays dividends of $1,000 on December 31, 2012.

c. Common stock is $15,000 at the beginning of the year, and additional shares are issued for $4,000 during 2012.

Suggested Homework:
BE1-5, BE1-6;
E1-6, E1-7, E1-8;
P1-3A&B, P1-5A&B

Required:

Prepare the (1) income statement, (2) statement of stockholders' equity, and (3) balance sheet.

Solution:

1. Income statement:

THE COMPUTER SHOP
Income Statement
For the year ended Dec. 31, 2012

Revenues:	
Service revenue	$65,000
Expenses:	
Rent expense	6,000
Supplies expense	14,000
Salaries expense	40,000
Net income	$ 5,000

2. Statement of stockholders' equity:

THE COMPUTER SHOP
Statement of Stockholders' Equity
For the year ended Dec. 31, 2012

	Common Stock	Retained Earnings	Total Stockholders' Equity
Beginning balance (Jan. 1)	$15,000	$ 7,000	$22,000
Issuance of common stock	4,000		4,000
Add: Net income		5,000	5,000
Less: Dividends		(1,000)	(1,000)
Ending balance (Dec. 31)	$19,000	$11,000	$30,000

3. Balance sheet:

THE COMPUTER SHOP
Balance Sheet
December 31, 2012

Assets		Liabilities	
Cash	$10,000	Accounts payable	$ 4,000
Supplies	8,000	Notes payable	10,000
Equipment	26,000	**Stockholders' Equity**	
		Common stock	19,000
		Retained earnings	11,000
Total assets	$44,000	Total liabilities and stockholders' equity	$44,000

FINANCIAL ACCOUNTING INFORMATION

To this point, you've had a simple, first look at how companies measure and communicate financial information to external users. Subsequent chapters will provide an even more detailed view of this measurement/communication process. However, before proceeding, it's important to first consider why we are studying financial accounting. Does it matter? In other words, does the use of financial accounting information result in better business decisions?

Is Financial Accounting Important?

One of the rewarding things about studying financial accounting is that it does matter! The concepts in this course have an impact on everyday business decisions as well as wide-ranging economic consequences. We'll see an example of this next and then more examples throughout the rest of this book.

■ LO4
Describe the role that financial accounting plays in the efficient distribution of society's resources.

Most prospering economies in the world today are structured around free markets. In free markets, firms are allowed to compete and customers are free to choose from a variety of products and services. From which company do you prefer to buy a notebook computer—**Dell**, **Hewlett-Packard**, or **Apple**? Competition among these companies helps determine the prices they charge customers and the amounts they spend on computer components, salaries, manufacturing and distribution facilities, warranties, research and development, and other business-related activities. Can these companies offer you the notebook computer you want for a price above their costs? If they can, they'll earn a profit and stay in business. If they cannot, they'll eventually go out of business. Because companies know they are directly competing with each other, they work harder and more efficiently to please you, the customer.

Successful companies use their resources efficiently to sell products and services for a profit. When a company is able to make a profit, investors and creditors are willing to transfer their resources to it, and the company will expand its profitable operations even further.

Unsuccessful companies either offer lower-quality products and services or do not efficiently keep their costs low. In either case, they are not profitable. When a company is unprofitable, investors will neither invest in nor lend to the firm. Without these sources of financing, eventually the company will fail. Clearly, you don't want to invest in an unsuccessful company and then watch your investment shrink as the company loses your money. But how do investors and creditors know the successful companies from the unsuccessful companies? Here's where financial accounting enters the picture. Investors and creditors rely heavily on financial accounting information in making investment and lending decisions.

As Illustration 1–12 demonstrates, investors and creditors have cash they are willing to invest. How do they decide which investment option provides the better opportunity? Most often, they analyze companies' financial accounting information in making their decision. In fact, **financial accounting information is essential to making good business decisions.**

ILLUSTRATION 1–12

Use of Financial Accounting Information in Investing and Lending Decisions

KEY POINT

Financial accounting serves an important role by providing information useful in investment and lending decisions.

To demonstrate the importance of financial accounting information to investment decisions, we can look at the relationship between changes in stock prices and changes in net income over 20 years. As an investor, you will make money from an increase in the stock price of a company in which you invest (you can sell the stock for more than you bought it). So as an investor, you are looking for companies whose stock price is likely to increase. Is there a way to find such companies? Interestingly, there is: **No other single piece of company information better explains companies' stock price performance than does financial accounting net income,** the bottom line in the income statement.

What if you were able to accurately predict the direction of companies' changes in net income over the next year—that is, whether it would increase or decrease—and then you invested $1,000 in companies that were going to have an *increase?* In contrast, what if instead you invested in companies that would have a *decrease* in net income? Illustration 1–13 shows what would happen to your $1,000 investment over 20 years for each scenario.

ILLUSTRATION 1–13

Relationship between Changes in Stock Prices and Changes in Net Income over a 20-Year Period

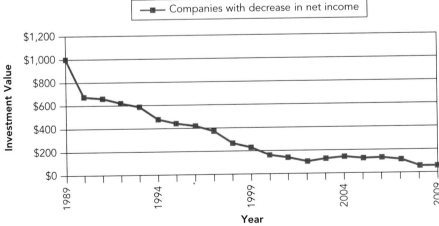

*Amounts in this chart represent the investment growth based on the median stock return of each group each year. Companies included in this analysis are all U.S. companies with listed stocks, which averages about 6,000 companies per year.

You can see that if you had invested $1,000 in companies with an increase in net income, your investment would have increased to $18,225 over the 20-year period. (The amount would have been much higher without the extraordinary events surrounding the financial crisis in 2008.) If instead you had invested $1,000 in companies with a decrease in net income, your $1,000 investment would have shrunk to $49 over this same period. This dramatic difference in the value of the investment demonstrates the importance of financial accounting information to investors. This book will provide you a thorough understanding of how net income is calculated and presented in financial statements. As you can see from the charts above, if you are able to predict the change in financial accounting's measure of profitability—net income—then you can predict the change in stock prices as well.

Investors and creditors also use information reported in the balance sheet. Consider a company's total liabilities, often referred to as *total debt*. Expanding debt levels limit management's ability to respond quickly and effectively to business situations. The "overhanging" debt, which involves legal obligation of repayment, restricts management's ability to engage in new profit-generating activities. Increased debt levels also increase interest payment burdens on the company. Failure to pay interest or to repay debt can result in creditors forcing the company to declare bankruptcy and go out of business. Understandably, then, investors and creditors keep a close eye on the company's debt level and its ability to repay.

KEY POINT

No single piece of company information better explains companies' stock price performance than does financial accounting net income. A company's debt level is an important indicator of management's ability to respond to business situations and the possibility of bankruptcy.

Rules of Financial Accounting

Recall that accounting serves two main functions in our society: It (1) measures business activities and (2) communicates those measurements to investors and creditors. Although this process might seem straightforward, it's not always. How do we measure assets? When do we record revenues? What do we classify as an expense? How should we present financial statements? These are all important issues, and the answers are not always simple.

■ LO5
Explain the term generally accepted accounting principles (GAAP) and describe the role of GAAP in financial accounting.

Because financial accounting information is so vital to investors and creditors, formal reporting standards have been established. All companies that sell their stock to the public must follow these rules and must publish financial statements in accordance with those rules. The rules of financial accounting are called generally accepted accounting principles, often abbreviated as GAAP (pronounced *gap*). The fact that all companies use these same rules is critical to financial statement users. It allows them to accurately *compare* financial information among companies when they are making decisions about where to lend or invest their resources.

CURRENT STANDARD SETTING

Today, financial accounting and reporting standards in the United States are established primarily by the Financial Accounting Standards Board (FASB) (pronounced either by the letters themselves or as *faz-be*). The FASB is an independent, private-sector body with full-time voting members and a very large support staff. Members include representatives from the accounting profession, large corporations, financial analysts, accounting educators, and government agencies.

Not all countries follow the same accounting and reporting standards. For example, accounting practices in the United Kingdom differ from those in the United States, and those in the United States differ from those in Japan. In recent years,

For information about the activities of the Financial Accounting Standards Board, see its website, *www.fasb.org*.

the accounting profession has undertaken a project whose goal is to eliminate differences in accounting standards around the world. The standard-setting body responsible for this convergence effort is the International Accounting Standards Board (IASB), as detailed in the following box.

 INTERNATIONAL FINANCIAL REPORTING STANDARDS (IFRS)

User's Guide Boxed sections on *International Financial Reporting Standards* (IFRS) are included throughout the text to emphasize the growing importance of international accounting standards throughout the world. They discuss specific instances in which U.S. GAAP and international standards differ. Appendix E at the back of the book provides more detail about differences between IFRS and U.S. GAAP.

For information about the activities of the International Accounting Standards Board, see its website, **www.iasb.org**.

The global counterpart to the FASB is the International Accounting Standards Board (IASB). In many ways, this organization functions like the FASB. The IASB's objectives are (1) to develop a single set of high-quality, understandable global accounting standards, (2) to promote the use of those standards, and (3) to bring about the convergence of national accounting standards and international accounting standards around the world. In 2002, the FASB and IASB signed the Norwalk Agreement, formalizing their commitment to convergence of U.S. and international accounting standards. The standards being developed and promoted by the IASB are called International Financial Reporting Standards (IFRS) (pronounced either by the letters or as *eye-furs*).

For more discussion, see Appendix E.

More than 100 countries have chosen to forgo their own country-specific standards and either require or allow International Financial Reporting Standards as their national standards. That movement, coupled with the convergence of U.S. GAAP and IFRS, has caused many to predict that soon both sets of rules, or perhaps only IFRS, will be acceptable for financial reporting in the United States.

 KEY POINT

The rules of financial accounting are called generally accepted accounting principles (GAAP). The Financial Accounting Standards Board (FASB) is an independent, private body that has primary responsibility for the establishment of GAAP in the United States.

HISTORICAL PERSPECTIVE ON STANDARD SETTING

Pressures on the accounting profession to establish uniform accounting standards began to surface after the stock market crash of 1929. The Dow Jones Industrial Average, a major stock market index in the United States, fell 40% over the period September 3 to October 29 that year. The Dow bottomed out in July 1932, after losing 89% of its value.

Many blamed financial accounting for the stock market crash and the ensuing Great Depression of the 1930s. At the time of the crash, accounting practices and reporting procedures were not well established, providing the opportunity for companies to engage in inaccurate financial reporting to enhance their reported performance. This led to many stocks being valued too highly. As investors began to recognize this, their confidence in the stock market fell. They panicked and sold stocks in a frenzy. The Dow did not reach precrash levels again until 1954.

The 1933 Securities Act and the 1934 Securities Exchange Act were designed to restore investor confidence in financial accounting. The 1933 act sets forth accounting and disclosure requirements for initial offerings of securities (stocks and bonds). The 1934 act created a government agency, the **Securities and Exchange Commission (SEC).** The 1934 act gives the SEC the power to require companies that publicly trade their stock to prepare periodic financial statements for distribution to investors and creditors.

While Congress has given the SEC both the power and the responsibility for setting accounting and reporting standards for publicly traded companies, the SEC has delegated the primary responsibility for setting accounting standards to the private sector, currently the FASB. Note that the SEC delegated only the responsibility, not the authority, to set these standards. The power still lies with the SEC. If the SEC does not agree with a particular standard issued by the FASB, it can force a change in the standard. In fact, it has done so in the past.

THE ROLE OF THE AUDITOR

It is the responsibility of management to apply GAAP when communicating with investors and creditors through financial statements. Unfortunately, however, sometimes those in charge of preparing financial statements do not always follow the rules. Instead, some purposely provide misleading financial accounting information, commonly referred to as "cooking the books." The phrase implies that the accounting records ("books") have been presented in an altered form ("cooked"). Managers may cook the books for several reasons, such as to hide the poor operating performance of the company or to increase their personal wealth at stockholders' expense.

To help ensure that management has in fact appropriately applied GAAP, the SEC requires independent outside verification of the financial statements of publicly traded companies. Such independent examination is done by auditors, who are hired by a company as an independent party to express a professional opinion of the accuracy of that company's financial statements. They are not employees of the company they are auditing. Auditors provide an independent opinion of the extent to which financial statements are prepared in compliance with GAAP. If they find mistakes or fraudulent reporting behavior, auditors require the company to correct all significant information before issuing financial statements.

Illustration 1–14 presents an excerpt from the report of the independent auditors for **Dell'**s financial statements. The auditor's report indicates that Dell's financial statements for the period mentioned have been prepared in conformity with GAAP.

DELL INCORPORATED
Report of Independent Registered Public Accounting Firm

To the Board of Directors and
Shareholders of Dell Inc.:

In our opinion, the consolidated financial statements listed in the accompanying index present fairly, in all material respects, the financial position of Dell Inc. and its subsidiaries at January 29, 2010, and January 30, 2009, and the results of their operations and their cash flows for each of the three years in the period ended January 29, 2010, in conformity with accounting principles generally accepted in the United States of America.

Our audits of financial statements included examining, on a test basis, evidence supporting the amounts and disclosures in the financial statements, assessing the accounting principles used and significant estimates made by management, and evaluating the overall financial statement presentation. We believe that our audits provide a reasonable basis for our opinion.

ILLUSTRATION 1–14

Excerpts from the 2009 Independent Auditor's Report of Dell Incorporated

User's Guide In this book, information from actual companies is illustrated using a flipped page in the lower-right corner.

Auditors play a major role in investors' and creditors' decisions by adding credibility to a company's financial statements.

OBJECTIVES OF FINANCIAL ACCOUNTING

After measuring business activities and communicating those measurements to investors and creditors, what do financial accountants hope to have achieved? What benefit will their services have brought to users of financial statements? The FASB has explicitly stated the specific objectives of financial accounting. These objectives are presented in Illustration 1–15.

ILLUSTRATION 1–15

Objectives of Financial Accounting

Financial accounting should provide information that:

1. Is useful to investors and creditors in making decisions.
2. Helps to predict cash flows.
3. Tells about economic resources, claims to resources, and changes in resources and claims.

The first objective is specific to investors and creditors. In addition to those users, though, financial accounting information is likely to have general usefulness to other groups of external users, who are interested in essentially the same financial aspects of a business as are investors and creditors. Some of these other groups were discussed in Illustration 1–1.

The second objective refers to the specific cash flow information needs of investors and creditors. The third objective emphasizes the need for information about economic resources (assets) and claims to those resources (liabilities and stockholders' equity) and their changes over time.

 KEY POINT

The primary objective of financial accounting is to provide useful information to investors and creditors in making decisions.

Underlying these three key objectives is a conceptual framework that is the foundation upon which financial accounting is built. We discuss the FASB's conceptual framework in detail in the appendix to this chapter.

An Ethical Foundation

Like all structures, accounting requires a strong foundation. For accounting, part of that foundation is the ethical behavior of those who practice its rules. You have probably encountered the topic of ethics in other business courses. Ethics refers to a code or moral system that provides criteria for evaluating right and wrong behavior. Investors, creditors, government, and the general public rely on general ethical behavior among those who record and report the financial activities of businesses. A lack of public trust in financial reporting can undermine business and the economy. Indeed, the dramatic collapse of **Enron** in 2001 and the dismantling of the international public accounting firm of **Arthur Andersen** in 2002 severely shook investors' confidence in the stock market. Some questioned the credibility of corporate America as well as the accounting profession itself.

Public outrage over accounting scandals at high-profile companies increased the pressure on lawmakers to pass measures that would restore credibility and investor confidence in the financial reporting process. These pressures resulted in the issuance of the Public Company Accounting Reform and Investor Protection Act of 2002, commonly referred to as the Sarbanes-Oxley Act (SOX), named for the two congressmen who sponsored the bill. The Sarbanes-Oxley Act provides for the regulation of auditors and the types of services they furnish to clients, increases accountability of corporate executives, addresses conflicts of interest for securities analysts, and provides for stiff criminal penalties for violators. These increased requirements have dramatically increased the need for good accounting and, at the same time, highlighted the value of accounting information to investors and creditors. We discuss the specific provisions of SOX in more detail in Chapter 4.

Important as such legislation is in supporting the ethical foundation of accounting, it is equally important that accountants themselves have their own personal standards for ethical conduct. You cannot, though, just go out and suddenly obtain ethics when you need them. ("I'd like a pound of ethics, please.") Rather, accountants need to *develop* their ability to identify ethical situations and know the difference between right and wrong in the context of the accounting topics you will learn in this course. One of the keys to ethical decision making is having an appreciation for how your actions affect others.

When you face ethical dilemmas in your professional life (and indeed in your personal life), you can apply the following simple framework as you think through what to do:

1. Identify the ethical situation and the people who will be affected (the stakeholders).
2. Specify the options for alternative courses of action.
3. Understand the impact of each option on the stakeholders.
4. Make a decision.

Throughout the book, we will discuss some ethical decisions relating to accounting and will make clear their financial impact. These discussions will give you opportunities to practice some ethical decision making in a classroom setting.

 ETHICAL DILEMMA

You have been the manager of a local restaurant for the past five years. Because of increased competition, you notice you're getting fewer customers. Despite all your attempts to attract new customers and cut costs, the restaurant's profitability continues to decline. The restaurant owner tells you that if this year's profit is lower than last year's, you'll lose your job.

When preparing financial statements at the end of the year, you notice that this year's profit *is* lower. You know that by purposely understating certain expenses, you can falsely report higher profits to the owner for this year. That will allow you to keep your job for at least one more year and look for a new job in the meantime.

What should you do? What if you really believe the lower profitability is caused by factors outside your control? Would this make the false reporting acceptable?

User's Guide
Throughout the book, you will see boxed discussions of *Ethical Dilemmas*. These dilemmas are designed to raise your awareness of accounting issues that have ethical ramifications.

CAREERS IN ACCOUNTING

PART C

At this point in your college career, you may be uncertain of your major. Here are three important questions to consider when you make your choice: (1) Will you enjoy your major as a career? (2) Will you be good at your chosen field? (3) Will you be well paid?

After completing the first course in accounting, you will have some idea of the answers to the first two questions. You will find out whether you might enjoy accounting. You will also find out through exams, quizzes, and homework whether you have the aptitude to be good at it. Realize, however, that besides being good at

CAREER CORNER

Over 20,000 employees join public accounting firms in entry-level jobs each year, and thousands more go into other areas of accounting. While financial accountants learn how to measure business transactions and prepare financial reports, they also learn a great deal about the business itself. Because of this widespread business knowledge, accountants often play a key role on the management team. In fact, it should come as no surprise to learn that most chief financial officers (CFOs) started their careers as accountants.

Accounting, because of its dynamic and professional nature, offers an attractive career option. You can learn more about a career in accounting by visiting the website of the American Institute of Certified Public Accountants (*www.aicpa.org*). There, you can look under the *Career Development and Workplace Issues* link to find current information about job opportunities, salaries, work life for women, how to write a resume, how to interview, and other general career advice. For salary and other job-related information, consult the website of the U.S. Bureau of Labor Statistics (*www.bls.gov/oco/ocos001.htm*) or go to *careers-in-accounting.com*.

In 2009, entry-level jobs ranged between $50,000 and $70,000, with $55,000 as the norm for Big-4 firms.

Is an accounting degree right for you?

the technical side of accounting, you will need interpersonal skills such as working well in teams, making presentations to clients, and leading co-workers in complex projects. As for the third question, someone definitely will pay you to be an accountant, as we discuss in the following section.

Demand for Accounting

One of the greatest benefits of an accounting degree is the wide variety of job opportunities it opens to you. With an accounting degree you can apply for almost any position available to finance majors. However, it doesn't work the other way: Finance majors often lack the accounting background necessary to apply for accounting positions.

For the past several years, accounting has ranked as one of the top majors on university campuses. Accounting firms are anticipating a 20% increase in new hires over the next several years. Because of their importance in our society, accountants are in high demand. And because of this high demand, accounting salaries are on the rise. Starting salaries are among the highest of all majors across the university.

Career Options in Accounting

User's Guide
Throughout the book, you will see sections titled *Career Corner*. These sections highlight a link between a particular topic and a career.

■ **LO6**
Identify career opportunities in accounting.

The first big decision a student makes as an accounting graduate is the choice between a career in public accounting and a career in private accounting.

PUBLIC ACCOUNTING

Public accounting firms are professional service firms that traditionally have focused on three areas: auditing, tax preparation/planning, and business consulting. We already have discussed the role of *auditors* in attesting to the accuracy of companies' financial statements. *Tax preparation/planning* is an increasingly important activity in the United States, as the complexity of tax laws related to personal and corporate taxes continues to increase. *Business consulting* is perhaps the most lucrative activity of accountants. Managers who want to better understand their companies' financial strengths and weaknesses often turn to public accountants for guidance. Who knows the business activities better than the one measuring and communicating them?

If you choose a career in public accounting, the next big decision is whether to work for one of the "Big 4" public accounting firms (**Deloitte**, **Ernst & Young**, **PricewaterhouseCoopers**, and **KPMG**) or one of the thousands of medium or smaller-sized firms. The Big 4 firms are huge, each having annual revenues in the billions. They audit almost all the Fortune 500 companies in the United States and most of the largest companies around the world, and they hire thousands of accounting majors each year. The thousands of smaller international, regional, and local accounting firms also hire thousands of accounting majors right out of college.

Most public accountants become *Certified Public Accountants (CPAs)*. You become a CPA by passing the four parts of the CPA exam and meeting minimum work experience requirements (in some states). Most states require that you have 150 semester hours (225 quarter hours) of college credit to take the exam. Becoming a CPA can provide a big boost in salary and long-term job opportunities.

PRIVATE ACCOUNTING

A career in **private accounting** means providing accounting services to the company that employs you. Every major company in the world hires accountants. Just think of all the accounting issues at **Dell**, for example. Dell, and all other large companies, need accountants with training and experience in financial accounting, management accounting, taxation, internal auditing, and accounting information systems. Whereas working as a public accountant provides the advantage of experience working with a number of different clients, private accountants sometimes earn higher starting salaries. In fact, many accounting students begin their careers in public accounting, gaining experience across a wide array of companies and industries, and then eventually switch over to one of their favorite clients as private accountants. Other students take positions directly in private accounting right out of college.

Because of their special training and valuable knowledge base, both public and private accountants are expanding their roles to include the following: financial planning, information technology development, financial analysis, forensic accounting, information risk management, investment banking, environmental accounting, tax law, FBI work, management consulting, and much, much more. Illustration 1–16 outlines just a few of the many career options in accounting.

	Public Accounting (Big 4 and Non-Big 4)	Private Accounting	
Clients	Corporations Governments Nonprofit organizations Individuals	Your particular employer	**ILLUSTRATION 1–16** Some of the Career Options in Accounting
Traditional roles	Auditors Tax preparers/planners Business consultants	Financial accountants Managerial accountants Budget analysts Internal auditors Tax preparers Payroll managers	
Expanding roles	Financial planners Information technology developers Financial analysts Forensic accountants Information risk managers Investment bankers Environmental accountants Financial advisors Tax lawyers	Information managers Management advisors Tax planners Acquisition specialists FBI agents Sports agents	
Other career options	Governmental accounting, sole proprietorships, and education.		

A recent survey by *BusinessWeek* on ideal employers for undergraduate business majors listed the Big 4 public accounting firms in the top 12 of all companies in the United States. Three of the Big 4 were in the top five. All of the firms in the list hire accountants. This is a great time to be an accounting major.

 KEY POINT

Because of the high demand for accounting graduates, wide range of job opportunities, and increasing salaries, this is a great time to obtain a degree in accounting.

APPENDIX   CONCEPTUAL FRAMEWORK

■ **LO7**
Explain the nature of the conceptual framework used to develop generally accepted accounting principles.

The FASB establishes financial accounting standards based on a **conceptual framework,** which you can think of as the "theory" of accounting. In much the same way that our nation's Constitution provides the underlying principles that guide the "correctness" of all laws, the FASB's conceptual framework prescribes the correctness of financial accounting rules. Having a conceptual framework provides standard setters with a benchmark for creating a consistent set of financial reporting rules now and in the future. It also provides others with a *written* framework so that everyone understands the underlying concepts that accountants are to consider in preparing and interpreting financial accounting information.

 KEY POINT

The conceptual framework provides an underlying foundation for the development of accounting standards and interpretation of accounting information.

In the chapter, we discussed the three objectives of financial accounting as outlined in the FASB's conceptual framework. To satisfy these stated objectives, accounting information should possess certain characteristics. What are the desired characteristics? Illustration 1–17 provides a graphical depiction of the qualitative characteristics of accounting information.

ILLUSTRATION 1–17   Qualitative Characteristics of Accounting Information

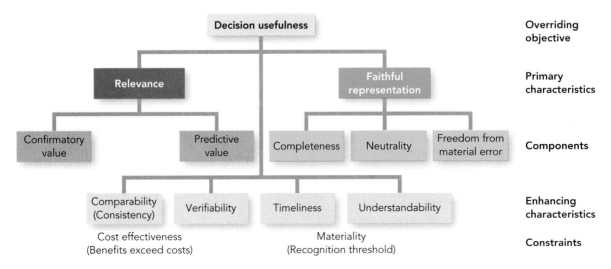

Notice that at the top of the figure is decision usefulness—the ability of the information to be useful in decision making. Accounting information should help investors, lenders, and other creditors make important decisions about providing funds to a company.

PRIMARY QUALITATIVE CHARACTERISTICS

The two primary decision-specific qualitative characteristics that make accounting information useful are *relevance* and *faithful representation*. Both are critical. No matter how representative, if information is not relevant to the decision at hand, it is useless. Conversely, relevant information is of little value if it does not accurately represent the underlying activity.

Relevance. To have relevance, accounting information should possess *confirmatory value* and/or *predictive value*. Generally, useful information will possess both of these components. For example, the ability of **Dell** to report a positive net income confirms that its management is effectively and efficiently using the company's resources to sell quality products. In this case, net income has *confirmatory value*. At the same time, reporting a positive and growing net income for several consecutive years should provide information that has *predictive value* for the company's future cash-generating ability.

Faithful representation. To be a faithful representation of business activities, accounting information should be complete, neutral, and free from material error. *Completeness* means including all information necessary for faithful representation of the business activity the firm is reporting. For example, when Dell reports inventory in its balance sheet, investors understand it to represent *all* items (and only those items) that are intended for sale to customers in the ordinary course of business. If the amount reported for inventory includes only some of the items to be sold, then it lacks completeness. Adequate note disclosure is another important component of completeness. Dell must disclose in the notes to the financial statements the method it used to calculate inventory reported on its balance sheet. (We discuss alternative inventory methods in Chapter 6.)

Neutrality means to be unbiased, and this characteristic is highly related to the establishment of accounting standards. Sometimes a new accounting standard may favor one group of companies over others. In such cases, the FASB must convince the financial community that this was a *consequence* of the standard, and not an *objective* used to set the standard. For example, the FASB requires that all research and development (R&D) costs be reported as an expense in the income statement, reducing the current year's net income. The FASB's objective in adopting this approach was not to weaken the financial appearance of those companies in R&D-intensive industries, such as telecommunications, pharmaceuticals, and software, even though that may have been the effect.

Freedom from material error indicates that reported amounts reflect the best available information. As you'll come to find out in this course, some amounts reported in the financial statements are based on estimates, and the accuracy of those estimates is subject to uncertainty. Because of this, financial statements are not expected to be completely free of error, but they are expected to reflect management's unbiased judgments.

KEY POINT

To be useful for decision making, accounting information should have relevance and faithful representation.

ENHANCING QUALITATIVE CHARACTERISTICS

Four enhancing qualitative characteristics are comparability, verifiability, timeliness, and understandability. Comparability refers to the ability of users to see similarities and differences between two different business activities. For example, how does **Dell's** net income compare with net income for other computer manufacturers such as **Hewlett-Packard** or **Gateway**? Comparability also refers to the ability of users to see similarities and differences in the same company over time. How does Dell's net income this year compare to last year's? Closely related to the notion of comparability is consistency. Consistency refers to the use of similar accounting procedures either over time for the same company, or across companies at the same point in time. Comparability of financial information is the overriding goal, while consistency of accounting procedures is a means of achieving that goal.

Verifiability implies a consensus among different measurers. For instance, different graders will arrive at the same exam score for multiple-choice tests, but they are more likely to differ in scoring essay exams. Multiple-choice tests are highly verifiable. The same idea holds in the business world. For example, the price Dell paid to purchase a patent from another company is usually highly verifiable because there is an exchange at a certain point in time. In contrast, the fair value of a patent for a product Dell developed internally over an extended period is more subjective and less verifiable.

Firms must also disclose information related to net income that is *timely*. Timeliness refers to information being available to users early enough to allow them to use it in the decision process. Large companies like Dell are required to report information related to net income within 40 days after the end of the quarter and within 60 days after the end of the year.

Understandability means that users must be able to understand the information within the context of the decision they are making. This is a user-specific quality because users will differ in their ability to comprehend any set of information.

PRACTICAL CONSTRAINTS ON ACHIEVING DESIRED QUALITATIVE CHARACTERISTICS

Sometimes, certain information involves more time and effort than the information is worth. For example, if a friend asks what you did today, she probably wants to know the general outline of your day, but does not want to hear a recital of every move you made. Similarly, there may be practical constraints (limits) on each of the qualitative characteristics of accounting information.

One such constraint is cost effectiveness, which suggests that financial accounting information is provided only when the benefits of doing so exceed the costs. For example, knowing the profit margin earned by Dell in each country provides decision-useful information to investors and creditors. However, this information is also helpful to the company's current and potential competitors such as Hewlett-Packard and Apple as they make their own expansion plans. The competitive costs of providing this information may outweigh the benefits.

A related constraint on the type of information we provide is the concept of materiality. Materiality reflects the impact of financial accounting information on investors' and creditors' decisions. Unless an item is *material* in amount or nature—that is, sufficient in amount or nature to affect a decision—it need not be reported in accordance with GAAP. Based on the concept of materiality, Dell probably does not record all its assets as assets. Most companies record assets such as wastebaskets and staplers as *expenses*, even though these items will benefit the company for a long period. Recording a $6 wastebasket as a current expense instead of a long-term asset for a multi-billion dollar company like Dell has no impact on investors' decisions.

UNDERLYING ASSUMPTIONS

Four basic assumptions underlie GAAP. As pictured in Illustration 1–18, they are (1) the economic entity assumption, (2) the monetary unit assumption, (3) the periodicity assumption, and (4) the going concern assumption.

GAAP

UNDERLYING ASSUMPTIONS			
Economic Entity	Monetary Unit	Periodicity	Going Concern

ILLUSTRATION 1-18

Assumptions That Underlie GAAP

Economic Entity Assumption. The economic entity assumption states that we can identify all economic events with a particular economic entity. In other words, only business transactions involving Dell should be reported as part of Dell's financial accounting information. Another key aspect of this assumption is the distinction between the economic activities of owners and those of the company. For example, Michael Dell's personal residence is not an asset of Dell Incorporated.

Monetary Unit Assumption. Information would be difficult to use if, for example, we listed assets as "three machines, two trucks, and a building." According to the monetary unit assumption, in order to *measure* financial statement elements, we need a unit or scale of measurement. The dollar in the United States is the most appropriate common denominator to express information about financial statement elements and changes in those elements. In Europe, the common denominator is the euro. Dell has operations throughout the world, so it must translate all its financial information to U.S. dollars under the monetary unit assumption.

Periodicity Assumption. The periodicity assumption relates to the qualitative characteristic of *timeliness*. External users need *periodic* information to make decisions. The periodicity assumption divides the economic life of an enterprise (presumed to be indefinite) into artificial time periods for periodic financial reporting. Corporations, like Dell, whose securities are publicly traded are required to provide financial information to the SEC on a quarterly *and* an annual basis.

Going Concern Assumption. The going concern assumption states that in the absence of information to the contrary, a business entity will continue to operate indefinitely. This assumption is critical to many broad and specific accounting principles. It provides justification for measuring many assets based on their original costs (a practice known as the *historical cost principle*). If we knew an enterprise was going to cease operations in the near future, we would measure assets and liabilities not at their original costs but at their current liquidation values.

In addition to the four basic assumptions that underlie GAAP are four principles (historical cost, full disclosure, realization, and matching) that guide the application of GAAP. We will explain each of these in an appropriate context in later chapters.

KEY POINTS BY LEARNING OBJECTIVE

LO1 Describe the two primary functions of financial accounting.

The functions of financial accounting are to measure business activities of a company and to communicate information about those activities to investors and creditors and other outside users for decision-making purposes.

LO2 Identify the three fundamental business activities that financial accounting measures.

Financing activities include transactions with lenders and owners. Investing activities generally include the purchase or disposal of productive assets. Operating activities relate to earning revenues and incurring expenses.

LO3 Discuss how financial accounting information is communicated through financial statements.

The income statement compares revenues and expenses for the current period to assess the company's ability to earn a profit from running its operations.

The statement of stockholders' equity reports information related to changes in common stock and retained earnings each period. The change in retained earnings equals net income less dividends for the period.

The balance sheet demonstrates that the company's resources (assets) equal creditors' claims (liabilities) plus owners' claims (stockholders' equity) to those resources.

The statement of cash flows reports cash transactions from operating, investing, and financing activities.

All transactions that affect revenues or expenses reported in the income statement ultimately affect the balance sheet through the balance in retained earnings.

LO4 Describe the role that financial accounting plays in the efficient distribution of society's resources.

Financial accounting serves an important role by providing information useful in investment and lending decisions.

No single piece of company information better explains companies' stock price performance than does financial accounting net income. A company's debt level is an important indicator of management's ability to respond to business situations and the possibility of bankruptcy.

LO5 Explain the term generally accepted accounting principles (GAAP) and describe the role of GAAP in financial accounting.

The rules of financial accounting are called generally accepted accounting principles (GAAP). The Financial Accounting Standards Board (FASB) is an independent, private body that has primary responsibility for the establishment of GAAP in the United States.

The primary objective of financial accounting is to provide useful information to investors and creditors in making decisions.

LO6 Identify career opportunities in accounting.

Because of the high demand for accounting graduates, the wide range of job opportunities, and increasing salaries, this is a great time to obtain a degree in accounting.

Appendix

LO7 Explain the nature of the conceptual framework used to develop generally accepted accounting principles.

The conceptual framework provides an underlying foundation for the development of accounting standards and interpretation of accounting information.

To be useful for decision making, accounting information should have relevance and faithful representation.

GLOSSARY

Accounting: A system of maintaining records of a company's operations and communicating that information to decision makers. **p. 4**

Accounting equation: Equation that shows a company's resources (assets) equal creditors' and owners' claims to those resources (liabilities and stockholders' equity). **p. 7**

Assets: Resources owned by a company. **p. 7**

Auditors: Trained individuals hired by a company as an independent party to express a professional opinion of the accuracy of that company's financial statements. **p. 23**

Balance sheet: A financial statement that presents the financial position of the company on a particular date. **p. 13**

Comparability: The ability of users to see similarities and differences between two different business activities. **p. 30**

Consistency: The use of similar accounting procedures either over time for the same company, or across companies at the same point in time. **p. 30**

Corporation: An entity that is legally separate from its owners. **p. 6**

Cost effectiveness: Financial accounting information is provided only when the benefits of doing so exceed the costs. **p. 30**

Decision usefulness: The ability of the information to be useful in decision making. **p. 29**

Dividends: Cash payments to stockholders. **p. 8**

Economic entity assumption: All economic events with a particular economic entity can be identified. **p. 31**

Ethics: A code or moral system that provides criteria for evaluating right and wrong behavior. **p. 24**

Expenses: Costs of providing products and services. **p. 8**

Faithful representation: Accounting information that is complete, neutral, and free from material error. **p. 29**

Financial accounting: Measurement of business activities of a company and communication of those measurements to external parties for decision-making purposes. **p. 5**

Financial Accounting Standards Board (FASB): An independent, private body that has primary responsibility for the establishment of GAAP in the United States. **p. 21**

Financial statements: Periodic reports published by the company for the purpose of providing information to external users. **p. 10**

Financing activities: Transactions involving external sources of funding. **p. 5**

Generally accepted accounting principles (GAAP): The rules of financial accounting. **p. 21**

Going concern assumption: In the absence of information to the contrary, a business entity will continue to operate indefinitely. **p. 31**

Income statement: A financial statement that reports the company's revenues and expenses over an interval of time. **p. 11**

International Accounting Standards Board (IASB): An international accounting standard-setting body responsible for the convergence of accounting standards worldwide. **p. 22**

International Financial Reporting Standards (IFRS): The standards being developed and promoted by the International Accounting Standards Board. **p. 22**

Investing activities: Transactions involving the purchase and sale of (1) long-term resources such as land, buildings, equipment, and machinery and (2) any resources not directly related to a company's normal operations. **p. 5**

Liabilities: Amounts owed to creditors. **p. 7**

Materiality: The impact of financial accounting information on investors' and creditors' decisions. **p. 30**

Monetary unit assumption: A unit or scale of measurement can be used to measure financial statement elements. **p. 31**

Net income: Difference between revenues and expenses. **p. 8**

Operating activities: Transactions involving the primary operations of the company, such as providing products and services to customers and the associated costs of doing so, like utilities, taxes, advertising, wages, rent, and maintenance. **p. 5**

Partnership: Business owned by two or more persons. **p. 9**

Periodicity assumption: The economic life of an enterprise (presumed to be indefinite) can be divided into artificial time periods for financial reporting. **p. 31**

Relevance: Accounting information that possesses confirmatory value and/or predictive value. **p. 29**

Retained earnings: Cumulative amount of net income earned over the life of the company that has not been distributed to stockholders as dividends. **p. 12**

Revenues: Amounts earned from selling products or services to customers. **p. 8**

Sarbanes-Oxley Act (SOX): Formally titled the Public Company Accounting Reform and Investor Protection Act of 2002, this act provides regulation of auditors and the types of services they furnish to clients, increases accountability of corporate executives, addresses conflicts of interest for securities analysts, and provides for stiff criminal penalties for violators. **p. 24**

Sole proprietorship: A business owned by one person. **p. 9**

Statement of cash flows: A financial statement that measures activities involving cash receipts and cash payments over an interval of time. **p. 15**

Statement of stockholders' equity: A financial statement that summarizes the changes in stockholders' equity over an interval of time. **p. 12**

Stockholder's equity: Stockholders', or owners', claims to resources, which equal the difference between total assets and total liabilities. **p. 7**

Timeliness: Information being available to users early enough to allow them to use it in the decision process. **p. 30**

Understandability: Users must understand the information within the context of the decision they are making. **p. 30**

Verifiability: A consensus among different measurers. **p. 30**

SELF-STUDY QUESTIONS

■ LO1

1. Based on the introductory section of this chapter, which course is most like financial accounting?
   a. College algebra.
   b. Foreign language.
   c. Molecular biology.
   d. Physical education.

■ LO2

2. Financial accounting serves which primary function(s)?
   a. Measures business activities.
   b. Communicates business activities to interested parties.
   c. Makes business decisions on behalf of interested parties.
   d. Both a. and b. are functions of financial accounting.

■ LO2

3. Financing activities of a company include which of the following?
   a. Selling products or services to customers.
   b. Using cash to purchase long-term assets such as machinery.
   c. Borrowing money from the bank.
   d. Paying salaries to employees.

■ LO2

4. Investing activities of a company include which of the following?
   a. Paying salaries to workers.
   b. Using cash to purchase long-term assets such as equipment.
   c. Issuing common stock to investors.
   d. Borrowing money from the bank.

■ LO3

5. Which financial statement conveys a company's ability to generate profits in the current period?
   a. Income statement.
   b. Statement of cash flows.
   c. Balance sheet.
   d. Statement of stockholders' equity.

■ LO3

6. Which financial statement shows that a company's resources equal claims to those resources?
   a. Income statement.
   b. Statement of stockholders' equity.
   c. Balance sheet.
   d. Statement of cash flows.

■ LO4

7. Why does financial accounting have a positive impact on our society?
   a. It entails a detailed transaction record necessary for filing taxes with the Internal Revenue Service (IRS).
   b. It allows investors and creditors to redirect their resources to successful companies and away from unsuccessful companies.
   c. It prevents competitors from being able to steal the company's customers.
   d. It provides a system of useful internal reports for management decision making.

■ LO5

8. The body of rules and procedures that guide the measurement and communication of financial accounting information is known as:
   a. Standards of Professional Compliance (SPC).
   b. Code of Ethical Decisions (COED).
   c. Rules of Financial Reporting (RFP).
   d. Generally Accepted Accounting Principles (GAAP).

9. What is a benefit to a career in accounting?   ■ LO6
   a. High salaries.
   b. Wide range of job opportunities.
   c. High demand for accounting graduates.
   d. All of the above.

10. What are the two primary qualitative characteristics identified by the Financial   ■ LO7
    Accounting Standards Board's (FASB) conceptual framework?
    a. Relevance and faithful representation.
    b. Materiality and efficiency.
    c. Comparability and consistency.
    d. Costs and benefits.

Answers to the Self-Study Questions
1. b   2. d   3. c   4. b   5. a   6. c   7. b   8. d   9. d   10. a

REVIEW QUESTIONS

1. Explain what it means to say that an accounting class is not the same as a math class.   ■ LO1

2. Identify some of the people interested in making decisions about a company.   ■ LO1

3. What is the basic difference between financial accounting and managerial accounting?   ■ LO1

4. What are the two primary functions of financial accounting?   ■ LO1

5. What are the three basic business activities that financial accounting seeks to   ■ LO2
   measure and communicate to external parties? Define each.

6. What are a few of the typical financing activities for a company like **United Parcel**   ■ LO2
   Service, Inc. (UPS), the world's largest package delivery company and a leading
   global provider of specialized transportation and logistics services?

7. What are a few of the typical investing activities for a company like **Trump**   ■ LO2
   Entertainment Resorts, Inc., a leading gaming company that owns and operates
   casinos, resorts, and hotels?

8. What are a few of the typical operating activities for a company like **Oracle**   ■ LO2
   Corporation, one of the world's leading suppliers of software for information
   management?

9. What are the three major legal forms of business organizations? Which one is   ■ LO2
   chosen by most of the largest companies in the United States?

10. Provide the basic definition for each of the account types: assets, liabilities,   ■ LO2
    stockholders' equity, dividends, revenues, and expenses.

11. What are the major advantages and disadvantages of each of the legal forms of   ■ LO2
    business organizations?

12. What are the four primary financial statements? What basic information is shown   ■ LO3
    on each?

13. What does it mean to say that the income statement, statement of stockholders'   ■ LO3
    equity, and statement of cash flows measure activity over an *interval of time,* but
    the balance sheet measures activity at a *point in time?*

14. Give some examples of the basic revenues and expenses for a company like   ■ LO3
    The Walt Disney Company.

15. What is the accounting equation? Which financial statement reports the   ■ LO3
    accounting equation?

16. Give some examples of the basic assets and liabilities of a company like **Walmart**   ■ LO3
    Stores, Inc.

■ LO3   17. "The retained earnings account is a link between the income statement and the balance sheet." Explain what this means.

■ LO3   18. What are the three types of cash flows reported in the statement of cash flows? Give an example of each type of activity for a company like **Oakley, Inc.**, a designer, manufacturer, and distributor of high-performance eyewear, footwear, watches, and athletic equipment.

■ LO3   19. In addition to financial statements, what are some other ways to disclose financial information to external users?

■ LO4   20. How does financial accounting have an impact on society?

■ LO5   21. What is meant by GAAP? Why should companies follow GAAP in reporting to external users?

■ LO5   22. Which body is primarily responsible for the establishment of GAAP in the United States? What body serves this function on an international basis?

■ LO5   23. In general terms, explain the terms U.S. GAAP and IFRS.

■ LO5   24. What was the primary reason for the establishment of the 1933 Securities Act and the 1934 Securities Exchange Act? What power does the Securities and Exchange Commission (SEC) have?

■ LO5   25. What is the role of the auditor in the financial reporting process?

■ LO5   26. What are the three primary objectives of financial reporting?

■ LO6   27. What are some of the benefits to obtaining a degree in accounting? What is the difference between a career in public accounting and private accounting? What are some of the traditional careers of accounting graduates? What new areas are accountants expanding into?

■ LO7   28. Discuss the terms *relevance* and *faithful representation* as they relate to financial accounting information.

■ LO7   29. What are the two components of relevance? What are the three components of faithful representation?

■ LO7   30. What is meant by the terms *cost effectiveness* and *materiality* in financial reporting?

■ LO7   31. Define the four basic assumptions underlying GAAP.

For the following, please visit your instructor's *Connect* site.

BRIEF EXERCISES	1-11
EXERCISES	1-16
PROBLEMS: SET A	1-7
PROBLEMS: SET B	1-7
GREAT ADVENTURES	

Mc Graw Hill **connect** |ACCOUNTING

Note: Additional Perspectives assignments for Financial Analysis, Comparative Analysis, Internet Research, and Written Communication are in Appendix F at the end of this book. For additional Exercises: Set B and for additional Problems: Set C, visit www.mhhe.com/spicelandMTC1e.

2

The Accounting Information System

AFTER STUDYING THIS CHAPTER, YOU SHOULD BE ABLE TO:

- **LO1** Identify the basic steps in measuring external transactions.
- **LO2** Analyze the impact of external transactions on the accounting equation.
- **LO3** Assess whether the impact of external transactions results in a debit or credit to an account balance.
- **LO4** Record transactions using debits and credits.
- **LO5** Post transactions to T-accounts in the general ledger.
- **LO6** Prepare a trial balance.

WALMART: **SHELVES OF BUSINESS TRANSACTIONS**

Walmart opened its first store in Rogers, Arkansas, in 1962. By 1967, the company had increased to 24 stores totaling $12,600,000 in sales, and the following year it expanded operations to Missouri and Oklahoma. Today, Wal-Mart Stores, Inc. (the parent company) is the world's largest retailer with over $400,000,000,000 in sales. (That's $400 billion!) With nearly 2 million employees worldwide, it's the largest private employer in the United States and Mexico and one of the largest in Canada. Each year Walmart purchases from over 60,000 vendors merchandise totaling $300 billion. More than 175 million customers visit Walmart stores each week.

With its huge numbers of financial transactions and relationships with customers, suppliers, employees, and government agencies, Walmart poses a challenge to potential investors and lenders who need to understand its financial position today. Obviously, its past performance represents a success story. Sam Walton, Walmart's founder, started his career at **J. C. Penney** in 1940, earning just $75 per month. In 2009, the Walton family's net worth totaled nearly $90 billion (*www.forbes.com*). If you had invested $1,000 in Walmart in 1970 when it first issued stock, your investment would have grown to more than $1 million by the end of 2009.

But is Walmart still a good investment? Would you want to invest $1,000 today? While the past provides useful information, what is the current financial position of Walmart? What is its potential for the future? For investors to fully understand the financial position and profitability of any company, a system must be in place that can summarize and communicate thousands (or even billions) of economic events.

As you may realize by now, summarizing and communicating economic events is the role of financial accounting. In this chapter, we review the process accountants use to identify, analyze, record, and summarize economic events affecting a company's financial position. Having a firm grasp of this process is key to your understanding of financial accounting.

MEASURING BUSINESS ACTIVITIES

In this chapter, we examine the accounting information process using a manual accounting system. Most business enterprises use a computerized accounting system due to the sheer volume of data they must process. Computerized data processing is fast, accurate, and affordable. Our focus on a manual accounting information system, though, will provide you an essential understanding of the basic model that underlies the computerized programs.

This chapter provides a foundation for the remaining chapters. We'll consider the *measurement role* of financial accounting and examine the process firms use to identify, analyze, record, and summarize the external economic events affecting their financial position.

Measurement of External Transactions

■ **LO1**
Identify the basic steps in measuring external transactions.

Recall from Chapter 1 that the two roles of financial accounting are to (1) measure business activities of the company and (2) communicate those measurements to external parties for decision-making purposes. The business activities, or transactions, we want to measure and communicate are classified as either external or internal. **External transactions** are transactions the firm conducts with a separate economic entity. Examples are selling products to a customer, purchasing supplies from a vendor, paying salaries to an employee, and borrowing money from a bank. **Internal transactions** are events that affect the financial position of the company but do not include an exchange with a separate economic entity. Examples are using supplies on hand and earning revenues after having received cash in advance from a customer. In this chapter, we focus on the measurement of external transactions. We save internal transactions for Chapter 3.

 KEY POINT

External transactions are transactions between the company and separate economic entities. Internal transactions do not include an exchange with a separate economic entity.

Measuring external transactions is a six-step process, as outlined in Illustration 2–1. These steps are the foundation for the remaining chapters in this book. Make sure you understand them before you proceed.

The first step in the measurement process involves gathering information about a transaction. Source documents such as sales invoices, bills from suppliers, and signed contracts provide information related to external transactions. These source documents usually identify the date and nature of each transaction, the participating parties, and the monetary terms. For example, a sales invoice might identify the date of sale, the customer, the specific items sold, the dollar amount of the sale, and the payment terms.

Companies record the effects of transactions in accounts. An **account** provides a summary of the effects of all transactions related to a particular item over a period of time. For instance, *asset accounts* include Cash, Supplies, and Equipment. All transactions affecting cash are summarized in the Cash account; all transactions affecting supplies are summarized in the Supplies account; and so on. Examples of *liability accounts* include Accounts Payable, Salaries Payable, Utilities Payable, and Taxes Payable. *Stockholders' equity accounts* include Common Stock and Retained Earnings. A list of all account names used to record transactions of a company is referred to as the **chart of accounts**. (Later in the chapter, we'll see a preliminary chart of accounts. A comprehensive chart of accounts provided at the back of the

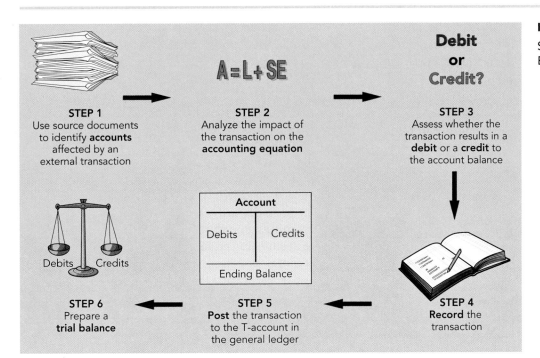

ILLUSTRATION 2–1

Six Steps in Measuring
External Transactions

book includes all accounts used in the book. Keep this handy for reference throughout the course.)

In this chapter and throughout the remainder of the book, you'll learn how to compute the balance of each account and eventually use these account balances to prepare the financial statements introduced in Chapter 1. But first, let's work through steps 2–6 of the measurement process to see how external business transactions are summarized in account balances.

 KEY POINT

The six-step measurement process (Illustration 2–1) is the foundation of financial accounting.

Effects of Transactions on the Basic Accounting Equation

The activities we want to record are those that affect the financial position of the company. That means they affect the accounting equation you learned about in Chapter 1. Remember, the basic accounting equation shows that resources of the company (asset accounts) are equal to claims to those resources by creditors (liability accounts) and owners (stockholders' equity accounts).

■ **LO2**
Analyze the impact of external transactions on the accounting equation.

$$\underbrace{\textbf{Assets}}_{\text{(resources)}} \quad = \quad \underbrace{\textbf{Liabilities} \quad + \quad \textbf{Stockholders' Equity}}_{\text{(claims to resources)}}$$

The basic accounting equation

When **Walmart** borrows cash from a bank, its financial position is affected because assets (cash) increase and liabilities (the loan payable to the bank) increase. So, Walmart records that event in its accounting records. On the other hand, when

Walmart hires Ralph as a front-door greeter, that action doesn't change the company's assets, liabilities, or stockholders' equity; Walmart's financial position is unaffected the day Ralph is hired, and until he begins work. Yes, Walmart hopes that hiring Ralph will favorably affect its financial position in the future, but the hiring itself does not.

Recall that the basic accounting equation must always remain in balance: The left side (assets) equals the right side (liabilities plus stockholders' equity). **Each transaction will have a dual effect.** If an economic event increases one side of the equation, then it also increases the other side of the equation by the same amount. That's what happens, for example, when Walmart borrows cash.

Sometimes, though, a transaction will not affect the *total* of either side. Let's say **Wendy's** buys new cash registers for its stores, paying cash. One asset (equipment) goes up; another asset (cash) goes down by the same amount. There's no change to assets *as a whole*. The accounting equation remains in balance. You can tell whether a transaction affects the accounting equation by considering its impact on the company's total resources—its total assets.

As the balance in an account changes, we record the increase or decrease in that specific account. Let's say we have $50,000 in cash. That's the *balance* in the Cash account. Now say a transaction causes cash to increase by $1,000. The balance in the Cash account is now $51,000.

To see the effect of each transaction, ask yourself these questions:

1. **"What is one account in the accounting equation affected by the transaction? Does that account increase or decrease?"**
2. **"What is a second account in the accounting equation affected by the transaction? Does that account increase or decrease?"**

After noting the effects of the transaction on the accounting equation, ask yourself this:

3. **"Do assets equal liabilities plus stockholders' equity?"**

The answer to the third question must be "yes." **At least two accounts will be affected by every transaction or economic event.** While some economic events will affect *more* than two accounts, most events we record affect only two accounts.

The best way to understand the impact of a transaction on the accounting equation is to see it demonstrated by a few examples. Let's return to the Eagle Golf Academy from Chapter 1. Illustration 2–2 (next page) summarizes the external transactions for Eagle in January, the first month of operations. (You may also want to refer back to the financial statements in Illustrations 1–6, 1–8, and 1–9 to remind yourself how the transactions will eventually be reported.) Note that business activities usually occur in this same order for a new company—obtain external *financing*, use those funds to *invest* in long-term productive assets, and then begin normal *operations*. We discussed these business activities in Chapter 1.

On the following pages, we discuss the impact of these 10 transactions on the accounting equation.

TRANSACTION (1): ISSUE COMMON STOCK

To begin operations, Eagle Golf Academy needs cash. To generate cash from external sources, Eagle sells shares of common stock for $25,000. Let's reflect on this for a moment. Imagine being the sole owner of Eagle Golf Academy. To get your business going, you take $25,000 from your personal funds and invest it in your business. Although your personal cash decreased, the cash of your company *increased*, and so did your equity or ownership interest in the company's assets. Now, imagine instead

Transaction	Date	External Transactions in January	Type of Activity
(1)	Jan. 1	Sell shares of common stock for $25,000 to obtain the funds necessary to start the business.	Financing
(2)	Jan. 1	Borrow $10,000 from the local bank and sign a note promising to repay the full amount of the debt in three years.	Financing
(3)	Jan. 1	Purchase equipment necessary for giving golf training, $24,000 cash.	Investing
(4)	Jan. 1	Pay one year of rent in advance, $6,000 ($500 per month).	Operating
(5)	Jan. 6	Purchase supplies on account, $2,300.	Operating
(6)	Jan. 12	Provide golf training to customers for cash, $3,600.	Operating
(7)	Jan. 17	Provide golf training to customers on account, $2,500.	Operating
(8)	Jan. 23	Receive cash in advance for 10 golf training sessions to be given in the future, $600.	Operating
(9)	Jan. 28	Pay salaries to employees, $2,800.	Operating
(10)	Jan. 30	Pay cash dividends of $200 to shareholders.	Financing

ILLUSTRATION 2–2

External Transactions of Eagle Golf Academy

that the company is organized as a corporation and that by investing $25,000 in it you are becoming one of its many stockholders or owners.

Eagle Golf Academy

Stock Certificate

Investors

(1) Issue common stock

It's time to ask the three questions we asked earlier:

1. **"What is one account in the accounting equation affected by the transaction? Does that account increase or decrease?"**

Answer: **Cash.** Cash is a resource owned by the company, which makes it an asset. The company receives cash from you, so cash and total assets **increase** by $25,000.

2. **"What is a second account in the accounting equation affected by the transaction? Does that account increase or decrease?"**

Answer: **Common Stock.** Common Stock is a stockholders' equity account. Issuing common stock to you in exchange for your $25,000 increases the amount of common stock owned by stockholders, so common stock and total stockholders' equity both **increase.**

Issuing common stock for cash increases both sides of the accounting equation:

Assets	=	Liabilities	+	Stockholders' Equity
Cash ↑ +$25,000	=			Common Stock ↑ +$25,000

TRANSACTION (1)

Initial investment of $25,000 by stockholders

3. "Do assets equal liabilities plus stockholders' equity?"

Answer: **Yes.**

Note that the accounting equation balances. If one side of the equation increases, so does the other side. We can use this same series of questions to understand the effect of *any* business transaction. Let's try another one.

 COMMON MISTAKE

It's sometimes tempting to *decrease* cash as a way of recording an investor's initial investment. However, we account for transactions *from the company's perspective*, and the company *received* cash from the stockholder—an increase in cash.

TRANSACTION (2): BORROW FROM THE BANK

Seeking cash from another external source, Eagle Academy borrows $10,000 from the bank and signs a note promising to repay it in the future.

(2) Borrow from bank

Eagle Golf Academy   IOU   Bank

1. "What is one account in the accounting equation affected by the transaction? Does that account increase or decrease?"

Answer: **Cash.** Cash is a resource owned by the company, which makes it an asset. The company receives cash, so cash and total assets **increase.**

2. "What is a second account in the accounting equation affected by the transaction? Does that account increase or decrease?"

Answer: **Notes Payable.** Notes payable represent amounts owed to creditors (the bank in this case), which makes them a liability. The company incurs debt when signing the note, so notes payable and total liabilities **increase.**

Borrowing by signing a note causes both assets and liabilities to increase:

TRANSACTION (2)

Borrow $10,000 from the bank and sign a long-term note

Assets	=	Liabilities	+	Stockholders' Equity
Cash ↑ +$10,000	=	Notes Payable ↑ +$10,000		

3. "Do assets equal liabilities plus stockholders' equity?"

Answer: **Yes.**

After these two transactions, the accounting equation remains in balance. The total resources of the company equal $35,000. Creditors' claims to those resources total $10,000, and the remaining resources of $25,000 were provided by stockholders. Illustration 2–3 summarizes the effects of the two financing activities we've analyzed so far.

Assets	=	Liabilities	+	Stockholders' Equity	
Financing Activities:					
(1) Cash ↑ +$ 25,000				Common Stock ↑ +$ 25,000	
(2) Cash ↑ +$ 10,000		Notes Payable ↑ +$ 10,000			
Total **$35,000** =		**$10,000** +		**$25,000**	

ILLUSTRATION 2–3

Summary of Initial Financing Transactions of Eagle Golf Academy

Regardless of the number of transactions occurring during the period, the accounting equation always must remain in balance. For brevity, we do not address the three-question process for Eagle's remaining eight transactions, but you should ask yourself those questions until you feel comfortable with the process.

KEY POINT

After each transaction, the accounting equation must always remain in balance. In other words, assets must always equal liabilities plus stockholders' equity.

TRANSACTION (3): PURCHASE EQUIPMENT

Once Eagle obtains financing by issuing common stock and borrowing from the bank, the company can invest in long-term assets necessary to operate the business.

Eagle Golf Academy   Supplier

(3) Purchase equipment

Buying equipment from a supplier causes one asset to increase and another asset to decrease:

Assets	=	Liabilities	+	Stockholders' Equity	
Equipment ↑ +$24,000					
Cash ↓ −$24,000					

TRANSACTION (3)

Purchase equipment with cash, $24,000

Notice that purchasing one asset (equipment) with another asset (cash) has no effect on the category totals in the accounting equation. One asset increases, while another asset decreases. Once we add transaction (3) to the accounting equation, we see in Illustration 2–4 (next page) that the accounting equation remains in balance.

TRANSACTIONS (4) AND (5): INCUR COSTS FOR RENT AND SUPPLIES

Eagle Academy now engages in some operating transactions: It pays one year of rent in advance, $6,000, and purchases supplies on account, $2,300. Because the rent paid is for occupying space in the future, we don't want to record it as an expense immediately. Instead, we record it as an asset representing the right to occupy the space in the future. We call the asset *prepaid rent* and, as we discuss later in the course, we'll report this amount as expense over the next 12 months, as the time we've prepaid

ILLUSTRATION 2–4

Summary of Initial Financing and Investing Transactions of Eagle Golf Academy

Assets		=	Liabilities		+	Stockholders' Equity	
Financing Activities:							
(1) Cash ↑	+$25,000					Common Stock ↑	+$25,000
(2) Cash ↑	+$10,000		Notes Payable ↑	+$10,000			
Subtotal	$35,000	=		$10,000	+		$25,000
Investing Activities:							
(3) Equipment ↑	+$24,000						
Cash ▼	−$24,000						
Total	$35,000	=		$10,000	+		$25,000

expires. Other common examples of prepaid assets include prepaid insurance and prepaid advertising. These items often are purchased prior to their use.

(4) Incur costs for rent

Purchasing rent in advance causes one asset to increase and one asset to decrease:

TRANSACTION (4)

Pay one year of rent in advance, $6,000

Assets		=	Liabilities	+	Stockholders' Equity
Prepaid Rent ↑	+$6,000	=			
Cash ▼	−$6,000				

Next, Eagle purchases supplies with the promise to pay cash in the future. This promise creates a liability. We refer to a liability of this type, in which we purchase something on account, as an *account payable*.

(5) Incur costs for supplies

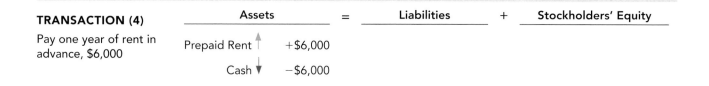

Purchasing supplies with the promise to pay cash in the future causes an asset (supplies) to increase and also causes a liability (accounts payable) to increase:

TRANSACTION (5)

Purchase supplies on account, $2,300

Assets		=	Liabilities		+	Stockholders' Equity
Supplies ↑	+$2,300	=	Accounts Payable ↑	+$2,300		

Effects of Transactions on the Expanded Accounting Equation

To better understand how revenues increase stockholders' equity, let's expand the accounting equation. As discussed in Chapter 1, we can divide stockholders' equity into its two components—common stock and retained earnings. Common stock represents investments by stockholders. Retained earnings represents net income earned over the life of the company that has *not* been distributed to stockholders as dividends. Both of these amounts represent stockholders' claims to the company's resources. Next, we can split retained earnings into its three components—revenues, expenses, and dividends. Illustration 2–5 presents the expanded accounting equation, which shows these components.

ILLUSTRATION 2–5

Expanded Accounting Equation

Be sure to notice the effects of revenues, expenses, and dividends on retained earnings (and therefore on total stockholders' equity) in the expanded accounting equation:

1. We *add* revenues to calculate retained earnings. That's because revenues increase net income, and net income increases stockholders' claims to resources. **Therefore, an *increase* in revenues has the effect of *increasing* stockholders' equity in the basic accounting equation.**

2. We *subtract* expenses and dividends to calculate retained earnings. Expenses reduce net income, and dividends represent a distribution of net income to stockholders. Both expenses and dividends reduce stockholders' claims to the company's resources. **Therefore, an *increase* in expenses or dividends has the effect of *decreasing* stockholders' equity in the basic accounting equation.**

 KEY POINT

The expanded accounting equation demonstrates that revenues increase retained earnings while expenses and dividends decrease retained earnings. Retained earnings is a component of stockholders' equity.

TRANSACTIONS (6) AND (7): PROVIDE SERVICES TO CUSTOMERS

To see an example of how revenue affects the expanded accounting equation, let's look at the two revenue transactions for Eagle Golf Academy. In transaction (6), Eagle provides golf training to customers who pay cash at the time of the service, $3,600.

(6) Provide golf training for cash

Eagle Golf Academy   Training   Customers

Providing training to customers for cash causes both assets and stockholders' equity to increase:

TRANSACTION (6)

Provide golf training to customers for cash, $3,600

Assets	=	Liabilities	+	Stockholders' Equity
				Common Stock + Retained Earnings
Cash ↑ +$3,600 =				+$3,600
				Revenues − Expenses − Dividends
				Service Revenue ↑

Notice that an increase in Service Revenue (↑) increases stockholders' equity by increasing the Retained Earnings account (+$3,600). Therefore, the basic accounting equation remains in balance (Assets = Liabilities + Stockholders' Equity).

As shown in Illustration 2–5, revenues are a component of retained earnings. When a company earns revenue, the amount of retained earnings (or net income) in the business increases. We can increase retained earnings by increasing its revenue component. Stated another way, an increase in revenues increases net income, which increases retained earnings, which increases total stockholders' equity:

Revenues → **Net Income** → **Retained Earnings** → **Stockholders' Equity**

In transaction (7), other customers receive golf training but promise to pay $2,500 cash at some time in the future. The fact that some customers do not pay cash at the time of the service doesn't prevent Eagle from recording revenue. Eagle has *earned* the revenue by providing services. In addition, the *right* to receive cash from a customer is something of value the company owns, and therefore is an asset. When a customer does not immediately pay for services with cash, we traditionally say the services are performed "on account," and we record an *account receivable*.

(7) Provide golf training on account

IOU

Eagle Golf Academy   Training   Customers

Providing services to customers on account causes both assets and stockholders' equity to increase:

TRANSACTION (7)

Provide golf training to customers on account, $2,500

TRANSACTION (8): RECEIVE CASH IN ADVANCE FROM CUSTOMERS

Companies sometimes receive cash in advance from customers. Let's assume that Eagle receives $600 from customers for golf training to be provided later. In this case, Eagle cannot now report revenue from training because it has yet to provide the training to *earn* those revenues. Instead, the advance payment from customers creates an obligation for the company to perform services in the future. This future obligation is a liability (or debt), most commonly referred to as *unearned revenue.*

(8) Receive cash in advance

Receiving cash in advance causes both assets and liabilities to increase:

TRANSACTION (8)

Receive cash in advance from customers, $600

 COMMON MISTAKE

Don't let the account name fool you. Even though the term *revenue* appears in the account title for *unearned revenue,* this is not a revenue account. *Unearned* indicates that the company has yet to earn this revenue and therefore is still obligated to provide the service in the future. This current obligation creates a liability.

TRANSACTION (9): INCUR COSTS FOR SALARIES

Companies incur a variety of expenses in generating revenues. Eagle Academy incurs salaries expense of $2,800.

(9) Incur salary costs

Paying salaries for the current period causes assets and stockholders' equity to decrease:

TRANSACTION (9)

Pay salaries to workers, $2,800

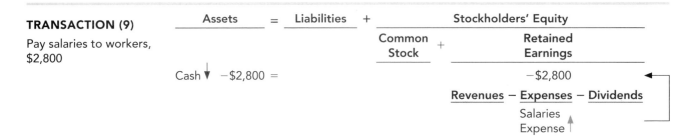

Notice that an *increase* in Salaries Expense (↑) results in a *decrease* in Retained Earnings (−$2,800). As a result, the accounting equation remains in balance, with both sides decreasing by $2,800. The concept of expenses flowing into retained earnings is the same concept that we see in transactions (6) and (7) where revenues also flow into retained earnings, but in the opposite direction. **Expenses *reduce* net income and therefore *reduce* the amount of retained earnings,** a stockholders' equity account. Stated another way, an increase in expenses decreases net income, which decreases retained earnings, which decreases total stockholders' equity:

spiceland.mhhe.com/c4

Beyond salaries expense, companies have a number of other expenses. Most expense accounts are labeled with the *expense* title. For instance, common expense accounts include Supplies Expense, Utilities Expense, Rent Expense, Advertising Expense, Interest Expense, and Insurance Expense.

TRANSACTION (10): PAY DIVIDENDS

The final financing transaction of Eagle Golf Academy for the month is the payment of a $200 cash dividend to stockholders. Recall from the previous chapter that a dividend represents a payment of cash to the owners (stockholders) of the company. Normally a company wouldn't pay dividends after only a month in business, but we make this assumption here for purposes of illustration.

(10) Pay dividends

Paying dividends causes assets and stockholders' equity to decrease:

TRANSACTION (10)

Pay dividends to stockholders, $200

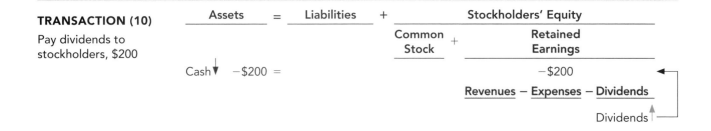

Like expenses, dividends *reduce* retained earnings, but dividends are *not* expenses. Instead, dividends are distributions of part of the company's net income to the owners, reducing the amount of earnings that have been retained in the business. Therefore, an *increase* in Dividends (↑) results in a *decrease* in Retained Earnings (−$200). The accounting equation remains in balance, with both sides decreasing by $200. Because retained earnings is a stockholders' equity account, when retained earnings decreases, so does stockholders' equity.

 COMMON MISTAKE

Students often believe a payment of dividends to owners increases stockholders' equity. Remember, you are accounting for the resources *of the company*. While stockholders have more personal cash after dividends have been paid, the company in which they own stock has *fewer* resources (less cash).

Illustration 2–6 summarizes all 10 of the month's transactions we just analyzed for Eagle Golf Academy.

Assets		=	Liabilities		+	Stockholders' Equity	
Financing Activities:							
(1) Cash ↑	+$ 25,000					Common Stock ↑	+$ 25,000
(2) Cash ↑	+$ 10,000		Notes Payable ↑	+$ 10,000			
Subtotal	$35,000	=		$10,000	+		$25,000
Investing Activities:							
(3) Equipment ↑	+$ 24,000						
Cash ↓	−$ 24,000						
Subtotal	$35,000	=		$10,000	+		$25,000
Operating Activities:							
(4) Prepaid Rent ↑	+$ 6,000						
Cash ↓	−$ 6,000						
(5) Supplies ↑	+$ 2,300		Accounts Payable ↑	+$ 2,300			
(6) Cash ↑	+$ 3,600					Service Revenue ↑	+$ 3,600
(7) Accounts Receivable ↑	+$ 2,500					Service Revenue ↑	+$ 2,500
(8) Cash ↑	+$ 600		Unearned Revenue ↑	+$ 600			
(9) Cash ↓	−$ 2,800					Salaries Expense ↑	−$ 2,800
Subtotal	$41,200	=		$12,900	+		$28,300
Financing Activity:							
(10) Cash ↓	−$ 200					Dividends ↑	−$ 200
Total	$41,000	=		$12,900	+		$28,100

ILLUSTRATION 2–6

Summary of All 10 External Transactions of Eagle Golf Academy

Let's Review

spiceland.mhhe.com/t2

Bogey Incorporated has the following transactions during May:

May 1 Purchase a storage building by obtaining a loan of $5,000.
May 6 Provide services on account to customers, $1,800.
May 12 Pay $1,200 cash for advertising in May.
May 17 Repay $1,000 of the amount borrowed on May 1.
May 25 Purchase office supplies for $800 cash.

Required:

Indicate how each transaction affects the accounting equation.

Solution:

	Assets	=	Liabilities	+	Stockholders' Equity
May 1	+$5,000		+$5,000		
May 6	+$1,800				+$1,800
May 12	−$1,200				−$1,200
May 17	−$1,000		−$1,000		
May 25	+$ 800				
	−$ 800				
	+$4,600	=	+$4,000	+	+$ 600

Suggested Homework:
BE2-2, BE2-3;
E2-2, E2-3, E2-4;
P2-1A&B, P2-2A&B

PART B

DEBITS AND CREDITS

As we saw in the previous section, external transactions have the effect of increasing or decreasing account balances. While the terms *increase* and *decrease* are well understood, accountants more often use the terms *debit* and *credit* to indicate whether an account balance has increased or decreased. Here, we introduce those terms, discuss their effect on account balances, and show how we record transactions using debits and credits.

Effects on Account Balances in the Basic Accounting Equation

■ **LO3**
Assess whether the impact of external transactions results in a debit or credit to an account balance.

You will need to learn how to increase and decrease account balances using the terms debit and credit because that's the language of accounting. Although debit and credit are derived from Latin terms, today *debit* simply means "left" and *credit* means "right." Their use dates back to 1494 and a Franciscan monk by the name of Luca Pacioli. It is easy to visualize the use of these directional signals by means of an accounting convention called a "T-account."

A **T-account** is a simplified presentation of an account, in the shape of the letter T. Across the top, we show the account title. On the two sides created by the vertical rule, we record debits and credits, as Illustration 2–7 shows. The left side of the T-account is the debit column. The right side is the credit column.

ILLUSTRATION 2–7
T-Account Format

Account Title	
Debit	Credit

The effect that debits and credits have on various accounts depends on the nature of the specific account. Illustration 2–8 summarizes the effects that debits and credits have on the accounts in the basic accounting equation.

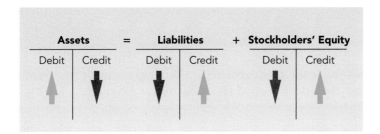

ILLUSTRATION 2–8

Debit and Credit Effects on Accounts in the Basic Accounting Equation

We refer to *increases* in accounts on the left side of the accounting equation—assets—as debits. Just the opposite is true for accounts on the right-hand side of the accounting equation: **We refer to *increases* in liabilities and stockholders' equity as credits.**

The rules reverse for *decreases* in accounts: Assets decrease with a credit. Liabilities and stockholders' equity decrease with a debit.

 COMMON MISTAKE

Students sometimes hear the phrase "assets are the debit accounts" and believe it indicates that assets can only be debited. This is incorrect! Assets, or any account, can be *either* debited or credited. Rather, this phrase indicates that debiting the asset account will increase the balance, and that an asset account normally will have a debit balance. Similarly, the phrase "liabilities and stockholders' equity are the credit accounts" does *not* mean that these accounts cannot be debited. They will be debited when their balances decrease. Rather, the phrase means that crediting the liabilities and stockholders' equity accounts increases their balances, and they normally will have a credit balance.

 KEY POINT

For the basic accounting equation (Assets = Liabilities + Stockholders' Equity), accounts on the left side are increased with *debits*. Accounts on the right side are increased with *credits*. The opposite is true to decrease any of these accounts.

Now, let's look again at the transactions of Eagle Golf Academy, but this time using debits and credits rather than increases and decreases to record the account changes. As we do, ask yourself these three questions for each transaction:

1. **"Is there an increase or decrease in the *first* account involved in the transaction? Should I record that increase or decrease with a debit or a credit?"**
2. **"Is there an increase or decrease in the *second* account involved in the transaction? Should I record that increase or decrease with a debit or a credit?"**
3. **"Do total debits equal total credits?"**

The answer to this last question must be "yes."

Recall our first example: Eagle issues common stock for cash of $25,000 in transaction (1).

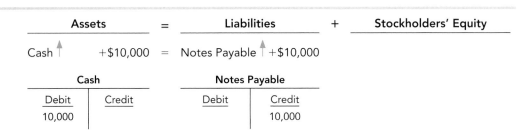

TRANSACTION (1)

Initial investment of $25,000 by stockholders

	Assets		=		Liabilities		+		Stockholders' Equity	
Cash	+$25,000		=					Common Stock	+$25,000	

Cash	
Debit	Credit
25,000	

Common Stock	
Debit	Credit
	25,000

1. **"Is there an increase or decrease in the *first* account involved in the transaction? Should I record that increase or decrease with a debit or a credit?"**

   Answer: **Cash increases.** Cash is an asset, and assets have a debit balance. We record an increase in cash with a **debit** to the Cash account.

2. **"Is there an increase or decrease in the *second* account involved in the transaction? Is that increase or decrease recorded with a debit or a credit?"**

   Answer: **Common Stock increases.** Common Stock is a stockholders' equity account, and stockholders' equity has a credit balance. We record an increase in common stock with a **credit** to the Common Stock account.

3. **Do total debits equal total credits?**

   Answer: **Yes.**

   The bank borrowing of $10,000 in transaction (2) has the following effects:

TRANSACTION (2)

Borrow $10,000 from the bank and sign a long-term note

	Assets		=		Liabilities		+		Stockholders' Equity
Cash	+$10,000		=	Notes Payable	+$10,000				

Cash	
Debit	Credit
10,000	

Notes Payable	
Debit	Credit
	10,000

1. **"Is there an increase or decrease in the *first* account involved in the transaction? Should I record that increase or decrease with a debit or a credit?"**

   Answer: **Cash increases.** Cash is an asset, and assets have a debit balance. We record an increase in cash with a **debit** to the Cash account.

2. **"Is there an increase or decrease in the *second* account involved in the transaction? Should I record that increase or decrease with a debit or a credit?"**

   Answer: **Notes Payable increases.** Notes payable are liabilities, and liabilities have a credit balance. We record an increase to notes payable with a **credit** to the Notes Payable account.

3. **Do total debits equal total credits?**

   Answer: **Yes.**

   To record a decrease in an account, see transaction (3), in which Eagle pays cash to purchase equipment. Recall that this transaction results in an increase in equipment and a decrease in cash, both asset accounts.

Assets	=	Liabilities	+	Stockholders' Equity
Equipment ↑ +$24,000				
Cash ↓ −$24,000				

TRANSACTION (3)

Purchase equipment with cash, $24,000

Equipment

Debit	Credit
24,000	

Cash

Debit	Credit
	24,000

1. **"Is there an increase or decrease in the *first* account involved in the transaction? Should I record that increase or decrease with a debit or a credit?"**

   Answer: **Equipment increases.** Equipment is an asset, and assets have a debit balance. We record an increase in equipment with a **debit** to the Equipment account.

2. **"Is there an increase or decrease in the *second* account involved in the transaction? Should I record that increase or decrease with a debit or a credit?"**

   Answer: **Cash decreases.** Cash is an asset, and assets have a debit balance. We record a decrease in cash with a **credit** to the Cash account.

3. **Do total debits equal total credits?**

   Answer: **Yes.**

spiceland.mhhe.com/c5

Effects on Account Balances in the Expanded Accounting Equation

Remember that accounts on the *left* side of the accounting equation (assets) increase with debits or the *left* side of an account. Accounts on the *right* side of the accounting equation (liabilities and stockholders' equity) increase with credits or the *right* side of an account. This was demonstrated in Illustration 2–8.

As we discussed previously in Illustration 2–5, we can expand the basic accounting equation to include the components of stockholders' equity (common stock and retained earnings) and the components of retained earnings (revenues, expenses, and dividends). Because common stock and retained earnings are part of stockholders' equity, it follows directly that we increase both with a credit. We saw this demonstrated for transaction (1) in the section above: Common stock increased, so we credited that account.

Revenues *increase* retained earnings ("there's more to keep"). Retained Earnings is a credit account, so we increase revenues with a credit. Expenses, on the other hand, *decrease* retained earnings ("there's less to keep"). Thus, we do the opposite of what we do with revenues: We increase expenses with a debit. **A debit to an expense is essentially a debit to Retained Earnings, decreasing the account.** Similarly, dividends *decrease* retained earnings, so we also record an increase in dividends with a debit. In Illustration 2–9 (next page) we show the effects of debits and credits on the components of stockholders' equity in the expanded accounting equation.

ILLUSTRATION 2–9 Debit and Credit Effects on Accounts in the Expanded Accounting Equation

 KEY POINT

The Retained Earnings account is a stockholders' equity account that normally has a credit balance. The Retained Earnings account has three components—revenues, expenses, and dividends. Revenues increase the balance of retained earnings. Expenses and dividends decrease the balance of retained earnings. Therefore, we increase revenues with a credit (similar to retained earnings) and increase expenses and dividends with a debit (opposite of retained earnings).

To see an example of the revenue, expense, and dividend components of retained earnings, let's refer back to transactions (6), (9), and (10) for Eagle Golf Academy: When providing services to customers for cash, in transaction (6), the company earns revenue. The impact of this revenue transaction on the related accounts is shown below.

TRANSACTION (6)

Provide training to customers for cash, $3,600

Paying workers' salaries for the current period in transaction (9) represents an expense and looks like this:

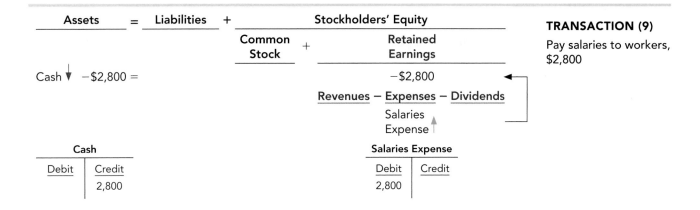

TRANSACTION (9)

Pay salaries to workers, $2,800

Eagle will record the payment of dividends in transaction (10) as:

TRANSACTION (10)

Pay dividends to stockholders, $200

In the last two transactions, both expenses and dividends are increasing. These accounts have debit balances, so we increase their account balances with *debits*. However, retained earnings (a component of stockholders' equity) has a *credit* balance. A debit to an expense or a debit to Dividends is the same as a debit to Retained Earnings, reducing the balance of stockholders' equity.

Decision Point

Question	Accounting information	Analysis
How much profit has a company earned over its lifetime for its owners and retained for use in the business?	Retained earnings	The balance of retained earnings provides a record of all revenues and expenses (which combine to make net income) less dividends over the life of the company.

Illustration 2–10 (next page) provides a simple memory aid that can help you remember debits and credits. Remember the acronym **DEALOR** and you'll be able to recall the effect that debits and credits have on account balances.

ILLUSTRATION 2–10

Effects of Debit and Credit on Each Account Type

DEALOR

Dividends	Liabilities
Expenses	Owners' equity
Assets	Revenues

Debit and Credit Rules: Debit ↑   Debit ↓
                           Credit ↓   Credit ↑

Common Terms Another common name for stockholders' equity is *owners' equity,* since stockholders are the owners of a corporation.

The three accounts on the left, or debit, side of **DEALOR**—**D**ividends, **E**xpenses, and **A**ssets—increase with a debit. The three accounts on the right, or credit, side—**L**iabilities, **O**wners' (stockholders') equity, and **R**evenues—increase with a credit.

Let's Review

Bogey Incorporated has the following transactions during May:

May 1 Purchase a storage building by obtaining a loan of $5,000.

May 6 Provide services on account to customers, $1,800.

May 12 Pay $1,200 cash for advertising in May.

May 17 Repay $1,000 of the amount borrowed on May 1.

May 25 Purchase office supplies for $800 cash.

Required:

For each transaction, (1) identify the two accounts involved, (2) the type of account, (3) whether the transaction increases or decreases the account balance, and (4) whether the increase or decrease would be recorded with a debit or credit.

Solution:

Date	(1) Accounts Involved	(2) Account Type	(3) Increase or Decrease	(4) Debit or Credit
May 1	Buildings	Asset	Increase	Debit
	Notes Payable	Liability	Increase	Credit
May 6	Accounts Receivable	Asset	Increase	Debit
	Service Revenue	Revenue	Increase	Credit
May 12	Advertising Expense	Expense	Increase	Debit
	Cash	Asset	Decrease	Credit
May 17	Notes Payable	Liability	Decrease	Debit
	Cash	Asset	Decrease	Credit
May 25	Supplies	Asset	Increase	Debit
	Cash	Asset	Decrease	Credit

Suggested Homework:
BE2-5, BE2-6;
E2-6, E2-7;
P2-3A&B

Recording Transactions

■ **LO4**

Record transactions using debits and credits.

We have just seen how to assess whether the impact of an external transaction results in a debit or credit to an account balance. Next, we'll learn how to formally record transactions using those same debits and credits in a journal. A journal provides a chronological record of all transactions affecting a firm. Prior to the widespread use of computers, companies recorded their transactions in paper-based journals. Thus, the term *journal entry* was used to describe the format for recording a transaction. Today, nearly all companies have easy access to computers, and paper-based journals have become obsolete, but the term *journal entry* continues to be commonly used. Illustration 2–11 shows the format we'll use throughout the book to record a company's transactions.

Date	Debit	Credit
Account Name	Amount	
Account Name		Amount
(Description of transaction)		

ILLUSTRATION 2–11

Format for a Recorded Transaction, or Journal Entry

The entry that records a transaction has a place for the date of the transaction, the relevant account names, debit amounts, credit amounts, and a description of the transaction. We first list the account to be debited; below that, and indented to the right, we list the account to be credited. The entry has two amount columns—one for debits, one for credits. Because the amounts always represent dollar amounts (not number of units, for example), the dollar sign ($) is not used. As you might expect, the left-hand column is for debits, the right-hand column is for credits. **The amount of the debit must always equal the amount of the credit.** It is acceptable to include a description of the transaction at the bottom. (For learning purposes, we include descriptions.)

spiceland.mhhe.com/c6

 COMMON MISTAKE

Many students forget to indent the credit account names. For the account credited, be sure to indent both the account name and the amount.

Think of recording a transaction as if you're writing a sentence form of the "accounting language." For example, "On January 1, Eagle Golf Academy issues shares of common stock for cash of $25,000." Here is this same sentence about transaction (1) written in the language of accounting:

January 1	Debit	Credit
Cash (+A)	**25,000**	
Common Stock (+SE)		**25,000**
(Issue common stock for cash)		

TRANSACTION (1)

Initial investment of $25,000 by stockholders

Just as every English sentence uses at least one noun and one verb, every accounting sentence includes at least one debit and one credit. While not a formal part of recording transactions, we'll use a notation in parentheses beside the account name in the first few chapters of this book to help you get more familiar with the effect of debits and credits on the account balance. Thus, the entry shows that transaction (1) causes total assets to increase (+A) and total stockholders' equity to increase (+SE). You will need to learn to read and write in the language of accounting as this is the language used throughout the business world.

Accounting is the language of business.

Let's try a few more transactions. In transaction (2), Eagle Academy borrows $10,000 from the bank. Eagle records the transaction as:

TRANSACTION (2)

Borrow $10,000 from the bank and sign a long-term note

January 1	Debit	Credit
Cash (+A)	10,000	
Notes Payable (+L)		10,000
(Borrow by signing long-term note)		

Both total assets and total liabilities increase by $10,000.

In transaction (3), Eagle Academy purchases equipment for $24,000 cash. Eagle records the transaction as:

TRANSACTION (3)

Purchase equipment with cash, $24,000

January 1	Debit	Credit
Equipment (+A)	24,000	
Cash (−A)		24,000
(Purchase equipment for cash)		

Here, one asset increases, while another asset decreases. We record the remaining transactions of Eagle Academy later in the chapter.

KEY POINT

For each transaction, total debits must equal total credits.

Let's Review

spiceland.mhhe.com/t3

Bogey Incorporated has the following transactions during May:

May 1 Purchase a storage building by obtaining a loan of $5,000.

May 6 Provide services on account to customers, $1,800.

May 12 Pay $1,200 cash for advertising in May.

May 17 Repay $1,000 of the amount borrowed on May 1.

May 25 Purchase office supplies for $800 cash.

Required:

Record each transaction.

Solution:

May 1	Debit	Credit
Buildings (+A)	5,000	
Notes Payable (+L)		5,000
(Purchase building with note payable)		

May 6	Debit	Credit
Accounts Receivable (+A)	1,800	
Service Revenue (+R, +SE)		1,800
(Provide services on account)		

May 12	Debit	Credit
Advertising Expense (+E, −SE)	1,200	
Cash (−A)..		1,200
(Pay advertising)		

May 17	Debit	Credit
Notes Payable (−L)	1,000	
Cash (−A)...		1,000
(Repay portion of note)		

May 25	Debit	Credit
Supplies (+A)	800	
Cash (−A)...		800
(Purchase supplies for cash)		

Suggested Homework:
BE2-7, BE2-8;
E2-8, E2-10, E2-11;
P2-5A&B, P2-6A&B

Posting

The journal provides in a single location a chronological listing of every transaction affecting a company. As such, it serves as a handy way to review specific transactions and to locate any accounting errors at their original source. But it's not a convenient format for calculating account balances to use in preparing financial statements. You don't need to stretch your imagination too far to see that even for a very small company with few transactions, calculating account balances from a journal would very soon become unmanageable. Just imagine how lengthy the journal would be for **Walmart**. If each sales transaction with a customer took about one inch of space, the journal would be over 150,000 miles long by the end of the year.

To make the process more efficient, we transfer information about transactions recorded in the journal to the specific accounts in the general ledger. The general ledger includes all accounts used to record the company's transactions. The names of these accounts are listed in the *chart of accounts*. Illustration 2–12 provides the chart of accounts for Eagle Golf Academy based on the 10 transactions we've covered to this point. Later, we'll introduce other transactions and accounts for Eagle. In addition, at the back of the book, you'll see a comprehensive chart of accounts that includes *all accounts* used throughout the book.

■ **LO5**
Post transactions to T-accounts in the general ledger.

EAGLE GOLF ACADEMY Chart of Accounts (preliminary)		
Assets	**Liabilities**	**Stockholders' Equity**
Cash	Accounts Payable	Common Stock
Accounts Receivable	Unearned Revenue	
Supplies	Notes Payable	Dividends:
Prepaid Rent		Dividends
Equipment		
		Revenues:
		Service Revenue
		Expenses:
		Salaries Expense

ILLUSTRATION 2–12

Preliminary Chart of Accounts for Eagle Golf Academy

The process of transferring the debit and credit information from the journal to individual accounts in the general ledger is called **posting**. **Since we post all transactions to the general ledger, each account provides in one location a collection of all transactions that affect that account.** Computerized systems automatically and instantly post information from the journal to the general ledger accounts.

A formal general ledger account includes an account title, account number, date, and columns for increases, decreases, and the cumulative balance. As described earlier, accounts are easier to visualize if we use the T-account format. With the additional information learned since we first discussed T-accounts, we can now more formally define a **T-account** as a simplified form of a general ledger account with space at the top for the account title and two sides for recording debits and credits. Consistent with our previous discussion of debits and credits, the left side of the T-account is the debit column. The right side is the credit column.

Let's see how debits and credits are posted to a T-account by looking at Illustration 2–13, where we have posted the cash transactions of Eagle Golf Academy. (The corresponding transaction numbers are included in parentheses, simply for teaching purposes.) For each transaction that involves cash, we post the debit in the journal as a debit to the T-account. Similarly, we post every credit in the journal as a credit to the T-account. Note that we do not have to put "+" signs or "−" signs beside the numbers in the T-account. With all transactions collected in one place, we can now easily calculate the *ending balance* of cash. We calculate the ending balance of $6,200 by totaling all debits and subtracting the total of all credits.

ILLUSTRATION 2–13

Cash T-Account for Transactions of Eagle Golf Academy

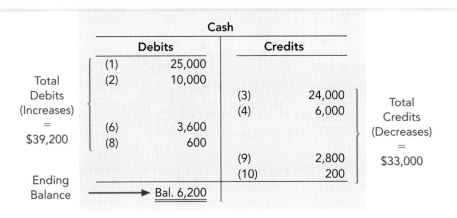

To review:

- For assets (such as cash), an amount in the debit or left column *always* means an increase in the balance. An amount in the credit or right column *always* means a decrease in the balance.
- Just the opposite is true for liabilities and stockholders' equity: A debit to a liability or stockholders' equity T-account *always* means a decrease, and a credit *always* means an increase.

Also, notice that transactions (5) and (7) are not posted to Eagle's Cash T-account. These transactions did not include the receipt or payment of cash, and therefore they do not affect the balance of cash. Only transactions that involve cash affect the balance of cash and are posted to the Cash T-account.

 COMMON MISTAKE

Some students think the term "debit" *always* means increase and "credit" *always* means decrease. While this is true for assets, it is *not* true for liabilities and stockholders' equity. Liabilities and stockholders' equity are increased by credits and decreased by debits.

KEY POINT

Posting is the process of transferring the debit and credit information from transactions recorded in the journal to the T-accounts in the general ledger.

Summary of the Measurement Process

To better understand the measurement of external transactions, let's apply the first five steps outlined in Illustration 2–1 to each of the 10 transactions of Eagle Golf Academy. These steps are detailed in Illustrations 2–14 through 2–23.

Step 1: Use source documents to analyze **accounts** affected.	**Cash** (asset) and **common stock** (stockholders' equity) both increase by $25,000.

Assets	=	Liabilities	+	Stockholders' Equity
+$25,000	=			+$25,000
(Cash ↑)				(Common Stock ↑)

Step 2: Determine impact on **accounting equation.**

Step 3: Determine **debits** and **credits** for accounts.

1. Assets increase with a debit, so **debit** Cash, $25,000.
2. Stockholders' equity increases with a credit, so **credit** Common Stock, $25,000.

Step 4: **Record** transaction.

January 1		Debit	Credit
Cash		25,000	
Common Stock			25,000

Step 5: **Post** to T-accounts.

Cash		Common Stock	
(1) **25,000**			(1) **25,000**
Bal. 25,000			Bal. 25,000

ILLUSTRATION 2–14

Transaction (1): Issue Shares of Common Stock for $25,000

Step 1: Use source documents to analyze **accounts.**	**Cash** (asset) and **notes payable** (liability) increase by $10,000.

Assets	=	Liabilities	+	Stockholders' Equity
+$10,000	=	+$10,000		
(Cash ↑)		(Notes Payable ↑)		

Step 2: Determine impact on **accounting equation.**

Step 3: Determine **debits** and **credits** for accounts.

1. Assets increase with a debit, so **debit** Cash for $10,000.
2. Liabilities increase with a credit, so **credit** Notes Payable for $10,000.

Step 4: **Record** transaction.

January 1		Debit	Credit
Cash		10,000	
Notes Payable			10,000

Step 5: **Post** to T-accounts.

Cash		Notes Payable	
(1) 25,000			(2) **10,000**
(2) **10,000**			
Bal. 35,000			Bal. 10,000

ILLUSTRATION 2–15

Transaction (2): Borrow $10,000 from the Bank and Sign a Long-Term Note

ILLUSTRATION 2–16

Transaction (3): Purchase Equipment with Cash, $24,000

| Step 1: Use source documents to analyze **accounts.** | **Equipment** (asset) increases and **cash** (asset) decreases by $24,000. |

Step 2: Determine impact on **accounting equation.**

$$
\underline{\text{Assets}} \quad = \quad \underline{\text{Liabilities}} \quad + \quad \underline{\text{Stockholders' Equity}}
$$

+$24,000   −$24,000 =
(Equipment ↑) (Cash ↓)

Step 3: Determine **debits** and **credits** for accounts.

1. Assets increase with a debit, so **debit** Equipment, $24,000.
2. Assets decrease with a credit, so **credit** Cash, $24,000.

Step 4: **Record** transaction.

January 1	Debit	Credit
Equipment	24,000	
Cash		24,000

Step 5: **Post** to T-accounts.

Equipment		Cash	
(3) **24,000**		(1) 25,000	(3) **24,000**
		(2) 10,000	
Bal. 24,000		Bal. 11,000	

ILLUSTRATION 2–17

Transaction (4): Pay One Year of Rent in Advance, $6,000

| Step 1: Use source documents to analyze **accounts.** | **Prepaid rent** (asset) increases and **cash** (asset) decreases by $6,000. |

Step 2: Determine impact on **accounting equation.**

$$
\underline{\text{Assets}} \quad = \quad \underline{\text{Liabilities}} \quad + \quad \underline{\text{Stockholders' Equity}}
$$

+$6,000   −$6,000 =
(Prepaid Rent ↑) (Cash ↓)

Step 3: Determine **debits** and **credits** for accounts.

1. Assets increase with a debit, so **debit** Prepaid Rent for $6,000.
2. Assets decrease with a credit, so **credit** Cash for $6,000.

Step 4: **Record** transaction.

January 1	Debit	Credit
Prepaid Rent	6,000	
Cash		6,000

Step 5: **Post** to T-accounts.

Prepaid Rent		Cash	
(4) **6,000**		(1) 25,000	(3) 24,000
		(2) 10,000	(4) **6,000**
Bal. 6,000		Bal. 5,000	

ILLUSTRATION 2–18

Transaction (5): Purchase Supplies on Account, $2,300

| Step 1: Use source documents to analyze **accounts.** | **Supplies** (asset) increases and **accounts payable** (liability) increases by $2,300. |

Step 2: Determine impact on **accounting equation.**

$$
\underline{\text{Assets}} \quad = \quad \underline{\text{Liabilities}} \quad + \quad \underline{\text{Stockholders' Equity}}
$$

+$2,300 =   +$2,300
(Supplies ↑)   (Accounts Payable ↑)

Step 3: Determine **debits** and **credits** for accounts.

1. Assets increase with a debit, so **debit** Supplies for $2,300.
2. Liabilities increase with a credit, so **credit** Accounts Payable for $2,300.

(continued)

Step 4: Record transaction.	January 6		Debit	Credit
	Supplies		2,300	
		Accounts Payable		2,300

Step 5: Post to T-accounts.

Supplies			Accounts Payable		
(5) **2,300**				(5) **2,300**	
Bal. 2,300				Bal. 2,300	

ILLUSTRATION 2–18
(concluded)

Step 1: Use source documents to analyze accounts.

Cash (asset) and **service revenue** (revenue) increase by $3,600.

Step 2: Determine impact on accounting equation.

Assets	=	Liabilities	+	Stockholders' Equity
+$3,600	=			+$3,600
(Cash ↑)				(Service Revenue ↑)

Step 3: Determine debits and credits for accounts.

1. Assets increase with a debit, so **debit** Cash for $3,600.
2. Revenues increase with a credit, so **credit** Service Revenue for $3,600. The increase in revenues increases stockholders' equity.

Step 4: Record transaction.	January 12		Debit	Credit
	Cash		3,600	
		Service Revenue		3,600

Step 5: Post to T-accounts.

Cash			Service Revenue		
(1) 25,000	(3) 24,000			(6) **3,600**	
(2) 10,000	(4) 6,000				
(6) **3,600**					
Bal. 8,600				Bal. 3,600	

ILLUSTRATION 2–19

Transaction (6): Provide Golf Training to Customers for Cash, $3,600

Step 1: Use source documents to analyze accounts.

Accounts receivable (asset) and **service revenue** (revenue) increase by $2,500.

Step 2: Determine impact on accounting equation.

Assets	=	Liabilities	+	Stockholders' Equity
+$2,500	=			+$2,500
(Accounts Receivable ↑)				(Service Revenue ↑)

Step 3: Determine debits and credits for accounts.

1. Assets increase with a debit, so **debit** Accounts Receivable for $2,500.
2. Revenues increase with a credit, so **credit** Service Revenue for $2,500. The increase in revenues increases stockholders' equity.

Step 4: Record transaction.	January 17		Debit	Credit
	Accounts Receivable		2,500	
		Service Revenue		2,500

Step 5: Post to T-accounts.

Accounts Receivable			Service Revenue		
(7) **2,500**				(6) 3,600	
				(7) **2,500**	
Bal. 2,500				Bal. 6,100	

ILLUSTRATION 2–20

Transaction (7): Provide Golf Training to Customers on Account, $2,500

ILLUSTRATION 2–21

Transaction (8): Receive Cash in Advance for Golf Training to Be Given Next Month, $600

| Step 1: Use source documents to analyze **accounts**. | **Cash** (asset) and **unearned revenue** (liability) increase by $600. |

| Step 2: Determine impact on **accounting equation**. |

Assets	=	Liabilities	+	Stockholders' Equity
+$600	=	+$600		
(Cash ↑)		(Unearned Revenue ↑)		

| Step 3: Determine **debits** and **credits** for accounts. | 1. Assets increase with a debit, so **debit** Cash for $600.
 2. Liabilities increase with a credit, so **credit** Unearned Revenue for $600. |

Step 4: Record transaction.

January 23	Debit	Credit
Cash	600	
Unearned Revenue		600

Step 5: Post to T-accounts.

Cash		Unearned Revenue	
(1) 25,000	(3) 24,000		(8) **600**
(2) 10,000	(4) 6,000		
(6) 3,600			
(8) **600**			
Bal. 9,200			Bal. 600

ILLUSTRATION 2–22

Transaction (9): Pay Salaries to Employees for Work during the Month, $2,800

| Step 1: Use source documents to analyze **accounts**. | **Cash** (asset) decreases and **salaries expense** (expense) increases by $2,800. |

Step 2: Determine impact on **accounting equation**.

Assets	=	Liabilities	+	Stockholders' Equity
– $2,800	=			– $2,800
(Cash ↓)				(Salaries Expense ↑)

| Step 3: Determine **debits** and **credits** for accounts. | 1. Assets decrease with a credit, so **credit** Cash for $2,800.
 2. Expenses increase with a debit, so **debit** Salaries Expense for $2,800. The increase in expenses decreases stockholders' equity. |

Step 4: Record transaction.

January 28	Debit	Credit
Salaries Expense	2,800	
Cash		2,800

Step 5: Post to T-accounts.

Cash		Salaries Expense	
(1) 25,000	(3) 24,000	(9) **2,800**	
(2) 10,000	(4) 6,000		
(6) 3,600	(9) **2,800**		
(8) 600			
Bal. 6,400		Bal. 2,800	

ILLUSTRATION 2–23

Transaction (10): Pay Cash Dividends of $200 to Shareholders

| Step 1: Use source documents to analyze **accounts**. | **Cash** (asset) decreases and **dividends** (dividends) increase by $200. |

Step 2: Determine impact on **accounting equation**.

Assets	=	Liabilities	+	Stockholders' Equity
–$200	=			–$200
(Cash ↓)				(Dividends ↑)

| Step 3: Determine **debits** and **credits** for accounts. | 1. Assets decrease with a credit, so **credit** Cash for $200.
 2. Dividends increase with a debit, so **debit** Dividends for $200. The increase in dividends decreases stockholders' equity. |

(continued)

Step 4: Record transaction.	January 30 Dividends Cash	Debit 200	Credit 200

ILLUSTRATION 2–23
(concluded)

Step 5: Post to T-accounts.

Dividends		Cash	
(10) **200**		(1) 25,000	(3) 24,000
		(2) 10,000	(4) 6,000
		(6) 3,600	(9) 2,800
		(8) 600	(10) **200**
Bal. 200		Bal. 6,200	

A summary of the external transactions recorded for Eagle Golf Academy is provided in Illustration 2–24.

	Debit	Credit
January 1		
Cash (+A)	25,000	
Common Stock (+SE)		25,000
(*Issue common stock for cash*)		
January 1		
Cash (+A)	10,000	
Notes Payable (+L)		10,000
(*Borrow by signing long-term note*)		
January 1		
Equipment (+A)	24,000	
Cash (−A)		24,000
(*Purchase equipment for cash*)		
January 1		
Prepaid Rent (+A)	6,000	
Cash (−A)		6,000
(*Prepay rent with cash*)		
January 6		
Supplies (+A)	2,300	
Accounts Payable (+L)		2,300
(*Purchase supplies on account*)		
January 12		
Cash (+A)	3,600	
Service Revenue (+R, +SE)		3,600
(*Provide training to customers for cash*)		
January 17		
Accounts Receivable (+A)	2,500	
Service Revenue (+R, +SE)		2,500
(*Provide training to customers on account*)		
January 23		
Cash (+A)	600	
Unearned Revenue (+L)		600
(*Receive cash in advance from customers*)		
January 28		
Salaries Expense (+E, −SE)	2,800	
Cash (−A)		2,800
(*Pay workers' salaries*)		
January 30		
Dividends (+D, −SE)	200	
Cash (−A)		200
(*Pay cash dividends*)		

ILLUSTRATION 2–24

Summary of External Transactions Recorded for Eagle Golf Academy

Illustration 2–25 provides the general ledger accounts after posting the external transactions summarized in Illustration 2–24. Account balances are in bold, and transaction numbers are shown in parentheses.

ILLUSTRATION 2–25   Posting of External Transactions of Eagle Golf Academy to General Ledger Accounts

| Assets | = | Liabilities | + | Stockholders' Equity |

Cash

(1) 25,000	(3) 24,000
(2) 10,000	(4) 6,000
(6) 3,600	(9) 2,800
(8) 600	(10) 200
Bal. 6,200	

Accounts Receivable

| (7) 2,500 | |
| **Bal. 2,500** | |

Accounts Payable

| | (5) 2,300 |
| | **Bal. 2,300** |

Common Stock

| | (1) 25,000 |
| | **Bal. 25,000** |

Retained Earnings

| | 0 |
| | 0 |

Supplies

| (5) 2,300 | |
| **Bal. 2,300** | |

Prepaid Rent

| (4) 6,000 | |
| **Bal. 6,000** | |

Unearned Revenue

| | (8) 600 |
| | **Bal. 600** |

Service Revenue

	(6) 3,600
	(7) 2,500
	Bal. 6,100

Salaries Expense

| (9) 2,800 | |
| **Bal. 2,800** | |

Equipment

| (3) 24,000 | |
| **Bal. 24,000** | |

Notes Payable

| | (2) 10,000 |
| | **Bal. 10,000** |

Dividends

| (10) 200 | |
| **Bal. 200** | |

Transaction numbers are shown in parentheses. Account balances are in bold.

Trial Balance

After we've posted transactions to the general ledger accounts, **the sum of the accounts with debit balances should equal the sum of the accounts with credit balances.** This is expected because debits were equal to credits for every transaction posted to those ledger accounts. To prove this to be the case and to check for completeness, we prepare a trial balance. A trial balance is a list of all accounts and their balances at a particular date, showing that total debits equal total credits. Another purpose of the trial balance is to assist us in preparing adjusting entries (for *internal* transactions). We discuss adjusting entries in Chapter 3.

Using the account balances calculated in Illustration 2–25, we can now prepare the trial balance of Eagle Golf Academy. The trial balance appears in Illustration 2–26 (next page). Notice that accounts are listed with the debit balances in one column and the credit balances in another column. Asset, expense, and dividend accounts normally have debit balances. Liability, stockholders' equity, and revenue accounts normally have credit balances.

 COMMON MISTAKE

Be careful. Just because the debits and credits are equal in a trial balance does not necessarily mean that all balances are correct. A trial balance could contain offsetting errors. For example, if we overstate cash and revenue each by $1,000, both accounts will be in error, but the trial balance will still balance, since the overstatement to cash increases debits by $1,000 and the overstatement to revenue increases credits by $1,000.

EAGLE GOLF ACADEMY
Trial Balance
January 31

Accounts	Debit	Credit
Cash	$ 6,200	
Accounts Receivable	2,500	
Supplies	2,300	
Prepaid Rent	6,000	
Equipment	24,000	
Accounts Payable		$ 2,300
Unearned Revenue		600
Notes Payable		10,000
Common Stock		25,000
Retained Earnings		0
Dividends	200	
Service Revenue		6,100
Salaries Expense	2,800	
Totals	$44,000	$44,000

ILLUSTRATION 2–26
Trial Balance of Eagle Golf Academy

Total debits equal total credits.

It may seem unusual that the Retained Earnings account has a balance of $0. As we explained earlier, retained earnings is a composite of three other types of accounts—revenues, expenses, and dividends. Those three accounts have balances at this point, but those balances haven't yet been transferred to retained earnings. This transfer is known as the *closing process,* and we will discuss it in Chapter 3. Since this is the first period of the company's operations, retained earnings will start at $0. As time goes by, the retained earnings balance will be the accumulated net amount of revenues minus expenses and dividends.

Decision Point

Question	Accounting information	Analysis
How does the accounting system capture the effects of a company's external transactions?	Account balances	The effects of external transactions are summarized by recording increases and decreases to account balances during the year.

ORDER OF ACCOUNTS

The trial balance is used *for internal purposes only* and provides a check on the equality of the debits and credits. Since the trial balance is not a published financial statement to be used by external parties, there is no required order for listing accounts in the trial balance. However, most companies list accounts in the following order: assets, liabilities, stockholders' equity, dividends, revenues, and expenses. As we'll see in Chapter 3, the trial balance simplifies preparation of the published financial statements. Asset, liability, and stockholders' equity accounts are reported in the balance sheet. Dividends are reported in the statement of stockholders'

The accuracy of account balances is essential for providing useful information to decision makers, such as investors and creditors. That's why the Securities and Exchange Commission (SEC) requires all companies with publicly traded stock to have their reported account balances verified by an independent auditor. Independent auditors use their understanding of accounting principles and business practices to provide reasonable assurance that account balances are free from material misstatements resulting from errors and fraud. Tens of thousands of audits are conducted each year. Because of the huge demand for auditors, many accounting majors choose auditing, also referred to as public accounting, as their first career. For an auditor to legally certify a company's account balances, the auditor must be designated as a Certified Public Accountant (CPA).

equity. Revenue and expense accounts are reported in the income statement. Having the accounts listed in order of those classifications in the trial balance makes it easier to prepare the financial statements.

 KEY POINT

A trial balance is a list of all accounts and their balances at a particular date. Debits must equal credits, but that doesn't necessarily mean that all account balances are correct.

KEY POINTS BY LEARNING OBJECTIVE

LO1 Identify the basic steps in measuring external transactions.

External transactions are transactions between the company and separate economic entities. Internal transactions do not include an exchange with a separate economic entity.

The six-step measurement process (Illustration 2–1) is the foundation of financial accounting.

LO2 Analyze the impact of external transactions on the accounting equation.

After each transaction, the accounting equation must always remain in balance. In other words, assets always must equal liabilities plus stockholders' equity.

The expanded accounting equation demonstrates that revenues increase retained earnings while expenses and dividends decrease retained earnings. Retained earnings is a component of stockholders' equity.

LO3 Assess whether the impact of external transactions results in a debit or credit to an account balance.

For the basic accounting equation (Assets = Liabilities + Stockholders' Equity), accounts on the left side are increased with *debits*. Accounts on the right side are increased with *credits*. The opposite is true to decrease any of these accounts.

The Retained Earnings account is a stockholders' equity account that normally has a credit balance. The Retained Earnings account has three components—revenues, expenses, and dividends. Revenues increase the balance of Retained Earnings, while expenses and dividends decrease the balance of Retained Earnings. Therefore, we increase revenues with a credit (similar to retained earnings) and increase expenses and dividends with a debit (opposite of retained earnings).

LO4 Record transactions using debits and credits.

For each transaction, total debits must equal total credits.

LO5 Post transactions to T-accounts in the general ledger.

Posting is the process of transferring the debit and credit information from transactions recorded in the journal to the T-accounts in the general ledger.

LO6 Prepare a trial balance.

A trial balance is a list of all accounts and their balances at a particular date. Debits must equal credits, but that doesn't necessarily mean that all account balances are correct.

GLOSSARY

Account: A summary of the effects of all transactions related to a particular item over a period of time. **p. 40**

Chart of accounts: A list of all account names used to record transactions of a company. **p. 40**

External transactions: Transactions the firm conducts with a separate economic entity. **p. 40**

General ledger: All accounts used to record the company's transactions. **p. 61**

Internal transactions: Events that affect the financial position of the company but do not include an exchange with a separate economic entity. **p. 40**

Journal: A chronological record of all transactions affecting a firm. **p. 58**

Posting: The process of transferring the debit and credit information from the journal to individual accounts in the general ledger. **p. 62**

T-account: A simplified form of a general ledger account with space at the top for the account title and two sides for recording debits and credits. **pp. 52 and 62**

Trial balance: A list of all accounts and their balances at a particular date, showing that total debits equal total credits. **p. 68**

SELF-STUDY QUESTIONS

1. Which of the following represents an external transaction? ■ LO1
   a. Lapse of insurance due to passage of time.
   b. Use of office supplies by workers over time.
   c. Payment of utility bill.
   d. Depreciation of equipment.

2. Which of the following is *not* a step in the process of measuring external transactions? ■ LO1
   a. Analyze the impact of the transaction on the accounting equation.
   b. Record the transaction using debits and credits.
   c. Post the transaction to the T-account in the general ledger.
   d. All of the above are steps in the measurement process of external transactions.

3. Which of the following transactions causes an increase in total assets? ■ LO2
   a. Pay workers' salaries for the current month.
   b. Receive cash payment from a customer billed in the previous period.
   c. Issue common stock in exchange for cash.
   d. Purchase office equipment for cash.

4. Which of the following transactions causes an increase in stockholders' equity? ■ LO2
   a. Pay dividends to stockholders.
   b. Obtain cash by borrowing from a local bank.
   c. Provide services to customers on account.
   d. Purchase advertising on a local radio station.

5. Which of the following causes the accounting equation *not* to balance? ■ LO2
   a. Increase assets; increase liabilities.
   b. Decrease assets; increase expenses.
   c. Increase assets; increase dividends.
   d. Decrease liabilities; increase revenues.

6. A debit is used to increase which of the following accounts? ■ LO3
   a. Utilities Expense.
   b. Accounts Payable.
   c. Service Revenue.
   d. Common Stock.

■ LO3

7. A credit is used to increase which of the following accounts?
   a. Dividends.
   b. Insurance Expense.
   c. Cash.
   d. Service Revenue.

■ LO4

8. Providing services to customers on account for $100 is recorded as:

a. Accounts Receivable	100	
Service Revenue................................		100
b. Cash...	100	
Accounts Receivable............................		100
c. Service Revenue	100	
Accounts Receivable............................		100
d. Service Expense	100	
Accounts Payable...............................		100

■ LO5

9. Posting is the process of:
   a. Analyzing the impact of the transaction on the accounting equation.
   b. Obtaining information about external transactions from source documents.
   c. Transferring the debit and credit information from the journal to individual accounts in the general ledger.
   d. Listing all accounts and their balances at a particular date and showing the equality of total debits and total credits.

■ LO6

10. A trial balance can best be explained as a list of:
    a. The income statement accounts used to calculate net income.
    b. Revenue, expense, and dividend accounts used to show the balances of the components of retained earnings.
    c. The balance sheet accounts used to show the equality of the accounting equation.
    d. All accounts and their balances at a particular date.

Answers to the Self-Study Questions
1. c   2. d   3. c   4. c   5. c   6. a   7. d   8. a   9. c   10. d

REVIEW QUESTIONS

■ LO1

1. Explain the difference between external transactions and internal transactions. If a company purchases supplies from a local vendor, would this be classified as an external or internal transaction?

■ LO1

2. List the steps we use to measure external transactions.

■ LO2

3. Each external transaction will have a dual effect on the company's financial position. Explain what this means.

■ LO2

4. Describe the impact of each of these external transactions on the accounting equation.
   a. Receive a loan from the bank.
   b. Pay employee salaries for the current period.
   c. Receive cash from customers for services provided in the current period.
   d. Purchase equipment by paying cash.

■ LO2

5. Jerry believes that "dual effect" indicates that, for all transactions, one account will increase and one account will decrease. Is Jerry correct? Explain.

■ LO3

6. What is the normal balance (debit or credit) of assets, liabilities, stockholders' equity, revenues, and expenses?

■ LO3

7. Jenny has learned that assets have debit balances, while liabilities have credit balances. Based on this, she believes that asset accounts can only be debited and liabilities can only be credited. Is Jenny correct? When would we credit an asset and when would we debit a liability?

8. For each of the following accounts, indicate whether we use a debit or a credit to *increase* the balance of the account.

   a. Cash.
   b. Salaries Payable.
   c. Utilities Expense.
   d. Service Revenue.

   ■ **LO3**

9. For each of the following accounts, indicate whether we use a debit or a credit to *decrease* the balance of the account. (Compare your answers to those for Question 8.)

   a. Cash.
   b. Salaries Payable.
   c. Utilities Expense.
   d. Service Revenue.

   ■ **LO3**

10. Suzanne knows that an increase to an expense reduces retained earnings (a stockholders' equity account). However, she also knows that expense accounts have a *debit* balance, while retained earnings normally has a *credit* balance. Are these two pieces of information consistent? Explain.

   ■ **LO3**

11. What is a journal? What is a journal entry?

   ■ **LO4**

12. Provide the proper format for recording a transaction.

   ■ **LO4**

13. Explain the phrase "debits equal credits."

   ■ **LO4**

14. Record each of the following external transactions using debits and credits.

   a. Receive cash of $1,200 for providing services to a customer.
   b. Pay rent of $500 for the current month.
   c. Purchase a building for $10,000 by signing a note with the bank.

   ■ **LO4**

15. Describe the events that correspond to the following transactions.

   ■ **LO4**

	Debit	Credit
a. Supplies	20,000	
Cash		20,000
b. Accounts Receivable	30,000	
Service Revenue		30,000
c. Accounts Payable	10,000	
Cash		10,000

16. What does a T-account represent? What is the left side of the T-account called? What is the right side called?

   ■ **LO5**

17. Describe what we mean by posting. Post the transactions in Question 15 to appropriate T-accounts.

   ■ **LO5**

18. What is a general ledger? How does it relate to the chart of accounts?

   ■ **LO6**

19. What is a trial balance? To what does the term "balance" refer?

   ■ **LO6**

20. If total debits equal total credits in the trial balance, does this indicate that all transactions have been properly accounted for? Explain.

   ■ **LO6**

For the following, please visit your instructor's *Connect* site.

BRIEF EXERCISES	1-12
EXERCISES	1-16
PROBLEMS: SET A	1-9
PROBLEMS: SET B	1-9
GREAT ADVENTURES	

Note: Additional Perspectives assignments for Financial Analysis, Comparative Analysis, Internet Research, and Written Communication are in Appendix F at the end of this book. For additional Exercises: Set B and for additional Problems: Set C, visit www.mhhe.com/spicelandMTC1e.

The Financial Reporting Process

AFTER STUDYING THIS CHAPTER, YOU SHOULD BE ABLE TO:

- **LO1** Record revenues using the revenue recognition principle and expenses using the matching principle.
- **LO2** Distinguish between accrual-basis and cash-basis accounting.
- **LO3** Demonstrate the purposes and recording of adjusting entries.
- **LO4** Post adjusting entries and prepare an adjusted trial balance.
- **LO5** Prepare financial statements using the adjusted trial balance.
- **LO6** Demonstrate the purposes and recording of closing entries.
- **LO7** Post closing entries and prepare a post-closing trial balance.

FEDERAL EXPRESS: DELIVERING PROFITS TO INVESTORS

Wouldn't it be great to put $1,000 into the stock market and watch your investment really grow? As a student, you may not have a lot of extra money right now, but someday you will. Which stock should you buy? Where should you buy it?

The largest stock exchange in the world in terms of value traded each day is the New York Stock Exchange (NYSE), nicknamed the "Big Board." The value of shares traded on the NYSE was approximately $20 trillion in 2009. Another popular place to find stocks is the NASDAQ (an acronym for National Association of Securities Dealers Automated Quotations system). This is an electronic stock exchange in the United States that lists more companies and, on average, trades more shares per day than any other securities market in the world. Together, the NYSE and NASDAQ offer investors thousands of stocks from which to choose. Thousands more are listed on other stock exchanges throughout the world.

With so many choices, how do you tell the winning stocks from the losing stocks? The single piece of information that best distinguishes them is *net income*. Recall that net income equals revenues minus expenses for each reporting period. It measures how profitable the business is. Since stockholders are the owners of the business, any profits of the company belong solely to them (and not to creditors). Therefore, as net income increases, so does the value of the company to its stockholders.

To see the power of net income in explaining movements in stock prices, consider the following information for **Federal Express (FedEx)**. Over the 20-year period from 1990–2009, FedEx's net income increased in 14 of 20 years. For the other six years, net income decreased. What happened to FedEx's stock price in each of these years? In the years that net income increased, FedEx's stock price *rose* an average of 21.0%. In contrast, in the years that net income decreased, FedEx's stock price *fell* an average of 9.6%. The goal is clear: Predict the direction of the change in net income and you'll predict the change in stock prices.

PART A

ACCRUAL-BASIS ACCOUNTING

Net income, while certainly not the only consideration, is an essential aspect of good investment decisions. Investors know that any information they gather to help in predicting net income will lead to more profitable investments. Given the importance of net income to investors, standard setters have devoted considerable attention to the proper measurement of the two primary components of net income—revenues and expenses. In this section, we look at important principles behind reporting of revenues and expenses and at their effect on accounting.

Revenue and Expense Reporting

■ **LO1**
Record revenues using the revenue recognition principle and expenses using the matching principle.

If accounting information is to be useful in making decisions, accountants must measure and report revenues and expenses in a way that clearly reflects the ability of the company to create value for its owners, the stockholders. To do this, we use *accrual-basis accounting*, in which we record revenues when we earn them (the revenue recognition principle) and we record expenses with related revenues (the matching principle). We discuss these two principles next.

REVENUE RECOGNITION PRINCIPLE

Recognize revenue when it is earned.

A company records revenues when it sells its product or provides its service to a customer. For example, revenues are recorded when **Federal Express** delivers a package, **Reebok** sells a pair of shoes, **AMC Theatres** sells a movie ticket, **American Eagle** sells a shirt, or **GEICO** provides insurance coverage. The overriding concept in understanding how to properly record revenue is the revenue recognition principle. The *revenue recognition principle* states that we record revenue in the period in which we *earn* it. If a company sells products or provides services to a customer in 2012, the firm should report the revenue in its 2012 income statement. If the company sells products or provides services to a customer in 2013, it should report the revenue in the 2013 income statement, and so on.

To illustrate, suppose Calvin wants to surprise his wife Ruby with a 12-day, Hawaiian cruise to celebrate their 35th wedding anniversary. He books the cruise with **Carnival Cruise Lines**. He makes reservations and pays for the cruise in November 2012, but the cruise is not scheduled to sail until April 2013. When does Carnival report revenue from the ticket sale? Although the company receives Calvin's cash from the ticket sale in November 2012, it does not report revenue at this time because it has not substantially fulfilled its obligation to Calvin. It has not yet provided the services. Carnival will recognize the revenue in April 2013 when the cruise occurs.

It works the other way, too. Suppose that, anticipating the cruise, Calvin buys a Jimmy Buffett CD from **Best Buy**. Rather than paying cash, Calvin uses his Best Buy card to buy the CD on account. Even though Best Buy doesn't receive cash immediately from Calvin, it still records the revenue at the time it sells the CD.

 KEY POINT

The revenue recognition principle states that we should recognize revenue in the period in which we *earn* it, not necessarily in the period in which we receive cash.

MATCHING PRINCIPLE

You've heard it said, "It takes money to make money." That's true for all businesses. To make money from the sale of goods and services, companies must spend money on such essentials as advertising, workers' salaries, utilities, office rent, equipment, and business supplies. We've discussed how use of the revenue recognition principle affects when we record revenues. Now let's discuss when we record *expenses,* the costs associated with producing these revenues.

The **matching principle** states that we recognize expenses *in the same period as the revenues they help to generate.* Implied in this principle is a *cause-and-effect* relationship between revenue and expense recognition. In a given period, we report revenue as it is earned, according to the revenue recognition principle. It's logical, then, that in the same period we should also record all expenses incurred to generate that revenue. The result is a measure—net income—that matches current period accomplishments (revenues) and sacrifices (expenses). That's the matching principle.

To see how the matching principle is applied, let's look back at Calvin and Ruby's Hawaiian cruise. What costs does Carnival Cruise Lines incur in order to generate the revenue from providing a cruise in April 2013? Some of the costs necessary to operate a cruise ship include:

1. The purchase of supplies the month before the cruise to prepare for sailing.
2. The purchase of fuel in the month of the cruise.
3. The payment of the captain's and other crew members' salaries in the month after the cruise.

Regardless of when Carnival actually pays the cash for these costs, the company should "expense the costs"—report the costs as expenses—in April. By doing this, Carnival reports the expenses in the same period as the revenue the expenses helped to generate. Illustration 3–1 shows how these costs would be expensed using the matching principle.

Expenses are reported with the revenues they help to generate.

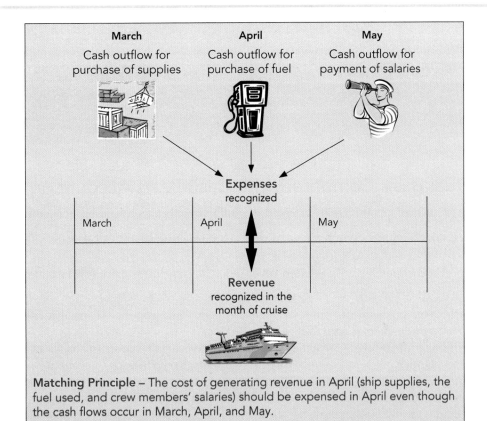

ILLUSTRATION 3–1

Matching Principle

Matching Principle – The cost of generating revenue in April (ship supplies, the fuel used, and crew members' salaries) should be expensed in April even though the cash flows occur in March, April, and May.

It's easy to see how these costs helped to generate the ticket revenue in April. Purchasing ship supplies is necessary for providing a cruise. Likewise, fuel is necessary for the ship to sail. Salaries are necessary to pay workers to operate the ship and serve the guests. All three costs are necessary to generate the ticket revenue in April, so we record them as expenses in April.

Of course, these are but a few of the costs of a cruise. Some costs are only indirectly related to producing revenue. For example, salaries paid in April 2013 to an office worker at Carnival's executive offices in Miami, Florida, are not directly related to the ticket revenue. But even such indirect costs contribute to overall operations, including cruise revenue, and so are expensed in April.

Sometimes it's impossible to determine in which period or periods, if any, revenues will occur. For example, consider the cost of advertising. Calvin may have booked the April 2013 cruise because of an advertisement (television, radio, print, Internet, cell phone) by Carnival back in November 2012. In theory, it would be ideal for Carnival to record the cost of this advertisement as an expense in April at the same time it records the revenue the advertisement helped to generate. However, it's difficult to determine when, how much, or even whether additional revenues occur as a result of a particular series of ads. Because of this obstacle, firms generally recognize advertising expenditures as expenses *in the period the ads are provided*, with no attempt made to match them with related revenues.

 KEY POINT

The matching principle states that we recognize expenses in the same period as the revenues they help to generate. Expenses include those directly and indirectly related to producing revenues.

Decision Point

Question	Accounting information	Analysis
Can the company earn revenues that exceed the cost of doing so?	Revenues and expenses reported in the income statement	Revenues measure the amount earned during the year. Expenses measure the cost of earning those revenues. Together, these two combine to measure net income, or profitability.

Accrual-Basis Compared with Cash-Basis Accounting

■ **LO2**
Distinguish between accrual-basis and cash-basis accounting.

In the preceding section, we discovered the following about accrual-basis accounting:

1. We record revenues when we earn them (the revenue recognition principle) and *not necessarily when we receive cash.*

2. We record expenses with related revenues (the matching principle) and *not necessarily when we pay cash.*

Under accrual-basis accounting, we record revenue and expense transactions *at the time the earnings-related activities occur.*

Cash-basis accounting provides an alternative way of recording revenues and expenses. Under **cash-basis accounting**, we record *revenues at the time we receive cash and expenses at the time we pay cash.* For example, recall in our Carnival example that Calvin purchased tickets in November 2012, for a Hawaiian cruise in April 2013. Under cash-basis accounting, the cruise line would report revenue in November 2012, at the time Calvin pays cash for the cruise, and it would record expenses as it pays cash for them over several months (rather than recording revenue in April 2013 in accord with the revenue recognition principle and related expenses in April 2013 in accord with the matching principle).

Cash-basis accounting is not part of generally accepted accounting principles (GAAP).

Cash-basis accounting may seem appealing because it is essentially how we think about the inflow and outflow of cash from our bank accounts. However, **because cash-basis accounting violates both the revenue recognition principle and the matching principle, it is generally not accepted in preparing financial statements.** We briefly study cash-basis accounting, though, to help provide a better understanding of the advantages and disadvantages of accrual-basis accounting.

Illustrations 3–2 and 3–3 demonstrate the timing difference between accrual-basis and cash-basis accounting by referring back to our example in Illustration 3–1 involving Ruby and Calvin's Hawaiian cruise.

		Recognize Revenue?		**ILLUSTRATION 3–2**
		Accrual-Basis	**Cash-Basis**	Accrual-Basis Revenue versus Cash-Basis Revenue
November 2012	Company receives cash from Ruby and Calvin for Hawaiian cruise next April.	No	Yes	
April 2013	Company provides cruise services to Ruby and Calvin.	Yes	No	

		Recognize Expense?		**ILLUSTRATION 3–3**
		Accrual-Basis	**Cash-Basis**	Accrual-Basis Expense versus Cash-Basis Expense
March 2013	Company pays cash for supplies to be used *next* month.	No	Yes	
April 2013	Company uses supplies purchased *last* month.	Yes	No	
	Company pays cash for fuel used during the cruise *this* month.	Yes	Yes	
	Employees earn salaries but will not be paid until *next* month.	Yes	No	
May 2013	Company pays cash to employees for salaries earned *last* month.	No	Yes	

Under both accrual-basis and cash-basis accounting, all revenues and expenses are eventually recorded for the same amount. In fact, over the life of the company, accrual-basis net income equals cash-basis net income. **The difference between the two methods is in the timing of when we record those revenues and expenses.** Under accrual-basis accounting, we record revenues when earned and expenses when we incur them. Under cash-basis accounting, we record revenues and expenses at the time we receive or pay cash.

spiceland.mhhe.com/c7

 KEY POINT

The difference between accrual-basis accounting and cash-basis accounting is *timing*. Under accrual-basis accounting, we record revenues when we earn them (revenue recognition principle) and record expenses with the revenue they help to generate (matching principle). Under cash-basis accounting, we record revenues when we receive cash and expenses when we pay cash. Cash-basis accounting is not allowed for financial reporting purposes.

Let's Review

Cavalier Company experienced the following set of events:

May: *Receives cash* from customers for services to be provided in June.
June: *Provides services* to customers who prepaid in May.
May: *Pays cash* for supplies but does not use them.
June: *Uses the supplies* purchased in May.

Required:

1. Indicate in which month Cavalier records revenues under:
    a. Accrual-basis accounting
    b. Cash-basis accounting

2. Indicate in which month Cavalier records expenses under:
    a. Accrual-basis accounting
    b. Cash-basis accounting

Suggested Homework:
BE3-4, BE3-5;
E3-3, E3-4;
P3-1A&B; P3-2A&B

Solution:

1a. June   1b. May   2a. June   2b. May

PART B   THE MEASUREMENT PROCESS

In Chapter 2, we discussed the initial part of the accounting cycle process, measurement of external transactions. In this chapter, we will complete the accounting cycle process summarized in Illustration 3–4. First we continue the measurement process by recording adjusting entries (or internal transactions). Following adjusting entries, we will prepare financial statements and then close the books at the end of the period.

ILLUSTRATION 3–4
Steps in the
Accounting Cycle

ACCOUNTING CYCLE

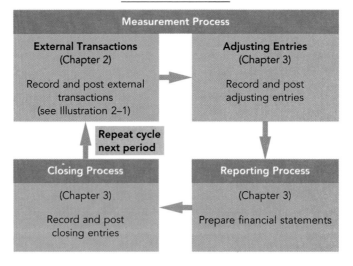

Adjusting Entries

■ **LO3**
Demonstrate the purposes and recording of adjusting entries.

At the end of a reporting period, even if we've accurately recorded every external transaction that occurred and accurately posted those transactions to appropriate accounts, our account balances are not updated for preparing financial statements. Before we can prepare the financial statements, we need to bring several of the accounts up-to-date. That's the purpose of adjusting entries. We use **adjusting entries** to record events that have occurred but that we have not yet recorded.

To envision the process, think of your auto insurance. Insurance companies require you to pay for insurance in advance. On the day you purchased the insurance, you actually bought an *asset* representing insurance coverage over a future period. With each passing day, however, the length of your policy is lapsing, decreasing your insurance asset. Tomorrow you will have one day less insurance coverage than you do today.

The same holds true for a business and its insurance coverage. Although it's true that the company's asset is declining daily, it is unnecessary (and in fact impractical) to record the lapsing of the insurance coverage each day. Recording the expense is necessary, though, when it's time to prepare financial statements at the end of the reporting period. Thus, we use an end-of-period *adjusting entry*. In the case of the insurance coverage, the business adjusts downward the balance of the asset (prepaid insurance) and records insurance expense for the amount of the policy that has lapsed.

If we do not record the adjusting entry for the part of the insurance policy that has lapsed, then total assets will be overstated and expenses will be understated, causing net income to be overstated. This kind of misstatement can mislead users of financial statements. Because adjusting entries allow for proper application of the revenue recognition principle (revenues) or the matching principle (expenses), they are a *necessary part of accrual-basis accounting*. They must be recorded at the end of each period before the company prepares its financial statements.

 KEY POINT

> Adjusting entries are a necessary part of accrual-basis accounting. They help to record revenues in the period earned and expenses in the period they are incurred to generate those revenues. Another benefit is that, by properly recording revenues and expenses, we correctly state assets and liabilities.

It is useful to group adjusting entries into two broad categories—prepayments and accruals—that can be further divided into four subcategories: prepaid expenses, unearned revenues, accrued expenses, and accrued revenues. These four occur as follows.

Prepayments
Prepaid expenses—We paid cash (or had an obligation to pay cash) for the purchase of an asset *before* we incurred the expense.
Unearned revenues—We received cash and recorded a liability *before* we earned the revenue.

Accruals
Accrued expenses—We paid cash *after* we incurred the expense and recorded a liability.
Accrued revenues—We received cash *after* we earned the revenue and recorded an asset.

Let's consider each of these situations. The easiest way to understand adjusting entries is to look at some examples. So, look back to the external transactions of Eagle Golf Academy from Chapter 2. For easy reference, we've restated these transactions in Illustration 3–5 (next page). We will prepare all adjusting entries on January 31, to account for revenue and expense transactions that have not been recorded by the end of the month.

PREPAID EXPENSES

Prepaid expenses are the costs of assets acquired in one period that will be expensed in a future period (like the insurance coverage mentioned previously). The cash outflow (or obligation to pay cash, in the case of assets bought on account)

ILLUSTRATION 3–5

External Transactions of Eagle Golf Academy

Transaction	Date	External Transactions in January	Type of Activity
(1)	Jan. 1	Sell shares of common stock for $25,000 to obtain the funds necessary to start the business.	Financing
(2)	Jan. 1	Borrow $10,000 from the local bank and sign a note promising to repay the full amount of the debt in three years.	Financing
(3)	Jan. 1	Purchase equipment necessary for giving golf training, $24,000 cash.	Investing
(4)	Jan. 1	Pay one year of rent in advance, $6,000 ($500 per month).	Operating
(5)	Jan. 6	Purchase supplies on account, $2,300.	Operating
(6)	Jan. 12	Provide golf training to customers for cash, $3,600.	Operating
(7)	Jan. 17	Provide golf training to customers on account, $2,500.	Operating
(8)	Jan. 23	Receive cash in advance for 10 golf training sessions to be given in the future, $600.	Operating
(9)	Jan. 28	Pay salaries to employees, $2,800.	Operating
(10)	Jan. 30	Pay cash dividends of $200 to shareholders.	Financing

from the purchase of an asset occurs before we record the expense. Examples are the purchase of equipment or supplies and the payment of rent or insurance in advance. These payments *create future benefits,* so we record them as assets at the time of purchase. The benefits provided by these assets *expire in future periods,* so we expense their cost in those future periods. **The adjusting entry for a prepaid expense always includes a debit to an expense account (increase an expense) and a credit to an asset account (decrease an asset).**

Eagle Golf Academy has three prepaid expenses during January: It purchases rent, supplies, and equipment. Each of these items provides future benefits and was recorded as an asset at the time of purchase. By the end of January, the company has used a portion of each asset, and that portion no longer represents a future benefit. The amount of the asset used represents an expense as well as a reduction of the asset. We'll look at each prepaid expense in turn.

Prepaid rent.   Let's begin with transaction (4) in which Eagle Golf Academy purchases one year of rent in advance for $6,000 ($500 per month). The benefits from using the rented space occur evenly over time, with one month's cost attributable to January, one month to February, and so on. Therefore, we need to record one month of the asset's cost as an expense in January and include it in that month's income statement, along with the revenue it helped to produce. At the same time, the asset account has one month's less benefit with each passing month, requiring us to reduce the balance of the asset.

The end-of-period **adjusting entry** for expiration of prepaid rent is below.

January 31	Debit	Credit
Rent Expense (+E, −SE)	500	
Prepaid Rent (−A)		500
(Reduce prepaid rent due to the passage of time)		

Balance Sheet						Income Statement		
				Stockholders' Equity				
				Common	**Retained**			**Net**
Assets	**=**	**Liabilities**	**+**	**Stock**	**+ Earnings**	**Revenues**	**− Expenses**	**= Income**
−500	=				−500		+500	= −500

User's Guide At this point in the book, below each journal entry we begin to include simple accounting equation analyses, to show the effects of the journal entry on the balance sheet and income statement.

Notice that the adjusting entry includes a $500 expense (+E), which reduces net income and stockholders' equity (−SE). At the same time, the balance in the asset account, Prepaid Rent, decreases (−A) by $500 and will now have a balance of $5,500 (= $6,000 − $500). We adjust any other assets that expire over time (such as prepaid insurance) in a similar manner.

Supplies. In transaction (5), Eagle purchases supplies for $2,300 on account on January 6. Even though cash will be paid later, the cost of supplies (or obligation to pay cash for supplies) is incurred on January 6. Suppose that at the end of January a count of supplies reveals that only $1,500 of supplies remains. What happened to the other $800 of supplies? Apparently, this is the amount of supplies used during the month. Since it's not cost-efficient to record the consumption of supplies every day, we make a single adjusting entry at the end of the month for the total amount used during the period.

The end-of-period **adjusting entry** for supplies is below.

January 31	Debit	Credit
Supplies Expense (+E, −SE)	800	
Supplies (−A)		800
(Consume supplies during the current period)		

Balance Sheet						Income Statement		
				Stockholders' Equity				
				Common	**Retained**			**Net**
Assets	**=**	**Liabilities**	**+**	**Stock**	**+ Earnings**	**Revenues**	**− Expenses**	**= Income**
−800	=				−800		+800	= −800

This entry simultaneously records the $800 of supplies used as an expense and reduces the balance of the Supplies account to the $1,500 amount that still remains.

Depreciable assets.   In transaction (3), Eagle purchases equipment for $24,000 cash. Let's assume that, at the time of purchase, Eagle estimates the equipment will be useful for the next five years (60 months). Because one month (January) has passed since the purchase of this asset, Eagle has used one month of the asset's estimated 60-month useful life. In addition, the company has used one month of the asset's cost to produce revenue in January. Therefore, we should *match* the cost (expense) with the revenue it helps to produce. Although this creates a situation much like that of prepaid rent or of supplies, we record the reduction in the cost of assets with longer lives using a concept called depreciation.

Depreciation is the process of allocating the cost of an asset, such as equipment, to expense. We discuss it in detail in Chapter 7; here we will cover only the basics.

The end-of-period **adjusting entry** to record one month of depreciation for equipment is below.

January 31	Debit	Credit
Depreciation Expense (+E, −SE)	400	
Accumulated Depreciation (−A)		400
(*Depreciate equipment = $24,000 ÷ 60 months = $400 per month*)		

This entry reduces the Equipment account by $400. Notice, however, that we didn't reduce Equipment directly, by crediting the asset account itself. Instead, we reduced the asset *indirectly* by crediting an account called *Accumulated Depreciation*. The Accumulated Depreciation account is called a *contra account*. A contra account is an account with a balance that is opposite, or "contra," to that of its related accounts.

The normal balance in the Accumulated Depreciation contra asset account is a *credit*, which is opposite to the normal *debit* balance in an asset account. The reason we use a contra account is to keep the original balance of the asset intact while reducing its current balance indirectly. In the balance sheet, we report equipment at its current *book value*, which equals its original cost less accumulated depreciation.

Illustration 3–6 shows how **American Airlines** records accumulated depreciation for its property and equipment. The net amount of property and equipment represents the book value, or amount of the assets' original costs less accumulated depreciation. As you will see in Chapter 7, depreciation is an *estimate* based on expected useful life and is an attempt to *allocate the cost of the asset over the useful life*. It is a calculation internal to the company and does not necessarily represent market value (what the asset could be sold for in the market).

ILLUSTRATION 3–6

Reporting Depreciation of Property and Equipment for American Airlines

AMERICAN AIRLINES Balance Sheet (partial) ($ in millions)		
Assets		
Flight equipment, at cost	$19,601	
Less: Accumulated depreciation	(7,147)	
Book value of flight equipment		$12,454
Other equipment and property, at cost	5,132	
Less: Accumulated depreciation	(2,762)	
Book value of other equipment and property		2,370

 ETHICAL DILEMMA

You have recently been employed by a large retail chain that sells sporting goods. One of your tasks is to help prepare financial statements for external distribution. The chain's largest creditor, National Savings & Loan, requires that financial statements be prepared according to generally accepted accounting principles (GAAP). During the months of November and December 2012, the company spent $1 million on a major TV advertising campaign. The $1 million included the costs of producing the commercials as well as the broadcast time purchased to run them. Because the advertising will be aired in 2012 only, you decide to charge all the costs to advertising expense in 2012, in accordance with requirements of GAAP.

The company's chief financial officer (CFO), who hired you, asks you for a favor. Instead of charging the costs to advertising expense, he asks you to set up an asset called prepaid advertising and to wait until 2013 to record any expense. The CFO explains, "This ad campaign has produced significant sales in 2012; but I think it will continue to bring in customers throughout 2013. By recording the ad costs as an asset, we can match the cost of the advertising with the additional sales in 2013. Besides, if we expense the advertising in 2012, we will show an operating loss in our income statement. The bank requires that we continue to show profits in order to maintain our loan in good standing. Failure to remain in good standing could mean we'd have to fire some of our recent hires." What should you do?

UNEARNED REVENUES

We record unearned revenues when a company receives cash in advance from a customer for products or services to be provided in the future. When customers pay cash in advance, we debit cash and credit a liability. This liability reflects the company's obligation to provide goods or services to the customer in the future. Once it has provided these products or services, the company can record revenue earned and reduce its obligation to the customer. **The adjusting entry for an unearned revenue always includes a debit to a liability account (decrease a liability) and a credit to a revenue account (increase a revenue).**

In transaction (8), Eagle receives $600 in advance from customers who will be given 10 golf lessons ($60 per lesson) in the future. Later, as Eagle provides that training to customers, it reduces the liability to customers and can record the service revenue because it now has earned it. Assume that by the end of January Eagle has provided one of the 10 training sessions paid for in advance.

The end-of-period **adjusting entry** to account for the revenue earned is below.

January 31	Debit	Credit
Unearned Revenue (−L)	60	
Service Revenue (+R, +SE)		60
(*Provide services to customers who paid in advance*)		

Illustration 3–7 shows an example of unearned revenue for **Apple Inc.**

ILLUSTRATION 3–7

Reporting Unearned Revenues and Other Current Liabilities for Apple Inc.

Common Terms
Another common name for unearned revenue is *deferred revenue*.

APPLE INC. Balance Sheet (partial) ($ in thousands)	
Current liabilities:	
Accounts payable	$ 5,601
Unearned revenue	10,305
Other current liabilities*	3,376
Total current liabilities	$19,282

*Includes amounts owed for taxes, salaries, advertising, and other operating costs.

Most of Apple's unearned revenue comes from sales of the popular iPhone. When you purchase an iPhone, Apple does not immediately record revenue from the sale. Instead, the company spreads this revenue over the next 24 months (the life of a typical iPhone contract). In other words, if you purchase an iPhone today, Apple initially records the entire sale as unearned revenue and then begins to recognize revenue (and decrease unearned revenue) as the company earns this revenue each month for the next 24 months.

Now that we've discussed prepaid expenses and unearned revenues (prepayments), let's look at the two other categories of adjusting entries—accrued expenses and accrued revenues. Accruals are the opposite of prepayments. **Accruals occur when the cash flow occurs *after* either the expense is incurred or the revenue is earned.** Walking through some examples using our Eagle Golf Academy illustration will demonstrate both types of accruals.

ACCRUED EXPENSES

When a company has incurred an expense but hasn't yet paid cash or recorded an obligation to pay, it still should record the expense. This is referred to as an accrued expense. **The adjusting entry for an accrued expense always includes a debit to an expense account (increase an expense) and a credit to a liability account (increase a liability).**

Accrued salaries.   Eagle pays total salaries to its employees of $100 per day. For the first four weeks (28 days), Eagle pays $2,800 cash to employees. For simplicity, we combined each of these four weeks in transaction (9) in Illustration 3–5. For the remaining three days in January, employees earn additional salaries of $300, but Eagle doesn't plan to pay the employees until the end of the week, February 4. However, Eagle must record the $300 salaries expense in the month employees worked (January). Stated differently, the salaries expense *accrues* during January even though the company won't pay the expense until February.

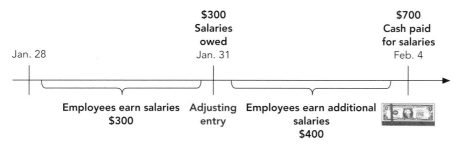

The end-of-period **adjusting entry** for accrued salaries is below.

January 31	Debit	Credit
Salaries Expense (+*E*, −*SE*)	300	
Salaries Payable (+*L*)		300
(*Owe for salaries earned by employees in the current period*)		

Accrued utility costs.   At the end of January, Eagle receives a utility bill for $960 associated with operations in January. Eagle plans to pay the bill on February 6. Even though it won't pay the cash until February, Eagle must record the utility costs for January as an expense in January. The firm records the corresponding obligation to the utility company at the same time.

The end-of-period **adjusting entry** is below.

	Debit	Credit
January 31		
Utilities Expense (+E, −SE)	960	
Utilities Payable (+L)		960
(Owe for utilities costs in the current period)		

Balance Sheet						Income Statement		
			Stockholders' Equity					**Net**
			Common	Retained				
Assets	=	**Liabilities** +	**Stock** +	**Earnings**		**Revenues** −	**Expenses** =	**Income**
	=	+960		−960			+960 =	−960

Accrued interest.   In transaction (2), Eagle borrows $10,000 from the bank to begin operations. Assume the bank charges Eagle annual interest of 12% (or 1% per month) on the borrowed amount. Interest is due by the end of the year, but repayment of the $10,000 borrowed is not due for three years. By the end of the first month, the loan has accrued interest of $100, calculated as follows:

Amount of note payable	×	**Annual interest rate**	×	**Fraction of the year**	=	**Interest**
$10,000	×	12%	×	1/12	=	$100

Notice that we multiplied by 1/12 to calculate the interest for one month (out of 12). If we had calculated interest for a two-month period, we would have multiplied by 2/12; for three months we would have multiplied by 3/12; and so on.

Although Eagle won't pay the $100 until the end of the year, it is a cost of using the borrowed funds during January and therefore is an expense for January.

The end-of-period **adjusting entry** for interest payable is below.

January 31	Debit	Credit
Interest Expense (+E, −SE)	100	
Interest Payable (+L)		100
(*Owe for interest charges in the current period*)		

Balance Sheet

Assets	=	Liabilities	+	Common Stock	+	Retained Earnings
	=	+100				−100

Income Statement

Revenues	−	Expenses	=	Net Income
		+100	=	−100

 COMMON MISTAKE

When recording the interest payable on a borrowed amount, students sometimes mistakenly credit the liability associated with the principal amount (Notes Payable). We record interest payable in a *separate account* (Interest Payable), to keep the balance owed for principal separate from the balance owed for interest.

ACCRUED REVENUES

When a company has earned revenue but hasn't yet received cash or recorded an amount receivable, it still should record the revenue. This is referred to as an accrued revenue. **The adjusting entry for an accrued revenue always includes a debit to an asset account (increase an asset) and a credit to a revenue account (increase a revenue).**

Interest receivable. We can see an example of accrued revenues if we review the flip side of transaction (2), which we discussed in the previous section. The bank lends Eagle Golf Academy $10,000 and charges Eagle annual interest of 12% (or 1% per month) on the borrowed amount. By the end of the month, interest has been earned each day, but the bank has not yet recorded the interest because it is impractical to record interest on a daily basis. At the end of January, the bank records interest revenue earned of $100 (= $10,000 × 12% × 1/12). The bank's adjusting entry for January will include a debit to Interest Receivable and a credit to Interest Revenue for $100. Note that this is the same amount that Eagle Golf Academy, the borrower, records as Interest Expense.

 Flip Side

Accounts receivable. Revenue also accrues when a firm performs services but has not yet collected cash or billed the customer. Suppose, for instance, that Eagle provides $200 of golf training to customers from January 28 to January 31. However, it usually takes Eagle one week to mail bills to customers and another week for customers to pay. Therefore, Eagle expects to receive cash from these customers during February 8–14. Because Eagle earned the revenue in January (regardless of when cash receipt takes place), Eagle should recognize in January the service revenue and the amount receivable from those customers.

The end-of-period **adjusting entry** is below.

January 31	Debit	Credit
Accounts Receivable (+A)	**200**	
Service Revenue (+R, +SE)		**200**
(Bill customers for services provided during the current period)		

Balance Sheet					Income Statement		
			Stockholders' Equity				
			Common	**Retained**			**Net**
Assets	=	**Liabilities** +	**Stock** +	**Earnings**	**Revenues** −	**Expenses** =	**Income**
+200	=			+200	+200		= +200

KEY POINT

Adjusting entries are needed when cash flows or obligations occur *before* the earnings-related activity (prepayment) or when cash flows occur *after* the earnings-related activity (accrual).

spiceland.mhhe.com/c8

NO ADJUSTMENT NECESSARY

Notice that we did not make any adjusting entries associated with transaction (1) or (10) for Eagle Golf Academy. Transaction (1) is the sale of common stock, and transaction (10) is the payment of dividends to common stockholders. **Neither of these transactions involves the recognition of revenues or expenses and therefore will not require month-end adjusting entries.**

Similarly, **transactions in which we (1) receive cash at the same time we earn revenue or (2) pay cash at the same time we incur an expense will not require adjusting entries.** For example, when Eagle provides golf training to customers for cash [transaction (6)], the company records revenue at the same time it records the cash received, and no corresponding month-end adjusting entry is needed.

KEY POINT

Adjusting entries are *unnecessary* in two cases: (1) for transactions that do not involve revenue or expense activities and (2) for transactions that result in revenues or expenses being recorded at the same time as the cash flow.

Below are four scenarios for a local **Midas Muffler** shop for the month of September.

spiceland.mhhe.com/t4

Let's Review

Scenario 1: On September 1, the balance of maintenance supplies totals $400. On September 15, the shop purchases an additional $200 of maintenance supplies. By the end of September, only $100 of maintenance supplies remains.

Scenario 2: On September 4, Midas receives $6,000 cash from a local moving company in an agreement to provide truck maintenance of $1,000 each month for the next six months, beginning in September.

Scenario 3: Mechanics have worked the final four days in September, earning $600, but have not yet been paid. Midas plans to pay its mechanics on October 2.

Scenario 4: Customers receiving $250 of maintenance services from Midas on September 29 have not been billed as of the end of the month. These customers will be billed on October 3 and are expected to pay the full amount owed on October 6.

Required:

For each of the scenarios:

1. Indicate the type of adjusting entry needed.
2. Record the transaction described and the month-end adjusting entry.

Solution:

Scenario 1: Adjusting entry type: Prepaid expense.

September 15 (external transaction)	Debit	Credit
Supplies (+A)	200	
Cash (−A)		200
(*Purchase maintenance supplies for cash*)		

September 30 (month-end adjusting entry)	Debit	Credit
Supplies Expense (+E, −SE)	500	
Supplies (−A)		500
(*Consume supplies*)		
(*$400 + $200 − $100 = $500*)		

Scenario 2: Adjusting entry type: Unearned revenue.

September 4 (external transaction)	Debit	Credit
Cash (+A)	6,000	
Unearned Revenue (+L)		6,000
(*Receive cash in advance from customers*)		

September 30 (month-end adjusting entry)	Debit	Credit
Unearned Revenue (−L)	1,000	
Service Revenue (+R, +SE)		1,000
(*Provide first of six months of services*)		

Scenario 3: Adjusting entry type: Accrued expense.

September 30 (month-end adjusting entry)	Debit	Credit
Salaries Expense (+E, −SE)	600	
Salaries Payable (+L)		600
(Owe for salaries earned by employees in the current period)		

October 2 (external transaction)	Debit	Credit
Salaries Payable (−L)	600	
Cash (−A)		600
(Pay salaries owed)		

Scenario 4: Adjusting entry type: Accrued revenue.

September 30 (month-end adjusting entry)	Debit	Credit
Accounts Receivable (+A)	250	
Service Revenue (+R, +SE)		250
(Provide maintenance service on account)		

October 6 (external transaction)	Debit	Credit
Cash (+A)	250	
Accounts Receivable (−A)		250
(Collect cash from customers previously billed)		

Suggested Homework:
**BE3-6, BE3-10;
E3-7, E3-8;
P3-3A&B, P3-4A&B**

Post Adjusting Entries

■ **LO4**

Post adjusting entries and prepare an adjusted trial balance.

To complete the measurement process, we need to update balances of assets, liabilities, revenues, and expenses for adjusting entries. In Illustration 3–8, we summarize the eight adjusting entries of Eagle Golf Academy recorded earlier. To update balances, we post the adjustments to the appropriate accounts in the general ledger, as demonstrated in Illustration 3–9.

ILLUSTRATION 3–8

Summary of Adjusting Entries for Eagle Golf Academy

January 31	Debit	Credit
(a) Rent Expense (+E, −SE)	500	
Prepaid Rent (−A)		500
(Reduce prepaid rent due to the passage of time)		
(b) Supplies Expense (+E, −SE)	800	
Supplies (−A)		800
(Consume supplies during the current period)		
(c) Depreciation Expense (+E, −SE)	400	
Accumulated Depreciation (−A)..		400
(Depreciate equipment)		
($24,000 ÷ 60 months = $400 per month)		
(d) Unearned Revenue (−L)	60	
Service Revenue (+R, +SE)		60
(Provide services to customers who paid in advance)		
(e) Salaries Expense (+E, −SE)	300	
Salaries Payable (+L)		300
(Owe for salaries earned by employees in the current period)		

ILLUSTRATION 3–8

Summary of Adjusting Entries for Eagle Golf Academy *(continued)*

(f) **Utilities Expense** (+E, −SE)	960	
Utilities Payable (+L)		960
(Owe for utilities costs in the current period)		
(g) **Interest Expense** (+E, −SE)	100	
Interest Payable (+L)		100
(Owe for interest charges in the current period)		
(h) **Accounts Receivable** (+A)	200	
Service Revenue (+R, +SE)		200
(Bill customers for services provided during the month)		

ILLUSTRATION 3–9   Posting Adjusting Entries (in red) of Eagle Golf Academy to General Ledger Accounts

Assets	=	Liabilities	+	Stockholders' Equity

Cash

(1)	25,000	(3)	24,000
(2)	10,000	(4)	6,000
(6)	3,600	(9)	2,800
(8)	600	(10)	200
Bal.	**6,200**		

Accounts Payable

	(5)	2,300
	Bal.	**2,300**

Common Stock

	(1)	25,000
	Bal.	**25,000**

Retained Earnings

	0
Bal.	**0**

Accounts Receivable

(7)	2,500
(h)	200
Bal.	**2,700**

Unearned Revenue

	(8)	600
(d)	60	
	Bal.	**540**

Dividends

(10)	200
Bal.	**200**

Service Revenue

	(6)	3,600
	(7)	2,500
	(d)	60
	(h)	200
	Bal.	**6,360**

Supplies

(5)	2,300		
		(b)	800
Bal.	**1,500**		

Salaries Payable

	(e)	300
	Bal.	**300**

Supplies Expense

(b)	800
Bal.	**800**

Rent Expense

(a)	500
Bal.	**500**

Prepaid Rent

(4)	6,000		
		(a)	500
Bal.	**5,500**		

Utilities Payable

	(f)	960
	Bal.	**960**

Depreciation Expense

(c)	400
Bal.	**400**

Salaries Expense

(9)	2,800
(e)	300
Bal.	**3,100**

Equipment

(3)	24,000
Bal.	**24,000**

Interest Payable

	(g)	100
	Bal.	**100**

Utilities Expense

(f)	960
Bal.	**960**

Interest Expense

(g)	100
Bal.	**100**

Accumulated Depreciation

	(c)	400
	Bal.	**400**

Notes Payable

	(2)	10,000
	Bal.	**10,000**

- Amounts in black represent external transactions in January. Numbers in parentheses refer to transaction numbers in Illustration 3–5.
- Amounts in red represent month-end adjusting entries. Letters in parentheses refer to adjusting entries in Illustration 3–8.
- Amounts in **bold** represent ending balances.

COMMON MISTAKE

Students sometimes mistakenly include the Cash account in an adjusting entry. An adjusting entry will never include the Cash account. Note that no adjusting entries are posted to the Cash account in Illustration 3–9.

KEY POINT

We post adjusting entries to the T-accounts in the general ledger to update the account balances.

ADJUSTED TRIAL BALANCE

After we have posted the adjusting entries to the general ledger accounts, we're ready to prepare an *adjusted* trial balance. An adjusted trial balance is a list of all accounts and their balances *after we have updated account balances for adjusting entries.* Illustration 3–10 shows the relationship between an unadjusted trial

ILLUSTRATION 3–10

Unadjusted Trial Balance and Adjusted Trial Balance for Eagle Golf Academy

EAGLE GOLF ACADEMY
Unadjusted Trial Balance and Adjusted Trial Balance
January 31

Accounts	Unadjusted Trial Balance Debit	Unadjusted Trial Balance Credit	Adjustments Debit	Adjustments Credit	Adjusted Trial Balance Debit	Adjusted Trial Balance Credit
Cash	$ 6,200				$ 6,200	
Accounts Receivable	2,500		(h) 200		2,700	
Supplies	2,300			(b) 800	1,500	
Prepaid Rent	6,000			(a) 500	5,500	
Equipment	24,000				24,000	
Accumulated Depreciation				(c) 400		$ 400
Accounts Payable		$ 2,300				2,300
Unearned Revenue		600	(d) 60			540
Salaries Payable				(e) 300		300
Utilities Payable				(f) 960		960
Interest Payable				(g) 100		100
Notes Payable		10,000				10,000
Common Stock		25,000				25,000
Retained Earnings		0				0
Dividends	200				200	
Service Revenue		6,100		(d and h) 260		6,360
Supplies Expense			(b) 800		800	
Rent Expense			(a) 500		500	
Depreciation Expense			(c) 400		400	
Salaries Expense	2,800		(e) 300		3,100	
Utilities Expense			(f) 960		960	
Interest Expense			(g) 100		100	
Totals	**$44,000**	**$44,000**			**$45,960**	**$45,960**

Total debits equal total credits.

balance (before adjustments) and an adjusted trial balance (after adjustments). The unadjusted trial balance is the one shown in Chapter 2 in Illustration 2–26. The adjusted trial balance includes the adjusted balances of all general ledger accounts shown in Illustration 3–9.

KEY POINT

An adjusted trial balance is a list of all accounts and their balances at a particular date, after we have updated account balances for adjusting entries.

THE REPORTING PROCESS: FINANCIAL STATEMENTS

PART C

Once the adjusted trial balance is complete, we prepare financial statements. Illustration 3–11 describes the relationship between the adjusted trial balance and the financial statements. Notice the color coding of the accounts, to indicate their relationships to the financial statements.

■ **LO5**
Prepare financial statements using the adjusted trial balance.

EAGLE GOLF ACADEMY
Adjusted Trial Balance
January 31

Accounts	Debit	Credit
Cash	$ 6,200	
Accounts Receivable	2,700	
Supplies	1,500	
Prepaid Rent	5,500	
Equipment	24,000	
Accumulated Depreciation		$ 400
Accounts Payable		2,300
Unearned Revenue		540
Salaries Payable		300
Interest Payable		100
Utilities Payable		960
Notes Payable		10,000
Common Stock		25,000
Retained Earnings		0
Dividends	200	
Service Revenue		6,360
Supplies Expense	800	
Rent Expense	500	
Depreciation Expense	400	
Salaries Expense	3,100	
Utilities Expense	960	
Interest Expense	100	
Totals	$45,960	$45,960

ILLUSTRATION 3–11
Relationship between Adjusted Trial Balance and Financial Statements

BALANCE SHEET
Assets
=
Liabilities
+
Stockholders'
Equity

STATEMENT OF STOCKHOLDERS' EQUITY

Common Stock
+
Retained Earnings
(= RE, Jan. 1 + NI − Divs)
=
Stockholders' Equity

INCOME STATEMENT
Revenues
−
Expenses
=
Net Income

Revenue and expense accounts are reported in the income statement. The difference between total revenues and total expenses equals net income. All asset, liability, and stockholders' equity accounts are reported in the balance sheet. The balance sheet confirms the equality of the basic accounting equation.

Income Statement

Illustration 3–12 shows the income statement of Eagle Golf Academy for the month of January. Note that, unlike the income statements shown in Chapter 1, this income statement has a *multicolumn* format: Amounts for individual items are placed in the left column, and subtotals are placed in the right column. Presenting the income statement in this manner makes it easier to see that net income equals the difference between total revenues and total expenses.

The income statement demonstrates that Eagle Golf Academy earned a profit of **$500** in the month of January. The revenues earned from providing training to customers exceed the costs of providing that training.

ILLUSTRATION 3–12

Income Statement for Eagle Golf Academy

Revenues minus expenses equal net income.

EAGLE GOLF ACADEMY		
Income Statement		
For the month ended January 31		
Revenues:		
Service revenue		$6,360
Expenses:		
Salaries expense	$3,100	
Rent expense	500	
Supplies expense	800	
Depreciation expense	400	
Interest expense	100	
Utilities expense	960	
Total expenses		5,860
Net income		$ 500

Statement of Stockholders' Equity

The statement of stockholders' equity summarizes the changes in each stockholders' equity account as well as in total stockholders' equity and the accounting value of the company to stockholders (owners). Illustration 3–13 shows the statement of stockholders' equity for Eagle Golf Academy.

ILLUSTRATION 3–13

Statement of Stockholders' Equity for Eagle Golf Academy

Retained earnings includes net income from the income statement.

EAGLE GOLF ACADEMY			
Statement of Stockholders' Equity			
For the month ended January 31			
	Common Stock	Retained Earnings	Total Stockholders' Equity
Balance at January 1	$ -0-	$ -0-	$ -0-
Issuance of common stock	25,000		25,000
Add: Net income for January		500	500
Less: Dividends		(200)	(200)
Balance at January 31	$25,000	$300	$25,300

Total stockholders' equity increases from **$0** at the beginning of January to **$25,300** by the end of January. The increase occurs as a result of a **$25,000** investment by the owners (stockholders) when they bought common stock plus an increase of **$300** when the company earned a profit of $500 on behalf of its stockholders and distributed $200 of dividends.

You've seen that retained earnings has three components: revenues, expenses, and dividends. In the adjusted trial balance, the balance of the Retained Earnings account is its balance at the beginning of the accounting period—the balance *before* all revenue, expense, and dividend transactions. For Eagle Golf Academy, the beginning balance of Retained Earnings equals $0 since this is the first month of operations. Ending Retained Earnings equals its beginning balance of $0 plus the effects of all revenue and expense transactions (net income of $500) less dividends of **$200** paid to stockholders. Since dividends represent the payment of company resources (cash), they will have a negative effect on the stockholders' equity (retained earnings) of the company.

Classified Balance Sheet

The balance sheet you saw in Chapter 1 contained the key asset, liability, and stockholders' equity accounts, presented as a rather simple list. Here, we introduce a slightly more complex form of the balance sheet, with many more accounts. To put those accounts in an order that enables ease of understanding, we use a format called the classified balance sheet.

Common Terms Another common name for current assets and liabilities is *short-term assets and liabilities.*

A classified balance sheet groups a company's assets, liabilities, and stockholders' equity accounts into several standard categories: We can separate assets into those that provide a benefit over the next year (*current assets*) and those that provide a benefit for more than one year (*long-term assets*). More precisely, the distinction between current and long-term assets is whether the asset will benefit the firm for more than one year or an *operating cycle*, whichever is longer. The operating cycle is the average time between purchasing or acquiring inventory and receiving cash proceeds from its sale. For nearly all firms, the operating cycle is shorter than one year. Similarly, we can divide liabilities into those due during the next year (*current liabilities*) and those due in more than one year (*long-term liabilities*).

Illustration 3–14 (next page) presents a classified balance sheet for Eagle Golf Academy. As we discuss later in the book, long-term assets are further classified into groups. Long-term asset categories include investments; property, plant, and equipment; and intangible assets:

- *Long-term investments* involve a company paying cash to invest in another company's debt or stock. We discuss long-term investments in debt and equity securities in Appendix D.
- *Property, plant, and equipment* items include long-term productive assets used in the normal course of business, such as land, buildings, equipment, and machinery. Eagle's purchase of training equipment is an example of a purchase of property, plant, and equipment. We discuss property, plant, and equipment in Chapter 7.
- *Intangible assets* are assets that lack physical substance but have long-term value to a company, such as patents, copyrights, franchises, and trademarks. We discuss intangible assets in Chapter 7.

ILLUSTRATION 3–14

Classified Balance Sheet for Eagle Golf Academy

Total **assets** equal current plus long-term assets.

Total **liabilities** equal current plus long-term liabilities.

Total **stockholders' equity** includes common stock and retained earnings from the statement of stockholders' equity.

Total assets must equal total liabilities plus stockholders' equity.

EAGLE GOLF ACADEMY Classified Balance Sheet January 31				
Assets			**Liabilities**	
Current assets:			Current liabilities:	
Cash	$ 6,200		Accounts payable	$ 2,300
Accounts receivable	2,700		Unearned revenue	540
Supplies	1,500		Salaries payable	300
Prepaid rent	5,500		Utilities payable	960
Total current assets	15,900		Interest payable	100
			Total current liabilities	4,200
Long-term assets:				
Equipment	24,000		Long-term liabilities:	
Less: Accum. depr.	(400)		Notes payable	10,000
			Total liabilities	14,200
Total long-term assets	23,600			
			Stockholders' Equity	
			Common stock	25,000
			Retained earnings	300
			Total stockholders' equity	25,300
			Total liabilities and	
Total assets	$39,500		stockholders' equity	$39,500

In Illustration 3–14, notice that total assets of $39,500 equal total liabilities and stockholders' equity of $39,500. We achieve this equality only by including the correct balance of **$300** for retained earnings from the statement of stockholders' equity, *not* the balance of $0 from the adjusted trial balance.

KEY POINT

We prepare the income statement, statement of stockholders' equity, and balance sheet from the adjusted trial balance. The income statement provides a measure of net income (profitability), calculated as revenues minus expenses. The balance sheet demonstrates that assets equal liabilities plus stockholders' equity (the basic accounting equation).

Statement of Cash Flows

The final financial statement we need to prepare is the statement of cash flows. As discussed in Chapter 1, the statement of cash flows measures activities involving cash receipts and cash payments, reflecting a company's operating, investing, and financing activities. We'll take another brief look at the statement of cash flows in the next chapter and then discuss it in detail in Chapter 11.

THE CLOSING PROCESS

■ **LO6**
Demonstrate the purposes and recording of closing entries.

Recall that revenues, expenses, and dividends are components of retained earnings. Notice that Eagle's balance sheet reports retained earnings of $300, as if all net income transactions (revenues and expenses) and dividend transactions had been recorded directly in Retained Earnings. However, instead of recording revenue, expense, and dividend transactions directly to the Retained Earnings account during the period, we recorded them to the three component accounts. This allows us to maintain individual measures of revenues, expenses, and dividends for preparing financial statements at the end of the period.

After we have reported revenues and expenses in the income statement and dividends in the statement of stockholders' equity, it's time to transfer these amounts to the Retained Earnings account itself. These three accounts—revenues, expenses, and dividends—are termed temporary accounts: We keep them for each period and then transfer the balances of revenues, expenses, and dividends to the Retained Earnings account. All accounts that appear in the balance sheet, including Retained Earnings, are permanent accounts, and we carry forward their balances from period to period. We treat only revenues, expenses, and dividends as temporary, *so it will appear as if we had recorded all these types of transactions directly in Retained Earnings* during the year. We accomplish this with closing entries.

Closing Entries

Closing entries **transfer the balances of all temporary accounts (revenues, expenses, and dividends) to the balance of the Retained Earnings account.** Here's how:

- All revenue accounts have credit balances. To transfer these balances to the Retained Earnings account, we debit each of these revenue accounts for its balance and credit Retained Earnings for the total.
- Similarly, all expense and dividend accounts have debit balances. So, we credit each of these accounts for its balance and debit Retained Earnings for the total.

By doing this, we accomplish two necessary tasks: First, we *update the balance in the Retained Earnings account to reflect transactions related to revenues, expenses, and dividends in the current period.* Second, we *reduce the balances of all revenue, expense, and dividend accounts to zero* so we can start from scratch in measuring those amounts in the next accounting period. After all, revenues, expenses, and dividends are temporary accounts, which means their balances each period must start at zero.

Closing entries serve two purposes.

KEY POINT

Closing entries serve two purposes: (1) to transfer the balances of temporary accounts (revenues, expenses, and dividends) to the Retained Earnings account, and (2) to reduce the balances of these temporary accounts to zero to prepare them for measuring activity in the next period.

For demonstration, refer back to Eagle Golf Academy. We can transfer the balances of all revenue, expense, and dividend accounts to the balance of the Retained Earnings account with the closing entries shown in Illustration 3–15.

ILLUSTRATION 3–15

Closing Entries for
Eagle Golf Academy

January 31	Debit	Credit
(a) Service Revenue	6,360	
Retained Earnings		6,360
(Close revenues to retained earnings)		
(b) Retained Earnings	5,860	
Supplies Expense		800
Rent Expense		500
Depreciation Expense		400
Salaries Expense		3,100
Utilities Expense		960
Interest Expense		100
(Close expenses to retained earnings)		
(c) Retained Earnings	200	
Dividends		200
(Close dividends to retained earnings)		

Note that closing entries transfer the balances of the components of retained earnings (revenues, expenses, and dividends) to the balance of Retained Earnings itself. Retained Earnings is credited (increased) in the first entry and then debited (decreased) in the second and third entries. Posting these amounts to the Retained Earnings account will result in the following ending balance:

	Retained Earnings		
		0	Beginning balance
		6,360	Total revenues
Total expenses	5,860		
Total dividends	200		
		300	Ending balance

spiceland.mhhe.com/c9

The ending balance of Retained Earnings now includes all transactions affecting the components of the account. The ending balance of **$300** represents all revenues and expenses over the life of the company (just the first month of operations in this example) less dividends. Another way to think about the balance of Retained Earnings is that it's the amount of net income earned by the company for its owners but that has not been paid to owners in the form of dividends.

The ending balance of Retained Earnings in January will be its beginning balance in February. Then we'll close February's revenues, expenses, and dividends to Retained Earnings, and this cycle will continue each period.

 COMMON MISTAKE

Students sometimes believe that closing entries are meant to reduce the balance of Retained Eearnings to zero. Retained Earnings is a *permanent account*, representing the accumulation of all revenues, expenses, and dividends over the life of the company.

In summary, the key points about closing entries are as follows.

- We *transfer the balance of all revenue, expense, and dividend accounts to the balance of Retained Earnings.* Dollar-for-dollar, every credit to revenues is now a credit to Retained Earnings, and every debit to expenses or dividends is now a debit to Retained Earnings.
- Closing entries *increase the Retained Earnings account by the amount of revenues and decrease Retained Earnings by the amount of expenses and dividends.*
- The balance of *each revenue, expense, and dividend account equals zero after closing entries.* These accounts have temporary balances and must be closed, or "zeroed out," to prepare them for measuring activity in the next period.
- Closing entries *do not affect the balances of permanent accounts* (assets, liabilities, and permanent stockholders' equity accounts) *other than retained earnings.* Permanent accounts carry a cumulative balance throughout the life of the company.

Illustration 3–16 shows retained earnings, net income, and dividends for **Coca-Cola** over a three-year period. Notice that the balance of retained earnings increases each year by the amount of net income less dividends. Retained earnings is a permanent account and represents the cumulative total of net income less dividends over the life of the company.

THE COCA-COLA COMPANY ($ in millions)							
Year	Beginning Retained Earnings*	+	Net Income**	−	Dividends	=	Ending Retained Earnings
2005							$31,299
2006	$31,299	+	$5,080	−	$2,911	=	33,468
2007	33,468	+	5,981	−	3,149	=	36,300
2008	36,300	+	5,807	−	3,521	=	38,586

*Beginning retained earnings is the ending retained earnings from the previous year.
**Net income equals total revenues minus total expenses.

ILLUSTRATION 3–16

Relation between Retained Earnings, Net Income, and Dividends for Coca-Cola

KEY POINT

Closing entries increase retained earnings by the amount of revenues for the period and decrease retained earnings by the amount of expenses and dividends for the period.

Post Closing Entries

■ **LO7**
Post closing entries
and prepare a post-
closing trial balance.

After we have prepared closing entries, we post amounts to the accounts in the general ledger. Illustration 3–17 demonstrates the process of posting the closing entries. The current balance of each account reflects transactions during the period (in black), adjusting entries (in **red**), and closing entries (in blue).

ILLUSTRATION 3–17   Posting Closing Entries to Adjusted Balances of Ledger Accounts

Assets	=	Liabilities	+	Stockholders' Equity

Assets

Cash

(1)	25,000	(3)	24,000
(2)	10,000	(4)	6,000
(6)	3,600	(9)	2,800
(8)	600	(10)	200
Bal.	**6,200**		

Accounts Receivable

(7)	2,500		
(h)	200		
Bal.	**2,700**		

Supplies

(5)	2,300		
		(b)	800
Bal.	**1,500**		

Prepaid Rent

(4)	6,000		
		(a)	500
Bal.	**5,500**		

Equipment

(3)	24,000		
Bal.	**24,000**		

Accumulated Depreciation

		(c)	400
		Bal.	**400**

Liabilities

Accounts Payable

		(5)	2,300
		Bal.	**2,300**

Unearned Revenue

		(8)	600
(d)	60		
		Bal.	**540**

Salaries Payable

		(e)	300
		Bal.	**300**

Utilities Payable

		(f)	960
		Bal.	**960**

Interest Payable

		(g)	100
		Bal.	**100**

Notes Payable

		(2)	10,000
		Bal.	**10,000**

Stockholders' Equity

Common Stock

		(1)	25,000
		Bal.	**25,000**

Retained Earnings

			0
		(a)	6,360
(b)	5,860		
(c)	200		
		Bal.	**300**

Dividends

(10)	200		
		(c)	200
Bal.	**0**		

Service Revenue

		(6)	3,600
		(7)	2,500
		(d)	60
		(h)	200
(a)	6,360		
		Bal.	**0**

Supplies Expense

(b)	800		
		(b)	800
Bal.	**0**		

Rent Expense

(a)	500		
		(b)	500
Bal.	**0**		

Depreciation Expense

(c)	400		
		(b)	400
Bal.	**0**		

Salaries Expense

(9)	2,800		
(e)	300		
		(b)	3,100
Bal.	**0**		

Utilities Expense

(f)	960		
		(b)	960
Bal.	**0**		

Interest Expense

(g)	100		
		(b)	100
Bal.	**0**		

- Amounts in black represent external transactions during January. Numbers in parentheses refer to transaction numbers in Illustration 3–5.
- Amounts in red represent month-end adjusting entries. Letters in parentheses refer to adjusting entries in Illustration 3–8.
- Amounts in blue represent month-end closing entries. Letters in parentheses refer to closing entries in Illustration 3–15.

After we post the closing entries, the **$300** balance of Retained Earnings now equals the amount shown in the balance sheet. In addition, the ending balances of all revenue, expense, and dividend accounts are now zero and ready to begin the next period.

After we post the closing entries to the ledger accounts, we can prepare a post-closing trial balance. The post-closing trial balance is a list of all accounts and their balances at a particular date *after we have updated account balances for closing entries.* The post-closing trial balance helps to verify that we prepared and posted closing entries correctly and that the accounts are now ready for the next period's transactions.

Illustration 3–18 shows the post-closing trial balance for Eagle Golf Academy as of January 31.

Amounts in bold represent ending balances.

EAGLE GOLF ACADEMY
Post-Closing Trial Balance
January 31

Accounts	Debit	Credit
Cash	$ 6,200	
Accounts Receivable	2,700	
Supplies	1,500	
Prepaid Rent	5,500	
Equipment	24,000	
Accumulated Depreciation		$ 400
Accounts Payable		2,300
Unearned Revenue		540
Salaries Payable		300
Interest Payable		100
Utilities Payable		960
Notes Payable		10,000
Common Stock		25,000
Retained Earnings		300
Totals	$39,900	$39,900

ILLUSTRATION 3–18

Post-Closing Trial Balance for Eagle Golf Academy

Notice that the post-closing trial balance does not include any revenues, expenses, or dividends, because these accounts all have zero balances after closing entries. The balance of Retained Earnings has been updated from the adjusted trial balance to include all revenues, expenses, and dividends for the period.

Decision Point

Question	Accounting information	Analysis
The amounts reported for revenues and expenses represent activity over what period of time?	Income statement	Revenue and expense accounts measure activity only for the current reporting period (usually a month, quarter, or year). At the end of each period, they are closed and begin the next period at zero.

Let's Review

spiceland.mhhe.com/t5

Below is the adjusted trial balance of Beckham Soccer Academy for October 31.

BECKHAM SOCCER ACADEMY Adjusted Trial Balance October 31		
Accounts	**Debit**	**Credit**
Cash	$ 2,600	
Supplies	3,900	
Accounts Payable		$ 1,000
Salaries Payable		300
Common Stock		3,000
Retained Earnings		1,700
Dividends	200	
Service Revenue		4,300
Salaries Expense	2,400	
Supplies Expense	700	
Rent Expense	500	
Totals	$10,300	$10,300

Required:

1. Prepare closing entries.
2. Prepare a post-closing trial balance.
3. Compare the balances of Retained Earnings in the adjusted trial balance and the post-closing trial balance.

Solution:

1. Closing entries.

October 31	Debit	Credit
Service Revenue	4,300	
Retained Earnings		4,300
(Close revenues to retained earnings)		
Retained Earnings	3,600	
Salaries Expense		2,400
Supplies Expense		700
Rent Expense		500
(Close expenses to retained earnings)		
Retained Earnings	200	
Dividends		200
(Close dividends to retained earnings)		

2. Post-closing trial balance.

BECKHAM SOCCER ACADEMY Post-Closing Trial Balance October 31		
Accounts	**Debit**	**Credit**
Cash	$2,600	
Supplies	3,900	
Accounts Payable		$1,000
Salaries Payable		300
Common Stock		3,000
Retained Earnings		2,200
Totals	$6,500	$6,500

3. The balance of Retained Earnings increases by $500 from the adjusted trial balance to the post-closing trial balance. The balance increases by the amount of net income ($700) and decreases by the amount of dividends ($200).

Suggested Homework:
**BE3-19, BE3-20;
E3-17, E3-18;
P3-7A&B; P3-8A&B**

KEY POINT

After we post the closing entries to the T-accounts in the general ledger, the balance of Retained Earnings equals the amount shown in the balance sheet. The balances of all revenue, expense, and dividend accounts are zero at that point.

KEY POINTS BY LEARNING OBJECTIVE

LO1 Record revenues using the revenue recognition principle and expenses using the matching principle.

The revenue recognition principle states that we should recognize revenue in the period in which we *earn* it, not necessarily in the period in which we receive cash.

The matching principle states that we recognize expenses in the same period as the revenues they help to generate. Expenses include those directly and indirectly related to producing revenues.

LO2 Distinguish between accrual-basis and cash-basis accounting.

The difference between accrual-basis accounting and cash-basis accounting is *timing*. Under accrual-basis accounting, we record revenues when we earn them (revenue recognition principle) and record expenses with the revenue they help to generate (matching

principle). Under cash-basis accounting, we record revenues when we receive cash and expenses when we pay cash. Cash-basis accounting is not allowed for financial reporting purposes.

LO3 Demonstrate the purposes and recording of adjusting entries.

Adjusting entries are a necessary part of accrual-basis accounting. They help to record revenues in the period earned and expenses in the period they are incurred to generate those revenues. Another benefit is that, by properly recording revenues and expenses, we correctly state assets and liabilities.

Adjusting entries are needed when cash flows or obligations occur *before* the earnings-related activity (prepayment) or when cash flows occur *after* the earnings-related activity (accrual).

Adjusting entries are unnecessary in two cases: (1) for transactions that do not involve revenue or expense activities and (2) for transactions that result in revenues or expenses being recorded at the same time as the cash flow.

LO4 Post adjusting entries and prepare an adjusted trial balance.

We post adjusting entries to the T-accounts in the general ledger to update the account balances.

An adjusted trial balance is a list of all accounts and their balances at a particular date after we have updated account balances for adjusting entries.

LO5 Prepare financial statements using the adjusted trial balance.

We prepare the income statement, statement of stockholders' equity, and balance sheet from the adjusted trial balance. The income statement provides a measure of net income (profitability), calculated as revenues minus expenses. The balance sheet demonstrates that assets equal liabilities plus stockholders' equity (the basic accounting equation).

LO6 Demonstrate the purposes and recording of closing entries.

Closing entries serve two purposes: (1) to transfer the balances of temporary accounts (revenues, expenses, and dividends) to the retained earnings account and (2) to reduce the balances of these temporary accounts to zero to prepare them for measuring activity in the next period.

Closing entries increase the balance of retained earnings by the amount of revenues for the period and decrease retained earnings by the amount of expenses and dividends for the period.

LO7 Post closing entries and prepare a post-closing trial balance.

After we post the closing entries to the T-accounts in the general ledger, the balance of Retained Earnings equals the amount shown in the balance sheet. The balances of all revenue, expense, and dividend accounts are zero at that point.

GLOSSARY

Accrual-basis accounting: Record revenues when earned (the revenue recognition principle) and expenses with related revenues (the matching principle). **p. 78**

Accrued expense: When a company has incurred an expense but hasn't yet paid cash or recorded an obligation to pay. **p. 89**

Accrued revenue: When a company has earned revenue but hasn't yet received cash or recorded an amount receivable. **p. 91**

Adjusted trial balance: A list of all accounts and their balances after we have updated account balances for adjusting entries. **p. 96**

Adjusting entries: Entries used to record events that occur during the period but that have not yet been recorded by the end of the period. **p. 82**

Cash-basis accounting: Record revenues at the time cash is received and expenses at the time cash is paid. **p. 80**

Classified balance sheet: Balance sheet that groups a company's assets into current assets and long-term assets and that separates liabilities into current liabilities and long-term liabilities. **p. 99**

Closing entries: Entries that transfer the balances of all temporary accounts (revenues, expenses, and dividends) to the balance of the Retained Earnings account. **p. 101**

Contra account: An account with a balance that is opposite, or "contra," to that of its related accounts. **p. 86**

Matching principle: Recognize expenses in the same period as the revenues they help to generate. **p. 79**

Operating cycle: The average time between purchasing or acquiring inventory and receiving cash proceeds from its sale. **p. 99**

Permanent accounts: All accounts that appear in the balance sheet; account balances are carried forward from period to period. **p. 101**

Post-closing trial balance: A list of all accounts and their balances at a particular date after we have updated account balances for closing entries. **p. 105**

Prepaid expenses: The costs of assets acquired in one period that will be expensed in a future period. **p. 83**

Revenue recognition principle: Record revenue in the period in which it's earned. **p. 78**

Temporary accounts: All revenue, expense, and dividend accounts; account balances are maintained for a single period and then closed (or zeroed out) and transferred to the balance of the Retained Earnings account at the end of the period. **p. 101**

Unearned revenues: When a company receives cash in advance from a customer for products or services to be provided in the future. **p. 87**

SELF-STUDY QUESTIONS

1. On May 5, Johnson Plumbing receives a phone call from a customer needing a new water heater and schedules a service visit for May 7. On May 7, Johnson installs the new water heater. The customer pays for services on May 10. According to the *revenue recognition principle,* on which date should Johnson record service revenue?   ■ **LO1**
   a. May 5 (date of phone call).
   b. May 7 (date of service).
   c. May 10 (date of cash receipt).
   d. Evenly over the three dates.

2. On January 17, Papa's Pizza signs a contract with Bug Zappers for exterminating services related to a recent sighting of cockroaches in the restaurant. Papa's pays for the extermination service on January 29, and Bug Zappers sprays for bugs on February 7. According to the *matching principle,* on which date should Papa's Pizza record the extermination expense?   ■ **LO1**
   a. January 17 (date of the contract).
   b. January 29 (date of cash payment).
   c. February 7 (date of extermination service).
   d. Evenly over the three dates.

3. Refer to the information in self-study question 1. Using *cash-basis accounting,* on which date should Johnson record service revenue?   ■ **LO2**
   a. May 5 (date of phone call).
   b. May 7 (date of service).
   c. May 10 (date of cash receipt).
   d. Evenly over the three dates.

4. Refer to the information in self-study question 2. Using *cash-basis accounting,* on which date should Papa's Pizza record the extermination expense?   ■ **LO2**
   a. January 17 (date of the contract).
   b. January 29 (date of cash payment).
   c. February 7 (date of extermination service).
   d. Evenly over the three dates.

5. Which of the following is *not* a characteristic of adjusting entries?   ■ **LO3**
   a. Reduce the balances of revenue, expense, and dividend accounts to zero.
   b. Allow for proper application of the revenue recognition principle (revenues) or the matching principle (expenses).
   c. Are part of accrual-basis accounting.
   d. Are recorded at the end of the accounting period.

6. Ambassador Hotels purchases one year of fire insurance coverage on December 1 for $24,000 ($2,000 per month), debiting prepaid insurance. On December 31, Ambassador would record the following year-end adjusting entry: ■ **LO3**

	Debit	Credit
a. Insurance Expense	24,000	
Prepaid Insurance		24,000
b. Insurance Expense	2,000	
Prepaid Insurance		2,000
c. Insurance Expense	22,000	
Prepaid Insurance		22,000
d. No entry is required on December 31 because full cash payment was made on December 1 and the insurance does not expire until the following November 30.		

■ LO4

7. An adjusted trial balance:
    a. Lists all accounts and their balances at a particular date after updating account balances for adjusting entries.
    b. Is used to prepare the financial statements.
    c. Includes balances for revenues, expenses, and dividends.
    d. All the above.

■ LO5

8. Which of the following describes the information reported in the statement of stockholders' equity?
    a. Net income for the period calculated as revenues minus expenses.
    b. Equality of total assets with total liabilities plus stockholders' equity.
    c. Change in stockholders' equity through changes in common stock and retained earnings.
    d. Net cash flows from operating, investing, and financing activities.

■ LO6

9. Which of the following describes the purpose(s) of closing entries?
    a. Adjust the balances of asset and liability accounts for unrecorded activity during the period.
    b. Transfer the balances of temporary accounts (revenues, expenses, and dividends) to Retained Earnings.
    c. Reduce the balances of the temporary accounts to zero to prepare them for measuring activity in the next period.
    d. Both *b*. and *c*.

■ LO7

10. Which of the following accounts is *not* listed in a post-closing trial balance?
    a. Prepaid Rent.
    b. Accounts Payable.
    c. Salaries Expense.
    d. Retained Earnings.

Answers to the Self-Study Questions
1. b   2. c   3. c   4. b   5. a   6. b   7. d   8. c   9. d   10. c

REVIEW QUESTIONS

■ LO1

1. Discuss the major principle that describes recording revenues.

■ LO1

2. Discuss the major principle that describes recording expenses.

■ LO1

3. Samantha is a first-year accounting student. She doesn't think it matters that expenses are reported in the same period's income statement with the related revenues (matching principle). She feels that "as long as revenues and expenses are recorded in any period, that's good enough." Help her understand why the matching principle is important.

■ LO2

4. Describe when revenues and expenses are recognized using cash-basis accounting. How does this differ from accrual-basis accounting?

■ LO2
Flip Side of Question 7

5. Executive Lawn provides $100 of landscape maintenance to Peterson Law on April 10. Consider three scenarios:

    a. Peterson pays for the lawn service in advance on March 28.
    b. Peterson pays for the lawn service on April 10, the day of service.
    c. Peterson pays for the lawn service the following month on May 2.

    If Executive Lawn uses accrual-basis accounting, on which date would Executive Lawn record the $100 revenue for each scenario?

6. Consider the information in question 5. Using cash-basis accounting, on which date would Executive Lawn record the $100 revenue for each scenario?

■ LO2
Flip Side of Question 8

7. Peterson Law asks Executive Lawn to provide $100 of landscape maintenance. Executive Lawn provides the service on April 10. Consider three scenarios:
   a. Peterson pays for the lawn service in advance on March 28.
   b. Peterson pays for the lawn service on April 10, the day of service.
   c. Peterson pays for the lawn service the following month on May 2.

   If Peterson Law uses accrual-basis accounting, on which date would Peterson Law record the $100 expense for each scenario?

■ LO2
Flip Side of Question 5

8. Consider the information in question 7. Using cash-basis accounting, on which date would Peterson Law record the $100 expense for each scenario?

■ LO2
Flip Side of Question 6

9. Why are adjusting entries necessary under accrual-basis accounting?

10. There are two basic types of adjusting entries—prepayments and accruals. Describe each in terms of the timing of revenue and expense recognition versus the flow of cash.

■ LO3
■ LO3

11. Provide an example of a prepaid expense. The adjusting entry associated with a prepaid expense always includes a debit and credit to which account classifications?

■ LO3

12. Provide an example of an unearned revenue. The adjusting entry associated with an unearned revenue always includes a debit and credit to which account classifications?

■ LO3

13. Provide an example of an accrued expense. The adjusting entry associated with an accrued expense always includes a debit and credit to which account classifications?

■ LO3

14. Provide an example of an accrued revenue. The adjusting entry associated with an accrued revenue always includes a debit and credit to which account classifications?

■ LO3

15. Sequoya Printing purchases office supplies for $75 on October 2. The staff uses the office supplies continually on a daily basis throughout the month. By the end of the month, office supplies of $25 remain. Record the month-end adjusting entry for office supplies (assuming the balance of Office Supplies at the beginning of October was $0).

■ LO3

16. Jackson Rental receives its September utility bill of $320 on September 30 but does not pay the bill until October 10. Jackson's accountant records the utility expense of $320 on October 10 at the time of payment. Will this cause any of Jackson's accounts to be misstated at the end of September? If so, indicate which ones and the direction of the misstatement.

■ LO3

17. Global Printing publishes several types of magazines. Customers are required to pay for magazines in advance. On November 5, Global receives cash of $120,000 for prepaid subscriptions. By the end of November, Global has distributed $20,000 of magazines to customers. Record the month-end adjusting entry.

■ LO3

18. At the end of May, Robertson Corporation has provided services to customers, but it has not yet billed these customers nor have any of them paid for those services. If Robertson makes no adjusting entry associated with these unpaid services provided, will any accounts be misstated? If so, indicate which ones and the direction of the misstatement.

■ LO3

19. Fill in the blank associated with each adjusting entry:
   a. *Prepaid expense:* Debit Supplies Expense; credit _____.
   b. *Unearned revenue:* Debit _____; credit Service Revenue.
   c. *Accrued expense:* Debit _____; credit Salaries Payable.
   d. *Accrued revenue:* Debit Accounts Receivable; credit _____.

■ LO3

■ **LO4**   20. What is the purpose of the adjusted trial balance? How do the adjusted trial balance and the (unadjusted) trial balance differ?

■ **LO5**   21. Explain what is meant by the term *classified* when referring to a balance sheet.

■ **LO5**   22. At the end of the period, Sanders Company reports the following amounts: Assets = $12,000; Liabilities = $8,000; Revenues = $5,000; Expenses = $3,000. Calculate stockholders' equity.

■ **LO6**   23. What are the two purposes of preparing closing entries?

■ **LO6**   24. What does it mean to close temporary accounts? Which of the following account types are closed: assets, liabilities, dividends, revenues, and expenses?

■ **LO6**   25. Describe the debits and credits for the three closing entries required at the end of a reporting period.

■ **LO6**   26. In its first four years of operations, Chance Communications reports net income of $300, $900, $1,500, and $2,400, respectively, and pays dividends of $200 per year. What would be the balance of Retained Earnings at the end of the fourth year?

■ **LO6**   27. Matt has been told by his instructor that dividends reduce retained earnings (and therefore stockholders' equity). However, since he knows that stockholders are receiving the dividend, Matt doesn't understand how paying a dividend would *decrease* stockholders' equity. Explain this to Matt.

■ **LO7**   28. How do the adjusted trial balance and the post-closing trial balance differ? Which accounts are shown in the adjusted trial balance but not in the post-closing trial balance? Which account is shown in both trial balances but with a different balance on each?

For the following, please visit your instructor's *Connect* site.

BRIEF EXERCISES	1-20
EXERCISES	1-19
PROBLEMS: SET A	1-8
PROBLEMS: SET B	1-8
GREAT ADVENTURES	

Note: Additional Perspectives assignments for Financial Analysis, Comparative Analysis, Internet Research, and Written Communication are in Appendix F at the end of this book. For additional Exercises: Set B and for additional Problems: Set C, visit www.mhhe.com/spicelandMTC1e.

4

Cash and Internal Controls

AFTER STUDYING THIS CHAPTER, YOU SHOULD BE ABLE TO:

- **LO1** Discuss the impact of accounting scandals and the passage of the Sarbanes-Oxley Act.
- **LO2** Identify the components, responsibilities, and limitations of internal control.
- **LO3** Define cash and cash equivalents.
- **LO4** Understand controls over cash receipts and cash disbursements.
- **LO5** Reconcile a bank statement.
- **LO6** Account for petty cash.
- **LO7** Identify the major inflows and outflows of cash.

Analysis

- **LO8** Assess earnings quality by comparing net income and cash flows.

REGAL ENTERTAINMENT: INTERNAL CONTROLS ARE A BOX-OFFICE HIT

Feature Story

According to research conducted by the Association of Certified Fraud Examiners (ACFE, *www.acfe.com*), U.S. organizations lose an estimated $1 *trillion* (or 7% of their total revenue) to employee fraud each year. This occurs despite increased corporate emphasis on antifraud controls and recent legislation to combat fraud. While some employees steal office supplies, inventory, and equipment, the asset most often targeted is cash. Cash fraud includes skimming cash receipts before they are recorded, stealing cash that has already been recorded, and falsely disbursing cash through fraudulent billing, expense reimbursement, or payroll.

Companies that rely heavily on cash transactions are especially susceptible to employee fraud. For example, consider a company like **Regal Entertainment Group** (NYSE: **RGC**), one of the world's largest motion picture exhibitors. The company operates almost 7,000 screens and sells about 250 million tickets per year, generating revenues each year of nearly $3 billion. The company states, "Revenues are generated principally through admissions and concessions sales with proceeds received in cash at the point of sale." The primary way a company like RGC can minimize cash losses due to employee fraud is to establish strong systems for internal control.

Toward that end, RGC makes extensive use of its point-of-service information technology for managing its theatres. The revenue streams generated by admissions and concessions are fully supported by information systems to monitor cash flow and to detect fraud and inventory theft. Simpler approaches to internal control include *separation of duties:* For example, one person sells tickets, and another collects the tickets. This prevents the ticket seller from pocketing a moviegoer's cash and then allowing admission without a ticket being produced by the ticket machine. At the end of the day, the number of tickets produced by the machine should exactly match the cash collected.

PART A

INTERNAL CONTROLS

We're all familiar, more or less, with the concept of fraud. Fraud occurs when a person intentionally deceives another person for personal gain or to damage that person. More specifically related to business activities, the Association of Certified Fraud Examiners (ACFE) defines occupational fraud as the use of one's occupation for personal enrichment through the deliberate misuse or misapplication of the employing organization's resources. As discussed in the chapter-opening Feature Story, occupational fraud is big business, with companies expecting to lose on average 7% of their total revenues to fraud each year. For a company like **Regal Entertainment Group**, 7% of total revenues would equal nearly $200 million lost to fraud in a single year. Given the high cost of occupational fraud, it's not surprising that companies are willing to spend significant amounts to prevent it.

To minimize occupational fraud, companies implement formal procedures known as internal controls. These represent a company's plan to (1) safeguard the company's assets and (2) improve the accuracy and reliability of accounting information. To accomplish this broad goal, all companies institute a variety of specific internal controls, which we discuss in this chapter.

The ACFE, the world's largest antifraud organization (*www.acfe.com*), reports that theft or the misuse of the company's resources occurs in 90% of all fraud cases. Common examples include stealing cash or inventory or using the company's resources for non–work-related purposes. Because cash is the asset most commonly misappropriated, a significant portion of this chapter discusses the procedures implemented by businesses to maintain control over cash receipts and cash disbursements. We'll also work through two specific examples of cash controls: the bank reconciliation and the petty cash fund.

A second source of occupational fraud involves financial statement manipulation. Here, those in charge of communicating financial accounting information falsify reports. You may have heard the phrase "cooking the books." The phrase implies that the accounting records ("books") have been presented in an altered form ("cooked"). Managers have a variety of reasons for manipulating the numbers in financial statements, such as maximizing their compensation, increasing the company's stock price, and preserving their jobs. Strong internal controls help to minimize financial statement manipulation.

To set the stage for the importance of internal controls in general, we discuss the impact of recent accounting scandals, and the response by Congress.

Recent Accounting Scandals and Response

■ **LO1**

Discuss the impact of accounting scandals and the passage of the Sarbanes-Oxley Act.

Managers are entrusted with the resources of both the company's lenders (liabilities) and its owners (stockholders' equity). In this sense, managers of the company act as stewards or caretakers of the company's assets. However, in recent years some managers shirked their ethical responsibilities and misused or misreported the company's funds. In many cases, top executives misreported accounting information to cover up their company's poor operating performance. Such fraudulent activity is costly: The ACFE reports that the median loss caused by fraudulent financial statement schemes, for example, is $2,000,000 per instance. As you become more familiar with specific accounting topics throughout the remainder of this book, you'll begin to understand how amounts reported in the financial statements can be manipulated by managers.

Two of the highest-profile cases of accounting fraud in U.S. history are the collapses of **Enron** and **WorldCom**. Enron used questionable accounting practices to avoid reporting billions in debt and losses in its financial statements. WorldCom misclassified certain expenditures to overstate assets and profitability by $11 billion. Both companies hoped to fool investors into overvaluing the company's stock. Other common types of financial statement fraud include creating fictitious revenues from a fake customer, improperly valuing assets, hiding liabilities, and mismatching revenues and expenses.

As the Enron and WorldCom frauds (as well as several others) were being uncovered in 2001 and 2002, the stock prices of these companies plummeted. Investors lost nearly $200 billion as a result. Employees of these companies also suffered. Both firms declared bankruptcy, resulting in employee termination; reduced salaries and increased workloads for those who were left; and loss of employee retirement funds, stock options, and health benefits.

Recall from Chapter 1 that all public companies are required to have an independent party, an auditor, provide reasonable assurance that financial statements are free of material misstatements. So where were the auditors in the cases of Enron and WorldCom, when the external audits failed to detect billions of dollars of fraud? Both companies had the same audit firm, **Arthur Andersen**. At the time, many would have argued that Arthur Andersen was the most prestigious and most trusted audit firm in the world. How did billions of dollars of fraud go unreported?

The high-profile scandals led to an extensive investigation of Arthur Andersen by the Securities and Exchange Commission (SEC). This action, along with subsequent events, damaged the auditor's reputation so severely that most of its clients fled to other auditors to avoid being associated with the Andersen name. By the end of 2002, Arthur Andersen was no longer in business.

SARBANES-OXLEY ACT OF 2002

In response to these corporate accounting scandals and to public outrage over seemingly widespread unethical behavior of top executives, Congress passed the Sarbanes-Oxley Act, also known as the *Public Company Accounting Reform and Investor Protection Act of 2002* and commonly referred to as *SOX*. SOX applies to all companies that are required to file financial statements with the SEC and represents one of the greatest reforms in business practices in U.S. history. The act established a variety of new guidelines related to auditor-client relations and internal control procedures. Illustration 4–1 lists and discusses some of the major provisions of SOX.

ILLUSTRATION 4–1

Major Provisions of the Sarbanes-Oxley Act of 2002

Oversight board. The Public Company Accounting Oversight Board (PCAOB) has the authority to establish standards dealing with auditing, quality control, ethics, independence, and other activities relating to the preparation of audited financial reports. The board consists of five members who are appointed by the Securities and Exchange Commission.

Corporate executive accountability. Corporate executives must personally certify the company's financial statements and financial disclosures. Severe financial penalties and the possibility of imprisonment are consequences of fraudulent misstatement.

Nonaudit services. It's unlawful for the auditors of public companies to also perform certain nonaudit services, such as consulting, for their clients.

Retention of work papers. Auditors of public companies must retain all work papers for seven years or face a prison term for willful violation.

Auditor rotation. The lead auditor in charge of auditing a particular company (referred to as the *audit partner*) must rotate off that company within five years and allow a new audit partner to take the lead.

Conflicts of interest. Audit firms are not allowed to audit public companies whose chief executives worked for the audit firm and participated in that company's audit during the preceding year.

Hiring of auditor. Audit firms are hired by the audit committee of the board of directors of the company, not by company management.

Internal control. Section 404 of the act requires (a) that company management document and assess the effectiveness of all internal control processes that could affect financial reporting and (b) that company auditors express an opinion on whether management's assessment of the effectiveness of internal control is fairly stated.

The last provision listed in Illustration 4–1, internal controls under Section 404, is worth pausing over for a moment, given the topic of this chapter. Section 404 requires company management and auditors to document and assess the effectiveness of a company's internal controls—processes that could affect financial reporting. PCAOB chairman William McDonough explained the significance of this part of the law: "In the past, internal controls were merely considered by auditors; now they will have to be tested and examined in detail" (*PCAOBUS.org,* June 18, 2004). Whether you are an investor, an employee, a manager, or an auditor, understanding a company's internal controls is important.

 KEY POINT

The accounting scandals in the early 2000s prompted passage of the Sarbanes-Oxley Act (SOX). Among other stipulations, SOX sets forth a variety of new guidelines related to auditor-client relations and additional internal controls. Section 404, in particular, requires company management and auditors to document and assess the effectiveness of a company's internal controls.

Framework for Internal Control

■ LO2
Identify the components, responsibilities, and limitations of internal control.

As noted above, internal control is a company's plan to (1) safeguard the company's assets and (2) improve the accuracy and reliability of accounting information. Effective internal control builds a wall to prevent misuse of company funds by employees and fraudulent or errant financial reporting. Strong internal control systems allow greater reliance by investors on reported financial statements.

COMPONENTS OF INTERNAL CONTROL

A framework for designing an internal control system was provided by the *Committee of Sponsoring Organizations (COSO)* of the Treadway Commission. Formed in 1985, COSO (*www.coso.org*) is dedicated to improving the quality of financial reporting through, among other things, effective internal controls. COSO suggests that internal control consists of five components, displayed in Illustration 4–2.

ILLUSTRATION 4–2

Components of Internal Control

Methods for collection of relevant **information and communication** in a timely manner, enabling people to carry out their responsibilities.

Continual **monitoring** of internal activities and reporting of deficiencies is required. Monitoring includes formal procedures for reporting control deficiencies.

Control activities are the policies and procedures that help ensure that management's directives are being carried out. These activities include authorizations, reconciliations, and separation of duties.

Risk assessment identifies and analyzes internal and external risk factors that could prevent a company's objectives from being achieved.

The **control environment** sets the overall ethical tone of the company with respect to internal control. It includes formal policies related to management's philosophy, assignment of responsibilities, and organizational structure.

The components of internal control are built on the foundation of the ethical tone set by top management in its control environment. From there, management assesses risks, implements specific control activities, and continuously monitors all systems. Running throughout this structure is the need for timely information and communication. Employees at all levels must understand the importance of high-quality information. Lower-level employees must report information accurately and in a timely manner to those higher in the organization. Top executives of a company then must effectively communicate this information to external parties such as investors and creditors through financial statements.

To see an example of how internal controls are linked to the information provided in financial statements, let's look at the description given by Regal Entertainment Group in its annual report (see Illustration 4–3).

ILLUSTRATION 4–3

Regal Entertainment's Discussion of Internal Controls and Financial Reporting

> **REGAL ENTERTAINMENT GROUP**
> **Notes to the Financial Statements (excerpt)**
>
> A company's internal control over financial reporting includes those policies and procedures that (1) pertain to the maintenance of records that, in reasonable detail, accurately and fairly reflect the transactions and dispositions of the assets of the company; (2) provide reasonable assurance that transactions are recorded as necessary to permit preparation of financial statements in accordance with generally accepted accounting principles, and that receipts and expenditures of the company are being made only in accordance with authorizations of management and directors of the company; and (3) provide reasonable assurance regarding prevention or timely detection of unauthorized acquisition, use, or disposition of the company's assets that could have a material effect on the financial statements.

Movie theatre example. Let's look at how the five components of internal control apply in actual practice. Here, we apply them to operating a movie theatre.

The overall attitudes and actions of management greatly affect the *control environment*. If employees notice unethical behavior or comments by management, they are more likely to behave in a similar manner, wasting the company's resources. Wouldn't you be more comfortable investing in or lending to a movie theatre if it were run by a highly ethical person, rather than someone of questionable character?

Risk assessment includes careful consideration of internal and external risk factors. Internal risks include issues such as unsafe lighting, faulty video projectors, unsanitary bathrooms, and employee incompetence with regard to food preparation. Common examples of external risks include a vendor supplying lower-grade or unsafe popcorn, moviegoers' security in the parking lot, or perhaps the decline in customer demand from DVD rentals or On Demand at home. These internal and external risk factors put the company's objectives in jeopardy.

Control activities include a variety of policies and procedures used to protect a company's assets. There are two general types of control activities: preventive and detective. *Preventive controls* are designed to keep errors or fraud from occurring in the first place. *Detective controls* are designed to detect errors or fraud that already have occurred.

Common examples of preventive controls include:

1. **Separation of duties.** Authorizing transactions, recording transactions, and maintaining control of the related assets should be separated among employees. The employee selling the movie ticket should not also be the employee in charge of collecting the tickets. The accountant at the movie theatre should not also have direct access to company cash by filling in as a ticket cashier or being

responsible for the daily cash deposits. Employees who have physical control of theatre inventory (candy bars, T-shirts, and so on) should not also be in charge of accounting for that inventory.

2. **Physical controls** over assets and accounting records. Each night, money from ticket sales should be placed in the theatre's safe or deposited at the bank. Important documents should be kept in fireproof files, and electronic records should be backed up daily and require user-ID and password for access. Concession supplies should be kept in a locked room with access allowed only to authorized personnel.

3. **Proper authorization** to prevent improper use of the company's resources. The theatre should establish formal guidelines on how to handle cash receipts and make purchases. For example, only management should be authorized to make purchases over a certain amount.

4. **Employee management.** The company should provide employees with appropriate guidance to ensure they have the knowledge necessary to carry out their job duties. Employees should be made fully aware of the company's internal control procedures, ethical responsibilities, and channels for reporting irregular activities.

Some examples of detective controls include:

1. **Reconciliations.** Management should periodically determine whether the amount of physical assets of the company (cash, supplies, inventory, and other property) match—reconcile with—the accounting records. For example, accounting personnel should routinely reconcile the company's cash records with those of its bank, and any discrepancy should be investigated. Later in this chapter we'll see an example of how to prepare a bank reconciliation for Starlight Drive-In.

2. **Performance reviews.** The actual performance of individuals or processes should be checked against their expected performance. For example, the amount of food sold should be compared to the number of tickets sold over a period of time. If food sales are lower than expected for a given number of tickets, employees could be wasting food, stealing food, or giving it to their friends for free. Alternatively, vendors may be supplying lower-quality food, driving down sales. Management may also wish to evaluate the overall performance of the theatre by comparing ticket sales for the current year with ticket sales for the previous year.

Monitoring of internal controls needs to occur on an ongoing basis. The theatre manager needs to actively review daily operations to ensure that control procedures work effectively. For instance, the manager should compare daily cash from ticket sales with the number of tickets issued, compare concession sales with units purchased, and make sure employees are paid only for actual hours worked.

Information and communication depend on the reliability of the accounting information system itself. If the accountant's office has papers scattered everywhere, and you learn the company still does all its accounting by hand without a computer, wouldn't you, as an investor or lender, be a bit worried? A system should be in place to ensure that current transactions of the company are reflected in current reports. Employees also should be aware of procedures in place to deal with any perceived internal control failures. For example, an anonymous tip hotline should be in place to encourage communication about unethical activities, such as an employee giving concession items for free to her friends. Employee tips historically have been the most common means of detecting employee fraud.

RESPONSIBILITIES FOR INTERNAL CONTROL

Everyone in a company has an impact on the operation and effectiveness of internal controls, but **the top executives are the ones who must take final responsibility for their establishment and success.** The CEO and CFO sign a report each year assessing whether the internal controls are adequate. Section 404 of SOX requires not only that companies document their internal controls and assess their adequacy, but that the company's auditors provide an opinion on management's assessment. A recent survey by the Financial Executives Institute of 247 executives reports that the total cost to a company of complying with Section 404 averages nearly $4 million.

The Public Company Accounting Oversight Board (PCAOB) further requires the auditor to express its own opinion on whether the company has maintained effective internal control over financial reporting. To see how this information gets reported, look at Illustration 4–4, which provides an excerpt from Regal Entertainment's auditor's report.

REGAL ENTERTAINMENT GROUP
Auditor's Report (excerpt)
In our opinion, management's assessment that Regal Entertainment Group maintained effective internal control over financial reporting is fairly stated, in all material respects, based on criteria established in *Internal Control—Integrated Framework* issued by the Committee of Sponsoring Organizations of the Treadway Commission (COSO). Also, in our opinion, Regal Entertainment Group maintained, in all material respects, effective internal control over financial reporting, based on criteria established in *Internal Control—Integrated Framework* issued by the Committee of Sponsoring Organizations of the Treadway Commission (COSO).

ILLUSTRATION 4–4

Excerpt from Regal Entertainment's Auditor's Report Related to Effectiveness of Internal Controls

LIMITATIONS OF INTERNAL CONTROL

Unfortunately, even with the best internal control systems, financial misstatements can occur. While better internal control systems will more likely detect operating and reporting errors, no internal control system can turn a bad employee into a good one.

Internal control systems are especially susceptible to collusion. Collusion occurs when two or more people act in coordination to circumvent internal controls. Going back to our movie theatre example, if the ticket cashier and the ticket taker, or the ticket cashier and the accountant, decide to work together to steal cash, theft will be much more difficult to detect. Fraud cases that involve collusion are typically several times more severe than are fraud cases involving a single perpetrator. This suggests that collusion is effective in circumventing control procedures.

Top-level employees who have the ability to override internal control features also have opportunity to commit fraud. For example, managers may be required to obtain approval from the chief financial officer (CFO) for all large purchases. However, if the CFO uses the company's funds to purchase a boat for personal use at a lake home, fewer controls are in place to detect this misappropriation. Even if lower-level employees suspect wrongdoing, they may feel intimidated to confront the issue.

Finally, because there are natural risks to running any business, **effective internal controls and ethical employees alone cannot ensure a company's success, or even survival.** Regal Entertainment recognizes the limitations of internal controls and provides an explicit discussion of this issue in its annual report, as shown in Illustration 4–5 (next page).

spiceland.mhhe.com/c10

ILLUSTRATION 4–5

Regal Entertainment's Discussion of Limitations of Internal Controls

> **REGAL ENTERTAINMENT GROUP**
> **Management Discussion and Analysis (excerpt)**
>
> Management recognizes that there are inherent limitations in the effectiveness of any internal control over financial reporting, including the possibility of human error and the circumvention or overriding of internal control. Accordingly, even effective internal control over financial reporting can provide only reasonable assurance with respect to financial statement preparation. Further, because of changes in conditions, the effectiveness of internal control over financial reporting may vary over time.

KEY POINT

Internal control refers to a company's plan to improve the accuracy and reliability of accounting information and safeguard the company's assets. Five key components to an internal control system are (1) control environment, (2) risk assessment, (3) control activities, (4) monitoring, and (5) information and communication.

Decision Point

Question	Accounting information	Analysis
Does the company maintain adequate internal controls?	Management's discussion, auditor's opinion	If management or the auditor notes any deficiencies in internal controls, financial accounting information may be unreliable.

PART B

CASH

Among all of the company's assets, cash is the one most susceptible to employee fraud. The obvious way that employees steal cash is by physically removing it from the company, such as pulling it out of the cash register and walking out the door. However, there are other, less obvious ways to commit fraud with a company's cash. An employee could falsify documents, causing the company to overreimburse the employee for certain expenses, to issue an inflated paycheck, or to make payment to a fictitious company. Because of these possibilities, companies develop strict procedures to maintain control of cash. Before discussing some of these controls, let's first get a good understanding of what "cash" includes.

Cash and Cash Equivalents

■ LO3
Define cash and cash equivalents.

The amount of **cash** recorded in a company's balance sheet includes currency, coins, and balances in savings and checking accounts, as well as items acceptable for deposit in these accounts, such as checks received from customers. *Checks* are written instruments instructing a bank to pay a specific amount from the check maker's account.

The balance of cash also includes **cash equivalents**, which are defined as short-term investments that have a maturity date no longer than three months *from the date of purchase*. Common examples of such investments are money market funds, Treasury bills, and certificates of deposit. The important point to understand is that cash and cash equivalents usually are combined and reported as a single asset in the balance sheet of most companies.

KEY POINT

Cash includes not only currency, coins, balances in checking accounts, and checks and money orders received from customers, but also cash equivalents, defined as investments that mature within three months (such as money market funds, Treasury bills, and certificates of deposit).

Whether a customer uses cash or a check to make a purchase, the company records the transaction as a cash sale. Let's assume a local theatre sells tickets for the entire day totaling $3,000. Some customers pay cash for those tickets, while others use a check. (Others will use credit cards or debit cards, which we discuss later.) Regardless of which method of payment customers use, the theatre records all of those ticket sales as cash sales.

User's Guide Below is a shorthand way of showing the effects of transactions on assets, liabilities, and stockholders' equity. We use these throughout the book.

	Debit	Credit	A	=	L	+	SE
Cash	3,000		+3,000				
Service Revenue		3,000					+3,000 Rev↑
(Sell tickets with cash or check)							

How Much Cash Is Enough?

Investors and creditors closely monitor the amount of cash a company holds. The company needs enough cash, or enough other assets that can quickly be converted to cash, to pay obligations as they become due. Available cash also helps a company respond quickly to new, profitable opportunities before competitors do. On the other hand, having too much cash leads to inefficient use of funds and could be a signal that a company's management does not see additional opportunities for profitable expansion. Investors usually view excess cash as a negative. ●

Decision Maker's Perspective

Cash Controls

Management must safeguard all assets against possible misuse. Again, because cash is especially susceptible to theft, internal control of cash is a key issue.

CONTROLS OVER CASH RECEIPTS

Most businesses receive payment from the sale of products and services either in the form of cash or as a check received immediately or through the mail. Internal control over cash receipts could include the following steps:

■ **LO4**
Understand controls over cash receipts and cash disbursements.

1. Record all cash receipts as soon as possible. Theft is more difficult once a record of the cash receipt has been made.
2. Open mail each day, and make a list of checks received, including the amount and payer's name.
3. Designate an employee to deposit cash and checks into the company's bank account each day, different from the person who receives cash and checks.
4. Have another employee record cash receipts in the accounting records. Verify cash receipts by comparing the bank deposit slip with the accounting records.
5. Accept credit cards or debit cards, to limit the amount of cash employees handle.

Because acceptance of credit cards and debit cards is so widespread, let's look at those controls in a bit more detail.

Acceptance of credit cards. The acceptance of credit cards provides an additional control by reducing employees' need to directly handle cash. The term *credit card* is derived from the fact that the issuer, such as **Visa** or **MasterCard**, extends credit (lends money) to the cardholder each time the cardholder uses the card. Cash in the amount of the sale automatically is deposited in the company's bank.

Credit card companies earn revenues primarily in two ways. First, the cardholder has a specified grace period before he or she has to pay the credit card balance in full. If the balance is not paid by the end of the grace period, the issuing company will charge a fee (interest). Second, credit card companies charge the *retailer,* not the customer, for the use of the credit card. This charge generally ranges from 2% to 4% of the amount of the sale.

For example, suppose a movie theatre accepts MasterCard as payment for $2,000 worth of movie tickets, and MasterCard charges the movie theatre a service fee of 3% (or $60 on sales of $2,000). Moviegoers don't pay cash to the theatre at the time of sale, but MasterCard deposits cash, less the service fee expense, into the theatre's account usually within 24 hours. Therefore, the theatre records the $2,000 credit card transaction as $1,940 cash received and $60 service fee expense.

	Debit	Credit
Cash	**1,940**	
Service Fee Expense...	**60**	
Service Revenue		**2,000**
(Sell tickets with credit card and 3% service fee)		

A = L + SE
+1,940
−60 Exp↑
+2,000 Rev↑

From the seller's perspective, the only difference between a cash sale and a credit card sale is that the seller must pay a fee to the credit card company for allowing the customer to use a credit card.

Decision Point

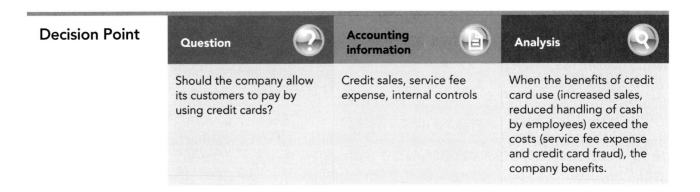

Question	Accounting information	Analysis
Should the company allow its customers to pay by using credit cards?	Credit sales, service fee expense, internal controls	When the benefits of credit card use (increased sales, reduced handling of cash by employees) exceed the costs (service fee expense and credit card fraud), the company benefits.

Acceptance of debit cards. *Debit cards* also provide an additional control for cash receipts. Like credit cards, debit cards offer customers a way to purchase goods and services without a physical exchange of cash. They differ, however, in that most debit cards (sometimes referred to as *check cards*) work just like a check and withdraw funds directly from the cardholder's bank account at the time of use. (Recall that credit cards don't remove cash from the cardholder's account after each transaction.)

Similar to credit cards, the use of debit cards by customers results in a fee being charged to the retailer. However, the fees charged for debit cards are typically much lower than those charged for credit cards. Debit card transactions are recorded similar to credit card transactions.

COMMON MISTAKE

The term *debit card* can cause some confusion for someone in the first accounting course. Throughout this course, we refer to an increase in cash as a *debit* to cash. However, using your *debit card* will result in a decrease in your cash account. It's the *merchant's* cash account, not yours, that increases and is debited. Don't let this confuse you.

ETHICAL DILEMMA

Jill is starting her sophomore year of college. The only way she can pay for tuition and school supplies is to take out a student loan. To make living costs more affordable, she shares an apartment with two other students. One week after Jill starts classes, her car breaks down. She pays a $120 towing bill to get the car to the service station, and the mechanic tells her the car has suffered major engine failure. The cost to fix the car will be $1,600, which is a fair price for such damage. Jill has enough money from her student loan to pay the bill, but she knows this will put her behind for the next several months' rent. The mechanic tells her that if she pays cash, instead of writing a check or paying with a debit card or credit card, he will charge her only $1,300. When she asks the reason for the $300 discount, he tells her, "If you pay cash, there's no record of our transaction, and I won't have to pay taxes. This will save money for both of us." What should Jill do? Another mechanic is likely to charge her full price, and she would have to pay an additional towing charge to get the car to a different mechanic.

CONTROLS OVER CASH DISBURSEMENTS

Managers should design proper controls for cash disbursements to prevent any unauthorized payments and ensure proper recording. Consistent with our discussion of cash receipts, cash disbursements include not only disbursing physical cash, but also writing checks and using credit cards and debit cards to make payments. All these forms of payment constitute cash disbursement and require formal internal control procedures. Important elements of a cash disbursement control system include the following steps:

1. Make all disbursements, other than very small ones, by check, debit card, or credit card. This provides a permanent record of all disbursements.
2. Authorize all expenditures before purchase and verify the accuracy of the purchase itself. The employee who authorizes payment should not also be the employee who prepares the check.

3. Make sure checks are serially numbered and signed only by authorized employees. Require two signatures for larger checks.

4. Periodically check amounts shown in the debit card and credit card statements against purchase receipts. The employee verifying the accuracy of the debit card and credit card statements should not also be the employee responsible for actual purchases.

5. Set maximum purchase limits on debit cards and credit cards. Give approval to purchase above these amounts only to upper-level employees.

6. Employees responsible for making cash disbursements should not also be in charge of cash receipts.

When the movie theatre pays $1,000 to advertise its show times, it records the following transaction, regardless of whether it pays with cash, a check, or a debit card.

	Debit	Credit
Advertising Expense	1,000	
Cash		1,000
(Purchase advertising with cash, check, or debit card)		

A = L + SE
−1,000 Exp↑
−1,000

Because credit cards allow the purchaser to delay payment for several weeks or even months, if the theatre uses a credit card to pay for the $1,000 worth of advertising, it would record the purchase as follows.

	Debit	Credit
Advertising Expense	1,000	
Accounts Payable		1,000
(Purchase advertising with credit card)		

A = L + SE
−1,000 Exp↑
+1,000

spiceland.mhhe.com/c11

 KEY POINT

Because cash is the asset of a company most susceptible to employee fraud, controls over cash receipts and cash disbursements are an important part of a company's overall internal control system. Important controls over cash receipts include separation of duties for those who handle cash and independent verification of cash receipts. Important controls over cash disbursements include payment by check, credit card, or debit card, separation of duties, and various authorization and documentation procedures.

Bank Reconciliation

■ LO5
Reconcile a bank statement.

Another important control used by nearly all companies to help maintain control of cash is a bank reconciliation. A **bank reconciliation** matches the balance of cash in the bank account with the balance of cash in the company's own records. If you have your own checking account, you know that the balance of cash in your checkbook often does not equal the balance of cash in your bank account. Why is that? One possibility is that you (or your bank) made a recording error. More likely, though, you've written a check or have cash receipts that haven't yet reached the bank, or maybe the bank has made an adjustment you haven't yet recorded.

It's the same for a business. A company's cash balance as recorded in its books rarely equals the cash balance reported in the bank statement. The reasons for the differences are the same as those for your personal checking account: Differences in these balances most often occur because of either timing differences or errors. It is the *possibility* of these errors, or even outright fraudulent activities, that makes the bank reconciliation a useful cash control tool.

***Timing differences* in cash occur when the company records transactions either before or after the bank records the same transaction.** For example, when a movie theatre pays its popcorn supplier $200 by check, the company records a decrease in cash immediately, but the bank doesn't record a decrease in cash until the popcorn supplier later deposits the check. If the supplier waits a week before depositing the check, the balance of cash in the company's records will be reduced one week earlier than will the bank's.

Other times, the bank is the first to record a transaction. The bank could charge a $50 service fee for processing the company's transaction, immediately reducing the bank's record of the company's balance for cash. However, the company may not be immediately aware of this fee. Only when the monthly bank statement is sent will the company become aware of the cash reduction. In this case, the bank's balance for cash reflects a cash transaction before the company's balance can reflect the same transaction.

***Errors* can be made either by the company or its bank and may be accidental or intentional.** An *accidental* error might occur if the company mistakenly were to record a check being written for $117 as $171 in its records, or if the bank improperly processed a deposit of $1,100 as a $1,010 deposit. An *intentional* error is the result of theft. If the company records a daily deposit of $5,000 but an employee deposits only $500 into the bank account and pockets the rest, the bank reconciliation will reveal the missing $4,500.

A bank reconciliation connects the company's cash balance to the bank's cash balance by identifying differences due to timing and errors. This concept is shown in Illustration 4–6.

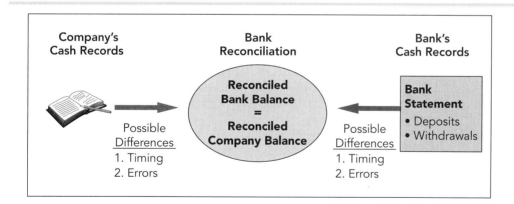

ILLUSTRATION 4–6
Bank Reconciliation

To see how a bank reconciliation is prepared, let's start by examining the bank statement of Starlight Drive-In. At the end of March, First Bank sends the bank statement in Illustration 4–7 (next page) to Starlight. Compare the bank statement with Starlight's own records of cash activity over the same period, as shown in Illustration 4–8 (next page).

First Bank's ending balance of cash ($4,100) differs from Starlight's ending balance of cash ($2,880). To understand why these two cash balances differ, we need to identify (1) timing differences created by cash activity reported by either First Bank or Starlight but not recorded by the other and (2) any errors.

ILLUSTRATION 4–7

Bank Statement

P.O. Box 26788	*First Bank*	Member FDIC
Odessa, TX 79760	*A Name You Can Trust*	
(432) 799-BANK		

Account Holder:	Starlight Drive-In	Account Number:	4061009619
	221B Baker Street		
	Odessa, TX 79760	Statement Date:	March 31, 2012

Account Summary

Beginning Balance	Deposits and Credits		Withdrawals and Debits		Ending Balance
March 1, 2012	No.	Total	No.	Total	March 31, 2012
$3,800	4	$8,600	7	$8,300	$4,100

Account Details

Deposits and Credits			Withdrawals and Debits				Daily Balance	
Date	Amount	Desc.	Date	No.	Amount	Desc.	Date	Amount
3/5	$3,600	DEP	3/8	293	$2,100	CHK	3/5	$7,400
3/9	3,000	NOTE	3/12	294	2,900	CHK	3/8	5,300
3/22	1,980	DEP	3/15		400	EFT	3/9	8,300
3/31	20	INT	3/22		750	NSF	3/12	5,400
			3/26	296	1,900	CHK	3/15	5,000
			3/28		200	DC	3/22	6,230
			3/31		50	SF	3/26	4,330
							3/28	4,130
	$8,600				$8,300		3/31	$4,100

Desc.	**DEP** Customer deposit	**INT** Interest earned	**SF** Service fees
	NOTE Note collected	**CHK** Customer check	**NSF** Nonsufficient funds
	EFT Electronic funds transfer	**DC** Debit card	

ILLUSTRATION 4–8

Company Records of
Cash Activities

STARLIGHT DRIVE-IN
Cash Account Records
March 1, 2012, to March 31, 2012

Deposits			Checks			
Date	Desc.	Amount	Date	No.	Desc.	Amount
3/5	Sales receipts	$3,600	3/6	293	Salaries	$2,100
3/22	Sales receipts	1,980	3/11	294	Rent	2,600
3/31	Sales receipts	2,200	3/21	295	Utilities	1,200
			3/24	296	Insurance	1,900
			3/30	297	Supplies	900
		$7,780				$8,700

SUMMARY OF TRANSACTIONS

Beginning Cash Balance March 1, 2012	+	Deposits	−	Checks	=	Ending Cash Balance March 31, 2012
$3,800		$7,780		$8,700		$2,880

COMMON MISTAKE

Notice that bank statements refer to an increase (or deposit) in the cash balance as a *credit* and a decrease (or withdrawal) as a *debit*. This terminology is the opposite of that used in financial accounting, where *debit* refers to an increase in cash and *credit* refers to a decrease in cash. The reason for the difference in terminology is a difference in perspective: The financial accounting records are prepared *from a company's perspective*, while the bank statement is prepared *from a bank's perspective*. When a company makes a deposit, the bank's liability to the company (a credit account) increases. When a company withdraws cash from its bank account, the bank's liability to the company decreases.

Reconciling the bank account involves three steps: (1) reconciling the bank's cash balance, (2) reconciling the company's cash balance, and (3) adjusting the company's cash balance. In the first two steps, we should catch timing differences (such as for deposits outstanding, checks outstanding, and bank memoranda) as well as errors made by either the company or the bank. In the third step, we update the company's accounting records for cash transactions that have occurred but have not yet been recorded.

STEP 1: RECONCILING THE BANK'S CASH BALANCE

First, we will reconcile the bank's cash balance. Cash transactions recorded by a company, but not yet recorded by its bank, include deposits outstanding and checks outstanding. **Deposits outstanding** are cash receipts of the company that have not been added to the bank's record of the company's balance. **Checks outstanding** are checks the company has written that have not been subtracted from the bank's record of the company's balance.

Timing differences

For example, comparing cash receipts recorded by Starlight (Illustration 4–8) to those reported as deposits in the bank statement (Illustration 4–7) reveals that cash sales receipts of $2,200 on March 31 are not yet reflected in the bank's balance by the end of March. This is a deposit outstanding.

Comparing the checks written by Starlight to those reported in the bank statement shows that the bank received checks #293, #294, and #296 by the end of March. This means checks #295 (for $1,200) and #297 (for $900) remain outstanding and are not yet reflected in the bank's balance.

Once the bank receives the deposits outstanding, the bank's cash balance will increase. Similarly, once the bank receives the checks outstanding, the bank's cash balance will decrease. We also need to check for and correct any bank errors.

The reconciled bank balance is calculated on the left side of Illustration 4–9 (next page).

STEP 2: RECONCILING THE COMPANY'S CASH BALANCE

Next, we need to reconcile the company's cash balance. What are some examples of cash transactions recorded by the bank but not yet recorded by the company? These would include items such as interest earned by the company, collections made by the bank on the company's behalf, service fees, and charges for **NSF checks**—customers' checks written on "nonsufficient funds," otherwise known as "bad" checks. In addition, we adjust the company's balance for any recording errors made by the company.

Six cash transactions recorded by First Bank (Illustration 4–7) are not reported in Starlight's cash records (Illustration 4–8) by the end of March:

1. Note received by First Bank on Starlight's behalf ($3,000 consisting of $2,800 plus related interest received of $200).
2. Interest earned by Starlight on its bank account ($20).

Timing differences

3. NSF check ($750).
4. Debit card purchase of office equipment by an employee ($200).
5. Electronic funds transfer (EFT) related to the payment of advertising ($400).
6. Service fee ($50).

COMMON MISTAKE

Students sometimes mistake an NSF check as a bad check written *by* the company instead of one written *to* the company. When an NSF check occurs, the company must adjust its balance of cash downward to reverse the increase in cash it recorded at the time it received the check from the customer, because the customer did not have enough funds to cover the check. This bounced check will create an account receivable for the company until the customer pays the funds it owes.

Company error

In addition to the amounts related to timing differences, we need to address one other reconciling item. Comparing Starlight's record of checks written to those in the bank statement reveals an error by Starlight. Check #294 for rent was written for $2,900, but Starlight's accountant recorded it incorrectly as $2,600. First Bank processed the check for the correct amount of $2,900. This means Starlight needs to reduce its cash balance by an additional $300 for rent expense. The reconciled company balance is calculated on the right side of Illustration 4–9. (Note that the illustration shows additions to the company's account in green and subtractions from the account in red.)

ILLUSTRATION 4–9

Reconciling the Bank Statement

STARLIGHT DRIVE-IN
Bank Reconciliation
March 31, 2012

Bank's Cash Balance		*Company's* Cash Balance	
Before reconciliation	$4,100	Before reconciliation	$2,880
Deposits outstanding:	+2,200	Note received	+2,800
3/31 = $2,200		Interest earned from note	+200
		Interest earned on bank account	+20
Checks outstanding:	−2,100	NSF check	−750
#295 = $1,200		Debit card for office equipment	−200
#297 = $ 900		EFT for advertising	−400
		Service fee	−50
		Corrected rent expense error	−300
After reconciliation	$4,200	After reconciliation	$4,200

Reconciled

If the bank were aware of all deposits made and all checks written by the company, the bank's cash balance would be $4,200. Similarly, once the company adjusts its balance for information revealed in the bank statement, its cash balance is $4,200. The fact that the two balances match provides some indication that cash is not being mishandled by employees.

STEP 3: ADJUSTING THE COMPANY'S CASH BALANCE

As a final step in the reconciliation process, a company must update the balance in its Cash account, to adjust for the items used to reconcile the *company's* cash balance. We record these adjustments once the bank reconciliation is complete. Remember, these are amounts the company didn't know until it received the bank statement.

We record items that increase the company's cash by a debit to Cash. Similarly, we record items that decrease the company's cash by a credit to Cash. The entries needed to adjust Starlight's cash balance for reconciliation items are as follows.

March 31, 2012	Debit	Credit	A	=	L	+	SE
Cash	3,020		+3,020				
Notes Receivable		2,800	−2,800				
Interest Revenue		220					+220 Rev↑
(Reconcile cash increases)			A	=	L	+	SE
Accounts Receivable	750		+750				
Equipment	200		+200				
Advertising Expense	400						−400 Exp↑
Service Fee Expense	50						−50 Exp↑
Rent Expense	300						−300 Exp↑
Cash		1,700	−1,700				
(Reconcile cash decreases)							

Most of the accounts are easy to understand. We credit Notes Receivable because the note has been received, decreasing that asset account (−$2,800). We recognize interest revenue (+$220) as earned. We need to record cash outflows related to expenses (advertising, service fee, and rent) and asset purchases need to be recorded. Finally, we debit Accounts Receivable, increasing that asset account (+$750) to show that the customer who paid with an NSF check still owes the company money.

spiceland.mhhe.com/c12

COMMON MISTAKE

Some students try to prepare adjusting entries for deposits outstanding, checks outstanding, or a bank error. The company does *not* need to adjust for these items related to reconciling the bank's balance because they are already properly recorded in the company's accounting records.

In the uncommon event that the two reconciled balances do not equal, management investigates the discrepancy to check for wrongdoing or errors by company employees or the bank. If the company cannot resolve the discrepancy, it records the difference to either Miscellaneous Expense or Miscellaneous Revenue, depending on whether it has a debit or credit balance. For example, suppose a company is unable to account for $100 of missing cash. In this event, the company records the following transaction, increasing Miscellaneous Expense and decreasing Cash.

	Debit	Credit	A	=	L	+	SE
Miscellaneous Expense	100						−100 Exp↑
Cash		100	−100				
(Record loss of $100 cash)							

KEY POINT

In a bank reconciliation we adjust the *bank's* balance for (1) cash transactions already recorded by the company but not yet recorded by the bank and (2) bank errors. Similarly, we adjust the *company's* balance for (1) cash transactions already recorded by the bank but not yet recorded by the company and (2) company errors. After we adjust both the bank balance and the company balance, the two should equal.

Let's Review

spiceland.mhhe.com/t6

At the end of April 2012, Showtime Theatre's accounting records show a cash balance of $4,800. The April bank statement reports a cash balance of $3,700. The following information is gathered from the bank statement and company records:

Checks outstanding	$1,900	Customer's NSF check	$1,300
Deposits outstanding	1,600	Service fee	200
Interest earned	70		

In addition, Showtime discovered it correctly paid for advertising with a check for $220 but incorrectly recorded the check in the company's records for $250. The bank correctly processed the check for $220.

Required:

1. Prepare a bank reconciliation for the month of April 2012.
2. Prepare entries to adjust the balance of cash in the company's records.

Solution:

1. Bank reconciliation:

SHOWTIME THEATRE
Bank Reconciliation
April 30, 2012

Bank's Cash Balance		Company's Cash Balance	
Before reconciliation	$3,700	Before reconciliation	$4,800
Deposits outstanding	+1,600	Interest earned	+70
		Company error	+30
Checks outstanding	−1,900	Service fee	−200
		NSF check	−1,300
After reconciliation	$3,400	After reconciliation	$3,400

2. Entries to adjust cash balance:

April 30, 2012	Debit	Credit
Cash	100	
Interest Revenue		70
Advertising Expense		30
(Reconcile cash increases)		
Service Fee Expense	200	
Accounts Receivable	1,300	
Cash		1,500
(Reconcile cash decreases)		

Suggested Homework:
BE4-8, BE4-9;
E4-12, E4-13;
P4-2A&B, P4-3A&B

Petty Cash

■ **LO6**
Account for petty cash.

You probably pay for most of your purchases with a debit card, credit card, or check. However, it's nice to have a little cash in your wallet for emergency or impulse expenditures. For example, you might decide to buy a box of Girl Scout cookies from your neighbor or soda from a machine. In the same way, most companies like to keep a small amount of cash on hand at the company's location for minor purchases such as postage, office supplies, delivery charges, and entertainment expenses. If the office manager orders a $10 pizza for a staff meeting, it would be inconvenient and costly to write and process a check for such a small amount. Furthermore, it would be time-consuming to run to the bank for a $10 cash withdrawal. To pay for these minor purchases, companies keep some minor amount of cash on hand in a **petty cash fund**.

Accounting for the petty cash fund involves recording transactions to (1) establish the fund, (2) recognize expenditures from the fund, and (3) replenish the fund as the cash balance becomes sufficiently low. Management establishes a petty cash fund by writing a check for cash against the company's checking account and putting that amount of withdrawn cash in the hands of an employee who becomes responsible for it. This employee is often referred to as the *petty-cash custodian*. The fund should have just enough cash to make minor expenditures over a reasonable period (such as a week or a month). Given appropriate documentation, such as a receipt for the purchase of the $10 pizza for the staff meeting or of office supplies, the petty-cash custodian will disburse cash to reimburse the purchaser. At any given time, the cash remaining in the fund plus all receipts should equal the amount of the fund. The receipts are important to ensure proper use of the funds and for recording expenditures each time the fund is replenished.

Suppose that at the beginning of May, Starlight Drive-In establishes a petty cash fund of $500 to pay for minor purchases. Starlight establishes the fund by recording:

May 1	Debit	Credit	A	=	L	+	SE
Petty Cash (on hand)	500		+500				
Cash (checking account)		500	−500				
(Establish the petty cash fund)							

Assume Starlight has the following expenditures from the petty cash fund during May:

Date	Expenditure	Amount
May 7	Postage	$ 75
May 16	Delivery charges	85
May 20	Office group lunch	50
May 26	Office supplies	120
		$330

By the end of May, the petty cash fund has distributed $330, leaving $170 in the fund, along with receipts for $330. However, the company did not record these transactions at the time these expenditures were made. By the end of the period, the expenditures from the petty cash fund must be recorded.

May 31	Debit	Credit	A	=	L	+	SE
Postage Expense	75						−75 Exp↑
Delivery Expense	85						−85 Exp↑
Entertainment Expense	50						−50 Exp↑
Supplies	120		+120				
Petty Cash (on hand)		330	−330				
(Recognize expenditures from the petty cash fund)							

Also at the end of the period, the petty cash fund may need to be replenished. Management can withdraw cash of $330 from the checking account and give it to the petty-cash custodian so the fund's balance will once again be $500.

A	=	L	+	SE	May 31		Debit	Credit
+330					**Petty Cash** (on hand)		330	
−330					**Cash** (checking account)			330
					(Replenish the petty cash fund at the end of the period)			

To maintain the control objective of separation of duties, the petty-cash custodian should not be involved in accounting for, nor in the process of writing or approving, replenishment checks.

What if only $150 is left in the petty cash fund, when there should be $170? It could be that $20 was stolen from the fund, or the fund could be missing a receipt for $20. If the question is not resolved, the firm will likely charge the $20 to Miscellaneous Expense.

 KEY POINT

> To pay for minor purchases, companies keep some cash on hand in a petty cash fund. At the end of the period, expenditures from the petty cash fund are recorded, and the fund is replenished.

Reporting Cash

To this point, we've considered several internal controls related to cash. Here, we discuss how companies report cash activities. Cash activities of a business enterprise are the most fundamental events upon which investors and lenders base their decisions: Where does a company get its cash? Where does a company usually spend its cash? These are important issues in determining management's efficient use of a company's resources and in predicting future performance. Companies report cash in two ways—in the balance sheet and in the statement of cash flows.

BALANCE SHEET

As we discussed in Chapter 3, companies report cash as an asset in the balance sheet. The amount is typically reported as a current asset and represents cash available for spending at the end of the reporting period. The balance sheet provides only the final balance for cash. It does not provide any details regarding cash receipts and payments during the period.

STATEMENT OF CASH FLOWS

■ **LO7**
Identify the major inflows and outflows of cash.

Companies report information about cash receipts and payments during the period in a statement of cash flows. **From the statement of cash flows, investors know a company's cash inflows and cash outflows related to (1) operating activities, (2) investing activities, and (3) financing activities.** We'll provide a complete discussion of the statement of cash flows in Chapter 11. Here, we briefly introduce the basics of the statement to help you understand that its purpose is to report activity related to the key topic of this chapter—cash.

Recall from Chapter 1 the three fundamental types of business activities relating to cash:

- *Operating activities* include cash transactions involving revenue and expense events during the period. In other words, operating activities include the cash effect of the same activities that are reported in the income statement.
- *Investing activities,* as the name implies, include cash investments in long-term assets and investment securities. When the firm later sells those assets, we consider those transactions investing activities also. So, investing activities tend to involve long-term assets.

- *Financing activities* include transactions designed to raise cash or finance the business. There are two ways to do this: borrow cash from lenders or raise cash from stockholders. We also consider cash outflows to repay debt and cash dividends to stockholders to be financing activities. So, financing activities involve liabilities and stockholders' equity.

It's easiest to understand cash flow information by looking at the underlying transactions. To do this, we'll refer back to the external transactions of Eagle Golf Academy introduced in Chapters 1 through 3. For convenience, Illustration 4–10 lists those transactions and analyzes their effects on the company's cash.

Transaction	External Transactions in January	Type of Activity	Is Cash Involved?	Inflow or Outflow?	
(1)	Sell shares of common stock for $25,000 to obtain the funds necessary to start the business.	Financing	Yes	Inflow	**ILLUSTRATION 4–10** External Transactions of Eagle Golf Academy
(2)	Borrow $10,000 from the local bank and sign a note promising to repay the full amount of the debt in three years.	Financing	Yes	Inflow	
(3)	Purchase equipment necessary for giving golf training, $24,000 cash.	Investing	Yes	Outflow	Which transactions involve the exchange of cash?
(4)	Pay one year of rent in advance, $6,000 ($500 per month).	Operating	Yes	Outflow	
(5)	Purchase supplies on account, $2,300.	Operating	No	—	
(6)	Provide golf training to customers for cash, $3,600.	Operating	Yes	Inflow	
(7)	Provide golf training to customers on account, $2,500.	Operating	No	—	
(8)	Receive cash in advance for 10 golf training sessions to be given in the future, $600.	Operating	Yes	Inflow	
(9)	Pay salaries to employees, $2,800.	Operating	Yes	Outflow	
(10)	Pay cash dividends of $200 to shareholders.	Financing	Yes	Outflow	

Which transactions involve the exchange of cash? All transactions except (5) and (7) involve either the receipt (inflow) or payment (outflow) of cash. **Only transactions involving *cash* affect a company's *cash* flows.**

Illustration 4–11 (next page) presents the statement of cash flows for Eagle Golf Academy using what's called the *direct method* of reporting operating activities. Corresponding transaction numbers are in brackets. (In Chapter 11 we'll discuss the *indirect method.*)

From the statement of cash flows, investors and creditors can see that the major source of cash inflow for Eagle is the issuance of common stock, a financing activity. Eagle has also received cash from bank borrowing, which must be repaid. The company is also investing heavily in its future by purchasing equipment. Eagle reports this amount as an investing outflow.

With regard to the three types of business activities, the cash flow that's related most directly to the company's profitability is net cash flows from operating activities. For Eagle Golf Academy, net cash flows from operating activities are –$4,600. This means that cash *outflows* related to operating activities exceed inflows. Stated another way, cash outflows related to expense activities exceed cash inflows related to revenue activities. While Eagle reports net income of $500 in its income statement (see Illustration 3–12 in Chapter 3), these same activities are not able to generate positive cash flows for the company. Ultimately, companies must be able to generate positive operating cash flows to maintain long-term success.

ILLUSTRATION 4–11

Statement of Cash Flows for Eagle Golf Academy

Numbers in brackets correspond to the external transaction numbers of Eagle Golf Academy in Illustration 4–10.

Only transactions that involve the exchange of cash are included in the statement of cash flows.

EAGLE GOLF ACADEMY
Statement of Cash Flows
For the month ended January 31, 2012

Cash Flows from Operating Activities

Cash inflows:		
From customers [6 and 8]	$ 4,200	
Cash outflows:		
For salaries [9]	(2,800)	
For rent [4]	(6,000)	
Net cash flows from operating activities		$ (4,600)

Cash Flows from Investing Activities

Purchase equipment [3]	(24,000)	
Net cash flows from investing activities		(24,000)

Cash Flows from Financing Activities

Issue common stock [1]	25,000	
Borrow from bank [2]	10,000	
Pay dividends [10]	(200)	
Net cash flows from financing activities		34,800
Net increase in cash		6,200
Cash at the beginning of the month		-0-
Cash at the end of the month		$ 6,200

The final amount reported in the statement of cash flows, **$6,200**, is the same amount of cash reported in the balance sheet. You can verify this is the case for Eagle Golf Academy by referring back to the balance sheet reported in Illustration 3–14 in Chapter 3.

KEY POINT

The statement of cash flows reports all cash activities for the period. *Operating activities* include those transactions involving revenue and expense activities. *Investing activities* include cash investments in long-term assets and investment securities. *Financing activities* include transactions designed to finance the business through borrowing and owner investment.

Decision Point

Question	Accounting information	Analysis
Is the company able to generate enough cash from internal sources to sustain daily operations?	Statement of cash flows	Cash flows generated from internal sources include operating and investing activities. For established companies, the sum of these amounts should be positive. Otherwise, the company will need to rely on external funding (lenders and stockholders), which is not sustainable in the long term.

Let's Review

A company reports in its current year each of the transactions listed below.

Required:

Indicate whether each transaction should be reported as an operating, investing, or financing cash flow in the company's statement of cash flows, and whether each is a cash inflow or outflow.

Transaction	Type of Cash Flow	Inflow or Outflow
1. Pay employees' salaries.	_____	_____
2. Obtain a loan at the bank.	_____	_____
3. Purchase a building with cash.	_____	_____
4. Purchase equipment with a note payable.	_____	_____

Solution:

1. Operating—outflow.   2. Financing—inflow.   3. Investing—outflow.
4. Not reported as a cash flow because no cash is involved in the transaction.

Suggested Homework:
BE4-11, BE4-12;
E4-16, E4-17;
P4-4A&B, P4-5A&B

CASH ANALYSIS
Krispy Kreme vs. Starbucks

ANALYSIS

We now look at how decision makers analyze and use information about cash. Krispy Kreme and Starbucks provide some interesting comparisons.

The difference between revenues and expenses—net income—provides an accrual-basis measure of the company's ability to create wealth for its stockholders. In general, the greater a company's net income, the greater will be the value of the company to stockholders. However, the *timing* of revenues and expenses recorded under accrual-basis accounting may differ from the timing of operating cash flows.

Earlier, we discussed an example of such a timing difference, by comparing the net income of Eagle Golf Academy ($500) to its net cash flows from operations (−$4,600). If you were considering an investment in Eagle Golf Academy, would you consider net income of $500 to be a reliable indicator of the profit-generating potential of the company, given that it has net cash flows from operating activities of −$4,600? Which number is more useful in helping us to predict the long-term profitability of the company? We refer to the ability of current net income to help us predict the future performance of a company as earnings quality. When net income does not provide a good indicator of future performance, its earnings quality is said to be low.

COMPARING NET INCOME TO CASH FLOW

One of the more common techniques used by investors for measuring earnings quality relies on comparing the trend in a company's reported net income to its trend in free cash flow. A simple way to calculate a company's free cash flow is to consider its operating cash flows plus investing cash flows during the period. This measure represents the cash that is *free* to repay debt and distribute to stockholders. Companies whose free cash flow is declining relative to the trend in net income are likely to have lower-quality earnings.

Let's look at an example: In 1937, Vernon Rudolph bought a secret doughnut recipe from a French chef in New Orleans, rented a building in Winston-Salem, North Carolina, and began selling doughnuts. Since then, Mr. Rudolph's company,

■ **LO8**
Assess earnings quality by comparing net income and cash flows.

Financial analysts offer investment advice to their clients—banks, insurance companies, mutual funds, securities firms, and individual investors. This advice usually comes in the form of a formal recommendation (buy, hold, or sell). Before giving an opinion, analysts develop a detailed understanding of a company's operations through discussions with management, analysis of competitors, and projections of industry trends. They also develop a detailed understanding of a company's financial statements, including its earnings quality. Analysts typically do not recommend companies with lower-quality earnings.

Understanding a company's earnings quality comes from having a good grasp of accrual-basis accounting. This is why many finance majors and MBA students, pursuing careers as financial analysts, take additional accounting-related courses when earning their degrees and even after graduation.

Comparing free cash flow with net income can help in measuring the quality of earnings.

Krispy Kreme, grew into a leading branded specialty retailer across the country, producing over a billion doughnuts a year. To illustrate the preference of not relying on a single measure like net income in isolation, we compare Krispy Kreme with **Starbucks Corporation**.

As Illustrations 4–12 and 4–13 show, both Krispy Kreme and Starbucks enjoyed explosive increases in net income over the 1999–2004 period. However, their free cash flows (or strict cash-basis net incomes) tell a very different story. Notice that Krispy Kreme's free cash was falling through 2004, while Starbucks' was increasing. The pattern should have raised concerns about the long-term profit-generating ability of Krispy Kreme. Indeed, in 2005, Krispy Kreme's growth in net income could no longer be sustained and decreased dramatically because the company did not have sufficient cash to maintain profitable operations.

In comparison, Starbucks' upward trend in net income through 2004 showed no signs of slowing. However, that trend would last for only a few more years. Notice that Starbucks' free cash flow began falling in 2006, while net income continued to rise. Again, the difference in trends between net income and free cash flow should have been a warning to investors.

ILLUSTRATION 4–12

Net Income and Free Cash Flow for Krispy Kreme, 1999–2009

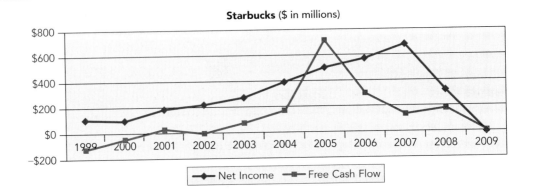

ILLUSTRATION 4–13

Net Income and Free Cash Flow for Starbucks Corporation, 1999–2009

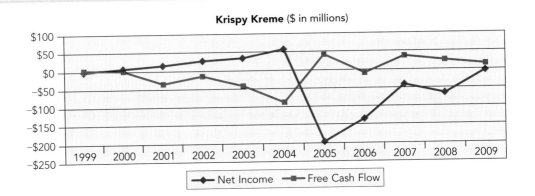

An upward trend in net income cannot be sustained indefinitely without a sufficient supply of cash. As predicted by the falling trend in free cash flow in 2006 and 2007, Starbucks' net income experienced a sharp decline beginning in 2008. These examples demonstrate the predictive ability of comparing a company's trend in net income and free cash flow. **When the trend in net income is upward while the trend in free cash flow is downward, a company is more likely to experience falling profits in the coming years.**

 KEY POINT

Companies whose free cash flow is decreasing relative to net income are likely to have lower earnings quality than are other companies, all else being equal.

Decision Point

Question	Accounting information	Analysis
How does free cash flow predict a company's net income?	Net income from the income statement and free cash flow (operating and investing) from the statement of cash flows	When free cash flow and net income have similar trends, net income is more likely to continue that trend in the future.

 KEY POINTS BY LEARNING OBJECTIVE

LO1 Discuss the impact of accounting scandals and the passage of the Sarbanes-Oxley Act.

The accounting scandals in the early 2000s prompted passage of the Sarbanes-Oxley Act (SOX). Among other stipulations, SOX sets forth a variety of new guidelines related to auditor-client relations and additional internal controls. Section 404, in particular, requires company management and auditors to document and assess the effectiveness of a company's internal controls.

LO2 Identify the components, responsibilities, and limitations of internal control.

Internal control refers to a company's plan to improve the accuracy and reliability of accounting information and safeguard the company's assets. Five key components to an internal control system are (1) control environment, (2) risk assessment, (3) control activities, (4) monitoring, and (5) information and communication.

LO3 Define cash and cash equivalents.

Cash includes not only currency, coins, balances in checking accounts, and checks and money orders received from customers, but also cash equivalents, defined as investments that mature within three months (such as money

market funds, Treasury bills, and certificates of deposit).

LO4 Understand controls over cash receipts and cash disbursements.

Because cash is the asset of a company most susceptible to employee fraud, controls over cash receipts and cash disbursements are an important part of a company's overall internal control system. Important controls over cash receipts include segregation of duties for those who handle cash and independent verification of cash receipts. Important controls over cash disbursements include payment by check, credit card, or debit card, segregation of duties, and various authorization and documentation procedures.

LO5 Reconcile a bank statement.

In a bank reconciliation we adjust the *bank's* balance for (1) cash transactions already recorded by the company but not yet recorded by the bank and (2) bank errors. Similarly, we adjust the *company's* balance for (1) cash transactions already recorded by the bank but not yet recorded by the company and (2) company errors. After we adjust both the bank balance and the company balance, the two should equal.

LO6 Account for petty cash.

To pay for minor purchases, companies keep some cash on hand in a petty cash fund. At the end of the period, expenditures from the petty cash fund are recorded, and the fund is replenished.

LO7 Identify the major inflows and outflows of cash.

The statement of cash flows reports all cash activities for the period. *Operating activities* include those transactions and events involving revenues and expenses. *Investing activities* include cash investments in long-term assets

and investment securities. *Financing activities* include transactions designed to finance the business through borrowing and owner investment.

Analysis

LO8 Assess earnings quality by comparing net income and cash flows.

Companies whose free cash flow is decreasing relative to net income are likely to have lower earnings quality than are other companies, all else being equal.

GLOSSARY

Bank reconciliation: Matching the balance of cash in the bank account with the balance of cash in the company's own records. **p. 126**

Cash: Currency, coins, balances in savings and checking accounts, items acceptable for deposit in these accounts (such as checks received from customers), and cash equivalents. **p. 122**

Cash equivalents: Short-term investments that have a maturity date no longer than three months from the date of purchase. **p. 122**

Checks outstanding: Checks the company has written that have not been subtracted from the bank's record of the company's balance. **p. 129**

Collusion: Two or more people acting in coordination to circumvent internal controls. **p. 121**

Deposits outstanding: Cash receipts of the company that have not been added to the bank's record of the company's balance. **p. 129**

Earnings quality: The ability of net income to help predict future performance of the company. **p. 137**

Free cash flow: Operating cash flows plus investing cash flows during the period. **p. 137**

Internal controls: A company's plans to (1) safeguard the company's assets and (2) improve the accuracy and reliability of accounting information. **p. 116**

NSF checks: Checks drawn on nonsufficient funds, or "bad" checks from customers. **p. 129**

Occupational fraud: The use of one's occupation for personal enrichment through the deliberate misuse or misapplication of the employing organization's resources. **p. 116**

Petty cash fund: Small amount of cash kept on hand to pay for minor purchases. **p. 133**

Sarbanes-Oxley Act: Known as the *Public Company Accounting Reform and Investor Protection Act of 2002* and commonly referred to as *SOX*; the act established a variety of new guidelines related to auditor-client relations and internal control procedures. **p. 117**

Separation of duties: Authorizing transactions, recording transactions, and maintaining control of the related assets should be separated among employees. **p. 119**

SELF-STUDY QUESTIONS

■ **LO1**   1. Fraudulent reporting by management could include:
  a. Fictitious revenues from a fake customer.
  b. Improper asset valuation.
  c. Mismatching revenues and expenses.
  d. All of the above.

■ **LO1**   2. The Sarbanes-Oxley Act (SOX) mandates which of the following?
  a. Increased regulations related to auditor-client relations.
  b. Increased regulations related to internal control.
  c. Increased regulations related to corporate executive accountability.
  d. All of the above.

3. What is the concept behind *separation of duties* in establishing internal control?   ■ **LO2**
   a. Employee fraud is less likely to occur when access to assets and access to accounting records are separated.
   b. The company's financial accountant should not share information with the company's tax accountant.
   c. Duties of middle-level managers of the company should be clearly separated from those of top executives.
   d. The external auditors of the company should have no contact with managers while the audit is taking place.

4. Which of the following is considered cash for financial reporting purposes?   ■ **LO3**
   a. Accounts receivable.
   b. Investments with maturity dates greater than three months.
   c. Checks received from customers.
   d. Accounts payable.

5. Which of the following generally would *not* be considered good internal control of cash receipts?   ■ **LO4**
   a. Allowing customers to pay with a debit card.
   b. Requiring the employee receiving the cash from the customer to also deposit the cash into the company's bank account.
   c. Recording cash receipts as soon as they are received.
   d. Allowing customers to pay with a credit card.

6. Which of the following adjusts the bank's balance of cash in a bank reconciliation?   ■ **LO5**
   a. NSF checks.
   b. Service fees.
   c. An error by the company.
   d. Checks outstanding.

7. Which of the following adjusts the company's balance of cash in a bank reconciliation?   ■ **LO5**
   a. Interest earned.
   b. Checks outstanding.
   c. Deposits outstanding.
   d. An error by the bank.

8. The purpose of a petty cash fund is to: ■ **LO6**
   a. Provide a convenient form of payment for the company's customers.
   b. Pay employee salaries at the end of each period.
   c. Provide cash on hand for minor expenditures.
   d. Allow the company to save cash for major future purchases.

9. Operating cash flows would include which of the following?   ■ **LO7**
   a. Repayment of borrowed money.
   b. Payment for employee salaries.
   c. Services provided to customers on account.
   d. Payment for a new operating center.

10. A company's free cash flow is calculated as: ■ **LO8**
   a. The amount of cash reporting in the balance sheet.
   b. Net income less investing cash flows.
   c. Operating cash flows plus investing cash flows.
   d. Net income plus operating cash flows.

Answers to the Self-Study Questions
1. d   2. d   3. a   4. c   5. b   6. d   7. a   8. c   9. b   10. c

REVIEW QUESTIONS

■ LO1   1. Define occupational fraud. Describe two common means of occupational fraud.

■ LO1   2. What is internal control? Why should a company establish an internal control system?

■ LO1   3. "Managers are stewards of the company's assets." Discuss what this means.

■ LO1   4. Why are some managers motivated to manipulate amounts reported in the financial statements?

■ LO1   5. What are some of the consequences to employees when managers engage in fraudulent financial reporting?

■ LO1   6. What are some of the major provisions of the Sarbanes-Oxley Act?

■ LO2   7. Briefly describe the five components of internal control outlined by the Committee of Sponsoring Organizations (COSO).

■ LO2   8. Describe the difference between preventive controls and detective controls. What are examples of each?

■ LO2   9. What is meant by separation of duties?

■ LO2   10. Who has responsibility for internal control in an organization? According to guidelines set forth in Section 404 of the Sarbanes-Oxley Act, what role does the auditor play in internal control?

■ LO2   11. What are some limitations of internal control?

■ LO2   12. To what does collusion refer?

■ LO2   13. Is fraud more likely to occur when it is being committed by top-level employees? Explain.

■ LO3   14. Define cash and cash equivalents.

■ LO3   15. Describe how the purchase of items with a check is recorded.

■ LO4   16. Discuss basic controls for cash receipts.

■ LO4   17. What is a credit card? How are credit card sales reported?

■ LO4   18. What is a debit card? How are debit card sales reported?

■ LO4   19. Discuss basic controls for cash disbursements.

■ LO4   20. How are credit card purchases reported?

■ LO5   21. What is a bank reconciliation? How can it help in determining whether proper control of cash has been maintained?

■ LO5   22. What are two primary reasons that the company's balance of cash will differ between its own records and those of the bank?

■ LO5   23. Give some examples of timing differences in cash transactions that firms need to account for in a bank reconciliation.

■ LO5   24. After preparing a bank reconciliation, what adjustments does the company need to make to its records?

■ LO6   25. What is a petty cash fund?

■ LO6   26. Describe how management maintains control over the petty cash fund.

■ LO7   27. The change in cash for the year can be calculated by comparing the balance of cash reported in this year's and last year's balance sheet. Why is the statement of cash flows needed?

■ LO7   28. Describe the operating, investing, and financing sections of the statement of cash flows.

29. How does the relationship between net income and cash flows for the period provide an indication of the quality of earnings?　　■ LO8

30. We compared **Krispy Kreme** and **Starbucks** at the end of this chapter. What was the difference between the two companies, and why did that matter?　　■ LO8

For the following, please visit your instructor's *Connect* site.

BRIEF EXERCISES	1-15
EXERCISES	1-21
PROBLEMS: SET A	1-5
PROBLEMS: SET B	1-5
GREAT ADVENTURES	

McGraw Hill connect™
|ACCOUNTING

Note: Additional Perspectives assignments for Financial Analysis, Comparative Analysis, Internet Research, and Written Communication are in Appendix F at the end of this book. For additional Exercises: Set B and for additional Problems: Set C, visit www.mhhe.com/spicelandMTC1e.

Receivables and Sales

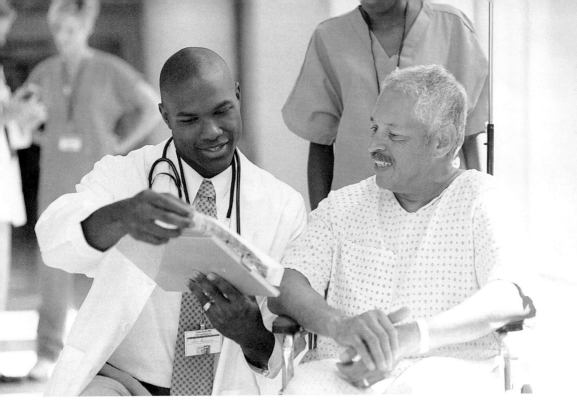

TENET HEALTHCARE: **BAD DEBTS CAUSE PAIN TO INVESTORS**

Tenet Healthcare Corporation is one of the largest hospital chains in the United States. The company operates 50 hospitals in 12 states, employs over 57,000 people, admits more than 500,000 patients, and has nearly 4,000,000 outpatient visits each year. For the period 2007–2009, the company reported net operating revenues of $26 billion. Everything seems fine, right?

Wrong. Over this same period, Tenet reported profits of only $145 million. That's a profit of only one-half of a penny for every dollar of revenue. One of the reasons for Tenet's poor operating performance was the cost of "uncompensated care." Uncompensated care occurs when patients receive services but are either unwilling or unable to pay. Though hospitals try to minimize these costs, federal law requires that patients not be denied emergency treatment due to inability to pay. Uncompensated care is a problem for the entire health-care industry.

Tenet reports uncompensated care in three ways: (1) as charity care, (2) as discounted services, and (3) as provisions for bad debts. For patients who are financially unable to pay for their health-care services, Tenet does not pursue collection of amounts that qualify as charity care. Also, it offers discounted services to patients who have no insurance or are underinsured. The company instituted a program of discounted services to reduce the reported amounts of bad debts. Bad debts occur when customers have been billed but never pay, and the company decides to recognize that fact in its accounting records. In reality, the three types of uncompensated care are difficult to separate, and all have a negative economic impact on the company's operations.

Over the period 2007–2009, Tenet reported the following amounts (in millions) for each of these categories of uncompensated care:

Year	Charity Care	Discounted Services	Provision for Bad Debts	Total
2007	$121	$ 342	$ 555	$1,018
2008	113	359	628	1,100
2009	118	365	697	1,180
Total	$352	$1,066	$1,880	$3,298

Tenet's profits would have been dramatically higher without the cost of more than $3 billion in uncompensated care. Tenet states in its annual report, ". . . unless our business mix shifts toward a greater number of insured patients or the trend of higher co-payments and deductibles reverses, we anticipate this high level of uncollectible accounts to continue." In 2010, health-care industry troubles, such as Tenet's, sparked a heated national debate over the need for health-care reform in the United States.

PART A

RECOGNIZING ACCOUNTS RECEIVABLE

As you learned in Chapter 2, companies sometimes provide goods or services to customers, not for cash, but on account. Formally, **accounts receivable** represent the amount of cash owed to a company by its customers from the sale of products or services on account. To understand accounts receivable, we need to start with *credit sales*, from which accounts receivable originate.

Credit Sales and Accounts Receivable

■ LO1
Recognize accounts receivable.

Have you ever sold a product or service to someone and accepted that person's promise to pay you in the future? For example, did you ever sell a candy bar as part of a fund-raiser and have the person promise to pay you later? If so, you made a credit sale. **Credit sales** transfer products and services to a customer today while bearing the risk of collecting payment from that customer in the future. Credit sales transactions are also known as *sales on account* or *services on account*. As we saw in the opening story, Tenet Healthcare provides a considerable number of credit sales for health care–related services, but many of its credit customers never pay. In this chapter, we focus on recording credit sales and dealing with the likelihood that some customers will not pay as promised.

Credit sales are common for large business transactions in which buyers don't have sufficient cash available or in which credit cards cannot be used because the transaction amount exceeds typical credit card limits. They typically include an informal credit agreement supported by an invoice and require payment within 30 to 60 days after the sale. **Even though the seller does not receive cash at the time of the credit sale, the firm records revenue immediately, as long as future collection from the customer is reasonably certain.**

Along with the recognized revenue, at the time of sale the seller also obtains a legal right to receive cash from the buyer. **The legal right to *receive* cash is valuable and represents an asset of the company.** This asset is referred to as accounts receivable (sometimes called *trade receivables*), and the firm records it at the time of a credit sale.

To see how companies record credit sales, consider an example. Suppose Link's Dental charges $500 for teeth whitening. Dee Kay decides to have her teeth whitened on March 1 but doesn't pay cash at the time of service. She promises to pay the $500 whitening fee to Link by March 31. Link's Dental records the following at the time of the whitening.

A = L + SE	March 1	Debit	Credit
+500	Accounts Receivable	500	
+500 Rev↑	Service Revenue		500
	(Provide services on account)		

Notice that instead of debiting Cash, as in a cash sale, Link's Dental debits another asset—Accounts Receivable—for the credit sale.

 KEY POINT

Companies record an asset (accounts receivable) and revenue when they sell products and services to their customers on account, expecting payment in the future.

As you study receivables, realize that one company's right to *collect* cash corresponds to another company's (or individual's) obligation to *pay* cash. One company's account receivable is the flip side of another company's account payable. In Chapter 6 we discuss accounts payable in the context of inventory purchases on account. In Chapter 8 we again discuss accounts payable, but in the context of current liabilities.

Flip Side

OTHER TYPES OF RECEIVABLES

Other types of receivables are less common than accounts receivable. *Nontrade receivables* are receivables that originate from sources other than customers. They include tax refund claims, interest receivable, and loans by the company to other entities, including stockholders and employees. When receivables are accompanied by formal credit arrangements made with written debt instruments (or notes), we refer to them as *notes receivable*. We'll consider notes receivable later in this chapter.

Net Revenues

From time to time, companies offer discounts to customers. These discounts offer ways to quickly sell old inventory, attract new customers, reward long-term loyal customers, and encourage customers to pay quickly on their accounts. However, while these discounts may be beneficial to the company's long-term success, they can reduce the amount of revenue reported in the current period. In addition, the company's revenues are reduced when customers return unsatisfactory products or demand allowances for inferior services. Therefore, it is important for managers to consider not only their companies' total revenues, but also net revenues. Net revenues refer to a company's total revenues less any amounts for discounts, returns, and allowances. We discuss these items next.

■ **LO2**
Calculate net revenues using discounts, returns, and allowances.

TRADE DISCOUNTS

Trade discounts represent a reduction in the listed price of a product or service. Companies typically use trade discounts to provide incentives to larger customers or consumer groups to purchase from the company. Trade discounts also can be a way to change prices without publishing a new price list or to disguise real prices from competitors.

When recording a transaction, companies don't recognize trade discounts *directly*. Instead, they recognize trade discounts *indirectly* by recording the sale at the discounted price. For example, let's go back to Link's Dental, which typically charges $500 for teeth whitening. Assume that in order to entice more customers, Dr. Link offers a 20% discount on teeth whitening to any of his regular patients. Since Dee Kay is one of Dr. Link's regular patients, she can take advantage of the special discount and have her teeth whitened for only $400.

March 1	Debit	Credit
Accounts Receivable	400	
Service Revenue		400
(Make credit sale of $500 with a 20% trade discount)		

A	=	L	+	SE
+400				
				+400 Rev↑

Notice that Link's Dental records the trade discount *indirectly* by recognizing revenue equal to the discounted price, which is $500 less the trade discount of $100 (= $500 × 20%).

SALES DISCOUNTS

Unlike a trade discount, a sales discount represents a reduction, not in the selling price of a product or service, but in the amount to be paid by a credit customer if payment is made within a specified period of time. It's a discount intended to provide incentive for quick payment.

Discount terms, such as 2/10, n/30, are a shorthand way to communicate the amount of the discount and the time period within which it's available. The term "2/10," pronounced "two ten," for example, indicates the customer will receive a 2% discount if the amount owed is paid within 10 days. The term "n/30," pronounced "net thirty," means that if the customer does *not* take the discount, full payment is due within 30 days.

Assume Link's Dental wants Dee to pay quickly on her teeth whitening bill and offers her terms of 2/10, n/30. This means that if Dee pays within 10 days, the amount due ($400 after the trade discount) will be reduced by 2% (or $8 = $400 × 2%). Let's consider two alternatives—taking or not taking the sales discount.

With the sales discount. Let's see what happens when Dee pays within 10 days: Assume that Dee pays on March 10, which is within the 10-day discount period. Link's Dental records the following transaction when it receives payment.

March 10	Debit	Credit
Cash	392	
Sales Discounts	8	
Accounts Receivable		400
(Collect cash on account with a 2% sales discount)		

Balance Sheet					Income Statement		
			Stockholders' Equity				
			Common	**Retained**			**Net**
Assets	=	**Liabilities** +	**Stock** +	**Earnings**	**Revenues** −	**Expenses** =	**Income**
+392	=			−8	−8		= −8
−400							
−8							

Notice that Link receives only $392 cash, the full amount owed less the 2% sales discount. **We record the sales discount as a** contra revenue account. A contra revenue account is an account with a balance that is opposite, or "contra," to that of its related revenue account. The reason we use a contra revenue account is to be able to keep a record of the total revenue separate from the reduction in that revenue due to quick payment. In this case, Service Revenue has a credit balance of $400, and its related contra revenue account—Sales Discounts—has a debit balance of $8. The net effect is that sales discounts increase, reducing net revenues of the company to $392. It's easier to see the relationship between these two accounts by looking at the partial income statement of Link's Dental in Illustration 5–1.

ILLUSTRATION 5–1

Partial Income Statement Reporting Revenues Net of Sales Discounts

LINK'S DENTAL		
Income Statement (partial)		
Service revenues	$400	
Less: Sales discounts	(8)	
Net service revenues		$392

Link provides a service with a normal price of $500. However, after the trade discount of $100 and the sales discount of $8, Link's income statement reports net revenue of $392.

Also notice that Link's Dental credits Accounts Receivable for $400, even though it receives only $392 cash. The reason is that the $400 balance in Accounts Receivable is "paid in full" by the combination of the $392 cash payment and the $8 sales discount. Dee owes $0 after paying $392. The balance of Accounts Receivable now equals $0, as demonstrated in Illustration 5–2.

	Accounts Receivable		
Credit sale	Mar. 1 400		Collection of $392
		Mar. 10 400	on account
Ending balance	Bal. 0		

ILLUSTRATION 5–2

Balance of Accounts Receivable after Credit Sale and Subsequent Collection on Account

Without the sales discount.   For our second scenario, assume that Dee waits until March 31 to pay, which is *not* within the 10-day discount period. Link's Dental records the following transaction at the time it collects cash from Dee.

March 31	Debit	Credit
Cash	400	
Accounts Receivable		400
(Collect cash on account)		

A	=	L	+	SE
+400				
−400				

Notice that there is no indication in recording the transaction that the customer does not take the sales discount. This is the typical way to record a cash collection on account when no sales discounts are involved. Accounts Receivable is credited for $400 to reduce its balance to $0, representing the amount owed by the customer after payment.

SALES RETURNS AND ALLOWANCES

In some cases, customers may not be satisfied with a product or service purchased. If a customer returns a product, we call that a **sales return**. After a sales return, (a) we reduce the customer's account balance if the sale was on account or (b) we issue a cash refund if the sale was for cash.

Sometimes, because of a deficiency in the company's product or service, the seller reduces the customer's balance owed or provides at least a partial refund while allowing the customer to keep the product. Such a reduction or partial refund is called a **sales allowance**. Suppose on March 5, after she gets her teeth whitened but before she pays, Dee notices that another local dentist is offering the same procedure for $350, which is $50 less than Link's discounted price of $400. Dee brings this to Dr. Link's attention and because his policy is to match any competitor's pricing, he offers to reduce Dee's account balance by $50. Link's Dental records the following sales allowance.

March 5	Debit	Credit
Sales Allowances	50	
Accounts Receivable		50
(Make sales allowance for credit sale)		

This reduction of accounts receivable indicates that Dee owes less after the allowance—she now owes only $350.

Firms sometimes combine their sales returns and sales allowances in a *single* Sales Returns and Allowances account. **Like sales discounts, sales returns and allowances are contra revenue accounts.** We report both sales discounts and sales returns and allowances as reductions in the related revenue account, causing a reduction in net income.

KEY POINT

Sales discounts, returns, and allowances are contra revenue accounts. We subtract the balances in these accounts from total revenues when calculating net revenues.

Decision Point

Question	Accounting information	Analysis
Does a company have a recurring problem with customer satisfaction?	Total sales and sales returns and allowances	If sales returns and allowances are routinely high relative to total sales, this might indicate that customers are not satisfied with the company's products or services.

COMMON MISTAKE

Students sometimes misclassify contra revenue accounts—sales discounts, returns, and allowances—as expenses. Like expenses, contra revenues have normal debit balances and reduce the reported amount of net income. However, contra revenues represent *direct reductions* of revenues, whereas expenses represent the separate costs of generating revenues. Misclassifying contra revenue accounts as expenses overstates revenues and expenses but leaves bottom-line net income unaffected.

Let's Review

spiceland.mhhe.com/t7

Snap-Crackle-Pop (SCP) Chiropractic normally charges $120 for a full spinal adjustment. Currently, the company is offering a $20 discount to senior citizens. In addition, SCP offers terms 2/10, n/30 to all customers receiving services on account. The following events occur.

June 18   David, age 72, calls to set up an appointment.
June 20   David visits SCP and receives a spinal adjustment for the discounted price.
June 29   David pays for his office visit.

Required:

1. On what date should SCP record patient revenue?
2. Record patient revenue for SCP.
3. Record the cash collection for SCP assuming SCP receives David's payment in full on June 29 (within the discount period).
4. Calculate the balance of Accounts Receivable using a T-account format, and then calculate the balance of net revenue as shown in the income statement after the cash payment is received.

Solution:

1. SCP should record patient revenue on June 20—the date the service is provided.

2. Record patient revenue:

June 20	Debit	Credit
Accounts Receivable	100	
Service Revenue		100
(Provide services on account)		
(Revenue = $120 less $20 trade discount)		

3. Record receipt of David's payment in full within the discount period:

June 29	Debit	Credit
Cash	98	
Sales Discounts	2	
Accounts Receivable		100
(Collect cash on account with a 2% sales discount)		
(Sales discount = $100 × 2%)		

4. Balance of Accounts Receivable and calculation of net revenue after receipt of cash payment:

Accounts Receivable		
Jun. 20 100		
	Jun. 29 100	
Bal. 0		

Service revenue (from *Requirement 2*)	$100
Less: Sales discounts (from *Requirement 3*)	(2)
Net revenue	$ 98

Suggested Homework:
BE5-1, BE5-2;
E5-2, E5-3;
P5-2A&B

VALUING ACCOUNTS RECEIVABLE

PART B

The right to receive cash from a customer is a valuable resource for the company. **This is why accounts receivable is an asset, reported in the company's balance sheet.** If the company expects to receive the cash within one year, it classifies the receivable as a current asset; otherwise it classifies the receivable as a long-term asset.

What, though, is the *value* of being owed $100? If you are confident the person will actually pay you $100 in the near future, then you might consider the right to receive the money to be worth $100. However, if the person is unable to pay you anything, then your right to collect $100 is worth $0. Of course there are many possibilities in between. To be useful to decision makers, accounts receivable should be reported at the amount of cash the firm *expects* to collect, an amount known as net realizable value.

 KEY POINT

We recognize accounts receivable as assets in the balance sheet and report them at their *net realizable value*, that is, the amount of cash we expect to collect.

Allowance Method

■ **LO3**

Record an allowance for future uncollectible accounts.

We know that companies often are not able to collect all of their accounts receivable from customers. Rather than accept only cash payment at the time of sale, should companies extend credit to their customers by allowing them to purchase on account? **The upside of extending credit to customers is that it boosts sales by allowing customers the ability to purchase on account and pay cash later.** Just think of how many times you wanted to buy food, clothes, electronics, or other items that you could afford, but you didn't have cash with you. You're not alone. Many customers may not have cash readily available to make a purchase or, for other reasons, simply prefer to buy on credit.

The downside of extending credit to customers is that not all customers will pay fully on their accounts. Even the most well-meaning customers may find themselves in difficult financial circumstances beyond their control, limiting their ability to repay debt. Customers' accounts that we no longer consider collectible are uncollectible accounts, or *bad debts.*

The allowance method estimates future uncollectible accounts.

We account for uncollectible accounts using what's called the allowance method. This method involves *allowing for the possibility* that some accounts will be uncollectible at some point in the future.[1] Be sure to understand this key point. Using the allowance method we account for events (customers' bad debts) that have *not yet* occurred but that are likely to occur. This is different from other transactions you've learned about to this point. Those earlier transactions involved recording events that have already occurred, such as purchasing supplies, paying employees, and providing services to customers. **Under the allowance method, companies are required to *estimate* future uncollectible accounts and record those estimates in the current year.**

Before seeing exactly how to record the allowance method, let's first think about the effects that uncollectible accounts should have on the financial position of the company. Uncollectible accounts have the effect of (1) reducing assets (accounts receivable) by an estimate of the amount we don't expect to collect and (2) increasing expenses (bad debt expense) to reflect the cost of offering credit to customers. Illustration 5–3 demonstrates how the effects of uncollectible accounts should therefore be reflected in the financial statements.

ILLUSTRATION 5–3

The Financial Statement Effects of Accounting for Future Uncollectible Accounts

An account we do not expect to collect has no value. Thus, we need to reduce assets because we don't expect to collect the entire accounts receivable (assets). At the same time, failure to collect a customer's cash represents a cost inherent in using credit sales. The cost of uncollectible accounts is an operating expense, decreasing net income by the uncollectible amount. Next, let's see how to record bad debts so that both of these effects are captured in the financial statements—the reduction in assets and the increase in operating expenses.

---

[1]Later in the chapter, we'll look at a second method—the direct write-off method. The direct write-off method is used for tax purposes but is generally not permitted for financial reporting.

KEY POINT

Under the allowance method, companies are required to *estimate* future uncollectible accounts and record those estimates in the current year. Estimated uncollectible accounts reduce assets and increase expenses.

ESTIMATING UNCOLLECTIBLE ACCOUNTS

Now that we have discussed the impact of uncollectible accounts in the financial statements, let's see how we record them. To use the allowance method, a company first estimates at the end of the *current* year how much in uncollectible accounts will occur in the *following* year. Consider an example of future uncollectible accounts for Kimzey Medical Clinic, which specializes in emergency outpatient care. Because it doesn't verify the patient's health insurance before administering care, Kimzey knows that a high proportion of fees for emergency care provided will not be collected.

In 2012, Kimzey bills customers $50 million for emergency care it provided. By the end of the year, $20 million remains due from customers, but how much of this amount does Kimzey expect *not* to collect in the following year? Let's suppose that in previous years approximately 30% of accounts receivable were not collected; Kimzey decides to base this year's estimate on that same percentage. Estimating uncollectible accounts based on the percentage of accounts receivable expected not to be collected is known as the percentage-of-receivables method. This method sometimes is referred to as the *balance sheet method*, because we base the estimate of bad debts on a balance sheet amount—accounts receivable.[2]

Using the 30% estimate, Kimzey expects that $6 million of its accounts receivable (or 30% of $20 million) likely will never be collected. It makes the following year-end adjustment to allow for these future uncollectible accounts.

December 31, 2012 ($ in millions)	Debit	Credit
Bad Debt Expense	6	
Allowance for Uncollectible Accounts		6
(*Estimate future bad debts*)		
($20 million × 30% = $6 million)		

Balance Sheet						Income Statement			
			Stockholders' Equity						
Assets	=	Liabilities	+	Common Stock	+	Retained Earnings	Revenues	− Expenses	= Net Income
−6	=					−6		+6	= −6

The effect of the adjustment in the financial statements reflects the impact of the transaction on the financial position of the company. Because the nature of the accounts in this adjusting entry differs somewhat from those in other year-end adjusting entries we covered in Chapter 3, let's look closer.

Bad debt expense.   First, bad debt expense represents the cost of the estimated future bad debts. Kimzey estimates that it will not collect 30% of its accounts receivable, and so records Bad Debt Expense of $6 million. We include this expense

Common Terms Bad debt expense sometimes is referred to as *uncollectible accounts expense.*

[2]In the appendix to this chapter, we'll consider a second method, the *percentage-of-credit-sales method* (also referred to as the *income statement method*). In practice, companies are required to follow the percentage-of-receivables method, so that will be our focus here.

in the same income statement as the credit sales with which these bad debts are associated. By doing so, we properly "match" expenses (bad debts) with the revenues (credit sales) they help to generate. Illustration 5–4 shows the partial income statement for Kimzey Medical Clinic after estimating bad debt expense.

ILLUSTRATION 5–4

Partial Income Statement Showing Estimated Bad Debt Expense

KIMZEY MEDICAL CLINIC Income Statement (partial) For the year ended 2012	
($ in millions)	
Credit sales	$50
Bad debt expense	(6)
	$44

Match expenses with their related revenues.

In the 2012 income statement, we reduce the $50 million of revenue from credit sales by $6 million for estimated future bad debts. Even though the company reports credit sales of $50 million, the expected profits on these sales, after considering the cost of future bad debts, is only $44 million.

 KEY POINT

Adjusting for estimates of future uncollectible accounts matches expenses (bad debts) in the same period as the revenues (credit sales) they help to generate.

Common Terms The allowance for uncollectible accounts is sometimes referred to as the *allowance for doubtful accounts.*

spiceland.mhhe.com/c13

Report accounts receivable at net realizable value.

Allowance for uncollectible accounts.   Second, we adjust for future bad debts by making an allowance for uncollectible accounts. The contra asset account Allowance for Uncollectible Accounts represents the amount of accounts receivable we do not expect to collect. Earlier in the chapter, we discussed *contra revenue* accounts—sales discounts, returns, and allowances. Recall that these accounts provide a way to *reduce revenue indirectly.* In the same way, the allowance account provides a way to *reduce accounts receivable indirectly* to its *net realizable value,* rather than decreasing the accounts receivable balance itself.

We report the allowance for uncollectible accounts in the asset section of the balance sheet, but it represents a reduction in the balance of accounts receivable. The difference between total accounts receivable and the allowance for uncollectible accounts is referred to as net accounts receivable, which is net realizable value. Illustration 5–5 (next page) demonstrates the concept behind accounting for future uncollectible accounts and how the accounts receivable portion of Kimzey's year-end balance sheet appears.

After we estimate uncollectible accounts to be $6 million, we reduce the $20 million balance of accounts receivable and report them at their net realizable value of $14 million. But is this estimate correct? Only time will tell. Kimzey's prediction of $6 million for uncollectible accounts might be too high, or it might be too low. In either case, it's generally more informative than making no estimate at all. (Later in the chapter, we'll find out how close the estimate is.)

 KEY POINT

Recording an allowance for uncollectible accounts correctly reports accounts receivable at their net realizable value.

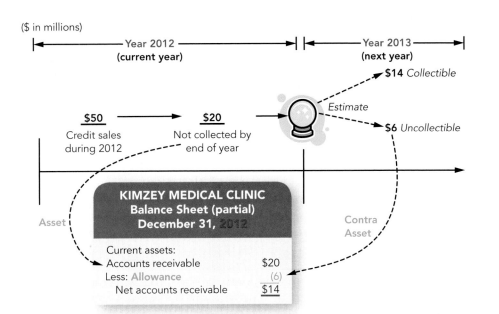

ILLUSTRATION 5–5

Accounting for Uncollectible Accounts and the Accounts Receivable Portion of the Balance Sheet

 COMMON MISTAKE

Because Allowance for Uncollectible Accounts has a normal credit balance, students sometimes misclassify this account as a liability, which also has a normal credit balance. Instead, a contra asset represents a reduction in a related asset.

Question		Accounting information		Analysis	
Are the company's credit sales policies too lenient?		Accounts receivable and the allowance for uncollectible accounts		A high ratio of the allowance for uncollectible accounts to total accounts receivable could be an indication that the company extends too much credit to high-risk customers.	

Decision Point

WRITING OFF ACCOUNTS RECEIVABLE

To continue with our example of Kimzey Medical Clinic, let's suppose that on February 23, 2013 (the following year), Kimzey receives notice that one of its former patients, Bruce Easley, has filed for bankruptcy protection against all creditors. Based on this information, Kimzey believes it is unlikely Bruce will pay his account of $4,000. Remember, Kimzey previously allowed for the likelihood that *some* of its customers would not pay, though it didn't know which ones. Now that it *knows* a specific customer will not pay, it can adjust the allowance and reduce the accounts receivable balance itself. Upon receiving news of this *actual* bad debt, Kimzey records the following.

■ **LO4**
Apply the procedure to write off accounts receivable as uncollectible.

February 23, 2013	Debit	Credit
Allowance for Uncollectible Accounts	4,000	
Accounts Receivable		4,000
(Write off a customer's account)		

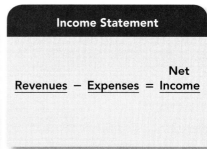

Balance Sheet					Income Statement		
			Stockholders' Equity				
			Common	Retained			Net
Assets	=	**Liabilities** +	**Stock** +	**Earnings**	**Revenues** −	**Expenses** =	**Income**
+4,000	=						
−4,000							
0							

What is the effect in Kimzey's financial statements when writing off Bruce's account receivable? **Overall, the write-off of the account receivable has no effect on total amounts reported in the balance sheet or in the income statement.** Notice that there is no decrease in total assets and no decrease in net income with the write-off. Here's why: **We have already recorded the negative effects of the bad news.** Kimzey recorded those effects when it *estimated* future bad debts at the end of 2012 and both reduced assets and recorded the bad debt expense. Now, when Bruce declares bankruptcy in the following year, 2013, we have already established the allowance for this bad debt. The write-off on February 23, 2013, reduces both an asset account (Accounts Receivable) and its contra asset account (Allowance for Uncollectible Accounts), leaving the *net* receivable unaffected. Thus, the write-off results in no change to total assets.

 COMMON MISTAKE

Students often mistakenly record bad debt expense when they write off an uncollectible account. The bad debt expense was recorded in a prior year at the time of estimating uncollectible accounts.

COLLECTION OF ACCOUNTS PREVIOUSLY WRITTEN OFF

Later in 2013, on September 8, Bruce's bankruptcy proceedings are complete. Kimzey had expected to receive none of the $4,000 Bruce owed. However, after liquidating all assets, Bruce is able to pay each of his creditors 25% of the amount due them. So, when Kimzey receives payment of $1,000 (= $4,000 × 25%), it makes the following two entries.

September 8, 2013	Debit	Credit
Accounts Receivable	1,000	
Allowance for Uncollectible Accounts		1,000
(Reestablish portion of account previously written off)		
Cash	1,000	
Accounts Receivable		1,000
(Collect cash on account)		

Balance Sheet					Income Statement		
			Stockholders' Equity				
			Common	Retained			Net
Assets	=	**Liabilities** +	**Stock** +	**Earnings**	**Revenues** −	**Expenses** =	**Income**
+1,000	=						
−1,000							
+1,000							
−1,000							
0							

The first entry simply reverses a portion of the previous entry that Kimzey made on February 23 to write off the account. The second entry records the collection of the account receivable. Notice that in both entries the debit entry increases total assets by the same amount that the credit entry decreases total assets. **Therefore, collecting cash on an account previously written off has no effect on total assets and no effect on net income.**

Let's assume that total accounts written off by Kimzey during 2013 equaled $5 million but that $1 million of this amount was ultimately collected by the end of the year. The time line of events related to accounts receivable of Kimzey during 2012 and 2013 is this:

1. At the end of 2012, accounts receivable total $20 million.
2. Kimzey makes an adjustment at the end of 2012 for *estimated* bad debts of $6 million.
3. In 2013, *actual* accounts Kimzey writes off as uncollectible total $5 million.
4. Of the $5 million in accounts written off earlier, $1 million later appears receivable.
5. Kimzey receives $1 million cash for the accounts reestablished in (4).

Illustration 5–6 summarizes the impact of each of these events (also numbered 1–5 there) in calculating net accounts receivable.

($ in millions)	2012		2013		
	(1) Accounts Receivable Total $20	**(2)** *Estimate* Bad Debts in 2013 to Be $6	**(3)** Write Off *Actual* Bad Debts of $5	**(4)** Reestablish Previous Write-offs of $1	**(5)** Collect Cash from Previous Write-offs of $1
Accts. receiv.	$20	$20	$15	$16	$15
Less: Allowance	(0)	(6)	(1)	(2)	(2)
Net accts. receiv.	$20	$14	$14	$14	$13

ILLUSTRATION 5–6

Balance of Kimzey's Net Accounts Receivable

Net accounts receivable decline for two of these events. First, as we *estimate* future bad debts, we recognize the likelihood that we will not collect cash for some accounts. Second, once the company receives payment from customers, their account balances are no longer receivable.

On the other hand, writing off *actual* bad debts and reestablishing those previous write-offs when it appears that customers will pay has no effect on net accounts receivable.

Notice that the balance of the allowance account is $2 million at the end of 2013. Does the fact that the allowance account has a nonzero ending balance mean that Kimzey's estimate of uncollectible accounts for 2013 was *wrong*? Perhaps. On the other hand, it may only mean that some of the $15 million in accounts receivable has not yet proven uncollectible but eventually will. In any case, when we make estimates in accounting, it's highly unlikely they will prove exactly correct.

Users of financial statements must realize that some of the amounts reported in financial statements are estimates, and estimating the future almost always results in some inaccuracy. Illustration 5–7 (next page) provides an excerpt from the annual report of **Tenet Healthcare Corporation.**

KEY POINT

Writing off a customer's account as uncollectible reduces the balance of accounts receivable but also reduces the contra asset—allowance for uncollectible accounts. The net effect is that there is no change in the *net* receivable (accounts receivable less the allowance) or in total assets. We recorded the decrease to assets as a result of the bad debt when we established the allowance for uncollectible accounts in a prior year.

TENET HEALTHCARE CORPORATION
Notes to the Financial Statements (excerpt)

The preparation of financial statements, in conformity with accounting principles generally accepted in the United States of America, requires us to make estimates and assumptions that affect the amounts reported in the Consolidated Financial Statements and these accompanying notes. We regularly evaluate the accounting policies and estimates we use. In general, we base the estimates on historical experience and on assumptions that we believe to be reasonable given the particular circumstances in which we operate. Although we believe all adjustments considered necessary for fair presentation have been included, actual results may vary from those estimates.

ESTIMATING UNCOLLECTIBLE ACCOUNTS IN THE FOLLOWING YEAR

At the end of 2013, Kimzey must once again estimate uncollectible accounts and make a year-end adjustment. Suppose that in 2013 Kimzey bills customers for services totaling $80 million, and $30 million is still receivable at the end of the year. Of the $30 million still receivable, let's say Kimzey again uses the percentage-of-receivables method and estimates 30% (or $9 million) will not be collected. For what amount would Kimzey record the year-end adjustment for bad debts in 2013? Before answering, let's first examine the current balance of the allowance account, as shown in Illustration 5–8.

ILLUSTRATION 5–8

Balance of Kimzey's
Allowance for
Uncollectible Accounts

Allowance for Uncollectible Accounts
($ in millions)

Write off account	5	6	Beginning balance for 2013
		1	Collection of previous write-off
		2	Balance before adjustment
		?	Year-end adjustment
		9	Estimated ending balance for 2013

Notice that the balance before the year-end adjustment in this example is a $2 million *credit*. **A credit balance before adjustment indicates that last year's estimate of uncollectible accounts may have been too high.** However, it's possible that some of the estimated uncollectible accounts have not proven bad yet. **A *debit* balance before adjustment indicates that last year's estimate was too low.**

Based on all available information at the end of 2013, Kimzey estimates that the allowance for uncollectible accounts should be $9 million. This means the allowance account needs to increase from its current balance of $2 million credit to the estimated ending balance of $9 million credit. Kimzey can accomplish this by adjusting the account for $7 million as follows:

A = L + SE		December 31, 2013	Debit	Credit
	−7 Exp↑	**Bad Debt Expense**	7	
−7		**Allowance for Uncollectible Accounts**		7
		(*Estimate future bad debts*)		

In its 2013 income statement, Kimzey will report bad debt expense of $7 million along with other operating expenses of, say, $50 million. This is shown in Illustration 5–9.

KIMZEY MEDICAL CLINIC
Income Statement
For the year ended 2013

($ in millions)

Revenue from credit sales		$80
Expenses:		
Bad debt expense	$ 7	
Other operating expenses	50	
Net income		57
		$23

ILLUSTRATION 5–9

Bad Debt Expense in the Income Statement

In the 2013 balance sheet, Kimzey will report the allowance account at the best estimate of its appropriate balance, $9 million. This is shown in Illustration 5–10.

KIMZEY MEDICAL CLINIC
Balance Sheet (partial)
December 31, 2013

Assets

Current assets ($ in millions):	
Accounts receivable	$30
Less: Allowance for uncollectible accounts	(9)
Net accounts receivable	$21

ILLUSTRATION 5–10

Accounts Receivable Portion of the Balance Sheet

The process of estimating an allowance for uncollectible accounts, writing off bad debts in the following period, and then reestimating the allowance at the end of the period is one that occurs throughout the company's life.

AGING OF ACCOUNTS RECEIVABLE

In our example for Kimzey Medical Clinic, we estimated future uncollectible accounts by applying a *single* estimated percentage to total accounts receivable (30%). Management can estimate this percentage using historical averages, current economic conditions, industry comparisons, or other analytical techniques. A more accurate method than assuming a single percentage uncollectible for all accounts is to consider the *age* of various accounts receivable, and use a higher percentage for "old" accounts than for "new" accounts. This is known as the aging method. For instance, accounts that are 60 days past due are older than accounts that are 30 days past due. **The older the account, the less likely it is to be collected.**

Let's return to Kimzey Medical Clinic to see how an aging of accounts receivable can be used to estimate uncollectible accounts. Recall that accounts receivable at the end of 2013 totaled $30 million. Illustration 5–11 (next page) shows Kimzey's accounts receivable aging schedule at the end of 2013.

Each age group has its own estimate of the percent uncollectible. Summing the estimated allowance for each age group results in a total estimated allowance of **$8** million. Because the allowance has a balance of $2 million before adjustment at the end of 2013 (refer back to Illustration 5–8), it needs a **$6** million adjustment. In other words, the $2 million current balance in the allowance account needs an upward adjustment of $6 million to reach the $8 million estimated ending balance for 2013. Illustration 5–12 (next page) demonstrates this calculation.

■ **LO5**
Use the aging method to estimate future uncollectible accounts.

ILLUSTRATION 5–11

Kimzey's Accounts
Receivable Aging
Schedule

($ in millions)

Age Group (days past due)	Accounts Receivable	×	Estimated Percent Uncollectible	=	Estimated Allowance
0–60	$20		20%		$4.0
61–120	5		30%		1.5
121–180	4		40%		1.6
More than 180	1		90%		0.9
Total	$30				$8.0

ILLUSTRATION 5–12

Balance of Kimzey's
Allowance for
Uncollectible Accounts

spiceland.mhhe.com/c14

A = L + SE
              –6 Exp↑
–6

Allowance for Uncollectible Accounts
($ in millions)

Write off account	5	6	Beginning balance for 2013
		1	Collection of previous write-off
		2	Balance before adjustment
		?	Year-end adjustment
		8	Estimated ending balance for 2013

To adjust the allowance from its current balance of $2 million credit to the estimated balance of $8 million credit, we record the following:

December 31, 2013	Debit	Credit
Bad Debt Expense	6	
Allowance for Uncollectible Accounts		6
(*Estimate future bad debts*)		

Illustration 5–13 presents **Tenet Healthcare**'s policy of estimating uncollectible accounts.

ILLUSTRATION 5–13

Excerpt from
Tenet Healthcare
Corporation's Annual
Report

TENET HEALTHCARE CORPORATION
Notes to the Financial Statements (excerpt)

We provide for an allowance against accounts receivable that could become uncollectible by establishing an allowance to reduce the carrying value of such receivables to their estimated net realizable value. We estimate this allowance based on the aging of our accounts receivable by hospital, our historical collection experience by hospital and for each type of payer over an 18-month look-back period, and other relevant factors. There are various factors that can impact collection trends, such as changes in the economy, which in turn have an impact on unemployment rates and the number of uninsured and underinsured patients, the volume of patients through the emergency department, the increased burden of co-payments and deductibles to be made by patients with insurance, and business practices related to collection efforts. These factors continuously change and can have an impact on collection trends and our estimation process.

The following tables present the approximate aging by payer of our continuing operations' net accounts receivable.

Age	Medicare	Medicaid	Managed Care	Indemnity, Self-pay, and Other	Total
0–60 days	94%	63%	78%	26%	69%
61–120 days	3	24	12	27	15
121–180 days	3	11	5	13	6
Over 180 days	0	2	5	34	10
Total	100%	100%	100%	100%	100%

KEY POINT

Using the aging method to estimate uncollectible accounts is more accurate than applying a single percentage to all accounts receivable. The aging method recognizes that the longer accounts are past due, the less likely they are to be collected.

Decision Point

Question		Accounting information		Analysis	
How likely is it that the company's accounts receivable will be collected?		Notes to the financial statements detailing the age of individual accounts receivable		Older accounts are less likely to be collected.	

Let's Review

spiceland.mhhe.com/t8

Community Medical is an outpatient health facility that provides minor surgical and other health-related services to the local community. Many of the patients do not have medical insurance. These customers are required to pay for services within 30 days of receiving treatment. At the beginning of 2012, Community Medical's allowance for uncollectible accounts was a $100,000 credit.

Required:

1. Record the write-off of $120,000 of accounts receivable during 2012.

2. Estimate the allowance for future uncollectible accounts using the following ages and estimated percentage uncollectible at the end of 2012:

Age Group	Amount Receivable	Estimated Percent Uncollectible	Estimated Amount Uncollectible
Not yet due	$600,000	10%	
1–45 days past due	200,000	20	
More than 45 days past due	50,000	60	
Total	$850,000		

3. Use a T-account to determine the year-end adjustment to the allowance account.

4. Record the year-end adjustment for bad debts expense.

5. Prepare a partial balance sheet showing accounts receivable and the allowance for uncollectible accounts.

Solution:

1. Write-off of accounts receivable during 2012:

	Debit	Credit
Allowance for Uncollectible Accounts	120,000	
Accounts Receivable		120,000

2. Estimate of the allowance for future uncollectible accounts:

Age Group	Amount Receivable	Estimated Percent Uncollectible	Estimated Amount Uncollectible
Not yet due	$600,000	10%	$ 60,000
1–45 days past due	200,000	20%	40,000
More than 45 days past due	50,000	60%	30,000
Total	$850,000		$130,000

3. Year-end adjustment to the allowance account:

	Allowance for Uncollectible Accounts		
		100,000	Beginning balance
Write-offs	120,000		
Balance before adjustment	20,000		
		?	Year-end adjustment
		130,000	Estimated ending balance

4. Year-end adjustment for bad debt expense:

December 31, 2012	Debit	Credit
Bad Debt Expense	150,000	
Allowance for Uncollectible Accounts		150,000*

*Notice from the T-account in *Requirement* 3 that the balance of the allowance account before adjustment is a $20,000 *debit*. Based on the estimated allowance of a $130,000 *credit*, we need a credit adjustment of $150,000. Of this adjustment, $20,000 is needed to get the allowance account to a zero balance, and the remaining $130,000 credit adjusts the account to the estimated ending balance.

5. Balance sheet:

COMMUNITY MEDICAL
Balance Sheet (partial)
December 31, 2012

Assets		
Current assets:		
Accounts receivable	$850,000	
Less: Allowance for uncollectible accounts	(130,000)	
Net accounts receivable		$720,000

Suggested Homework:
BE5-5, BE5-8;
E5-11, E5-12;
P5-4A&B, P5-6A&B

Direct Write-Off Method

■ **LO6**
Contrast the allowance method and direct write-off method when accounting for uncollectible accounts.

We've just seen how the allowance method of accounting for uncollectible accounts works. However, if uncollectible accounts are not anticipated or are immaterial, or if it's not possible to reliably estimate them, we need not make an allowance for them. **In these rare situations, we do not estimate uncollectible accounts, but we write off any bad debts that do arise as bad debt expense at that time.**

For example, suppose a company provides services for $10,000 on account in 2012, but makes no allowance for uncollectible accounts at the end of the year. On September 17, 2013, an account of $2,000 is considered uncollectible. The company records the write-off as follows.

A	=	L	+	SE
				−2,000 Exp↑
−2,000				

September 17, 2013	Debit	Credit
Bad Debt Expense	2,000	
Accounts Receivable		2,000
(*Write off uncollectible account directly*)		

The direct write-off method typically is not acceptable for financial reporting.

Recording bad debt expense at the time we know the account to be uncollectible is known as the direct write-off method. **The direct write-off method is used for tax purposes but is generally not permitted for financial reporting.** Can you guess why? Accounts receivable generated from the credit sales in 2012 are recorded in 2012, but no allowance is made for the possibility that some of these accounts will not be collected. As a result, in 2012 assets are overstated and operating expenses are understated. This is why the direct write-off method of accounting for uncollectible accounts is not permitted for financial reporting purposes except in limited circumstances. Specifically, **a firm must use the allowance method if it is probable that the firm will not collect a material amount of receivables and it can reasonably estimate that amount.**

Illustration 5–14 highlights the difference between the allowance method and the direct write-off method for our example.

	2012 (Year-end estimated bad debts = $2,000)	2013 (Actual bad debts = $2,000)
	Year-end adjustment	**Write-off**

Allowance method (estimate)	Bad Debt Expense 2,000
	  Allowance 2,000
		Allowance 2,000
		  Accounts Receivable 2,000

Direct write-off method	No Adjustment	Bad Debt Expense 2,000 Accounts Receivable 2,000

ILLUSTRATION 5–14

Comparing the Allowance Method and the Direct Write-off Method for Recording Uncollectible Accounts

Assume that at the end of 2012 we *estimate* $2,000 of accounts receivable won't be collected. For simplicity, also assume that our estimate of future bad debts turns out to be correct, and actual bad debts in 2013 total $2,000.

Under the allowance method, future bad debts are *estimated* and recorded as an expense and a reduction in assets in 2012. Under the direct write-off method, though, we make no attempt to estimate future bad debts. We record bad debt expense in the period the account proves uncollectible. In this case, we report the bad debt expense and reduction in assets in 2013. Notice that, either way, the ultimate effect is a $2,000 debit to Bad Debt Expense and a $2,000 credit to Accounts Receivable. **The difference is in the timing.**

COMMON MISTAKE

Some students erroneously think firms should reduce total assets and record bad debt expense at the time the bad debt actually occurs. However, companies *anticipate* future bad debts and establish an allowance for those estimates.

KEY POINT

The direct write-off method reduces accounts receivable and records bad debt expense at the time the account receivable proves uncollectible. If the credit sale occurs in a prior reporting period, bad debt expense is not properly matched with revenues (credit sales). Also, accounts receivable will be overstated in the prior period. The direct write-off method typically is not acceptable for financial reporting.

Managing Bad Debt Estimates

Decision Maker's Perspective

While the allowance method is conceptually superior to the direct write-off method and more accurately reports assets and matches revenues and expenses, it does have one disadvantage. This disadvantage arises from the fact that reported amounts under the allowance method represent management estimates. If so inclined, management could use these estimates to manipulate reported earnings.[3] For example, if management wants to boost earnings in the current year, it can intentionally

[3]M. McNichols, G. P. Wilson, and L. De Angelo. 1988. Evidence of Earnings Management from the Provision for Bad Debts. *Journal of Accounting Research* (26): 1–40.

underestimate future uncollectible accounts. Similarly, if a company is having an especially good year and management wants to "reserve" earnings for the future, it can intentionally *overestimate* future uncollectible accounts. Having a large expense in the current year means there is less of a charge to bad debt expense in a future year, increasing future earnings. Other expenses, such as rent expense, are much more difficult to manipulate because their reported amounts don't rely on management estimates. These expenses are evidenced by past transactions, and their amounts are verifiable to the penny using a receipt or an invoice.

HealthSouth Corporation appears to have used estimates of uncollectible accounts to manipulate earnings. In the early 1990s, HealthSouth reported large amounts of bad debt expense, building large reserves in the allowance account. Then in the mid-1990s, as additional earnings were needed to meet analysts' expectations, HealthSouth was able to report low amounts for bad debt expense because of the previously inflated allowance account. In 1999, when it became apparent that HealthSouth's earnings were falling dramatically, the company took a "big bath" by reporting a very large charge to bad debt expense. Some companies feel that if they are going to have a bad year, they might as well release all the bad news at once. This makes it possible to report better news in future years. ●

 ETHICAL DILEMMA

 Philip Stanton, the executive manager of Thomson Pharmaceutical, receives a bonus if the company's net income in the current year exceeds net income in the past year. By the end of 2012, it appears that net income for 2012 will easily exceed net income for 2011. Philip has asked Mary Beth Williams, the company's controller, to try to reduce this year's income and "bank" some of the profits for future years. Mary Beth suggests that the company's bad debt expense as a percentage of accounts receivable for 2012 be increased from 10% to 15%. She believes 10% is the more accurate estimate but knows that both the corporation's internal and external auditors allow some flexibility in estimates. What is the effect of increasing the estimate of bad debts from 10% to 15% of accounts receivable? Does Mary Beth's proposal present an ethical dilemma?

PART C

NOTES RECEIVABLE

Notes receivable are similar to accounts receivable but are more formal credit arrangements evidenced by a written debt instrument, or *note*. Notes receivable typically arise from loans to other entities (including affiliated companies); loans to stockholders and employees; and occasionally the sale of merchandise, other assets, or services.

Accounting for Notes Receivable

■ **LO7**
Apply the procedure to account for notes receivable, including interest calculation.

Like accounts receivable, notes receivable are assets and therefore have a normal debit balance. We classify notes receivable as either *current* or *noncurrent*, depending on the expected collection date. If the time to maturity is longer than one year, the note receivable is a long-term asset.

As an example, let's say that, on February 1, 2012, Kimzey Medical Clinic provides services of $10,000 to a patient, Justin Payne, who is not able to pay immediately. In place of payment, Justin offers Kimzey a six-month, 12% promissory note. Because of the large amount of the receivable, Kimzey agrees to accept the promissory note as a way to increase the likelihood of eventually receiving payment. In addition, because of the delay in payment, Kimzey would like to charge interest on the outstanding balance. A formal promissory note provides an explicit statement of the interest charges. Illustration 5–15 shows an example of a typical note receivable.

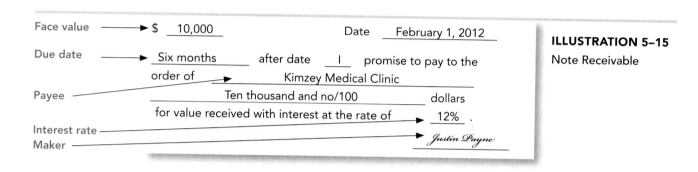

ILLUSTRATION 5–15

Note Receivable

Kimzey records the note as follows.

February 1, 2012	Debit	Credit
Notes Receivable	10,000	
Service Revenue		10,000
(Accept a six-month, 12% note receivable for services provided)		

A = L + SE
+10,000
+10,000 Rev↑

Another example of the use of notes receivable is to replace existing accounts receivable. For example, suppose that Justin received $10,000 of services on account, but Kimzey originally recorded the amount due as a typical account receivable. Over time, it became apparent that Justin would not be able to pay quickly, so Kimzey required Justin to sign a six-month, 12% promissory note on February 1, 2012. When Justin signs the note, Kimzey records the following transaction to reclassify the existing account receivable as a note receivable.

February 1, 2012	Debit	Credit
Notes Receivable	10,000	
Accounts Receivable		10,000
(Reclassify an existing account receivable as a six-month, 12% note receivable)		

A = L + SE
+10,000
−10,000

Recognize that the transaction has no impact on the accounting equation; it is simply a matter of reclassifying assets. One asset (notes receivable) increases, while another asset (accounts receivable) decreases.

How would the patient, Justin Payne, record the previous transaction? By signing the note, Justin has an account payable that becomes reclassified as a note payable. He records the issuance of the note payable on February 1 as follows.

Flip Side

February 1, 2012	Debit	Credit
Accounts Payable	10,000	
Notes Payable		10,000
(Reclassify account payable as a six-month, 12% note payable)		

A = L + SE
−10,000
+10,000

Flip Side

Just as one company's account payable is another company's account receivable, there is also a note payable for every note receivable. For every dollar a company earns in interest revenue, another company incurs a dollar of interest expense. We address notes payable in Chapter 8, but if you have a good understanding of notes receivable, then you have a head start with its flip side—notes payable.

KEY POINT

Notes receivable are similar to accounts receivable except that notes receivable are more formal credit arrangements made with a written debt instrument, or *note*.

INTEREST CALCULATION

Many of the same issues we discussed concerning accounts receivable, such as allowing for uncollectible accounts, apply also to notes receivable. The one issue that usually applies to notes receivable but not to accounts receivable is interest. You're probably familiar with the concept of interest. You may be earning interest on money in a savings account or checking account, and you might be paying interest on student loans, a car loan, or a credit card.

In the previous example, Kimzey issued a six-month, 12% promissory note. The "12%" indicates the *annual* interest rate charged by the payee. The terms of the six-month note mean that Kimzey will charge Justin Payne one-half year of interest, or 6%, on the face value. Interest on Kimzey's note receivable is calculated as follows.

Interest calculation

		Face value	×	Annual interest rate	×	Fraction of the year
Interest	=	**value**	×	**interest rate**	×	**of the year**
$600	=	$10,000	×	12%	×	6/12

KEY POINT

We calculate interest as the face value of the note multiplied by the stated annual interest rate multiplied by the appropriate fraction of the year that the note is outstanding.

COLLECTION OF NOTES RECEIVABLE

We record the collection of notes receivable the same way as collection of accounts receivable, except that we also record interest earned as interest revenue in the income statement.

Continuing the previous example, suppose that on August 1, 2012, the maturity date, Justin repays the note and interest in full as promised. Kimzey will record the following.

A = L + SE	August 1, 2012	Debit	Credit
+10,600	Cash	10,600	
−10,000	Notes Receivable		10,000
+600 Rev↑	Interest Revenue		600
	(Collect note receivable and interest)		
	(Interest revenue = $10,000 × 12% × 6/12)		

Over the six-month period, Kimzey earns interest revenue of $600. The credit to Notes Receivable reduces the balance in that account to $0, which is the amount Justin owes after payment to Kimzey.

ACCRUED INTEREST

It frequently happens that a note is issued in one year and the maturity date occurs in the following year. For example, what if Justin Payne issued the previous six-month note to Kimzey on November 1, 2012, instead of February 1, 2012? In that case, the $10,000 face value (principal) and $600 interest on the six-month note are not due until May 1, 2013. The length of the note (six months) and interest rate (12%) remain the same, and so the total interest charged to Justin remains the same. However, Kimzey will earn interest revenue in two separate accounting periods (assuming Kimzey uses a calendar year): for two months of the six-month note in 2012 (November and December), and for four months in the next year (January through April). Illustration 5–16 demonstrates the calculation of interest revenue over time. Interest receivable from Kimzey's six-month, $10,000, 12% note is $100 per month (= $10,000 × 12% × 1/12).

spiceland.mhhe.com/c15

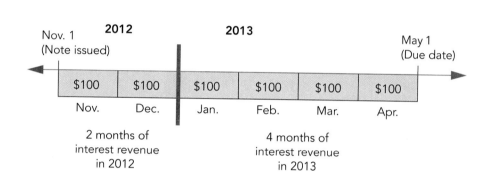

ILLUSTRATION 5–16

Calculating Interest Revenue over Time for Kimzey Medical Clinic

Because Kimzey earns two months of interest in 2012, it must accrue that interest as revenue on December 31, 2012 (even though no cash has been collected). The adjustment to accrue interest revenue follows.

December 31, 2012	Debit	Credit
Interest Receivable	200	
Interest Revenue		200
(Accrue interest revenue)		
(Interest revenue = $10,000 × 12% × 2/12)		

A = L + SE
+200
+200 Rev↑

On May 1, 2013, the maturity date, Kimzey records the collection of the note receivable and interest receivable from 2012 as well as the revenue related to the remaining four months' interest earned in 2013.

May 1, 2013	Debit	Credit
Cash	10,600	
Notes Receivable		10,000
Interest Receivable		200
Interest Revenue		400
(Collect note receivable and interest)		
(Interest revenue = $10,000 × 12% × 4/12)		

A = L + SE
+10,600
−10,000
−200
+400 Rev↑

On May 1, 2013, Kimzey has received the note receivable recorded on November 1, 2012, and the interest receivable recorded on December 31, 2012, and has eliminated their balances. The remaining four months' interest occurs in 2013, and Kimzey recognizes it as revenue in 2013.

KEY POINT

We record interest earned on notes receivable but not yet collected by the end of the year as interest receivable and interest revenue.

Let's Review

spiceland.mhhe.com/t9

General Hospital has a policy of lending any employee up to $3,000 for a period of 12 months at a fixed interest rate of 9%. Chevy Chase has worked for General Hospital for more than 10 years and wishes to take his family on a summer vacation. On May 1, 2012, he borrows $3,000 from General Hospital to be repaid in 12 months.

Required:

1. Record the loan of cash and acceptance of the note receivable by General Hospital.

2. Record General Hospital's year-end adjustment to accrue interest revenue.

3. Record the collection of the note with interest from Chevy Chase on May 1, 2013.

Solution:

1. Acceptance of the note receivable:

May 1, 2012	Debit	Credit
Notes Receivable	3,000	
Cash		3,000
(*Accept note receivable*)		

2. Year-end adjustment to accrue interest revenue:

December 31, 2012	Debit	Credit
Interest Receivable	180	
Interest Revenue (8 months' interest)		180
(*Accrue interest revenue*)		
(*Interest revenue = $3,000 × 9% × 8/12*)		

3. Collection of the note with interest:

May 1, 2013	Debit	Credit
Cash	3,270	
Notes Receivable		3,000
Interest Receivable		180
Interest Revenue (4 months' interest)		90
(*Collect note receivable and interest*)		
(*Interest revenue = $3,000 × 9% × 4/12*)		

Suggested Homework:
BE5-10, BE5-11;
E5-15, E5-17;
P5-8A&B

ANALYSIS

RECEIVABLES ANALYSIS
Tenet vs. LifePoint

The amount of a company's accounts receivable is influenced by a variety of factors, including the level of sales, the nature of the product or service sold, and credit and collection policies. These factors are, of course, related. For example, a change in credit policies could affect sales. More liberal credit policies—allowing customers a longer time to pay or offering cash discounts for early payment—often are initiated with the specific objective of increasing sales volume.

Management's choice of credit and collection policies results in trade-offs. For example, when a company attempts to boost sales by allowing customers more time to pay, that policy also creates an increase in the required investment in receivables and may increase bad debts because older accounts are less likely to be collected. Offering discounts for early payment may increase sales volume, accelerate customer payment, and reduce bad debts, but at the same time it reduces the amount of cash collected from customers who take advantage of the discounts.

CAREER CORNER

Investors, creditors, and financial analysts can gain important insights by monitoring a company's investment in receivables. Two important ratios that help in understanding the company's effectiveness in managing receivables are the *receivables turnover ratio* and the *average collection period*. We discuss those measures and then compare them for **Tenet Healthcare Corporation** and **LifePoint Hospitals**.

■ **LO8**
Calculate key ratios investors use to monitor a company's effectiveness in managing receivables.

RECEIVABLES TURNOVER RATIO

The receivables turnover ratio shows the number of times during a year that the average accounts receivable balance is collected (or "turns over"). We calculate it as follows:

$$\text{Receivables turnover ratio} = \frac{\textbf{Net credit sales}}{\textbf{Average accounts receivable}}$$

Let's say net credit sales are $400,000 for the year and the average accounts receivable balance is $40,000. In that case, we could say the turnover ratio is 10 ($400,000/$40,000), or that average receivables were collected 10 times during the year.

Note that the lower half of the receivables turnover ratio—average accounts receivable—is typically measured as the beginning accounts receivable plus the ending accounts receivable divided by two. So, our average of $40,000 might be the result of having a $35,000 balance at the beginning of the year and a $45,000 balance at the end of the year.

$$\text{Receivables turnover ratio} = \frac{\$400,000}{(\$35,000 + \$45,000)/2} = 10$$

AVERAGE COLLECTION PERIOD

The average collection period is another way to express the same efficiency measure. We calculate the average collection period as:

$$\text{Average collection period} = \frac{\textbf{365 days}}{\textbf{Receivables turnover ratio}}$$

169

It shows the approximate number of days the average accounts receivable balance is outstanding. If the turnover is 10 times a year (365 days), then the average balance is collected every 36.5 days.

$$\text{Average collection period} = \frac{365 \text{ days}}{10} = 36.5 \text{ days}$$

Companies typically strive for a high receivables turnover ratio and a correspondingly low average collection period. As a company's sales increase, receivables also likely will increase. If the percentage increase in receivables is greater than the percentage increase in sales, the receivables turnover ratio will decline (and the average collection period will increase). This could indicate that customers are dissatisfied with the product or that the company's payment terms for attracting new customers are too generous, which, in turn, could increase sales returns and bad debts.

Of course, what's "high" and what's "low" for these ratios depends on the situation. Companies may wish to evaluate these ratios relative to the prior year's ratios, ratios of other firms in the same industry, or specific targets set by management.

Decision Point

Question	Accounting information	Analysis
Is the company effectively managing its receivables?	Receivables turnover ratio and average collection period	A high receivables turnover ratio (or low average collection period) generally indicates that the company's credit sales and collection policies are effective.

Now let's compare **Tenet Healthcare Corporation** to **LifePoint Hospitals**. The calculations of the receivables turnover ratio and average collection period for each company for 2008 and 2009, along with their net income for those years, are shown in Illustration 5–17.

ILLUSTRATION 5–17

Comparison of Receivables Ratios between Tenet Healthcare Corporation and LifePoint Hospitals

TENET HEALTHCARE CORPORATION

	Net Sales (in millions)	Average Accounts Receivable (in millions)	Receivables Turnover Ratio	Average Collection Period	Net Income
2008	$8,585	$1,361	$\frac{\$8,585}{\$1,361} = 6.31$	$\frac{365}{6.31} = 57.8$	$ 32
2009	$9,014	$1,248	$\frac{\$9,014}{\$1,248} = 7.22$	$\frac{365}{7.22} = 50.6$	$197

LIFEPOINT HOSPITALS

2008	$2,701	$ 310	$\frac{\$2,701}{\$310} = 8.71$	$\frac{365}{8.71} = 41.9$	$103
2009	$2,963	$ 321	$\frac{\$2,963}{\$321} = 9.23$	$\frac{365}{9.23} = 39.5$	$134

From Illustration 5–17, we see that LifePoint has a much higher receivables turnover, indicating that the company more efficiently collects cash from patients than does Tenet. The average collection period is much longer for Tenet. Better management of receivables by LifePoint may help explain the company's more profitable operations. Over the two-year period, LifePoint's net income is greater than that of Tenet, even though its revenue is only about one-third.

Having enough cash is important to running any business. The more quickly a company can collect its receivables, the more quickly it can use that cash to generate even more cash by reinvesting in the business and generating additional sales.

 KEY POINT

The receivables turnover ratio and average collection period can provide an indication of management's ability to collect cash from customers in a timely manner.

PERCENTAGE-OF-CREDIT-SALES METHOD

APPENDIX

In the chapter, we estimated uncollectible accounts based on a percentage of accounts receivable at the end of the period. You learned that this method is the *percentage-of-receivables method* or the *balance sheet method*, because we base the estimate of bad debts on a balance sheet amount—accounts receivable.

As an alternative, we can estimate uncollectible accounts based on the percentage of credit sales for the year, aptly referred to as the *percentage-of-credit-sales method* or the *income statement method*, because we base the estimate of bad debts on an income statement amount—credit sales. In this appendix, we consider the percentage-of-credit-sales method.

Let's rework the example in the chapter for Kimzey Medical Clinic (see Illustrations 5–8 to 5–10 and their discussion). During 2013, Kimzey bills customers $80 million for services, with $30 million in accounts receivable remaining at the end of the year. The balance of the allowance account, before adjustment, is a $2 million credit. For the percentage-of-receivables method, we'll use the estimate for uncollectible accounts used in the chapter—30% of receivables. For the percentage-of-credit-sales method, let's assume Kimzey expects 10% of credit sales to be uncollectible. Kimzey bases the 10% estimate on a number of factors, such as the average percentage of uncollectibles each year over the past several years.

Illustration 5–18 demonstrates the differences in the two methods when adjusting for estimates of uncollectible accounts.

■ **LO9**
Estimate uncollectible accounts using the percentage-of-credit-sales method.

Percentage-of-Receivables Method (repeated from chapter)	Percentage-of-Credit Sales Method
Estimate of Uncollectible Accounts	Estimate of Uncollectible Accounts
• 30% of ending accounts receivable will not be collected.	• 10% of credit sales will not be collected.
• 30% of $30 million = $9 million.	• 10% of $80 million = $8 million.
• Adjust from $2 million existing balance.	• Ignore $2 million existing balance.

Adjustment ($ in millions)			Adjustment ($ in millions)		
Bad Debt Expense	7		Bad Debt Expense	8	
Allowance for Uncoll. Accts.		7	Allowance for Uncoll. Accts.		8

ILLUSTRATION 5–18

Adjusting for Estimates of Uncollectible Accounts

Notice that the two methods for estimating uncollectible accounts result in different adjustments. Because the amounts of the adjustments differ, the effects on the financial statements differ. Recall that the balance of the allowance account before adjustment is a $2 million credit. After adjustment, the balance of the allowance account will differ between the two methods, as will the amount of bad debt expense. Illustration 5–19 summarizes the differences in financial statement effects.

ILLUSTRATION 5–19

Financial Statement Effects of Estimating Uncollectible Accounts

Percentage-of-Receivables Method
($ in millions)

Income Statement Effect

Revenues	$80
Bad debt expense	(7)
Net income	$73

Balance Sheet Effect

Accounts receivable	$30
Less: Allowance	(9)*
Net accounts receivable	$21

* $9 = $2 + $7 (adjustment)

Percentage-of-Credit-Sales Method
($ in millions)

Income Statement Effect

Revenues	$80
Bad debt expense	(8)
Net income	$72

Balance Sheet Effect

Accounts receivable	$30
Less: Allowance	(10)*
Net accounts receivable	$20

* $10 = $2 + $8 (adjustment)

From an income statement perspective, some argue that the percentage-of-credit-sales method provides a better method for estimating bad debts because expenses (bad debts) are better matched with revenues (credit sales). A better matching of expenses and revenues results in a more accurate measure of net income for the period. From a balance sheet perspective, though, the percentage-of-receivables method is preferable because assets (net accounts receivable) are reported closer to their net realizable value.

The current emphasis on better measurement of assets (balance sheet focus) outweighs the emphasis on better measurement of net income (income statement focus). **This is why the percentage-of-receivables method (balance sheet method) is the preferable method, while the percentage-of-credit-sales method (income statement method) is allowed only if amounts do not differ significantly from estimates using the percentage-of-receivables method.**

KEY POINT

When applying the percentage-of-credit-sales method, we adjust the allowance for uncollectible accounts for the current year's credit sales that we don't expect to collect (rather than adjusting at the end of the year for the percentage of accounts receivable we don't expect to collect).

 KEY POINTS BY LEARNING OBJECTIVE

LO1 Recognize accounts receivable.

Companies record an asset (accounts receivable) and revenue when they sell products and services to their customers on account, expecting payment in the future.

LO2 Calculate net revenues using discounts, returns, and allowances.

Sales discounts, returns, and allowances are contra revenue accounts. We subtract the balances in these accounts from total revenues when calculating net revenues.

LO3 Record an allowance for future uncollectible accounts.

We recognize accounts receivable as assets in the balance sheet and record them at their net realizable values, that is, the amount of cash we expect to collect.

Under the allowance method, companies are required to *estimate* future uncollectible accounts and record those estimates in the current year. Estimated uncollectible accounts reduce assets and increase expenses.

Adjusting for estimates of future uncollectible accounts matches expenses (bad debts) in the same period as the revenues (credit sales) they help to generate.

Recording an allowance for uncollectible accounts correctly reports accounts receivable at their net realizable value.

LO4 Apply the procedure to write off accounts receivable as uncollectible.

Writing off a customer's account as uncollectible reduces the balance of accounts receivable but also reduces the contra asset—allowance for uncollectible accounts. The net effect is that there is no change in the *net* receivable (accounts receivable less the allowance) or in total assets. We recorded the decrease to assets as a result of the bad debt when we established the allowance for uncollectible accounts in a prior year.

LO5 Use the aging method to estimate future uncollectible accounts.

Using the aging method to estimate uncollectible accounts is more accurate than applying a single percentage to all accounts receivable. The aging method recognizes that the longer accounts are past due, the less likely they are to be collected.

LO6 Contrast the allowance method and direct write-off method when accounting for uncollectible accounts.

The direct write-off method reduces accounts receivable and records bad debt expense at the time the account receivable proves uncollectible. If the credit sale occurs in a prior reporting period, bad debt expense is not properly matched with revenues (credit sales). Also, accounts receivable will be overstated in the prior period. The direct write-off method typically is not acceptable for financial reporting.

LO7 Apply the procedure to account for notes receivable, including interest calculation.

Notes receivable are similar to accounts receivable except that notes receivable are more formal credit arrangements made with a written debt instrument, or *note*.

We calculate interest as the face value of the note multiplied by the stated annual interest rate multiplied by the appropriate fraction of the year.

We record interest earned on notes receivable but not yet collected by the end of the year as interest receivable and interest revenue.

Analysis

LO8 Calculate key ratios investors use to monitor a company's effectiveness in managing receivables.

The receivables turnover ratio and average collection period can provide an indication of management's ability to collect cash from customers in a timely manner.

Appendix

LO9 Estimate uncollectible accounts using the percentage-of-credit-sales method.

When applying the percentage-of-credit-sales method, we adjust the allowance for uncollectible accounts for the current year's credit sales that we don't expect to collect (rather than adjusting at the end of the year for the percentage of accounts receivable we don't expect to collect).

GLOSSARY

Accounts receivable: The amount of cash owed to the company by its customers from the sale of products or services on account. **p. 146**

Aging method: Using a higher percentage for "old" accounts than for "new" accounts when estimating uncollectible accounts. **p. 159**

Allowance for uncollectible accounts: Contra asset account representing the amount of accounts receivable that we do not expect to collect. **p. 154**

Allowance method: Recording an adjustment at the end of each period to allow for the possibility of future uncollectible accounts. The adjustment has the effects of reducing assets and increasing expenses. **p. 152**

Average collection period: Approximate number of days the average accounts receivable balance is outstanding. It equals 365 divided by the receivables turnover ratio. **p. 169**

Bad debt expense: The amount of the adjustment to the allowance for uncollectible accounts, representing the cost of estimated future bad debts charged to the current period. **p. 153**

Contra revenue account: An account with a balance that is opposite, or "contra," to that of its related revenue account. **p. 148**

Credit sales: Transfer of products and services to a customer today while bearing the risk of collecting payment from that customer in the future. Also known as *sales on account* or *services on account.* **p. 146**

Direct write-off method: Recording bad debt expense at the time we know the account is uncollectible. **p. 162**

Net accounts receivable: The difference between total accounts receivable and the allowance for uncollectible accounts. **p. 154**

Net realizable value: The amount of cash the firm expects to collect. **p. 151**

Net revenues: A company's total revenues less any discounts, returns, and allowances. **p. 147**

Notes receivable: Formal credit arrangements evidenced by a written debt instrument, or *note.* **p. 164**

Percentage-of-receivables method: Method of estimating uncollectible accounts based on the percentage of accounts receivable expected not to be collected. **p. 153**

Receivables turnover ratio: Number of times during a year that the average accounts receivable balance is collected (or "turns over"). It equals net credit sales divided by average accounts receivable. **p. 169**

Sales allowance: Seller reduces the customer's balance owed or provides at least a partial refund because of some deficiency in the company's product or service. **p. 149**

Sales discount: Reduction in the amount to be paid by a credit customer if payment on account is made within a specified period of time. **p. 147**

Sales return: Customer returns a product. **p. 149**

Trade discount: Reduction in the listed price of a product or service. **p. 147**

Uncollectible accounts: Customers' accounts that no longer are considered collectible. **p. 152**

SELF-STUDY QUESTIONS

■ **LO1**

1. Accounts receivable are best described as:
   a. Liabilities of the company that represent the amount owed to suppliers.
   b. Amounts that have previously been received from customers.
   c. Assets of the company representing the amount owed by customers.
   d. Amounts that have previously been paid to suppliers.

■ **LO2**

2. On March 17, Fox Lumber sells materials to Whitney Construction for $12,000, terms 2/10, n/30. Whitney pays for the materials on March 23. What amount would Fox record as revenue on March 17?
   a. $12,400.
   b. $11,760.
   c. $12,000.
   d. $12,240.

■ **LO2**

3. Refer to the information in the previous question. What is the amount of net revenues (sales minus sales discounts) as of March 23?
   a. $0.
   b. $11,760.
   c. $12,000.
   d. $12,240.

■ **LO3**

4. Suppose the balance of Allowance for Uncollectible Accounts at the end of the current year is $400 (*credit*) before any adjustment. The company estimates future uncollectible accounts to be $3,200. At what amount would bad debt expense be reported in the current year's income statement?
   a. $400.
   b. $2,800.
   c. $3,200.
   d. $3,600.

■ **LO3**

5. Suppose the balance of Allowance for Uncollectible Accounts at the end of the current year is $400 (*debit*) before any adjustment. The company estimates future

uncollectible accounts to be $3,200. At what amount would bad debt expense be reported in the current year's income statement?

a. $400.

b. $2,800.

c. $3,200.

d. $3,600.

6. The entry to record a write-off of accounts receivable will include: ■ LO4

a. A debit to Bad Debt Expense.

b. A debit to Allowance for Uncollectible Accounts.

c. No entry because an allowance for uncollectible accounts was established in an earlier period.

d. A debit to Service Revenue.

7. Kidz Incorporated reports the following aging schedule of its accounts receivable   ■ LO5
with the estimated percent uncollectible. What is the total estimate of uncollectible accounts using the aging method?

Age Group	Amount Receivable	Estimated Percent Uncollectible
0–60 days	$20,000	2%
61–90 days	6,000	15%
More than 90 days past due	2,000	50%
Total	$28,000	

a. $1,150.

b. $1,900.

c. $2,300.

d. $5,900.

8. The direct write-off method is generally not permitted for financial reporting   ■ LO6
purposes because:

a. Compared to the allowance method, it would allow greater flexibility to managers in manipulating reported net income.

b. This method is primarily used for tax purposes.

c. It is too difficult to accurately estimate future bad debts.

d. Expenses (bad debts) are not properly matched with the revenues (credit sales) they help to generate.

9. On January 1, 2012, Roberson Supply borrows $10,000 from Nees Manufacturing   ■ LO7
by signing a 9% note due in eight months. Calculate the amount of interest revenue Nees will record on September 1, 2012, the date that the note is due.

a. $300.

b. $600.

c. $900.

d. $1,000.

10. At the beginning of 2012, Clay Ventures has total accounts receivable of $100,000.   ■ LO8
By the end of 2012, Clay reports net credit sales of $900,000 and total accounts receivable of $200,000. What is the receivables turnover ratio for Clay Ventures?

a. 2.0.

b. 4.5.

c. 6.0.

d. 9.0.

Answers to the Self-Study Questions

1. c   2. c   3. b   4. b   5. d   6. b   7. c   8. d   9. b   10. c

REVIEW QUESTIONS

■ LO1
1. When recording a credit sale, what account do we debit? Describe where this account is reported in the financial statements.

■ LO1
2. What is the difference between a trade receivable and a nontrade receivable?

■ LO2
3. Explain the difference between a trade discount and a sales discount. Where are sales discounts reported in the income statement?

■ LO2
4. Briefly explain the accounting treatment for sales returns and allowances. Where are these accounts reported in the income statement?

■ LO2
5. Revenue can be earned at one point or over a period. Provide an example of each.

■ LO3
6. Explain the correct way companies should account for uncollectible accounts receivable (bad debts).

■ LO3
7. What two purposes do firms achieve by estimating future uncollectible accounts?

■ LO3
8. How does accounting for uncollectible accounts conform to the concept of the matching principle?

■ LO3
9. What are the financial statement effects of establishing an allowance for uncollectible accounts?

■ LO3
10. Describe the year-end adjustment to record the allowance for uncollectible accounts.

■ LO3
11. Allowance for Uncollectible Accounts is a contra asset account, which means that its normal balance is a credit. However, it is possible for the account to have a debit balance before year-end adjustments are recorded. Explain how this could happen.

■ LO3
12. We report accounts receivable in the balance sheet at their *net realizable value*. Explain what this term means.

■ LO4
13. When we have established an allowance for uncollectible accounts, how do we write off an account receivable as uncollectible? What effect does this write-off have on the reported amount of total assets and net income at the time of the write-off?

■ LO4
14. If at the end of the year Allowance for Uncollectible Accounts has a credit balance before any adjustment, what might that tell us about last year's estimate of future uncollectible accounts?

■ LO5
15. What does the *age* of accounts receivable refer to? How can we use an aging method to estimate uncollectible accounts receivable?

■ LO6
16. Discuss the differences between the allowance method and the direct write-off method for recording uncollectible accounts. Which of the two is acceptable under financial accounting rules?

■ LO7
17. Notes receivable differ from accounts receivable in that notes receivable represent *written* debt instruments. What is one other common difference between notes receivable and accounts receivable?

■ LO7
18. With respect to notes receivable, explain what each of these represent: (a) face value, (b) annual interest rate, and (c) fraction of the year.

■ LO7
19. What will be the total interest earned on a 6%, $2,000 note receivable that is due in nine months?

■ LO7
20. Interest on a note receivable typically is due along with the face value at the note's maturity date. If the end of the accounting period occurs before the maturity date, how do we record interest earned but not yet collected?

■ LO8
21. How is the receivables turnover ratio measured? What does this ratio indicate? Is a higher or lower receivables turnover preferable?

22. How is the average collection period of receivables measured? What does this ratio indicate? Is a higher or lower average collection period preferable? ■ LO8

23. How can effectively managing receivables benefit a company? ■ LO8

24. Which method, the percentage-of-receivables method or the percentage-of-credit-sales method, is typically used in practice? Why? ■ LO9

25. Explain why the percentage-of-receivables method is referred to as the *balance sheet method* and the percentage-of-credit-sales method is referred to as the *income statement method*. ■ LO9

For the following, please visit your instructor's *Connect* site.

BRIEF EXERCISES	1-13
EXERCISES	1-20
PROBLEMS: SET A	1-8
PROBLEMS: SET B	1-8
GREAT ADVENTURES	

Mc Graw Hill **connect** |ACCOUNTING

Note: Additional Perspectives assignments for Financial Analysis, Comparative Analysis, Internet Research, Written Communication, and Earnings Management are in Appendix F at the end of this book. For additional Exercises: Set B and for additional Problems: Set C, visit www.mhhe.com/spicelandMTC1e.

Inventory and Cost of Goods Sold

Learning Objectives

AFTER STUDYING THIS CHAPTER, YOU SHOULD BE ABLE TO:

- ■ **LO1** Trace the flow of inventory costs from manufacturing companies to merchandising companies.
- ■ **LO2** Calculate cost of goods sold.
- ■ **LO3** Determine the cost of goods sold and ending inventory using different inventory cost methods.
- ■ **LO4** Explain the financial statement effects and tax effects of inventory cost flow assumptions.
- ■ **LO5** Record inventory transactions using a perpetual inventory system.
- ■ **LO6** Prepare a multiple-step income statement.
- ■ **LO7** Apply the lower-of-cost-or-market method for inventories.

Analysis

- ■ **LO8** Analyze management of inventory using the inventory turnover ratio and gross profit ratio.

Appendix

- ■ **LO9** Record inventory transactions using a periodic inventory system.
- ■ **LO10** Determine the financial statement effects of inventory errors.

BEST BUY: **TAKING INVENTORY OF ELECTRONICS SOLD**

Best Buy Co., Inc., is the largest specialty retailer of consumer goods in the United States, accounting for 17% of the specialty retail market. You are probably familiar with most of the products offered by Best Buy—computers, computer software, video games, music, DVDs, mobile phones, digital and video cameras, home appliances (washing machines, dryers, and refrigerators), and other related merchandise.

Merchandise inventory for sale to customers is the single largest asset owned by Best Buy, as it is for many retail companies. At any given time, Best Buy holds about $3 billion in inventory, or about 30% of the company's total assets. Proper management of inventory is key to the company's success.

Management of Best Buy knows there is a fine line between having too little and too much inventory. Having too little inventory reduces the selection of products available to customers, ultimately reducing sales revenue. On the other hand, in a technology-based industry where changes occur rapidly, having too much inventory can leave the store holding outdated inventory. Just think of what happens to the value of computers when the next generation becomes available. Managers don't want to get stuck with old inventory that is decreasing in value. Besides obsolescence, other costs associated with holding large inventories are storage, insurance, and shrinkage (theft). Holding less inventory provides access to money that can be invested elsewhere within the company.

For now, Best Buy seems to be taking the right steps with its inventory. Look below at the company's revenues from inventory sales compared to the cost of the inventory sold. These amounts are reported in the company's income statement. The difference between revenues and cost of goods sold (an expense) is called *gross profit,* and it has been steadily increasing over time.

	2006	2007	2008	2009
Revenues	$30,848	$35,934	$40,023	$45,015
Cost of goods sold	23,122	27,165	30,477	34,017
Gross profit	$ 7,726	$ 8,769	$ 9,546	$10,998

In this chapter, we explore how to account for the purchase and sale of inventory items. We'll see how inventory (an asset in the balance sheet) turns into cost of goods sold (an expense in the income statement) once it is sold, and how these amounts can affect business decisions.

UNDERSTANDING INVENTORY AND COST OF GOODS SOLD

In preceding chapters, we dealt mostly with companies that provide a service. *Service companies* such as **UPS**, **United Healthcare**, **Allstate Insurance**, and **Marriott Hotels** earn revenues by providing services to their customers. UPS delivers your packages, United Healthcare treats your medical needs, Allstate provides insurance coverage, and Marriott offers you a place to stay the night. Many companies, though, earn revenues by selling inventory rather than a service.

Part A of this chapter introduces the concept of inventory and demonstrates the different methods used to calculate the cost of inventory for external reporting. Once you understand this, then you're ready to see, in Part B and Part C, how companies actually maintain their own (internal) records of inventory transactions and the adjustments that are sometimes needed to prepare financial statements.

Inventory

■ LO1
Trace the flow of inventory costs from manufacturing companies to merchandising companies.

Companies that earn revenue by selling inventory are either *manufacturing* or *merchandising companies*. Inventory includes items a company intends for sale to customers. You already are familiar with several types of inventory—clothes at **The Limited**, shoes at **Payless ShoeSource**, grocery items at **Publix Super Markets**, digital equipment at **Best Buy**, building supplies at **The Home Depot**, and so on. Inventory also includes items that are not yet finished products. For instance, lumber at a cabinet manufacturer, steel at a construction firm, and rubber at a tire manufacturer are part of inventory because the firm will use them to make a finished product for sale to customers.

We report inventory as a current asset in the balance sheet—an *asset* because it represents a valuable resource the company owns, and *current* because the company expects to convert it to cash in the near term. At the end of the period, the amount the company reports for inventory is the cost of inventory *not yet sold*. What happens to the cost of the inventory sold during the period? The company reports the cost of the inventory it sold as cost of goods sold in the income statement.

Common Terms Cost of goods sold is also referred to as *cost of sales, cost of merchandise sold*, or *cost of products sold*.

As we'll see, determining these two amounts is a critical task in accounting for inventory. For companies that earn revenues by selling inventory, cost of goods sold often is the largest expense in the income statement. Before we explore how companies calculate cost of goods sold, we first need to consider the differences between merchandising and manufacturing companies, so that we understand the types of inventory each holds.

MERCHANDISING COMPANIES

Merchandising companies purchase inventories that are primarily in finished form for resale to customers. These companies may assemble, sort, repackage, redistribute, store, refrigerate, deliver, or install the inventory, but they do not manufacture it. They simply serve as intermediaries in the process of moving inventory from the manufacturer, the company that actually makes the inventory, to the end user.

We can broadly classify merchandising companies as wholesalers or retailers. *Wholesalers* resell inventory to retail companies or to professional users. For example, a wholesale food service company like **Sysco Corporation** supplies food to restaurants, schools, and sporting events but generally does not sell food directly to the public. Also, Sysco does not transform the food prior to sale; it just stores the food, repackages it as necessary, and delivers it.

Retailers purchase inventory from manufacturers or wholesalers and then sell this inventory to end users. You probably are more familiar with retail companies because these are the companies from which you buy products. **Best Buy**, **Target**,

Lowe's, Macy's, Gap, Sears, and McDonald's are retailers. Merchandising companies typically hold their inventories in a single category simply called *inventory*.

Common Terms
Inventory is also referred to as *merchandise inventory*.

MANUFACTURING COMPANIES

Manufacturing companies manufacture the inventories they sell, rather than buying them in finished form from suppliers. **Apple Inc., Coca-Cola, Sara Lee, Harley-Davidson, ExxonMobil, Ford, Sony,** and **Dell** are manufacturers. Manufacturing companies buy the inputs for the products they manufacture. Thus, we classify inventory for a manufacturer into three categories: (1) raw materials, (2) work in process, and (3) finished goods:

- **Raw materials** inventory includes the cost of components that will become part of the finished product but have not yet been used in production. (Raw materials sometimes are called *direct materials*.)
- **Work-in-process** inventory refers to the products that have started the production process but are not yet complete at the end of the period.
- **Finished goods** inventory consists of items for which the manufacturing process is complete.

Each of these inventory accounts includes its own costs. For example, Dell's raw materials inventory includes the costs of the semiconductors, circuit boards, and plastic parts that go into the production of personal computers. For its work-in-process inventory, Dell includes the cost of *raw materials* used in production, the cost of *direct labor* that we can trace directly to the goods in process, and an allocated portion of other manufacturing costs, called *overhead*. Overhead costs include costs to operate the manufacturing facility, depreciation of manufacturing equipment, and many other costs that we cannot directly link to the production of specific inventories. Once the manufacturing process is complete, Dell transfers to finished goods inventory the total cost of fully assembled but unshipped computers at the end of the reporting period. Illustration 6–1 shows inventory amounts for **Dell Computers**.

DELL COMPUTERS Notes to the Financial Statements (excerpt)		
($ in millions)	2009	2008
Raw materials	$454	$ 714
Work in process	150	144
Finished products	263	322
Total inventories	$867	$1,180

ILLUSTRATION 6–1

Types of Inventory for Dell Computers

At any given time, Dell holds around 70% of its inventory in a form other than finished products ready for sale to customers. Once inventory products are finished, Dell hopes to sell them as soon as possible.

 KEY POINT

Service companies earn revenues by providing services to customers. Merchandising and manufacturing companies earn revenues by selling inventory to customers.

FLOW OF INVENTORY COSTS

As you might guess, the flow of inventory costs differs depending on the type of company. Illustration 6–2 (next page) shows the flow of inventory costs for the three types of companies—service, merchandising, and manufacturing.

ILLUSTRATION 6–2

Types of Companies
and Flow of Inventory
Costs

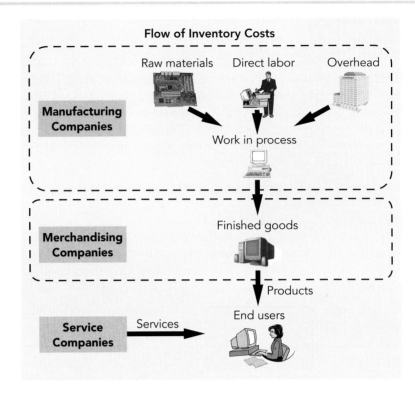

Inventory's journey begins when manufacturing companies purchase raw materials, hire workers, and incur manufacturing overhead during production. Once the products are finished, manufacturers normally pass inventories to merchandising companies, whether wholesalers or retailers. Merchandising companies then sell inventories to you, the end user. In some cases, manufacturers may sell directly to end users.

Some companies provide both services and inventories to customers. For example, **IBM** generates about half its revenues from selling its inventories of hardware and software, and the other half from providing services like consulting, systems maintenance, and financing.

In this chapter, we focus on merchandising companies, both wholesalers and retailers. Still, most of the accounting principles and procedures discussed here also apply to manufacturing companies. We do not attempt to address all the unique problems of accumulating the direct costs of raw materials and labor and allocating manufacturing overhead. We leave those details for managerial and cost accounting courses. In this course, we focus on the financial reporting implications of inventory cost flows.

Cost of Goods Sold

■ **LO2**
Calculate cost of goods
sold.

Let's think a little more about the relationship between ending inventory in the balance sheet and cost of goods sold in the income statement. Remember that inventory represents the cost of inventory *not sold*, and cost of goods sold represents the cost of inventory *sold*. Thus, we can see that, once the inventory is sold, the amount reported for inventory becomes the amount reported for cost of goods sold. This relationship is depicted at the bottom of Illustration 6–3. Note, too, the two inventory inputs at the top of the figure: beginning inventory and purchases during the year. **The costs of *beginning inventory* plus the *additional purchases during the year* make up the cost of inventory (cost of goods) available for sale.**

ILLUSTRATION 6–3

Relationship between Inventory and Cost of Goods Sold

To demonstrate these relationships using numbers, assume a local **Best Buy** store begins the year with $20,000 of DVD player inventory. That amount represents how much Best Buy spent to purchase the inventory of DVD players on hand at the beginning of the year. During the year, the company purchases additional DVD players for $90,000. What is the total cost of goods (DVD players) available for sale? Illustration 6–4 shows the answer: $110,000 (= $20,000 + $90,000). Now, assume that by the end of the year, the purchase cost of the remaining DVD player inventory is $30,000. What is the cost of goods sold? As Illustration 6–4 shows, the cost of the DVD players sold is $80,000 (= $110,000 − $30,000).

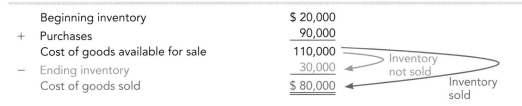

	Beginning inventory	$ 20,000
+	Purchases	90,000
	Cost of goods available for sale	110,000
−	Ending inventory	30,000
	Cost of goods sold	$ 80,000

ILLUSTRATION 6–4

Numerical Illustration of the Relationship between Inventory and Cost of Goods Sold

Of the $110,000 of goods available for sale during the year, some were not sold (ending inventory = $30,000) and some were sold (cost of goods sold = $80,000). The cost of the inventory sold (cost of goods sold) is an expense, which the company reports in the income statement (as we will see in more detail later).

 KEY POINT

> Inventory is a current asset reported in the balance sheet and represents the cost of inventory *not yet sold* at the end of the period. Cost of goods sold is an expense reported in the income statement and represents the cost of inventory *sold*.

Inventory Cost Methods

To this point, we've discussed the cost of inventory without considering how we determine that cost. We do that now by considering four methods for inventory costing:

1. Specific identification
2. First-in, first-out (FIFO)
3. Last-in, first-out (LIFO)
4. Weighted-average cost

■ **LO3**

Determine the cost of goods sold and ending inventory using different inventory cost methods.

SPECIFIC IDENTIFICATION

The specific identification method is the method you might think of as the most logical. It matches—identifies—each unit of inventory with its actual cost. For example, an automobile has a unique serial number that we can match to an invoice identifying the actual purchase price. Fine jewelry and pieces of art are other possibilities. Specific identification works well in such cases. However, the specific identification method is practicable only for companies selling unique, expensive products. Consider the inventory at **The Home Depot** or **Sally Beauty Supply**: numerous items, many of which are relatively inexpensive. Specific identification would be very difficult for such merchandisers. Although bar codes and RFID tags now make it possible to identify and track each unit of inventory, the costs of doing so outweigh the benefits for multiple, small inventory items. For that reason, the specific identification method is used primarily by companies with unique, expensive products with low sales volume.

FIRST-IN, FIRST-OUT

For practical reasons, most companies use one of the other three inventory cost flow assumptions—FIFO, LIFO, or weighted-average cost—to determine cost of goods sold and inventory. Note the use of the word *assumptions:* Each of these three inventory cost methods *assumes* a particular pattern of inventory cost flows. However, the *actual* flow of inventory does not need to match the *assumed* cost flow in order for the company to use a particular method.

To see how the three cost flow assumptions work, let's begin with FIFO. We'll examine the inventory transactions in Illustration 6–5 for Mario's Game Shop, which sells video game cartridges. Mario has 100 units of inventory at the beginning of the year and then makes two purchases during the year—one on April 25 and one on October 19. (Note the different unit costs at the time of each purchase.) There are **1,000** game cartridges available for sale.

ILLUSTRATION 6–5

Inventory Transactions for Mario's Game Shop

Date	Transaction	Number of Units	Unit Cost	Total Cost
Jan. 1	Beginning inventory	100	$ 7	$ 700
Apr. 25	Purchase	300	9	2,700
Oct. 19	Purchase	600	11	6,600
	Total goods available for sale	1,000		$10,000
Jan. 1–Dec. 31	Total sales to customers	800		
Dec. 31	Ending inventory	200		

During the year, Mario sells **800** video game cartridges for $15 each. This means that **200** cartridges remain in ending inventory at the end of the year. But which 200? Do they include some of the $7 units from beginning inventory? Are they 200 of the $9 units from the April 25 purchase? Or, do they include some $11 units from the October 19 purchase? We consider these questions below.

Using the first-in, first-out (FIFO) method, we assume that the first units purchased (the first in) are the first ones sold (the first out). We assume that beginning inventory sells first, followed by the inventory from the first purchase during the year, followed by the inventory from the second purchase during the year, and so on.

In our example, which 800 units did Mario's Game Shop sell? Using the FIFO method, we *assume* they were the *first* 800 units purchased, and that all other units remain in ending inventory. These calculations are shown in Illustration 6–6.

We assume that all units from beginning inventory (100 units) and the April 25 purchase (300 units) were sold. For the final 400 units sold, we split the October 19

Inventory Transactions for Mario's Game Shop—FIFO METHOD

ILLUSTRATION 6–6

Inventory Calculation Using the FIFO Method

Purchases	Cost of Goods Available for Sale			=		Cost of Goods Sold	+	Ending Inventory
	Number of Units ×	Unit Cost =	Total Cost					
Jan. 1	100	$ 7	$ 700		Sold first 800 units	$ 700		
Apr. 25	300	9	2,700			2,700		
Oct. 19	400	11	4,400			4,400		
	200	11	2,200		Not sold			$2,200
	1,000		$10,000	=		$7,800	+	$2,200

purchase of 600 units into two groups—400 units assumed sold and 200 units assumed not sold. We calculate cost of goods sold as the units of inventory assumed sold times their respective unit costs. [That is: $(100 \times \$7) + (300 \times \$9) + (400 \times \$11)$ in our example.] Similarly, ending inventory equals the units assumed not sold times *their* respective unit costs ($200 \times \$11$ in our example). The amount of cost of goods sold Mario reports in the income statement will be **$7,800**. The amount of ending inventory in the balance sheet will be **$2,200**.

You may have realized that we don't actually need to directly calculate both cost of goods sold and inventory. Once we calculate one, the other is apparent. Because the two amounts always add up to the cost of goods available for sale (**$10,000** in our example), knowing either amount allows us to subtract to find the other.

Realize, too, that the amounts reported for ending inventory and cost of goods sold do *not* represent the actual cost of inventory sold and not sold. That's okay. **Companies are allowed to report inventory costs by *assuming* which units of inventory are sold and not sold, even if this does not match the *actual* flow.**

LAST-IN, FIRST-OUT

Using the last-in, first-out (LIFO) method, we assume that the last units purchased (the last in) are the first ones sold (the first out). If Mario sold 800 units, we assume all the 600 units purchased on October 19 (the last purchase) were sold, along with 200 units from the April 25 purchase. That leaves 100 of the units from the April 25 purchase and all 100 units from beginning inventory assumed to remain in ending inventory (not sold). Illustration 6–7 shows calculations of cost of goods sold and ending inventory for the LIFO method.

Inventory Transactions for Mario's Game Shop—LIFO METHOD

ILLUSTRATION 6–7

Inventory Calculation Using the LIFO Method

Purchases	Cost of Goods Available for Sale			=		Cost of Goods Sold	+	Ending Inventory
	Number of Units ×	Unit Cost =	Total Cost					
Jan. 1	100	$ 7	$ 700		Not sold			$ 700
Apr. 25	100	9	900					900
	200	9	1,800		Sold last 800 units	$1,800		
Oct. 19	600	11	6,600			6,600		
	1,000		$10,000			$8,400	+	$1,600

COMMON MISTAKE

Many students find it surprising that companies are allowed to report inventory costs using assumed amounts rather than actual amounts. Nearly all companies sell their actual inventory in a FIFO manner, but they are allowed to report it as if they sold it in a LIFO manner. Later, we'll see why that's advantageous.

WEIGHTED-AVERAGE COST

spiceland.mhhe.com/c16

Using the weighted-average cost method, we assume that both cost of goods sold and ending inventory consist of a random mixture of all the goods available for sale. We assume each unit of inventory has a cost equal to the weighted-average unit cost of all inventory items. We calculate that cost at the end of the year as:

$$\text{Weighted-average unit cost} = \frac{\text{Cost of goods available for sale}}{\text{Number of units available for sale}}$$

Illustration 6–8 demonstrates the calculation of cost of goods sold and ending inventory using the weighted-average cost method. Notice that the weighted-average cost of each game cartridge is $10, even though none of the game cartridges actually cost $10. However, on average, all the game cartridges cost $10, and this is the amount we use to calculate cost of goods sold and ending inventory under the weighted-average cost method.

ILLUSTRATION 6–8

Inventory Calculation Using the Weighted-Average Cost Method

**Inventory Transactions for Mario's Game Shop—
WEIGHTED-AVERAGE COST METHOD**

		Cost of Goods Available for Sale		
Date	Transaction	Number of Units	× Unit Cost	= Total Cost
Jan. 1	Beginning inventory	100	$ 7	$ 700
Apr. 25	Purchase	300	9	2,700
Oct. 19	Purchase	600	11	6,600
		1,000		$10,000

Weighted-average unit cost	=	$\dfrac{\$10,000}{1,000 \text{ units}}$	=	$10 per unit
Cost of goods sold	=	800 sold	× $10	= $ 8,000
Ending inventory	=	200 not sold	× 10	= 2,000
				$10,000

 COMMON MISTAKE

In calculating the weighted-average unit cost, be sure to use a *weighted* average of the unit cost instead of the *simple* average. In the example above, there are three unit costs: $7, $9, and $11. A simple average of these amounts is $9 [= (7 + 9 + 11) ÷ 3]. The simple average, though, fails to take into account that several more units were purchased at $11 than at $7 or $9. So we need to *weight* the unit costs by the number of units purchased. We do that by taking the total cost of goods available for sale ($10,000) divided by total number of units available for sale (1,000) for a weighted average of $10.

Illustration 6–9 depicts the concept behind the three inventory cost flow assumptions. A company begins the year with one unit of inventory and then purchases three units of inventory during the year. If the company sells two units of inventory, which two are they? Using FIFO, we assume inventory is sold in the order

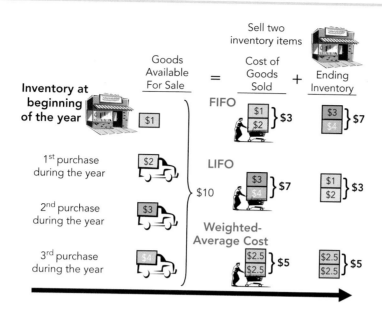

ILLUSTRATION 6–9

Comparison of Cost of Goods Sold and Ending Inventory under the Three Inventory Cost Flow Assumptions

purchased: Beginning inventory is sold first, and then the first purchase during the year is sold second. Using LIFO, we assume inventory is sold in the *opposite* order that we purchased it: The last unit purchased is sold first, and the second-to-last unit purchased is sold second. Using average cost, we assume inventory is sold using an average of all inventory purchased, including the beginning inventory.

COMMON MISTAKE

Students sometimes answer FIFO and LIFO backwards when calculating ending inventory. The reason is that these acronyms describe more directly the calculation of *cost of goods sold,* rather than ending inventory. For example, FIFO (first-in, first-out) directly suggests which inventory units are assumed sold (the first ones in) and therefore used to calculate cost of goods sold. It is implicit that the inventory units *not* sold are the last ones in and are used to calculate ending inventory.

KEY POINT

Companies are allowed to report inventory costs by *assuming* which specific units of inventory are sold and not sold, even if this does not match the *actual* flow. The three major inventory cost flow assumptions are FIFO (first-in, first-out), LIFO (last-in, first-out), and weighted-average cost.

NASCAR Unlimited sells remote-control cars. For 2012, the company has the following beginning inventory and purchase.

Let's Review

spiceland.mhhe.com/t10

Date	Transaction	Number of Units	Unit Cost	Total Cost
Jan. 1	Beginning inventory	120	$20	$2,400
Aug. 15	Purchase	180	15	2,700
	Total	300		$5,100

Because of technological advances, NASCAR Unlimited has seen a decrease in the unit cost of its inventory. Throughout the year, the company maintained a selling price of $30 for each remote-control car and sold a total of 280 units, which leaves 20 units in ending inventory.

Required:

1. Calculate cost of goods sold and ending inventory using the FIFO method.
2. Calculate cost of goods sold and ending inventory using the LIFO method.
3. Calculate cost of goods sold and ending inventory using the weighted-average cost method.

Solution:

1. Cost of goods sold and ending inventory using the **FIFO method:**

Purchases	Number of Units	×	Unit Cost	=	Total Cost		Cost of Goods Sold	+	Ending Inventory
				Cost of Goods Available for Sale		**=**			
Jan. 1	120		$20		$2,400	Sold first 280 units	$2,400		
Aug. 15	160		15		2,400		2,400		
	20		15		300 }	Not sold			$300
	300				$5,100	=	$4,800	+	$300

2. Cost of goods sold and ending inventory using the **LIFO method:**

Purchases	Number of Units	×	Unit Cost	=	Total Cost		Cost of Goods Sold	+	Ending Inventory
				Cost of Goods Available for Sale		**=**			
Jan. 1	20		$20		$ 400 }	Not sold			$400
	100		20		2,000	Sold last 280 units	$2,000		
Aug. 15	180		15		2,700		2,700		
	300				$5,100	=	$4,700	+	$400

3. Cost of goods sold and ending inventory using the **weighted-average cost method:**

$$\text{Weighted-average unit cost} = \frac{\$5,100}{300} = \$17$$

Cost of goods sold	= 280 sold	×	$17 =	$4,760
Ending inventory	= 20 not sold	×	17 =	340
	300			$5,100

Suggested Homework:
BE6-4, BE6-5;
E6-2, E6-3;
P6-1A&B, P6-2A&B

Effects of Managers' Choice of Inventory Reporting Methods

■ **LO4**
Explain the financial statement effects and tax effects of inventory cost flow assumptions.

Companies are free to choose FIFO, LIFO, or weighted-average cost to report inventory and cost of goods sold. However, because inventory costs generally change over time, the reported amounts for ending inventory and cost of goods sold will not be the same across inventory reporting methods. These differences could cause investors and creditors to make bad decisions if they are not aware of differences in inventory assumptions.

Illustration 6–10 compares the FIFO, LIFO, and weighted-average cost methods for Mario's Game Shop (assuming rising costs). (Recall from the Feature Story at the start of the chapter, that *gross profit* is a key measure of profitability, calculated as the difference between revenues and cost of goods sold.)

	FIFO	LIFO	Weighted-Average
Balance sheet:			
Ending inventory	$ 2,200	$ 1,600	$ 2,000
Income statement:			
Sales revenue (800 × $15)	$12,000	$12,000	$12,000
Cost of goods sold	7,800	8,400	8,000
Gross profit	$ 4,200	$ 3,600	$ 4,000

ILLUSTRATION 6–10

Comparison of Inventory Cost Flow Assumptions, When Costs Are Rising

When inventory costs are rising, Mario's Game Shop will report both higher inventory in the balance sheet and higher gross profit in the income statement if it chooses FIFO. The reason is that FIFO assumes the lower costs of the earlier purchases become cost of goods sold first, leaving the higher costs of the later purchases in ending inventory. Under the same assumption (rising inventory costs), LIFO will produce the *opposite* effect: LIFO will report both the lowest inventory and the lowest gross profit. The weighted-average cost method typically produces amounts that fall between the FIFO and LIFO amounts for both cost of goods sold and ending inventory.

Accountants often call FIFO the *balance-sheet approach:* The amount it reports for ending inventory (which appears in the *balance sheet*) better approximates the current cost of inventory. The ending inventory amount reported under LIFO, in contrast, generally includes "old" inventory costs that do not realistically represent the cost of today's inventory.

FIFO has a balance-sheet focus.

Accountants often call LIFO the *income-statement approach:* The amount it reports for cost of goods sold (which appears in the *income statement*) more realistically matches the current costs of inventory needed to produce current revenues. Recall that LIFO assumes the last purchases are sold first, reporting the most recent inventory cost in cost of goods sold. However, also note that the most recent cost is not the same as the actual cost. FIFO better approximates actual cost of goods sold for most companies, since most companies' actual physical flow follows FIFO.

LIFO has an income-statement focus.

FIFO or LIFO?

Management must weigh the benefits of FIFO and LIFO when deciding which inventory cost flow assumption will produce a better outcome for the company. Here we review the logic behind that decision.

Decision Maker's Perspective

Why Choose FIFO?

Most companies' actual physical flow follows FIFO. Think about a supermarket, car dealership, clothing shop, electronics store, or just about any company you're familiar with. These companies generally sell their oldest inventory first (first-in, first-out). If a company wants to choose an inventory method that most closely approximates its *actual physical flow* of inventory, then for most companies FIFO makes the most sense.

FIFO matches physical flow for most companies.

Another reason managers may want to use FIFO relates to its effect on the financial statements. **During periods of rising costs, which is the case for most companies (including our example for Mario's Game Shop), FIFO results in a (1) *higher* ending inventory, (2) *lower* cost of goods sold, and**

FIFO generally results in higher assets and higher net income when inventory costs are rising.

Many career opportunities are available in tax accounting. Because tax laws constantly change and are complex, tax accountants provide services to their clients not only through income tax statement preparation but also by formulating tax strategies to minimize tax payments. The choice of LIFO versus FIFO is one such example.

Tax accountants need a thorough understanding of legal matters, business transactions, and the tax code. Large corporations increasingly are looking to hire individuals with both an accounting and a legal background in tax. For example, someone who is a Certified Public Accountant (CPA) and has a law degree is especially desirable in the job market. In addition, people in nonaccounting positions also benefit greatly from an understanding of tax accounting. Whether you work in a large corporation or own a small business, virtually all business decisions have tax consequences.

(3) *higher* reported profit than does LIFO. Managers may want to report higher assets and profitability to increase their bonus compensation, decrease unemployment risk, satisfy shareholders, meet lending agreements, or increase stock price.

Why Choose LIFO?

If FIFO results in higher total assets and higher net income and produces amounts that most closely follow the actual flow of inventory, why would any company choose LIFO? **The primary benefit of choosing LIFO is tax savings.** LIFO results in the lowest amount of reported profits (when inventory costs are rising). While that might not look so good in the income statement, it's a welcome outcome in the tax return. When taxable income is lower, the company owes less in taxes to the Internal Revenue Service (IRS).

LIFO generally results in tax savings.

Can a company have its cake and eat it too by using FIFO for the income statement and LIFO for the tax return? No. The IRS established the LIFO conformity rule, which requires a company that uses LIFO for tax reporting to also use LIFO for financial reporting. ●

REPORTING THE LIFO DIFFERENCE

As Mario's Game Shop demonstrates, the choice between FIFO and LIFO results in different amounts for ending inventory in the balance sheet and cost of goods sold in the income statement. This complicates the way we compare financial statements: One company may be using FIFO, while a competing company may be using LIFO. To determine which of the two companies is more profitable, investors must adjust for the fact that managers' choice of inventory method has an effect on reported performance.

Because of the financial statement effects of different inventory methods, companies that choose LIFO must report the difference in the amount of inventory a company would report *if* it used FIFO instead of LIFO. (This difference is sometimes referred to as the LIFO reserve.) For some companies that have been using LIFO for a long time or for companies that have seen dramatic increases in inventory costs, the LIFO difference can be substantial. For example, Illustration 6–11 shows the effect of the LIFO difference reported by **Rite Aid Corporation**, which uses LIFO to account for most of its inventory.

ILLUSTRATION 6–11

Impact of the LIFO Difference on Reported Inventory of Rite Aid Corporation

RITE AID CORPORATION Notes to the Financial Statements (partial)		
($ in millions)	2009	2008
Reported inventory under LIFO	$3,509	$3,937
LIFO difference	746	563
Inventory assuming FIFO	$4,255	$4,500

If Rite Aid had used FIFO instead of LIFO, reported inventory amounts would have been $746 million greater and $563 million greater in 2009 and 2008, respectively. The magnitude of these effects can have a significant influence on investors' decisions.

Decision Point

Question	Accounting information	Analysis
When comparing inventory amounts between two companies, does the choice of inventory method matter?	The LIFO difference reported in the footnotes to the financial statements	When inventory costs are rising, FIFO results in a *higher* reported inventory. The LIFO difference can be used to compare inventory of two companies if one uses FIFO and the other uses LIFO.

CONSISTENCY IN REPORTING

Companies can choose which inventory method they prefer, even if the method does not match the actual physical flow of goods. However, once the company chooses a method, it is not allowed to frequently change to another one.[1] For example, a retail store cannot use FIFO in the current year because inventory costs are rising and then switch to LIFO in the following year because inventory costs are now falling.

However, a company need not use the same method for all its inventory. **International Paper Company**, for instance, uses LIFO for its raw materials and finished pulp and paper products, and both FIFO and weighted-average cost for other inventories. Because of the importance of inventories and the possible differential effects of different methods on the financial statements, a company informs its stockholders of the inventory method(s) being used in a note to the financial statements.

KEY POINT

Generally, FIFO more closely resembles the actual physical flow of inventory. When inventory costs are rising, FIFO results in higher reported inventory in the balance sheet and higher reported income in the income statement. Conversely, LIFO results in a lower reported inventory and net income, reducing the company's income tax obligation.

INTERNATIONAL FINANCIAL REPORTING STANDARDS (IFRS)

LIFO is not allowed under IFRS because it tends not to match the actual physical flow of inventory. FIFO and weighted-average cost are allowable inventory cost methods under IFRS. This distinction will become increasingly important as the United States moves closer to accepting IFRS for financial reporting. Will LIFO eventually disappear as a permitted inventory cost flow method? Perhaps so . . . stay tuned.

For more discussion, see Appendix E.

---

[1]When a company changes from LIFO for tax purposes, it cannot change back to LIFO until it has filed five tax returns using the non-LIFO method.

PART B

RECORDING INVENTORY TRANSACTIONS

So far, we've talked about purchases and sales of inventories and how to track their costs. We have not yet discussed how to *record* inventory transactions. We turn to that topic now.

Most companies, with the help of scanners and bar codes, keep a continual record of inventory using a **perpetual inventory system**. The continual—that is, perpetual—tracking of inventory helps a company to better manage its inventory levels. Just think of the losses that might occur at a video game store if the manager has no clear idea of the store's inventory and orders too many of a particular game that soon becomes obsolete when the next version or next hottest game comes out.

In contrast, a **periodic inventory system** does not continually modify inventory amounts, but instead *periodically* adjusts for purchases and sales of inventory at the end of the reporting period, based on a physical count of inventory on hand. Because this system does not provide a useful, continuing record of inventory, very few companies actually use the periodic inventory system in practice to maintain their own (internal) records of inventory transactions. Therefore, in this section, we will focus on how to record inventory transactions using a perpetual inventory system. Appendix A to the chapter covers the periodic system.

Perpetual Inventory System

■ LO5
Record inventory transactions using a perpetual inventory system.

To see how to record inventory transactions using a perpetual inventory system, we will look again at the inventory transactions for Mario's Game Shop. Recall that from January 1 through December 31, Mario sold 800 games. Now let's modify the example by giving exact dates for the sale of the 800 games—300 on July 17 and 500 on December 15. Illustration 6–12 shows the order of inventory transactions for Mario's Game Shop, including the total cost of the inventory and the total revenue from the sale of the 800 games.

ILLUSTRATION 6–12

Inventory Transactions for Mario's Game Shop

Date	Transaction	Details	Total Cost	Total Revenue
Jan. 1	Beginning inventory	100 units for $7 each	$ 700	
Apr. 25	Purchase	300 units for $9 each	2,700	
Jul. 17	Sale	300 units for $15 each		$ 4,500
Oct. 19	Purchase	600 units for $11 each	6,600	
Dec. 15	Sale	500 units for $15 each		7,500
	Totals		$10,000	$12,000

Using this information, let's see how Mario would record purchases and sales of inventory.

INVENTORY PURCHASES AND SALES

To record the purchase of new inventory, we debit Inventory (an asset) to show that the company's balance of this asset account has increased. At the same time, if the purchase was paid in cash, we credit Cash. Or more likely, if the company made the purchase on account, we credit Accounts Payable, increasing total liabilities. Thus, Mario records the first purchase of 300 units for $2,700 on April 25 as:

April 25	Debit	Credit
Inventory	2,700	
Accounts Payable		2,700
(Purchase inventory on account)		

Balance Sheet					Income Statement		
			Stockholders' Equity				
			Common	Retained			Net
Assets	=	Liabilities +	Stock	+ Earnings	Revenues	− Expenses =	Income
+2,700	=	+2,700					

On July 17, Mario sold 300 units of inventory on account for $15 each, resulting in total sales of $4,500. We make two entries to record the sale: (1) The first entry shows an increase to the asset account (in this case, Accounts Receivable) and an increase to Sales Revenue. (2) The second entry adjusts the Inventory and Cost of Goods Sold accounts.

Mario records as revenue the $4,500 from the July 17 sale. That amount is the price Mario charges to customers, but what did that inventory *cost* Mario? (That is, what is the cost of the goods sold?) Under the assumption that Mario uses FIFO to calculate inventory, the cost of the *first* 300 units purchased is $2,500, which is $700 of beginning inventory (100 units × $7) plus $1,800 of the April 25 purchase (200 units × $9). We record this amount as the cost of goods sold for the July 17 sale. At the same time, we maintain a continual (perpetual) record of inventory by reducing the Inventory balance by the cost of the amount sold, $2,500, as shown below.

July 17	Debit	Credit
Accounts Receivable	4,500	
Sales Revenue		4,500
(Sell inventory on account)		
($4,500 = 300 units × $15)		
Cost of Goods Sold	2,500	
Inventory		2,500
(Record cost of inventory sold)		
($2,500 = [100 units × $7] + [200 units × $9])		

Balance Sheet					Income Statement		
			Stockholders' Equity				
			Common	Retained			Net
Assets	=	Liabilities +	Stock	+ Earnings	Revenues	− Expenses =	Income
+4,500	=			+2,000	+4,500	− +2,500 =	+2,000
−2,500							
+2,000							

By recording the sales revenue and the cost of goods sold at the same time, we can see that Mario's profit on the sale is $2,000.

On October 19, Mario purchased 600 additional units of inventory for $6,600 on account. We record that purchase as:

A	=	L	+	SE
+6,600				
		+6,600		

October 19	Debit	Credit
Inventory	6,600	
Accounts Payable		6,600
(Purchase inventory on account)		

On December 15, Mario sold another 500 units for $15 each on account. Again, we make two entries to record the sale. The first increases Accounts Receivable and Sales Revenue. The second adjusts the Cost of Goods Sold and Inventory accounts. What did the inventory sold on December 15 cost Mario? On the FIFO basis, the cost of goods sold is $5,300 (100 units × $9 plus 400 units × $11). Mario increases Cost of Goods Sold and decreases Inventory by that amount. Thus, we record the sale on December 15 as:

A	=	L	+	SE
+7,500				
				+7,500 Rev↑

December 15	Debit	Credit
Accounts Receivable	7,500	
Sales Revenue		7,500
(Sell inventory on account)		
($7,500 = 500 units × $15)		

A	=	L	+	SE
				−5,300 Exp↑
−5,300				

	Debit	Credit
Cost of Goods Sold	5,300	
Inventory		5,300
(Record cost of inventory sold)		
($5,300 = [100 units × $9] + [400 units × $11])		

After recording all purchases and sales of inventory for the year, we can determine the ending balance of Inventory by examining the postings to the account. Thus, Mario's ending Inventory balance is $2,200, as shown in Illustration 6–13.

ILLUSTRATION 6–13

Inventory Account for Mario's Game Shop

	Inventory		
Jan. 1 Beginning	700		
Apr. 25 Purchase	2,700	2,500	Jul. 17 Sale
Oct. 19 Purchase	6,600	5,300	Dec. 15 Sale
	10,000	7,800	
Dec. 31 Ending FIFO amount	Bal. 2,200		

KEY POINT

The perpetual inventory system maintains a continual—or *perpetual*—record of inventory purchased and sold. When companies *purchase* inventory using a perpetual inventory system, they increase the Inventory account and either decrease Cash or increase Accounts Payable. When companies *sell* inventory, they make two entries: (1) They increase an asset account (Cash or Accounts Receivable) and increase Sales Revenue, and (2) they increase Cost of Goods Sold and decrease Inventory.

Simple adjustment from FIFO to LIFO. In the example above, we recorded inventory transactions using the FIFO assumption. Thus, Mario assumed that the 800 units sold during the year came from the first 800 units purchased. **In practice, virtually all companies maintain their own inventory records using the FIFO assumption, because that's how they typically sell their actual inventory.** However, as discussed earlier in the chapter, for preparing financial statements, many companies choose to report their inventory using the LIFO assumption. So, how does a company adjust its own inventory records maintained on a FIFO basis to a LIFO basis for preparing financial statements? The adjustment is referred to as the LIFO adjustment, and you'll see that this involves a *very simple* adjustment.

spiceland.mhhe.com/c17

To see how easy the LIFO adjustment can be, let's refer back to our example involving Mario's Game Shop. As summarized in Illustration 6–13, Mario's ending balance of Inventory using FIFO is $2,200. Under LIFO, it is only $1,600 (see Illustration 6–7). As a result, if Mario's wants to adjust its FIFO inventory records to LIFO for preparing financial statements, it needs to adjust Inventory downward by $600 (decreasing the balance from $2,200 to $1,600). In this case, we record the LIFO adjustment at the end of the period through a decrease to Inventory and an increase to Cost of Goods Sold:

December 31	Debit	Credit
Cost of Goods Sold	600	
Inventory		600
(Record the LIFO adjustment)		

In rare situations where the LIFO Inventory balance is *greater* than the FIFO Inventory balance (such as when inventory costs are declining), the entry for the LIFO adjustment would be reversed.

Illustration 6–14 shows the Inventory account for Mario's Game Shop after the LIFO adjustment. Notice that the balance of Inventory has decreased to reflect the amount reported under the LIFO method.

Inventory			
Jan. 1 Beginning	700		
Apr. 25 Purchase	2,700	2,500	Jul. 17 Sale
Oct. 19 Purchase	6,600	5,300	Dec. 15 Sale
	10,000	7,800	
FIFO amount	2,200		
		600	LIFO
Dec. 31 Ending			adjustment
LIFO amount	Bal. 1,600		

ILLUSTRATION 6–14

Inventory Account for Mario's Game Shop, after LIFO Adjustment

 KEY POINT

Nearly all companies maintain their own inventory records on a FIFO basis, and then some prepare financial statements on a LIFO basis. To adjust their FIFO inventory records to LIFO for financial reporting, companies use a simple LIFO adjustment at the end of the period.

ADDITIONAL INVENTORY TRANSACTIONS

To this point, we've recorded inventory purchases and inventory sales transactions. So that we can discuss additional inventory topics, let's add three more inventory-related transactions to our Mario's example. Let's assume Mario also:

1. On April 25, pays freight charges of $300 for inventory purchased on April 25.
2. On April 30, pays for the units purchased on April 25, less a 2% purchase discount.
3. On October 22, returns 50 defective units from the October 19 purchase.

Next, we discuss how to record each of these three transactions.

Freight charges.   A significant cost associated with inventory for most merchandising companies includes freight (also called shipping) charges. This includes the cost of shipments of inventory from suppliers, as well as the cost of shipments to customers. When goods are shipped, they are shipped with terms *FOB shipping point* or *FOB destination*. FOB stands for "free on board" and indicates *when* title (ownership) passes from the seller to the buyer. FOB *shipping point* means title passes when the seller *ships* the inventory, not when the buyer receives it. The fact that a buyer does not have actual physical possession of the inventory does not prevent transfer of title to the buyer's inventory. In contrast, if the seller ships the inventory FOB *destination*, then title does not transfer to the buyer when the inventory is shipped. The buyer would not record the purchase transaction until the shipped inventory reached its *destination*, the buyer's location.

Freight charges on incoming shipments from suppliers are commonly referred to as freight-in. **We add the cost of freight-in to the balance of Inventory.** In this case, the cost of freight is considered a cost of the purchased inventory. When Mario pays $300 for freight charges associated with the purchase of inventory on April 25, those charges would be recorded as part of the inventory cost.

			Debit	Credit
A = L + SE	**April 25**			
+300	**Inventory**		300	
−300	**Cash**			300
	(Pay freight-in charges)			

Later, when that inventory is sold, those freight charges become part of the cost of goods sold. In Mario's case, all of the units purchased on April 25 are sold by the end of the year, so the $300 freight charge would be reported as part of cost of goods sold in the income statement at the end of the year.

The cost of freight on shipments *to* customers is called freight-out. Shipping charges for outgoing inventory are reported in the income statement either as part of cost of goods sold or as an operating expense, usually among selling expenses. If a company adopts a policy of not including shipping charges in cost of goods sold, both the amounts incurred during the period as well as the income statement classification of the expense must be disclosed.[2]

To see an example of how **Amazon.com** accounts for freight charges, look at Illustration 6–15 (next page).

Purchase discounts.   As discussed in Chapter 5, sellers often encourage prompt payment by offering *discounts* to buyers. From the seller's point of view, these are sales

---

[2]FASB ASC 605–45–50–2: Revenue Recognition–Principal Agent Considerations–Disclosure–Shipping and Handling Fees and Costs (previously "Accounting for Shipping and Handling Fees and Costs," *EITF Issue No. 00-10* [Norwalk, Conn.: FASB, 2000] par. 6).

AMAZON.COM, INC.
Notes to the Financial Statements (excerpt)

Shipping charges to receive products from our suppliers are included in our inventory, and recognized as "Cost of sales.". . . Outbound shipping-related costs are included in "Cost of sales" and totaled $1.5 billion, $1.2 billion, and $884 million for 2008, 2007, and 2006.

ILLUSTRATION 6–15

Accounting for Shipping Costs by Amazon.com

discounts; from the buyer's point of view, they are *purchase discounts*. Purchase discounts allow buyers to trim a portion of the cost of the purchase in exchange for payment within a certain period of time. Buyers are not required to take purchase discounts, but many find it advantageous to do so.

Let's assume that Mario's supplier, Luigi Software, Inc., offers terms 2/10, n/30 for the April 25 purchase on account. This means that Mario can receive a 2% discount if payment is made within 10 days, but the total invoice is due within 30 days. Mario's policy is to take advantage of discounts offered.

For a review of credit terms, look back at page 216.

Recall that on April 25 Mario purchased 300 units on account for $9 each (or $2,700 total). When Mario makes payment on April 30, the discount would be $54 (= $2,700 × 2%). Mario has to pay only $2,646 (= $2,700 − $54) to eliminate the $2,700 amount owed. To account for the purchase discount, we subtract the discount from the balance in the Inventory account:

April 30	Debit	Credit	A	=	L	+	SE
Accounts Payable	2,700				−2,700		
Inventory		54	−54				
Cash		2,646	−2,646				
(Pay on account with a 2% purchase discount of $54)							
($54 = $2,700 × 2%)							

Just as freight charges *add* to the cost of inventory and therefore increase the cost of goods sold once those items are sold, purchase discounts *subtract* from the cost of inventory and therefore reduce cost of goods sold once those items are sold. When Mario sells the 300 units purchased on April 25, the cost of goods sold associated with those items will be the cost of the actual units ($2,700) plus freight charges ($300) less the purchase discount ($54), totaling $2,946.

Purchase returns. Occasionally, a company will find inventory items to be unacceptable for some reason—perhaps they are damaged or are different from what was ordered. In those cases, the company returns the items to the supplier and records the purchase return as a reduction in both Inventory and Accounts Payable. For example, when Mario decides on October 22 to return 50 defective units from the 600 units purchased on October 19 for $11 each, the company would record the following transaction:

October 22	Debit	Credit	A	=	L	+	SE
Accounts Payable	550				−550		
Inventory		550	−550				
(Return inventory previously purchased on account)							
($550 = 50 defective units × $11)							

Let's Review

spiceland.mhhe.com/t11

Camcorder Central sells high-end **Sony** camcorders and accounts for its inventory using FIFO with a perpetual system. At the beginning of March 2012, the company has camcorder inventory of $24,000 (= $240 × 100 units).

Required:

Record the following inventory transactions for Camcorder Central.

1. On March 7, Camcorder Central purchases on account 210 camcorders from Sony Corporation for $250 each, terms 2/10, n/30.
2. On March 8, Camcorder Central pays $2,000 for freight charges associated with the 210 camcorders purchased on March 7.
3. On March 10, Camcorder Central returns to Sony 10 defective camcorders from the March 7 purchase, receiving a credit of $250 for each camcorder.
4. On March 16, Camcorder Central makes full payment for inventory purchased on March 7, excluding the 10 defective camcorders returned and the 2% discount received.
5. On March 20, Camcorder Central sells 300 camcorders for $90,000 ($300 each). All sales are for cash.

Solution:

1. Camcorder Central's March 7 purchase on account of 210 camcorders from Sony Corporation for $250 each, terms 2/10, n/30:

March 7	Debit	Credit
Inventory	52,500	
Accounts Payable		52,500
(Purchase camcorders on account)		
($52,500 = $250 × 210 camcorders)		

2. Camcorder's March 8 payment for freight charges associated with the camcorders purchased on March 7:

March 8	Debit	Credit
Inventory	2,000	
Cash		2,000
(Pay for freight charges)		

3. Camcorder's March 10 return of 10 defective camcorders from the March 7 purchase, for a credit of $250 per camcorder:

March 10	Debit	Credit
Accounts Payable	2,500	
Inventory		2,500
(Return defective camcorders)		

4. Camcorder's March 16 payment for inventory purchased on March 7, excluding the returned camcorders and less the 2% discount:

March 16	Debit	Credit
Accounts Payable	50,000	
Inventory		1,000
Cash		49,000
(Make full payment for March 7 purchase)		
($1,000 = $50,000 × 2%)		

5. Camcorder's cash sale on March 20 of 300 camcorders for $300 each:

March 20	Debit	Credit
Cash	90,000	
Sales Revenue		90,000
(Sell 300 camcorders for cash)		
($90,000 = $300 × 300 camcorders)		
Cost of Goods Sold	75,000	
Inventory		75,000
(Record cost of camcorders sold)		
(Cost of 100 camcorders in beginning inventory = $24,000)		
(Cost of 200 camcorders purchased = $52,500 + $2,000 − $2,500 − $1,000 = $51,000)		

Suggested Homework:
BE6-9, BE6-11;
E6-7, E6-8;
P6-3A&B, P6-6A&B

SALES TRANSACTIONS: THE OTHER SIDE OF PURCHASE TRANSACTIONS

Flip Side

For every purchase transaction, there is a sales transaction for another party. Sometimes, seeing the other side of the transaction helps us understand the economic events we are recording. In the Let's Review exercise above, Camcorder Central made a $52,500 purchase of inventory on account from Sony Corporation. Camcorder Central then returned inventory of $2,500 and received a $1,000 purchase discount for quick payment. Camcorder Central is the purchaser and Sony is the seller. We discussed returns and discounts from the seller's viewpoint in Chapter 5; here, let's briefly reexamine the transactions between Sony and Camcorder Central so we can see a side-by-side comparison of purchase and sales transactions. Illustration 6–16 shows these entries.

Purchaser			Seller		
Camcorder Central			Sony Corporation		
Purchase on Account			**Sale on Account***		
Inventory	52,500		Accounts Receivable	52,500	
Accounts Payable		52,500	Sales Revenue		52,500
Purchase Return			**Sales Return**		
Accounts Payable	2,500		Sales Return	2,500	
Inventory		2,500	Accounts Receivable		2,500
Payment on Account with Discount			**Receipt on Account with Discount**		
Accounts Payable	50,000		Cash	49,000	
Inventory		1,000	Sales Discounts	1,000	
Cash		49,000	Accounts Receivable		50,000

ILLUSTRATION 6–16

Comparison of Purchase and Sale of Inventory Transactions

*In practice, Sony also records the cost of inventory sold at the time of the sale. For simplicity, we omit this part of the transaction since Camcorder Central has no comparable transaction. We have also omitted Camcorder Central's March 20 sale of camcorders, since Sony is not party to that transaction.

KEY POINT

For most companies, freight charges are added to the cost of inventory, whereas purchase returns and purchase discounts are deducted from the cost of inventory. Some companies choose to report freight charges on outgoing shipments as part of selling expenses instead of cost of goods sold.

Multiple-Step Income Statement

■ **LO6**
Prepare a multiple-step income statement.

In Chapters 1 through 5, we presented a form of the income statement with two main categories: total revenues and total expenses. Look back at Illustration 3–12 (page 128) for an example. That format involves essentially a single calculation—total revenues minus total expenses—to get to net income. Not surprisingly, such an income statement is called a *single-step income statement.*

In this chapter, we have seen that sales and purchases of inventory typically are the most important transactions for a merchandising company. As a result, in their income statements, merchandisers report revenues and expenses from these transactions separately from other revenues and expenses. Because of this separate reporting, merchandising companies usually use a different format, called a **multiple-step income statement**, referring to the fact that the income statement reports *multiple* levels of income (or profitability).

Gross profit.   The multiple-step income statement begins by reporting that a company's sales revenue minus cost of goods sold equals gross profit. Illustration 6–17 shows these amounts for our continuing example of Mario's Game Shop. Recall that Mario sold 800 units during the year for $15 each (or $12,000 total). This amount is reported as sales revenue.

ILLUSTRATION 6–17

Multiple-Step Income Statement

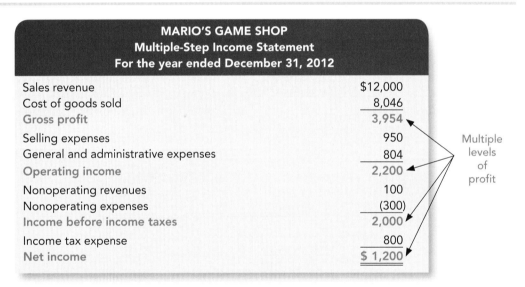

MARIO'S GAME SHOP
Multiple-Step Income Statement
For the year ended December 31, 2012

Sales revenue	$12,000
Cost of goods sold	8,046
Gross profit	3,954
Selling expenses	950
General and administrative expenses	804
Operating income	2,200
Nonoperating revenues	100
Nonoperating expenses	(300)
Income before income taxes	2,000
Income tax expense	800
Net income	$ 1,200

Multiple levels of profit

From sales revenue, we subtract the cost of the 800 units sold. Again, to calculate this balance, we can look back to our transactions involving goods sold, including the cost of freight charges and the purchase discount associated with the purchase on April 25. The 800 units sold consist of the following:

	Units Sold	Unit Cost	Total Cost
Beginning inventory	100	$ 7	$ 700
Purchase on April 25	300	9	2,700
Freight charges			300
Purchase discount			(54)
Purchase on October 19	400	11	4,400
	800		$8,046

Mario would report $8,046 as the cost of goods sold.

The difference between sales of inventory and the cost of that inventory is the company's *gross profit.* Gross profit is one of the profitability measures investors use to evaluate the performance of a merchandising company. As Illustration 6–17 shows, Mario's gross profit is $3,954.

Operating income. After gross profit, the next items reported are selling expenses and general and administrative expenses, often referred to as **operating expenses**. We discussed several types of operating expenses in earlier chapters—salaries, utilities, advertising, supplies, rent, insurance, and bad debts. These costs are normal for operating most companies. Gross profit reduced by these operating expenses is referred to as operating income (or sometimes referred to as *income from operations*). It measures profitability from *normal* operations, a key performance measure for predicting the future profit-generating ability of the company.

After operating income, a company reports **nonoperating revenues and expenses**. Nonoperating revenues and expenses arise from activities that are *not* part of the company's primary operations. Interest revenue and interest expense are examples. (In Chapter 7, we will discuss another common nonoperating item—gains and losses on the sale of long-term assets.) Investors focus less on nonoperating items than on income from operations, as these nonoperating activities often do not have long-term implications on the company's profitability.

Income before income taxes. Combining operating income with nonoperating revenues and expenses yields income before income taxes. For Mario's Game Shop, the amount of nonoperating expenses exceeds the amount of nonoperating revenues, so income before income taxes is lower than operating income.

Net income. Next, the company subtracts income tax expense to find its bottom-line net income. At the bottom line, net income represents the difference between all revenues and all expenses for the period. Note in Illustration 6–17 that the multiple-step income statement, unlike the single-step format, reports *multiple levels of profit*—gross profit, operating income, income before income taxes, and net income. We'll examine the multiple-step income statement again in Chapter 12, when we discuss additional income statement activities such as discontinued operations and extraordinary items.

 KEY POINT

A multiple-step income statement reports multiple levels of profitability. **Gross profit** equals sales revenue minus cost of goods sold. **Operating income** equals gross profit minus operating expenses. **Income before income taxes** equals operating income plus nonoperating revenues and minus nonoperating expenses. **Net income** equals all revenues minus all expenses.

Illustration 6–18 presents an example of a multiple-step income statement for **hhgregg, Inc.**, a specialty retailer of consumer electronics and home appliances.

hhgregg, INC. Multiple-Step Income Statement For the year ended March 31, 2009 ($ in millions)	
Sales revenue, net	$1,397
Cost of goods sold	962
Gross profit	435
Selling, general, and administrative expenses	287
Advertising expenses	62
Other operating expenses	16
Operating income	70
Interest expense	7
Income before income taxes	63
Income tax expense	26
Net income	$ 37

Multiple levels of profit

ILLUSTRATION 6–18

Multiple-Step Income Statement for hhgregg, Inc.

The company has sales revenue of $1,397 million and cost of goods sold of $962 million, resulting in a gross profit of $435 million. After subtracting normal operating expenses, operating income is $70 million. Income before taxes equals $63 million after subtracting interest expense. The company's after-tax net income equals $37 million.

PART C

LOWER-OF-COST-OR-MARKET METHOD

■ **LO7**
Apply the lower-of-cost-or-market method for inventories.

Think about the store where you usually buy your clothes. You've probably noticed the store selling leftover inventory at deeply discounted prices after the end of each selling season to make room for the next season's clothing line. The value of the company's old clothing inventory has likely fallen below its original cost. Is it appropriate to report the reduced-value inventory at its original cost? The answer to that question has motivated accountants to use the lower-of-cost-or-market method.

When the market value of inventory falls below its original cost, companies are required to report inventory at the lower market value. Normally, the market value of inventory is considered to be the replacement cost of that inventory. In other words, what is the cost to replace the inventory item in its identical form? The cost of inventory is the amount initially recorded in the accounting records based on methods we discussed in the previous section (specific identification, FIFO, LIFO, or weighted-average cost). Once it has determined both the cost and market value of inventory, the company reports ending inventory in the balance sheet at the *lower* of the two amounts. This is known as the lower-of-cost-or-market (LCM) method to valuing inventory.

Illustration 6–19 demonstrates the concept behind the lower-of-cost-or-market method.

ILLUSTRATION 6–19

Lower-of-Cost-or-Market Method

To see how we apply the lower-of-cost-or-market method to inventory amounts, assume Mario's Game Shop sells FunStation 2 and FunStation 3. Illustration 6–20 shows information related to ending inventory at the end of 2012.

ILLUSTRATION 6–20

Calculating the Lower-of-Cost-or-Market

Inventory Items	Cost per Unit	Market per Unit	Lower-of-Cost-or-Market per Unit		Quantity		Total Lower-of-Cost-or-Market
FunStation 2	$300	$200	→ $200	×	15	=	$ 3,000
FunStation 3	400	450	→ 400	×	20	=	8,000
			Reported ending inventory			=	$11,000

Mario reports the FunStation 2 in ending inventory at market value ($200 per unit) because that's lower than its original cost ($300 per unit). The 15 FunStation 2s were originally reported in inventory at their cost of $4,500 (= 15 × $300). To reduce the inventory from that original cost of $4,500 to its lower market value of $3,000 (= 15 × $200), Mario records a $1,500 reduction in inventory with the following year-end adjustment.

December 31, 2012	Debit	Credit
Cost of Goods Sold	1,500	
Inventory		1,500
(Adjust inventory down to market value)		

Notice that the write-down of inventory has the effect not only of reducing total assets, but also of reducing net income and retained earnings.

The FunStation 3 inventory, on the other hand, remains on the books at its original cost of $8,000 (= $400 × 20), since cost is less than market value. Mario does not need to make any adjustment for these inventory items.

After adjusting inventory to the lower-of-cost-or-market, the store calculates its ending Inventory balance as:

spiceland.mhhe.com/c20

	Inventory		
Balance before LCM adjustment	12,500		
		1,500	LCM adjustment
Ending balance	Bal. 11,000		

Conservatism and the Lower-of-Cost-or-Market Method

Firms are required to report the falling value of inventory, but they are not allowed to report any increasing value of inventory. Why is this? The answer lies in the conservative nature of some accounting procedures. A *conservative* approach in accounting implies that there is more potential harm to users of financial statements if estimated *gains* turn out to be wrong than if estimated *losses* turn out to be wrong. It also guides companies, when faced with a choice, to select accounting methods that are less likely to overstate assets and net income. Therefore, companies typically do not report estimated gains. ●

Decision Maker's Perspective

KEY POINT

We report inventory at the lower-of-cost-or-market; that is, at cost (specific identification, FIFO, LIFO, or weighted-average cost) or market value (replacement cost), whichever is lower. When market value falls below cost, we adjust downward the balance of inventory from cost to market value.

Let's Review

spiceland.mhhe.com/t12

Auto Adrenaline provides specialty car products—satellite radios, GPS navigation systems, and subwoofers. At the end of 2012, the company's records show the following amounts in ending inventory.

Inventory Items	Quantity	Cost per Unit	Market per Unit
Satellite radios	10	$100	$120
GPS navigators	20	300	350
Subwoofers	40	70	50

Required:

1. Determine ending inventory using the lower-of-cost-or-market method.
2. Record any necessary year-end adjustment entry associated with the lower-of-cost-or-market method.

Solution:

1. Ending inventory, lower-of-cost-or-market:

Inventory Items	Cost per Unit	Market per Unit	Lower-of-Cost-or-Market per Unit		Quantity		Total Lower-of-Cost-or-Market
Satellite radios	$100	$120	→ $100	×	10	=	$1,000
GPS navigators	300	350	→ 300	×	20	=	6,000
Subwoofers	70	50	→ 50	×	40	=	2,000
							$9,000

Cost is lower than market for satellite radios and GPS navigators. We get lower-of-cost-or-market by multiplying the *cost* per unit times the quantity. However, market is lower than cost for subwoofers. In that case, we get lower-of-cost-or-market by multiplying the *market* per unit times quantity.

2. Year-end adjustment associated with the lower-of-cost-or-market method:

December 31, 2012	Debit	Credit
Cost of Goods Sold	800	
Inventory		800
(Adjust inventory down to market value)		
($800 = 40 subwoofers × $20 decline in market below cost)		

Suggested Homework:
BE6-14, BE6-15;
E6-13, E6-14;
P6-4A&B

We need the $800 adjustment to reduce the reported Inventory balance of the 40 subwoofers by $20 each (from $70 to $50).

ETHICAL DILEMMA

Diamond Computers, which is owned and operated by Dale Diamond, manufactures and sells different types of computers. The company has reported profits every year since its inception in 2000 and has applied for a bank loan near the end of 2012 to upgrade manufacturing facilities. These upgrades should significantly boost future productivity and profitability.

In preparing the financial statements for the year, the chief accountant, Sandy Walters, mentions to Dale that approximately $80,000 of computer inventory has become obsolete and a write-down of inventory should be recorded in 2012.

Dale understands that the write-down would result in a net loss being reported for company operations in 2012. This could jeopardize the company's application for the bank loan, which would lead to employee layoffs. Dale is a very kind, older gentleman who cares little for his personal wealth but who is deeply devoted to his employees' well-being. He truly believes the loan is necessary for the company's sustained viability. Dale suggests Sandy wait until 2013 to write down the inventory so that profitable financial statements can be presented to the bank this year.

What should Sandy do?

INVENTORY ANALYSIS
Best Buy vs. Radio Shack

ANALYSIS

As discussed in the previous section, if managers purchase too much inventory, the company runs the risk of the inventory becoming obsolete and market value falling below cost, resulting in inventory write-downs. Outside analysts as well as managers often use the *inventory turnover ratio* to evaluate a company's effectiveness in managing its investment in inventory. In addition, investors often rely on the *gross profit ratio* to determine the core profitability of a merchandising company's operations. We discuss these ratios next.

■ **LO8**
Analyze management of inventory using the inventory turnover ratio and gross profit ratio.

INVENTORY TURNOVER RATIO

The inventory turnover ratio shows the number of times the firm sells its average inventory balance during a reporting period. It is calculated as cost of goods sold divided by average inventory.

$$\text{Inventory turnover ratio} = \frac{\text{Cost of goods sold}}{\text{Average inventory}}$$

The more frequently a business is able to sell or "turn over" its average inventory balance, the less the company needs to invest in inventory for a given level of sales. Other things equal, a higher ratio indicates greater effectiveness of a company in managing its investment in inventory.

AVERAGE DAYS IN INVENTORY

Another way to measure the same activity is to calculate the *average days in inventory*. This ratio indicates the approximate number of days the average inventory is held. It is calculated as 365 days divided by the inventory turnover ratio.

$$\text{Average days in inventory} = \frac{365}{\text{Inventory turnover ratio}}$$

We can analyze the inventory of **Best Buy** and **Radio Shack Corporation** by calculating these ratios for both companies. Best Buy sells a large volume of commonly purchased products. In contrast, Radio Shack sells more distinct electronic items. Below are relevant amounts for each company as of February 2009 for Best Buy and December 2008 for Radio Shack.

($ in millions)	Cost of Goods Sold	Beginning Inventory	Ending Inventory
Best Buy	$34,017	$4,708	$4,753
Radio Shack	2,302	705	636

To compute the inventory turnover ratio we need the *average* inventory, which is the beginning amount of inventory plus the ending amount, divided by 2.

Best Buy   Average inventory = ($4,708 + $4,753) ÷ 2 = $4,730.5

Radio Shack   Average inventory = ($705 + $636) ÷ 2 = $670.5

We put average inventory in the denominator to compute the inventory turnover ratio, as shown in Illustration 6–21.

ILLUSTRATION 6–21

Inventory Turnover Ratios for Best Buy and Radio Shack

	Inventory Turnover Ratio	Average Days in Inventory
Best Buy	$34,017 ÷ $4,730.5 = 7.2 times	$\frac{365}{7.2}$ = 51 days
Radio Shack	$2,302 ÷ $670.5 = 3.4 times	$\frac{365}{3.4}$ = 107 days

The turnover ratio is more than twice as high for Best Buy. On average, it takes Radio Shack an additional 56 days to sell its inventory. If the two companies had the same business strategies, this would indicate that Best Buy is better at managing inventory. In this case, though, the difference in inventory turnover more likely is related to the products the two stores sell. Specialty items are not expected to sell as quickly. As we see in the next section, Radio Shack offsets its relatively low inventory turnover with a relatively high profit margin.

Decision Point

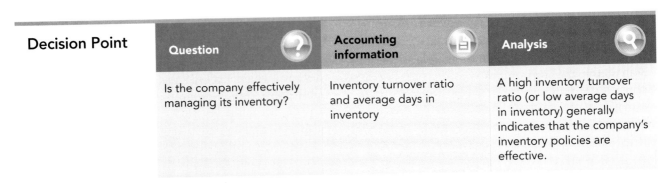

Question	Accounting information	Analysis
Is the company effectively managing its inventory?	Inventory turnover ratio and average days in inventory	A high inventory turnover ratio (or low average days in inventory) generally indicates that the company's inventory policies are effective.

COMMON MISTAKE

Many students use ending inventory rather than average inventory in calculating the inventory turnover ratio. Generally, when you calculate a ratio that includes an income statement item (an amount generated over a period) with a balance sheet item (an amount at a particular date), the balance sheet item needs to be converted to an amount *over the same period*. This is done by averaging the beginning and ending balances of the balance sheet item.

GROSS PROFIT RATIO

Another important indicator of the company's successful management of inventory is the gross profit ratio. It measures the amount by which the sale price of inventory exceeds its cost per dollar of sales. We calculate the gross profit ratio as gross profit divided by net sales. (Net sales equal total sales revenue less sales discounts, returns, and allowances).

$$\text{Gross profit ratio} = \frac{\text{Gross profit}}{\text{Net sales}}$$

The higher the gross profit ratio, the higher is the "markup" a company is able to achieve on its inventories. Best Buy and Radio Shack report the following information.

($ in millions)	Net Sales	–	Cost of Goods Sold	=	Gross Profit
Best Buy	$45,015		$34,017		$10,998
Radio Shack	4,225		2,302		1,923

Illustration 6–22 shows calculation of the gross profit ratio for Best Buy and Radio Shack.

	Gross Profit ÷ Net Sales	=	Gross Profit Ratio
Best Buy	$10,998 ÷ $45,015	=	24%
Radio Shack	$1,923 ÷ $4,225	=	46%

ILLUSTRATION 6–22

Gross Profit Ratios for Best Buy and Radio Shack

For Best Buy, this means that for every $1 of sales revenue, the company spends $0.76 on inventory, resulting in a gross profit of $0.24. In contrast, the gross profit ratio for Radio Shack is 46%. We saw earlier that Radio Shack's inventory turnover is about half that of Best Buy. But, we see now that Radio Shack makes up for that lower turnover with a gross profit margin about twice that of Best Buy. The products Best Buy sells are familiar goods, and competition from companies like **Dell**, **Target**, and **Walmart** for these high-volume items keeps sale prices low compared to costs. Because Radio Shack specializes in unique lower-volume products, there is less competition, allowing greater price markups.

As products become more highly specialized, gross profit ratios typically increase even further. For example, consider a company like **Blue Coat Systems**, a company that specializes in unique products and services that optimize and secure information sent over business networks or the Internet. In 2009, the company reported gross profit of $314 million on net sales of $445 million—a gross profit ratio of 71%.

KEY POINT

The inventory turnover ratio indicates the number of times the firm sells, or turns over, its average inventory balance during a reporting period. The gross profit ratio measures the amount by which the sale price of inventory exceeds its cost per dollar of sales.

Decision Point

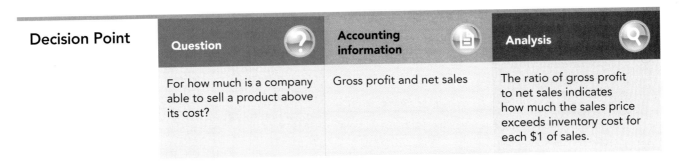

Question	Accounting information	Analysis
For how much is a company able to sell a product above its cost?	Gross profit and net sales	The ratio of gross profit to net sales indicates how much the sales price exceeds inventory cost for each $1 of sales.

APPENDIX A
RECORDING INVENTORY TRANSACTIONS USING A PERIODIC INVENTORY SYSTEM

■ **LO9**
Record inventory transactions using a periodic inventory system.

In this chapter, we discussed how to record inventory transactions using a *perpetual* inventory system. Here we discuss how to record inventory transactions using a *periodic* inventory system.

Recall that under a **perpetual inventory system** we maintain a continual—or *perpetual*—record of inventory purchased and sold. In contrast, using a **periodic inventory system** we do not continually modify inventory amounts. Instead, we *periodically* adjust for purchases and sales of inventory at the end of the reporting period, based on a physical count of inventory on hand.

To demonstrate the differences in these two systems, let's record inventory transactions under the periodic system using the same information (from Illustration 6–12) that we used to demonstrate the perpetual inventory system. We repeat those transactions in Illustration 6–23.

ILLUSTRATION 6–23

Inventory Transactions for Mario's Game Shop

Date	Transaction	Details	Total Cost	Total Revenue
Jan. 1	Beginning inventory	100 units for $7 each	$ 700	
Apr. 25	Purchase	300 units for $9 each	2,700	
Jul. 17	Sale	300 units for $15 each		$ 4,500
Oct. 19	Purchase	600 units for $11 each	6,600	
Dec. 15	Sale	500 units for $15 each		7,500
	Totals		$10,000	$12,000

To make the distinction between the perpetual system and periodic system easier, let's look at side-by-side comparisons. The perpetual entries are repeated from those in the chapter.

INVENTORY PURCHASES AND SALES

The first transaction on April 25 involves the purchase of $2,700 of inventory on account. Under the periodic system, instead of debiting the Inventory account, we debit a Purchases account. Remember, we're not continually adjusting the Inventory account under the periodic method. We use the Purchases account to temporarily track increases in inventory.

Purchase inventory on account

Perpetual System			Periodic System		
Inventory	2,700		Purchases	2,700	
Accounts Payable		2,700	Accounts Payable		2,700

The transaction on July 17 involves the sale on account of 300 units of inventory for $4,500. We record that transaction as follows.

Perpetual System			Periodic System			
Accounts Receivable	4,500		Accounts Receivable	4,500		Sell inventory on account
Sales Revenue		4,500	Sales Revenue		4,500	
Cost of Goods Sold	2,500					
Inventory		2,500	No entry for cost of goods sold			

Notice that under the periodic system, we record the revenue earned, but we don't record the reduction in inventory or the increase in cost of goods sold at the time of the sale. Instead, we will record these at the end of the period.

The final two transactions are (1) the purchase of 600 additional units of inventory for $6,600 on account on October 19 and (2) the sale of 500 units for $7,500 on account on December 15.

Perpetual System			Periodic System			
Inventory	6,600		Purchases	6,600		Purchase inventory on account
Accounts Payable		6,600	Accounts Payable		6,600	

Perpetual System			Periodic System			
Accounts Receivable	7,500		Accounts Receivable	7,500		Sell inventory on account
Sales Revenue		7,500	Sales Revenue		7,500	
Cost of Goods Sold	5,300					
Inventory		5,300	No entry for cost of goods sold			

In addition to purchases and sales of inventory, we also looked at additional inventory transactions for Mario's Game Shop that related to freight charges, purchase discounts, and purchase returns:

1. On April 25, Mario pays freight charges of $300 for inventory purchased on April 25.
2. On April 30, Mario pays for the units purchased on April 25, less a 2% purchase discount.
3. On October 22, Mario returns 50 defective units from the October 19 purchase.

Next, let's compare the perpetual system and periodic system for these transactions.

FREIGHT CHARGES

Under the perpetual system discussed in the chapter, we saw that freight charges are included as an additional cost of inventory. Here we'll see that under the periodic system, we record these charges in a separate account called Freight-in. That account will later be closed in a period-end adjustment. For freight charges of $300 associated with the April 25 purchase, we record the following transaction.

Perpetual System			Periodic System			
Inventory	300		Freight-in	300		Pay freight-in charges
Cash		300	Cash		300	

PURCHASE DISCOUNTS AND RETURNS

Under the perpetual system, purchase discounts and purchase returns are recorded as a reduction in inventory cost. Under the periodic system, these transactions are recorded in separate accounts—Purchase Discounts and Purchase Returns. In the perpetual system, we credit purchase returns and purchase discounts to Inventory. The Purchase Returns and Purchase Discounts accounts used in the periodic system are referred to as *contra purchases accounts*.

For our examples in the chapter, Mario (1) makes payment on April 30 for inventory purchased on April 25 for $2,700, receiving a $54 discount and (2) returns 50 defective units on October 22 from the 600 units purchased on account on October 19 for $11 each.

Pay on account with a 2% purchase discount of $54

Perpetual System			Periodic System		
Accounts Payable	2,700		Accounts Payable	2,700	
Inventory		54	Purchase Discounts		54
Cash		2,646	Cash		2,646

Return inventory previously purchased on account

Perpetual System		Periodic System	
Accounts Payable	550	Accounts Payable	550
Inventory	550	Purchase Returns	550

PERIOD-END ADJUSTMENT

A period-end adjustment is needed only under the periodic system. The adjustment serves the following purposes:

1. Adjusts the balance of inventory to its proper ending balance.
2. Records the cost of goods sold for the period, to match inventory costs with the related sales revenue.
3. Closes (or zeros out) the temporary purchases accounts (Purchases, Freight-in, Purchase Discounts, and Purchase Returns).

Let's see what the period-end adjustment would look like for Mario's Game Shop using the transactions described in this appendix. In addition, recall that beginning inventory equals $700 (= 100 units × $7 unit cost) and ending inventory equals $1,650 (= 150 units × $11 unit cost).

Adjust inventory and cost of goods sold at the end of the period

Perpetual System	Periodic System		
No entry	Inventory (ending)	1,650	
	Cost of Goods Sold	8,046	
	Purchase Discounts	54	
	Purchase Returns	550	Temporary accounts closed
	Purchases		9,300
	Freight-In		300
	Inventory (beginning)		700

Notice that (1) the balance of Inventory is updated for its ending amount of $1,650, while its beginning balance of $700 is eliminated, (2) Cost of Goods Sold is recorded for $8,046, and (3) temporary accounts related to purchases are closed to zero.

If you look carefully, you may notice that the amount of cost of goods sold above calculated under the periodic system is the same as that calculated under the perpetual system (in Illustration 6–17). To see a detailed example of this, let's reexamine the first section of the multiple-step income statement, shown again in Illustration 6–24.

The periodic system and perpetual system will always produce the same amounts for cost of goods sold and inventory when the FIFO inventory method is used.

MARIO'S GAME SHOP
Multiple-Step Income Statement (partial)
For the year ended December 31, 2012

Sales revenue		$12,000
Cost of goods sold:		
Beginning inventory	$ 700	
Add: Purchases	9,300	
Freight-in	300	
Less: Purchase discounts	(54)	
Purchase returns	(550)	
Cost of goods available for sale	9,696	
Less: Ending inventory	(1,650)	
Cost of goods sold		8,046
Gross profit		$ 3,954

ILLUSTRATION 6–24

Calculation of Gross Profit in a Multiple-Step Income Statement

However, when using LIFO, the amounts for cost of goods sold and ending inventory may differ between the two systems. The reason for this difference is discussed further in more advanced accounting courses; it occurs because determining which "last" units of inventory are sold first occurs multiple times using a perpetual system but just once using a periodic system.

In practice, very few companies report inventory and cost of goods sold using the LIFO perpetual system. Instead, as discussed in Part B of the chapter, nearly all companies that report using LIFO maintain their own records on a FIFO basis and then adjust for the LIFO difference for preparing financial statements. **The inventory recording and reporting procedures discussed in Part B of the chapter reflect those used in actual practice.**

 KEY POINT

Using the periodic inventory system, we record purchases of inventory, freight-in, purchase returns, and purchase discounts to *temporary accounts* rather than directly to Inventory. These temporary accounts are closed in a period-end adjustment. In addition, at the time inventory is sold, we do not record a decrease in inventory sold; instead, we update the balance of Inventory in the period-end adjustment.

INVENTORY ERRORS

Nobody's perfect, and even accountants make mistakes. When we discover accounting errors, we always correct them. However, we don't always know when we've made an error. Errors can unknowingly occur in inventory amounts if there are mistakes in a physical count of inventory or in the pricing of inventory quantities.

APPENDIX B

■ **LO10**
Determine the financial statement effects of inventory errors.

EFFECTS IN THE CURRENT YEAR

To understand the effects of an inventory error in the financial statements, let's think again about the formula for cost of goods sold, shown in Illustration 6–25.

Beginning Inventory	
+ Purchases	
− Ending Inventory	Asset; Balance sheet
Cost of Goods Sold	Expense; Income statement

ILLUSTRATION 6–25

Calculation of Cost of Goods Sold

Notice that an error in calculating ending inventory (an asset in the balance sheet) causes an error in calculating cost of goods sold (an expense in the income statement). If cost of goods sold is misstated, gross profit will be misstated as well, but in the opposite direction. This is true because gross profit equals sales *minus* cost of goods sold. The effect of the inventory error in the current year is summarized in Illustration 6–26.

ILLUSTRATION 6–26

Summary of Effects of Inventory Error in the Current Year

Inventory Error	Ending Inventory	Cost of Goods Sold	Gross Profit
Overstate ending inventory	Overstate	Understate	Overstate
Understate ending inventory	Understate	Overstate	Understate

EFFECTS IN THE FOLLOWING YEAR

To understand the effects of a current-year inventory error on financial statements in the following year, remember that the amount of ending inventory this year is the amount of beginning inventory next year. An error in ending inventory this year will create an error in beginning inventory next year. This is demonstrated in Illustration 6–27.

ILLUSTRATION 6–27

Relationship between Cost of Goods Sold in the Current Year and the Following Year

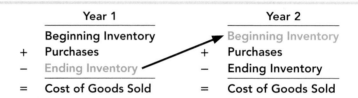

Notice that ending inventory is *subtracted* in calculating cost of goods sold in year 1 (the year of the inventory error). That same amount becomes beginning inventory in the following year and is *added* in calculating cost of goods sold. Because of this, **an error in calculating ending inventory in the current year will automatically affect cost of goods sold in the following year** *in the opposite direction.*

Consider a simple example to see how this works. Illustration 6–28 shows the correct inventory amounts for 2012 and 2013.

ILLUSTRATION 6–28

Correct Inventory Amounts

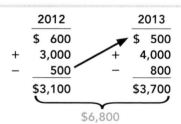

Now, assume the company mistakenly reports ending inventory in 2012 as $400, instead of $500. The effect of the mistake is shown in Illustration 6–29.

ILLUSTRATION 6–29

Incorrect Inventory Amounts

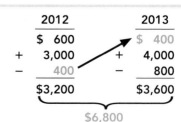

Notice three things: First, the amount reported for inventory is correct by the end of the second year, $800. This is true *even if the company had never discovered its inventory mistake* in 2012.

Second, the total amount reported for cost of goods sold over the two-year period from 2012 to 2013 is the same ($6,800) whether the error occurs or not. That's because the overstatement to cost of goods sold of $100 in 2012 is offset by an understatement of $100 in 2013. This also means that the inventory error affects gross profit in each of the two years, but the combined two-year gross profit amount is unaffected.

Third, if the combined two-year gross profit is correct, then retained earnings will also be correct by the end of 2013. Thus, the inventory error in 2012 has no effect on the accounting equation at the end of 2013. Assets (inventory) and stockholders' equity (retained earnings) are correctly stated.

 KEY POINT

In the current year, inventory errors affect the amounts reported for inventory and retained earnings in the balance sheet and amounts reported for cost of goods sold and gross profit in the income statement. At the end of the following year, the error has no effect on ending inventory or retained earnings but reverses for cost of goods sold and gross profit.

 ## KEY POINTS BY LEARNING OBJECTIVE

LO1 Trace the flow of inventory costs from manufacturing companies to merchandising companies.

Service companies earn revenues by providing services to customers. Manufacturing and merchandising companies earn revenues by selling inventory to customers.

LO2 Calculate cost of goods sold.

Inventory is a current asset reported in the balance sheet and represents the cost of inventory *not yet sold* at the end of the period. Cost of goods sold is an expense reported in the income statement and represents the cost of inventory *sold*.

LO3 Determine the cost of goods sold and ending inventory using different inventory cost methods.

Companies are allowed to report inventory costs by *assuming* which units of inventory are sold and not sold, even if this does not match the *actual* flow. The three major inventory cost flow assumptions are FIFO (first-in, first-out), LIFO (last-in, first-out), and weighted-average cost.

LO4 Explain the financial statement effects and tax effects of inventory cost flow assumptions.

Generally, FIFO more closely resembles the actual physical flow of inventory. When inventory costs are rising, FIFO results in higher reported inventory in the balance sheet and higher reported income in the income statement. Conversely, LIFO results in a lower reported inventory and net income, reducing the company's income tax obligation.

LO5 Record inventory transactions using a perpetual inventory system.

The perpetual inventory system maintains a continual—or *perpetual*—record of inventory purchased and sold. When companies *purchase* inventory using a perpetual inventory system, they increase the Inventory account and either decrease Cash or increase Accounts Payable. When companies *sell* inventory, they make two entries: (1) They increase an asset account (Cash or Accounts Receivable) and increase Sales Revenue, and (2) they increase Cost of Goods Sold and decrease Inventory.

Nearly all companies maintain their own inventory records on a FIFO basis, and then some prepare financial statements on a LIFO basis. To adjust their FIFO inventory records to LIFO for financial reporting, companies use a simple LIFO adjustment at the end of the period.

For most companies, freight charges are added to the cost of inventory, whereas purchase returns and purchase discounts are deducted from the cost of inventory. Some companies choose to report freight charges on outgoing shipments as part of selling expenses instead of cost of goods sold.

LO6 Prepare a multiple-step income statement.

A multiple-step income statement reports multiple levels of profitability. *Gross profit* equals sales revenue minus cost of goods sold. *Operating income* equals gross profit minus operating expenses. *Income before income taxes* equals operating income plus nonoperating revenues and minus nonoperating expenses. *Net income* equals all revenues minus all expenses.

LO7 Apply the lower-of-cost-or-market method for inventories.

We report inventory at the lower-of-cost-or-market; that is, at cost (specific identification, FIFO, LIFO, or weighted-average cost) or market value (replacement cost), whichever is lower. When market value falls below cost, we adjust downward the balance of inventory from cost to market value.

Analysis

LO8 Analyze management of inventory using the inventory turnover ratio and gross profit ratio.

The inventory turnover ratio indicates the number of times the firm sells, or turns over, its average inventory balance during a reporting period. The gross profit ratio measures the amount by which the sale price of inventory exceeds its cost per dollar of sales.

Appendixes

LO9 Record inventory transactions using a periodic inventory system.

Using the periodic inventory system, we record purchases of inventory, freight-in, purchase returns, and purchase discounts to *temporary accounts* rather than directly to Inventory. These temporary accounts are closed in a period-end adjustment. In addition, at the time inventory is sold, we do not record a decrease in inventory sold; instead, we update the balance of Inventory in the period-end adjustment.

LO10 Determine the financial statement effects of inventory errors.

In the current year, inventory errors affect the amounts reported for inventory and retained earnings in the balance sheet and amounts reported for cost of goods sold and gross profit in the income statement. At the end of the following year, the error has no effect on ending inventory or retained earnings but reverses for cost of goods sold and gross profit.

GLOSSARY

Average days in inventory: Approximate number of days the average inventory is held. It equals 365 days divided by the inventory turnover ratio. **p. 206**

Cost of goods sold: Cost of the inventory that was sold during the period. **p. 180**

Finished goods: Inventory items for which the manufacturing process is complete. **p. 181**

First-in, first-out method (FIFO): Inventory costing method that assumes the first units purchased (the first in) are the first ones sold (the first out). **p. 184**

Freight-in: Cost to transport inventory to the company, which is included as part of inventory cost. **p. 196**

Freight-out: Cost of freight on shipments to customers, which is included in the income statement either as part of cost of goods sold or as a selling expense. **p. 196**

Gross profit: The difference between sales revenue and cost of goods sold. **p. 200**

Gross profit ratio: Measure of the amount by which the sale price of inventory exceeds its cost per dollar of sales. It equals gross profit divided by net sales. **p. 207**

Income before income taxes: Operating income plus nonoperating revenues less nonoperating expenses. **p. 201**

Inventory: Items a company intends for sale to customers. **p. 180**

Inventory turnover ratio: The number of times a firm sells its average inventory balance during a reporting period. It equals cost of goods sold divided by average inventory. **p. 205**

Last-in, first-out method (LIFO): Inventory costing method that assumes the last units purchased (the last in) are the first ones sold (the first out). **p. 185**

LIFO adjustment: An adjustment used to convert a company's own inventory records maintained on a FIFO basis to LIFO basis for preparing financial statements. **p. 195**

LIFO conformity rule: IRS rule requiring a company that uses LIFO for tax reporting to also use LIFO for financial reporting. **p. 190**

Lower-of-cost-or-market (LCM) method: Method where companies report inventory in the balance sheet at the lower of cost or market value, where market value equals replacement cost. **p. 202**

Multiple-step income statement: An income statement that reports *multiple* levels of income (or profitability). **p. 200**

Net income: Difference between all revenues and all expenses for the period. **p. 201**

Operating income: Profitability from normal operations that equals gross profit less operating expenses. **p. 201**

Periodic inventory system: Inventory system that periodically adjusts for purchases and sales of inventory at the end of the reporting period based on a physical count of inventory on hand. **p. 192**

Perpetual inventory system: Inventory system that maintains a continual record of inventory purchased and sold. **p. 192**

Raw materials: Components that will become part of the finished product but have not yet been used in production. **p. 181**

Replacement cost: The cost to replace an inventory item in its identical form. **p. 202**

Specific identification method: Inventory costing method that matches or identifies each unit of inventory with its actual cost. **p. 184**

Weighted-average cost method: Inventory costing method that assumes both cost of goods sold and ending inventory consist of a random mixture of all the goods available for sale. **p. 186**

Work-in-process: Products that have started the production process but are not yet complete at the end of the period. **p. 181**

SELF-STUDY QUESTIONS

1. Which of following companies earn revenues by selling inventory?   ■ LO1
   a. Service companies.
   b. Manufacturing companies.
   c. Merchandising companies.
   d. Both manufacturing and merchandising companies.

2. At the beginning of the year, Bennett Supply has inventory of $3,500. During the   ■ LO2
   year, the company purchases an additional $12,000 of inventory. An inventory count
   at the end of the year reveals remaining inventory of $4,000. What amount will
   Bennett report for cost of goods sold?
   a. $11,000.
   b. $11,500.
   c. $12,000.
   d. $12,500.

3. Madison Outlet has the following inventory transactions for the year: ■ LO3

Date	Transaction	Number of Units	Unit Cost	Total Cost
Jan. 1	Beginning inventory	10	$200	$2,000
Mar. 14	Purchase	15	300	4,500
				$6,500
Jan. 1–Dec. 31	Total sales to customers	12		

What amount would Madison report for *cost of goods sold* using FIFO?
   a. $2,600.
   b. $2,900.
   c. $3,600.
   d. $3,900.

4. Which inventory cost flow assumption generally results in the lowest reported   ■ LO4
   amount for cost of goods sold when inventory costs are rising?
   a. Lower-of-cost-or-market.
   b. First-in, first-out (FIFO).
   c. Last-in, first-out (LIFO).
   d. Weighted-average cost.

5. Using a *perpetual* inventory system, the purchase of inventory on account would be   ■ LO5
   recorded as:
   a. Debit Cost of Goods Sold; credit Inventory.
   b. Debit Inventory; credit Sales Revenue.

c. Debit Purchases; credit Accounts Payable.

d. Debit Inventory; credit Accounts Payable.

■ LO6

6. Which of the following levels of profitability in a multiple-step income statement represents revenues from the sale of inventory less the cost of that inventory?

a. Gross profit.

b. Operating income.

c. Income before income taxes.

d. Net income.

■ LO7

7. At the end of a reporting period, Maxwell Corporation determines that its ending inventory has a cost of $1,000 and a market value of $800. What would be the effect(s) of the adjustment to write down inventory to market value?

a. Decrease total assets.

b. Decrease net income.

c. Decrease retained earnings.

d. All of the above.

■ LO8

8. For the year, Simmons Incorporated reports net sales of $100,000, cost of goods sold of $80,000, and an average inventory balance of $40,000. What is Simmons' gross profit ratio?

a. 20%.

b. 25%.

c. 40%.

d. 50%.

■ LO9

9. Using a *periodic* inventory system, the purchase of inventory on account would be recorded as:

a. Debit Cost of Goods Sold; credit Inventory.

b. Debit Inventory; credit Sales Revenue.

c. Debit Purchases; credit Accounts Payable.

d. Debit Inventory; credit Accounts Payable.

■ LO10

10. Suppose Ajax Corporation overstates its ending inventory amount. What effect will this have on the reported amount of cost of goods sold in the year of the error?

a. Overstate cost of goods sold.

b. Understate cost of goods sold.

c. Have no effect on cost of goods sold.

d. Not possible to determine with information given.

Answers to the Self-Study Questions

1. d   2. b   3. a   4. b   5. d   6. a   7. d   8. a   9. c   10. b

REVIEW QUESTIONS

■ LO1

1. What is inventory? Where in the financial statements is inventory reported?

■ LO1

2. What is the primary distinction between a service company and a manufacturing or merchandising company?

■ LO1

3. What is the difference among raw materials inventory, work-in-process inventory, and finished goods inventory?

■ LO2

4. Define the cost of goods available for sale. How does it relate to cost of goods sold and ending inventory?

■ LO2

5. For a company like **Radio Shack**, what does the balance of Cost of Goods Sold in the income statement represent? What does the balance of Inventory in the balance sheet represent?

6. Cheryl believes that companies report cost of goods sold and ending inventory based on *actual* units sold and not sold. Her accounting instructor explains that most companies account for cost of goods sold and ending inventory based on *assumed* units sold and not sold. Help her understand why companies are allowed to do this.   ■ **LO3**

7. What are the three primary cost flow assumptions? How does the specific identification method differ from these three primary cost flow assumptions?   ■ **LO3**

8. Which cost flow assumption generally results in the highest reported amount for ending inventory when inventory costs are rising? Explain.   ■ **LO4**

9. Which cost flow assumption generally results in the highest reported amount of net income when inventory costs are rising? Explain.   ■ **LO4**

10. What does it mean that FIFO has a balance-sheet focus and LIFO has an income-statement focus?   ■ **LO4**

11. Explain how LIFO generally results in lower income taxes payable when inventory costs are increasing. What is the LIFO conformity rule?   ■ **LO4**

12. What is the difference between the *timing* of recording inventory transactions under the perpetual and periodic inventory systems?   ■ **LO5**

13. Explain how freight charges, purchase returns, and purchase discounts affect the cost of inventory.   ■ **LO5**

14. What is a multiple-step income statement? What information does it provide beyond "bottom-line" net income?   ■ **LO6**

15. Explain the lower-of-cost-or-market method of reporting inventory.   ■ **LO7**

16. How is cost determined under the lower-of-cost-or-market method? How is market value determined for this purpose?   ■ **LO7**

17. Describe the entry to adjust from cost to market for inventory write-downs. What effects does this adjustment have on (a) assets, (b) liabilities, (c) stockholders' equity (or retained earnings), (d) revenues, (e) expenses, and (f) net income?   ■ **LO7**

18. What is meant by the assertion that the lower-of-cost-or-market method is an example of conservatism in accounting?   ■ **LO7**

19. What is the inventory turnover ratio? What is it designed to measure?   ■ **LO8**

20. How is gross profit calculated? What is the gross profit ratio? What is it designed to measure?   ■ **LO8**

21. Explain how the sale of inventory on account is recorded under a periodic system. How does this differ from the recording under a perpetual system?   ■ **LO9**

22. What are the purposes of the period-end adjustment under the periodic inventory system?   ■ **LO9**

23. Jeff is the new inventory manager for Alan Company. During the year-end inventory count, Jeff forgets that the company stores additional inventory in a back room, causing his final ending inventory count to be understated. Explain what effect this error will have on the reported amounts for (a) assets, (b) liabilities, (c) stockholders' equity (or retained earnings), (d) revenues, (e) expenses, and (f) net income in the current year.   ■ **LO10**

24. Refer to the inventory error in *Question* 23. Explain what effect Jeff's error will have on reported amounts at the end of the following year, assuming the mistake is not corrected and no further mistakes are made.   ■ **LO10**

For the following, please visit your instructor's *Connect* site.

BRIEF EXERCISES	1-22
EXERCISES	1-20
PROBLEMS: SET A	1-10
PROBLEMS: SET B	1-10
GREAT ADVENTURES	

Note: Additional Perspectives assignments for Financial Analysis, Comparative Analysis, Internet Research, Written Communication, and Earnings Management are in Appendix F at the end of this book. For additional Exercises: Set B and for additional Problems: Set C, visit www.mhhe.com/spicelandMTC1e.

Long-Term Assets

AFTER STUDYING THIS CHAPTER, YOU SHOULD BE ABLE TO:

- **LO1** Identify and record the major types of property, plant, and equipment.
- **LO2** Identify and record the major types of intangible assets.
- **LO3** Discuss the accounting treatment of expenditures after acquisition.
- **LO4** Calculate depreciation of property, plant, and equipment.
- **LO5** Calculate amortization of intangible assets.
- **LO6** Account for the disposal of long-term assets.

Analysis

- **LO7** Describe the relationship among return on assets, profit margin, and asset turnover.

Appendix

- **LO8** Identify impairment situations and describe the two-step impairment process.

WORLDCOM: **EXPENSES CALLED ASSETS**

WorldCom was the parent company of **MCI** and recognized as the leading telecommunications company in North America. Then in 2002, a routine internal audit uncovered massive accounting fraud. The firm had recorded assets in the balance sheet that should have been recorded as *expenses* in the income statement. Although this kind of fraudulent reporting was not new, the sheer volume of the fraud set new records. By failing to record expenses, WorldCom overstated its income and assets by about $11 billion (not $11 million, but $11 *billion!*). Estimates of investor losses from the resulting bankruptcy exceeded $100 billion.

How was the fraud accomplished? When WorldCom used the telecommunication lines of another company, it paid a fee. This fee is part of normal operating costs, and it should have been recorded as an expense of the current period, to properly match the expense with the revenues it helped to generate. Instead, WorldCom recorded these operating expenses as long-term assets in the balance sheet. Failure to report these operating expenses caused net income to be overstated by billions; operating expenses were purposely misstated as assets.

What motivated WorldCom's management to commit this fraud? It appears the intention was to hide operating losses and maintain a strong stock price. If investors had known the true operating performance of WorldCom, the stock price would have tumbled.

For his role in the accounting scandal that led to the largest bankruptcy in U.S. history, Bernard Ebbers, the 63-year-old CEO of WorldCom, was sentenced to 25 years in a low-security federal prison.[1] Ebbers, who took the stand in his own defense, insisted that he knew nothing of WorldCom's fraudulent accounting, but had left the accounting to Scott Sullivan, the company's former chief financial officer (CFO). The jury did not buy Ebbers's hands-off defense. They concluded that the CEO, as head of the company, is ultimately responsible for the firm's accounting.

[1]J. Sandberg, D. Solomon, and R. Blumenstein. "Inside WorldCom's Unearthing of a Vast Accounting Scandal." *The Wall Street Journal* (June 27, 2002); K. Eichenwald and S. Romero. "Inquiry Finds Effort to Delay at WorldCom." *The New York Times* (July 4, 2002); K. Crawford. "Ex-WorldCom CEO Ebbers Guilty." *CNNMoney.com* (March 15, 2005); and "Bernard Ebbers Given 25-year Prison Sentence." CBC News (July 13, 2005).

Winnebago cannot make campers without its manufacturing facilities and the equipment in those facilities. In contrast, it's not physical assets, but copyrights on its computer software that give **Google** the ability to generate billions of dollars in revenue each year. Both of these types of revenue-producing assets are considered *long-term assets,* the topic of this chapter.

We classify long-term assets into two major categories:

Common Terms Tangible assets are also called *property, plant, and equipment; plant assets;* or *fixed assets.*

1. **Tangible assets.** Assets in this category include land, land improvements, buildings, equipment, and natural resources. Winnebago's land, buildings, and equipment fall into this category.

2. **Intangible assets.** Assets in this category include patents, trademarks, copyrights, franchises, and goodwill. We distinguish these assets from property, plant, and equipment by their lack of physical substance. The evidence of their existence often is based on a legal contract. Google's copyrights are intangible assets.

Long-term assets often represent a significant portion of the total assets of a company. Illustration 7–1 presents a breakdown of the total assets for **Darden Restaurants**, a publicly traded company that owns and operates restaurant chains such as Red Lobster, Olive Garden, and Longhorn Steakhouse. Notice that current assets represent only about 11% of total assets, and long-term assets make up the remaining 89%. Accounting for long-term assets, both tangible (property, plant, and equipment) and intangible, is important and is the primary focus in this chapter.

ILLUSTRATION 7–1

Balance Sheet for Darden Restaurants

DARDEN RESTAURANTS Balance Sheet (partial) May 31, 2009 and 2008 ($ in thousands)		
	2009	**2008**
Cash	$ 62,900	$ 43,200
Receivables	147,500	161,300
Inventory	247,000	216,700
Other current assets	97,400	46,700
Total current assets	554,800	467,900
Property, plant, and equipment	3,306,700	3,066,000
Intangible assets	1,058,200	1,040,800
Other long-term assets and investments	105,500	155,900
Total assets	$5,025,200	$4,730,600

To properly report both tangible and intangible assets, we need to address a variety of issues including (1) which amounts to include in their cost, (2) how to expense their costs while using them, and (3) how to record their sale or disposal at the end of their useful life. These three are the basis for the three major parts of the chapter.

PART A

ACQUISITIONS

The first issue to consider in accounting for long-term assets is how to identify them and measure their costs. To do this, we need to understand the major types of tangible and intangible assets. We begin with tangible assets, also referred to as property, plant, and equipment.

Property, Plant, and Equipment

The property, plant, and equipment category consists of land, land improvements, buildings, equipment, and natural resources. The general rule for recording all such long-term assets can be stated rather simply: **We record a long-term asset at its cost *plus* all expenditures necessary to get the asset ready for use.** Thus, the initial cost of a long-term asset might be more than just its purchase price; it also will include any additional amounts the firm paid to bring the asset to its desired condition and location for use. We use the term capitalize to describe recording an expenditure as an asset.

When we make an expenditure, we have the choice of recording it as an expense of the current period or recording it as an asset and then allocating that cost as an expense over future periods. The choice depends on when the company benefits from having the asset: in the current period or over future periods. Determining which costs to record as expenses and which to record as long-term assets is crucial. Several infamous accounting frauds were the result of inflating net income by improperly recording current expenses as long-term assets.

We look at the proper recording of land, land improvements, buildings, basket purchases, equipment, and natural resources next.

■ **LO1**
Identify and record the major types of property, plant, and equipment.

LAND

The Land account represents land a company is using in its operations. (In contrast, land purchased for investment purposes is recorded in a separate investment account.) We capitalize to Land all expenditures necessary to get the land ready for its intended use.

Such capitalized costs include the purchase price of the land plus closing costs such as fees for the attorney, real estate agent commissions, title, title search, and recording fees. If the property is subject to back taxes or other obligations, we include these amounts as well. In fact, any additional expenditure such as clearing, filling, and draining the land, or even removing old buildings to prepare the land for its intended use, become part of the land's capitalized cost. If we receive any cash from selling salvaged materials from old buildings torn down, we reduce the cost of land by that amount.

Assume, for instance, that Kyoto's Sushi Bar purchases a two-acre tract of land and an existing building for $500,000. The company plans to remove the old building and construct a new restaurant on the site. In addition to the purchase price, the company pays a sales commission of $30,000 to the real estate agent and title insurance of $3,000. Kyoto also pays $8,000 in property taxes, which includes $6,000 of back taxes (unpaid taxes from previous years) paid by Kyoto on behalf of the seller and $2,000 due for the current fiscal year after the purchase date. Shortly after closing, the company pays a contractor $50,000 to tear down the old building and remove it from the site. Kyoto is able to sell salvaged materials from the old building for $5,000 and pays an additional $6,000 to level the land.

Using the guideline of **cost *plus* all expenditures necessary to get the asset ready for use,** at what amount should Kyoto record as the cost of the land? Illustration 7–2 (next page) shows the computation for the cost of Kyoto's land.

You may wonder why Kyoto recorded only $6,000 for property taxes. That was the amount required to get the asset ready for use—Kyoto could not use the land until it paid the back taxes. The additional $2,000 in property taxes, though, relates only to the current period, and so Kyoto records that amount as an expense in the current period. All of the other costs, including the $6,000 in back property taxes, are necessary to acquire the land, so Kyoto capitalizes them. Note that the salvaged materials that were sold for $5,000 reduce the overall cost of the land.

ILLUSTRATION 7–2

Computation of the
Cost of Land

Purchase price of land (and building to be removed)	$500,000
Commissions	30,000
Back property taxes	6,000
Title insurance	3,000
Cost of removing old building	50,000
Less: Salvaged materials from old building	(5,000)
Cost of leveling the land	6,000
Total cost	$590,000

COMMON MISTAKE

Many students incorrectly add or ignore the cash received from the sale of salvaged materials. Cash received from the sale of salvaged materials *reduces* the total cost of land.

LAND IMPROVEMENTS

Beyond the cost of the land, Kyoto likely will spend additional amounts to improve the land by adding a parking lot, sidewalks, driveways, landscaping, lighting systems, fences, sprinklers, and similar additions. These are land improvements.

In Chapter 3, we briefly discussed *depreciation* as the process of allocating the cost of an asset over its life. We will discuss depreciation in detail later in this chapter. When we do so, you will discover that land is an asset we do not depreciate because its life is indefinite. However, we do depreciate land improvements. For example, the paved parking lot Kyoto adds to its new property will eventually deteriorate and be replaced. Because land improvements have limited lives, we record them separately from the land itself.

BUILDINGS

Buildings include administrative offices, retail stores, manufacturing facilities, and storage warehouses. The cost of acquiring a building usually includes realtor commissions and legal fees in addition to the purchase price. The new owner sometimes needs to remodel or otherwise modify the building to suit its needs. These additional costs are part of the building's acquisition cost.

Unique accounting issues arise when a firm constructs a building rather than purchasing it. Of course the cost of construction includes architect fees, material costs, and construction labor. New building construction likely also includes costs such as officer supervision, overhead (costs indirectly related to the construction), and capitalized interest.

Capitalized interest refers to interest costs we add to the asset account rather than recording them as interest expense. In keeping with the idea that the cost of an asset includes *all* costs of making the asset ready for its intended use, if a company borrows money to finance the construction of an asset, the interest paid to borrow the funds logically is part of the asset's cost. Capitalizing interest also is in keeping with the *matching principle*. The matching principle states that expenses are to be matched with (included on the same income statement as) the revenues they help to create. During construction of a building, no revenues are created. Revenues won't be created until after the asset is fully constructed and placed into service. Therefore, interest represents a cost similar to materials, labor, and overhead necessary in preparing an asset for use.

EQUIPMENT

Equipment is a broad term that includes machinery used in manufacturing, computers and other office equipment, vehicles, furniture, and fixtures. The cost of equipment is the actual purchase price plus all other costs necessary to prepare the asset for use. These can be any of a variety of other costs including sales tax, shipping, delivery insurance, assembly, installation, testing, and even legal fees incurred to establish title.

What about recurring costs related to equipment, such as annual property insurance and annual property taxes on vehicles? Rather than including recurring costs as part of the cost of the equipment, we expense them as we incur them, in order to properly match them with revenues generated during the same period. The question to ask yourself when deciding whether to add a cost to the asset account or record it as an expense of the current period is, *"Is this a cost of acquiring this asset and getting it ready for use, or is it a recurring cost that benefits the company in the current period?"*

Assume now that Kyoto's Sushi Bar purchases new restaurant equipment for $82,000 plus $6,500 in sales tax. Kyoto pays a freight company $800 to transport the equipment and $200 shipping insurance. The firm also pays $1,600 for one year of liability insurance on the equipment in advance. The equipment was also installed at an additional cost of $1,500. Illustration 7–3 shows the calculation of the amount at which Kyoto should record the cost of the equipment.

Purchase price	$82,000	**ILLUSTRATION 7–3**
Sales tax	6,500	Computation of the
Transportation	800	Cost of Equipment
Shipping insurance	200	
Installation	1,500	
Total cost	$91,000	

Thus, Kyoto should record the equipment at a total cost of $91,000. With the exception of the $1,600 annual insurance on the equipment, each of the expenditures described was necessary to bring the equipment to its condition and location for use. Kyoto will report the $1,600 insurance amount as insurance expense over the first year of coverage.

BASKET PURCHASES

Sometimes companies purchase more than one asset at the same time for one purchase price. This is known as a basket purchase. For example, assume Kyoto purchases land, building, and equipment together for $900,000. How much should we record in the separate accounts for the land, the building, and the equipment? The simple answer is that we allocate the total purchase price of $900,000 based on the estimated fair values of each of the individual assets.

The difficulty, though, is that the estimated fair values of the individual assets often exceed the total purchase price, in this case, $900,000. Let's say the estimated fair values of the land, buildings, and equipment are $200,000, $700,000, and $100,000, respectively, for a total estimated fair value of $1 million. In that case, Kyoto's total purchase of $900,000 will be allocated to the separate accounts for Land, Building, and Equipment based on their relative fair values as shown in Illustration 7–4.

	Estimated Fair Value	Allocation Percentage		Amount of Basket Purchase	Recorded Amount	
Land	$ 200,000	$200,000/$1,000,000 = 20%	×	$900,000	$180,000	**ILLUSTRATION 7–4**
Building	700,000	$700,000/$1,000,000 = 70%	×	$900,000	630,000	Allocation of Cost in a Basket Purchase
Equipment	100,000	$100,000/$1,000,000 = 10%	×	$900,000	90,000	
Total	$1,000,000				$900,000	

NATURAL RESOURCES

In addition to land, buildings, and equipment, many companies depend heavily on natural resources, such as oil, natural gas, timber, and even salt. **ExxonMobil**, for example, maintains oil and natural gas deposits on six of the world's seven continents. **Weyerhaeuser** is one of the largest pulp and paper companies in the world with major investments in soft timber forests. Even salt is a natural resource, with the largest supply in the United States mined directly under the Great Lakes of North America.

We can distinguish natural resources from other property, plant, and equipment by the fact that we can physically use up, or *deplete,* natural resources. ExxonMobil's oil reserves are a natural resource that decreases as the firm extracts oil. Similarly, timber is used extensively to provide materials in the construction industry. Salt is used as a food additive and to melt icy roads in the winter.

A primary concern with regard to natural resources is sustainability. A common definition of sustainability is "meeting the needs of the present without compromising the ability of future generations to meet their own needs." The oil and gas industry is developing new sources of energy based on solar, wind, and hydro power. Another example is the timber industry, in which companies plant three new trees for every tree cut down. Companies need to find ways of replenishing the natural resources used so that we do not leave future generations without these valuable resources.

 KEY POINT

Tangible assets include land, land improvements, buildings, equipment, and natural resources.

Intangible Assets

■ LO2
Identify and record the major types of intangible assets.

The other major category of long-term assets, intangible assets, have no physical substance. Assets in this category include patents, trademarks, copyrights, franchises, and goodwill.

Despite their lack of physical substance, intangible assets can be very valuable indeed. One of the most valuable intangible assets for many companies is their trademark or brand. *BusinessWeek* publishes an annual list of the 100 most valuable brands. Illustration 7–5 summarizes the top 10 most valuable brands in 2009. As you can see, the **Coca-Cola** brand has an estimated value of $68.7 billion. Despite this value, Coca-Cola reports trademarks on its balance sheet at only $2 billion. Later, we'll see why many intangible assets are *not* recorded on the balance sheet at their estimated values.

ILLUSTRATION 7–5

World's Top 10 Brands

Rank	Company	Country	Estimated Value
1	Coca-Cola	United States	$68.7 billion
2	IBM	United States	60.2 billion
3	Microsoft	United States	56.6 billion
4	GE	United States	47.8 billion
5	Nokia	Finland	34.9 billion
6	McDonald's	United States	32.3 billion
7	Google	United States	32.0 billion
8	Toyota	Japan	31.3 billion
9	Intel	United States	30.6 billion
10	Disney	United States	28.4 billion

Source: *BusinessWeek* (September 2009), *http://businessweek.com/go/brand/.*

Companies acquire intangible assets in two ways: (1) They *purchase* intangible assets like patents, copyrights, trademarks, or franchise rights from other entities, or (2) they *create* intangible assets internally, by developing a new product or process and obtaining a protective patent. The reporting rules for intangible assets vary depending on whether the company purchased or acquired the asset.

Reporting *purchased* intangibles is similar to reporting purchased property, plant, and equipment. **We record purchased intangible assets at their original cost plus all other costs, such as legal and filing fees, necessary to get the asset ready for use.** Filing fees include items such as the fee to record a copyright with the U.S. Copyright Office or the various fees to record a patent with the U.S. Patent and Trademark Office.

Reporting intangible assets that are *developed internally* is quite different. Rather than recording these on the balance sheet as intangible assets, **we expense to the income statement most of the costs for internally developed intangible assets as we incur those costs.** For example, the research and development (R&D) costs incurred in developing a patent internally are not recorded as an intangible asset in the balance sheet. Instead, they are expensed directly in the income statement. The reason we expense all R&D costs is the difficulty in determining the portion of R&D that benefits future periods. Conceptually, we should record as an intangible asset the portion that benefits future periods. Due to the difficulties in arriving at this estimate, current U.S. accounting rules require firms to expense all R&D costs as incurred.

INTERNATIONAL FINANCIAL REPORTING STANDARDS (IFRS)

International accounting standards differ from U.S. accounting standards in the treatment of R&D costs. U.S. GAAP requires that we expense all research and development expenditures in the period incurred. IFRS makes a distinction between *research* activities and *development* activities. Under IFRS, research expenditures are expensed in the period incurred, consistent with U.S. GAAP. However, development costs that benefit future periods can be recorded as an intangible asset.

For more discussion, see Appendix E.

A similar argument about the difficulty of estimating benefits in future periods can be made for advertising expenses. Advertising at **Coca-Cola** clearly has made its trademark more valuable. Because we cannot tell what portion of today's advertising benefits future periods and how many periods it might benefit, advertising costs are not recorded as an intangible asset on the balance sheet. Instead, advertising costs are recorded as expenses in the income statement.

KEY POINT

We record (capitalize) purchased intangible assets at their purchase price plus all costs necessary to get the asset ready for use. We expense internally generated intangible assets, such as R&D and advertising costs, as we incur them.

Let's look in more detail at how we report specific types of intangible assets.

PATENTS

A patent is an exclusive right to manufacture a product or to use a process. The U.S. Patent and Trademark Office grants this right for a period of 20 years. When a firm *purchases* a patent, it records the patent at its purchase price plus such other costs as legal and filing fees to secure the patent.

In contrast, when a firm *develops a patent internally*, it expenses the research and development costs as it incurs them. An exception to this rule is legal fees. The firm will record in the Patent asset account the legal and filing fees to secure the patent, even if it developed the patented item or process internally.

Holders of patents often need to defend their exclusive rights in court. For example, The **J.M. Smucker Company** obtained a patent on a round, crustless, frozen peanut butter and jelly sandwich sealed in an airtight foil wrapper, marketed under the name "Uncrustables." Smucker's later had to defend its patent by attempting to stop another company from making similar sandwiches. The costs of successfully defending a patent, including attorneys' fees, are added to the Patent account.

COPYRIGHTS

A copyright is an exclusive right of protection given by the U.S. Copyright Office to the creator of a published work such as a song, film, painting, photograph, book, or computer software. Copyrights are protected by law and give the creator (and his or her heirs) the exclusive right to reproduce and sell the artistic or published work for the life of the creator plus 70 years. A copyright also allows the copyright holder to pursue legal action against anyone who attempts to infringe the copyright. Accounting for the costs of copyrights is virtually identical to that of patents.

TRADEMARKS

A trademark, like the name **Coca-Cola**, is a word, slogan, or symbol that distinctively identifies a company, product, or service. The firm can register its trademark with the U.S. Patent and Trademark Office to protect it from use by others for a period of 10 years. The registration can be renewed for an indefinite number of 10-year periods, so a trademark is an example of an intangible asset whose useful life can be indefinite.

Firms often acquire trademarks through acquisition. As an example, **Hewlett-Packard (HP)** acquired all the outstanding stock of **Compaq Computer Corporation** for $24 billion, of which $1.4 billion was assigned to the Compaq trademark.

Advertising costs can factor into the cost of a trademark in a big way. For example, **Subway** aired a series of commercials featuring Jared Fogle, a student at Indiana University who lost 245 pounds eating Subway sandwiches. Certainly these ads benefited Subway. But what was the value to the company of the advertising? And for how many years will Subway receive that value? These are difficult questions. Thus, when a firm develops a trademark internally through advertising, it doesn't record the advertising costs as part of the cost of the intangible asset. Instead, it expenses the advertising costs in the income statement. Even though some advertising costs meet the definition of an asset by providing future benefits, due to the difficulty in estimating these amounts, financial accounting rules require advertising costs to be expensed as incurred.

A firm can record attorney fees, registration fees, design costs, successful legal defense, and other costs directly related to securing the trademark as an intangible asset in the Trademark asset account. This is how Coca-Cola can have a trademark valued at $67 billion, but reported in the balance sheet at only $2 billion. The estimated value of the trademark is not recorded on the balance sheet; instead, only the legal, registration, and design fees are recorded. The advertising costs that create value for the trademark are recorded as advertising expense.

FRANCHISES

The last time you ordered a sandwich at Subway, you probably dealt with a franchise. Many popular retail businesses such as restaurants, auto dealerships, and hotels are set up as franchises. These are local outlets that pay for the exclusive right to use the franchisor company's name and to sell its products within a specified geographical area. Many franchisors provide other benefits to the franchisee,

Names can lose their trademarked status if their owners fail to prevent improper use by others. All of the following were once valuable trademarks in the United States: *aspirin, escalator, cellophane, zipper, shredded wheat, corn flakes,* and *kerosene.*

such as participating in the construction of the retail outlet, training employees, and purchasing national advertising.

To record the cost of a franchise, the franchisee records the initial fee as an intangible asset and then expenses that cost over the life of the franchise agreement. Additional periodic payments to the franchisor usually are for services the franchisor provides on a continuing basis, and the franchisee will expense them as incurred.

GOODWILL

Goodwill often is the largest, yet the most confusing, intangible asset recorded in the balance sheet. While most long-term assets, even intangible ones, can be separated from the company and sold individually, goodwill cannot. Goodwill represents the value of a company as a whole, over and above the value of its identifiable net assets. That value can emerge from a company's reputation, its trained employees and management team, its favorable business location, and any other unique features of the company that we are unable to associate with a specific asset.

We record goodwill as an intangible asset in the balance sheet *only* when we purchase it as part of the acquisition of another company. In this case, the acquiring company records goodwill equal to the purchase price less the fair value of the net assets acquired. The fair value of the net assets is equal to the value of all identifiable assets acquired, minus the value of all liabilities assumed.

To see how this works, assume that Enriched White Bread Company (EWB) acquires Whole Wheat Bread Company (WWB) by paying $36 million in cash. The fair values of all identifiable assets acquired are as follows ($ in millions):

Receivables	$10
Inventory	14
Property, plant, and equipment	18
Patent	8
Total	$50

In the purchase, EWB also assumes all of WWB's long-term debt, which has a fair value of $24 million at the date of acquisition. Illustration 7–6 shows how to calculate the amount EWB would report as goodwill ($10 million).

($ in millions)		
Purchase price		$36
Less:		
Fair value of assets acquired	$ 50	
Less: Fair value of liabilities assumed	(24)	
Fair value of identifiable net assets		(26)
Goodwill		$10

ILLUSTRATION 7–6

Business Acquisition with Goodwill

EWB records the acquisition as follows:

	Debit	Credit	A	=	L	+	SE
Receivables (at fair value)	10		+10				
Inventory (at fair value)	14		+14				
Property, Plant, and Equipment (at fair value)	18		+18				
Patent (at fair value)	8		+8				
Goodwill (remaining purchase price)	10		+10				
Long-Term Debt (at fair value)		24			+24		
Cash (at purchase price)		36	−36				
(*Acquire Whole Wheat Bread Company*)							

Most companies also create goodwill to some extent through advertising, training, and other efforts. However, as it does for other internally generated intangibles, a company must *expense* any costs it incurs in the internal generation of goodwill. Imagine how difficult it would be to estimate the amount and future benefits of internally generated goodwill. Due to this difficulty, we record goodwill only when it is acquired as part of the purchase of another business.

 KEY POINT

Intangible assets include patents, copyrights, trademarks, franchises, and goodwill.

Expenditures after Acquisition

■ LO3
Discuss the accounting treatment of expenditures after acquisition.

Over the life of a long-term asset, the owners often incur additional expenditures for repairs and maintenance, additions, improvements, or litigation costs. We credit these costs to Cash or perhaps to Accounts Payable or Notes Payable, but what account do we debit? As with any other expenditure, the choice is to debit either an asset or an expense. Recall that an asset is a probable future benefit. **We capitalize an expenditure as an asset if it increases future benefits. We expense an expenditure if it benefits only the current period.** To see the choice more clearly, let's look at repairs and maintenance, additions, improvements, and litigation costs in more detail.

REPAIRS AND MAINTENANCE

The cost of an engine tune-up or the repair of an engine part for a delivery truck allows the truck to continue its productive activity. We expense repairs and maintenance expenditures like these because they maintain a given level of benefits in the period incurred. We capitalize as assets more extensive repairs that *increase* the future benefits of the delivery truck, such as a new transmission or an engine overhaul.

ADDITIONS

An addition occurs when we add a new major component to an existing asset. We should capitalize the cost of additions because they increase, rather than maintain, the future benefits from the expenditure. For example, adding a refrigeration unit to a delivery truck increases the capability of the truck beyond that originally anticipated, thus increasing its future benefits.

IMPROVEMENTS

An improvement is the cost of replacing a major component of an asset. The replacement can be a new component with the same characteristics as the old component, or a new component with enhanced operating capabilities. For example, we could replace an existing refrigeration unit in a delivery truck with a new but similar unit or with a new and improved refrigeration unit. In either case, the cost of the improvement usually increases future benefits, and we should capitalize it to the Equipment account.

LEGAL DEFENSE OF INTANGIBLE ASSETS

The expenditures after acquisition mentioned so far—repairs and maintenance, additions, and improvements—generally relate to property, plant, and equipment. Intangible assets, though, also can require expenditures after their acquisition, the most frequent being the cost of legally defending the right that gives the asset its value. For example, when The J.M. Smucker Company attempted to prevent another company from copying its peanut butter and jelly sandwich patent, it incurred legal costs. If a firm successfully defends an intangible right, it should capitalize the litigation costs and amortize them over the remaining useful life of the related intangible. However, if the defense of an intangible right is unsuccessful, then the firm should expense the litigation costs as incurred because they provide no future benefit.

MATERIALITY

Materiality relates to the size of an item that is likely to influence a decision. An item is said to be material if it is large enough to influence a decision. Materiality is an important consideration in the "capitalize versus expense" decision. There often are practical problems in capitalizing small expenditures. For example, a stapler may have a 20-year service life, but it would not be practical to capitalize and then allocate that small of a cost to expense over 20 years. Companies generally expense all costs under a certain dollar amount, say $1,000, regardless of whether future benefits are increased. It's important for a company to establish a policy for treating these expenditures and apply the policy consistently.

Illustration 7–7 provides a summary of expenditures after acquisition.

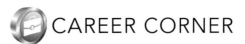
Type of Expenditure	Definition	Period Benefited	Usual Accounting Treatment
Repairs and maintenance	Maintaining a given level of benefits	Current	Expense
Repairs and maintenance	Making major repairs that increase future benefits	Future	Capitalize
Additions	Adding a new major component	Future	Capitalize
Improvements	Replacing a major component	Future	Capitalize
Legal defense of intangible assets	Incurring litigation costs to defend the legal right to the asset	Future	Capitalize (Expense if defense is unsuccessful)

ILLUSTRATION 7–7

Expenditures after Acquisition

spiceland.mhhe.com/c19

KEY POINT

Capital expenditures (recorded as assets) benefit *future* periods. Expenses typically benefit only the *current* period.

COST ALLOCATION

PART B

When people talk about a car depreciating, they usually are talking about how much the value of the car has decreased. Depreciation in accounting, though, is different. The primary dictionary definition of depreciation differs from the definition of depreciation used in accounting:

Dictionary definition = Decrease in value (or selling price) of an asset.

Accounting definition = Allocation of an asset's cost to an expense over time.

COMMON MISTAKE

Students sometimes mistake accounting depreciation as recording the decrease in value of an asset. Depreciation in accounting is *not* a valuation process. Rather, depreciation in accounting is an allocation of an asset's cost to expense over time.

In this section, we discuss the allocation of an asset's cost over time. We use the term *depreciation* to describe that process when it applies to property, plant, and equipment. You will see that we use a different term, *depletion*, to describe the cost allocation process when it applies to natural resources. For intangible assets, the term we use is *amortization*.

Depreciation of Property, Plant, and Equipment

■ **LO4**
Calculate depreciation of property, plant, and equipment.

Depreciation in accounting is the process of allocating to an expense the cost of an asset over its service life. An asset provides benefits (revenues) to a company in future periods. To properly match the cost (expense) with the revenues it helps to generate, we allocate a portion of the asset's cost to an expense in each year that the asset provides a benefit. If the asset will provide benefits to the company for four years, for example, then we allocate a portion of the asset's cost to depreciation expense in each year for four years. Illustration 7–8 portrays this concept of depreciating an asset's original purchase cost over the periods benefited.

ILLUSTRATION 7–8

Depreciation of Long-Term Assets

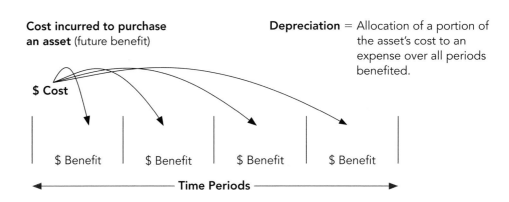

For demonstration, let's assume the local **Starbucks** pays $1,200 for equipment—say, an espresso machine. The machine is expected to have a useful life of four years. We record annual depreciation as shown below.

	Debit	Credit
Depreciation Expense	300	
Accumulated Depreciation		300
(*Depreciate equipment*)		
(*$300 = $1,200 ÷ 4 years*)		

A = L + SE
−300 Exp
−300

ACCUMULATED DEPRECIATION

The credit portion of the entry requires some explanation. **Accumulated Depreciation** is a contra asset account, meaning that it reduces an asset account. Rather than credit the Equipment account directly, we instead credit its contra account, which we offset against the Equipment account in the balance sheet. The name of the account comes from the fact that the depreciation we record each period *accumulates* in the account. After one year, for instance, we have:

Equipment (cost)	$1,200
Less: Accumulated depreciation ($300 × 1 year)	(300)
= Book value	$ 900

Common Terms Book value sometimes is called *carrying value*.

Book value equals the original cost of the asset minus the current balance in Accumulated Depreciation. Note that by increasing accumulated depreciation each period, we are reducing the book value of equipment. The Accumulated Depreciation account allows us to reduce the book value of assets through depreciation, while maintaining the original cost of each asset in the accounting records.

After two years, we have:

Equipment (cost)	$1,200
Less: Accumulated depreciation ($300 × 2 years)	(600)
= Book value	$ 600

KEY POINT

Depreciation refers to the allocation of the asset's original cost to an expense during the periods benefited. Depreciation does *not* refer to the change in value or selling price.

Depreciation requires accountants to estimate the *service life* of the asset, or its *useful life*, as well as its residual value at the end of that life. The **service life** is how long the company expects to receive benefits from the asset before disposing of it. We can measure service life in units of time or in units of activity. For example, the estimated service life of a delivery truck might be either five years or 100,000 miles. We use the terms service life and useful life interchangeably, because both terms are used in practice.

Common Terms Service life often is called *useful life*.

Depreciation also requires accountants to estimate what an asset's value will be at the end of its service life. Called **residual value**, or *salvage value*, it is the amount the company expects to receive from selling the asset at the end of its service life. A company might estimate residual value from prior experience or by researching the resale values of similar types of assets. Due to the difficulty in estimating residual value, it's not uncommon to assume a residual value of zero.

Common Terms Residual value often is called *salvage value*.

Remember: We record depreciation for land improvements, buildings, and equipment, but we *don't* record depreciation for land. Unlike other long-term assets, land is not "used up" over time.

COMMON MISTAKE

A common mistake is to depreciate land. Land is *not* depreciated, because its service life never ends.

Generally accepted accounting principles allow us to use various methods to calculate depreciation. In the following sections, we illustrate the three most common depreciation methods used in practice: straight-line, declining-balance, and activity-based.[2] All three illustrations are based on the same business situation: Little King Sandwiches, a local submarine sandwich restaurant, purchased a new delivery truck. The specific details of that purchase are described in Illustration 7–9.

ILLUSTRATION 7–9

Data for Little King Sandwiches's Delivery Truck Purchase, to Illustrate Depreciation Methods

Cost of the new truck	$40,000
Estimated residual value	$5,000
Estimated service life	5 years or 100,000 miles

STRAIGHT-LINE DEPRECIATION

By far the most easily understood and widely used depreciation method is straight-line. With the straight-line method we allocate an *equal* amount of the depreciable cost to each year of the asset's service life. The *depreciable cost* is the asset's cost minus its estimated residual value. We simply divide the depreciable cost by the number of years in the asset's life, as shown in Illustration 7–10.

ILLUSTRATION 7–10

Formula for Straight-Line Method

$$\text{Depreciation expense} = \frac{\text{Asset's cost} - \text{Residual value}}{\text{Service life}} = \frac{\text{Depreciable cost}}{\text{Service life}}$$

$$\text{Depreciation expense} = \frac{\$40,000 - \$5,000}{5 \text{ years}} = \$7,000 \text{ per year}$$

Note that dividing the depreciable cost each year by five is the same as multiplying the depreciable cost each year by 20% ($1/5 = 0.20$).

Illustration 7–11 provides a depreciation schedule using the straight-line method.

ILLUSTRATION 7–11

Straight-Line Depreciation Schedule

LITTLE KING SANDWICHES
Depreciation Schedule—Straight-Line

Year	Depreciable Cost	×	Depreciation Rate	=	Depreciation Expense	Accumulated Depreciation	Book Value*
							$40,000
1	$35,000		0.20		$ 7,000	$ 7,000	33,000
2	35,000		0.20		7,000	14,000	26,000
3	35,000		0.20		7,000	21,000	19,000
4	35,000		0.20		7,000	28,000	12,000
5	35,000		0.20		7,000	35,000	5,000
Total					$35,000		

*Book value is the cost of the asset ($40,000) minus accumulated depreciation. Book value of $33,000 at the end of year 1, for example, is $40,000 minus $7,000 in accumulated depreciation.

---

[2]Some introductory financial accounting textbooks illustrate a fourth depreciation method called *sum-of-the-years'-digits*. However, use of this method has decreased dramatically over the years to the point that this method is now rarely seen in actual practice. A recent survey of depreciation methods used by large public companies is provided in Illustration 7–17.

Partial-year depreciation. We assume Little King Sandwiches bought the delivery truck at the beginning of year 1. What if it bought the truck sometime during the year instead? Then, it will record depreciation for only the portion of the first year that it owned the truck. For example, if Little King bought the truck on November 1 and its year-end is December 31, it will record depreciation for only two of the 12 months in year 1. So, depreciation expense in year 1 is $1,167 (= $7,000 × 2/12). If instead Little King bought the truck back on March 1, it will record depreciation for 10 of the 12 months in year 1. In that case, depreciation expense in year 1 is $5,833 (= $7,000 × 10/12).

In both cases, depreciation for the second, third, fourth, and fifth years still is $7,000. The partial-year depreciation for the first year does not affect the depreciation in those subsequent years. However, it does affect the depreciation treatment in the asset's final year of service life: Since the firm didn't take a full year of depreciation in year 1, it needs to record a partial year of depreciation in year 6 in order to fully depreciate the truck from its cost of $40,000 down to its residual value of $5,000. Depreciation in year 6 is $5,833 for the truck purchased on November 1 (= $7,000 − $1,167). For the truck purchased on March 1, depreciation in year 6 is $1,167 (= $7,000 − $5,833).

 COMMON MISTAKE

Many students think March 1 to the end of the year is nine months because December is the twelfth month and March is the third month. March 1 to the end of the year is actually *ten* months; it is every month except January and February.

Change in depreciation estimate. Depreciation is an *estimate.* Remember that the amount of depreciation allocated to each period is produced by two estimates—management's estimates of service life and of residual value—as well as the depreciation method chosen. Management needs to periodically review these estimates. When a change in estimate is required, the company changes depreciation in current and future years, but not in prior periods.

For example, assume that at the end of the third year Little King Sandwiches estimates the remaining service life of the delivery truck to be four more years, for a total service life of seven years rather than the original five. At this time, Little King also changes the estimated residual value to $3,000 from the original estimate of $5,000. How much should Little King record each year for depreciation in years 4 to 7? Take the book value at the end of year 3 ($19,000), subtract the new estimated residual value ($3,000), and then divide by the new remaining service life (four more years). Little King Sandwiches will record depreciation in years 4 to 7 as $4,000 per year. Illustration 7–12 shows the calculations.

Book value, end of year 3	$19,000
− New residual value	(3,000)
New depreciable cost	16,000
÷ Remaining service life	÷ 4
Annual depreciation in years 4 to 7	$ 4,000

ILLUSTRATION 7–12

Change in Depreciation Estimate

Notice that Little King Sandwiches makes all the changes in years 4 to 7. The company does not go back and change the calculations for depreciation already recorded in years 1 to 3.

ETHICAL DILEMMA

James Wright is the chief financial officer (CFO) for The Butcher Block, a major steakhouse restaurant chain. As CFO, James has the final responsibility for all aspects of financial reporting. The company is publicly traded and followed closely by the investment community. James holds regular teleconference discussions with financial analysts; in the most recent teleconference, he indicated the company is emerging nicely from the economic recession. He told the analysts that The Butcher Block should post earnings per share (net income divided by the number of shares of common stock) of at least $1.25. The analysts now expect that amount.

A couple months later, James is examining the preliminary year-end numbers. He notices that earnings per share are coming in at $1.23, two cents per share under target. He also is aware that The Butcher Block has been depreciating most of its restaurant equipment conservatively over a five-year useful life. In some cases, the equipment is used by the company for 10 years or more. He proposes to change the estimated useful life for a subset of the equipment to a more reasonable useful life of seven, rather than five, years. By depreciating over a longer useful life, depreciation expense will be lower in the current year, increasing earnings per share for the year to $1.26. It looks like The Butcher Block is going to meet analyst expectations after all.

Do you think James Wright's proposal to more accurately reflect the true depreciable life of assets is ethical? What concerns might you have?

Straight-line depreciation assumes that the benefits we derive from the use of an asset are the same each year. In some situations it might be more reasonable to assume that the asset will provide greater benefits in the earlier years of its life than in the later years. In these cases, we achieve a better matching of depreciation with revenues by using an accelerated depreciation method, with higher depreciation in the earlier years of the asset's life and lower depreciation in later years. We look at one such method next.

DECLINING-BALANCE DEPRECIATION

The declining-balance method is an accelerated depreciation method. Declining-balance depreciation will be higher than straight-line depreciation in earlier years, but lower in later years. **However, both declining-balance and straight-line will result in the same total depreciation over the asset's service life.** No matter what allocation method we use, total depreciation over the asset's service life will be equal to the depreciable cost (asset cost minus residual value).

The depreciation rate we use under the declining-balance method is a multiple of the straight-line rate, such as 125%, 150%, or 200% of the straight-line rate. The most common declining-balance rate is 200%, which we refer to as the *double*-declining-balance method since the rate is double the straight-line rate. In our illustration for Little King Sandwiches, the double-declining-balance rate would be 40% (two times the straight-line rate of 20%). Illustration 7–13 provides a depreciation schedule using the double-declining-balance method.

LITTLE KING SANDWICHES
Depreciation Schedule—Double-Declining-Balance

ILLUSTRATION 7–13
Double-Declining-
Balance Depreciation
Schedule

Year	Beginning Book Value	×	Depreciation Rate	=	Depreciation Expense	Accumulated Depreciation	Book Value*
			Calculation			**End-of-Year Amounts**	
							$40,000
1	$40,000		0.40		**$16,000**	$16,000	24,000
2	24,000		0.40		**9,600**	25,600	14,400
3	14,400		0.40		**5,760**	31,360	8,640
4	8,640		0.40		**3,456**	34,816	5,184
5	5,184				**184****	35,000	**5,000**
Total					**$35,000**		

*Book value is the cost of the asset minus accumulated depreciation. Book value at the end of year 1 is $24,000, equal to the cost of $40,000 minus accumulated depreciation of $16,000. Book value at the end of **year 1** in the last column is equal to book value at the beginning of **year 2** in the second column of the schedule.
**Amount necessary to reduce book value to residual value.

A simple way to get the depreciation rate for double-declining-balance is to divide the number 2 by the estimated service life (2/5 year service life = 0.40). If the service life had been four years instead of five, what depreciation rates would we use under straight-line and under double-declining-balance? The straight-line rate is 1 divided by the four-year service life, or 1/4 = 0.25. The double-declining-balance rate is 2 divided by the four-year service life, or 2/4 = 0.50.

Notice two unusual features of declining-balance depreciation. First, we multiply the rate by *book value* (cost minus accumulated depreciation), rather than by the depreciable cost (cost minus residual value). Second, in year 5 we are not able to record depreciation expense for the entire $5,184 times 0.40, because doing so would cause the book value to fall below the expected residual value. Instead, depreciation expense in the final year is the amount that reduces book value to the expected residual value (book value beginning of year, $5,184, minus estimated residual value, $5,000, = $184).

 COMMON MISTAKE

Mistakes are commonly made in the first and last year of the calculation. In the first year, students sometimes calculate depreciation incorrectly as cost minus residual value times the depreciation rate. The correct way in the first year is to simply multiply cost times the depreciation rate. In the final year, some students incorrectly calculate depreciation expense in the same manner as in earlier years, multiplying book value by the depreciation rate. However, under the declining-balance method, depreciation expense in the final year is the amount necessary to reduce book value down to residual value.

If the estimated residual value is high enough, the asset will reach its residual value in fewer years than its expected service life. For instance, if the estimated residual value had been $10,000 rather than $5,000, the delivery truck would be fully depreciated under the double-declining-balance method in only three years, even though we used a five-year life in determining the depreciation rate.

ACTIVITY-BASED DEPRECIATION

Straight-line and declining-balance methods measure depreciation based on time. In an **activity-based method**, we instead allocate an asset's cost based on its *use*. For example, we could measure the service life of a machine in terms of its output

Common Terms
Activity-based depreciation is also called *units of production* or *units of output.*

(units, pounds, barrels). This method also works for vehicles such as our delivery truck, whose use we measure in miles.

We first compute the average *depreciation rate per unit* by dividing the depreciable cost (cost minus residual value) by the number of units expected to be produced. In our illustration, the depreciation rate is $0.35 per mile, calculated as shown in Illustration 7–14.

ILLUSTRATION 7–14

Formula for Depreciation Rate per Unit in Activity-Based Method

$$\text{Depreciation rate per unit} = \frac{\text{Depreciable cost}}{\text{Total units expected to be produced}}$$

$$\text{Depreciation rate} = \frac{\$40,000 - \$5,000}{100,000 \text{ expected miles}} = \$0.35 \text{ per mile}$$

To calculate the depreciation expense for the reporting period, we then multiply the per-unit rate by the number of units of activity each period. Illustration 7–15 shows a depreciation schedule using the activity-based method. The actual miles driven in years 1 to 5 were 30,000, 22,000, 15,000, 20,000, and 13,000. Notice that the activity-based method is very similar to the straight-line method, except that rather than dividing the depreciable cost by the service life in years, we divide it by the service life in expected miles.

ILLUSTRATION 7–15

Activity-Based Depreciation Schedule

spiceland.mhhe.com/c21

LITTLE KING SANDWICHES
Depreciation Schedule—Activity-Based

Year	Miles Driven	×	Depreciation Rate	=	Depreciation Expense	Accumulated Depreciation	Book Value*
							$40,000
1	30,000		$0.35		$10,500	$10,500	29,500
2	22,000		0.35		7,700	18,200	21,800
3	15,000		0.35		5,250	23,450	16,550
4	20,000		0.35		7,000	30,450	9,550
5	13,000		0.35		4,550	35,000	5,000
Total	100,000				$35,000		

*Book value is the cost of the asset ($40,000) minus accumulated depreciation. Book value of $29,500 in year 1 is $40,000 minus $10,500 in accumulated depreciation.

In our illustration, the delivery truck is driven exactly 100,000 miles over the five years. What if we drive the delivery truck *less than* 100,000 miles by the end of the fifth year? Then we will continue to depreciate the truck past five years until we reach 100,000 miles. Similarly, if we drive the delivery truck more than 100,000 miles in less than five years, we will stop depreciating the truck at 100,000 miles before the five years are up. In either case, we need to depreciate the asset until the book value (cost minus accumulated depreciation) declines to the estimated residual value.

Decision Maker's Perspective

Selecting a Depreciation Method

Assume you are the chief financial officer (CFO) responsible for your company's accounting and reporting policies. Which depreciation method would you choose? Illustration 7–16 compares annual depreciation under the three alternatives we discussed.

Year	Straight-Line	Double-Declining-Balance	Activity-Based
1	$ 7,000	$16,000	$10,500
2	7,000	9,600	7,700
3	7,000	5,760	5,250
4	7,000	3,456	7,000
5	7,000	184	4,550
Total	$35,000	$35,000	$35,000

ILLUSTRATION 7–16

Comparison of Depreciation Methods

Comparing methods, we see that all three alternatives result in total depreciation of $35,000 ($40,000 cost minus $5,000 residual value). Straight-line creates an equal amount of depreciation each year. Double-declining-balance creates more depreciation in earlier years and less depreciation in later years. Activity-based depreciation varies depending on the miles driven each year.

Companies are free to choose the depreciation method they believe best reflects the pattern of an asset's use and the revenues it creates. Illustration 7–17 shows the results of a recent survey of depreciation methods used by large public companies.

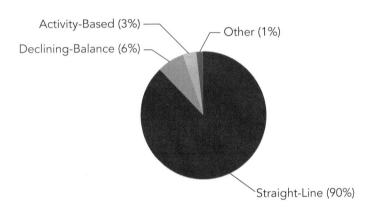

ILLUSTRATION 7–17

Use of Various Depreciation Methods

Activity-Based (3%)
Other (1%)
Declining-Balance (6%)
Straight-Line (90%)

Source: Accounting Trends and Techniques (New York: AICPA, 2009).

Why do so many companies use the straight-line method? Many probably believe they realize benefits from their plant assets approximately evenly over these assets' service lives. Certainly another motivating factor is that straight-line is the easiest method to apply. One more important motivation is straight-line's positive effect on reported income. Straight-line produces a higher net income than accelerated methods in the earlier years of an asset's life. Higher net income can improve bonuses paid to management, increase stock prices, and reduce the likelihood of violating debt agreements with lenders. ●

DEPLETION

Earlier in the chapter we discussed natural resources like oil, natural gas, and timber. We allocate natural resources to expense through a process known as **depletion**. The process of recording depletion expense for natural resources is nearly identical to the activity-based method of recording depreciation. Specific details for recording depletion are covered in more advanced accounting courses.

TAX DEPRECIATION

Conflicting with the desire to report higher net income is the desire to reduce taxes by *reducing* taxable income. An accelerated method serves this objective by reducing taxable income more in the earlier years of an asset's life than does straight-line.

As a result, most companies use the straight-line method for financial reporting and the Internal Revenue Service's prescribed accelerated method (called MACRS[3]) for income tax purposes. Thus, companies record higher net income using straight-line depreciation and lower taxable income using MACRS depreciation. MACRS combines declining-balance methods in earlier years with straight-line in later years to allow for a more advantageous tax depreciation deduction. Congress, not accountants, approved MACRS rules to encourage greater investment in long-term assets by U.S. companies.

 KEY POINT

Straight-line, declining-balance, and activity-based depreciation all are acceptable depreciation methods for financial reporting. Most companies use straight-line depreciation for financial reporting and an accelerated method called MACRS for tax reporting.

Let's Review

spiceland.mhhe.com/t13

University Hero purchases new bread ovens at a cost of $110,000. On the date of purchase, the company estimates the ovens will have a residual value of $20,000. University Hero expects to use the ovens for four years or about 9,000 total hours.

Required:

Prepare a depreciation schedule using each of the following methods:

1. Straight-line.
2. Double-declining-balance.
3. Activity-based.

Actual oven use per year was as follows:

Year	Hours Used
1	2,200
2	2,600
3	2,300
4	2,100
Total	9,200

Solution:

1. Straight-line:

UNIVERSITY HERO
Depreciation Schedule—Straight-Line

	Calculation				End-of-Year Amounts	
Year	Depreciable Cost	×	Depreciation Rate*	=	Depreciation Expense	Accumulated Depreciation	Book Value**
1	$90,000		0.25		**$22,500**	$22,500	$87,500
2	90,000		0.25		**22,500**	45,000	65,000
3	90,000		0.25		**22,500**	67,500	42,500
4	90,000		0.25		**22,500**	90,000	**20,000**
Total					**$90,000**		

*1 ÷ 4 years = 0.25 per year
**$110,000 cost minus accumulated depreciation.

[3]Modified Accelerated Cost Recovery System.

2. Double-declining-balance:

UNIVERSITY HERO
Depreciation Schedule—Double-Declining-Balance

	Calculation				End-of-Year Amounts	
Year	Beginning Book Value	×	Depreciation Rate*	= Depreciation Expense	Accumulated Depreciation	Book Value**
1	$110,000		0.50	$55,000	$55,000	$55,000
2	55,000		0.50	27,500	82,500	27,500
3	27,500		0.50	7,500***	90,000	20,000
4				0	90,000	20,000
Total				$90,000		

*2 ÷ 4 years = 0.50 per year
**$110,000 cost minus accumulated depreciation.
***Amount needed to reduce book value to residual value.

3. Activity-based:

UNIVERSITY HERO
Depreciation Schedule—Activity-Based

	Calculation				End-of-Year Amounts	
Year	Hours Used	×	Depreciation Rate*	= Depreciation Expense	Accumulated Depreciation	Book Value**
1	2,200		$10	$22,000	$22,000	$88,000
2	2,600		10	26,000	48,000	62,000
3	2,300		10	23,000	71,000	39,000
4	2,100			19,000***	90,000	20,000
Total	9,200			$90,000		

*$90,000 ÷ 9,000 hours = $10/hour
**$110,000 cost minus accumulated depreciation.
***Amount needed to reduce book value to residual value.

Suggested Homework:
BE7-7, BE7-8;
E7-10, E7-11;
P7-5A&B, P7-7A&B

Amortization of Intangible Assets

Allocating the cost of property, plant, and equipment to expense is called depreciation. Allocating the cost of natural resources to expense is called depletion. Similarly, allocating the cost of *intangible* assets to expense is called amortization.

INTANGIBLE ASSETS SUBJECT TO AMORTIZATION

Most intangible assets have a finite useful life that we can estimate. For these, we allocate the asset's cost less any estimated residual value to periods in which we expect the intangible asset to contribute to the company's revenue-generating activities. This requires that we estimate the intangible asset's service life and its residual value.

■ **LO5**
Calculate amortization of intangible assets.

The service life of an intangible asset usually is limited by legal, regulatory, or contractual provisions. For example, the legal life of a patent is 20 years. However, the estimated useful life of a patent often is less than 20 years if the benefits are not expected to continue for the patent's entire legal life. The patent for **Apple's** iPad, for example, is amortized over fewer than 20 years, since new technology will cause the iPad to become outdated in a much shorter period.

The expected residual value of most intangible assets is zero. This might not be the case, though, if at the end of its useful life to the reporting entity the asset will benefit another entity. For example, if **Microsoft** has a commitment from another company to purchase one of its patents at the end of the patent's useful life at a determinable price, we use that price as the patent's residual value.

The method of amortization should reflect the pattern of use of the asset in generating benefits. Most companies use *straight-line amortization* for intangibles. Also, many companies credit amortization to the intangible asset account itself rather than to accumulated amortization. However, using a contra account such as Accumulated Amortization also is acceptable.

Let's look at an example: In early January, Little King Sandwiches acquires franchise rights from University Hero for $800,000. The franchise agreement is for a period of 20 years. In addition, Little King purchases a patent for a meat-slicing process for $72,000. The original legal life of the patent was 20 years, and there are 12 years remaining. However, due to expected technological obsolescence, the company estimates that the useful life of the patent is only 8 more years. Little King uses straight-line amortization for all intangible assets. The company's fiscal year-end is December 31. Little King records the amortization expense for the franchise and the patent as follows.

	Debit	Credit
Amortization Expense	40,000	
Franchises		40,000
(*Amortize franchise*)		
(*$40,000 = $800,000 ÷ 20 years*)		
Amortization Expense	9,000	
Patents		9,000
(*Amortize patent*)		
(*$9,000 = $72,000 ÷ 8 years*)		

INTANGIBLE ASSETS NOT SUBJECT TO AMORTIZATION

We don't depreciate land because it has an unlimited life. Similarly, we do *not* amortize intangible assets with indefinite useful lives. An asset's useful life is indefinite if there is no foreseeable limit on the period of time over which we expect it to contribute to the cash flows of the entity. For example, suppose Little King acquired a trademark for a line of sandwiches. Registered trademarks have a legal life of 10 years, but the trademark registration is renewable for an indefinite number of 10-year periods. We consider the life of Little King's trademark to be indefinite, so we don't amortize it.

Goodwill is the most common intangible asset with an indefinite useful life. Recall that we measure goodwill as the difference between the purchase price of a company and the fair value of all its identifiable net assets (tangible and intangible assets minus the fair value of liabilities assumed). Does this mean that goodwill and other intangible assets with indefinite useful lives will remain on a company's balance sheet at their original cost forever? Probably not. Management must review long-term assets for a potential write-down when events or changes in circumstances indicate the amount recorded for an asset in the accounting records might not be recoverable. All long-term assets are subject to these "impairment" rules, which we discuss in more detail in the appendix to this chapter.

KEY POINT

Amortization is a process, similar to depreciation, in which we allocate the cost of intangible assets over their estimated service lives. Intangible assets with an indefinite useful life (goodwill and most trademarks) are *not* amortized.

ASSET DISPOSITION: SALE, RETIREMENT, OR EXCHANGE

■ **LO6**
Account for the disposal of long-term assets.

Few things last forever. In this section we discuss what to do when we no longer use a long-term asset. A *sale* is a possibility. When a long-term asset is no longer useful but cannot be sold, we have a *retirement*. For example, Little King Sandwiches might physically remove a baking oven that no longer works and also remove it from the accounting records through a retirement entry. An *exchange* occurs when two companies trade assets. In a trade, we often use cash to make up for any difference in fair value between the assets.

Selling a long-term asset can result in either a gain or a loss. We record a *gain* if we sell the asset for *more* than its book value. Similarly, we record a *loss* if we sell the asset for *less* than its book value. A gain is a credit balance account like other revenue accounts; a loss is a debit balance account like other expense accounts. Remember, book value is the cost of the asset minus accumulated depreciation. In order to have the correct book value, it's important to record depreciation up to the date of the sale.

ⓧ COMMON MISTAKE

Some students forget to update depreciation prior to recording the disposal of the asset. Depreciation must be recorded up to the date of the sale, retirement, or exchange. Otherwise, the book value will be overstated, and the resulting gain or loss on disposal will be in error as well.

To illustrate the recording of disposals, let's return to our delivery truck example for Little King Sandwiches. Assume Little King uses straight-line depreciation and records the delivery truck in the Equipment account. The specific details are summarized again in Illustration 7–18.

Original cost of the truck	$40,000
Estimated residual value	$5,000
Estimated service life	5 years

ILLUSTRATION 7–18

Data for Little King Sandwiches's Delivery Truck Purchase, to Illustrate Long-Term Asset Disposals

Sale of Long-Term Assets

If we assume that Little King sells the delivery truck at the end of year 3 for $22,000, we can calculate the gain as $3,000. Note that both the delivery truck and the related accumulated depreciation are removed. Illustration 7–19 shows the calculation.

Sale amount		$22,000
Less:		
Original cost of the truck	$40,000	
Less: Accumulated depreciation (3 years × $7,000/year)	(21,000)	
Book value at the end of year 3		19,000
Gain on sale		$ 3,000

ILLUSTRATION 7–19

Gain on Sale

We record the gain on sale as:

	Debit	Credit	A	=	L	+	SE
Cash	22,000		+22,000				
Accumulated Depreciation	21,000		+21,000				
Equipment		40,000	−40,000				
Gain		3,000					+3,000 Rev↑
(Sell equipment for a gain)							

COMMON MISTAKE

Be careful not to combine the delivery truck ($40,000) and accumulated deprecia-tion ($21,000) and credit the $19,000 difference to the Equipment account. Instead, remove the delivery truck and accumulated depreciation from the accounting records separately. Otherwise, the Equipment and the Accumulated Depreciation accounts will incorrectly have a remaining balance after the asset has been sold.

If we assume that Little King sells the delivery truck at the end of year 3 for only $17,000 instead of $22,000, we have a $2,000 loss as calculated in Illustration 7–20.

ILLUSTRATION 7–20

Loss on Sale

Sale amount		$17,000
Less:		
Original cost of the truck	$40,000	
Less: Accumulated depreciation (3 years × $7,000/year)	(21,000)	
Book value at the end of year 3		19,000
Loss on sale		$ (2,000)

We record the loss on sale as:

	Debit	Credit
A = L + SE			

		Debit	Credit
+17,000	Cash	17,000	
+21,000	Accumulated Depreciation	21,000	
−2,000 Exp↑	Loss	2,000	
−40,000	Equipment		40,000
	(Sell equipment for a loss)		

Decision Point

Question	Accounting information	Analysis
How different is the company's recorded book value from its actual fair value?	Gain or loss on sale	A gain on sale indicates the actual fair value is more than the recorded book value. A loss on sale indicates the opposite.

Retirement of Long-Term Assets

Now assume that Little King retires the delivery truck instead of selling it. If, for example, the truck is totaled in an accident at the end of year 3, we have a $19,000 loss on retirement as calculated in Illustration 7–21.

ILLUSTRATION 7–21

Loss on Retirement

Sale amount		$ 0
Less:		
Original cost of the truck	$40,000	
Less: Accumulated depreciation (3 years × $7,000/year)	(21,000)	
Book value at the end of year 3		19,000
Loss on retirement		$(19,000)

We record the loss on retirement as:

	Debit	Credit		A	=	L	+	SE
Accumulated Depreciation	**21,000**			+21,000				
Loss	**19,000**							−19,000 Exp↑
Equipment		**40,000**		−40,000				
(*Retire equipment for a loss*)								

The above entry assumes Little King did not have collision insurance coverage. If Little King had insured the truck and collected $17,000 in insurance money for the totaled vehicle, the entry would be identical to the sale for $17,000 in Illustration 7–20.

Exchange of Long-Term Assets

Now assume that Little King exchanges the delivery truck at the end of year 3 for a new truck valued at $45,000. The dealership gives Little King a trade-in allowance of $23,000 on the exchange, with the remaining $22,000 paid in cash. We have a $4,000 gain, as calculated in Illustration 7–22.

Trade-in allowance		$23,000	**ILLUSTRATION 7–22**
Less:			Gain on Exchange
Original cost of the truck	$40,000		
Less: Accumulated depreciation (3 years × $7,000/year)	(21,000)		
Book value at the end of year 3		19,000	
Gain on exchange		$ 4,000	

We record the gain on exchange as:

	Debit	Credit		A	=	L	+	SE
Equipment (new)	**45,000**			+45,000				
Accumulated Depreciation	**21,000**			+21,000				
Cash		**22,000**		−22,000				
Equipment (old)		**40,000**		−40,000				
Gain		**4,000**						+4,000 Rev↑
(*Exchange equipment for a gain*)								

KEY POINT

If we dispose of an asset for *more* than book value, we record a gain. If we dispose of an asset for *less* than book value, we record a loss.

spiceland.mhhe.com/c18

ASSET ANALYSIS
Walmart vs. Abercrombie

We have discussed the purchase, depreciation, and disposal of long-term assets. In this final section, we see how to use actual financial statement information to analyze the profitability of a company's assets. Illustration 7–23 (next page) provides selected financial data reported by **Walmart** and **Abercrombie** for use in our analysis.

ANALYSIS

■ **LO7**
Describe the relation among return on assets, profit margin, and asset turnover.

ILLUSTRATION 7–23

Selected Financial Data for Walmart and Abercrombie

($ in millions) Walmart	2009	2008
Net sales	$405,607	$378,799
Net income	13,400	12,731
Total assets	163,429	163,514

Abercrombie	2009	2008
Net sales	$3,540	$3,750
Net income	272	476
Total assets	2,848	2,568

RETURN ON ASSETS

Common Terms Return on assets is often just called *ROA.*

Walmart had net income of $13,400 million and Abercrombie had net income of $272 million in 2009. Since Walmart's net income is so much larger, does that mean Walmart is more profitable? Not necessarily. Walmart is also a much larger company, as indicated by total assets. Walmart's total assets were $163,429 million compared to $2,848 million for Abercrombie. A more comparable measure of profitability than income is return on assets, which equals net income divided by *average* total assets. Dividing net income by average total assets adjusts net income for differences in company size.

 COMMON MISTAKE

Students sometimes divide by ending total assets rather than by *average* total assets. We measure net income over time, whereas we measure total assets at a *point* in time. Therefore, whenever we divide a number in the income statement by a number in the balance sheet, it's more meaningful to use an *average* balance sheet number.

The return on assets ratio is calculated for Walmart and Abercrombie in Illustration 7–24.

ILLUSTRATION 7–24

Return on Assets for Walmart and Abercrombie

($ in millions)	Net Income	÷	Average Total Assets	=	Return on Assets
Walmart	$13,400	÷	($163,429 + $163,514)/2	=	8.2%
Abercrombie	$ 272	÷	($2,848 + $2,568)/2	=	10.0%

Although Walmart has a much higher net income, Abercrombie actually is more profitable, with a higher return on assets. Return on assets indicates the amount of net income generated for each dollar invested in assets.

Decision Point

Question	Accounting information	Analysis
How effectively is the company using its assets?	Return on assets ratio	A higher return on assets generally indicates a more effective use of assets.

PROFIT MARGIN AND ASSET TURNOVER

We can explore profitability further by separating return on assets into two components: profit margin and asset turnover, as shown in Illustration 7–25.

Return on assets	=	Profit margin	×	Asset turnover
$\dfrac{\text{Net income}}{\text{Average total assets}}$	=	$\dfrac{\text{Net income}}{\text{Net sales}}$	×	$\dfrac{\text{Net sales}}{\text{Average total assets}}$

ILLUSTRATION 7–25

Components of Return on Assets

Profit margin is net income divided by net sales. This ratio indicates the earnings per dollar of sales. Asset turnover is net sales divided by average total assets. This ratio measures the sales per dollar of assets invested.

Strategies for Increasing Return on Assets

Decision Maker's Perspective

Companies have two primary strategies for increasing their return on assets. Some companies, like Walmart, pursue a high sales volume by charging *lower prices.* Walmart is profitable as long as it can maintain or increase its asset turnover. Other companies, like Abercrombie, pursue a higher profit margin through *product differentiation* and *premium pricing.* Abercrombie is profitable as long as it can maintain or increase its high profit margins. In Illustrations 7–26 and 7–27 we calculate profit margin and asset turnover, respectively, for both companies. We then can see if our expectations regarding Walmart and Abercrombie are supported.

($ in millions)	Net Income	÷	Net Sales	=	Profit Margin
Walmart	$13,400	÷	$405,607	=	3.3%
Abercrombie	$272	÷	$ 3,540	=	7.7%

ILLUSTRATION 7–26

Profit Margin for Walmart and Abercrombie

($ in millions)	Net Sales	÷	Average Total Assets	=	Asset Turnover
Walmart	$405,607	÷	($163,429 + $163,514)/2	=	2.5 times
Abercrombie	$3,540	÷	($2,848 + $2,568)/2	=	1.3 times

ILLUSTRATION 7–27

Asset Turnover for Walmart and Abercrombie

Illustration 7–26 indicates that Abercrombie's profit margin is more than twice that for Walmart. Illustration 7–27, however, shows that Walmart has the higher asset turnover. These accounting ratios support our expectations regarding the different business strategies Walmart and Abercrombie are pursuing. To maximize profitability, a company ideally strives to increase *both* net income per dollar of sales (profit margin) and sales per dollar invested in assets (asset turnover). ●

KEY POINT

Return on assets indicates the amount of net income generated for each dollar invested in assets. Return on assets can be separated to examine two important business strategies: profit margin and asset turnover.

Decision Point

Question	Accounting information	Analysis
How much profit is being generated from sales?	Profit margin	A higher profit margin indicates a company generates a higher net income per dollar of sales.
Is the company effectively generating sales from its assets?	Asset turnover ratio	A higher asset turnover indicates a company generates a higher sales volume per dollar of assets invested.

APPENDIX

ASSET IMPAIRMENT

■ LO8
Identify impairment situations and describe the two-step impairment process.

Management must review long-term assets for impairment when events or changes in circumstances indicate that book value might not be recoverable. Impairment occurs when the future cash flows (future benefits) generated for a long-term asset fall below its book value (cost minus accumulated depreciation). The relationship among future cash flows, fair value, and book value can be confusing. Illustration 7–28 displays the normal relationship and the impaired relationship among these three values.

ILLUSTRATION 7–28

Relationship among Future Cash Flows, Fair Value, and Book Value

	Normal Relationship		Impaired Relationship
Largest:	Future cash flows	*Largest:*	Book value
Middle:	Fair value	*Middle:*	Future cash flows
Smallest:	Book value	*Smallest:*	Fair value

Note that future cash flows always exceed fair value. This is true since the present value of future cash flows are used in determining fair value and the present value of an amount is always less than the total of its future cash flows. If estimated future cash flows from the asset are below the book value (as in the impaired relationship column), we record an impairment loss. The *impairment loss* is equal to the difference between the asset's book value and its fair value. Thus, reporting for impairment losses is a two-step process summarized in Illustration 7–29.

ILLUSTRATION 7–29

Two-Step Impairment Process

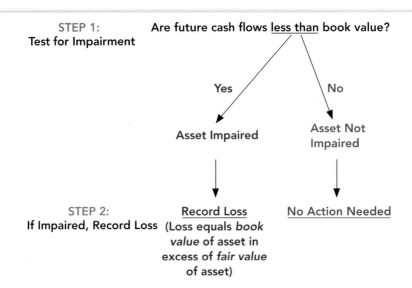

STEP 1: Test for Impairment — Are future cash flows <u>less than</u> book value?

Yes → Asset Impaired

No → Asset Not Impaired

STEP 2: If Impaired, Record Loss — Record Loss (Loss equals *book value* of asset in excess of *fair value* of asset)

No Action Needed

To illustrate asset impairment, suppose Little King pays $50,000 for the trademark rights to a line of specialty sandwiches. This intangible asset is not amortized because management assumes the trademark has an indefinite useful life. After several years, sales for this line of specialty sandwiches are disappointing, and management estimates the total future cash flows from sales will be only $20,000. Due to the disappointing sales, the estimated fair value of the trademark is now about $12,000. Here's how Little King determines and records the impairment loss.

STEP 1: TEST FOR IMPAIRMENT

The long-term asset is impaired since future cash flows ($20,000) are less than book value ($50,000).

STEP 2: IF IMPAIRED, RECORD THE LOSS

The loss is $38,000, calculated as the amount by which book value ($50,000) exceeds fair value ($12,000). We record the impairment loss as follows:

	Debit	Credit	A	=	L	+	SE
Loss	38,000		−38,000				
Trademarks		38,000					−38,000 Exp↑
(Record impairment of trademark)							

 COMMON MISTAKE

> Some students forget step 1 when considering impairment. Record an impairment loss only when book value exceeds *both* future cash flows and fair value.

What is the overall financial statement effect of an impairment loss? The impairment entry reduces net income in the income statement by $38,000 and reduces total assets in the balance sheet by $38,000. The new balance in the Trademarks account is $12,000, which equals its current fair value. We can write down the trademark further through impairment in future years, but we cannot write it back up under current accounting rules.

 INTERNATIONAL FINANCIAL REPORTING STANDARDS (IFRS)

International accounting standards also record impairments based on a two-step impairment process. The details are covered in more advanced accounting courses. However, one important difference is this: Impairments under U.S. GAAP are permanent—the asset cannot be written back up in future periods. In contrast, impairments under IFRS rules can be reversed. Thus, under IFRS a company can record an impairment loss in one period and then write the asset back up with a corresponding gain in a later period.

For more discussion, see Appendix E.

 KEY POINT

> Impairment is a two-step process: **Step 1: Test for impairment:** The long-term asset is impaired if future cash flows are less than book value. **Step 2: If impaired, record impairment loss:** The impairment loss is the amount by which book value exceeds fair value.

Decision Maker's Perspective   Taking a Big Bath

In practice, determining impairment losses can be subjective. Accounting research suggests that managers sometimes use the recording of impairment losses to their advantage. Some companies time their impairment losses with other one-time losses such as losses on sales of assets, inventory write-downs, and restructuring charges, to record a big loss in one year. We refer to this practice as taking a big bath—recording all losses in one year to make a bad year even worse. Management thus cleans its slate and is able to report higher earnings in future years. Future earnings are higher because the write-down of assets in this year results in lower depreciation and amortization charges in the future. When analyzing financial statements, investors should be alert to this kind of manipulation. ●

KEY POINTS BY LEARNING OBJECTIVE

LO1 Identify and record the major types of property, plant, and equipment.

Tangible assets include land, land improvements, buildings, equipment, and natural resources.

LO2 Identify and record the major types of intangible assets.

We record (capitalize) purchased intangible assets at their purchase price plus all costs necessary to get the asset ready for use. We expense internally generated intangible assets, such as R&D and advertising costs, as we incur those costs.

Intangible assets include patents, copyrights, trademarks, franchises, and goodwill.

LO3 Discuss the accounting treatment of expenditures after acquisition.

Capital items (recorded as assets) benefit *future* periods. Expenses benefit only the *current* period.

LO4 Calculate depreciation of property, plant, and equipment.

Depreciation refers to the allocation of an asset's original cost to an expense during the periods benefited. Depreciation does *not* refer to the change in value or selling price.

Straight-line, declining-balance, and activity-based depreciation all are acceptable depreciation methods for financial reporting. Most companies use straight-line depreciation for financial reporting and an accelerated method called MACRS for tax reporting.

LO5 Calculate amortization of intangible assets.

Amortization is a process, similar to depreciation, in which we allocate the cost of intangible assets over their estimated service life. Intangible assets with an indefinite useful life (goodwill and most trademarks) are *not* amortized.

LO6 Account for the disposal of long-term assets.

If we dispose of an asset for more than book value, we record a gain. If we dispose of an asset for less than book value, we record a loss.

Analysis

LO7 Describe the relationship among return on assets, profit margin, and asset turnover.

Return on assets indicates the amount of net income generated for each dollar invested in assets. Return on assets can be separated to examine two important business strategies: profit margin and asset turnover.

Appendix

LO8 Identify impairment situations and describe the two-step impairment process.

Impairment is a two-step process. **Step 1: Test for impairment:** The long-term asset is impaired if future cash flows are less than book value. **Step 2: If impaired, record loss:** The impairment loss is the amount book value exceeds fair value.

GLOSSARY

Accelerated depreciation method: Allocates a higher depreciation in the earlier years of the asset's life and lower depreciation in later years. **p. 236**

Accumulated Depreciation: A contra asset account representing the total depreciation taken to date. **p. 232**

Activity-based method: Allocates an asset's cost based on its use. **p. 237**

Addition: Occurs when a new major component is added to an existing asset. **p. 230**

Amortization: Allocation of the cost of an intangible asset over its service life. **p. 241**

Asset turnover: Net sales divided by average total assets, which measures the sales per dollar of assets invested. **p. 247**

Basket purchase: Purchase of more than one asset at the same time for one purchase price. **p. 225**

Big bath: Recording all losses in one year to make a bad year even worse. **p. 250**

Book value: Equal to the original cost of the asset minus the current balance in Accumulated Depreciation. **p. 233**

Capitalize: Record an expenditure as an asset. **p. 223**

Capitalized interest: Interest costs recorded as assets rather than interest expense. **p. 224**

Copyright: An exclusive right of protection given to the creator of a published work such as a song, film, painting, photograph, book, or computer software. **p. 228**

Declining-balance method: An accelerated depreciation method that records more depreciation in earlier years and less depreciation in later years. **p. 236**

Depletion: Allocation of the cost of a natural resource over its service life. **p. 239**

Depreciation: Allocation of the cost of a tangible asset over its service life. **p. 232**

Franchise: Local outlets that pay for the exclusive right to use the franchisor company's name and to sell its products within a specified geographical area. **p. 228**

Goodwill: The value of a company as a whole, over and above the value of its identifiable net assets. Goodwill equals the purchase price less the fair value of the net assets acquired. **p. 229**

Impairment: Occurs when the future cash flows (future benefits) generated for a long-term asset fall below its book value (cost minus accumulated depreciation). **p. 248**

Improvement: The cost of replacing a major component of an asset. **p. 230**

Intangible assets: Long-term assets that lack physical substance, and whose existence is often based on a legal contract. **p. 226**

Land improvements: Improvements to land such as paving, lighting, and landscaping that, unlike land itself, are subject to depreciation. **p. 224**

Material: Large enough to influence a decision. **p. 231**

Natural resources: Assets like oil, natural gas, and timber that we can physically use up or deplete. **p. 226**

Patent: An exclusive right to manufacture a product or to use a process. **p. 227**

Profit margin: Net income divided by net sales; indicates the earnings per dollar of sales. **p. 247**

Repairs and maintenance: Expenses that maintain a given level of benefits in the period incurred. **p. 230**

Residual value: The amount the company expects to receive from selling the asset at the end of its service life; also referred to as *salvage value*. **p. 233**

Return on assets: Net income divided by average total assets; measures the amount of net income generated for each dollar invested in assets. **p. 246**

Service life: How long the company expects to receive benefits from the asset before disposing of it; also referred to as *useful life*. **p. 233**

Straight-line method: Allocates an equal amount of depreciation to each year of the asset's service life. **p. 234**

Trademark: A word, slogan, or symbol that distinctively identifies a company, product, or service. **p. 228**

SELF-STUDY QUESTIONS

1. We normally record a long-term asset at the: ■ LO1
   a. Cost of the asset only.
   b. Cost of the asset plus all costs necessary to get the asset ready for use.
   c. Appraised value.
   d. Cost of the asset, but subsequently adjust it up or down to appraised value.

2. Sandwich Express incurred the following costs related to its purchase of a bread machine. ■ LO1

Cost of the equipment	$20,000
Sales tax (8%)	1,600
Shipping	2,200
Installation	1,400
Total costs	$25,200

At what amount should Sandwich Express record the bread machine?
a. $20,000.
b. $21,600.
c. $23,800.
d. $25,200.

■ LO2

3. Research and development costs generated internally:
a. Are recorded as research and development assets.
b. Are capitalized and then amortized.
c. Should be included in the cost of the patent they relate to.
d. Should be expensed.

■ LO3

4. Which of the following expenditures should be recorded as an expense?
a. Repairs and maintenance that maintain current benefits.
b. Adding a major new component to an existing asset.
c. Replacing a major component of an existing asset.
d. Successful legal defense of an intangible asset.

■ LO4

5. Which of the following will maximize net income by minimizing depreciation expense in the first year of the asset's life?
a. Short service life, high residual value, and straight-line depreciation.
b. Long service life, high residual value, and straight-line depreciation.
c. Short service life, low residual value, and double-declining-balance depreciation.
d. Long service life, high residual value, and double-declining-balance depreciation.

■ LO4

6. The book value of an asset is equal to the:
a. Replacement cost.
b. Asset's cost less accumulated depreciation.
c. Asset's fair value less its historical cost.
d. Historical cost plus accumulated depreciation.

■ LO4

7. The balance in the Accumulated Depreciation account represents:
a. The amount charged to expense in the current period.
b. A contra expense account.
c. A cash fund to be used to replace plant assets.
d. The amount charged to depreciation expense since the acquisition of the plant asset.

■ LO5

8. Which of the following statements is *true* regarding the amortization of intangible assets?
a. Intangible assets with a limited useful life are not amortized.
b. The service life of an intangible asset is always equal to its legal life.
c. The expected residual value of most intangible assets is zero.
d. In recording amortization, Accumulated Amortization is always credited.

■ LO6

9. Equipment originally costing $95,000 has accumulated depreciation of $30,000. If it sells the equipment for $55,000, the company should record:
a. No gain or loss.
b. A gain of $10,000.
c. A loss of $10,000.
d. A loss of $40,000.

■ LO7

10. The return on assets is equal to the:
a. Profit margin plus asset turnover.
b. Profit margin minus asset turnover.
c. Profit margin times asset turnover.
d. Profit margin divided by asset turnover.

Answers to the Self-Study Questions
1. b   2. d   3. d   4. a   5. b   6. b   7. d   8. c   9. c   10. c

REVIEW QUESTIONS

1. **WorldCom** committed the largest fraud in U.S. history. What was the primary method WorldCom's management used to carry out the fraud?   ■ **LO1**

2. What are the two major categories of long-term assets? How do these two categories differ?   ■ **LO1**

3. Explain how we initially record a long-term asset.   ■ **LO1**

4. If University Hero initially records an expense incorrectly as an asset, how does this mistake affect the income statement and the balance sheet?   ■ **LO1**

5. Little King acquires land and an old building across the street from Northwestern State University. Little King intends to remove the old building and build a new sandwich shop on the land. What costs might the firm incur to make the land ready for its intended use?   ■ **LO1**

6. Why don't we depreciate land? What are land improvements? Why do we record land and land improvements separately?   ■ **LO1**

7. Equipment includes machinery used in manufacturing, computers and other office equipment, vehicles, furniture, and fixtures. What costs might we incur to get equipment ready for use?   ■ **LO1**

8. Where in the balance sheet do we report natural resources? Provide at least three examples of natural resource assets.   ■ **LO1**

9. Explain how the accounting treatment differs between purchased and internally developed intangible assets.   ■ **LO2**

10. What are the differences among a patent, a copyright, and a trademark?   ■ **LO2**

11. What is goodwill and how do we measure it? Can we sell goodwill separately from the business?   ■ **LO2**

12. How do we decide whether to capitalize (record as an asset) or expense a particular cost?   ■ **LO3**

13. Explain the usual accounting treatment for repairs and maintenance, additions, and improvements.   ■ **LO3**

14. Are litigation costs to defend an intangible asset capitalized or expensed? Explain your answer.   ■ **LO3**

15. How is the dictionary definition different from the accounting definition of depreciation?   ■ **LO4**

16. What factors must we estimate in allocating the cost of a long-term asset over its service life?   ■ **LO4**

17. What is the service life of an asset? How do we determine service life under the straight-line and the activity-based depreciation methods?   ■ **LO4**

18. What is residual value? How do we use residual value in calculating depreciation under the straight-line method?   ■ **LO4**

19. Contrast the effects of the straight-line, declining-balance, and activity-based methods on annual depreciation expense.   ■ **LO4**

20. Assume that Little King Sandwiches uses straight-line depreciation and University Hero uses double-declining-balance depreciation. Explain the difficulties in comparing the income statements and balance sheets of the two companies.   ■ **LO4**

21. Assume Little King Sandwiches depreciates a building over 40 years and University Hero depreciates a similar building over 20 years, and both companies use the straight-line depreciation method. Explain the difficulties in comparing the income statements and balance sheets of the two companies.   ■ **LO4**

■ LO4   22. Which depreciation method is most common for financial reporting? Which depreciation method is most common for tax reporting? Why do companies choose these methods?

■ LO5   23. Justin Time is confident that firms amortize all intangible assets. Is he right? If amortized, are intangible assets always amortized over their legal life? Explain.

■ LO6   24. What is book value? How do we compute the gain or loss on the sale of long-term assets?

■ LO7   25. Describe return on assets, profit margin, and asset turnover.

■ LO7   26. Provide an example of a company like **Abercrombie** with a high profit margin. Provide an example of a company like **Walmart** with high asset turnover.

■ LO8   27. What is an asset impairment? Describe the two-step process for recording impairments. How does recording an impairment loss affect the income statement and the balance sheet?

■ LO8   28. How do companies take a *big bath?* Explain the effect of a big bath on the current year's and future years' net income.

For the following, please visit your instructor's *Connect* site.

Mc Graw Hill **connect** |ACCOUNTING

BRIEF EXERCISES	1-15
EXERCISES	1-20
PROBLEMS: SET A	1-10
PROBLEMS: SET B	1-10
GREAT ADVENTURES	

Note: Additional Perspectives assignments for Financial Analysis, Comparative Analysis, Internet Research, Written Communication, and Earnings Management are in Appendix F at the end of this book. For additional Exercises: Set B and for additional Problems: Set C, visit www.mhhe.com/spicelandMTC1e.

8

Current Liabilities

Learning Objectives

AFTER STUDYING THIS CHAPTER, YOU SHOULD BE ABLE TO:

- ■ **LO1** Distinguish between current and long-term liabilities.
- ■ **LO2** Account for notes payable and interest expense.
- ■ **LO3** Account for employee and employer payroll liabilities.
- ■ **LO4** Demonstrate the accounting for other current liabilities.
- ■ **LO5** Apply the appropriate accounting treatment for contingencies.

Analysis

- ■ **LO6** Assess liquidity using current liability ratios.

UNITED AIRLINES: A FUTURE UP IN THE AIR

Feature Story

Have you ever considered buying stock in an airline? Do you think companies like **American**, **Delta**, or **United** would be a good investment? Think again. Warren Buffett, a self-made billionaire based in Omaha, Nebraska, is regarded as one of the world's top investors. In 1991 he observed that the airline industry had not made a dime for investors in a century of manned flight. Buffett acknowledged his mistake in buying stock in **US Airways**, which later filed for Chapter 11 bankruptcy along with Delta, **Northwest**, United, and others.

Companies must file for bankruptcy protection when they no longer are able to pay their liabilities as they become due. By carefully examining information in financial statements, investors and creditors can assess a company's profitability and its *liquidity*—its ability to pay currently maturing debt. Both profitability and liquidity help indicate a company's risk of filing for bankruptcy. Wise investors, like Warren Buffett, pay careful attention to these warning signs.

What are some of the current liabilities reported by companies in the airline industry? The airline industry is very labor-intensive, resulting in extensive payroll liabilities. Another substantial current liability for airlines is advance ticket sales. This liability, representing tickets sold for future flights, is in the billions of dollars for several major U.S. airlines. Airlines are well known for their frequent-flier programs. These programs have created liabilities for frequent-flier incentives exceeding $100 million. Finally, a somewhat different type of liability airlines face is contingent liabilities. A *contingent liability* is a possible liability for which payment is contingent upon another event. An example is pending litigation. All of the major airlines report contingent liabilities related to unsettled litigation.

With airlines incurring so many types of liabilities, it is no wonder many airlines have filed for bankruptcy. However, there is one shining star among companies in the airline industry—**Southwest Airlines**. Known as the airline where your "bags fly free," it is recognized in the investment community for its strong financial performance. At the end of the chapter, we compare liquidity ratios between United Airlines and Southwest Airlines, to explore whether the financial reputation of Southwest Airlines is for real.

PART A

■ **LO1**
Distinguish between
current and long-term
liabilities.

CURRENT LIABILITIES

In the four preceding chapters, we worked our way down the asset side of the balance sheet, examining cash, accounts receivable, inventory, and long-term assets. We now turn to the liabilities side of the balance sheet. In the next three chapters, we discuss how companies finance their operations through borrowing (liabilities) or additional investment by owners (stockholders' equity). Chapter 8 focuses on current liabilities and Chapter 9 on long-term liabilities. In Chapter 10, we look at stockholders' equity.

Liabilities have three essential characteristics. Liabilities are: (1) probable *future* sacrifices of economic benefits, (2) arising from *present* obligations to other entities, (3) resulting from *past* transactions or events.[1] The definition of liabilities touches on the present, the future, and the past: A liability is a present responsibility to sacrifice assets in the future due to a transaction or other event that happened in the past.

Recall that assets represent probable future *benefits*. In contrast, liabilities represent probable future *sacrifices* of benefits. What benefits are sacrificed? Most liabilities require the future sacrifice of cash. For instance, accounts payable, notes payable, and salaries payable usually are paid in cash.

Can you think of a liability that requires paying something other than cash? One such liability is unearned revenue. Remember (from Chapter 3) that this liability arises when a company receives payment in advance of providing the product or service it's selling. This obligation requires giving up inventory or services rather than cash to satisfy the debt.

Current vs. Long-Term Classification

In a classified balance sheet, we categorize liabilities as either current or long-term. **In most cases, current liabilities are payable within one year, and long-term liabilities are payable more than one year from now.**

Common Terms Current liabilities are also sometimes called *short-term liabilities.*

 COMMON MISTAKE

Current liabilities are *usually*, but not always, due within one year. But for some companies (a winery, for example), it takes longer than a year to perform the activities that produce revenue. We call the time it takes to produce revenue—from "cash to cash" as the saying goes (i.e., initial investment to revenue)—the *operating cycle.* If a company has an operating cycle longer than one year, its current liabilities are defined by the operating cycle rather than by the length of a year. For now, remember that in most cases (but not all) current liabilities are due within one year.

Distinguishing between current and long-term liabilities is important in helping investors and creditors assess risk. Given a choice, most companies would prefer to report a liability as long-term rather than current, because doing so may cause the firm to appear less risky. In turn, less-risky firms may enjoy lower interest rates on borrowing and command higher stock prices for new stock listings.

The Feature Story at the beginning of this chapter pointed out that the U.S. airline industry has experienced financial difficulties in recent years, resulting in greater risk to investors. Several major airlines have been forced into bankruptcy because they were unable to pay current liabilities as they became due. In Illustration 8–1 an excerpt from the annual report of **United Airlines** discusses the problem.

spiceland.mhhe.com/c22

---

[1]"Elements of Financial Statements." 1985. *Statement of Financial Accounting Concepts No. 6* (Stamford, Conn.: FASB), par. 38.

> **UNITED AIRLINES**
> **Management Discussion and Analysis (excerpt)**
>
> Over the past several years, United and indeed the entire airline industry have faced severe business challenges and fundamental industry changes which have produced material adverse impacts on earnings, financial position and liquidity. The Company had been operating under Chapter 11 bankruptcy protection since December 9, 2002, and emerged on February 1, 2006.
>
> Operating revenues for the airline industry in general, as well as for United, have been adversely impacted by several factors. The growth of low cost carriers; excess seat capacity; pricing transparency; reduced demand for high-yield business travel; global events such as the war in Iraq, the outbreak of disease as well as the fear of terrorist attacks since September 11, 2001; and the enactment of federal taxes on ticket sales to fund additional airport security measures, have caused earnings to decline.

ILLUSTRATION 8–1

Bankruptcy of United Airlines

What obligations do firms most frequently report as current liabilities? Notes payable, accounts payable, and payroll liabilities are three main categories. In addition, companies report a variety of other current liabilities, including unearned revenue, sales tax payable, and the current portion of long-term debt.

There is no prescribed order for presenting accounts within the current liabilities section of the balance sheet. However, many companies list notes payable first, followed by accounts payable, and then other current liabilities from largest to smallest. *Follow this order when preparing your homework assignments.* In keeping with this order, we discuss notes payable in the next section.

 KEY POINT

In most cases, current liabilities are payable within one year, and long-term liabilities are payable more than one year from now.

Notes Payable

In Chapter 5, we saw how companies account for notes receivable. Here, we discuss the flip side of notes receivable—notes payable. Recall that notes receivable is an asset that creates interest revenue. In contrast, notes payable is a *liability* that creates interest *expense.*

Very often, small firms are unable to tap into the major sources of long-term financing (such as bonds) to the extent necessary to provide for their capital needs, so they must rely heavily on short-term financing. When a company borrows cash from a bank, the bank requires the firm to sign a note promising to repay the amount borrowed plus interest. The borrower reports its liability as notes payable. About two-thirds of bank loans are short-term. Even large companies use short-term debt as a significant part of their capital structure. A major reason is that short-term funds usually offer lower interest rates than long-term debt.

Assume **Southwest Airlines** borrows $100,000 from **Bank of America** on September 1, 2012, signing a 6%, six-month note for the amount borrowed plus accrued interest due six months later on March 1, 2013. On September 1, 2012, Southwest will receive $100,000 in cash and record the following:

■ LO2
Account for notes payable and interest expense.

September 1, 2012	Debit	Credit
Cash	100,000	
Notes Payable		100,000
(Issue notes payable)		

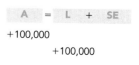

When a company borrows money, it pays the lender **interest** in return for using the lender's money during the term of the loan. Interest is stated in terms of an annual percentage rate to be applied to the face value of the loan. Because the stated interest rate is an *annual* rate, when calculating interest for a current note payable we must adjust for the fraction of the annual period the loan spans. We calculate interest on notes as:

$$\text{Interest} = \text{Face value} \times \frac{\text{Annual}}{\text{interest rate}} \times \frac{\text{Fraction}}{\text{of the year}}$$

In the example above, how much interest cost does Southwest incur for the six-month period of the note from September 1, 2012, to March 1, 2013?

$$\$3,000 = \$100,000 \times 6\% \times 6/12$$

However, if Southwest's reporting period ends on December 31, 2012, the company can't wait until March 1, 2013, to record interest. Instead, the company records the four months' interest incurred during 2012 in an adjustment prior to preparing the 2012 financial statements. Since the firm will not pay the 2012 interest until the note becomes due (March 1, 2013), it records the $2,000 interest as **interest payable,** as follows:

A = L + SE	December 31, 2012	Debit	Credit
−2,000 Exp↑	**Interest Expense** (= $100,000 × 6% × 4/12)	2,000	
+2,000	**Interest Payable**		2,000
	(*Record interest incurred, but not paid*)		

 COMMON MISTAKE

When calculating the number of months of interest, students sometimes mistakenly subtract December (month 12) from September (month 9) and get three months. However, the time from September 1 to December 31 includes both September and December, so there are four months. If you are ever in doubt, count out the months on your fingers. Your fingers never lie.

The purpose of the adjusting entry is to report four months' interest (September, October, November, and December) in 2012. Southwest will report the remaining $1,000 of interest (for January and February) in 2013. Since the firm won't actually pay the 2012 interest until March 1, 2013, its financial statements for the year ended December 31, 2012, will show interest payable of $2,000 along with notes payable of $100,000 as a current liability on the balance sheet, and the "other expenses" section of the income statement will report interest expense of $2,000.

When the note comes due on March 1, 2013, Southwest Airlines will pay the face value of the loan ($100,000) plus the entire $3,000 interest incurred ($100,000 × 6% × 6/12). The $3,000 represents six months of interest—the four months of interest ($2,000) in 2012 previously recorded as interest payable and two months of interest ($1,000) in 2013. Southwest records these transactions on March 1, 2013, as follows:

A = L + SE	March 1, 2013	Debit	Credit
−100,000	**Notes Payable** (face value)	100,000	
−1,000 Exp↑	**Interest Expense** (= $100,000 × 6% × 2/12)	1,000	
−2,000	**Interest Payable** (= $100,000 × 6% × 4/12)	2,000	
−103,000	**Cash**		103,000
	(*Pay notes payable and interest*)		

The entry on March 1 does the following:

- Removes the note payable ($100,000).
- Records interest expense for January and February 2013 ($1,000).
- Removes the interest payable recorded in the December 31, 2012, entry ($2,000).
- Reduces cash ($103,000).

Notice that we record interest expense incurred for four months in 2012 and two months in 2013, rather than recording all six months' interest expense in 2013 when we pay it. This is consistent with the matching principle.

spiceland.mhhe.com/c23

 KEY POINT

We record interest expense in the period in which we *incur* it, rather than in the period in which we pay it.

How would the lender, Bank of America, record this note? For the bank it's a **note receivable** rather than a note payable, and it generates **interest revenue** rather than interest expense. (You may want to review the discussion on notes receivable in Chapter 5.) The entries for Bank of America's loan are as follows:

Flip Side

September 1, 2012	Debit	Credit	A	=	L	+	SE
Notes Receivable	100,000		+100,000				
Cash		100,000	−100,000				
(*Issue notes receivable*)							

December 31, 2012	Debit	Credit	A	=	L	+	SE
Interest Receivable	2,000		+2,000				
Interest Revenue (= $100,000 × 6% × 4/12)		2,000					+2,000 Rev↑
(*Record interest earned, but not received*)							

March 1, 2013	Debit	Credit	A	=	L	+	SE
Cash	103,000		+103,000				
Interest Revenue (= $100,000 × 6% × 2/12)		1,000					+1,000 Rev↑
Interest Receivable (= $100,000 × 6% × 4/12)		2,000	−2,000				
Notes Receivable (face value)		100,000	−100,000				
(*Collect notes receivable and interest*)							

Assume **Delta Airlines** borrows $500,000 from **Chase Bank** on November 1, 2012, signing a 9%, six-month note payable.

Let's Review

Required:

1. Record the issuance of the note payable.
2. Record the adjustment for the note payable on December 31, 2012.
3. Record the payment of the note payable at maturity.

spiceland.mhhe.com/t14

Solution:

1. Issuance of note payable:

November 1, 2012	Debit	Credit
Cash	500,000	
Notes Payable		500,000
(Issue note payable)		

2. Adjustment for interest expense at the end of the period:

December 31, 2012	Debit	Credit
Interest Expense (= $500,000 × 9% × 2/12)	7,500	
Interest Payable		7,500
(Record interest incurred, but not paid)		

3. Payment of note at maturity:

May 1, 2013	Debit	Credit
Notes Payable	500,000	
Interest Expense (= $500,000 × 9% × 4/12)	15,000	
Interest Payable (= $500,000 × 9% × 2/12)	7,500	
Cash		522,500
(Pay note payable and interest)		

Suggested Homework:
BE8-1, BE8-2;
E8-2, E8-3;
P8-2A&B

Rather than wait until borrowing becomes necessary, many companies pre-arrange the terms of a note payable by establishing a line of credit with a bank. A line of credit is an informal agreement that permits a company to borrow up to a prearranged limit without having to follow formal loan procedures and prepare paperwork. The line of credit works like a note payable except the company is able to borrow without having to go through a formal loan approval process each time it borrows money. Banks sometimes require the company to maintain a cash balance on deposit with the bank, say, 5% of the line of credit. The recording for a line of credit is exactly the same as the recording for notes payable described earlier.

Decision Point

Question	Accounting information	Analysis
How can you tell the amount and interest rate of a company's line of credit?	Notes to the financial statements	Companies are required to disclose the terms of available lines of credit such as the amounts, maturity dates, and interest rates.

If a company borrows from another company rather than from a bank, the note is referred to as commercial paper. Commercial paper is sold with maturities ranging from 30 to 270 days. (Beyond 270 days, the issuing firm is required to file a registration statement with the SEC.) Since a company is borrowing directly from another company, the interest rate on commercial paper is usually lower than on a bank loan. Commercial paper has thus become an increasingly popular way for large companies to raise funds, so much so that the total dollar value of commercial paper loans outstanding has multiplied five times in the last decade.

KEY POINT

Many short-term loans are arranged under an existing line of credit with a bank, or for larger corporations in the form of commercial paper, a loan from one company to another.

Accounts Payable

Accounts payable, sometimes called *trade accounts payable,* are amounts the company owes to suppliers of merchandise or services that it has bought on credit. We discussed accounting for this very common form of current liability when we discussed inventory purchases in Chapter 6. Briefly, recall that when a company purchases items on account (if it does not pay immediately with cash), it increases a liability called Accounts Payable. Later, when the company pays the amount owed, it decreases both Cash and Accounts Payable.

Payroll Liabilities

Many companies, including those in the airline industry, are very labor-intensive. Payroll liabilities make up a significant portion of current liabilities for these companies. Here, we will look at how payroll is calculated for both the employee and the employer.

■ LO3
Account for employee and employer payroll liabilities.

Let's assume you are hired at a $60,000 annual salary with salary payments of $5,000 per month. Before you make any spending plans, though, you need to realize that your payroll check will be much *less* than $5,000 a month. Before depositing your monthly payroll check in your bank account, your employer will "withhold" amounts for (1) federal and state income taxes; (2) Social Security and Medicare; (3) health, dental, disability, and life insurance premiums; and (4) *employee* investments to retirement or savings plans. Realistically, then, your $5,000 monthly salary translates to less than $4,000 in actual take-home pay.

Now assume you are an employer. You hire an employee at a starting annual salary of $60,000. Your costs for this employee will be much *more* than $5,000 per month. Besides the $5,000 monthly salary, you will incur significant costs for (1) federal and state unemployment taxes; (2) the *employer* portion of Social Security and Medicare; (3) *employer* contributions for health, dental, disability, and life insurance; and (4) *employer* contributions to retirement or savings plans. With these additional costs, a $5,000 monthly salary could very easily create total costs in excess of $6,000 per month. Illustration 8–2 summarizes payroll costs for employees and employers. We discuss these costs below.

Employee Payroll Costs	Employer Payroll Costs
Federal and state income taxes	Federal and state unemployment taxes
Employee portion of Social Security and Medicare	Employer matching portion of Social Security and Medicare
Employee contributions for health, dental, disability, and life insurance	Employer contributions for health, dental, disability, and life insurance
Employee investments in retirement or savings plans	Employer contributions to retirement or savings plans

ILLUSTRATION 8–2

Payroll Costs for Employees and Employers

EMPLOYEE COSTS

Employers are required by law to withhold federal and state income taxes from employees' paychecks and remit these taxes to the government. The amount withheld varies according to the amount the employee earns and the number of exemptions

CAREER CORNER

When comparing compensation among different career opportunities, don't base your final decision on salary alone. Fringe benefits can sometimes make up for a lower annual salary. Various employers offer *fringe benefits*—also called "perquisites," or "perks"—that catch the attention of would-be employees: a pound of coffee every month at Starbucks, free skiing for employees at Vail Ski Resort, or scuba and kayaking in the pool at Nike's Athletic Village in Beaverton, Oregon. More common fringe benefits, and ones that many people appreciate in the long run, include employer coverage of family health insurance, educational benefits, and contributions to retirement plans.

However, remember that even more important than either salary *or* benefits are the training and experience the position offers. Training and experience can provide you with the skills necessary to land that big promotion or dream job in the future.

the employee claims. The IRS furnishes tax tables that assist in determining the amount withheld. If you are able to claim more exemptions, you will have less tax withheld from your paycheck. Not all states require the payment of personal income taxes: Alaska, Florida, Nevada, South Dakota, Texas, Washington, and Wyoming have no state income tax. Two others, New Hampshire and Tennessee, tax only dividend and interest income.

Employers also withhold Social Security and Medicare taxes from employees' paychecks. Collectively, Social Security and Medicare taxes are referred to as FICA taxes, named for the Federal Insurance Contribution Act (FICA). This act requires employers to withhold a 6.2% Social Security tax up to a maximum base amount plus a 1.45% Medicare tax with no maximum. Therefore, the total FICA tax is 7.65% (6.2% + 1.45%) on income up to a base amount ($106,800 in 2010) and 1.45% on all income above the base amount. For example, if you earn less than $106,800, you will have 7.65% withheld from your check all year. However, if you earn, let's say, $156,800, you would have 7.65% withheld for FICA on the first $106,800 of your annual salary and then only 1.45% withheld on the remaining $50,000 earned during the rest of the year.

Besides the required deductions for income tax and FICA taxes, employees may opt to have additional amounts withheld from their paychecks. These might include the employee portion of insurance premiums, employee investments in retirement or savings plans, and contributions to charitable organizations such as **United Way**. The employer records the amounts deducted from employee payroll as liabilities until it pays them to the appropriate organizations.

EMPLOYER COSTS

By law, the employer pays an additional (matching) FICA tax on behalf of the employee. The employer's limits on FICA tax are the same as the employee's. Thus, the government actually collects 15.3% (7.65% employee + 7.65% employer) on each employee's salary.

In addition to FICA, the employer also must pay federal and state unemployment taxes on behalf of its employees. The *Federal Unemployment Tax Act* (FUTA) requires a tax of 6.2% on the first $7,000 earned by each employee. This amount is reduced by a 5.4% (maximum) credit for contributions to state unemployment programs, so the net federal rate often is 0.8%. Under the *State Unemployment Tax Act* (SUTA), in many states the maximum state unemployment tax rate is 5.4%, but many companies pay a lower rate based on past employment history.

 COMMON MISTAKE

Many people think FICA taxes are paid only by the employee. The employer is required to match the amount withheld for each employee, effectively doubling the amount paid into Social Security.

Additional employee benefits paid for by the employer are referred to as fringe benefits. Employers often pay all or part of employees' insurance premiums and make contributions to retirement or savings plans. Many companies provide additional fringe benefits specific to the company or the industry, as discussed in the nearby Career Corner. For instance, an important additional fringe benefit in the airline industry is the ability for the employee and family to fly free.

To understand how employee and employer payroll costs are recorded, assume that Hawaiian Travel Agency has a total payroll for the month of January of $100,000 for its 20 employees. Its withholdings and payroll taxes are shown in Illustration 8–3.

Federal and state income tax withheld	$24,000	**ILLUSTRATION 8–3**
Health insurance premiums (Blue Cross) paid by employer	5,000	Payroll Example,
Contribution to retirement plan (Fidelity) paid by employer	10,000	Hawaiian Travel
FICA tax rate (Social Security and Medicare)	7.65%	Agency
Federal and state unemployment tax rate	6.2%	

Hawaiian Travel Agency records the *employee* salary expense, withholdings, and salaries payable on January 31 as follows:

January 31	Debit	Credit	A	=	L	+	SE
Salaries Expense	**100,000**						−100,000 Exp↑
Income Tax Payable		**24,000**			+24,000		
FICA Tax Payable (= 0.0765 × $100,000)		**7,650**			+7,650		
Salaries Payable (to balance)		**68,350**			+68,350		
(*Record employee salary expense and withholdings*)							

Hawaiian Travel Agency records its employer-provided fringe benefits as follows:

January 31	Debit	Credit	A	=	L	+	SE
Salaries Expense (fringe benefits)	**15,000**						−15,000 Exp↑
Accounts Payable (to Blue Cross)		**5,000**			+5,000		
Accounts Payable (to Fidelity)		**10,000**			+10,000		
(*Record employer-provided fringe benefits*)							

Hawaiian Travel Agency pays employer's FICA taxes at the same rate that the employees pay (7.65%) and also pays unemployment taxes at the rate of 6.2%. The agency records its *employer's* payroll taxes as follows:

January 31	Debit	Credit	A	=	L	+	SE
Payroll Tax Expense (total)	**13,850**						−13,850 Exp↑
FICA Tax Payable (= 0.0765 × $100,000)		**7,650**			+7,650		
Unemployment Tax Payable (= 0.062 × $100,000)		**6,200**			+6,200		
(*Record employer payroll taxes*)							

Hawaiian Travel Agency incurred an additional $28,850 in expenses ($15,000 for fringe benefits plus $13,850 for employer payroll taxes) beyond the $100,000 salary expense. Also notice that the FICA tax payable in the *employee* withholding is the same amount recorded for *employer* payroll tax. That's because the employee pays 7.65% and the employer matches this amount with an additional 7.65%. The amounts withheld are then transferred at regular intervals, monthly or quarterly, to their designated recipients. Income taxes, FICA taxes, and unemployment taxes are transferred to various government agencies, and fringe benefits are paid to the company's contractual suppliers.

KEY POINT

Employee salaries are reduced by withholdings for federal and state income taxes, FICA taxes, and the employee portion of insurance and retirement contributions. The employer, too, incurs additional payroll expenses for unemployment taxes, the employer portion of FICA taxes, and employer insurance and retirement contributions.

Other Current Liabilities

■ LO4
Demonstrate the accounting for other current liabilities.

Additional current liabilities companies might report include unearned revenues, sales tax payable, the current portion of long-term debt, and deferred taxes. We explore each of these in more detail below.

UNEARNED REVENUES

United Airlines sells tickets and collects the cash price several days, weeks, or sometimes months before the actual flight. When does United Airlines record the revenue—when it sells the ticket, or when the flight actually takes place? Illustration 8–4 provides the answer, in United's disclosure of its revenue recognition policies.

ILLUSTRATION 8–4
Revenue Recognition Policy of United Airlines

> **UNITED AIRLINES**
> **Notes to the Financial Statements (excerpt)**
>
> ***Airline Revenues***—We record passenger fares and cargo revenues as operating revenues when the transportation is provided. The value of unused passenger tickets is included in current liabilities as advance ticket sales. We periodically evaluate the balance in advance ticket sales and record any adjustments in the period the evaluation is completed.

As you can see, United waits until the actual flight occurs to record the revenues. Since the flights have not taken place, the airline has not yet earned the revenue.

United's situation is not unique. It's not uncommon for companies to require advance payments from customers that will be applied to the purchase price when they deliver goods or provide services. You've likely been one of these customers. Examples of advance payments are gift cards from clothing stores like **American Eagle** or restaurants like **Chili's**, movie tickets from **Fandango**, room deposits at hotels like **Embassy Suites**, and subscriptions for magazines like *Sports Illustrated*.

How do these companies account for the cash they receive in advance? We initially discussed unearned revenue in Chapter 3, but let's review with an example. Assume **Apple Inc.** sells an iTunes gift card to a customer for $100. Apple records the sale of the gift card as follows:

				Debit	Credit
A	=	L	+	SE	
+100					
		+100			

	Debit	Credit
Cash	100	
Unearned Revenue		100
(Receive cash for gift card)		

As you can see, Apple Inc. records the receipt of cash, but does not credit Sales Revenue. Rather, since the iTunes have not been downloaded yet, the company credits Unearned Revenue, a liability account. While it may seem unusual for an account called Unearned Revenue to be a liability, think of it this way: Having already collected the cash, the company now has the obligation to earn it.

When the customer purchases and downloads, say, $15 worth of music, Apple records the following:

	Debit	Credit
Unearned Revenue	15	
Sales Revenue		15
(Earn revenue from music downloaded)		

A	=	L	+	SE
		−15		
				+15 Rev↑

As the company earns revenue from music downloads, it decreases (debits) Unearned Revenue and increases (credits) Sales Revenue. The customer has a balance of $85 on his gift card, and Apple Inc. has a balance in Unearned Revenue, a liability account, of $85 for music downloads.

KEY POINT

When a company receives cash in advance, it debits Cash and credits Unearned Revenue, a current liability account. When it earns the revenue, the company debits Unearned Revenue and credits Sales Revenue.

Let's Review

spiceland.mhhe.com/t15

The new **Dallas Cowboys** football stadium has a seating capacity of 80,000, expandable to 111,000 with standing-room-only capacity. The new stadium cost $1.15 billion, making it one of the most expensive sports stadiums ever built. The Cowboys hold eight regular season games at home; an average ticket sells for about $100 a game. Assume the Cowboys collect $48 million in season ticket sales prior to the beginning of the season. For eight home games, that's $6 million per game ($48 million ÷ 8 games).

Required:

1. Record the sale of $48 million in season tickets prior to the beginning of the season.
2. Record the $6 million in revenue recognized after the first game.

Solution:

1. Sale of $48 million in season ticket sales:

($ in millions)	Debit	Credit
Cash	48	
Unearned Revenue		48
(Sell season tickets prior to the beginning of the season)		

2. $6 million in revenue recognized after the first game:

($ in millions)	Debit	Credit
Unearned Revenue	6	
Sales Revenue		6
(Earn revenue for each home game played)		

The Cowboys would make similar entries after each home game.

Suggested Homework:
BE8-6,
E8-10;
P8-5A&B

SALES TAX PAYABLE

Most states impose a state sales tax, and many areas include a local sales tax as well. Yet, some states do not have a sales tax. Upon arriving in Oregon for the first time, Don ordered lunch at a fast-food restaurant. His meal cost $4.99. When the employee at the counter said, "You're not from Oregon, are you?", Don wondered aloud how the sales clerk could tell. The clerk politely replied, "You have five dollars and some change in your hand, but in Oregon there's no sales tax." States that currently don't impose a general state sales tax are Alaska, Delaware, Montana, New Hampshire, and Oregon. However, many cities in Alaska have *local* sales taxes. The other four states impose sales-type taxes on specific transactions such as lodging, tobacco, or gasoline sales.

Each company selling products subject to sales tax is responsible for collecting the sales tax directly from customers and periodically sending the sales taxes collected to the state and local governments. The selling company records sales revenue in one account and sales tax payable in another. **When the company collects the sales taxes, it increases (debits) Cash and increases (credits) Sales Tax Payable.**

Suppose you buy lunch in the airport for $15 plus 9% sales tax. The airport restaurant records the transaction this way:

	Debit	Credit
Cash	16.35	
Sales Revenue		15.00
Sales Tax Payable (= $15 × 0.09)		1.35
(Record sales and sales tax)		

A   =   L   +   SE
+16.35
        +15.00 Rev↑
    +1.35

Some companies don't separately record sales and sales tax with each sale. Instead, they choose to separate the two amounts later. Suppose you buy lunch in the airport for $21.80 that includes a 9% sales tax. How much did the restaurant charge you for the lunch, and how much does it owe the state for sales tax? If we divide the total cash paid by 1.09 (1 + 9% sales tax rate), we get $20 (= $21.80 ÷ 1.09) as the sales price, leaving $1.80 as sales tax payable. If the entire amount collected is recorded initially as sales, at some point the company will separate the sales tax portion from sales and record that amount as sales tax payable.

 KEY POINT

Sales taxes collected from customers by the seller are not an expense. Instead, they represent current liabilities payable to the government.

CURRENT PORTION OF LONG-TERM DEBT

Distinguishing between the current portion of long-term debt and long-term debt is important to management, investors, and lenders. The current portion of long-term debt is the amount that will be paid within the next year. Management needs to know this amount in order to budget the cash flow necessary to pay the current portion as it becomes due. Investors and lenders also pay attention to current debt because it provides information about a company's liquidity, a useful indicator of risk.

Long-term obligations (notes, mortgages, bonds) usually are reclassified and reported as current liabilities when they become payable within the upcoming year (or operating cycle, if longer than a year). For example, a firm reports a 10-year note payable as a long-term liability for nine years but as a current liability on the balance sheet prepared during the tenth year of its term to maturity. As another example, **Southwest Airlines** had total borrowings of $3,515 million at December 31, 2009, of which $190 million was payable in 2010 and the remaining $3,325 million is due after 2010. In its 2009 balance sheet, the company records the $3,515 million in current and long-term debt, as shown in Illustration 8–5.

spiceland.mhhe.com/c24

ILLUSTRATION 8–5

Current Portion of Long-Term Debt

SOUTHWEST AIRLINES	
Balance Sheet (partial)	
December 31, 2009	
($ in millions)	
Current liabilities:	
Current portion of long-term debt	$ 190
Long-term liabilities:	
Long-term debt	3,325
Total borrowings	$3,515

KEY POINT

We report the currently maturing portion of a long-term debt as a current liability on the balance sheet.

Current or Long-Term?

**Decision Maker's
Perspective**

Given a choice, do you suppose management would prefer to report an obligation as a current liability or a long-term liability? Other things being equal, most managers would choose the long-term classification. The reason is that outsiders like banks, bondholders, and shareholders usually consider debt that is due currently to be riskier than debt that is not due for some time. Riskier debt means paying higher interest rates for borrowing. So, be aware that management has incentives to report current obligations as long-term. ●

DEFERRED TAXES

Net income in the income statement is *not* the same amount as taxable income reported to the Internal Revenue Service (IRS). Net income is based on financial accounting rules, while taxable income in the corporate tax return is based on tax accounting rules. There are many differences between financial accounting rules and tax accounting rules. For instance, most companies use straight-line depreciation in financial accounting, but a different depreciation method (called MACRS) for tax accounting. You will learn more about tax accounting rules in an individual or corporate income tax class.

Differences between financial accounting and tax accounting can result in a company recording financial income now, but deferring payment of some of its income tax expense to future years. In such a case, it will report a *deferred tax liability*. (Or the company may record an expense now, but deduct it for taxes in future years, in which case it will report a deferred tax asset.) As you might guess, deferred taxes can get pretty complex. For now, just remember that there are differences between net income reported on the income statement and taxable income reported on the tax return, and these differences can result in deferred tax liabilities, both current and long-term.

KEY POINT

Net income and taxable income often differ because of differences in financial accounting and tax accounting rules. These differences can result in deferred tax liabilities, in which income is reported now but the tax on the income will not be paid until future years.

PART B

■ **LO5**
Apply the appropriate accounting treatment for contingencies.

CONTINGENCIES

Many companies are involved in litigation disputes, in which the final outcome is uncertain. In its financial statements, does the company wait until the lawsuit is settled, or does it go ahead and report the details of the unsettled case? In this section, we discuss how to report these uncertain situations, which are broadly called contingencies. We look at both contingent liabilities and their flip side, contingent gains.

Contingent Liabilities

A contingent liability may not be a liability at all. Whether it is depends on whether an uncertain event that might result in a loss occurs or not. Examples include lawsuits, product warranties, environmental problems, and premium offers. **Philip Morris**'s tobacco litigation, **Motorola**'s cell phone warranties, **BP**'s environmental obligations, and **United**'s frequent-flier program are all contingent liabilities. To demonstrate, let's consider a litigation example.

LITIGATION AND OTHER CAUSES

Deloitte was the auditor for a client we'll call Jeeps, Inc. The client sold accessories for jeeps, such as tops, lights, cargo carriers, and hitches. One of the major issues that appeared in Deloitte's audit of Jeeps, Inc., was outstanding litigation. Several lawsuits against the company alleged that the jeep top (made of vinyl) did not hold during a major collision. The jeep manufacturer, **Chrysler**, also was named in the lawsuits. The damages claimed were quite large, about $100 million. Although the company had litigation insurance, there was some question whether the insurance company could pay because the insurance carrier was undergoing financial difficulty. The auditor discussed the situation with the outside legal counsel representing Jeeps, Inc. Legal counsel indicated that the possibility of payment was remote and that if the case went to trial, Jeeps, Inc., would almost surely win.

As the auditor, you could choose one of three options to report the situation. You could: (1) report a liability for the full $100 million or for some lesser amount, (2) provide full disclosure in a note to the financial statements but not report a liability in the balance sheet, or (3) provide no disclosure at all.

Whether we report a contingent liability (option 1) depends on two criteria: (1) the likelihood of payment and (2) the ability to estimate the amount of payment. Let's look at the options for each:

1. The likelihood of payment can be:
    a. *Probable*—likely to occur;
    b. *Reasonably possible*—more than remote but less than probable; or
    c. *Remote*—the chance is slight.

2. The ability to estimate the payment amount is either:
    a. Known or reasonably estimable; or
    b. Not reasonably estimable.

A contingent liability is recorded only if a loss is *probable* **and** the amount can be *reasonably estimated*. We record this with a debit to Loss (which acts like an expense account) and a credit to Contingent Liability.

	Debit	Credit
Loss	**x,xxx**	
Contingent Liability		**x,xxx**
(Record a contingent liability)		

INTERNATIONAL FINANCIAL REPORTING STANDARDS (IFRS)

We record a contingent liability under U.S. GAAP if it's both probable and can be reasonably estimated. IFRS rules are similar, but the threshold is "more likely than not." This is a lower threshold than "probable," and thus, contingent liabilities are more likely to be recorded under IFRS rules than under U.S. GAAP.

For more discussion, see Appendix E.

If the likelihood of payment is probable and if one amount within a range appears more likely, we record that amount. When no amount within the range appears more likely than others, we record the *minimum* amount and disclose the potential additional loss. If the likelihood of payment is *reasonably possible* rather than probable, we record no entry but make full disclosure in a note to the financial statements to describe the contingency. Finally, if the likelihood of payment is *remote*, disclosure usually is not required. Illustration 8–6 provides a summary of the accounting for contingent liabilities.

If payment is:	Known or Reasonably Estimable	Not Reasonably Estimable
Probable	Liability recorded and disclosure required	Disclosure required
Reasonably possible	Disclosure required	Disclosure required
Remote	Disclosure not required	Disclosure not required

ILLUSTRATION 8–6

Accounting Treatment of Contingent Liabilities

 KEY POINT

A contingent liability is recorded only if a loss is *probable* **and** the amount can be *reasonably estimated*.

Back to the example of Jeeps, Inc.: How do you think **Deloitte**, as the auditor of Jeeps, Inc., treated the litigation described earlier? Based on the response of legal counsel, the likelihood of the payment occurring was considered to be remote, so disclosure was not required. However, because the amount was so large, and because there were concerns about the firm's primary insurance carrier undergoing financial difficulty, Deloitte insisted on full disclosure of the litigation in the notes to the financial statements.

Decision Point

Question ?	Accounting information 📄	Analysis 🔍
Is the company involved in any litigation?	Notes to the financial statements	Companies are required to disclose all contingencies, including litigation, with at least a reasonable possibility of payment. This information can then be used to help estimate their potential financial impact.

Illustration 8–7 provides excerpts from the disclosure of contingencies made by **United Airlines**.

ILLUSTRATION 8–7

Disclosure of Contingencies by United Airlines

UNITED AIRLINES
Notes to the Financial Statements (excerpts)

Legal and Environmental Contingencies. United Airlines has certain contingencies resulting from litigation and claims (including environmental issues) incident to the ordinary course of business. Management believes, after considering a number of factors, including (but not limited to) the views of legal counsel, the nature of contingencies to which we are subject and prior experience, that the ultimate disposition of these contingencies will not materially affect the Company's consolidated financial position or results of operations.

Contingency for Frequent-Flyer Program Awards. United's Mileage Plus frequent-flyer program awards mileage credits to passengers who fly on United, United Express, and certain other airlines that participate in the program. When a travel award level is attained by a Mileage Plus member, we record a liability for the estimated cost of such awards. The Company had recorded a liability and deferred revenue for its frequent-flyer program totaling $1.6 billion (consisting of $679 million for prepaid miles and $923 million related to award travel).

WARRANTIES

Warranties are perhaps the most common example of contingent liabilities. When you buy a new **Dell** notebook, it comes with a warranty covering the hardware from defect for either a 90-day, one-year, or two-year period depending on the product. Why does Dell offer a warranty? To increase sales, of course.

Based on the matching principle, the company needs to record the warranty expense in the same accounting period in which it sells you the product. The warranty for the computer represents an expense and a liability for Dell at the time of the sale because it meets the criteria for recording a contingent liability: Because warranties almost always entail an eventual expenditure, it's *probable* that a cost will be incurred. And even though Dell doesn't know exactly what that cost will be, it can, based on experience, *reasonably estimate* the amount. Let's look at a warranty example in more detail.

Dell introduces a new notebook computer in December that carries a one-year warranty against manufacturer's defects. Based on industry experience with similar product introductions, Dell expects warranty costs will be an amount equal to approximately 3% of sales. New notebook sales for the month of December are $1.5 million. Dell records the warranty liability on December 31 as follows:

December 31	Debit	Credit
Warranty Expense ($1.5 million × 3%)	45,000	
Warranty Liability		45,000
(Record liability for warranties)		

A = L + SE
−45,000 Exp↑
+45,000

When customers make warranty claims and Dell incurs costs to satisfy those claims, the liability is reduced. Let's say that customers make claims costing $12,000 in December. We record the warranty expenditures as follows:

December 31	Debit	Credit
Warranty Liability	12,000	
Cash		12,000
(Record actual warranty expenditures)		

A = L + SE
−12,000
−12,000

Any time you need to calculate a balance, it's often helpful to make a T-account and record the transactions. Remember, journal entries show the transaction, while T-accounts give you the balance. The balance in the Warranty Liability account at the end of December is $33,000 as follows:

	Warranty Liability		
Payment	12,000	45,000	Expense
		33,000	Balance

COMMON MISTAKE

Some students think the balance in the Warranty Liability account is equal to Warranty Expense, $45,000 in this example. Remember, the liability is increased by warranty expense but then is reduced over time by actual warranty expenditures.

Flip Side

Contingent Gains

A contingent gain is an existing uncertain situation that might result in a gain, which often is the flip side of contingent liabilities. In a pending lawsuit, one side—the defendant—faces a contingent liability, while the other side—the plaintiff—has a contingent gain. For example, **Polaroid** sued **Kodak** for patent infringement of its instant photography technology. Polaroid had a potential gain, while Kodak faced a potential loss.

As discussed earlier, we record contingent liabilities when the loss is probable and the amount is reasonably estimable. However, **we do not record contingent gains until the gain is certain.** The nonparallel treatment of contingent gains follows the same conservative reasoning that motivates reporting some assets (like inventory) at lower-of-cost-or-market. Specifically, it's desirable to anticipate losses, but recognizing gains should await their final settlement. Though firms do not record contingent gains in the accounts, they sometimes disclose them in notes to the financial statements.

KEY POINT

Unlike contingent liabilities, contingent gains are not recorded until the gain is certain and no longer a contingency.

ANALYSIS

LIQUIDITY ANALYSIS
United vs. Southwest

■ **LO6**
Assess liquidity using
current liability ratios.

Liquidity refers to having sufficient cash (or other current assets convertible to cash in a relatively short time) to pay currently maturing debts. Because a lack of liquidity can result in financial difficulties or even bankruptcy, it is critical that managers as well as outside investors and lenders maintain close watch on this aspect of a company's well-being. Here we look at three liquidity measures: working capital, the current ratio, and the acid-test ratio. All three measures are calculated using current assets and current liabilities.

WORKING CAPITAL

The concept of **working capital** is straightforward. It is simply the difference between current assets and current liabilities:

Working capital = Current assets − Current liabilities

Working capital answers the question, "After paying our current obligations, how much will we have to work with?" For example, if you have $20 in your pocket and you know that you still owe $10 to your friend and $3 for parking, your working capital is $7. A large positive working capital is an indicator of liquidity—whether a company will be able to pay its current debts on time.

However, working capital is not the best measure of liquidity when comparing one company with another, since it does not control for the relative size of each company. In comparing companies, the current ratio and the acid-test ratio are better measures of a company's ability to pay its debts on time.

CURRENT RATIO

We calculate the **current ratio** by dividing current assets by current liabilities:

$$\text{Current ratio} = \frac{\text{Current assets}}{\text{Current liabilities}}$$

A current ratio greater than 1 implies more current assets than current liabilities. Recall that current assets include cash, current investments, accounts receivable, inventories, and prepaid expenses. As a rule of thumb, a current ratio of 1 or higher often reflects an acceptable level of liquidity. A current ratio of 1 indicates that for every dollar of current liabilities, the company has an equal amount of current assets. A current ratio of, say, 1.5 indicates that for every dollar of current liabilities, the company has $1.50 of current assets.

In general, the higher the current ratio, the greater the company's liquidity. But we should evaluate the current ratio, like other ratios, in the context of the industry in which the company operates and other specific circumstances. Keep in mind, though, that not all current assets are equally liquid, which leads us to another, more specific ratio for measuring liquidity.

ACID-TEST RATIO

Common Terms The acid-test ratio is also called the *quick ratio*.

The **acid-test ratio**, or *quick ratio*, is similar to the current ratio but is based on a more conservative measure of current assets available to pay current liabilities. We calculate it by dividing "quick assets" by current liabilities. **Quick assets** include only cash, current investments, and accounts receivable. By eliminating current assets, such as inventory and prepaid expenses, that are less readily convertible into cash, the acid-test ratio may provide a better indication of a company's liquidity than does the current ratio.

$$\text{Acid-test ratio} = \frac{\text{Cash + Current investments + Accounts receivable}}{\text{Current liabilities}}$$

We interpret the acid-test ratio much like the current ratio, with one difference: We know that the current assets in the top half of the ratio are only those that can be quickly converted to cash. Thus, an acid-test ratio of, say, 1.5 would indicate that for every dollar of current liabilities, the company has $1.50 of current assets that are easily convertible to cash that might be used to help pay the current liabilities as they come due. As is true for other ratios, be sure to evaluate the acid-test ratio in the context of the industry in which the company operates.

KEY POINT

Working capital is the difference between current assets and current liabilities. The current ratio is equal to current assets divided by current liabilities. The acid-test ratio is equal to quick assets (cash, current investments, and accounts receivable) divided by current liabilities. Each measures a company's liquidity, its ability to pay currently maturing debts.

Decision Point

Question		Accounting information		Analysis	
Does the company have enough cash to pay current liabilities as they come due?		Working capital, current ratio, and acid-test ratio		A high working capital, current ratio, or acid-test ratio generally indicates the ability to pay current liabilities on a timely basis.	

Let's compare **United Airlines**'s liquidity ratios to those of **Southwest Airlines**, considered by many to be the airline industry leader in profitability and overall financial condition.

Let's Review

Selected financial data regarding current assets and current liabilities for United and Southwest Airlines are as follows.

spiceland.mhhe.com/t16

($ in millions)	United	Southwest
Current assets:		
Cash and cash equivalents	$3,046	$1,368
Current investments		435
Net receivables	977	574
Inventory	237	203
Other current assets	601	313
Total current assets	$4,861	$2,893
Current liabilities:		
Accounts payable	$3,231	$2,643
Short/current long-term debt	1,808	163
Other current liabilities	2,242	
Total current liabilities	$7,281	$2,806

Required:

1. Calculate working capital for United Airlines and Southwest Airlines. Is working capital adequate for each company?
2. Calculate the current ratio for United Airlines and Southwest Airlines. Which company has a better current ratio?
3. Calculate the acid-test (quick) ratio for United Airlines and Southwest Airlines. Which company has a better acid-test ratio?

Solution:

1. Working capital:

($ in millions)	Total Current Assets	−	Total Current Liabilities	=	Working Capital
United	$4,861	−	$7,281	=	$(2,420)
Southwest	$2,893	−	$2,806	=	$ 87

United Airlines actually has a negative working capital, in which its current liabilities exceed its current assets by $2.4 billion. Southwest Airlines, with positive working capital, has more liquidity.

2. Current ratio:

($ in millions)	Total Current Assets	÷	Total Current Liabilities	=	Current Ratio
United	$4,861	÷	$7,281	=	0.67
Southwest	$2,893	÷	$2,806	=	1.03

Southwest Airlines also has a higher current ratio, which would indicate better liquidity than United. Southwest has just above the "acceptable" liquidity level of 1.0.

3. Acid-test (quick) ratio:

Remember that *quick assets* equal cash + current investments + net receivables.

($ in millions)	Quick Assets	÷	Total Current Liabilities	=	Acid-Test Ratio
United	$4,023	÷	$7,281	=	0.55
Southwest	$2,377	÷	$2,806	=	0.85

Suggested Homework:
BE8-15;
E8-16;
P8-9A&B

By eliminating less-liquid current assets such as inventory, the acid-test ratio often provides a better indicator of liquidity. Once again, Southwest Airlines "wins" with an acid-test ratio of 0.85, compared to 0.55 for United Airlines.

What do the liquidity measures for United and Southwest tell us? Together, they provide an indication of a company's ability to pay its currently maturing debts. Looking at working capital, the current ratio, and the acid-test ratio, it appears that Southwest Airlines is in a better position than United to meet its current debt obligations. But remember that we should evaluate liquidity measures in the context of an industry. The airlines have faced tough times recently, between dampened demand resulting from 9/11, increasing fuel costs, and the recent recession. So, while Southwest has fared better than United, its liquidity still may not compare well with other industries.

Decision Maker's Perspective   Indicators of Liquidity

If the firm's current ratio or acid-test ratio is lower than that of the industry as a whole, does that mean liquidity is a problem? Perhaps, but perhaps not. It does, though, raise a red flag that suggests caution when assessing other aspects of the company.

It's important to remember that each ratio is but one piece of the puzzle. For example, profitability is probably the best long-run indicator of liquidity. It is difficult to maintain liquidity over a string of consecutive loss years. Another consideration is that management may be very efficient in managing current assets so that some current assets—receivables or inventory—remain at minimum amounts. This is good for the company overall, but it may result in less-impressive current and acid-test ratios. The turnover ratios we discussed in Chapters 5 and 6, such as receivables turnover and inventory turnover, help measure the efficiency of asset management in this regard. ●

 COMMON MISTAKE

> As a general rule, a higher current ratio is better. However, a high current ratio is not always a positive signal. Companies having difficulty collecting receivables or holding excessive inventory will also have a higher current ratio. Managers must balance the incentive for strong liquidity (yielding a high current ratio) with the need to minimize levels of receivables and inventory (yielding a lower current ratio).

Effect of Transactions on Liquidity Ratios

It also is important to understand the effect of specific transactions on the current ratio and acid-test ratio. Both ratios have the same denominator, current liabilities, so a decrease in current liabilities will increase the ratios (dividing by a smaller number makes the ratio bigger). Likewise, an increase in current liabilities will decrease the ratios (dividing by a bigger number makes the ratio smaller).

How are the ratios affected by changes in current assets? It depends on which current asset changes. Both ratios include cash, current investments, and accounts receivable. An increase in any of those will increase *both* ratios. However, only the current ratio includes inventory and other current assets. An increase to inventory or other current assets will increase the current ratio, but not the acid-test ratio.

Liquidity Management

Can management influence the ratios that measure liquidity? Yes, at least to some extent. A company can influence the timing of accounts payable recognition by asking suppliers to change their delivery schedules. For example, a large airplane manufacturer like **Boeing** or **McDonnell Douglas** might delay the shipment and billing of certain inventory parts from late December to early January, reducing accounts payable at its December year-end. Because accounts payable is included in calculating the current ratio, the timing of accounts payable recognition could mean the difference between an unacceptable ratio and an acceptable one, or between violating and complying with a debt covenant.

Suppose, for instance, a company with a current ratio of 1.25 (current assets of $5 million and current liabilities of $4 million) has entered into a *debt covenant* with its bank that requires a minimum current ratio of 1.25. A debt covenant is an agreement between a borrower and a lender that requires that certain minimum financial measures be met or the lender can recall the debt. By delaying the delivery of $1 million of inventory purchased on account, the company can increase the ratio to 1.33 (current assets of $4 million and current liabilities of $3 million). Investors and creditors should be aware of managerial activities that increase liquidity ratios, such as misclassification of current liabilities or unusual variations in accounts payable levels.

ETHICAL DILEMMA

Airport Accessories (AA) has several loans outstanding with a local bank. The loan contract contains an agreement that AA must maintain a current ratio of at least 0.90. Micah, the assistant controller, estimates that the year-end current assets and current liabilities will be $2,100,000 and $2,400,000, respectively. These estimates provide a current ratio of only 0.875. Violation of the debt agreement will increase AA's borrowing costs because the loans will be renegotiated at higher interest rates.

Micah proposes that AA purchase inventory of $600,000 on credit before year-end. This will cause both current assets and current liabilities to increase by the same amount, but the current ratio will increase to 0.90. The extra $600,000 in inventory will be used over the next year. However, the purchase will cause warehousing costs and financing costs to increase.

Micah is concerned about the ethics of his proposal. What do you think?

 KEY POINTS BY LEARNING OBJECTIVE

LO1 Distinguish between current and long-term liabilities.

In most cases, current liabilities are payable within one year and long-term liabilities are payable more than one year from now.

LO2 Account for notes payable and interest expense.

We record interest expense in the period we incur it, rather than in the period in which we pay it.

Many short-term loans are arranged under an existing line of credit with a bank, or for larger corporations in the form of commercial paper, a loan from one company to another.

LO3 Account for employee and employer payroll liabilities.

Employee salaries are reduced by withholdings for federal and state income taxes, FICA taxes, and the employee portion of insurance and retirement contributions. The employer, too, incurs additional payroll expenses for unemployment taxes, the employer portion of FICA taxes, and employer insurance and retirement contributions.

LO4 Demonstrate the accounting for other current liabilities.

When a company receives cash in advance, it debits Cash and credits Unearned Revenue, a current liability account. When it earns the revenue, the company debits Unearned Revenue and credits Sales Revenue.

Sales taxes collected from customers by the seller are not an expense. Instead, they represent current liabilities payable to the government.

We report the currently maturing portion of a long-term debt as a current liability on the balance sheet.

Net income and taxable income often differ because of differences between financial accounting and tax accounting rules. These differences can result in *deferred tax liabilities*, in which income is reported now but the tax on the income will not be paid until future years.

LO5 Apply the appropriate accounting treatment for contingencies.

A contingent liability is recorded only if a loss is *probable* **and** the amount can be *reasonably estimated*.

Unlike contingent liabilities, contingent gains are not recorded until the gain is certain and no longer a contingency.

Analysis

LO6 Assess liquidity using current liability ratios.

Working capital is the difference between current assets and current liabilities. The current ratio is equal to current assets divided by current liabilities. The acid-test ratio is equal to quick assets (cash, short-term investments, and accounts receivable) divided by current liabilities. Each measures a company's liquidity, its ability to pay currently maturing debts.

GLOSSARY

Acid-test ratio: Cash, current investments, and accounts receivable divided by current liabilities; measures the availability of liquid current assets to pay current liabilities. **p. 274**

Commercial paper: Borrowing from another company rather than from a bank. **p. 262**

Contingencies: Uncertain situations that can result in a gain or a loss for a company. **p. 270**

Contingent gain: An existing uncertain situation that might result in a gain. **p. 273**

Contingent liability: An existing uncertain situation that might result in a loss. **p. 270**

Current liabilities: Debts that, in most cases, are due within one year. However, when a company has an operating cycle of longer than a year, its current liabilities are defined by the length of the operating cycle, rather than by the length of one year. **p. 258**

Current portion of long-term debt: Debt that will be paid within the next year. **p. 268**

Current ratio: Current assets divided by current liabilities; measures the availability of current assets to pay current liabilities. **p. 274**

Debt covenant: An agreement between a borrower and a lender that requires that certain minimum financial measures be met or the lender can recall the debt. **p. 277**

FICA taxes: Based on the Federal Insurance Contribution Act; tax withheld from employees' paychecks and matched by employers for Social Security and Medicare. **p. 264**

Fringe benefits: Additional employee benefits paid for by the employer. **p. 265**

Liability: A present responsibility to sacrifice assets in the future due to a transaction or other event that happened in the past. **p. 258**

Line of credit: An informal agreement that permits a company to borrow up to a prearranged limit without having to follow formal loan procedures and prepare paperwork. **p. 262**

Liquidity: Having sufficient cash (or other assets convertible to cash in a relatively short time) to pay currently maturing debts. **p. 274**

Notes payable: Written promises to repay amounts borrowed plus interest. **p. 259**

Quick assets: Includes only cash, current investments, and accounts receivable. **p. 274**

Sales tax payable: Sales tax collected from customers by the seller, representing current liabilities payable to the government. **p. 268**

Unearned revenue: A liability account used to record cash received in advance of the sale or service. **p. 266**

Unemployment taxes: A tax to cover federal and state unemployment costs paid by the employer on behalf of its employees. **p. 264**

Working capital: The difference between current assets and current liabilities. **p. 274**

SELF-STUDY QUESTIONS

1. Which of the following statements regarding liabilities is *not* true? ■ LO1
   a. Liabilities can be for services rather than cash.
   b. Liabilities are reported in the balance sheet for almost every business.
   c. Liabilities result from future transactions.
   d. Liabilities represent probable future sacrifices of benefits.

2. Current liabilities: ■ LO1
   a. May include contingent liabilities.
   b. Include obligations payable within one year or one operating cycle, whichever is shorter.
   c. Can be satisfied only with the payment of cash.
   d. Are preferred by most companies over long-term liabilities.

3. If Express Jet borrows $100 million on October 1, 2012, for one year at 6% interest, how much interest expense does it record for the year ended December 31, 2012? ■ LO2
   a. $0.
   b. $1 million.
   c. $1.5 million.
   d. $6 million.

4. We record interest expense on a note payable in the period in which: ■ LO2
   a. We pay cash for interest.
   b. We incur interest.

c. We pay cash and incur interest.

d. We pay cash or incur interest.

■ LO3

5. Which of the following is *not* deducted from an employee's salary?

a. FICA taxes.

b. Unemployment taxes.

c. Income taxes.

d. Employee portion of insurance and retirement payments.

■ LO4

6. The seller collects sales taxes from the customer at the time of sale and reports the sales taxes as:

a. Sales tax expense.

b. Sales tax revenue.

c. Sales tax receivable.

d. Sales tax payable.

■ LO5

7. Management can estimate the amount of loss that will occur due to litigation against the company. If the likelihood of loss is reasonably possible, a contingent liability should be:

a. Disclosed but not reported as a liability.

b. Disclosed and reported as a liability.

c. Neither disclosed nor reported as a liability.

d. Reported as a liability but not disclosed.

■ LO5

8. Smith Co. filed suit against Western, Inc., seeking damages for patent infringement. Western's legal counsel believes it is probable that Western will settle the lawsuit for an estimated amount in the range of $75,000 to $175,000, with all amounts in the range considered equally likely. How should Western report this litigation?

a. As a liability for $75,000 with disclosure of the range.

b. As a liability for $125,000 with disclosure of the range.

c. As a liability for $175,000 with disclosure of the range.

d. As a disclosure only. No liability is reported.

■ LO6

9. The acid-test ratio is:

a. Current assets divided by current liabilities.

b. Cash and current investments divided by current liabilities.

c. Cash, current investments, and accounts receivable divided by current liabilities.

d. Cash, current investments, accounts receivable, and inventory divided by current liabilities.

■ LO6

10. Assuming a current ratio of 1.0 and an acid-test ratio of 0.75, how will the purchase of inventory with cash affect each ratio?

a. Increase the current ratio and increase the acid-test ratio.

b. No change to the current ratio and decrease the acid-test ratio.

c. Decrease the current ratio and decrease the acid-test ratio.

d. Increase the current ratio and decrease the acid-test ratio.

Answers to the Self-Study Questions

1. c   2. a   3. c   4. b   5. b   6. d   7. a   8. a   9. c   10. b

REVIEW QUESTIONS

■ LO1

1. What are the essential characteristics of liabilities for purposes of financial reporting?

■ LO1

2. How do we define current liabilities? Long-term liabilities?

■ LO1

3. Why is it important to distinguish between current and long-term liabilities?

4. **United Airlines** served as an example throughout the chapter. Provide several examples of current liabilities in the airline industry.   ■ LO1

5. Explain why we record interest in the period in which we incur it rather than in the period in which we pay it.   ■ LO2

6. Bank loans often are arranged under existing lines of credit. What is a line of credit? How does a line of credit work?   ■ LO2

7. How does commercial paper differ from a normal bank loan? Why is the interest rate often less for commercial paper?   ■ LO2

8. Name at least four items withheld from employee payroll checks. Which deductions are required by law and which are voluntary?   ■ LO3

9. Name at least four employer costs in addition to the employee's salary. Which costs are required by law and which are voluntary?   ■ LO3

10. Who pays Social Security taxes: the employer, the employee, or both? How is the deduction for Social Security and Medicare (FICA) computed?   ■ LO3

11. Retailers like **McDonald's**, **American Eagle**, and **Apple Inc.** sell quite a few gift cards. Explain how these companies account for the sale of gift cards.   ■ LO4

12. *BusinessWeek* sells magazine subscriptions in advance of their distribution. (a) What journal entry would the company make at the time it sells subscriptions? (b) What journal entry would the company make each time it distributes a magazine?   ■ LO4

13. Like all retailers, **Hollister** is required to collect sales tax to be remitted to state and local government authorities. Assume a local store has cash proceeds from sales of $5,325, including $325 in sales tax. What is the sales tax rate? Provide the journal entry to record the proceeds.   ■ LO4

14. If $10 million of **Dell Computer Corporation**'s $130 million notes payable is due in the next year, how will the firm present this debt within the current and long-term liabilities sections of the current year's balance sheet?   ■ LO4

15. Is net income reported in the income statement the same amount as taxable income in the corporate tax return? Why or why not?   ■ LO4

16. Define contingent liability. Provide three common examples.   ■ LO5

17. List and briefly describe the three categories of likelihood that a payment for a contingent liability will need to be made.   ■ LO5

18. Under what circumstances should a firm report a contingent liability?   ■ LO5

19. Suppose the firm's analysis of a contingent liability indicates that an obligation is not probable. What accounting treatment, if any, is warranted?   ■ LO5

20. If a contingent liability is probable but estimable only within a range, what amount, if any, should the firm report?   ■ LO5

21. Your company is the plaintiff in a lawsuit. Legal counsel advises you that your eventual victory is inevitable. "You will be awarded $2 million," your attorney confidently asserts. Describe the appropriate accounting treatment.   ■ LO5

22. Current liabilities affect a company's liquidity. What is liquidity, and how do we evaluate it?   ■ LO6

23. Explain the differences among working capital, the current ratio, and the acid-test ratio.   ■ LO6

24. How would the following transactions affect the current ratio and the acid-test ratio? (a) Purchase of inventory with cash; and (b) sale of inventory for more than its cost. Assume that prior to these transactions the current ratio and acid-test ratio are both less than one.   ■ LO6

For the following, please visit your instructor's *Connect* site.

BRIEF EXERCISES	**1-15**
EXERCISES	**1-16**
PROBLEMS: SET A	**1-9**
PROBLEMS: SET B	**1-9**
GREAT ADVENTURES	

McGraw Hill **connect**
|ACCOUNTING

Note: Additional Perspectives assignments for Financial Analysis, Comparative Analysis, Internet Research, Written Communication, and Earnings Management are in Appendix F at the end of this book. For additional Exercises: Set B and for additional Problems: Set C, visit www.mhhe.com/spicelandMTC1e.

Long-Term Liabilities

Learning Objectives

AFTER STUDYING THIS CHAPTER, YOU SHOULD BE ABLE TO:

- ■ **LO1** Explain financing alternatives.
- ■ **LO2** Identify the characteristics of bonds.
- ■ **LO3** Determine the price of a bond issue.
- ■ **LO4** Account for the issuance of bonds.
- ■ **LO5** Record the retirement of bonds.
- ■ **LO6** Identify other major long-term liabilities.

Analysis

- ■ **LO7** Make financial decisions using long-term liability ratios.

SIX FLAGS: **THE UPS AND DOWNS OF BORROWING**

Can you name the largest chain of amusement parks in the world? Would you guess **Disney**? **Six Flags** actually is larger, with over 20 amusement and water parks across North America. The first Six Flags amusement park, *Six Flags Over Texas,* was built in 1961 in Arlington, between Dallas and Fort Worth. The park is named for the six different flags that have flown over the state of Texas during its history—the flags of Spain, France, Mexico, the Republic of Texas, the United States, and the Confederate States of America.

What is the top-rated amusement park in the world? Six Flags? Disney? Guess again. Cedar Point, in Sandusky, Ohio, is known as the roller-coaster capital of the world and was rated the *Best Amusement Park in the World* for eleven consecutive years (*www.amusementtoday.com*). The park boasts an unheard-of 17 roller coasters! With a lineup that includes three of the top 10 steel roller coasters, Cedar Point is a coaster lover's dream come true. Its parent firm, **Cedar Fair Entertainment Company**, currently owns and operates 12 amusement parks in North America.

Comparing the financial information for Six Flags and Cedar Fair is revealing. Both companies are listed on the New York Stock Exchange, Six Flags under the ticker symbol SIX and Cedar Fair under the ticker symbol FUN. Both carry a very high level of long-term debt. However, the profitability of the two companies is quite different. From 2006–2008, Six Flags reported an average net loss each year of $238 million, and in 2009 Six Flags entered into bankruptcy proceedings. During this same time, Cedar Fair reported an average annual net income of about $30 million.

As you will learn in this chapter, assuming more debt can be either good or bad. If a company earns a rate of return higher than the interest rate on its debt, borrowing additional funds can increase overall profitability. On the other hand, if a company earns a rate of return lower than the interest rate on its debt, borrowing additional funds will further reduce profitability and may even result in bankruptcy proceedings.

OVERVIEW OF LONG-TERM DEBT

In the previous chapter, we discussed current liabilities. In this chapter we focus on long-term liabilities, primarily bonds. Parts A, B, and C deal with various aspects of bonds. Part D discusses other long-term liabilities such as installment notes and leases. We conclude the chapter by looking at how debt affects the riskiness and profitability of **Coca-Cola** and **Pepsi**.

Suppose you are the chief financial officer (CFO) for RC Enterprises, a company that designs, manufactures, and installs steel roller coasters. The executives at your company have an idea for a new ride that could revolutionize the amusement park industry. A ride like this could spur a huge increase in sales volume and create the opportunity to expand the idea to amusement parks around the world. But growth requires funding. What are RC Enterprises's choices? To answer that question, let's consider the financing alternatives available.

Financing Alternatives

■ **LO1**
Explain financing alternatives.

Some of the financing needed to fund a company's growth can come from the profits generated by operations. Frequently, though, companies must find additional external financing to meet their needs for cash. Let's look back at the basic accounting equation:

$$\underbrace{\text{Assets}}_{\text{(resources)}} = \underbrace{\text{Liabilities} + \text{Stockholders' Equity}}_{\text{(claims to resources)}}$$

The right side of the accounting equation reveals the two sources of external financing available to RC Enterprises: Debt financing refers to borrowing money (liabilities). Equity financing refers to obtaining additional investment from stockholders (stockholders' equity).

Companies in the auto industry, like **Ford**, typically lean toward liabilities for their financing. Companies in the computer industry, like **Microsoft**, use stockholders' equity to a greater extent to finance their asset growth. The mixture of liabilities and stockholders' equity a business uses is called its capital structure.

Decision Point	Question	Accounting information	Analysis
	How do you determine a company's capital structure?	Balance sheet	An equity capital structure would have fewer liabilities than stockholders' equity. A debt capital structure would have a higher portion of liabilities relative to stockholders' equity.

Why would a company choose to borrow money rather than issue additional stock in the company? One of the primary reasons relates to taxes. **Interest expense incurred when borrowing money is tax-deductible, whereas dividends paid to stockholders are *not* tax-deductible.** Interest expense incurred on debt reduces taxable income; paying dividends to stockholders does not reduce taxable income because dividends are not an expense. Therefore, debt can be a less costly source of external financing.

KEY POINT

Companies obtain external funds through debt financing (liabilities) and equity financing (stockholders' equity). One advantage of debt financing is that interest on borrowed funds is tax-deductible.

Companies have three primary sources of long-term debt financing: bonds, notes, and leases. Medium- and large-sized corporations often choose to borrow cash by issuing bonds. In fact, **bonds are the most common form of corporate debt.** A company also can borrow cash from a bank or other financial institution through notes payable. A third source of debt financing that continues to grow in popularity is leasing. We discuss each of these sources of long-term debt financing in this chapter.

What Are Bonds?

A bond is a formal debt instrument that obligates the borrower to repay a stated amount, referred to as the *principal* or *face amount,* at a specified maturity date. In return for the use of the money borrowed, the borrower also agrees to pay *interest* over the life of the bond. Sound familiar? It should. That's the way we described notes payable in the preceding chapter. Bonds are very similar to notes. Bonds, though, usually are issued to many lenders, while notes most often are issued to a single lender such as a bank. Traditionally, interest on bonds is paid twice a year (semiannually) on designated interest dates, beginning six months after the original bond issue date.

Perhaps your local school board issued bonds to build a new football stadium for the high school, or maybe your hometown issued bonds to build a new library. To build the stadium or library, a city needs external financing, so it borrows money from people in the community. Bonds provide a way to borrow the money needed from many community members, each willing to lend a small amount. In return, those investing in the bonds receive interest over the life of the bonds, say 20 years, and repayment of the principal amount at the end of the bonds' life.

For most large corporations, bonds are sold, or *underwritten,* by investment houses. The three largest bond underwriters are **JPMorgan**, **Citibank**, and **Bank of America**. The issuing company—the borrower—pays a fee for these underwriting services. Other costs include legal, accounting, registration, and printing fees. To keep costs down, the issuing company may choose to sell the debt securities directly to a single investor, such as a large investment fund or an insurance company. This is referred to as a private placement. Issue costs for private placements are lower because these bonds are not subject to the costly and lengthy process of registering with the SEC that is required of all public offerings.

Why do some companies issue bonds rather than borrow money directly from a bank? A company that borrows by issuing bonds is effectively bypassing the bank and borrowing directly from the investing public—usually at a lower interest rate than it would in a bank loan. However, issuing bonds entails significant bond issue costs that can exceed 5% of the amount borrowed. For smaller loans, the additional bond issuance costs exceed the savings from a lower interest rate, making it more economical to borrow from a bank. For loans of $20 million or more, the interest rate savings often exceed the additional bond issuance costs, making a bond issue more attractive.

A bond issue, in effect, breaks down a large debt into manageable parts—usually $1,000 units. This avoids the necessity of finding a single investor who is both willing and able to loan a large amount of money at a reasonable interest rate. So rather than signing a $50 million note to borrow cash, a company may find it more practicable to sell $1,000 bonds to as many as 50,000 separate investors.

Bond Characteristics

A **bond indenture** is a contract between a firm issuing bonds to borrow money (the issuer) and the corporations or individuals who purchase the bonds as investments (the investors). Because it would not be practical for the corporation to enter into a direct agreement with each of the many bondholders, the bond indenture is held by a trustee, usually a commercial bank or other financial institution, appointed by the issuing firm to represent the rights of the bondholders. If the firm fails to live up to the terms of the bond indenture, the trustee may bring legal action against the company on behalf of the bondholders.

For any particular bond, the bond may be secured or unsecured, term or serial, callable, or convertible. We'll discuss each of these characteristics below.

SECURED AND UNSECURED BONDS

LO2
Identify the characteristics of bonds.

When you buy a house and finance your purchase with a bank loan, you sign a mortgage agreement assigning your house as collateral. If later you are unable to make the payments, the bank is entitled to take your house. Secured bonds are similar. They are supported by specific assets the issuer has pledged as collateral. For instance, mortgage bonds are backed by specific real estate assets. If the borrower defaults on the payments, the lender is entitled to the real estate pledged as collateral.

However, **most bonds are unsecured.** Unsecured bonds, also referred to as *debentures*, are not backed by a specific asset. These bonds are secured only by the "full faith and credit" of the borrower.

TERM AND SERIAL BONDS

Term bonds require payment of the full principal amount of the bond at a single maturity date (the end of the loan term). Most bonds have this characteristic. Borrowers often plan ahead for the repayment by setting aside funds throughout the term to maturity. For example, let's say a city borrows $20 million to build a new sports park by issuing 7% term bonds due in 10 years. To ensure that sufficient funds are available to pay the $20 million 10 years later, the borrower sets aside money in a "sinking fund." A sinking fund is a designated fund to which an organization makes payments each year over the life of its outstanding debt. The city might put $2 million each year for 10 years into a sinking fund, so that $20 million is available to pay the bonds when they become due.

Serial bonds require payments in installments over a series of years. Rather than issuing $20 million in bonds that will be due at the *end* of the 10th year, the city may issue $20 million worth of 7% serial bonds, of which $2 million is due *each year* for the next 10 years. This makes it easier for the city to meet its bond obligations as they become due. Since **most bonds are term bonds,** we focus on term bonds in this chapter.

CALLABLE BONDS

Suppose your company issued bonds a few years ago that pay 10% interest. Now market interest rates have declined to 6%, but you're obligated to pay 10%

interest for the remaining time to maturity. How can you avoid this unfortunate situation?

Most corporate bonds are callable, or redeemable. This feature allows the borrower to repay the bonds before their scheduled maturity date at a specified call price. The *call price* is stated in the bond contract and usually exceeds the bond's face amount.

A call feature helps protect the borrower against future decreases in interest rates. If interest rates decline, the borrower can buy back the high-interest-rate bonds at a fixed price and issue new bonds at the new, lower interest rate. Just think about any loans that you may currently have, maybe a car loan or credit card balance. If interest rates drop, wouldn't it be nice to pay off your debt and reestablish it at the lower interest rate? Many home loans, in fact, provide the option to pay the loan early and refinance at a lower rate.

CONVERTIBLE BONDS

While a bond could be both callable and convertible, **a call feature is more common than a conversion feature.** Another important distinction is that callable bonds are designed to benefit the borrower, whereas convertible bonds benefit both the borrower and the lender. Convertible bonds allow the lender (the investor) to convert each bond into a specified number of shares of common stock. For example, let's say a $1,000 convertible bond can be converted into 20 shares of common stock. In this case, convertible bondholders benefit if the market price of the common stock goes above $50 per share (= $1,000 ÷ 20 shares), assuming the current market price of the bond is $1,000. If the company's stock price goes to $60 per share, the convertible bondholder can trade the $1,000 bond for 20 shares of stock worth $60 per share (or $1,200). Prior to conversion, the bondholder still receives interest on the convertible bond. The borrower also benefits. Convertible bonds sell at a higher price and require a lower interest rate than bonds without a conversion feature.

INTERNATIONAL FINANCIAL REPORTING STANDARDS (IFRS)

Using IFRS, we would divide the issue price of convertible debt into its liability (bonds) and equity (conversion option) elements. Under U.S. GAAP, the entire issue price is recorded as a liability.

For more discussion, see Appendix E.

Illustration 9–1 summarizes bond characteristics.

Bond Characteristic	Definition
Secured	Bonds are backed by collateral.
Unsecured	Bonds are not backed by collateral.
Term	Bond issue matures on a single date.
Serial	Bond issue matures in installments.
Callable	Borrower can pay off bonds early.
Convertible	Lender can convert bonds to common stock.

ILLUSTRATION 9–1

Summary of Bond Characteristics

KEY POINT

The distinguishing characteristics of bonds include whether they are backed by collateral (secured or unsecured), become due at a single specified date or over a series of years (term or serial), can be redeemed prior to maturity (callable), or can be converted into common stock (convertible).

Corporations normally issue bonds in the millions of dollars. However, to simplify the illustrations in this chapter, we drop three digits and illustrate the issuance of bonds in thousands rather than in millions. We begin with the following example and build upon it as we progress through the chapter.

Assume that on January 1, 2012, RC Enterprises decides to raise money for development of its new roller coaster by issuing $100,000 of bonds paying a stated interest rate of 7%. The bonds are due in 10 years, with interest payable semiannually on June 30 and December 31 each year. **In practice, most corporate bonds pay interest semiannually (every six months) rather than paying interest monthly, quarterly, or annually.** Thus, investors in RC Enterprises's bonds will receive (1) the *face amount* of $100,000 at the end of 10 years and (2) *interest payments* of $3,500 (= $100,000 × 7% × 1/2 year) every six months for 10 years. That's a total of 20 interest payments of $3,500 each (= $70,000). Illustration 9–2 provides a timeline of the cash flows related to the bond issue.

ILLUSTRATION 9–2

Timeline of a
Bond Issue

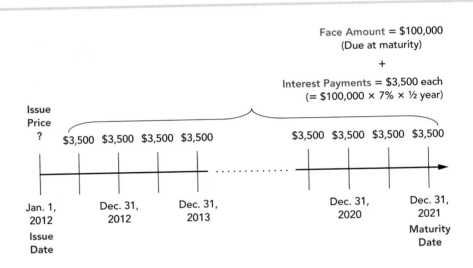

Over the 10-year period, bondholders will receive a total of $170,000, which is the face amount of $100,000 due at maturity plus semiannual interest payments totaling $70,000. How much are investors willing to pay the company today (January 1, 2012) for the right to receive $170,000 over the next 10 years? Certainly less than $170,000, because the cash flows are in the future. In the next section we see how to determine that price.

PART B

PRICING A BOND

■ **LO3**
Determine the price
of a bond issue.

We can calculate the issue price of a bond as the present value of the face amount *plus* the present value of the periodic interest payments. To calculate the issue price of RC Enterprises's $100,000 bonds, we need to determine the face amount of the bonds, the interest payment each period, the market interest rate per period, and the number of periods to maturity.

Bonds Issued at Face Amount

Common Terms The
market rate is also
known as the *effective
interest rate* or *yield rate.*

For RC, the face amount equals $100,000. The interest payment every six months is $3,500 (= $100,000 × 7% × 1/2 year). The market interest rate represents the true interest rate used by investors to value RC's bond issue. The market rate can be equal to, less than, or greater than the stated 7% interest rate paid to investors. As we will see later, the market rate is determined for each bond issue by the forces of supply and demand. The stated interest rate is the rate quoted in the bond contract used to calculate the cash payments for interest.

Let's first assume the market interest rate is 7%, the same as the stated interest rate. (Later we will calculate the bond issue price when the market interest rate is less than or greater than the stated interest rate.) The number of periods to maturity is the number of years to maturity multiplied by the number of interest payments per year. Since RC's bonds pay interest semiannually (twice per year) for 10 years, there are 20 periods to maturity.

One way to determine the issue price of bonds is to use your financial calculator. Illustration 9–3 shows the calculator inputs used to obtain an issue price at the face amount of $100,000.

CALCULATOR INPUT

Bond Characteristics	Key	Amount
1. Face amount	FV	$100,000
2. Interest payment each period	PMT	$3,500 = $100,000 × 7% × 1/2 year
3. Market interest rate each period	I	3.5% = 7% ÷ 2 semiannual periods
4. Periods to maturity	N	20 = 10 years × 2 periods each year

CALCULATOR OUTPUT

Issue price	PV	$100,000

ILLUSTRATION 9–3

Pricing Bonds Issued at Face Amount Using a Financial Calculator

An alternative to using a financial calculator is to calculate the price of bonds in Excel. Illustration 9–4 demonstrates the inputs and the formula used to calculate the issue price.

ILLUSTRATION 9–4

Pricing Bonds Issued at Face Amount Using Excel

	C7		f_x	=-PV(C4, C5, C3, C2, 0)			
	A	B	C	D	E	F	
1							
2	Face amount		$100,000.00				
3	Interest payment		$3,500.00				
4	Market interest rate		3.5%				
5	Number of periods		20				
6							
7	Issue price		$100,000.00				
8							
9							

Sheet1 / Sheet2 / Sheet3

Ready   100%

A third alternative is to calculate the price of the bonds using present value tables. In Illustration 9–5 we calculate the price of the bonds using the present value tables provided at the back of the textbook.

Present value of face amount	= $100,000 × 0.50257*	= $ 50,257
Present value of interest payments	= $3,500[1] × 14.21240**	= 49,743
Issue price of the bonds		$100,000

ILLUSTRATION 9–5

Pricing Bonds Issued at Face Amount Using Present Value Tables

[1]$100,000 × 7% × 1/2 year = $3,500
*Table 2, i = 3.5%, n = 20
**Table 4, i = 3.5%, n = 20

We use Table 2, the present value of $1, to calculate the present value of the face amount since it's just one amount ($100,000) due at maturity. We use Table 4, the present value of an ordinary annuity of $1, to calculate the present value of the interest payments since they are a series of equal amounts ($3,500 each) paid every semiannual interest period.

Using any of these three alternatives, the issue price of the bonds is equal to $100,000. All three methods have their advantages. A financial calculator and Excel are simple to use and provide greater flexibility regarding the choice of different interest rates and time periods. On the other hand, present value tables provide a better conceptual understanding of how bond prices are determined.

We assumed a market rate of 7%, which is exactly equal to the 7% stated rate of interest on the bond contract. The market rate is the interest rate investors determine for each bond issue through the forces of supply and demand. Market rates change continuously. Announcements by the Federal Reserve regarding its intentions to increase the federal funds rate (the interest rate the Federal Reserve charges to banks), political unrest, an increase in the price of oil, and fears of growing inflation, to name a few, can cause an increase in market interest rates.

Another important point to remember is that the market rate is not the same for all companies issuing bonds. Market rates vary based on the default risk of the company issuing the bonds. Default risk refers to the possibility that a company will be unable to pay the bond's face amount or interest payments as they become due. As a company's default risk increases, investors demand a higher market interest rate on their bond investments. For example, would you pay the same for a $1,000 bond paying 7% interest issued by **Six Flags** as you would for a $1,000 bond paying 7% interest issued by **Cedar Fair**? Probably not. As we discussed earlier, Six Flags lost money in each of the past three years. This means there is a greater chance of default by Six Flags. By paying less for Six Flags' $1,000, 7% bond, investors are effectively increasing their market rate of return. **The higher the market interest rate, the lower the bond issue price will be.**

Bonds Issued at a Discount

Now let's assume that RC Enterprises issues the same $100,000 of 7% bonds when other bonds of similar risk and maturity are paying 8%. RC's bonds are less attractive to investors, because investors can purchase bonds of similar risk that are paying the higher 8% rate. Because of this, to make the bonds more attractive, RC will have to issue its 7% bonds *below* its $100,000 face amount. Bonds issued *below* face amount are said to be issued at a discount.

In this instance, the bonds will be issued for less than the $100,000 face amount. How much less? Let's calculate the bond issue price using I = 4% (= 8% ÷ 2) rather than the 3.5% used in the previous example. In Illustration 9–6 we recalculate the issue price of the bonds, assuming the market rate of interest is now 8% per year (4% every semiannual period).

ILLUSTRATION 9–6

Pricing Bonds Issued at a Discount Using a Financial Calculator

CALCULATOR INPUT

Bond Characteristics	Key	Amount
1. Face amount	FV	$100,000
2. Interest payment each period	PMT	$3,500 = $100,000 × 7% × 1/2 year
3. Market interest rate each period	I	4% = 8% ÷ 2 semiannual periods
4. Periods to maturity	N	20 = 10 years × 2 periods each year

CALCULATOR OUTPUT

Issue price	PV	$93,205

Illustration 9–7 demonstrates how to use Excel to determine the issue price.

	C7			f_x	20		
	A	B	C	D	E	F	
1							
2	Face amount		$100,000.00				
3	Interest payment		$3,500.00				
4	Market interest rate		4%				
5	Number of periods		20				
6							
7	Issue price		$93,205.00				
8							
9							

Sheet1 / Sheet2 / Sheet3

Ready   100%

ILLUSTRATION 9–7

Pricing Bonds Issued at a Discount Using Excel

In Illustration 9–8 we calculate the price of the bonds using the present value tables provided at the back of the textbook, assuming the market rate of interest is 8% per year, or 4% every semiannual period.

Present value of principal	= $100,000 × 0.45639*	=	$45,639
Present value of interest payments	= $3,500[1] × 13.59033**	=	47,566
Issue price of the bonds			$93,205

[1]$100,000 × 7% × 1/2 year = $3,500
*Table 2, $i = 4\%$, $n = 20$
**Table 4, $i = 4\%$, $n = 20$

ILLUSTRATION 9–8

Pricing Bonds Issued at a Discount Using Present Value Tables

In practice, investors might refer to the bonds as being "issued at 93.2." This means the bonds were issued at approximately 93.2% of the $100,000 face value, or $93,200.

We see that in this instance the bond issue price is below the face amount of $100,000. The issuing company receives only $93,205 from investors, but will pay back $100,000 when the bonds mature in 10 years. Why? Because the bonds pay only 7% interest when the market rate for bonds of similar risk and maturity is 8%. By issuing the bonds for only $93,205, the issuer is effectively raising the interest earned by investors from the stated rate of 7% to the market rate of 8%. In other words, an investor paying $93,205 for the 7% bonds will earn the same rate of return on the investment (8%) as if he paid $100,000 for 8% bonds.

 COMMON MISTAKE

The interest rate we use to calculate the bond issue price is always the *market* rate, never the stated rate. Some students get confused and incorrectly use the stated rate to calculate present value. Use the stated rate to calculate the interest payment each period, but use the market rate to calculate the present value of the cash flows.

Bonds Issued at a Premium

Now let's assume that RC Enterprises issues $100,000 of 7% bonds when other bonds of similar risk and maturity are paying only 6%. Investors will pay *more* than $100,000 for these 7% bonds since they look relatively attractive compared with bonds paying only 6%. These bonds will sell at a premium. A **premium** occurs when the issue price of a bond is *above* its face amount. In this case, RC's bonds will sell for more than $100,000. How much more? In Illustration 9–9 we recalculate the issue price using a market rate of 6% (3% semiannually).

ILLUSTRATION 9–9

Pricing Bonds Issued at a Premium Using a Financial Calculator

CALCULATOR INPUT

Bond Characteristics	Key	Amount
1. Face amount	FV	$100,000
2. Interest payment each period	PMT	$3,500 = $100,000 × 7% × 1/2 year
3. Market interest rate each period	I	3% = 6% ÷ 2 semiannual periods
4. Periods to maturity	N	20 = 10 years × 2 periods each year

CALCULATOR OUTPUT

Issue price	PV	$107,439

Illustration 9–10 demonstrates how to use Excel to determine the issue price.

ILLUSTRATION 9–10

Pricing Bonds Issued at a Premium Using Excel

Illustration 9–11 calculates the price of the bonds using the present value tables provided at the back of the textbook, again assuming the market rate of interest is 6% (3% semiannually).

ILLUSTRATION 9–11

Pricing Bonds Issued at a Premium Using Present Value Tables

Present value of principal	= $100,000 × 0.55368*	=	$ 55,368
Present value of interest payments	= $3,500[1] × 14.87747**	=	52,071
Issue price of the bonds			$107,439

[1]$100,000 × 7% × 1/2 year = $3,500
*Table 2, i = 3%, n = 20
**Table 4, i = 3%, n = 20

In practice, investors might refer to these bonds as being "issued at 107.4." This means the bonds were issued at approximately 107.4% of the $100,000 face value, or $107,400.

Here, we see that the bond issue price is above the face amount of $100,000. RC Enterprises receives $107,439 from investors, but will need to pay back only $100,000 when the bonds mature in 10 years. Why? Because the bonds pay 7% interest when the market rate for bonds of similar risk is only 6%. By issuing the bonds for $107,439, the company is effectively lowering the interest earned by investors from the stated rate of 7% to the market rate of 6%.

Illustration 9–12 shows the relation between the stated interest rate, the market interest rate, and the bond issue price.

Stated Interest Rate		Market Interest Rate	Bonds Issued at
7%	<	8%	Discount
7%	=	7%	Face amount
7%	>	6%	Premium

ILLUSTRATION 9–12

Stated Rate, Market Rate, and the Bond Issue Price

If the bonds' stated interest rate is less than the market interest rate, then the bonds will issue below face amount (discount). If the bonds' stated interest rate equals the market interest rate, then the bonds will issue at face amount. Finally, if the bonds' stated interest rate is more than the market interest rate, the bonds will issue above face amount (premium).

Which is most common in practice—bonds issued at face amount, a discount, or a premium? Most bonds initially are issued at a slight discount. Because there is a delay between when the company determines the characteristics of the bonds and when the bonds actually are issued, the company must estimate the market rate of interest. Bond issuers usually adopt a stated interest rate that is close to, but just under, the expected market interest rate. However, in future periods, the bonds may trade at either a discount or a premium depending on changes in market interest rates.

KEY POINT

The price of a bond is equal to the present value of the face amount (principal) payable at maturity, plus the present value of the periodic interest payments. Bonds can be issued at face amount, below face amount (at a discount), or above face amount (at a premium).

Assume that on January 1, 2012, Wally World issues $200,000 of 9% bonds, due in 10 years, with interest payable semiannually on June 30 and December 31 each year.

Required:

1. If the market rate is 9%, will the bonds issue at face amount, a discount, or a premium? Calculate the issue price.
2. If the market rate is 10%, will the bonds issue at face amount, a discount, or a premium? Calculate the issue price.
3. If the market rate is 8%, will the bonds issue at face amount, a discount, or a premium? Calculate the issue price.

Let's Review

spiceland.mhhe.com/t17

Solution:

1. If the market rate is 9%, the bonds will issue at face amount.

CALCULATOR INPUT

Bond Characteristics	Key	Amount
1. Face amount	FV	$200,000
2. Interest payment each period	PMT	$9,000 = $200,000 × 9% × 1/2 year
3. Market interest rate each period	I	4.5% = 9% ÷ 2 semiannual periods
4. Periods to maturity	N	20 = 10 years × 2 periods each year

CALCULATOR OUTPUT

Issue price	PV	$200,000

	C7			f_x	=-PV(C4, C5, C3, C2, 0)	
	A	B	C	D	E	F
1						
2	Face amount		$200,000.00			
3	Interest payment		$9,000.00			
4	Market interest rate		4.5%			
5	Number of periods		20			
6						
7	Issue price		$200,000.00			
8						
9						

Sheet1 / Sheet2 / Sheet3

Ready — 100% —

PRESENT VALUE TABLES

Present value of principal	= $200,000 × 0.41464*	= $ 82,928
Present value of interest payments	= $9,000[1] × 13.00794**	= 117,072
Issue price of the bonds		$200,000

[1]$200,000 × 9% × 1/2 year = $9,000
*Table 2, i = 4.5%, n = 20
**Table 4, i = 4.5%, n = 20

2. If the market rate is 10%, the bonds will issue at a discount. The only change we make in the calculation is that now I = 5% rather than 4.5%.

CALCULATOR INPUT

Bond Characteristics	Key	Amount
1. Face amount	FV	$200,000
2. Interest payment each period	PMT	$9,000 = $200,000 × 9% × 1/2 year
3. Market interest rate each period	I	5% = 10% ÷ 2 semiannual periods
4. Periods to maturity	N	20 = 10 years × 2 periods each year

CALCULATOR OUTPUT

Issue price	PV	$187,538

C7			*fx*	=-PV(C4, C5, C3, C2, 0)	
	A	B	C	D	E	F
1						
2	Face amount		$200,000.00			
3	Interest payment		$9,000.00			
4	Market interest rate		5%			
5	Number of periods		20			
6						
7	Issue price		$187,538.00			
8						
9						

PRESENT VALUE TABLES

Present value of principal	= $200,000 × 0.37689*	= $ 75,378
Present value of interest payments	= $9,000[1] × 12.46221**	= 112,160
Issue price of the bonds		$187,538

[1]$200,000 × 9% × 1/2 year = $9,000
*Table 2, *i* = 5%, *n* = 20
**Table 4, *i* = 5%, *n* = 20

3. If the market rate is 8%, the bonds will issue at a premium. The only change we make in the calculation is that now I = 4%.

CALCULATOR INPUT

Bond Characteristics	Key	Amount
1. Face amount	FV	$200,000
2. Interest payment each period	PMT	$9,000 = $200,000 × 9% × 1/2 year
3. Market interest rate each period	I	4% = 8% ÷ 2 semiannual periods
4. Periods to maturity	N	20 = 10 years × 2 periods each year

CALCULATOR OUTPUT

Issue price	PV	$213,590

C7			*fx*	=-PV(C4, C5, C3, C2, 0)	
	A	B	C	D	E	F
1						
2	Face amount		$200,000.00			
3	Interest payment		$9,000.00			
4	Market interest rate		4%			
5	Number of periods		20			
6						
7	Issue price		$213,590.00			
8						
9						

Suggested Homework:
BE9-3, BE9-4;
E9-3, E9-4;
P9-1A&B

PRESENT VALUE TABLES

Present value of principal	= $200,000 × 0.45639* =	$ 91,278
Present value of interest payments	= $9,000[1] × 13.59033** =	122,312
Issue price of the bonds		$213,590

[1]$200,000 × 9% × 1/2 year = $9,000
*Table 2, $i = 4\%$, $n = 20$
**Table 4, $i = 4\%$, $n = 20$

PART C

RECORDING BONDS PAYABLE

Now that we have seen how companies price bonds, let's look at how they record the bond issue and the related interest.

Accounting for a Bond Issue

■ **LO4**
Account for the issuance of bonds.

To see how to record the issuance of bonds, let's return to our initial example. On January 1, 2012, RC Enterprises issues $100,000 of 7% bonds, due in 10 years, with interest payable semiannually on June 30 and December 31 each year.

RECORDING BONDS ISSUED AT FACE VALUE

The bonds issue for exactly $100,000, assuming a 7% market interest rate. RC Enterprises records the bond issue as:

A = L + SE
+100,000
        +100,000

January 1, 2012	Debit	Credit
Cash	100,000	
Bonds Payable		100,000
(Issue bonds at face amount)		

RC Enterprises reports bonds payable in the long-term liabilities section of the balance sheet. Nine years from now, when the bonds are within one year of maturity, the firm will reclassify the bonds as current liabilities.

On June 30, 2012, RC Enterprises records the first semiannual interest payment:

A = L + SE
        −3,500 Exp
−3,500

June 30, 2012	Debit	Credit
Interest Expense	3,500	
Cash		3,500
(Pay semiannual interest)		
($3,500 = $100,000 × 7% × 1/2)		

The firm will record another semiannual interest payment on December 31, 2012. In fact, it will record semiannual interest payments at the end of every six-month period for the next 10 years.

RECORDING BONDS ISSUED AT A DISCOUNT

In the preceding example we assumed the stated interest rate (7%) and the market interest rate (7%) were the same. How will the entries differ if the stated interest rate is less than the market rate of, say, 8%? The bonds will issue at only $93,205. This is less than $100,000 because the bonds are paying only 7%, while investors can purchase bonds of similar risk paying 8%. When bonds issue at less than face value, we say they issue at a discount. RC Enterprises records the bond issue at a discount as:

January 1, 2012	Debit	Credit	A	=	L	+	SE
Cash	93,205		+93,205				
Bonds Payable		93,205			+93,205		
(Issue bonds at a discount)							

We initially record the Bonds Payable account at $93,205.[1] The balance in the Bonds Payable account is the **carrying value**. The carrying value will increase from the amount originally borrowed ($93,205) to the amount due at maturity ($100,000) over the 10-year life of the bonds.

 INTERNATIONAL FINANCIAL REPORTING STANDARDS (IFRS)

Including the discount or premium as part of the carrying value of bonds payable (called the *net method*) is the preferred method of reporting under IFRS. This is also how companies in the United States report bonds payable on the balance sheet. An alternative approach (referred to as the *gross method*), in which bonds payable is recorded at face value and the discount or premium is recorded in a separate account, is covered in more advanced accounting courses.

For more discussion, see Appendix E.

We calculate each period's interest expense as the carrying value (the amount actually owed during that period) times the market rate (4% semiannually or 8% annually, in our example).[2] For the first interest payment, interest expense is:

$$\text{Interest expense} = \text{Carrying value of bond} \times \text{Market interest rate per period}$$
$$\$3,728 = \$93,205 \times 8\% \times 1/2$$

However, the bond agreement specifies that cash paid for interest is equal to the face amount times the stated rate (3.5% semiannually or 7% annually, in our example):

$$\text{Cash paid for interest} = \text{Face amount of bond} \times \text{Stated interest rate per period}$$
$$\$3,500 = \$100,000 \times 7\% \times 1/2$$

Notice that when the bond sells at a discount, interest expense ($3,728) is *more* than the cash paid for interest ($3,500). (The opposite is true when the bond sells at a premium: Interest expense is less than the cash paid for interest.) On June 30, 2012, RC Enterprises records interest expense, an increase in the carrying value of bonds payable, and the cash paid for interest as follows:

June 30, 2012	Debit	Credit	A	=	L	+	SE
Interest Expense (= $93,205 × 8% × 1/2)................	3,728						−3,728 Exp
Bonds Payable (difference)........................		228			+228		
Cash (= $100,000 × 7% × 1/2).....................		3,500	−3,500				
(Pay semiannual interest)							

[1]Recording bonds payable, net of the discount or plus the premium, is how companies report bonds payable on the balance sheet. Companies also record the flip side, investment in bonds, net of the discount or plus the premium. Using the net method to record both bonds payable and the investment in bonds is (1) consistent with the actual reporting used by companies in practice and (2) easier to understand than recording the discount or premium separately.

[2]We cover the effective interest method, as this is the generally accepted method under both U.S. GAAP and IFRS. The straight-line amortization method, which is allowed only if it does not materially differ from the effective interest method, is discussed as an alternative approach in more advanced accounting courses.

COMMON MISTAKE

Students sometimes incorrectly record interest expense using the stated rate rather than the market rate. Remember that interest expense is the carrying value times the market rate, while the cash paid for interest is the face amount times the stated rate.

Because the carrying value of debt issued at a discount increases over time, interest expense also will increase each semiannual interest period. We record interest for the next semiannual interest period on December 31, 2012, as:

December 31, 2012	Debit	Credit
Interest Expense (= [$93,205 + $228] × 8% × 1/2)...................	3,737	
Bonds Payable (difference)..		237
Cash (= $100,000 × 7% × 1/2)..		3,500
(Pay semiannual interest)		

An amortization schedule provides a convenient summary of the cash interest payments, interest expense, and changes in carrying value for each semiannual interest period. Illustration 9–13 provides an amortization schedule for the bonds issued at a discount. Note that the amounts for the June 30, 2012, and the December 31, 2012, semiannual interest payments shown above can be taken directly from the amortization schedule.

ILLUSTRATION 9–13

Amortization Schedule for Bonds Issued at a Discount

(1) Date	(2) Cash Paid for Interest	(3) Interest Expense	(4) Increase in Carrying Value	(5) Carrying Value
	Face Amount × Stated Rate	Carrying Value × Market Rate	(3)−(2)	Prior Carrying Value + (4)
1/1/12				$ 93,205
6/30/12	$3,500	$3,728	$228	93,433
12/31/12	3,500	3,737	237	93,670
*	*	*	*	*
*	*	*	*	99,057
6/30/21	3,500	3,962	462	99,519
12/31/21	3,500	3,981	481	100,000

The amortization schedule shows interest calculations every six months because interest is paid semiannually. The entire amortization schedule would be 20 rows long. To save space, we show only the amortization for the first and last years. The eight years in the middle are represented by asterisks. Cash paid is $3,500 (= $100,000 × 7% × 1/2) every six months. Interest expense is the carrying value times the market rate. Interest expense for the six months ended June 30, 2012, is $3,728 (= $93,205 × 4%). The difference between interest expense and the cash paid increases the carrying value of the bonds. At the maturity date, the carrying value will equal the face amount of $100,000.

Decision Maker's Perspective

Carrying Value and Market Value

Is the carrying value of bonds payable reported on the balance sheet really what the bonds are worth? Yes, but only on the date issued and on the final maturity date. Between these two dates, the carrying value of bonds payable reported on the balance sheet can vary considerably from the true underlying market value of the liability.

The reason is that the market interest rate is constantly changing. The market value of bonds moves in the opposite direction of interest rates: When market interest rates go up, the market value of bonds goes down. However, the carrying value of bonds is not adjusted for changes in market interest rates after the issue date.

Refer back to the amortization schedule for the bonds issued at a discount by RC Enterprises. The carrying value of $93,205 on the date of issue equals the market value of the bonds. However, the carrying value one year later on December 31, 2012 ($93,670), will equal market value *only* if the market rate of interest continues to be 8%. If market interest rates go up during the year, the value of bonds payable will fall. Similarly, if market rates go down during the year, the value of bonds payable will increase.

Current generally accepted accounting principles allow the option to report some or all of a company's financial assets and liabilities at fair value. If a company chooses to report a financial liability such as bonds payable at fair value, then it reports changes in fair value as gains and losses in the income statement. ●

RECORDING BONDS ISSUED AT A PREMIUM

Now assume RC Enterprises issues $100,000 of 7% bonds when other bonds of similar risk are paying only 6%. The bonds will issue at $107,439. Investors will pay more than $100,000 for these 7% bonds because bonds of similar risk are paying only 6% interest. When bonds issue at more than face value, we say they issue at a premium. RC Enterprises records the bond issue at a premium as:

January 1, 2012	Debit	Credit		A	=	L	+	SE
Cash	107,439			+107,439				
Bonds Payable		107,439				+107,439		
(*Issue bonds at a premium*)								

Initially, we record the Bonds Payable account at $107,439. However, RC Enterprises will need to pay back only $100,000 when the bonds mature in 10 years. Therefore, the carrying value will decrease from $107,439 (issue price) to $100,000 (face amount) over the 10-year life of the bonds. We still calculate interest expense as the carrying value times the market rate (3% semiannually). On June 30, 2012, RC Enterprises records interest, assuming the bonds were issued at a premium, as follows:

June 30, 2012	Debit	Credit		A	=	L	+	SE
Interest Expense (= $107,439 × 6% × 1/2)	3,223							−3,223 Exp↑
Bonds Payable (difference)	277					−277		
Cash (= $100,000 × 7% × 1/2)		3,500		−3,500				
(*Pay semiannual interest*)								

When bonds are issued at a premium, the carrying value of the debt decreases over time. That's why we *debit* Bonds Payable, because Bonds Payable is decreasing over time. Since the carrying value of the debt decreases over time, interest expense will also decrease each semiannual interest period. RC Enterprises records interest for the next semiannual interest period on December 31, 2012, as:

December 31, 2012	Debit	Credit		A	=	L	+	SE
Interest Expense (= [$107,439 − $277] × 6% × 1/2)	3,215							−3,215 Exp↑
Bonds Payable (difference)	285					−285		
Cash (= $100,000 × 7% × 1/2)		3,500		−3,500				
(*Pay semiannual interest*)								

The amortization schedule in Illustration 9–14 summarizes the recording of interest expense for the bonds issued at a premium.

ILLUSTRATION 9–14

Amortization Schedule for Bonds Issued at a Premium

(1) Date	(2) Cash Paid for Interest Face Amount × Stated Rate	(3) Interest Expense Carrying Value × Market Rate	(4) Decrease in Carrying Value (2) − (3)	(5) Carrying Value Prior Carrying Value − (4)
1/1/12				$107,439
6/30/12	$3,500	$3,223	$277	107,162
12/31/12	3,500	3,215	285	106,877
*	*	*	*	*
*	*	*	*	100,956
6/30/21	3,500	3,029	471	100,485
12/31/21	3,500	3,015	485	100,000

Just as in the discount example, the amounts for the June 30, 2012, and the December 31, 2012, semiannual interest payments can be obtained directly from the amortization schedule. Now, however, with a bond premium, the difference between cash paid and interest expense *decreases* the carrying value each period from $107,439 at bond issue down to $100,000 (the face amount) at bond maturity.

Illustration 9–15 shows how carrying value changes as a bond approaches its maturity date.

ILLUSTRATION 9–15

Changes in Carrying Value over Time

 KEY POINT

When bonds issue at face amount, the carrying value and the corresponding interest expense *remain constant* over time. When bonds issue at a discount (below face amount), the carrying value and the corresponding interest expense *increase* over time. When bonds issue at a premium (above face amount), the carrying value and the corresponding interest expense *decrease* over time.

Assume that on January 1, 2012, Wally World issues $200,000 of 9% bonds, due in 10 years, with interest payable semiannually on June 30 and December 31 each year.

Let's Review

spiceland.mhhe.com/t18

Required:

1. If the market rate is 9%, the bonds will issue at $200,000. Record the bond issue on January 1, 2012, and the first two semiannual interest payments on June 30, 2012, and December 31, 2012.

2. If the market rate is 10%, the bonds will issue at $187,538. Record the bond issue on January 1, 2012, and the first two semiannual interest payments on June 30, 2012, and December 31, 2012.

3. If the market rate is 8%, the bonds will issue at $213,590. Record the bond issue on January 1, 2012, and the first two semiannual interest payments on June 30, 2012, and December 31, 2012.

Solution:

1. Record the bonds issued at face amount and the first two semiannual interest payments:

January 1, 2012	Debit	Credit
Cash	200,000	
Bonds Payable		200,000
(Issue bonds at face amount)		
June 30, 2012		
Interest Expense	9,000	
Cash (= $200,000 × 9% × 1/2)		9,000
(Pay semiannual interest)		
December 31, 2012		
Interest Expense	9,000	
Cash (= $200,000 × 9% × 1/2)		9,000
(Pay semiannual interest)		

2. Record the bonds issued at a discount and the first two semiannual interest payments:

January 1, 2012	Debit	Credit
Cash	187,538	
Bonds Payable		187,538
(Issue bonds at a discount)		
June 30, 2012		
Interest Expense (= $187,538 × 10% × 1/2)	9,377	
Bonds Payable (difference)		377
Cash (= $200,000 × 9% × 1/2)		9,000
(Pay semiannual interest)		
December 31, 2012		
Interest Expense (= [$187,538 + $377] × 10% × 1/2)	9,396	
Bonds Payable (difference)		396
Cash (= $200,000 × 9% × 1/2)		9,000
(Pay semiannual interest)		

3. Record the bonds issued at a premium and the first two semiannual interest payments:

January 1, 2012	Debit	Credit
Cash	213,590	
Bonds Payable		213,590
(Issue bonds at a premium)		
June 30, 2012		
Interest Expense (= $213,590 × 8% × 1/2)	8,544	
Bonds Payable (difference)	456	
Cash (= $200,000 × 9% × 1/2)...		9,000
(Pay semiannual interest)		
December 31, 2012		
Interest Expense (= [$213,590 − $456] × 8% × 1/2)................	8,525	
Bonds Payable (difference)	475	
Cash (= $200,000 × 9% × 1/2)...		9,000
(Pay semiannual interest)		

Suggested Homework:
BE9-6, BE9-7;
E9-6, E9-7;
P9-2A&B, P9-4A&B

Accounting for Bond Retirements

■ **LO5**
Record the retirement of bonds.

When the issuing corporation buys back its bonds from the investors, we say the company has **retired** those bonds. The corporation can wait until the bonds mature to retire them, or frequently (for reasons we describe below), the issuer will choose to buy the bonds back from the bondholders early.

BOND RETIREMENTS AT MATURITY

Regardless of whether bonds are issued at face amount, a discount, or a premium, **their carrying value at maturity will equal their face amount.** RC Enterprises records the retirement of its bonds at maturity (December 31, 2021) as:

A = L + SE
    −100,000
−100,000

December 31, 2021	Debit	Credit
Bonds Payable	100,000	
Cash		100,000
(Retire bonds at maturity)		

BOND RETIREMENTS BEFORE MATURITY

Earlier we noted that a call feature accompanies most bonds, allowing the issuer to buy back bonds at a fixed price. Even when bonds are not callable in this way, the issuing company can retire bonds early by purchasing them on the open market. Regardless of the method, when the issuer retires debt of any type before its scheduled maturity date, the transaction is an early extinguishment of debt.

Let's return to our example of RC Enterprises issuing $100,000 of 7% bonds maturing in 10 years when other bonds of similar risk are paying 8%. The bonds were issued on January 1, 2012, below face amount (at a discount) at $93,205. Let's assume that market interest rates drop from 8% to 6% during 2012 and RC Enterprises decides to repurchase the bonds one year after issuance on December 31,

2012, when the carrying value of the bonds is now $93,670 (see the amortization table in Illustration 9–13).

When interest rates go down, bond prices go up. If the market rate drops to 6%, it will now cost $106,877 to retire the bonds on December 31, 2012.[3] The bonds have a carrying value on December 31, 2012, of only $93,670, but it will cost the issuing company $106,877 to retire them. RC Enterprises will record a loss for the difference. RC Enterprises records the retirement as:

December 31, 2012	Debit	Credit	A	=	L	+	SE
Bonds Payable (account balance)	93,670				−93,670		
Loss (difference)	13,207						−13,207 Exp↑
Cash (amount paid)		106,877	−106,877				
(*Retire bonds before maturity*)							

Losses (and gains) on the early extinguishment of debt are reported as nonoperating items (similar to losses and gains on the sale of long-term assets) in the income statement. Losses have the effect of reducing net income, while gains increase net income.

Why Buy Back Debt Early?

Decision Maker's Perspective

In the example above, RC Enterprises recorded a loss of $13,207 due to a decrease in market interest rates of 2%. One way a company can protect itself from decreases in interest rates is to include a call feature allowing the company to repurchase bonds at a fixed price (such as 2% over face amount, which in our example would be $102,000). When interest rates decrease, companies with a call provision are more likely to repurchase higher-cost debt and then reissue debt at new, lower interest rates. This type of buyback and reissue lowers future interest expense.

Another reason to repay debt early is to improve the company's debt ratios (discussed later in the chapter). **Six Flags** sold seven amusement parks for just over $300 million and used the proceeds to reduce its overall debt.

Early extinguishment of debt can also be timed to manage reported earnings. Since bonds payable are reported at carrying values and not market values, firms can time their repurchase of bonds to help meet earnings expectations. For instance, when interest rates go up, bond prices go down. In this case, RC Enterprises will record a gain rather than a loss on early extinguishment. ●

KEY POINT

No gain or loss is recorded on bonds retired at maturity. For bonds retired before maturity, we record a gain or loss on early extinguishment equal to the difference between the price paid to repurchase the bonds and the bonds' carrying value.

---

[3]The repurchase price of $106,877 is based on the following financial calculator inputs: future value, $100,000; interest payment each period, $3,500; market interest rate each period, 3% (6% ÷ 2 semiannual periods); and periods to maturity, 18 (9 years left × 2 periods each year).

ETHICAL DILEMMA

 On January 1, 2012, West-Tex Oil issued $50 million of 8% bonds maturing in 10 years. The market interest rate on the issue date was 9%, which resulted in the bonds being issued at a discount. In December 2013, Tex Winters, the company CFO, notes that in the two years since the bonds were issued, interest rates have fallen almost 3%. Tex suggests that West-Tex might consider repurchasing the 8% bonds and reissuing new bonds at the lower current interest rates.

Another executive, Will Bright, asks, "Won't the repurchase result in a large loss to our financial statements?" Tex agrees, indicating that West-Tex is likely to just meet earnings targets for 2013. It would probably not meet them with an added loss on bond repurchase in the millions. However, 2014 looks to be a record-breaking year. They decide that maybe they should wait until 2014 to repurchase the bonds.

How could the repurchase of debt cause a loss to be reported in net income? Explain how the repurchase of debt might be timed to manage reported earnings. Is it ethical to time the repurchase of bonds to help meet earnings targets?

PART D

■ **LO6**
Identify other major long-term liabilities.

OTHER LONG-TERM LIABILITIES

Companies report many long-term liabilities other than bonds payable. In this section, we briefly discuss two of them: installment notes and leases. (Deferred taxes, a third long-term liability, discussed in Chapter 8, are classified as either current or long-term.) The emphasis in this discussion is on the big picture, saving the details for more advanced accounting courses.

Installment Notes

You may have purchased a car, or maybe even a house. If so, unless you paid cash, you signed a note promising to pay the purchase price over, say, four years for the car or 30 years for the house. Car and house loans usually call for payment in monthly installments rather than by a single amount at maturity. Companies, too, often borrow using installment notes. **Each installment payment includes both an amount that represents interest and an amount that represents a reduction of the outstanding loan balance.** The periodic reduction of the balance is enough that at maturity the note is completely paid.

To illustrate, assume that RC Enterprises obtains a $25,000, 6%, four-year loan for a new truck on January 1, 2012. Payments of $587.13 are required at the end of each month for 48 months.[4] Illustration 9–16 (next page) provides an amortization schedule for the loan.

Notice that the carrying value begins at $25,000 and decreases each month to a final carrying value of $0 at the end of the four-year loan. Also, notice that interest

---

[4]The monthly payment of $587.13 is based on the following financial calculator inputs: future value, $0; present value, $25,000; market interest rate, 0.5% (6% ÷ 12 periods each year); periods to maturity, 48 (4 years × 12 periods each year)—and solving for the monthly payment (PMT).

(1) Date	(2) Cash Paid for Interest	(3) Interest Expense	(4) Decrease in Carrying Value	(5) Carrying Value
		Carrying Value × Market Rate	(2)−(3)	Prior Carrying Value − (4)
1/1/12				$25,000.00
1/31/12	$587.13	$125.00	$462.13	24,537.87
2/28/12	587.13	122.69	464.44	24,073.43
*	*	*	*	*
*	*	*	*	*
11/30/15	587.13	5.83	581.30	584.21
12/31/15	587.13	2.92	584.21	0

ILLUSTRATION 9–16

Amortization Schedule for an Installment Note

expense decreases with each monthly payment. In each of the following months, the amount that goes to interest expense becomes less and the amount that goes to decreasing the carrying value (referred to as the principal) becomes more. Why is this? Interest expense decreases over time because the carrying value decreases over time, and interest is a constant percentage of carrying value.

We record the note and the first two monthly installment payments as follows:

	Debit	Credit		A	=	L	+	SE
January 1, 2012								
Cash	25,000			+25,000				
Notes Payable		25,000					+25,000	
(*Issue a note payable*)								
January 31, 2012								
Interest Expense (= $25,000 × 6% × 1/12)	125.00							−125.00 Exp
Notes Payable (difference)	462.13					−462.13		
Cash (monthly payment)		587.13		−587.13				
(*Pay monthly installment on note*)								
February 28, 2012								
Interest Expense (= $24,537.87 × 6% × 1/12)	122.69							−122.69 Exp
Notes Payable (difference)	464.44					−464.44		
Cash (monthly payment)		587.13		−587.13				
(*Pay monthly installment on note*)								

KEY POINT

Most notes payable require periodic installment payments. Each installment payment includes an amount that represents interest expense and an amount that represents a reduction of the outstanding loan balance.

Leases

If you have ever leased a car or an apartment, you are familiar with leasing. A lease is a contractual arrangement by which the *lessor* (owner) provides the *lessee* (user) the right to use an asset for a specified period of time. For accounting purposes, we have two basic types of leases: operating leases and capital leases.

Operating leases are like rentals. If you lease a car for a week, you really have no intention of owning the car. Short-term car rentals and most apartment leases are operating leases. The lessor owns the asset, and the lessee simply uses the asset temporarily. Over the lease term, the lessee records rent expense and the lessor records rent revenue.

spiceland.mhhe.com/c27

However, not all leases are simply rentals. Capital leases occur when the lessee essentially buys an asset and borrows the money through a lease to pay for the asset. For example, let's say RC Enterprises leases rather than buys a truck, signing a four-year lease at 6% interest that automatically transfers ownership of the car to RC Enterprises at the end of the lease term. The dealership (the lessor) calculates the lease payments to cover the purchase price of the truck and 6% interest. In substance, RC Enterprises (the lessee) bought the car and borrowed the money at 6% interest to pay for it, even though RC signed a so-called lease agreement. RC would record the lease just as if it had bought the car and borrowed the money from the dealer—except "notes payable" would be labeled "lease payable." In turn, the dealership records the sale like other sales on credit.[5]

Decision Maker's Perspective

Why Do Some Companies Lease Rather Than Buy?

Leasing continues to grow in popularity. Approximately one-third of all debt financing in the United States is through leasing. Why do so many companies choose to lease rather than buy?

1. **Leasing improves cash flows through up to 100% financing.** In a purchase, most lenders require a down payment up to 20%. In contrast, leasing may allow you to finance up to the entire purchase price, freeing cash for other uses.

2. **Leasing improves the balance sheet by reducing long-term debt.** As long as the lessee can structure the lease as an operating lease, the lessee reports only rent expense, avoiding the reporting of long-term debt in a purchase with debt financing.

3. **Leasing can lower income taxes.** Many companies today find that purchasing equipment causes them to be faced with an extra income tax burden under the alternative minimum tax (AMT) calculations. Leasing is one way to help avoid these additional taxes. ●

 KEY POINT

An operating lease is recorded just like a rental. In a capital lease, the lessee essentially "buys" the asset and borrows the money to pay for it.

Decision Point

Question	Accounting information	Analysis
Does the company have significant obligations related to operating leases?	Disclosure of lease commitments in the notes to the financial statements	Operating lease commitments are not reported as liabilities on the balance sheet, but are disclosed in the notes to the financial statements. They need to be considered when calculating important debt ratios such as the debt to equity ratio.

---

[5]Lease accounting can be complex. Therefore, the details regarding the accounting for capital leases are covered in more advanced accounting classes.

DEBT ANALYSIS
Coca-Cola vs. PepsiCo

Business decisions include risk. Failure to properly consider risk in those decisions is one of the most costly, yet most common, mistakes investors and creditors make. Long-term debt is one of the first places decision makers should look when trying to get a handle on risk. As stated in the feature story at the beginning of the chapter, **Six Flags** entered into bankruptcy proceedings in 2009 due to difficulties in repaying its long-term debt. Illustration 9–17 describes steps taken by Six Flags to reduce its long-term debt.

■ **LO7**
Make financial decisions using long-term liability ratios.

SIX FLAGS, INC.
Notes to the Financial Statements (excerpt)

Six Flags, Inc., has entered into an agreement to sell three of its water parks and four of its theme parks to PARC 7F-Operations Corporation (PARC) of Jacksonville, Florida, for $312 million, consisting of $275 million in cash and a note receivable for $37 million.
     The disposition of these seven parks is a key component of the Company's overall strategy to reduce debt and enhance operational and financial flexibility. Company management stated that its intent was to reduce debt by several hundred million dollars over the next several years.

ILLUSTRATION 9–17

Six Flags's Disclosure of Long-Term Debt

Here, we look at two ratios frequently used to measure financial risk related to long-term liabilities: (1) debt to equity and (2) times interest earned.

DEBT TO EQUITY RATIO

To measure a company's risk, we often calculate the debt to equity ratio:

$$\text{Debt to equity ratio} = \frac{\text{Total liabilities}}{\text{Stockholders' equity}}$$

Debt requires payment on specific dates. Failure to repay debt or the interest associated with the debt on a timely basis may result in default and perhaps even bankruptcy. Other things being equal, the higher the debt to equity ratio, the higher the risk of bankruptcy. When a company assumes more debt, risk increases.

Debt also can be an advantage. It can enhance the return to stockholders. If a company earns a return in excess of the cost of borrowing the funds, shareholders are provided with a total return greater than what could have been earned with equity funds alone. Unfortunately, borrowing is not always favorable. Sometimes the cost of borrowing the funds exceeds the returns they generate. This illustrates the risk–reward trade-off faced by shareholders.

Have you ever ordered a Pepsi and then found out the place serves only Coke products? Amusement parks often have exclusive contracts for soft drinks. The official soft drink of **Six Flags** is Coca-Cola, while **Cedar Point** serves only Pepsi products. Illustration 9–18 provides selected financial data for **Coca-Cola** and **PepsiCo**.

ILLUSTRATION 9–18

Financial Information for Coca-Cola and PepsiCo

Selected Balance Sheet Data
December 31, 2008 and 2007
($ in millions)

	Coca-Cola		PepsiCo	
	2008	**2007**	**2008**	**2007**
Total assets	$40,519	$43,269	$35,994	$34,628
Total liabilities	$20,047	$21,525	$23,888	$17,394
Stockholders' equity	20,472	21,744	12,106	17,234
Total liabilities and equity	$40,519	$43,269	$35,994	$34,628

Income Statements
For the year ended December 31, 2008
($ in millions)

	Coca-Cola	PepsiCo
Net sales	$31,944	$43,251
Cost of goods sold	11,374	20,351
Gross profit	20,570	22,900
Operating expenses	12,693	15,550
Interest expense	438	329
Tax expense	1,632	1,879
Net income	$ 5,807	$ 5,142

Illustration 9–19 compares the 2008 debt to equity ratio for Coca-Cola and PepsiCo.

ILLUSTRATION 9–19

Debt to Equity Ratio for Coca-Cola and PepsiCo

($ in millions)	Total Liabilities	÷	Stockholders' Equity	=	Debt to Equity Ratio
Coca-Cola	$20,047	÷	$20,472	=	0.98
PepsiCo	$23,888	÷	$12,106	=	1.97

The debt to equity ratio is higher for PepsiCo. Debt to equity is a measure of financial leverage. Thus, PepsiCo has higher leverage than Coca-Cola. Leverage enables a company to earn a higher return using debt than without debt, in the same way a person can lift more weight with a lever than without it.

Decision Point

Question	Accounting information	Analysis
Which company has higher leverage?	Debt to equity ratio	Debt to equity is a measure of financial leverage. Companies with more debt will have a higher debt to equity ratio and higher leverage.

PepsiCo is assuming more debt, and therefore its investors are assuming more risk. Remember, this added debt could be good or bad depending on whether the company earns a return in excess of the cost of borrowed funds. Let's explore this further by revisiting the return on assets introduced in Chapter 7. Recall that return on assets measures the amount of income generated for each dollar invested in assets. In Illustration 9–20 we calculate the return on assets for Coca-Cola and PepsiCo.

$$\text{Return on assets} = \frac{\text{Net income}}{\text{Average total assets}}$$

($ in millions)	Net Income	÷	Average Total Assets	=	Return on Assets
Coca-Cola	$5,807	÷	$41,894*	=	13.9%
PepsiCo	$5,142	÷	$35,311**	=	14.6%

*($40,519 + $43,269) ÷ 2
**($35,994 + $34,628) ÷ 2

ILLUSTRATION 9–20

Return on Assets for Coca-Cola and PepsiCo

The return on assets indicates a company's overall profitability, ignoring specific sources of financing. PepsiCo's profitability slightly exceeds Coca-Cola's. Note that both Coca-Cola and PepsiCo have a strong return on assets.

What happens when we compare the companies' return on equity, which indicates their ability to generate earnings from the resources that *owners* provide? Illustration 9–21 shows the calculation for return on equity.

$$\text{Return on equity} = \frac{\text{Net income}}{\text{Average stockholders' equity}}$$

($ in millions)	Net Income	÷	Average Stockholders' Equity	=	Return on Equity
Coca-Cola	$5,807	÷	$21,108*	=	27.5%
PepsiCo	$5,142	÷	$14,670**	=	35.1%

*($20,472 + $21,744) ÷ 2
**($12,106 + $17,234) ÷ 2

ILLUSTRATION 9–21

Return on Equity for Coca-Cola and PepsiCo

The difference between the return on assets and return on equity measures is due to the difference in leverage: PepsiCo's higher leverage results in a 7.6% higher return on equity compared to only a 0.7% higher return on assets. PepsiCo increased its return on equity 2.4 times (35.1% ÷ 14.6%) the return on assets. Coca-Cola increased its return on equity only 2.0 times (27.5% ÷ 13.9%) the return on assets. So, as long as both companies have strong returns in excess of the rate charged on borrowed funds, the greater leverage of PepsiCo will result in a higher return to investors. However, if returns should fall below the rate charged on borrowed funds, PepsiCo's greater leverage will result in lower overall returns to PepsiCo than to Coca-Cola. That's where the risk comes in.

Decision Point

Question	Accounting information	Analysis
How does leverage affect a company's return on equity?	Debt to equity ratio; return on equity ratio	Leverage increases risk. In good times, higher leverage results in higher return on equity. In down times, higher leverage results in lower return on equity.

TIMES INTEREST EARNED RATIO

Lenders require interest payments in return for the use of their money. Failure to pay interest when it is due may invoke penalties, possibly leading to bankruptcy. A ratio often used to measure this risk is the times interest earned ratio. This ratio compares interest expense with income available to pay those charges.

At first glance, you might think we can calculate this simply by dividing net income by interest expense. But remember, interest is one of the expenses subtracted in determining net income. So to measure the amount available to pay interest, we need to add interest back to net income. Similarly, because interest is deductible for income tax purposes, we need to add back tax expense as well.

To illustrate the need to add back interest expense and tax expense, assume a company has the following income statement:

Income before interest and taxes	$100,000
Interest expense	(20,000)
Income before taxes	80,000
Income tax expense (40%)	(32,000)
Net income	$ 48,000

What's the maximum amount of interest the company *could have incurred* and still break even? Is it $48,000? No, it's $100,000:

Income before interest and taxes	$100,000
Interest expense	(100,000)
Income before taxes	0
Income tax expense (40%)	(0)
Net income	$ 0

Notice that the $100,000 is equal to net income plus income tax expense plus interest expense.

We compute the times interest earned ratio as:

$$\text{Times interest earned ratio} = \frac{\text{Net income} + \text{Interest expense} + \text{Tax expense}}{\text{Interest expense}}$$

Illustration 9–22 compares the times interest earned ratios for Coca-Cola and PepsiCo to see which company is better able to meet interest payments.

ILLUSTRATION 9–22

Times Interest Earned Ratio for Coca-Cola and PepsiCo

($ in millions)	Net Income + Interest Expense + Tax Expense	÷	Interest Expense	=	Times Interest Earned Ratio
Coca-Cola	$7,877	÷	$438	=	18.0
PepsiCo	$7,350	÷	$329	=	22.3

PepsiCo has a higher times interest earned ratio than Coca-Cola. However, both companies exhibit strong earnings in relation to their interest expense, and both companies appear well able to meet interest payments as they become due.

KEY POINT

The debt to equity ratio is a measure of financial leverage. Taking on more debt (higher leverage) can be good or bad depending on whether the company earns a return in excess of the cost of borrowed funds. The times interest earned ratio measures a company's ability to meet interest payments as they become due.

Question	Accounting information	Analysis	Decision Point
Can a company meet its interest obligations?	Times interest earned ratio	A high times interest earned ratio indicates the ability of a company to meet its interest obligations.	

KEY POINTS BY LEARNING OBJECTIVE

LO1 Explain financing alternatives.

Companies obtain external funds through debt financing (liabilities) and equity financing (stockholders' equity). One advantage of debt financing is that interest on borrowed funds is tax-deductible.

LO2 Identify the characteristics of bonds.

The distinguishing characteristics of bonds include whether they are backed by collateral (secured or unsecured), become due at a single specified date or over a series of years (term or serial), can be redeemed prior to maturity (callable), or can be converted into common stock (convertible).

LO3 Determine the price of a bond issue.

The price of a bond is equal to the present value of the face amount (principal) payable at maturity, plus the present value of the periodic interest payments. Bonds can be issued at face amount, below face amount (at a discount), or above face amount (at a premium).

LO4 Account for the issuance of bonds.

When bonds issue at face amount, the carrying value and the corresponding interest expense *remain constant* over time. When bonds issue at a discount (below face amount), the carrying value and the corresponding interest expense *increase* over time. When bonds issue at a premium (above face amount), the carrying value and the corresponding interest expense *decrease* over time.

LO5 Record the retirement of bonds.

No gain or loss is recorded on bonds retired at maturity. For bonds retired before maturity, we record a gain or loss on early extinguishment equal to the difference between the price paid to repurchase the bonds and the bonds' carrying value.

LO6 Identify other major long-term liabilities.

Most notes payable require periodic installment payments. Each installment payment includes an amount that represents interest expense and an amount that represents a reduction of the outstanding loan balance.

An operating lease is recorded just like a rental. In a capital lease, the lessee essentially "buys" the asset and borrows the money to pay for it.

Analysis

LO7 Make financial decisions using long-term liability ratios.

The debt to equity ratio is a measure of financial leverage. Assuming more debt (higher leverage) can be good or bad depending on whether the company earns a return in excess of the cost of borrowed funds. The times interest earned ratio measures a company's ability to meet interest payments as they become due.

GLOSSARY

Amortization schedule: Provides a summary of the cash interest payments, interest expense, and changes in carrying value for debt instruments. **p. 300**

Bond: A formal debt instrument that obligates the borrower to repay a stated amount, referred to as the principal or face amount, at a specified maturity date. **p. 287**

Bond indenture: A contract between a firm issuing bonds and the corporations or individuals who purchase the bonds. **p. 288**

Callable: A bond feature that allows the borrower to repay the bonds before their scheduled maturity date at a specified call price. **p. 289**

Capital lease: Contract in which the lessee essentially buys an asset and borrows the money through a lease to pay for the asset. **p. 308**

Capital structure: The mixture of liabilities and stockholders' equity in a business. **p. 286**

Carrying value: The balance in the bonds payable account, which equals the face value of bonds payable minus the discount or the face value plus the premium. **p. 299**

Convertible: A bond feature that allows the lender (or investor) to convert each bond into a specified number of shares of common stock. **p. 289**

Debt financing: Obtaining additional funding from lenders. **p. 286**

Debt to equity ratio: Total liabilities divided by total stockholders' equity; measures a company's risk. **p. 309**

Default risk: The risk that a company will be unable to pay the bond's face amount or interest payments as it becomes due. **p. 292**

Discount: A bond's issue price is below the face amount. **p. 292**

Early extinguishment of debt: The issuer retires debt before its scheduled maturity date. **p. 304**

Equity financing: Obtaining additional funding from stockholders. **p. 286**

Installment payment: Includes both an amount that represents interest and an amount that represents a reduction of the outstanding balance. **p. 306**

Lease: A contractual arrangement by which the lessor (owner) provides the lessee (user) the right to use an asset for a specified period of time. **p. 307**

Market interest rate: Represents the true interest rate used by investors to value a bond. **p. 290**

Operating lease: Contract in which the lessor owns the asset and the lessee simply uses the asset temporarily. **p. 307**

Premium: A bond's issue price is above the face amount. **p. 294**

Private placement: Sale of debt securities directly to a single investor. **p. 287**

Return on assets: Net income divided by average total assets; measures the income generated per dollar of assets. **p. 311**

Return on equity: Net income divided by average stockholders' equity; measures the income generated per dollar of equity. **p. 311**

Secured bonds: Bonds that are supported by specific assets pledged as collateral. **p. 288**

Serial bonds: Bonds that require payment of the principal amount of the bond over a series of maturity dates. **p. 288**

Sinking fund: An investment fund used to set aside money to be used to pay debts as they come due. **p. 288**

Stated interest rate: The rate quoted in the bond contract used to calculate the cash payments for interest. **p. 290**

Term bonds: Bonds that require payment of the full principal amount of the bond at a single maturity date. **p. 288**

Times interest earned ratio: Ratio that compares interest expense with income available to pay those charges. **p. 312**

Unsecured bonds: Bonds that are *not* supported by specific assets pledged as collateral. **p. 288**

SELF-STUDY QUESTIONS

■ LO1

1. Which of the following is *not* a primary source of corporate debt financing?
   a. Bonds.
   b. Notes.
   c. Leases.
   d. Receivables.

■ LO2

2. Serial bonds are:
   a. Bonds backed by collateral.
   b. Bonds that mature in installments.

c. Bonds the issuer can repurchase at a fixed price.

d. Bonds issued below the face amount.

3. Convertible bonds: ■ LO2

   a. Provide potential benefits only to the issuer.

   b. Provide potential benefits only to the investor.

   c. Provide potential benefits to both the issuer and the investor.

   d. Provide no potential benefits.

4. The price of a bond is equal to: ■ LO3

   a. The present value of the face amount plus the present value of the stated interest payments.

   b. The future value of the face amount plus the future value of the stated interest payments.

   c. The present value of the face amount only.

   d. The present value of the interest only.

5. Which of the following is true for bonds issued at a discount?   ■ LO4

   a. The stated interest rate is greater than the market interest rate.

   b. The market interest rate is greater than the stated interest rate.

   c. The stated interest rate and the market interest rate are equal.

   d. The stated interest rate and the market interest rate are unrelated.

6. Interest expense on bonds payable is calculated as: ■ LO4

   a. Face amount times the stated interest rate.

   b. Carrying value times the market interest rate.

   c. Face amount times the market interest rate.

   d. Carrying value times the stated interest rate.

7. When bonds are issued at a discount, what happens to the carrying value and   ■ LO4
   interest expense over the life of the bonds?

   a. Carrying value and interest expense increase.

   b. Carrying value and interest expense decrease.

   c. Carrying value decreases and interest expense increases.

   d. Carrying value increases and interest expense decreases.

8. Lincoln County retires a $50 million bond issue when the carrying value of the ■ LO5
   bonds is $48 million, but the market value of the bonds is $54 million. Lincoln
   County will record the retirement as:

   a. A debit of $6 million to Loss due to early extinguishment.

   b. A credit of $6 million to Gain due to early extinguishment.

   c. No gain or loss on retirement.

   d. A debit to Cash for $54 million.

9. Which of the following leases is essentially the purchase of an asset with debt ■ LO6
   financing?

   a. An operating lease.

   b. A capital lease.

   c. Both an operating lease and a capital lease.

   d. Neither an operating lease nor a capital lease.

10. Which of the following ratios measures financial leverage?   ■ LO7

   a. The return on assets ratio.

   b. The return on equity ratio.

   c. The times interest earned ratio.

   d. The debt to equity ratio.

Answers to the Self-Study Questions

1. d   2. b   3. c   4. a   5. b   6. b   7. a   8. a   9. b   10. d

REVIEW QUESTIONS

■ **LO1**   1. What is capital structure? How do the capital structures of **Ford** and **Microsoft** differ?

■ **LO1**   2. Why would a company choose to borrow money rather than issue additional stock?

■ **LO1**   3. What are bond issue costs? What is an underwriter?

■ **LO1**   4. Why do some companies issue bonds rather than borrow money directly from a bank?

■ **LO2**   5. Contrast the following types of bonds:
   a. Secured and unsecured.
   b. Term and serial.
   c. Callable and convertible.

■ **LO2**   6. What are convertible bonds? How do they benefit both the investor and the issuer?

■ **LO3**   7. How do we calculate the issue price of bonds? Is it equal to the present value of the principal? Explain.

■ **LO3**   8. Explain the difference in each of these terms used for bonds:
   a. Face amount and carrying value.
   b. Stated interest rate and market interest rate.

■ **LO3**   9. If bonds issue at a *discount,* is the stated interest rate less than, equal to, or more than the market interest rate? Explain.

■ **LO3**   10. If bonds issue at a *premium,* is the stated interest rate less than, equal to, or more than the market interest rate? Explain.

■ **LO3**   11. Extreme Motion issues $500,000 of 6% bonds due in 20 years with interest payable semiannually on June 30 and December 31. What is the amount of the cash payment for interest every six months? How many interest payments will there be?

■ **LO3**   12. Extreme Motion issues $500,000 of 6% bonds due in 20 years with interest payable semiannually on June 30 and December 31. Calculate the issue price of the bonds assuming a market interest rate of:
   a. 5%
   b. 6%
   c. 7%

■ **LO4**   13. If bonds issue at a *discount,* what happens to the carrying value of bonds payable and the amount recorded for interest expense over time?

■ **LO4**   14. If bonds issue at a *premium,* what happens to the carrying value of bonds payable and the amount recorded for interest expense over time?

■ **LO4**   15. Explain how each of the columns in an amortization schedule is calculated, assuming the bonds are issued at a discount. How is the amortization schedule different if bonds are issued at a premium?

■ **LO5**   16. Why would a company choose to buy back bonds before their maturity date?

■ **LO5**   17. If bonds with a carrying value of $280,000 are retired early at a cost of $330,000, is a gain or loss recorded by the issuer retiring the bonds? How does the issuer record the retirement?

■ **LO6**   18. How do interest expense and the carrying value of the note change over time for an installment note with fixed monthly loan payments?

■ **LO6**   19. Explain the difference between an operating lease and a capital lease.

■ **LO7**   20. What are the potential risks and rewards of carrying additional debt?

For the following, please visit your instructor's *Connect* site.

BRIEF EXERCISES	1-18
EXERCISES	1-17
PROBLEMS: SET A	1-7
PROBLEMS: SET B	1-7
GREAT ADVENTURES	

Note: Additional Perspectives assignments for Financial Analysis, Comparative Analysis, Internet Research, Written Communication, and Earnings Management are in Appendix F at the end of this book. For additional Exercises: Set B and for additional Problems: Set C, visit www.mhhe.com/spicelandMTC1e.

Stockholders' Equity

DECKERS OUTDOOR: FROM DOWN UNDER TO TOP TEN

David Letterman has made the "Top Ten" list famous. His top ten things you *don't* want to hear from your accountant include, "Listen, I'm not good with math," "The good news is you're getting a huge refund—the bad news is you'll have to hide in Costa Rica for a while," "Do you have any dedemptions or exuptions or whatever?," and "Relax, everything here will be fine—I used to work for Enron."

Wouldn't it be nice to know the top ten best stock investments for the future? Although we can't predict the future, we can learn from the past. The ten best stock investments and their investment return over the past decade from 2000 through 2009 were:

Company	Main Product or Service	Return, 2000–2009
Green Mountain Coffee	Coffee	7,434%
Hansen Natural	Beverages	6,455%
Terra Nitrogen	Fertilizers	6,156%
Bally	Slot machines	5,965%
Southwestern Energy	Natural gas	5,411%
Clean Harbors	Hazardous waste disposal	5,464%
Amedisys	Home health care	4,452%
Quality Systems	Accounting and other financial software	3,592%
Deckers Outdoor	Footwear	3,549%
XTO Energy	Oil and natural gas	3,533%

Green Mountain Coffee was the top investment over the past decade. You may be more familiar with Starbucks, but Green Mountain was the better investment. If you had invested $1,000 in the company in 2000, your investment would have grown to over $74,000 by the end of 2009. The second-place finisher, **Hansen Natural**, provides a variety of all-natural beverages such as soda, energy drinks like the Monster brand, juice, and tea. A $1,000 investment in Hansen Natural would have grown to over $64,000 ten years later. Another company you might be familiar with is **Deckers Outdoor**. The company designs and manufactures trendy footwear like Teva sandals and UGG sheepskin boots, available in most shopping malls.

What do these great stock investments have in common? They all were very profitable in relation to the initial investment made by stockholders. In this chapter you will learn how to compare earnings in relation to equity—both the stockholders' equity recorded in the company balance sheet and the market value of equity as determined by the price per share times the number of shares.

Recall from the accounting equation that assets equal liabilities plus stockholders' equity.

$$\underbrace{\text{Assets}}_{\text{(resources)}} = \underbrace{\text{Liabilities} + \text{Stockholders' Equity}}_{\text{(claims to resources)}}$$

In Chapters 4–7 we focused on assets and in Chapters 8–9 on liabilities. Here, in Chapter 10, we focus on the third component of the accounting equation—stockholders' equity. Because assets represent resources of the company and liabilities are creditors' claims to those resources, equity represents the owners' residual claim to those resources. Stated another way, equity is equal to what we own (assets) minus what we owe (liabilities). We use the term *stockholders'* equity (as opposed to *owners'* equity) because our focus throughout the book is on corporations.

Common Terms Stockholders' equity sometimes is referred to as *shareholders' equity*.

Stockholders' equity consists of three primary classifications: paid-in capital, retained earnings, and treasury stock. Paid-in capital is the amount stockholders have invested in the company. Retained earnings is the amount of earnings the corporation has kept or retained—that is, the earnings not paid out in dividends. Treasury stock is the corporation's own stock that it has reacquired. Illustration 10–1 shows those components in the stockholders' equity section of the balance sheet for **American Eagle**.

ILLUSTRATION 10–1

Stockholders' Equity Section for American Eagle

AMERICAN EAGLE
Balance Sheet
January 31, 2009

(Dollars and number of shares in thousands)

Total assets	$ 1,963,676
Total liabilities	$ 554,645
Stockholders' equity:	
Preferred stock, $0.01 par value	–0–
Common stock, $0.01 par value	2,485
Additional paid-in capital	513,574
Total paid-in capital	516,059
Retained earnings	1,679,772
Treasury stock, 43,248 (thousand) shares	(786,800)
Total stockholders' equity	$1,409,031
Total liabilities and stockholders' equity	$ 1,963,676

At this point, simply note that total stockholders' equity for American Eagle consists of total paid-in capital, retained earnings, and treasury stock. It is increased by paid-in capital and retained earnings and reduced by treasury stock. We'll fill in the details as we progress through the chapter.

In Part A of the chapter, we discuss transactions involving paid-in capital. A better description might be "invested capital" since it's the amount stockholders invest when they purchase a company's stock. In Part B, we examine transactions involving retained earnings. A better description might be "earned capital," since it's the amount the company has *earned* for the stockholders. In Part C, we look at the reporting of stockholders' equity.

INVESTED CAPITAL

Invested capital is the amount of money paid into a company by its owners. The owners of a corporation are its stockholders. Recall from Chapter 1 that a company can be formed as a sole proprietorship, a partnership, or a corporation. A sole proprietorship is a business owned by one person, whereas a partnership is a business owned by two or more persons. A **corporation** is an entity that is legally separate from its owners and even pays its own income taxes. Most corporations are owned by many stockholders, although some corporations are owned entirely by one individual.

While sole proprietorships are the most common form of business, corporations dominate in terms of total sales, assets, earnings, and employees. That's why we focus on corporations in this book. To better understand the composition of invested capital, it is helpful to know more about the corporate form of ownership.

Corporations

Corporations are formed in accordance with the laws of individual states. For instance, **American Eagle** is based in Pennsylvania but incorporated in the state of Delaware. Many corporations choose to incorporate in Delaware due to the favorable incorporation laws found there. State incorporation laws share many similarities, thanks to the widespread adoption of the Model Business Corporation Act. This act serves as a guide to states in the development of their corporate statutes.

The state incorporation laws, in turn, guide corporations as they write their articles of incorporation (sometimes called the *corporate charter*). The articles of incorporation describe (a) the nature of the firm's business activities, (b) the shares of stock to be issued, and (c) the initial board of directors. The board of directors establishes corporate policies and appoints officers who manage the corporation. Illustration 10–2 presents an organization chart tracing the line of authority for a typical corporation.

PART A

■ **LO1**
Identify the advantages and disadvantages of the corporate form of ownership.

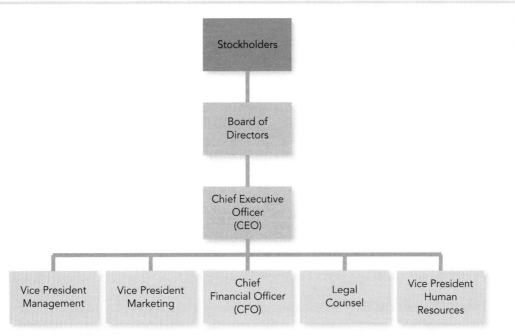

ILLUSTRATION 10–2
Organization Chart

Ultimately, a corporation's stockholders control the company. They are the owners of the corporation. By voting their shares, stockholders determine the makeup of the board of directors—which in turn appoints the management to run the company.

STAGES OF EQUITY FINANCING

Most corporations that end up selling stock to the general public don't begin that way. Instead, there's usually a progression of equity financing stages leading to a public offering, as summarized in Illustration 10–3.

ILLUSTRATION 10–3

Stages of Equity Financing

Stages of Equity Financing

The progression leading to a public offering might include some or all of these steps:

(1) Investment by the founders of the business.

(2) Investment by friends and family of the founders.

(3) Outside investment by "angel" investors and venture capital firms.

(4) Initial public offering (IPO).

Most corporations first raise money by selling stock to the founders of the business and to their friends and family. As the equity financing needs of the corporation grow, companies prepare a business plan and seek outside investment from "angel" investors and venture capital firms. Angel investors are wealthy individuals in the business community willing to risk investment funds on a promising business venture. Individual angel investors may invest from a few thousand dollars to over a million dollars in the corporation. Venture capital firms provide additional financing, often in the millions, for a percentage ownership in the company. Many venture capital firms look to invest in promising companies to which they can add value through business contacts, financial expertise, or marketing channels. Most corporations do not consider issuing stock to the general public ("going public") until their equity financing needs exceed $20 million.

The first time a corporation issues stock to the public is called an initial public offering (IPO). Future stock issues by the company are called *seasoned equity offerings (SEOs)*. Like the issuance of bonds in Chapter 9, the public issuance of stock is a major event requiring the assistance of an investment banking firm (underwriter), lawyers, and public accountants. Major investment bankers, such as **Citigroup**, **Morgan Stanley**, and **Goldman Sachs**, can charge up to 6 percent of the issue proceeds for their services. That's $6 million for a $100 million stock offering. Legal and accounting fees also are not cheap, often running over $200 an hour for services performed in preparation for a public stock offering.

PUBLIC OR PRIVATE

Corporations may be either public or private. The stock of a publicly held corporation trades on the New York Stock Exchange (NYSE) or National Association of Securities Dealers Automated Quotations (NASDAQ), or by over-the-counter (OTC) trading. Many of the largest companies in the world such as **Walmart**, **Exxon-Mobil**, and **General Electric** are traded on the NYSE. The NASDAQ is home to many of the largest high-tech companies, including **Microsoft**, **Intel**, and **Cisco**. Over-the-counter trading takes place outside one of the major stock exchanges. Because these trades are not on any major stock exchange and there is less research done on them in the financial market, they are considered to be more risky. All publicly held corporations are regulated by the Securities and Exchange Commission (SEC), resulting in significant additional reporting and filing requirements.

A privately held corporation does not allow investment by the general public and normally has fewer stockholders than a public corporation. Three of the largest private corporations in the United States are **Cargill** (agricultural commodities), **Koch Industries** (oil and gas), and **Chrysler** (cars). Corporations whose stock is privately held do not need to file financial statements with the SEC.

Frequently, companies begin as smaller, privately held corporations. Then, as success broadens opportunities for expansion, the corporation goes public. For example, **Google** was a private corporation until it decided to take the company public in order to raise large amounts of outside investment funds. The result was the largest technology IPO ever.

STOCKHOLDER RIGHTS

Whether public or private, stockholders are the owners of the corporation and have certain rights: the right to vote on certain matters (including electing the board of directors), the right to receive dividends, the right to share in the distribution of assets if the company is liquidated, and (sometimes) the right to maintain their percentage share of ownership (the *preemptive right*). Illustration 10–4 further explains these stockholder rights.

ILLUSTRATION 10–4

Stockholder Rights

(1)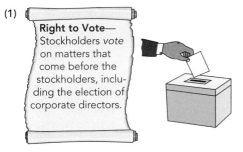

Right to Vote— Stockholders *vote* on matters that come before the stockholders, including the election of corporate directors.

(2) **Right to Receive Dividends**—Stockholders share in profits when the company declares *dividends*. The percentage of shares a stockholder owns determines his or her share of the dividends distributed.

(3) **Right to Share in the Distribution of Assets**—Stockholders share in *the distribution of assets* if the company is liquidated. The percentage of shares a stockholder owns determines his or her share of the assets, which are distributed after creditors and preferred stockholders are paid.

(4) **Preemptive Right**—The *preemptive right* allows a stockholder to maintain his or her percentage share of ownership when new shares are issued. Each stockholder can buy a percentage of any new shares issued equal to the percentage of shares he or she owns. However, most corporations have dropped this right due to difficulties it causes when corporations issue new shares.

ADVANTAGES OF A CORPORATION

A corporation offers three primary advantages over sole proprietorships and partnerships. These are: (1) limited liability, (2) ability to raise capital, and (3) lack of mutual agency.

Limited liability. Limited liability guarantees that stockholders in a corporation can lose no more than the amount they invested in the company, even in the event of bankruptcy. In contrast, owners in a sole proprietorship or a partnership can be held personally liable for debts the company has incurred, above and beyond the investment they have made.

Ability to raise capital. A corporation is better suited to raising capital than is a sole proprietorship or a partnership. Because corporations sell ownership interest in the form of shares of stock, ownership rights are easily transferred. An investor can sell his or her ownership interest (shares of stock) at any time and without affecting the structure of the corporation or its operations. As a result, attracting outside investment is easier for a corporation than for a sole proprietorship or a partnership.

Lack of mutual agency. Another favorable aspect of investing in a corporation is the *lack of mutual agency.* Mutual agency means that individual partners in a partnership each have the power to bind the business to a contract. Therefore, an investor in a partnership must be very careful to investigate the character and business savvy of his or her fellow partners. In contrast, stockholders' participation in the affairs of a corporation is limited to voting at stockholders' meetings (unless the stockholder also is a manager). For example, owning shares of **Microsoft** stock doesn't allow you to transact business or enter into a contract in Microsoft's name. Consequently, a stockholder needn't exercise the same degree of care that partners must in selecting co-owners.

DISADVANTAGES OF A CORPORATION

A corporation has two primary disadvantages relative to sole proprietorships and partnerships. These are (1) additional taxes and (2) more paperwork.

Additional taxes. Owners of sole proprietorships and partnerships are taxed once, when they include their share of earnings in their personal income tax returns. However, corporations have double taxation: As a legal entity separate from its owners, a corporation pays income taxes on its earnings. Then, when it distributes the earnings to stockholders in dividends, the stockholders—the company's owners—pay taxes a second time on the corporate dividends they receive. In other words, corporate income is taxed once on earnings at the corporate level and again on dividends at the individual level.

More paperwork. To protect the rights of those who buy a corporation's stock or who lend money to a corporation, the federal and state governments impose extensive reporting requirements on the company. The additional paperwork is intended to ensure adequate disclosure of the information investors and creditors need.

Illustration 10–5 summarizes the primary advantages and disadvantages of a corporation compared to a sole proprietorship or partnership.

ILLUSTRATION 10–5

Advantages and
Disadvantages of a
Corporation

Advantages

(1) **Limited liability**
A stockholder can lose no more than the amount invested.

(2) **Ability to raise capital**
Attracting outside investment is easier for a corporation.

(3) **Lack of mutual agency**
Stockholders cannot legally bind the corporation to a contract.

Disadvantages

(1) **Additional taxes**
Corporate earnings are taxed twice—at the corporate level and individual stockholder level.

(2) **More paperwork**
Federal and state governments impose additional reporting requirements.

Limited Liability *and* Beneficial Tax Treatment

Decision Maker's Perspective

Wouldn't it be nice to get the best of both worlds—enjoy the limited liability of a corporation and the tax benefits of a sole proprietorship or partnership? An S corporation allows a company to enjoy limited liability as a corporation, but tax treatment as a partnership. Because of these benefits, many companies that qualify choose to incorporate as S corporations. One of the major restrictions is that the corporation cannot have more than 100 stockholders, so S corporations appeal more to smaller, less widely held businesses.

Two additional business forms have evolved in response to liability issues and tax treatment—*limited liability companies* (LLCs) and *limited liability partnerships* (LLPs). Most accounting firms in the United States adopt one of these two business forms because they offer limited liability and avoid double taxation, but with no limits on the number of owners as in an S corporation. ●

KEY POINT

The primary advantages of the corporate form of business are limited liability, ability to raise capital, and lack of mutual agency. The primary disadvantages are additional taxes and more paperwork.

Common Stock

■ LO2
Record the issuance
of common stock.

If a corporation has only one kind of stock, it usually is labeled as common stock. We can think of the common stockholders as the "true owners" of the business. The number of shares of common stock in a corporation are described as being authorized, issued, or outstanding.

AUTHORIZED, ISSUED, AND OUTSTANDING STOCK

Authorized stock is the total number of shares available to sell, stated in the company's articles of incorporation. The authorization of stock is not recorded in the accounting records. However, the corporation is required to disclose the number of shares authorized. Issued stock is the number of shares that have been sold to investors. A company usually does not issue all its authorized stock. Outstanding stock is the number of shares held *by investors*. Issued and outstanding are the same amounts as long as the corporation has not repurchased any of its own shares. Repurchased shares, called *treasury stock,* are included as part of shares issued, but excluded from shares outstanding. We discuss treasury stock in more detail later in the chapter. Illustration 10–6 summarizes the differences between authorized, issued, and outstanding shares.

ILLUSTRATION 10–6

Authorized, Issued, and Outstanding Stock

spiceland.mhhe.com/c28

Type of Stock	Definition
Authorized	Shares available to sell (issued and unissued)
Issued	Shares actually sold (includes treasury stock)
Outstanding	Shares held by investors (excludes treasury stock)

$$\text{Authorized} - \text{Unissued} = \text{Issued}$$
$$\text{Issued} - \text{Treasury Stock} = \text{Outstanding}$$

Decision Point

Question		Accounting information		Analysis	
How many of a company's shares are authorized, issued, and outstanding?		Balance sheet		The number of authorized, issued, and outstanding shares is normally reported in the stockholders' equity section of the balance sheet. If the number of issued and outstanding shares differs, look for a separate line in the equity section called *treasury stock*.	

PAR VALUE

Par value is the legal capital per share of stock that's assigned when the corporation is first established. Par value originally indicated the real value of a company's shares of stock. During the late 19th and early 20th centuries, many cases of selling shares for *less* than par value (known as *watered shares*) triggered a number of lawsuits. To escape potential litigation, companies began issuing shares with very low par values—often pennies. Today, **par value has no relationship to the market value of the common stock.** For instance, **American Eagle**'s common stock has a par value of $0.01 per share but a market value over $15 per share.

Laws in some states permit corporations to issue no-par stock. No-par value stock is common stock that has not been assigned a par value. Most new corporations, and even some established corporations such as **Nike** or **Procter & Gamble**, issue no-par value common stock. In some cases, a corporation assigns a stated value to the shares. Stated value is treated and recorded in the same manner as par value shares.

 COMMON MISTAKE

Some students confuse par value with market value. Par value is the legal capital per share that is set when the corporation is first established and actually is unrelated to "value." The market value per share is equal to the current share price. In most cases, the market value per share will far exceed the par value.

ACCOUNTING FOR COMMON STOCK ISSUES

When a company receives cash from issuing common stock, it debits Cash. If it issues no-par value stock, the corporation credits the equity account entitled Common Stock. For example, let's assume Canadian Falcon, a specialty retailer of casual apparel and accessories, issues 1,000 shares of no-par value common stock at $30 per share. We record this transaction as:

	Debit	Credit	A	=	L	+	SE
Cash (= 1,000 shares × $30)	30,000		+30,000				
Common Stock		30,000					+30,000
(*Issue no-par value common stock*)							

If the company issues par value stock rather than no-par value stock, we record the transaction slightly differently. In that case, we credit two equity accounts. We credit the Common Stock account for the number of shares issued times the par value per share (as before), *and* we credit Additional Paid-in Capital for the portion of the cash proceeds above par value.

For example, assume that Canadian Falcon issues 1,000 shares of $0.01 par value common stock at $30 per share. The company credits the Common Stock account for par value. One thousand shares issued times $0.01 per share is $10. The company credits Additional Paid-in Capital for the portion of the cash proceeds above par value.

Common Terms
Additional paid-in capital is simply the amount paid for stock over par value. It is also called *paid-in capital in excess of par*.

A = L + SE		Debit	Credit
+30,000	**Cash** (= 1,000 shares × $30)	30,000	
+10	**Common Stock** (= 1,000 shares × $0.01)		10
+29,990	**Additional Paid-in Capital** (difference).................................		29,990
	(*Issue common stock above par*)		

What if the common stock had a *stated value* of $0.01, rather than a *par value* of $0.01? We would record the same entry as in the par value example. For accounting purposes, **stated value is treated in the same manner as par value.**

Occasionally, a company will issue shares of stock in exchange for noncash goods or services. For example, what if 1,000 shares of common stock were issued to an attorney in payment for $30,000 in legal services? We would record the transaction in the same way as above, except we debit Legal Fees Expense, rather than Cash, for $30,000. The noncash exchange of stock, in this case for legal services, must be recorded at the fair value of the goods or services received.

KEY POINT

If no-par value stock is issued, the corporation debits Cash and credits Common Stock. If par value or stated value stock is issued, the corporation debits Cash and credits two equity accounts—Common Stock at the par value or stated value per share and Additional Paid-in Capital for the portion above par or stated value.

Preferred Stock

■ **LO3**
Contrast preferred stock with common stock and bonds payable.

About 20% of the largest U.S. companies have preferred stock outstanding.

In order to attract wider investment, some corporations issue preferred stock in addition to common stock. **American Eagle** has been authorized to issue 5 million shares of preferred stock, but the company has yet to issue any of these shares. Preferred stock is "preferred" over common stock in two ways:

1. Preferred stockholders usually have first rights to a specified amount of dividends (a stated dollar amount per share or a percentage of par value per share). If the board of directors declares dividends, preferred shareholders will receive the designated dividend before common shareholders receive any.
2. Preferred stockholders receive preference over common stockholders in the distribution of assets in the event the corporation is dissolved.

However, unlike common stock, most preferred stock does not have voting rights, leaving control of the company to common stockholders.

COMPARISON OF FINANCING ALTERNATIVES

Preferred stock actually has a mixture of attributes somewhere between common stock (equity) and a bond (liability). Investors in common stock are the owners of the corporation because they have voting rights. Investors in bonds are creditors who have loaned money to the corporation. Preferred stockholders have characteristics of both. Illustration 10–7 provides a comparison of common stock, preferred stock, and bonds along several dimensions. Note that preferred stock falls in the middle between common stock and bonds for each of these factors.

Factor	Common Stock	Preferred Stock	Bonds
Voting rights	Yes	Usually no	No
Risk to the investor	Highest	Middle	Lowest
Expected return to the investor	Highest	Middle	Lowest
Risk of contract violations	Lowest	Middle	Highest
Preference for payments	Lowest	Middle	Highest
Tax deductibility of payments	No	Usually no	Yes

ILLUSTRATION 10–7

Comparison of Financing Alternatives

FEATURES OF PREFERRED STOCK

Preferred stock is especially interesting due to the flexibility allowed in its contractual provisions. For instance, preferred stock might be convertible, redeemable, and/or cumulative:

Convertible   Shares can be exchanged for common stock.

Redeemable   Shares can be returned to the corporation at a fixed price.

Cumulative   Shares receive priority for future dividends, if dividends are not paid in a given year.

Preferred stock may be convertible, which allows the stockholder to exchange shares of preferred stock for common stock at a specified conversion ratio. **Xerox Corporation** at one time had outstanding 6.4 million shares of convertible preferred stock.

Occasionally, preferred stock is redeemable at the option of either stockholders or the corporation. A redemption privilege might allow preferred stockholders the option, under specified conditions, to return their shares for a predetermined redemption price. Similarly, shares may be redeemable at the option of the issuing corporation.

 INTERNATIONAL FINANCIAL REPORTING STANDARDS (IFRS)

Under U.S. accounting rules, we usually record preferred stock in the stockholders' equity section of the balance sheet just above common stock. However, sometimes preferred stock shares features with debt. Redeemable preferred stock with a fixed redemption date (called *mandatorily redeemable*) is reported, like bonds payable, in the liability section of the balance sheet.[1] However, under IFRS, most preferred stock is reported as debt, with the dividends reported in the income statement as interest expense. Under U.S. GAAP, that's the case only for "mandatorily redeemable" preferred stock.

For more discussion, see Appendix E.

Preferred stock usually is cumulative: If the specified dividend is not paid in a given year, unpaid dividends (called dividends in arrears) accumulate, and the firm must pay them in a later year before paying any dividends on common stock. For instance, assume that a company issues 1,000 shares of 8%, $30 par value cumulative

[1]FASB ASC Topic 480: Distinguishing Liabilities from Equity.

preferred stock and 1,000 shares of $1 par value common stock. The company owes a dividend on the preferred stock of $2,400 each year (= 1,000 shares × 8% × $30 par value). If the dividend is not paid in 2010 or 2011, dividends in arrears for the two years will total $4,800. Now, let's say the company declares a dividend of $10,000 in 2012. Before it can pay dividends to common stockholders, it must pay the $4,800 in unpaid dividends for 2010 and 2011, and then the current dividend on preferred stock of $2,400 in 2012. After paying the preferred stock dividends, the company can pay the remaining balance of $2,800 (= $10,000 − $4,800 − $2,400) in dividends on common stock. However, if the preferred stock is noncumulative, any dividends in arrears are lost. The dividend of $10,000 in 2012 will be split, with $2,400 paid to preferred stockholders for the current year and the remaining $7,600 paid to common stockholders.

Because dividends are not an actual liability until they are declared by the board of directors, dividends in arrears are not reported as a liability in the balance sheet. However, information regarding any dividends in arrears is disclosed in the notes to the financial statements.

ACCOUNTING FOR PREFERRED STOCK ISSUES

We record the issuance of preferred stock similar to the way we did for the issue of common stock. Assume that Canadian Falcon issues 1,000 shares of $30 par value preferred stock for $40 per share. We record the transaction as:

	Debit	Credit
Cash (= 1,000 shares × $40)	40,000	
Preferred Stock (= 1,000 shares × $30)		30,000
Additional Paid-in Capital (difference)		10,000
(*Issue preferred stock above par*)		

A = L + SE

+40,000

+30,000
+10,000

Illustration 10–8 displays the stockholders' equity section of the balance sheet for Canadian Falcon following the issuance of both common and preferred stock. We discuss the retained earnings balance later in the chapter.

ILLUSTRATION 10–8

Stockholders' Equity Section

CANADIAN FALCON
Balance Sheet (partial)
December 31, 2012

Stockholders' equity:	
Preferred stock, $30 par value; 100,000 shares authorized; 1,000 shares issued and outstanding	$ 30,000
Common stock, $0.01 par value; 1 million shares authorized; 1,000 shares issued and outstanding	10
Additional paid-in capital	39,990
Total paid-in capital	70,000
Retained earnings	30,000
Total stockholders' equity	$100,000

 KEY POINT

Preferred stock has features of both common stock and bonds and is usually included in stockholders' equity. However, some preferred stock (mandatorily redeemable) is so similar to bonds that we include it with bonds payable in the liability section of the balance sheet.

Treasury Stock

■ **LO4**
Account for treasury stock.

We just examined the issuance of common and preferred stock. Next, we look at what happens when companies reacquire shares they have previously issued. Most medium- and large-size companies buy back some of their own shares. Many have formal share repurchase plans. **Treasury stock** is the name given to a corporation's own stock that it has reacquired.

Just as issuing shares increases stockholders' equity, buying those shares back decreases stockholders' equity. Buying back shares is quite different from buying the shares of another corporation. For example, when **Gap** buys its own stock, it decreases stockholders' equity and records the repurchase as treasury stock. On the other hand, if Gap purchases shares of **The Limited**, it records this transaction as an investment (an asset) and not as treasury stock (a reduction of stockholders' equity). We discuss equity investments in Appendix D.

Share buybacks are more common than ever. Over two-thirds of all publicly traded companies report treasury stock in their balance sheets. What would motivate a company to buy back its own stock?

Why Corporations Repurchase Their Stock

Decision Maker's Perspective

Companies buy back their own stock for various reasons:

1. **To boost underpriced stock.** When company management feels the market price of its stock is too low, it may attempt to support the price by decreasing the supply of stock in the marketplace. A **Johnson & Johnson** announcement that it planned to buy up to $5 billion of its outstanding shares triggered a public buying spree that pushed the stock price up by more than 3%.

2. **To distribute surplus cash without paying dividends.** While dividends usually are a good thing, investors do pay personal income tax on them. Another way for a firm to distribute surplus cash to shareholders without giving them taxable *dividend* income is to use the excess cash to repurchase its own stock.

3. **To boost earnings per share.** Earnings per share is calculated as earnings divided by the number of shares outstanding. Stock repurchases reduce the number of shares outstanding, thereby increasing earnings per share. However, with less cash in the company, it's more difficult for companies to maintain the same level of earnings following a share repurchase.

4. **To satisfy employee stock ownership plans.** Perhaps the primary motivation for stock repurchases is to acquire shares used in employee stock award and stock option compensation programs. **Microsoft**, for example, reported that its board of directors had approved a program to repurchase shares of its common stock to offset the increase in shares from stock option and stock purchase plans. ●

American Eagle reported its treasury stock transactions in the notes to its financial statements as shown in Illustration 10–9.

ILLUSTRATION 10–9

Disclosure of Treasury Stock Transactions by American Eagle

AMERICAN EAGLE OUTFITTERS, INC.
Notes to the Financial Statements (excerpt)

The Company's Board authorized an additional 60.0 million shares of its common stock to be repurchased under the Company's share repurchase program. Subsequent to this authorization, the Company repurchased 18.7 million shares of its common stock. The shares were repurchased for approximately $438.3 million, at a weighted average share price of $23.38. As of March 25, 2010, the Company had 30.0 million shares remaining authorized for repurchase.

ACCOUNTING FOR TREASURY STOCK

Treasury stock is the repurchase of a company's own issued stock. As noted above, buying back stock decreases stockholders' equity. Rather than reducing the stock accounts directly, though, we record treasury stock as a "negative" or "contra" account. Recall that liability and stockholders' equity accounts normally have credit balances. So, treasury stock is included in the stockholders' equity section of the balance sheet with an opposite, or debit, balance. When a corporation repurchases its own stock, it increases (debits) Treasury Stock, while it decreases (credits) Cash.

 COMMON MISTAKE

Sometimes students confuse the purchase of treasury stock with investments in another company. An equity investment is the purchase of stock *in another corporation,* and we record it as an increase in assets. Treasury stock is the repurchase of a *corporation's own stock,* and we record it as a reduction in stockholders' equity. It is not an asset; a company cannot invest in itself.

We record treasury stock at the *cost* of the shares reacquired. For example, let's assume that Canadian Falcon repurchases 100 shares of its own $0.01 par value common stock at $30 per share. We record this transaction as:

A	=	L	+	SE		Debit	Credit
				−3,000	Treasury Stock (= 100 shares × $30)	3,000	
−3,000					Cash		3,000
					(Repurchase treasury stock)		

Notice that the stock's par value has no effect on the entry to record treasury stock. We record treasury stock at its cost, which is $30 per share in this example. The debit to Treasury Stock reduces stockholders' equity. Illustration 10–10 displays the stockholders' equity section of the balance sheet following the repurchase of treasury stock.

ILLUSTRATION 10–10

Stockholders' Equity after Purchase of Treasury Stock

CANADIAN FALCON Balance Sheet (partial)	
Stockholders' equity:	
Preferred stock, $30 par value; 100,000 shares authorized; 1,000 shares issued and outstanding	$30,000
Common stock, $0.01 par value; 1 million shares authorized; 1,000 shares issued and 900 shares outstanding	10
Additional paid-in capital	39,990
Total paid-in capital	70,000
Retained earnings	30,000
Treasury stock, 100 shares	(3,000)
Total stockholders' equity	$97,000

Treasury stock is reported as a contra equity, or negative amount, since treasury stock reduces total stockholders' equity.

Now let's assume that Canadian Falcon later reissues the 100 shares of treasury stock for $35. Recall that these shares originally were purchased for $30 per share, so the $35 reissue price represents a $5 per share increase in additional paid-in capital. It's *not* recorded as a $5 per share gain in the income statement, as we would for the sale of an investment in another company, since the company is reissuing its own stock. We record this transaction as:

	Debit	Credit	A	=	L	+	SE
Cash (= 100 shares × $35)	3,500		+3,500				
Treasury Stock (= 100 shares × $30)		3,000					+3,000
Additional Paid-in Capital[2] (= 100 shares × $5)		500					+500
(Reissue treasury stock above cost)							

We debit Cash at $35 per share to record the inflow of cash from reissuing treasury stock. We recorded the 100 shares of treasury stock in the accounting records at a cost of $30 per share at the time of purchase. Now, when we reissue the treasury shares, we must reduce the Treasury Stock account at the same $30 per share. We record the $500 difference (= 100 shares × $5 per share) as Additional Paid-in Capital. Illustration 10–11 presents the stockholders' equity section of the balance sheet immediately after the sale of treasury stock.

spiceland.mhhe.com/c29

CANADIAN FALCON	
Balance Sheet (partial)	
Stockholders' equity:	
Preferred stock, $30 par value; 100,000 shares authorized; 1,000 shares issued and outstanding	$ 30,000
Common stock, $0.01 par value; 1 million shares authorized; 1,000 shares issued and outstanding	10
Additional paid-in capital	40,490
Total paid-in capital	70,500
Retained earnings	30,000
Treasury stock	0
Total stockholders' equity	$100,500

ILLUSTRATION 10–11

Stockholders' Equity after Sale of Treasury Stock

What if the stock price goes down, and we reissue the treasury stock for less than we paid to buy back the shares? Let's assume Canadian Falcon later reissues the 100 shares of treasury stock for only $25 rather than $35. It records this transaction as:

	Debit	Credit	A	=	L	+	SE
Cash (= 100 × $25)	2,500		+2,500				
Additional Paid-in Capital[3] (= 100 × $5)	500						−500
Treasury Stock (= 100 × $30)...................................		3,000					+3,000
(Reissue treasury stock below cost)							

By repurchasing 100 shares of its own stock for $30 per share and reselling them for only $25 per share, Canadian Falcon experienced a decrease in additional

---

[2]Some companies credit "Additional Paid-in Capital from Treasury Stock Transactions" as a separate account from "Additional Paid-in Capital from Common Stock Transactions." We combine all additional paid-in capital entries into one "Additional Paid-in Capital" account, similar to how most companies report additional paid-in capital on the balance sheet.
[3]Companies debit Retained Earnings rather than Additional Paid-in Capital if there is not a sufficient prior credit balance in Additional Paid-in Capital from treasury stock transactions. The details are covered in more advanced financial accounting courses.

paid-in capital. This is reflected in the entry as a debit to the Additional Paid-in Capital account. It's not recorded as a $5 per share loss in the income statement, as we would for the sale of an investment in another company, since the company is reissuing its own stock.

KEY POINT

We include treasury stock in the stockholders' equity section of the balance sheet as a reduction in stockholders' equity. When we reissue treasury stock, we report the difference between its cost and the cash received as an increase or decrease in additional paid-in capital.

PART B

■ **LO5**

Describe retained earnings and record cash dividends.

EARNED CAPITAL

In Part A of the chapter, we discussed transactions involving "invested capital," because when investors buy a corporation's stock, they are investing in the company. Here, in Part B, we examine transactions involving retained earnings. Similarly, we might refer to this source of stockholders' equity as "earned capital," because it represents the net assets of the company that have been *earned* for the stockholders rather than *invested* by the stockholders.

Retained Earnings and Dividends

As noted at the beginning of the chapter, retained earnings represent the earnings retained in the corporation—earnings not paid out as dividends to stockholders. In other words, the amount of retained earnings equals all net income, less all dividends, since the company began.

In a company's early years, the amount of retained earnings tends to be small, and total paid-in capital—money invested into the corporation—tends to be large. As the years go by, the earnings retained in the business continue to grow and, for many profitable companies, can exceed the total amount originally invested in the corporation. Unfortunately, for some companies, expenses sometimes are more than revenues, so a net loss rather than net income is recorded. Just as net income increases retained earnings, a net loss *decreases* retained earnings.

Retained Earnings has a normal credit balance, consistent with other stockholders' equity accounts. However, if losses exceed income since the company began, Retained Earnings will have a debit balance. A debit balance in Retained Earnings is called an accumulated deficit. We subtract an accumulated deficit from total paid-in capital in the balance sheet to arrive at total stockholders' equity. Many companies in the start-up phase or when experiencing financial difficulties report an accumulated deficit. For instance, **Amazon.com** had an accumulated deficit of $730 million at the end of 2008 due to net losses reported in earlier years.

COMMON MISTAKE

Some students think, incorrectly, that retained earnings represents a *cash* balance set aside by the company. In fact, the size of retained earnings has no relationship to the balance in the Cash account. **American Eagle** reported $1.3 billion in retained earnings, but only $60 million in cash.

Dividends are distributions by a corporation to its stockholders. Investors pay careful attention to cash dividends. A change in the quarterly or annual cash dividend paid by a company can provide useful information about its future prospects.

For instance, an increase in dividends often is perceived as good news. Companies tend to increase dividends when the company is doing well and future prospects look bright.

Many investors choose to automatically reinvest their dividends. Automatic dividend reinvestment works similar to compound interest in a savings account. The investor does not receive dividends directly as cash; instead, his or her dividends are directly reinvested into more shares of the company. This allows the investment to grow at a faster rate.

Why Don't Some Companies Pay Dividends?

Decision Maker's Perspective

Some companies are unprofitable and, therefore, unable to pay cash dividends. However, many profitable companies *choose* not to pay cash dividends. Companies with large expansion plans, called *growth companies,* prefer to reinvest earnings in the growth of the company rather than distribute earnings back to investors in the form of cash dividends. **Starbucks** is a nice example. As companies mature and their growth opportunities diminish, they tend to pay out more dividends. **Microsoft** and **Walmart** did not pay dividends in their early growth years, but began paying them in more recent years. ●

Why do investors buy stock in companies like **Starbucks** if they do not receive dividends? Investors make money through dividends, but they also make money when a company's share price increases. **American Eagle** has experienced tremendous increases in share price, but it has paid relatively small dividends. For instance, investors holding American Eagle stock in 2009 enjoyed a total return of 73%. This return includes a share price increase of about 71% and dividends of about 2%. Thus, the gains to American Eagle investors have come almost entirely from share price increases rather than dividend payments. Illustration 10–12 presents the disclosure of American Eagle's dividend policy.

ILLUSTRATION 10–12

American Eagle's Dividend Policy

AMERICAN EAGLE OUTFITTERS, INC.
Notes to the Financial Statements (excerpt)

Subsequent to the fourth quarter, our Board declared a quarterly cash dividend of $0.075 per share, payable on April 13, to stockholders of record at the close of business on March 30. The payment of future dividends is at the discretion of our Board and is based on future earnings, cash flow, financial condition, capital requirements, changes in U.S. taxation and other relevant factors. It is anticipated that any future dividends paid will be declared on a quarterly basis.

Note that it is the board of directors that declares the cash dividend to be paid. The day this occurs is known as the declaration date. The declaration of a cash dividend creates a binding legal obligation for the company declaring the dividend. On that date, we (a) increase Dividends, a temporary account that is closed into Retained Earnings at the end of each period, and (b) increase the liability account, Dividends Payable. The board of directors also indicates a specific date on which the company will determine the registered owners of stock and therefore who will receive the dividend. This date is called the record date. Investors who own stock on the date of record are entitled to receive the dividend. The date of the actual cash distribution is the payment date.

To illustrate the payment of a cash dividend, assume that on March 15 Canadian Falcon declares a $0.25 per share dividend on its 2,000 outstanding shares—1,000 shares of common stock and 1,000 shares of preferred stock. We record the declaration of cash dividends as:

March 15 (declaration date)	Debit	Credit
Dividends (= 2,000 shares × $0.25)	500	
Dividends Payable		500
(Declare cash dividends)		

−500
+500

The Dividends account is a *temporary* stockholders' equity account that is closed into Retained Earnings at the end of each period, as discussed in Chapter 3.

Let's continue our example and assume that the dividend declared by Canadian Falcon is paid on April 15 to stockholders of record at the close of business on March 31. We make no entry on March 31, the date of record. We record the payment of cash dividends on April 15 as:

April 15 (payment date)	Debit	Credit
Dividends Payable (= 2,000 shares × $0.25)	500	
Cash		500
(Pay cash dividends)		

−500
−500

As we will show in Part C later in the chapter, the amount of cash dividends the company declares and pays will be reported in the statement of stockholders' equity.

KEY POINT

The declaration of cash dividends decreases Retained Earnings and increases Dividends Payable. The payment of cash dividends decreases Dividends Payable and decreases Cash. The net effect, then, is a reduction in both retained earnings and cash.

Decision Point

Question	Accounting information	Analysis
How much did the company pay in cash dividends?	Statement of stockholders' equity	The statement of stockholders' equity provides a summary of the activity in each equity account during the period. Any dividends declared and paid during the year will be reported in this statement.

Let's Review

spiceland.mhhe.com/t19

Slacks 5th Avenue has two classes of stock authorized: $100 par preferred and $1 par common. As of the beginning of 2012, 1,000 shares of common stock and no preferred shares have been issued. The following transactions affect stockholders' equity during 2012:

January	15	Issue 2,000 additional shares of common stock for $20 per share.
February	1	Issue 100 shares of preferred stock for $110 per share.
June	1	Declare a cash dividend of $5 per share on preferred stock and $1 per share on common stock to all stockholders of record on June 15.
June	30	Pay the cash dividend declared on June 1.
October	1	Repurchase 200 shares of treasury stock for $25 per share.
November	1	Reissue 100 shares of the treasury stock purchased on October 1 for $28 per share.

Slacks 5th Avenue has the following beginning balances in its stockholders' equity accounts on January 1, 2012: Preferred Stock, $0: Common Stock, $1,000; Paid-in Capital, $14,000; and Retained Earnings, $5,000.

Required:

1. Record each transaction.
2. Indicate whether each transaction increases (+), decreases (−), or has no effect (NE), on total assets, total liabilities, and total stockholders' equity.

Solution:

1. Entries to record each transaction:

January 15, 2012	Debit	Credit
Cash (= 2,000 × $20)	40,000	
Common Stock (= 2,000 × $1)		2,000
Additional Paid-in Capital (difference).............................		38,000
(Issue common stock above par)		

February 1, 2012		
Cash (= 100 × $110)	11,000	
Preferred Stock (= 100 × $100)............................		10,000
Additional Paid-in Capital (difference)		1,000
(Issue preferred stock above par)		

June 1, 2012		
Dividends*	3,500*	
Dividends Payable		3,500
(Declare cash dividends)		
*=(100 preferred shares × $5) + (3,000 common shares × $1)		

June 30, 2012		
Dividends Payable	3,500	
Cash		3,500
(Pay cash dividends)		

October 1, 2012		
Treasury Stock (= 200 shares × $25)	5,000	
Cash		5,000
(Repurchase treasury stock)		

November 1, 2012		
Cash (= 100 shares × $28)	2,800	
Treasury Stock (= 100 shares × $25)		2,500
Additional Paid-in Capital (= 100 × $3)		300
(Reissue treasury stock above cost)		

2. Effects of transactions on the components of the accounting equation:

Transaction	Total Assets	Total Liabilities	Total Stockholders' Equity
Issue common stock	+	NE	+
Issue preferred stock	+	NE	+
Declare cash dividends	NE	+	−
Pay cash dividends	−	−	NE
Purchase treasury stock	−	NE	−
Reissue treasury stock	+	NE	+

Suggested Homework:
BE10-3, BE10-4;
E10-5, E10-6;
P10-2A&B

Stock Dividends and Stock Splits

■ **LO6**
Explain the effect of
stock dividends and
stock splits.

Sometimes corporations distribute to shareholders additional shares of the companies' own stock rather than cash. These are known as stock dividends or stock splits depending on the size of the stock distribution. Suppose you own 100 shares of stock. Assuming a 10% stock dividend, you'll get 10 additional shares. If it's a 20% stock dividend, you'll get 20 more shares. A 100% stock dividend, equivalent to a 2-for-1 stock split, means 100 more shares.

Large stock dividends (25% or higher) and stock splits are declared primarily due to the effect they have on stock prices. Let's say that before the 100% stock dividend, your shares are trading at $40 a share, so your 100 shares are worth $4,000. After the 100% stock dividend, you will have twice as many shares. It sounds good, but let's look closer. Since the company as a whole still has the same value, each share of stock is now worth one-half what it was worth before the stock dividend. Your 200 shares still have a value of $4,000, the same as your 100 shares before the stock dividend. However, now each share is worth half as much—$20 rather than $40 per share.

Think of the company as a pizza. A 100% stock dividend is like changing an 8-slice pizza into 16 slices by cutting each slice in half. You are no better off with 16 half-slices than with the original 8 slices. Whether it's cut in 8 large slices or 16 smaller slices, it's still the same-sized pizza. Whether a company is represented by 1 million shares worth $40 each or 2 million shares worth $20 each, it's the same $40 million company. **Total assets, total liabilities, and total stockholders' equity do not change as a result of a stock dividend.**

 COMMON MISTAKE

Unfortunately, people often misuse the term *stock dividends* to refer to cash dividends on stock. Stock dividends, though, as you've learned, are distributions of additional shares of stock to shareholders, unlike cash dividends, which are distributions of cash to shareholders.

STOCK DIVIDENDS

Accounting standards distinguish between stock splits, large stock dividends, and small stock dividends (less than 25%). We look first at the accounting for stock splits and large stock dividends because they are more common in practice.

Stock splits/Large stock dividends.   When a company declares a stock split, we do not record a transaction. After a 2-for-1 stock split, the Common Stock account balance (total par value) represents twice as many shares. For instance, assume Canadian Falcon declares a 2-for-1 stock split on its 1,000 shares of $0.01 par value common stock. The balance in the Common Stock account is 1,000 shares times $0.01 par value per share, which equals $10. With no journal entry, the balance remains $10 despite the number of shares doubling. As a result, the par value *per share* is reduced by one-half to $0.005 (2,000 shares times $0.005 par per share still equals $10).

As you might expect, having the par value per share change in this way is cumbersome and expensive. All records, printed or electronic, that refer to the previous amount must be changed to reflect the new amount. Fortunately there is an alternative: To avoid the inconvenience and added cost, a company can choose to account for the large stock distribution as a stock *dividend* rather than a stock *split*. We account for a large stock dividend by recording an increase in the Common

Stock account in the amount of the par value of the additional shares distributed, as presented below:

	Debit	Credit
Stock Dividends (= 1,000 shares × $0.01)	10	
Common Stock		10
(Declare 100% [large] stock dividend)		

A = L + SE
−10
+10

So, to avoid changing the par value per share, most companies report a 100% stock distribution as a *stock split to be recorded as a stock dividend.*

Similar to cash dividends, the Stock Dividends account is a temporary stockholders' equity account that is closed into Retained Earnings. Because an increase to stock dividends reduces retained earnings, we decrease one equity account, Retained Earnings, and increase another equity account, Common Stock. Note that the above entry does not change total assets, total liabilities, or total stockholders' equity. Illustration 10–13 presents the stockholders' equity section of the balance sheet for Canadian Falcon before and after the 2-for-1 stock split accounted for as a 100% stock dividend.

ILLUSTRATION 10–13

Stockholders' Equity before and after a 2-for-1 Stock Split Accounted for as a 100% Stock Dividend

CANADIAN FALCON
Balance Sheet (partial)

	Before 100% Stock Dividend	After 100% Stock Dividend
Stockholders' equity:		
Preferred stock, $30 par value	$ 30,000	$ 30,000
Common stock, $0.01 par value	10	20
Additional paid-in capital	40,490	40,490
Total paid-in capital	70,500	70,510
Retained earnings	29,500	29,490
Total stockholders' equity	$100,000	$100,000
Common shares outstanding	1,000	2,000
Par value per share	$0.01	$0.01
Share price	$30	$15

Notice that total stockholders' equity remains at $100,000 before and after the stock distribution. Common stock increased by $10, while retained earnings decreased by $10.

Why Declare a Stock Split?

Decision Maker's Perspective

Why would a company declare a 2-for-1 stock split when the stockholders are not really receiving anything of substance? The primary reason is to lower the trading price of the stock to a more acceptable trading range, making it attractive to a larger number of potential investors. Many companies like their stock to trade under $100 per share—$20 to $40 per share is common. For instance, after a company declares a 2-for-1 stock split with a per share market price of $80, it then has twice the number of shares outstanding, each with an approximate market value reduced to a more marketable trading range of $40.

However, there are exceptions to the normal trading range. **Google**'s stock trades in the several-hundred-dollars-per-share range. **Berkshire Hathaway**'s "A" shares trade at over $100,000 per share, making it accessible only to wealthier investors. Berkshire Hathaway is founded by billionaire investor Warren Buffett. While still an outspoken critic of stock dividends and stock splits, even Warren Buffett is giving in a little. In January 2010, Berkshire Hathaway's "B" shares, designed for general public investment, were split 50 to 1. The shares had a value of about $3,500 before the split and a value in a more acceptable trading range of about $70 ($3,500 ÷ 50) after the stock split. ●

Small stock dividends.   Let's also look briefly at small stock dividends. Recall that we record large stock dividends at the *par value* per share. We record small stock dividends at the *market value*, rather than the par value, per share. Assume, for example, the market value of Canadian Falcon common stock is $30 per share when Canadian Falcon declares a 10% dividend on its 1,000 shares outstanding of $0.01 par value common stock. After the 10% stock dividend, Canadian Falcon will have 1,100 shares outstanding. The company records this small stock dividend as:

A	=	L	+	SE		June 30, 2012	Debit	Credit
				−3,000		**Stock Dividends** (= 1,000 × 10% × $30)	**3,000**	
				+1		**Common Stock** (= 1,000 × 10% × $0.01)................................		**1**
				+2,999		**Additional Paid-in Capital** (difference)....................................		**2,999**
						(Pay 10% [small] stock dividend)		

So, small stock dividends are recorded at the market value per new share, while large stock dividends are recorded at the par value per share. Why the inconsistency? Some believe that a small stock dividend will have little impact on the market price of shares currently outstanding, arguing for the recording of small stock dividends at market value. However, this reasoning is contrary to research evidence, which finds the market price adjusts for both large and small stock dividends.[4] A 10% stock dividend will result in 10% more shares, but each share will be worth 10% less, so the investor is no better off. Note that the above entry still does not change total assets, total liabilities, or total stockholders' equity. The debit to Stock Dividends simply decreases one equity account, Retained Earnings, while the credits increase two other equity accounts, Common Stock and Additional Paid-in Capital.

American Eagle is a prime candidate for stock splits since its share price has risen dramatically in prior years. Illustration 10–14 presents the disclosure of American Eagle's 3-for-2 stock split.

ILLUSTRATION 10–14

American Eagle's Stock Split

AMERICAN EAGLE OUTFITTERS, INC.
Notes to the Financial Statements

On November 13, the Company's Board approved a 3-for-2 stock split. This stock split was distributed on December 18, to stockholders of record on November 24. All share amounts and per share data presented herein have been restated to reflect this stock split.

---

[4]Taylor W. Foster and Don Vickrey. 1978. "The Information Content of Stock Dividend Announcements." *Accounting Review 53*, no. 2 (April), pp. 360–70; and J. David Spiceland and Alan J. Winters. 1986. "The Market Reaction to Stock Distributions: The Effect of Market Anticipation and Cash Returns." *Accounting and Business Research 16*, no. 63 (Summer), pp. 211–25.

Intercontinental Clothing Distributors has paid cash dividends every year since the company was founded in 1990. The dividends have steadily increased from $0.05 per share to the latest dividend declaration of $1.00 per share. The board of directors is eager to continue this trend despite the fact that earnings fell significantly during the recent quarter as a result of worsening economic conditions and increased competition. The chair of the board proposes a solution. She suggests a 5% stock dividend in lieu of a cash dividend, to be accompanied by the following press announcement: "In place of our regular $1.00 per share cash dividend, Intercontinental will distribute a 5% stock dividend on its common shares, currently trading at $20 per share. Changing the form of the dividend will permit the company to direct available cash resources to the modernization of facilities in order to better compete in the 21st century."

Is a 5% stock dividend equivalent to a $1.00 per share cash dividend when shares are trading at $20 per share? Is the chair's suggestion ethical?

KEY POINT

Declaring stock dividends and stock splits is like cutting a pizza into more slices. Everyone has more shares, but each share is worth proportionately less than before.

REPORTING STOCKHOLDERS' EQUITY

PART C

We now can apply what we've learned so far in the chapter to analyze the stockholders' equity of an actual company—**American Eagle**. In this section, we show the financial statement presentation of stockholders' equity in the balance sheet and differentiate it from the statement of stockholders' equity.

Stockholders' Equity in the Balance Sheet

Illustration 10–15 (next page) presents the stockholders' equity section of the balance sheet for **American Eagle**, introduced briefly at the beginning of the chapter.

Preferred stock is listed before common stock in the balance sheet. American Eagle has 5 million shares of preferred stock authorized but has not yet issued any preferred shares. Can you determine how many shares of common stock the company has issued? Common stock is reported at its par value of $0.01 per share. If we take the Common Stock account balance of $2,485,000 ($2,485 in thousands) and divide it by $0.01 per share, we find that the company has issued just under 250 million shares (248,500,000). The number of shares outstanding is equal to the number of shares issued (248,500,000) minus the number of shares bought back (the 43,248,000 treasury shares), or 205,252,000 shares.

Notice that the Additional Paid-in Capital account balance is much larger than the Common Stock account balance. This is to be expected. Remember, American Eagle has a par value of only $0.01 per share, so most of the money invested in the company was credited to Additional Paid-in Capital rather than Common Stock.

■ **LO7**
Prepare and analyze the stockholders' equity section of a balance sheet and the statement of stockholders' equity.

ILLUSTRATION 10–15

Stockholders' Equity
Section of American
Eagle's Balance Sheet

AMERICAN EAGLE
Balance Sheet (partial)
January 31, 2009

(Dollars and number of shares in thousands)	
Total assets	$ 1,963,676
Total liabilities	$ 554,645
Stockholders' equity:	
Preferred stock, $0.01 par value	–0–
Common stock, $0.01 par value	2,485
Additional paid-in capital	513,574
Total paid-in capital	516,059
Retained earnings	1,679,772
Treasury stock, 43,248 (thousand) shares	(786,800)
Total stockholders' equity	$1,409,031
Total liabilities and stockholders' equity	$ 1,963,676

Now look at retained earnings. When a company is started, most of the equity is in the paid-in capital section because that's the amount invested by stockholders. But then, if a company is profitable, like American Eagle, and pays little in dividends, the retained earnings section of equity grows and often exceeds the amount invested by stockholders. For American Eagle, the amount of retained earnings is so large that it actually exceeds total stockholders' equity. How can this happen? American Eagle has been very profitable over the years, building retained earnings. It has used a portion of the company's earnings to buy back treasury shares, which decreases stockholders' equity. American Eagle has applied this strategy to such an extent that the balance in treasury stock (representing the cost of shares repurchased by the company) now exceeds total paid-in capital (representing the total cost of shares originally issued).

American Eagle has been very active in acquiring treasury shares. Has it benefited from the treasury stock repurchases? Dividing the treasury stock balance of $786,800 by the 43,248 shares repurchased, we can estimate an average purchase cost of $18.19 per share. That average repurchase price is nearly double the current trading price of $9 per share at January 31, 2009. Thus, at this point in time, it looks like American Eagle has not benefited from the treasury stock repurchase. However, if stock prices should again rise above $18.19 per share, the company could sell the treasury shares for more than the average purchase price.

Statement of Stockholders' Equity

The stockholders' equity section of the balance sheet, like the one we just examined for American Eagle, shows the balance in each equity account *at a point in time*. In contrast, the statement of stockholders' equity summarizes the *changes* in the balance in each stockholders' equity account *over a period of time*.

To contrast the stockholders' equity section of the balance sheet and the statement of stockholders' equity, let's compare both statements for our continuing example company—Canadian Falcon. Illustration 10–16 (next page) shows the stockholders' equity section reported in Canadian Falcon's balance sheet.

Compare that snapshot of stockholders' equity at the end of 2012 with Illustration 10–17 (next page) showing the statement of stockholders' equity for Canadian Falcon.

ILLUSTRATION 10–16

Stockholders' Equity Section—Canadian Falcon

CANADIAN FALCON
Balance Sheet (partial)
December 31, 2012

Stockholders' equity:

Preferred stock, $30 par value; 100,000 shares authorized; 1,000 shares issued and outstanding	$ 30,000
Common stock, $0.01 par value; 1 million shares authorized; 2,000 shares issued and outstanding	20
Additional paid-in capital	40,490
Total paid-in capital	70,510
Retained earnings	29,490
Treasury stock	–0–
Total stockholders' equity	$100,000

ILLUSTRATION 10–17

Statement of Stockholders' Equity— Canadian Falcon

CANADIAN FALCON
Statement of Stockholders' Equity
For the year ended December 31, 2012

	Preferred Stock	Common Stock	Additional Paid-in Capital	Retained Earnings	Treasury Stock	Total Stockholders' Equity
Balance, January 1	$ –0–	$–0–	$ –0–	$ –0–	$ –0–	$ –0–
Issued common stock		10	29,990			30,000
Issued preferred stock	30,000		10,000			40,000
Repurchase of treasury stock					(3,000)	(3,000)
Sale of treasury stock			500		3,000	3,500
Cash dividends				(500)		(500)
100% stock dividend		10		(10)		–0–
Net income				30,000		30,000
Balance, December 31	$30,000	$20	$40,490	$29,490	$ –0–	$100,000

   Each of the beginning balances in Illustration 10–17 is zero because this is the first year of operations. (The beginning balances for the following year, January 1, 2013, are the same as the ending balance this year, December 31, 2012.)

   The statement of stockholders' equity reports how each equity account changed during the year. For instance, the Common Stock account increased because Canadian Falcon issued common stock and declared a 100% stock dividend. The Additional Paid-in Capital account increased from the issuance of common stock, the issuance of preferred stock, and the sale of treasury stock for more than its original cost. Retained Earnings increased due to net income and decreased due to both cash and stock dividends. The repurchase of treasury stock is shown as a reduction because treasury stock reduces total stockholders' equity. The ending balance in Treasury Stock is zero, since all the treasury stock purchased was resold by the end of the year.

spiceland.mhhe.com/c30

KEY POINT

The stockholders' equity section of the balance sheet presents the balance of each equity account *at a point in time*. The statement of stockholders' equity shows the change in each equity account balance *over time*.

Let's Review

spiceland.mhhe.com/t20

This exercise is a continuation of the Let's Review exercise presented earlier. Recall that Slacks 5th Avenue has two classes of stock authorized: $100 par preferred and $1 par value common. As of the beginning of 2012, 1,000 shares of common stock have been issued and no shares of preferred stock have been issued. The following transactions affect stockholders' equity during 2012:

January	15	Issue 2,000 additional shares of common stock for $20 per share.
February	1	Issue 100 shares of preferred stock for $110 per share.
June	1	Declare a cash dividend of $5 per share on preferred stock and $1 per share on common stock to all stockholders of record on June 15.
June	30	Pay the cash dividend declared on June 1.
October	1	Repurchase 200 shares of common treasury stock for $25 per share.
November	1	Reissue 100 shares of treasury stock purchased on October 1 for $28 per share.

Slacks 5th Avenue has the following beginning balances in its stockholders' equity accounts on January 1, 2012: Preferred Stock, $0; Common Stock, $1,000; Paid-in Capital, $14,000; and Retained Earnings, $5,000. Net income for the year ended December 31, 2012, is $4,000.

Required:

Taking into consideration all of the transactions during 2012, prepare the following for Slacks 5th Avenue:

1. The stockholders' equity section as of December 31, 2012.
2. The statement of stockholders' equity for the year ended December 31, 2012.

Solution:

1. Stockholders' equity section:

SLACKS 5TH AVENUE Balance Sheet (partial) December 31, 2012	
Stockholders' equity:	
Preferred stock, $100 par value	$10,000
Common stock, $1 par value	3,000
Additional paid-in capital	53,300
Total paid-in capital	66,300
Retained earnings	5,500
Treasury stock	(2,500)
Total stockholders' equity	$69,300

2. Statement of stockholders' equity:

SLACKS 5TH AVENUE						
Statement of Stockholders' Equity						
For the year ended December 31, 2012						
	Preferred Stock	Common Stock	Additional Paid-in Capital	Retained Earnings	Treasury Stock	Total Stockholders' Equity
Balance, January 1	$ –0–	$1,000	$14,000	$5,000	$ –0–	$20,000
Issued common stock		2,000	38,000			40,000
Issued preferred stock	10,000		1,000			11,000
Cash dividends				(3,500)		(3,500)
Repurchase of treasury stock					(5,000)	(5,000)
Sale of treasury stock			300		2,500	2,800
Net income				4,000		4,000
Balance, December 31	$10,000	$3,000	$53,300	$5,500	$(2,500)	$69,300

Suggested Homework:
BE10-13, BE10-14;
E10-10, E10-11;
P10-5A&B

EQUITY ANALYSIS

Deckers Outdoor vs. Timberland

ANALYSIS

Earnings are the key to a company's long-run survival. However, we need to evaluate earnings in comparison to the size of the investment. For instance, earnings of $500,000 may be quite large for a small business, but would be a rather disappointing outcome for a major corporation like **American Eagle**. A useful summary measure of earnings that considers the relative size of the business is the return on equity.

■ **LO8**
Evaluate company performance using information on stockholders' equity.

RETURN ON EQUITY

The return on equity (ROE) measures the ability of company management to generate earnings from the resources that owners provide. We compute the ratio by dividing net income by average stockholders' equity.

$$\text{Return on equity} = \frac{\text{Net income}}{\text{Average stockholders' equity}}$$

Deckers Outdoor was listed at the beginning of the chapter as one of the top ten investments of the past decade. The company is probably best known for its footwear products such as Teva sandals and UGG sheepskin boots. We can compare its profitability with a close competitor in the footwear industry, **Timberland**. Illustration 10–18 (next page) provides selected financial data for Deckers Outdoor and Timberland.

ILLUSTRATION 10–18

Financial Information for Deckers Outdoor and Timberland

Selected Balance Sheet Data
December 31, 2009 and 2008
($ in thousands)

	Deckers Outdoor		Timberland	
	2009	**2008**	**2009**	**2008**
Total assets	$599,043	$483,721	$859,907	$849,399
Total liabilities	$107,685	$ 99,469	$264,290	$272,861
Stockholders' equity	491,358	384,252	595,617	576,538
Total liabilities and equity	$599,043	$483,721	$859,907	$849,399
Stock price, ending	$101.72		$17.83	
Shares outstanding (in thousands)	12,868		85,660	

Selected Income Statement Data
For the year ended December 31, 2009
($ in thousands)

	Deckers Outdoor	Timberland
Net sales	$813,177	$1,285,876
Net income	$116,786	$56,644

The return on equity for both companies is calculated in Illustration 10–19.

ILLUSTRATION 10–19

Return on Equity for Deckers Outdoor and Timberland

($ in thousands)	Net Income	÷	Average Stockholders' Equity	=	Return on Equity
Deckers Outdoor	$116,786	÷	($384,252 + $491,358)/2	=	26.7%
Timberland	$56,644	÷	($576,538 + $595,617)/2	=	9.7%

As might be expected for a top-10 investment, Deckers Outdoor has a significantly higher return on equity of 26.7% compared to a respectable 9.7% for Timberland. A return on equity of 26.7% suggests that for every $1 of investors' resources, the company has earned almost $0.27 for its investors. Similarly, a return on equity of 9.7% suggests that for every $1 of investors' resources, the company has earned almost $0.10 for its investors. Although the return on equity is useful when comparing the effectiveness of management in employing resources provided by owners, analysts must be careful not to view it in isolation or without considering how the ratio is derived.

RETURN ON THE MARKET VALUE OF EQUITY

To supplement the return on equity ratio, analysts often relate earnings to the market value of equity, which is calculated as the ending stock price times the number of shares outstanding. The return on the market value of equity is computed as net income divided by the market value of equity, as shown in Illustration 10–20 (next page).

Once again, Deckers Outdoor has a higher return than Timberland. Notice that the return on the market value of equity for both companies is much lower than their return on equity. The reason is that the average stockholders' equity for Deckers Outdoor and Timberland is much lower than the market value of equity. For

($ in thousands)	Net Income	÷	Market Value of Equity (Ending stock price × Number of shares)	=	Return on the Market Value of Equity
Deckers Outdoor	$116,786	÷	($101.72 × 12,868)	=	8.9%
Timberland	$56,644	÷	($17.83 × 85,660)	=	3.7%

ILLUSTRATION 10–20

Return on the Market Value of Equity for Deckers Outdoor and Timberland

some companies, the return on equity is a meaningful measure of earnings performance. For others, the return on the market value of equity is a better measure, especially when the recorded balance in stockholders' equity and the market value of equity differ greatly.

Why Doesn't Stockholders' Equity Equal the Market Value of Equity?

Decision Maker's Perspective

The *market* value of equity is the price investors are willing to pay for a company's stock. The market value of equity equals the stock price times the number of shares outstanding. On the other hand, the *book* value of equity equals total stockholders' equity reported in the balance sheet. Market value and book value generally are not the same, and often are vastly different. For example, Deckers Outdoor reported total stockholders' equity of $491 million in 2009, yet its market value at this same time was over $1.3 billion. Why?

Keep in mind that stockholders' equity is equal to assets minus liabilities. An asset's book value usually equals its market value *on the date it's purchased.* However, the two aren't necessarily the same after that. For instance, an asset such as a building might increase in value over time, but it continues to be reported in the balance sheet at historical cost minus accumulated depreciation. Consider another example: **Deckers Outdoor** creates brand awareness and increases market value through advertising, but under accounting rules, it expenses all its advertising costs as it incurs them. This causes the true market value of assets and stockholders' equity to be greater than the amount recorded for assets and stockholders' equity in the accounting records. ●

Question		Accounting information		Analysis		**Decision Point**
What is a company's return on investment?		Return on equity and return on market value of equity		A high return on equity or market value of equity in relation to industry competitors indicates a strong return on investment. Note the return on market value of equity will normally be lower than the return on equity.		

EARNINGS PER SHARE

Earnings per share (EPS) measures the net income earned per share of common stock. We calculate earnings per share as net income minus dividends on preferred stock divided by the average shares of common stock outstanding during the period:

$$\text{Earnings per share} = \frac{\text{Net income} - \text{Dividends on preferred stock}}{\text{Average shares of common stock outstanding}}$$

The upper half of the fraction measures the income available to common stockholders. We subtract any dividends paid to preferred stockholders from net income to arrive at the income available to the true owners of the company—the common stockholders. If a company does not issue preferred stock, the top half of the fraction is simply net income. We then divide income available to common stockholders by the average shares outstanding during the period to calculate earnings per share.

Earnings per share is useful in comparing earnings performance for the same company over time. It is *not* useful for comparing earnings performance of one company with another because of wide differences in the number of shares outstanding among companies. For instance, assume two companies, Alpha and Beta, both report net income of $1 million and are valued by the market at $20 million. Quite comparable, right? But, if Alpha has one million shares outstanding and Beta has two million shares outstanding, their earnings per share amounts will not be comparable. Alpha will have a share price of $20 (= $20 million ÷ 1 million shares) and an EPS of $1.00 (= $1 million in earnings ÷ 1 million shares). Beta, on the other hand, will have a share price of $10 (= $20 million ÷ 2 million shares) and an EPS of $0.50 (= $1 million in earnings ÷ 2 million shares). Is the earnings performance for Alpha better than that for Beta? Of course not. They both earned $1 million. Alpha's earnings per share is higher simply because it has half as many shares outstanding. (Same pizza, fewer slices.)

If Alpha declared a 2-for-1 stock split, its earnings per share would match Beta's exactly. The key point is that earnings per share is useful in comparing either Alpha's earnings over time, or Beta's earnings over time, but it is not useful in comparing the companies *with each other*.

Investors use earnings per share extensively in evaluating the earnings performance of a company over time. Investors are looking for companies with the potential to increase earnings per share. Analysts also forecast earnings on a per share basis. If reported earnings per share fall short of analysts' forecasts, this is considered negative news, usually resulting in a decline in a company's stock price.

PRICE-EARNINGS RATIO

Another measure analysts use extensively is the price-earnings ratio (PE ratio). It indicates how the stock is trading in relationship to current earnings. We calculate the PE ratio as the stock price divided by earnings per share, so that both stock price and earnings are expressed on a per share basis:

$$\text{Price-earnings ratio} = \frac{\text{Stock price}}{\text{Earnings per share}}$$

Price-earnings ratios are commonly in the range of 15 to 20. A high PE ratio indicates that the market has high hopes for a company's stock and has bid up the price. Growth stocks are stocks whose future earnings investors expect to be higher. Their stock prices are high in relation to current earnings because investors expect future earnings to be higher. On the other hand, value stocks are stocks that are priced low in relation to current earnings. The low price in relation to earnings may be justified due to poor future prospects, or it might suggest an underpriced "sleeper" stock. Illustration 10–21 calculates the price-earnings ratio for **Deckers Outdoor** and **Timberland**.

ILLUSTRATION 10–21	($ in thousands)	**Stock Price**	÷	**Earnings per Share**	=	**Price-Earnings Ratio**	
Price-Earnings Ratios for Deckers Outdoor and Timberland	Deckers Outdoor	$101.72	÷	$116,786/12,868	=	11.2	
	Timberland	$ 17.83	÷	$ 56,644/85,660	=	27.0	

The price-earnings ratio for Deckers Outdoor and Timberland is 11.2 and 27.0, respectively. A low price-earnings ratio indicates to investors that a stock is priced low in relation to its current earnings. Deckers Outdoor has a much lower stock price in relation to its current earnings, making it a potentially more attractive investment.

KEY POINT

The return on equity measures the ability to generate earnings from the owners' investment. It is calculated as net income divided by average stockholders' equity. The return on the market value of equity is another useful measure, especially when the recorded balance in stockholders' equity and the market value of equity differ substantially. Earnings per share measures the net income earned per share of common stock. The price-earnings ratio indicates how the stock is trading in relationship to current earnings.

Question	Accounting information	Analysis	**Decision Point**
Do investors expect future earnings to grow?	Price-earnings ratio (PE ratio)	A high PE ratio indicates investors expect future earnings to be higher. A low PE ratio indicates investors' lack of confidence in future earnings growth.	

KEY POINTS BY LEARNING OBJECTIVE

LO1 Identify the advantages and disadvantages of the corporate form of ownership.

The primary advantages of the corporate form of business are limited liability, ability to raise capital, and lack of mutual agency. The primary disadvantages are additional taxes and more paperwork.

LO2 Record the issuance of common stock.

If no-par value stock is issued, the corporation debits Cash and credits Common Stock. If par value or stated value stock is issued, the corporation debits Cash and credits two equity accounts—Common Stock at the par value or stated value per share and Additional Paid-in Capital for the portion above par or stated value.

LO3 Contrast preferred stock with common stock and bonds payable.

Preferred stock has features of both common stock and bonds and is usually included in stockholders' equity. However, mandatorily redeemable preferred stock is so similar to bonds that we include it with bonds payable in the liability section of the balance sheet.

LO4 Account for treasury stock.

We include treasury stock in the stockholders' equity section of the balance sheet as a reduction in stockholders' equity. When we reissue treasury stock, we report the difference between its cost and the cash received as an increase or decrease in Additional Paid-in Capital.

LO5 Describe retained earnings and record cash dividends.

The declaration of cash dividends decreases Retained Earnings and increases Dividends Payable. The payment of dividends decreases Dividends Payable and decreases Cash. The net effect, then, is a reduction in both retained earnings and cash.

LO6 Explain the effect of stock dividends and stock splits.

Declaring stock dividends and stock splits is like cutting a pizza into more slices. Everyone has more shares, but each share is worth proportionately less than before.

LO7 Prepare and analyze the stockholders' equity section of a balance sheet and the statement of stockholders' equity.

The stockholders' equity section of the balance sheet presents the balance of each equity account *at a point in time*. The statement of stockholders' equity shows the change in each equity account balance *over time*.

Analysis

LO8 Evaluate company performance using information on stockholders' equity.

The return on equity measures the ability to generate earnings from the owners' investment. It is calculated as net income divided by average stockholders' equity. The return on the market value of equity is another useful measure, especially when the recorded balance in stockholders' equity and the market value of equity differ substantially. Earnings per share measures the net income earned per share of common stock. The price-earnings ratio indicates how the stock is trading in relationship to current earnings.

GLOSSARY

Accumulated deficit: A debit balance in Retained Earnings. **p. 334**

Additional paid-in capital: The portion of the cash proceeds above par value. **p. 328**

Angel investors: Wealthy individuals in the business community willing to risk investment funds on a promising business venture. **p. 322**

Articles of incorporation: Describes the nature of the firm's business activities, the shares to be issued, and the composition of the initial board of directors. **p. 321**

Authorized stock: The total number of shares available to sell, stated in the company's articles of incorporation. **p. 326**

Convertible: Shares can be exchanged for common stock. **p. 329**

Cumulative: Shares receive priority for future dividends, if dividends are not paid in a given year. **p. 329**

Declaration date: The day on which the board of directors declares the cash dividend to be paid. **p. 335**

Dividends: Distributions by a corporation to its stockholders. **p. 334**

Dividends in arrears: Unpaid dividends on cumulative preferred stock. **p. 329**

Double taxation: A corporation pays income taxes on its earnings, and when dividends are distributed to stockholders, the stockholders pay taxes a second time on the corporate dividends they receive. **p. 324**

Earnings per share: Measures the net income earned per share of common stock. **p. 347**

Growth stocks: Stocks that tend to have higher price-earnings ratios and are expected to have higher future earnings. **p. 348**

Initial public offering: The first time a corporation issues stock to the public. **p. 322**

Issued stock: The number of shares sold to investors; includes treasury shares. **p. 326**

Limited liability: Stockholders in a corporation can lose no more than the amount they invested in the company. **p. 324**

Model Business Corporation Act: Serves as a guide to states in the development of their corporate statutes. **p. 321**

Mutual agency: Individual partners each have power to bind the partnership to a contract. **p. 324**

No-par value stock: Common stock that has not been assigned a par value. **p. 327**

Organization chart: Traces the line of authority for a typical corporation. **p. 321**

Outstanding stock: The number of shares held by investors; excludes treasury shares. **p. 326**

Paid-in capital: The amount stockholders have invested in the company. **p. 320**

Par value: The legal capital assigned per share of stock. **p. 327**

Payment date: The date of the actual cash distribution of dividends. **p. 335**

Preferred stock: Stock with preference over common stock in the payment of dividends and the distribution of assets. **p. 328**

Price-earnings ratio: The stock price divided by earnings per share so that both stock price and earnings are expressed on a per share basis. **p. 348**

Privately held corporation: Does not allow investment by the general public and normally has fewer stockholders. **p. 323**

Publicly held corporation: Allows investment by the general public and is regulated by the Securities and Exchange Commission. **p. 322**

Record date: A specific date on which the company will determine the registered owners of stock and, therefore, who will receive the dividend. **p. 335**

Redeemable: Shares can be returned to the corporation at a fixed price. **p. 329**

Retained earnings: Represents all net income, less all dividends, since the company began. **pp. 320, 334**

Return on equity: Net income divided by average stockholders' equity; measures the income generated per dollar of equity. **p. 345**

Return on the market value of equity: Net income divided by the market value of equity. **p. 346**

S corporation: Allows a company to enjoy limited liability as a corporation, but tax treatment as a partnership. **p. 325**

Stated value: The legal capital assigned per share to no-par stock. **p. 327**

Statement of stockholders' equity: Summarizes the changes in the balance in each stockholders' equity account over a period of time. **p. 342**

Stock dividends: Additional shares of a company's own stock given to stockholders. **p. 338**

Stock split: A large stock dividend that includes a reduction in the par or stated value per share. **p. 338**

Treasury stock: A corporation's own stock that it has reacquired. **p. 320**

Value stocks: Stocks that tend to have lower price-earnings ratios and are priced low in relation to current earnings. **p. 348**

Venture capital firms: Provide additional financing, often in the millions, for a percentage ownership in the company. **p. 322**

SELF-STUDY QUESTIONS

1. Which of the following is a publicly traded company? ■ LO1
   a. American Eagle.
   b. Cargill.
   c. Ernst & Young.
   d. Koch Industries.

2. The disadvantages of owning a corporation include: ■ LO1
   a. Lack of mutual agency.
   b. Additional taxes.
   c. Limited liability.
   d. Ability to raise capital.

3. The correct order from the smallest number of shares to the largest number of shares is: ■ LO2
   a. Authorized, issued, and outstanding.
   b. Outstanding, issued, and authorized.
   c. Issued, outstanding, and authorized.
   d. Issued, authorized, and outstanding.

4. Preferred stock: ■ LO3
   a. Is always recorded as a liability.
   b. Is always recorded as part of stockholders' equity.
   c. Can have features of both liabilities and stockholders' equity.
   d. Is not included in either liabilities or stockholders' equity.

5. Treasury stock: ■ LO4
   a. Has a normal credit balance.
   b. Decreases stockholders' equity.
   c. Is recorded as an investment.
   d. Increases stockholders' equity.

6. Retained earnings: ■ LO5
   a. Has a normal debit balance.
   b. Decreases stockholders' equity.
   c. Is equal to the balance in cash.
   d. Increases stockholders' equity.

7. We record cash dividends on the: ■ LO5
   a. Declaration date, record date, and payment date.
   b. Record date and payment date.
   c. Declaration date and payment date.
   d. Declaration date and record date.

8. Both cash dividends and stock dividends: ■ LO6
   a. Reduce total assets.
   b. Reduce total liabilities.
   c. Reduce total stockholders' equity.
   d. Reduce retained earnings.

■ LO7

9. How does the stockholders' equity section in the balance sheet differ from the statement of stockholders' equity?
    a. The stockholders' equity section shows balances at a point in time, whereas the statement of stockholders' equity shows activity over a period of time.
    b. The stockholders' equity section shows activity over a period of time, whereas the statement of stockholders' equity is at a point in time.
    c. There are no differences between them.
    d. The stockholders' equity section is more detailed than the statement of stockholders' equity.

■ LO8

10. The PE ratio:
    a. Tends to be lower for growth stocks.
    b. Tends to be higher for value stocks.
    c. Indicates how a stock is trading in relation to current earnings.
    d. Typically is less than 1.

Answers to the Self-Study Questions
1. a   2. b   3. b   4. c   5. b   6. d   7. c   8. d   9. a   10. c

REVIEW QUESTIONS

■ LO1

1. Corporations typically do not first raise capital by issuing stock to the general public. What are the common stages of equity financing leading to an initial public offering (IPO)?

■ LO1

2. What is the difference between a public and a private corporation? Provide an example of each.

■ LO1

3. What are the four basic ownership rights of common stockholders?

■ LO1

4. Which form of business organization is most common? Which form of business organization is larger in terms of total sales, total assets, earnings, and number of employees?

■ LO1

5. Describe the primary advantages and disadvantages of a corporation.

■ LO1

6. Explain how an LLC or an S corporation represents the "best of both worlds" in terms of business ownership.

■ LO2

7. Explain the difference between authorized, issued, and outstanding shares.

■ LO2

8. The articles of incorporation allow for the issuance of 1 million shares of common stock. During its first year, California Clothing issued 100,000 shares and reacquired 10,000 shares it held as treasury stock. At the end of the first year, how many shares are authorized, issued, and outstanding?

■ LO2

9. What is par value? How is it related to market value? How is it used in recording the issuance of stock?

■ LO3

10. What are the three potential features of preferred stock? Indicate whether each feature makes the preferred stock appear more like stockholders' equity or more like long-term liabilities.

■ LO3

11. Explain why preferred stock often is said to be a mixture of attributes somewhere between common stock and bonds.

■ LO4

12. What would motivate a company to buy back its own stock?

■ LO4

13. How is the accounting for a repurchase of a company's own stock (treasury stock) different from the purchase of stock in another corporation?

■ LO5

14. Explain why some companies choose not to pay cash dividends. Why do investors purchase stock in companies that do not pay cash dividends?

15. Describe the declaration date, record date, and payment date for a cash dividend.   ■ **LO5**

16. How does a 100% stock dividend or a 2-for-1 stock split affect total assets, total liabilities, and total stockholders' equity?   ■ **LO6**

17. Contrast the effects of a cash dividend and a stock dividend on total assets, total liabilities, and total stockholders' equity.   ■ **LO6**

18. What happens to the par value, the share's trading price, and the number of shares outstanding in a 2-for-1 stock split?   ■ **LO6**

19. Indicate the correct order in which to report the following accounts in the stockholders' equity section of the balance sheet: Additional Paid-in Capital, Common Stock, Preferred Stock, Treasury Stock, and Retained Earnings.   ■ **LO7**

20. How is the stockholders' equity section of the balance sheet different from the statement of stockholders' equity?   ■ **LO7**

21. Why doesn't total stockholders' equity equal the market value of the firm?   ■ **LO8**

22. Which tends to be larger, the return on equity or the return on the market value of equity? Explain why.   ■ **LO8**

23. What does "PE" stand for in the PE ratio, and how do investors use this ratio?   ■ **LO8**

For the following, please visit your instructor's *Connect* site.

BRIEF EXERCISES	1-15
EXERCISES	1-15
PROBLEMS: SET A	1-7
PROBLEMS: SET B	1-7
GREAT ADVENTURES	

Note: Additional Perspectives assignments for Financial Analysis, Comparative Analysis, Internet Research, Written Communication, and Earnings Management are in Appendix F at the end of this book. For additional Exercises: Set B and for additional Problems: Set C, visit www.mhhe.com/spicelandMTC1e.

Statement of Cash Flows

AFTER STUDYING THIS CHAPTER, YOU SHOULD BE ABLE TO:

- **LO1** Classify cash transactions as operating, investing, or financing activities.
- **LO2** Prepare the operating activities section of the statement of cash flows using the indirect method.
- **LO3** Prepare the investing activities section and the financing activities section of the statement of cash flows.

Analysis

- **LO4** Perform financial analysis using the statement of cash flows.

Appendix

- **LO5** Prepare the operating activities section of the statement of cash flows using the direct method.

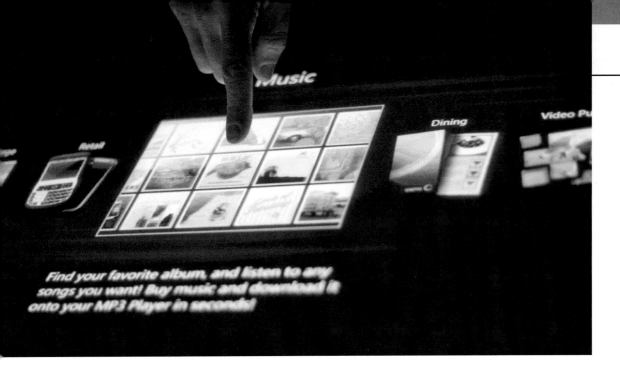

APPLE INC.: CASH FLOWS AT THE CORE

Net income represents all revenues less expenses of a company during a reporting period. Operating cash flows represent the cash inflows less cash outflows related to the very same revenue and expense activities. Although you might expect these two amounts to be similar, fairly large differences sometimes exist. For instance, here are the 2009 net income and operating cash flows for three well-known companies in the electronics industry ($ in millions):

Feature Story

Company Name	Net Income	Operating Cash Flows
Apple	$ 5,704	$10,159
Hewlett-Packard	7,660	13,379
Microsoft	14,569	19,037

All three companies report higher operating cash flows than net income. For **Apple** and **Hewlett-Packard**, operating cash flow is almost twice net income. One reason may be that certain items, like depreciation expense, decrease net income but have no effect on operating cash flows. Both net income and operating cash flows are important indicators in explaining stock prices. Which is more important to investors—net income or operating cash flows? The financial press discusses net income more than cash flows, but many finance courses emphasize that "cash is king."

However, in comparing net income with operating cash flows, research consistently finds that net income, not cash, is king. Net income works better than operating cash flow in forecasting not only future net income, but also future cash flow.[1] The research also finds that stock returns (the change in stock price plus dividends) are more closely related to net income than to operating cash flow.[2] Net income helps smooth out the unevenness or lumpiness in year-to-year operating cash flow, producing a better estimate of ongoing company profitability.

While net income may win in a direct competition with operating cash flow, it's important to remember that both net income and operating cash flow provide important information. An investor or creditor who analyzes both net income and operating cash flow will do better than one who focuses solely on net income. For instance, a company with increasing earnings but decreasing operating cash flow is probably not as good an investment as a company with increasing earnings and increasing operating cash flow. Net income and operating cash flows are each so valuable that we might think of them both as financial royalty.

---

[1]M. Barth, C. Cram, and K. Nelson. 2001. "Accruals and the Prediction of Future Cash Flows." *The Accounting Review* 76 (January), pp. 27–58; and C. Finger. 1994. "The Ability of Earnings to Predict Future Earnings and Cash Flow." *Journal of Accounting Research* 32 (Autumn), pp. 210–23.
[2]P. Dechow. 1994. "Accounting Earnings and Cash Flow as Measures of Firm Performance: The Role of Accounting Accruals." *Journal of Accounting and Economics* (July), pp. 3–42.

PART A   FORMATTING THE STATEMENT OF CASH FLOWS

A **statement of cash flows** provides a summary of cash inflows and cash outflows during the reporting period. Illustration 11–1 presents the statement of cash flows for E-Games, Inc.

ILLUSTRATION 11–1

Statement of Cash Flows

E-GAMES, INC. Statement of Cash Flows For the year ended December 31, 2012		
Cash Flows from Operating Activities		
Net income	$42,000	
Adjustments for noncash effects:		
Depreciation expense	9,000	
Loss on sale of land	4,000	
Changes in current assets and current liabilities:		
Increase in accounts receivable	(7,000)	
Decrease in inventory	10,000	
Increase in prepaid rent	(2,000)	
Decrease in accounts payable	(5,000)	
Increase in interest payable	1,000	
Decrease in income tax payable	(2,000)	
Net cash flows from operating activities		$50,000
Cash Flows from Investing Activities		
Purchase of investment	(35,000)	
Sale of land	6,000	
Net cash flows from investing activities		(29,000)
Cash Flows from Financing Activities		
Issuance of common stock	5,000	
Payment of cash dividends	(12,000)	
Net cash flows from financing activities		(7,000)
Net increase (decrease) in cash		14,000
Cash at the beginning of the period		48,000
Cash at the end of the period		$62,000
Note: Noncash Activities		
Purchased equipment by issuing a note payable		$20,000

We will use this statement as an example throughout the chapter. Don't be concerned about the details just yet. That's what the rest of the chapter is all about.

Classification of Transactions

LO1

Classify cash transactions as operating, investing, or financing activities.

The three primary categories of cash flows are (1) cash flows from operating activities, (2) cash flows from investing activities, and (3) cash flows from financing activities. Classifying each cash flow by source (operating, investing, or financing activities) is more informative than simply listing the various cash flows.

REPORTING CASH FLOW ACTIVITIES

Operating activities include cash receipts and cash payments for transactions relating to revenue and expense activities. These are essentially the very same activities reported on the income statement. In other words, cash flows from operating activities include the elements of net income, but reported on a cash basis. Common examples of operating activities include the collection of cash from customers or the payment of cash for inventory purchases, salaries, and rent.

Investing activities include cash transactions involving the purchase and sale of long-term assets and current investments. Companies periodically invest cash to replace or expand productive facilities such as buildings, land, and equipment. They might also invest in other assets, such as stocks or bonds of other firms, with the expectation of a return on those investments. Eventually, many of these assets are sold. Investment in and sale of long-term assets and investments are common examples of investing activities.

Financing activities are both inflows and outflows of cash resulting from the external financing of a business. A major portion of financing for many companies comes from external sources, specifically stockholders and lenders. Common financing activities are borrowing and repaying debt, issuing and repurchasing stock, and paying dividends.

 INTERNATIONAL FINANCIAL REPORTING STANDARDS (IFRS)

In a joint project on financial reporting presentation with the FASB, the IASB recently proposed extending the operating, investing, and financing classifications used in the statement of cash flows to the income statement and the balance sheet. If the proposal goes through, all the major financial statements will be organized along the lines of operating, investing, and financing activities.

For more discussion, see Appendix E.

Illustration 11–2 lists common cash receipts and cash payments for operating, investing, and financing activities. **Review this illustration carefully** (you may even want to bookmark it); it will come in handy in solving many of the questions, exercises, problems, and cases at the end of the chapter.

Cash Flows from Operating Activities

Cash Inflows	Cash Outflows
Sale of goods or services	Purchase of inventory
Receipt of interest and dividends	For operating expenses
	For interest
	For income taxes

Cash Flows from Investing Activities

Cash Inflows	Cash Outflows
Sale of investments	Purchase of investments
Sale of property, plant, and equipment or intangibles	Purchase of property, plant, and equipment or intangibles
Collection of notes receivable	Lending with notes receivable

Cash Flows from Financing Activities

Cash Inflows	Cash Outflows
Issuance of bonds or notes payable	Repayment of bonds or notes payable
Issuance of stock	Reacquisition of stock (treasury stock)
	Payment of dividends

ILLUSTRATION 11–2

Operating, Investing, and Financing Activities

Let's look at a few of the cash flows. For example, we report interest and dividends received from investments with operating activities rather than investing activities. Similarly, we report interest paid on bonds or notes payable with operating activities rather than financing activities. Why are these classified as operating activities? They are included in operating activities because each is a cash flow from an activity reported in the income statement—interest revenue, dividend revenue, and interest expense. As we discussed earlier, operating activities are those we report on the income statement.

On the other hand, we record dividends paid as a financing activity. Recall that dividends are not an expense and, therefore, paying dividends has no effect on net

spiceland.mhhe.com/c31

income. The payment of dividends simply reduces assets (cash) and stockholders' equity (retained earnings).

 COMMON MISTAKE

Students sometimes misclassify dividends in preparing the statement of cash flows. Dividends *received* are included in operating activities. Dividends *paid* are included in financing activities.

As we saw in Chapter 3, we prepare the income statement, the statement of stockholders' equity, and the balance sheet directly from the adjusted trial balance. Unfortunately, though, the accounts listed on the adjusted trial balance do not directly provide the cash inflows and cash outflows we report on the statement of cash flows. We need to rely on other sources to determine the amounts necessary to prepare the statement of cash flows. Illustration 11–3 outlines the three primary sources.

ILLUSTRATION 11–3

Information Sources for Preparing the Statement of Cash Flows

Information Sources	Explanation
1. Income statement	The income statement provides important information in determining cash flows from operating activities.
2. Balance sheet	We look at the change in asset, liability, and stockholders' equity accounts from the end of the last period to the end of this period to find cash flows from operating, investing, and financing activities.
3. Detailed accounting records	Sometimes we need additional information from the accounting records to determine specific cash inflows or cash outflows for the period.

 KEY POINT

Operating activities relate to income statement items. Investing activities primarily involve changes in long-term assets. Financing activities primarily involve changes in long-term liabilities and stockholders' equity.

Illustration 11–4 summarizes the relationship of the income statement and balance sheet to the operating, investing, and financing sections in the statement of cash flows.

ILLUSTRATION 11–4

Relationship of the Income Statement and Balance Sheet to the Statement of Cash Flows

REPORTING NONCASH ACTIVITIES

Suppose a company borrows $200,000 cash from a bank, issuing a long-term note payable for that amount. The firm reports this transaction in a statement of cash flows as a *financing activity*. Now suppose the company uses that cash to purchase new equipment. It reports this second transaction as an *investing activity*. But what if, instead of two separate transactions, the company acquired $200,000 of new equipment by issuing a $200,000 long-term note payable in a *single transaction?* Since this transaction does not affect cash, it is excluded from the statement of cash flows.

However, undertaking a significant investing activity and a significant financing activity as two parts of a single transaction does not lessen the value of reporting these activities. For that reason, transactions that do not increase or decrease cash, but that result in significant investing and financing activities, are reported as noncash activities either directly after the cash flow statement or in a note to the financial statements. Examples of significant noncash investing and financing activities include:

1. Purchase of long-term assets by issuing debt.
2. Purchase of long-term assets by issuing stock.
3. Conversion of bonds payable into common stock.
4. Exchange of long-term assets.

Having a better overall picture of total investing and financing activities is important for investors and creditors. Thus, they should consider both the investing and financing activities reported in the statement of cash flows and the noncash investing and financing activities reported in the notes to the financial statements.

Decision Point

Question ?	Accounting information	Analysis
Did the company have any significant noncash investing and financing activities?	Reported either directly after the cash flow statement or in a note to the financial statements	The disclosure of noncash investing and financing activities can be combined with information reported on the statement of cash flows to provide a better overall picture of total investing and financing activities.

Let's Review

Indicate whether each of the following items is classified as an operating activity, investing activity, financing activity, or a significant noncash activity.
1. Dividends received from an investment.
2. Dividends paid to shareholders.
3. Property, plant, and equipment purchased for cash.
4. Property, plant, and equipment purchased by issuing stock.
5. Notes receivable accepted for lending cash.
6. Notes payable issued for borrowing cash.

Solution:
1. Operating.
2. Financing.
3. Investing.
4. Noncash.
5. Investing.
6. Financing.

Suggested Homework:
BE11-1, BE11-2;
E11-3, E11-4;
P11-1A&B

OPERATING ACTIVITIES—INDIRECT AND DIRECT METHODS

We have two ways to determine and report cash flows from operating activities in a statement of cash flows—the indirect method and the direct method. The methods differ only in the presentation format for operating activities. **The total net cash flows from operating activities are identical under both methods.** Also, the two methods affect only the operating section. We report investing, financing, and noncash activities identically under both methods.

Using the indirect method, we begin with net income and then list adjustments to net income, in order to arrive at operating cash flows. The indirect method is more popular because it is generally easier and less costly to prepare. In fact, nearly all major companies in the United States (about 99%) prepare the statement of cash flows using the indirect method.[3] For this reason, we emphasize the indirect method.

Using the direct method, we adjust the items on the income statement to directly show the cash inflows and outflows from operations such as cash received from customers and cash paid for inventory, salaries, rent, interest, and taxes. If a company decides to use the direct method to report operating activities, it must also report the indirect method either along with the statement of cash flows or in a separate note to the financial statements.

We discuss the indirect method in the next section. We present the direct method using the same example in an appendix to this chapter.

KEY POINT

Companies choose between the indirect method and the direct method in reporting operating activities in the statement of cash flows. The indirect method is less costly to prepare and is used in practice by the majority of companies. The direct method more logically presents the cash inflows and outflows from operations. The investing and financing sections of the statement of cash flows are identical under both methods.

PART B   PREPARING THE STATEMENT OF CASH FLOWS

In this section, we first look at the steps involved in preparing the statement of cash flows, and its basic format. Then we work through these steps in preparing the operating, investing, and financing activities sections of the statement of cash flows.

Steps in Preparing the Statement of Cash Flows

Illustration 11–5 summarizes the four basic steps in preparing the statement of cash flows.

ILLUSTRATION 11–5

Steps in Preparing the Statement of Cash Flows

Step 1. Calculate net cash flows from *operating activities*, using information from the income statement and changes in current assets (other than cash) and current liabilities from the balance sheet.

Step 2. Determine the net cash flows from *investing activities*, by analyzing changes in long-term asset accounts from the balance sheet.

Step 3. Determine the net cash flows from *financing activities*, by analyzing changes in long-term liabilities and stockholders' equity accounts from the balance sheet.

Step 4. Combine the operating, investing, and financing activities, and make sure the total change from these three activities agrees with the net increase (decrease) in cash shown at the bottom of the statement of cash flows.

---

[3]*Accounting Trends and Techniques—2009.* 2009. (New York: American Institute of Certified Public Accountants).

Illustration 11–6 provides the income statement, balance sheet, and additional information for E-Games, Inc. We will use this information to prepare the statement of cash flows following the four basic steps.

ILLUSTRATION 11–6

Income Statement, Balance Sheet, and Additional Information for E-Games, Inc.

E-GAMES, INC.
Income Statement
For the year ended December 31, 2012

Revenues		$1,012,000
Expenses:		
Cost of goods sold	$650,000	
Operating expenses (salaries, rent, utilities)	286,000	
Depreciation expense	9,000	
Loss on sale of land	4,000	
Interest expense	5,000	
Income tax expense	16,000	
Total expenses		970,000
Net income		$ 42,000

E-GAMES, INC.
Balance Sheet
December 31, 2012 and 2011

	2012	2011	Increase (I) or Decrease (D)
Assets			
Current assets:			
Cash	$ 62,000	$ 48,000	$14,000 (I)
Accounts receivable	27,000	20,000	7,000 (I)
Inventory	35,000	45,000	10,000 (D)
Prepaid rent	4,000	2,000	2,000 (I)
Long-term assets:			
Investments	35,000	0	35,000 (I)
Land	70,000	80,000	10,000 (D)
Equipment	90,000	70,000	20,000 (I)
Accumulated depreciation	(23,000)	(14,000)	9,000 (I)
Total assets	$300,000	$251,000	
Liabilities and Stockholders' Equity			
Current liabilities:			
Accounts payable	$ 22,000	$ 27,000	$ 5,000 (D)
Interest payable	2,000	1,000	1,000 (I)
Income tax payable	5,000	7,000	2,000 (D)
Long-term liabilities:			
Notes payable	95,000	75,000	20,000 (I)
Stockholders' equity:			
Common stock	105,000	100,000	5,000 (I)
Retained earnings	71,000	41,000	30,000 (I)
Total liabilities and stockholders' equity	$300,000	$251,000	

(continued)

ILLUSTRATION 11–6
(*concluded*)

Additional Information for 2012:

1. Purchased stock in Intendo Corporation for $35,000.
2. Sold land originally costing $10,000 for $6,000, resulting in a $4,000 loss on sale of land.
3. Purchased $20,000 in equipment by issuing a $20,000 note payable due in three years. No cash was exchanged in the transaction.
4. Issued common stock for $5,000 cash.
5. Declared and paid a cash dividend of $12,000.

Basic Format

In preparing the statement of cash flows, it's helpful to first set up the basic format. As Illustration 11–7 shows, the last three lines of the statement of cash flows include amounts for the net increase (decrease) in cash, cash at the beginning of the period, and cash at the end of the period obtained from the E-Games balance sheet. Cash at the beginning of the period is $48,000 (the balance for cash in the 2011 balance sheet column), and cash at the end of the period is $62,000 (the balance for cash in the 2012 balance sheet column). The $14,000 change in the cash balance will be our "check figure," which means the cash inflows and cash outflows we identify must net to this amount. After all, the purpose of the statement of cash flows is to explain *why* cash increased by $14,000.

ILLUSTRATION 11–7

Basic Format for the Statement of Cash Flows

E-GAMES, INC. Statement of Cash Flows For the year ended December 31, 2012	
Cash Flows from Operating Activities	$_____
Cash Flows from Investing Activities	_____
Cash Flows from Financing Activities	_____
Net increase (decrease) in cash	14,000
Cash at the beginning of the period	48,000
Cash at the end of the period	$62,000
Note: Noncash Activities	
List of noncash transactions	_____

Operating Activities—Indirect Method

■ LO2
Prepare the operating activities section of the statement of cash flows using the indirect method.

As we learned in Illustration 11–5, the first step in preparing the statement of cash flows is to calculate net cash flows from *operating activities* using information from the income statement and changes in current assets (other than cash) and current liabilities from the balance sheet.

The key to understanding the operating activities section of the statement of cash flows is to understand that both net income and cash flows from operating activities represent the same operating activities: The income statement reports net income on an *accrual basis*. That is, we report revenues when we earn them, regardless of when cash is received, and expenses when we incur them, regardless of when cash is paid. On the other hand, the statement of cash flows reports the very same activities on a *cash basis*—revenues when we receive cash, and expenses when we pay cash.

Net income includes both cash and noncash components. *Our task, when preparing a statement of cash flows, is to convert net income from an accrual basis to a cash basis.* In other words, we remove noncash components from net income so that what's left is cash flows only. We can classify the noncash components as:

(a)   revenues and expenses that don't affect cash at all (adjustments for non-cash components of net income), and

(b)   revenues and expenses that do affect cash, but not by the amount reported as the revenue or expense (adjustments for changes in current assets and current liabilities).

We look at each of those two adjustments for noncash components in the sections that follow.

Decision Point

Question	Accounting information	Analysis
Is a company's net income supported by strong operating cash flows?	Operating activities section of the statement of cash flows using the indirect method	The operating activities section using the indirect method reconciles net income to operating cash flows. Net income is considered to be of higher quality when backed by strong operating cash flows.

ADJUSTMENTS FOR NONCASH COMPONENTS OF NET INCOME

Using the indirect method, we first adjust net income for revenues and expenses that don't affect cash at all. Here are two common examples.

Depreciation expense.   Depreciation expense reduces net income. Remember, though, depreciation expense does not correspond to a cash outflow in the current period. Recording depreciation expense results in increases to the Depreciation Expense and Accumulated Depreciation accounts. In recording depreciation, we're simply allocating the cost of an asset over the periods the asset is used. But since we deducted this noncash expense in the determination of net income, we need to add it back in order to eliminate it. Amortization of intangible assets is treated the same way as depreciation of tangible assets. We add back both depreciation expense and amortization expense to net income in arriving at cash flows from operating activities.

E-Games, Inc., reports net income of $42,000 and depreciation expense of $9,000 in its income statement. Since depreciation expense reduces net income by $9,000, E-Games will add the $9,000 back to net income as a step in arriving at net cash flows from operations. Illustration 11–8 shows how E-Games reports depreciation expense in the statement of cash flows under the indirect method.

E-GAMES, INC.
Statement of Cash Flows (partial)

Cash Flows from Operating Activities	
Net income	$42,000
Adjustments for noncash effects:	
Depreciation expense	9,000

ILLUSTRATION 11–8

Adjustment for Depreciation Expense

Loss on sale of land.   Gains on the sale of long-term assets increase net income, while losses on the sale of those assets decrease net income. E-Games, Inc., reports a $4,000 loss on sale of land in its income statement. To see how to treat the loss, let's re-create how E-Games recorded the sale of land. We see from additional-information item (2) that E-Games sold land originally costing $10,000 for only $6,000, resulting in a $4,000 loss.

	Debit	Credit
Cash	6,000	
Loss	4,000	
Land		10,000
(Record loss on sale of land)		

The cash effect of this transaction is a cash increase of $6,000. The sale of land, though, is an investing activity, so this cash inflow is reported in the investing section of the statement of cash flows. Note that the loss is simply the difference between cash received in the sale of land (reported as an investing activity) and the cost of the land. It is not a cash inflow or cash outflow. And yet, we subtracted the $4,000 loss on the income statement in the determination of net income, so we need to add it back in order to eliminate this noncash component of net income. Illustration 11–9 shows how E-Games adds back the loss on sale of land to net income in arriving at net cash flows from operating activities.

ILLUSTRATION 11–9

Adjustment for Loss on Sale of Land

E-GAMES, INC.	
Statement of Cash Flows (partial)	
Cash Flows from Operating Activities	
Net income	$42,000
Adjustments for noncash effects:	
Depreciation expense	9,000
Loss on sale of land	4,000

What if E-Games, Inc., had a gain of $4,000, rather than a loss, on the sale of land? Since we would have added the $4,000 gain in the determination of net income, we would need to subtract it from net income to eliminate it.

 COMMON MISTAKE

Students sometimes are unsure whether to add or subtract a loss on the sale of assets. Just remember that a loss is like an expense—both reduce net income. Treat a loss on the sale of assets like depreciation expense and add it back to net income. A gain on the sale of long-term assets is the opposite of an expense, so we subtract it from net income to arrive at net cash flows from operating activities.

ADJUSTMENTS FOR CHANGES IN CURRENT ASSETS AND CURRENT LIABILITIES

For components of net income that increase or decrease cash, but *by an amount different from that reported on the income statement,* we adjust net income for changes in the balances of related balance sheet accounts to convert the effects of those items to a cash basis. For example, E-Games reports sales revenue of $1,012,000 in its income statement. This does not mean, however, that E-Games collected $1,012,000 cash from its customers during the reporting period. Since accounts receivable increased during the year, some of the sales revenue the company earned must not yet have been collected. We need, then, to make an adjustment to net income for the change in accounts receivable to convert the sales revenue number to a cash basis. To similarly convert other income statement components from accrual basis to cash basis, we adjust net income for changes in all current assets (other than cash) and current liabilities. Let's look at the changes in current assets and current liabilities for E-Games to see how this works.

Increase in accounts receivable.   E-Games' accounts receivable increased $7,000 during the year (from $20,000 in 2011 to $27,000 in 2012). This tells us that the company must not have collected all of its $1,012,000 sales revenue in cash. Why? Because customers owe the company $7,000 more than before. Let's confirm this by recording the selling and collection activities during the year:

	Debit	Credit	A	=	L	+	SE
Cash (to balance)	1,005,000		+1,005,000				
Accounts Receivable (= $27,000 − $20,000)	7,000		+7,000				
Revenues (from income statement)		1,012,000					+1,012,000 Rev↑
(Record increase in accounts receivable)							

We record an increase in Revenues with a credit and an increase in Accounts Receivable with a debit. Cash received from customers of $1,005,000 is the number we need for the debits and credits to equal.

The $7,000 increase in accounts receivable represents $7,000 of credit sales that E-Games reported as part of net income but that did not result in operating cash inflows. Therefore, to adjust net income to operating cash flows, we need to eliminate $7,000 from net income, as shown in Illustration 11–10.

E-GAMES, INC.
Statement of Cash Flows (partial)

Cash Flows from Operating Activities	
Net income	$42,000
Adjustments for noncash effects:	
Depreciation expense	9,000
Loss on sale of land	4,000
Changes in current assets and current liabilities:	
Increase in accounts receivable	(7,000)

ILLUSTRATION 11–10

Adjustment for Change in Accounts Receivable

A decrease in accounts receivable would have the opposite effect. We would *add* a decrease in accounts receivable to net income to arrive at net cash flows from operating activities. A decrease in accounts receivable indicates that we collected more cash from customers than we recorded as credit sales.

Decrease in inventory.   E-Games' inventory balance decreased by $10,000 during the year. This tells us that the company purchased $10,000 less inventory than is reflected in cost of goods sold in the income statement. In other words, $10,000 of E-Games' cost of goods sold was a result of reducing its inventory, rather than a purchase of new inventory and a corresponding cash outflow. Therefore, we need to eliminate the noncash portion of cost of goods sold from net income as part of our conversion of net income to operating cash flows. To eliminate the effect of this $10,000 expense, we add the $10,000 decrease in inventory to net income. Illustration 11–11 shows this adjustment.

ILLUSTRATION 11–11

Adjustment for Change in Inventory

E-GAMES, INC.
Statement of Cash Flows (partial)

Cash Flows from Operating Activities

Net income	$42,000
Adjustments for noncash effects:	
Depreciation expense	9,000
Loss on sale of land	4,000
Changes in current assets and current liabilities:	
Increase in accounts receivable	(7,000)
Decrease in inventory	**10,000**

Increase in prepaid rent. E-Games' prepaid rent increased $2,000 during the year. The company paid $2,000 cash for an asset (prepaid rent) for which there is no corresponding expense (rent expense). In other words, the cash outflow for prepaid rent caused cash to decrease by $2,000, but net income remained unaffected. To adjust for this, we subtract the $2,000 increase in prepaid rent from net income to reflect the $2,000 cash outflow not reflected in net income. Illustration 11–12 shows this adjustment.

ILLUSTRATION 11–12

Adjustment for Change in Prepaid Rent

E-GAMES, INC.
Statement of Cash Flows (partial)

Cash Flows from Operating Activities

Net income	$42,000
Adjustments for noncash effects:	
Depreciation expense	9,000
Loss on sale of land	4,000
Changes in current assets and current liabilities:	
Increase in accounts receivable	(7,000)
Decrease in inventory	10,000
Increase in prepaid rent	**(2,000)**

Decrease in accounts payable. E-Games' accounts payable decreased $5,000 during the year. Reducing the amount owed to suppliers means the company paid $5,000 more cash than the cost of goods purchased. The decrease in accounts payable indicates that the company paid $5,000 cash to reduce its liability (accounts payable) but reported no corresponding expense (cost of goods sold) during the period. In other words, total cash outflows to reduce accounts payable were $5,000 greater than total related expenses. To adjust for the greater cash outflows, we subtract the $5,000 decrease in accounts payable from net income, as shown in Illustration 11–13.

ILLUSTRATION 11–13

Adjustment for Change in Accounts Payable

E-GAMES, INC.
Statement of Cash Flows (partial)

Cash Flows from Operating Activities

Net income	$42,000
Adjustments for noncash effects:	
Depreciation expense	9,000
Loss on sale of land	4,000
Changes in current assets and current liabilities:	
Increase in accounts receivable	(7,000)
Decrease in inventory	10,000
Increase in prepaid rent	(2,000)
Decrease in accounts payable	**(5,000)**

Increase in interest payable. E-Games' interest payable increased $1,000 during the year. That means the company owes $1,000 more than previously, so it must have paid $1,000 less cash than the interest expense included in net income. As shown in Illustration 11–14, the company adds the increase in interest payable to net income to adjust for the fact that cash outflows are less than interest expense, increasing overall cash flows.

Decrease in income tax payable. E-Games' income tax payable decreased $2,000 during the year. A change in income tax payable indicates a difference between income tax expense and income taxes paid. A $2,000 decrease in income tax payable indicates E-Games paid $2,000 more to reduce its tax liability (income tax payable) than it recorded as an expense (income tax expense) in net income. To adjust for the fact that cash outflow is greater than tax expense, we subtract $2,000 from net income to calculate operating cash flows. Illustration 11–15 shows this adjustment and calculates total net cash flows from operating activities of $50,000.

CAREER CORNER

Are you good at analyzing information? If so, you might consider a career as a financial analyst. A career in this field involves understanding the operations of companies, assessing the reasonableness of their stock price, and predicting their future performance. Investment analysts rely heavily on financial statements as a source of information in predicting stock price movements. Since financial statements, including the cash flow statement covered in this chapter, are accounting-based, it is no surprise that a strong background in accounting is necessary for a career as a financial analyst. A background in accounting is useful, not only in preparing accounting information, but analyzing and interpreting that information as well.

E-GAMES, INC.
Statement of Cash Flows (partial)

Cash Flows from Operating Activities

Net income	$42,000
Adjustments for noncash effects:	
Depreciation expense	9,000
Loss on sale of land	4,000
Changes in current assets and current liabilities:	
Increase in accounts receivable	(7,000)
Decrease in inventory	10,000
Increase in prepaid rent	(2,000)
Decrease in accounts payable	(5,000)
Increase in interest payable	1,000

ILLUSTRATION 11–14

Adjustment for Change in Interest Payable

E-GAMES, INC.
Statement of Cash Flows (partial)

Cash Flows from Operating Activities

Net income	$42,000	
Adjustments for noncash effects:		
Depreciation expense	9,000	
Loss on sale of land	4,000	
Changes in current assets and current liabilities:		
Increase in accounts receivable	(7,000)	
Decrease in inventory	10,000	
Increase in prepaid rent	(2,000)	
Decrease in accounts payable	(5,000)	
Increase in interest payable	1,000	
Decrease in income tax payable	(2,000)	
Net cash flows from operating activities		$50,000

ILLUSTRATION 11–15

Adjustment for Change in Income Tax Payable

Illustration 11–16 provides a summary of the adjustments we make to convert net income to net cash flows from operating activities.

ILLUSTRATION 11–16

Summary of Adjustments to Net Income

Cash Flows from Operating Activities

Net income
Adjustments for noncash effects:

For noncash components of income:
+ Depreciation expense
+ Amortization expense
+ Loss on sale of assets
− Gain on sale of assets

For changes in current assets and current liabilities:
− Increase in a current asset
+ Decrease in a current asset
+ Increase in a current liability
− Decrease in a current liability

= Net cash flows from operating activities

spiceland.mhhe.com/c32

This illustration is a helpful reference when completing the homework exercises at the end of the chapter. Remember that for noncash components of income, we add back expenses and losses and subtract gains. For changes in current liabilities, we add an increase in a current liability and subtract a decrease. We do just the opposite for changes in current assets.

 KEY POINT

Using the indirect method, we start with net income and adjust this number for (a) revenue and expense items that do not represent cash and (b) changes in current assets and current liabilities.

Investing and Financing Activities

■ **LO3**

Prepare the investing activities section and the financing activities section of the statement of cash flows.

As noted earlier, we prepare the investing and financing activities in the statement of cash flows the same whether we use the indirect or the direct method. Here, we take a detailed look at how investing and financing activities are determined in our E-Games, Inc., example.

INVESTING ACTIVITIES

As we learned in Illustration 11–5, the second step in preparing the statement of cash flows is to determine the net cash flows from *investing* activities by analyzing changes in long-term asset accounts from the balance sheet. The long-term assets section of the balance sheet is the place to look for investing activities.[4] Looking at that section of E-Games' balance sheet, we determine the following cash flows from investing activities.

---

[4]Although not used as an example in this chapter, it's also possible to have investing activities related to changes in current investments or current notes receivable.

Increase in investments. E-Games' investments in stock increased $35,000 during the year (from $0 in 2011 to $35,000 in 2012). In the absence of contrary evidence, it's logical to assume the increase is due to the purchase of investments during the year. Additional-information item (1) in Illustration 11–6 confirms this assumption. As Illustration 11–17 (see below) shows, we report the purchase of Intendo Corporation stock as a cash outflow of $35,000 from investing activities.

Decrease in land. The Land account decreased $10,000 during the year, indicating that E-Games sold land costing $10,000. Additional-information item (2) in Illustration 11–6 indicates that we originally recorded the land at a cost of $10,000 but sold it for only $6,000 (resulting in a loss on the sale of land of $4,000, as recorded in the operating activities section). We report $6,000 as a cash inflow from investing activities—the actual amount of cash proceeds received from the sale. (See Illustration 11–17, below.)

 COMMON MISTAKE

Some students mistakenly record a cash inflow from investing activities equal to the change in the asset account, $10,000 in this case. Remember, though, that the statement of cash flows reports the *actual* cash received or paid, which is not always the same as the change in the balance sheet accounts.

Increase in equipment. E-Games' Equipment account increased by $20,000 during the year. If E-Games purchased the equipment with cash, we would record a cash outflow from investing activities of $20,000. However, additional-information item (3) in Illustration 11–6 indicates that the firm paid for the equipment by issuing a $20,000 note payable. No cash was exchanged in the transaction. The increase in equipment therefore represents a noncash activity, which is disclosed in the cash flow footnote. Illustration 11–17 provides a summary of the cash flows from investing activities and disclosure of the noncash activity.

E-GAMES, INC. Statement of Cash Flows (partial)	
Cash Flows from Investing Activities	
Purchase of investment	$(35,000)
Sale of land	6,000
Net cash flows from investing activities	$ (29,000)
Note: Noncash Activities	
Purchased equipment by issuing a note payable	$ 20,000

ILLUSTRATION 11–17

Cash Flows from Investing Activities

FINANCING ACTIVITIES

The third step in preparing the statement of cash flows is to determine the net cash flows from *financing* activities. We can find a firm's financing activities by examining changes in long-term liabilities and stockholders' equity accounts from the balance sheet.[5] Referring back to E-Games' balance sheet, we find the following cash flows from financing activities.

---

[5]Although not used as an example in this chapter, it is also possible for financing activities to be indicated by changes in current liability accounts, such as current notes payable.

Increase in notes payable. E-Games has only one long-term liability. The company reports an increase in notes payable of $20,000. As we saw earlier, this was in payment for equipment and represents a noncash activity disclosed in a note to the cash flow statement.

Increase in common stock. Common stock increased by $5,000 during the year. Item (4) of the additional information in Illustration 11–6 confirms that this was the result of issuing $5,000 of common stock. As Illustration 11–18 (see below) shows, the $5,000 inflow of cash is reported as a financing activity.

Increase in retained earnings. E-Games' Retained Earnings balance increased by $30,000 during the year. Recall from earlier chapters that the balance of Retained Earnings increases with net income and decreases with dividends:

		Retained Earnings	
		41,000	Beginning balance
Dividends *(decreases RE)*	?	42,000	Net income *(increases RE)*
		71,000	Ending balance

Since net income is $42,000 and retained earnings increased by only $30,000, the company must have declared dividends of $12,000 during the year:

Retained earnings, beginning balance	$41,000
+ Net income	42,000
− Dividends	(12,000)
Retained earnings, ending balance	$71,000

Additional-information item (5) in Illustration 11–6 confirms that E-Games declared and paid dividends of $12,000 during the year. As shown in Illustration 11–18, we report the payment of cash dividends as a cash outflow from financing activities.

ILLUSTRATION 11–18

Cash Flows from Financing Activities

E-GAMES, INC. Statement of Cash Flows (partial)		
Cash Flows from Financing Activities		
Issuance of common stock	$ 5,000	
Payment of cash dividends	(12,000)	
Net cash flows from financing activities		(7,000)

Only the dividends actually paid in cash during the year are reported in the statement of cash flows. If the company declares dividends in 2012 but does not pay them until 2013, it will report the dividends paid as a cash outflow in 2013, not in 2012.

KEY POINT

Most investing activities can be explained by changes in long-term asset accounts. Most financing activities can be explained by changes in long-term liability and stockholders' equity accounts.

The fourth and final step in preparing the statement of cash flows (see Illustration 11–5) is to combine the operating, investing, and financing activities and make sure the total of these three activities *agrees* with the net increase (decrease) in cash. Illustration 11–19 shows the complete statement of cash flows for E-Games, with all three sections—operating, investing, and financing—included along with the note for noncash activities.

E-GAMES, INC. Statement of Cash Flows—Indirect Method For the year ended December 31, 2012		
Cash Flows from Operating Activities		
Net income	$42,000	
Adjustments for noncash effects:		
Depreciation expense	9,000	
Loss on sale of land	4,000	
Changes in current assets and current liabilities:		
Increase in accounts receivable	(7,000)	
Decrease in inventory	10,000	
Increase in prepaid rent	(2,000)	
Decrease in accounts payable	(5,000)	
Increase in interest payable	1,000	
Decrease in income tax payable	(2,000)	
Net cash flows from operating activities		$50,000
Cash Flows from Investing Activities		
Purchase of investment	(35,000)	
Sale of land	6,000	
Net cash flows from investing activities		(29,000)
Cash Flows from Financing Activities		
Issuance of common stock	5,000	
Payment of cash dividends	(12,000)	
Net cash flows from financing activities		(7,000)
Net increase (decrease) in cash		14,000
Cash at the beginning of the period		48,000
Cash at the end of the period		$62,000
Note: Noncash Activities		
Purchased equipment by issuing a note payable		$20,000

ILLUSTRATION 11–19

Complete Statement of Cash Flows for E-Games, Inc.

This is the moment of truth. The sum of the net cash flows from operating, investing, and financing activities should equal the net increase (decrease) in cash for the period. In Illustration 11–19, we see that the total of the cash flows from operating (+$50,000), investing (−$29,000), and financing (−$7,000) activities equals the net increase in cash of $14,000 for the year. This amount was the increase in cash from the balance sheet in Illustration 11–6.

Let's Review

spiceland.mhhe.com/t21

Provided below are the income statement, balance sheet, and additional information for E-Phones, Inc.

E-PHONES, INC. Income Statement For the year ended December 31, 2012		
Revenues		$2,200,000
Gain on sale of investment		5,000
Expenses:		
Cost of goods sold	$1,100,000	
Operating expenses	450,000	
Depreciation expense	25,000	
Income tax expense	217,000	
Total expenses		1,792,000
Net income		$ 413,000

E-PHONES, INC. Balance Sheet December 31, 2012 and 2011			
	2012	2011	Increase (I) or Decrease (D)
Assets			
Current assets:			
Cash	$ 32,000	$ 48,000	$ 16,000 (D)
Accounts receivable	32,000	40,000	8,000 (D)
Inventory	100,000	70,000	30,000 (I)
Long-term assets:			
Investments	0	50,000	50,000 (D)
Land	280,000	180,000	100,000 (I)
Equipment	200,000	140,000	60,000 (I)
Accumulated depreciation	(53,000)	(28,000)	25,000 (I)
Total assets	$591,000	$500,000	
Liabilities and Stockholders' Equity			
Current liabilities:			
Accounts payable	$ 52,000	$ 62,000	$ 10,000 (D)
Income tax payable	55,000	12,000	43,000 (I)
Long-term liabilities:			
Bonds payable	0	200,000	200,000 (D)
Stockholders' equity:			
Common stock	200,000	100,000	100,000 (I)
Retained earnings	284,000	126,000	158,000 (I)
Total liabilities and stockholders' equity	$591,000	$500,000	

Additional Information for 2012:

1. Sold an investment in stock costing $50,000 for $55,000, resulting in a $5,000 gain on sale of investment.
2. Purchased $100,000 in land, issuing $100,000 of common stock as payment. No cash was exchanged in the transaction.
3. Purchased equipment for $60,000 cash.
4. Retired the $200,000 balance in bonds payable at the beginning of the year.
5. Declared and paid a cash dividend of $255,000.

Required:

Prepare the statement of cash flows using the *indirect method.* Disclose any non-cash transactions in an accompanying note.

Solution:

E-PHONES, INC. Statement of Cash Flows—Indirect Method For the year ended December 31, 2012		
Cash Flows from Operating Activities		
Net income	$413,000	
Adjustments for noncash effects:		
Depreciation expense	25,000	
Gain on sale of investment	(5,000)	
Changes in current assets and current liabilities:		
Decrease in accounts receivable	8,000	
Increase in inventory	(30,000)	
Decrease in accounts payable	(10,000)	
Increase in income tax payable	43,000	
Net cash flows from operating activities		$444,000
Cash Flows from Investing Activities		
Sale of investment	55,000	
Purchase of equipment	(60,000)	
Net cash flows from investing activities		(5,000)
Cash Flows from Financing Activities		
Retirement of bonds payable	(200,000)	
Payment of cash dividends	(255,000)	
Net cash flows from financing activities		(455,000)
Net increase (decrease) in cash		(16,000)
Cash at the beginning of the period		48,000
Cash at the end of the period		$ 32,000
Note: Noncash Activities		
Purchased land by issuing common stock		$100,000

Suggested Homework:
**BE11-4, BE11-5;
E11-7, E11-8;
P11-2A&B; P11-4A&B**

CASH FLOW ANALYSIS
Apple vs. Dell

Throughout this text, we have emphasized the analysis of financial statements from a decision maker's perspective. Often that analysis includes the development and comparison of financial ratios. Each of the ratios discussed in Chapters 5 through 10 is based on income statement and balance sheet amounts.

■ **LO4**
Perform financial analysis using the statement of cash flows.

Cash Flow Ratios

Decision Maker's Perspective

Analysts often supplement their investigation of income statement and balance sheet amounts with cash flow ratios. Some cash flow ratios are derived by substituting net cash flows from operating activities in place of net income—not to replace those ratios but to complement them. Substituting cash flow from operations in place of net income offers additional insight in the evaluation of a company's profitability and financial strength.[6] Positive cash flow from operations is important to a company's survival in the long run. ●

Now we reexamine the financial ratios introduced in Chapter 7—return on assets, profit margin, and asset turnover—substituting net cash flows from operating activities, also called **operating cash flows**, in place of net income. Illustration 11–20 provides selected financial data for **Apple** and **Dell**.

ILLUSTRATION 11–20

Selected Financial Data for Apple and Dell

($ in millions)	2009	2008
Apple		
Net sales	$36,537	$32,479
Net income	5,704	4,834
Operating cash flows	10,159	9,596
Total assets	53,851	39,572
Dell		
Net sales	$61,101	$61,133
Net income	2,478	2,947
Operating cash flows	1,894	3,949
Total assets	26,500	27,561

RETURN ON ASSETS

Return on assets, introduced in Chapter 7, is calculated as net income divided by average total assets. Illustration 11–21 presents return on assets for Apple and Dell.

ILLUSTRATION 11–21

Return on Assets for Apple and Dell

($ in millions)	Net Income	÷	Average Total Assets	=	Return on Assets
Apple	$5,704	÷	($53,851 + $39,572)/2	=	12.2%
Dell	$2,478	÷	($26,500 + $27,561)/2	=	9.2%

Both Apple and Dell report strong return on assets, with Apple's return on assets of 12.2% being higher than Dell's at 9.2%. Thus, Apple generated more income for each dollar invested in assets.

CASH RETURN ON ASSETS

We can gain additional insights by examining a similar measure called the cash return on assets. We calculate it as:

Cash return on assets = Operating cash flows ÷ Average total assets

Illustration 11–22 presents the cash return on assets for Apple and Dell.

ILLUSTRATION 11–22

Cash Return on Assets for Apple and Dell

($ in millions)	Operating Cash Flows	÷	Average Total Assets	=	Cash Return on Assets
Apple	$10,159	÷	($53,851 + $39,572)/2	=	21.7%
Dell	$1,894	÷	($26,500 + $27,561)/2	=	7.0%

---

[6]Proposals for informative sets of cash flow ratios are offered by Charles A. Carslaw and John R. Mills. 1991. "Developing Ratios for Effective Cash Flow Statement Analysis." *Journal of Accountancy* 172 (November), pp. 63–70; Don E. Giacomino and David E. Mielke. 1993. "Cash Flows: Another Approach to Ratio Analysis." *Journal of Accountancy* 174 (March), pp. 55–58; and John Mills and Jeanne H. Yamamura. 1998. "The Power of Cash Flow Ratios." *Journal of Accountancy* 186 (October), pp. 53–61.

Apple's cash return on assets of 21.7% is much higher than Dell's cash return on assets of only 7.0%. Note that operating cash flows exceed net income for Apple, while operating cash flows are less than net income for Dell. This causes a greater difference in *cash* return on assets for Apple and Dell, in comparison to the spread between the two companies for return on assets presented in Illustration 11–21. Apple's net income is supported by even higher operating cash flows, while Dell's is not.

COMPONENTS OF CASH RETURN ON ASSETS

Let's explore the cash return on assets further by separating the ratio into two separate parts, as shown in Illustration 11–23.

$$\text{Cash return on assets} = \text{Cash flow to sales} \times \text{Asset turnover}$$

$$\frac{\text{Operating cash flows}}{\text{Average total assets}} = \frac{\text{Operating cash flows}}{\text{Net sales}} \times \frac{\text{Net sales}}{\text{Average total assets}}$$

ILLUSTRATION 11–23

Components of Cash Return on Assets

Cash return on assets can be separated into cash flow to sales and asset turnover. **Cash flow to sales** measures the operating cash flows generated for each dollar of sales. (It is the cash flow equivalent to profit margin, introduced in Chapter 7.) **Asset turnover**, also covered in Chapter 7, measures the sales revenue generated per dollar of assets. Cash flow to sales and asset turnover represent two primary strategies that companies have for increasing their cash return on assets. One strategy, used by Apple, is to sell highly innovative products that yield very high cash inflows from customers in relationship to the cash outflows to produce their products. Another strategy, which Dell uses, is to pursue high asset turnover by selling at lower prices than the competition. In Illustrations 11–24 and 11–25, we calculate cash flow to sales and asset turnover for both companies. We then can see whether our expectations regarding Apple and Dell are supported.

($ in millions)	Operating Cash Flows	÷	Net Sales	=	Cash Flow to Sales
Apple	$10,159	÷	$36,537	=	27.8%
Dell	$1,894	÷	$61,101	=	3.1%

ILLUSTRATION 11–24

Cash Flow to Sales for Apple and Dell

($ in millions)	Net Sales	÷	Average Total Assets	=	Asset Turnover
Apple	$36,537	÷	($53,851 + $39,572)/2	=	0.8 times
Dell	$61,101	÷	($26,500 + $27,561)/2	=	2.3 times

ILLUSTRATION 11–25

Asset Turnover for Apple and Dell

The cash flow ratios support our expectations regarding the different business strategies of Apple and Dell. Apple, with its innovative products such as the iPod, iPad, and the iPhone, generates higher cash flow from each dollar of sales than Dell, as Illustration 11–24 shows. However, Dell, with its innovative marketing, distribution, and discount pricing strategies, generates nearly three times the asset turnover of Apple, as Illustration 11–25 shows. To maximize cash flow from operations, a company strives to increase *both* cash flow per dollar of sales (cash flow to sales) and sales per dollar of assets invested (asset turnover).

KEY POINT

Cash return on assets indicates the amount of operating cash flow generated for each dollar invested in assets. We can separate cash return on assets into two components—cash flow to sales and asset turnover—to examine two important business strategies.

Decision Point

Question	Accounting information	Analysis
Are the company's cash flows based more on selling at higher prices or on increasing sales volume?	Cash flow to sales and asset turnover ratios	Companies with high cash flow to sales ratios obtain high cash inflows from sales to customers in relation to the cash outflows to produce the products. Companies with high asset turnover ratios may not make as much on each sale, but they make money through higher sales volume.

ETHICAL DILEMMA

Ebenezer is CEO of a successful small business. One day he stops by to see Tim Cratchit, the new branch manager at First National Bank. Ebenezer would like to double the size of his loan with the bank from $500,000 to $1 million. Ebenezer explains, "Business is booming, sales and earnings are up each of the past three years, and we could certainly use the funds for further business expansion." Tim Cratchit has a big heart, and Ebenezer has been a close friend of the family. He thinks to himself this loan decision will be easy, but he asks Ebenezer to e-mail the past three years' financial statements as required by bank policy.

In looking over the financial statements sent by Ebenezer, Tim becomes concerned. Sales and earnings have increased just as Ebenezer said. However, receivables, inventory, and accounts payable have grown at a much faster rate than sales. Furthermore, he notices a steady decrease in operating cash flows over the past three years, with negative operating cash flows in each of the past two years.

Who are the stakeholders, and what is the ethical dilemma? Do you think Tim should go ahead and approve the loan?

APPENDIX

OPERATING ACTIVITIES—DIRECT METHOD

■ **LO5**

Prepare the operating section of the statement of cash flows using the direct method.

The presentation of cash flows from operating activities in the chapter is referred to as the indirect method. By this method, we determine the cash effect of each operating activity or income statement item indirectly, starting with reported net income and working backward to convert to a cash basis.

An alternative is the **direct method,** by which we report the cash inflows and cash outflows directly on the statement of cash flows. For instance, we report *cash received from customers* as the cash effect of sales activities, and *cash paid to suppliers* as the cash effect of cost of goods sold. Income statement items that have *no* cash effect—such as depreciation expense or gains and losses on the sale of assets— are simply not reported under the direct method.

Here, we repeat the example for E-Games, Inc., this time presenting cash flows from operating activities using the direct method. For convenience, the income statement, balance sheet, and additional information for E-Games, Inc., are repeated in Illustration 11–26.

E-GAMES, INC.
Income Statement
For the year ended December 31, 2012

Revenues		$1,012,000
Expenses:		
Cost of goods sold	$650,000	
Operating expenses (salaries, rent, utilities)	286,000	
Depreciation expense	9,000	
Loss on sale of land	4,000	
Interest expense	5,000	
Income tax expense	16,000	
Total expenses		970,000
Net income		$ 42,000

ILLUSTRATION 11–26

Income Statement, Balance Sheet, and Additional Information for E-Games, Inc.

E-GAMES, INC.
Balance Sheet
December 31, 2012 and 2011

	2012	2011	Increase (I) or Decrease (D)
Assets			
Current assets:			
Cash	$ 62,000	$ 48,000	$14,000 (I)
Accounts receivable	27,000	20,000	7,000 (I)
Inventory	35,000	45,000	10,000 (D)
Prepaid rent	4,000	2,000	2,000 (I)
Long-term assets:			
Investments	35,000	0	35,000 (I)
Land	70,000	80,000	10,000 (D)
Equipment	90,000	70,000	20,000 (I)
Accumulated depreciation	(23,000)	(14,000)	9,000 (I)
Total assets	$300,000	$251,000	
Liabilities and Stockholders' Equity			
Current liabilities:			
Accounts payable	$ 22,000	$ 27,000	$ 5,000 (D)
Interest payable	2,000	1,000	1,000 (I)
Income tax payable	5,000	7,000	2,000 (D)
Long-term liabilities:			
Notes payable	95,000	75,000	20,000 (I)
Stockholders' equity:			
Common stock	105,000	100,000	5,000 (I)
Retained earnings	71,000	41,000	30,000 (I)
Total liabilities and stockholders' equity	$300,000	$251,000	

(*continued*)

ILLUSTRATION 11–26
(*concluded*)

Additional Information for 2012:

1. Purchased stock in Intendo Corporation for $35,000.
2. Land costing $10,000 was sold for only $6,000, resulting in a $4,000 loss on sale of land.
3. Purchased $20,000 in equipment by issuing a $20,000 note payable due in three years. No cash was exchanged in the transaction.
4. Issued common stock for $5,000 cash.
5. The company declared and paid a cash dividend of $12,000.

Remember from Illustration 11–5 that the first step in preparing the statement of cash flows is to calculate net cash flows from *operating* activities using information from the income statement and changes in current assets and current liabilities from the balance sheet.

The income statement reports revenues earned during the year, *regardless of when cash is received*, and the expenses incurred in generating those revenues, *regardless of when cash is paid*. This is the *accrual concept* of accounting that we've discussed throughout the book. Cash flows from operating activities, on the other hand, are both inflows and outflows of cash that result from activities reported in the income statement. In other words, it's the elements of net income, but **reported on a cash basis.** Using the direct method, we examine each account in the income statement and convert it from an accrual amount to a cash amount. We directly report the cash inflows and cash outflows from operations as shown in Illustration 11–27.

ILLUSTRATION 11–27

Operating Activities
Using the Direct
Method

Cash Flows from Operating Activities
Cash inflows:
    Cash received from customers
    Cash received from interest
    Cash received from dividends
Cash outflows:
    Cash paid to suppliers
    Cash paid for operating expenses
    Cash paid for interest
    Cash paid for income taxes

= Net cash flows from operating activities

The best way to apply the direct method is to convert each revenue and expense item to its cash-basis amount. We do this by considering how each income statement account is affected by related changes in current asset and current liability accounts.

Cash received from customers. E-Games reports revenues of $1,012,000 as the first item in its income statement. Did E-Games receive $1,012,000 in cash from those revenues? We can answer this by looking at the change in accounts receivable. If accounts receivable increases, this indicates that revenues exceed cash receipts from customers. That's why customers owe more than they did before. If accounts receivable decreases, the opposite will be true. Recall that accounts receivable increased $7,000. Therefore, we deduct the $7,000 increase in accounts receivable from revenues to obtain cash received from customers of $1,005,000, as shown in Illustration 11–28.

Revenues	$ 1,012,000
− Increase in accounts receivable	(7,000)
Cash received from customers	**$1,005,000**

ILLUSTRATION 11–28

Cash Received from Customers

Let's consider this again from a couple of different perspectives. Accounts receivable increases when customers buy on credit and decreases when we receive cash from customers. We can compare sales and the change in accounts receivable during the year to determine the amount of cash we received from customers. In T–account format the relationship looks like this:

Accounts Receivable

Beginning balance	20,000		
Credit sales	1,012,000	?	Cash received
(increases A/R)			(decreases A/R)
Ending balance	27,000		

We see from this analysis that *cash received from customers* must have been $1,005,000. Still another way to view the situation is to think about how E-Games recorded these selling and collection activities during the year:

	Debit	Credit		A	=	L	+	SE
Cash (to balance)	**1,005,000**			+1,005,000				
Accounts Receivable (= $27,000 − $20,000)	**7,000**			+7,000				
Revenues (from income statement)		**1,012,000**						+1,012,000 Rev↑
(*Receive cash from customers*)								

We record an increase in Revenues with a credit and an increase in Accounts Receivable with a debit. Cash received from customers must be $1,005,000 for debits to equal credits.

Cash paid to suppliers. Moving down the income statement, we see that E-Games reports cost of goods sold of $650,000. Did E-Games pay cash of $650,000 to suppliers of those goods during the year? To answer this, we look to the two current balance sheet accounts affected by merchandise purchases—Inventory and Accounts Payable.

First, compare cost of goods sold with the change in inventory to determine the cost of goods purchased (not necessarily cash paid) during the year. Inventory decreased by $10,000. We can visualize the relationship in T-account format:

Inventory

Beginning balance	45,000		
Cost of goods purchased	?	650,000	Cost of goods sold
(increases inventory)			(decreases inventory)
Ending balance	35,000		

The number needed to explain the change is $640,000. That's the cost of goods *purchased* during the year. It's not necessarily true, though, that E-Games paid $640,000 cash to suppliers of these goods. We need to look at the change in accounts payable to determine the cash paid to suppliers:

Accounts Payable

		27,000	Beginning balance
Cash paid to suppliers	?	640,000	Cost of goods purchased
(decreases A/P)			(increases A/P)
		22,000	Ending balance

We now see that cash paid to suppliers is $645,000. We can confirm this by looking at how E-Games recorded inventory purchases and sales during the year:

A	=	L	+	SE		Debit	Credit
				−650,000 Exp↑	**Cost of Goods Sold** (from income statement)............................	**650,000**	
		−5,000			**Accounts Payable** (= $27,000 − $22,000).................................	**5,000**	
−10,000					**Inventory** (= $45,000 − $35,000)..		**10,000**
−645,000					**Cash** (to balance)...		**645,000**
					(*Pay cash for inventory*)		

We record an increase in Cost of Goods Sold with a debit, a decrease in Inventory with a credit, and a decrease in Accounts Payable with a debit. Cash paid to suppliers is the "plug" figure we need for debits to equal credits in the journal entry.

Alternatively, we can analyze the situation this way: Inventory decreased $10,000 for the year, so E-Games needed to purchase only $640,000 of goods in order to sell $650,000 of goods; $10,000 came from existing inventory. Because accounts payable decreased by $5,000, cash paid to suppliers must have been $5,000 more than purchases, so we add the decrease in accounts payable to purchases of $640,000 to arrive at cash paid to suppliers of $645,000, as shown in Illustration 11–29.

ILLUSTRATION 11–29

Cash Paid to Suppliers

Cost of goods sold	$ 650,000
− Decrease in inventory	(10,000)
= Purchases	640,000
+ Decrease in accounts payable	5,000
= Cash paid to suppliers	$645,000

Cash paid for operating expenses.   Operating expenses of $286,000 appear next in the income statement. We examine the changes in current assets and current liabilities for any accounts related to operating expenses. Rent expense is included in operating expenses, so we must consider the change in prepaid rent. Increasing prepaid rent takes additional cash. Prepaid rent increased by $2,000, so we need to add this change to operating expenses to determine the cash paid for operating expenses, as shown in Illustration 11–30.

ILLUSTRATION 11–30

Cash Paid for
Operating Expenses

Operating expenses	$ 286,000
+ Increase in prepaid rent	2,000
= Cash paid for operating expenses	$288,000

We see no current assets or current liabilities associated with other operating expenses such as salaries expense or utilities expense, so we make no adjustments to these expenses. Therefore, the amounts we report for these expenses in the income statement must equal the amount of cash we paid for these items.

Let's check our calculation by recording the payment for operating expenses during the year:

	Debit	Credit	A	=	L	+	SE
Operating Expenses (from the income statement)......................	**286,000**						−286,000 Exp↑
Prepaid Rent (= $4,000 − $2,000)...	**2,000**		+2,000				
Cash (to balance)...		**288,000**	−288,000				
(*Pay operating expenses*)							

Depreciation expense and loss on sale of land.   The next expense listed in the income statement is depreciation expense of $9,000. Depreciation expense has no effect on cash flows. It is merely an allocation in the current period of a prior cash expenditure (to acquire the depreciable asset). Therefore, unlike the other expenses to this point, depreciation is *not* reported on the statement of cash flows under the direct method.

Similar to depreciation expense, the loss on sale of land is *not* reported because it, too, has no effect on *operating* cash flows. Additional-information item (2) in Illustration 11–26 indicates that land we originally purchased at a cost of $10,000 was sold for $6,000, resulting in a loss on the sale of land of $4,000. E-Games records the sale as:

	Debit	Credit	A	=	L	+	SE
Cash (selling price)	**6,000**		+6,000				
Loss (difference)	**4,000**						−4,000 Exp↑
Land (cost)		**10,000**	−10,000				
(*Receive cash from sale of land*)							

As we discussed previously, we report the $6,000 cash inflow as an investing activity, because both investing in land and later selling it are considered investing activities. The original cost of the land, and thus the loss, has no effect on operating cash flows.

Cash paid for interest.   E-Games next reports interest expense of $5,000 in the income statement. The related current asset or current liability in the balance sheet is interest payable. If interest payable increases, interest expense exceeds cash paid for interest. Interest payable increases $1,000. As shown in Illustration 11–31, we deduct the increase in interest payable from interest expense to arrive at cash paid for interest.

Interest expense	$ 5,000
− Increase in interest payable	(1,000)
= Cash paid for interest	$4,000

ILLUSTRATION 11–31

Cash Paid for Interest

We can check our calculation by recording the payment for interest during the year:

	Debit	Credit	A	=	L	+	SE
Interest Expense (from income statement).................................	**5,000**						−5,000 Exp↑
Interest Payable (= $2,000 − $1,000).....................................		**1,000**			+1,000		
Cash (to balance)...		**4,000**	−4,000				
(*Pay interest*)							

Cash paid for income taxes. The final item reported in the income statement is income tax expense of $16,000. The related current asset or current liability in the balance sheet is income tax payable. Income tax payable decreased $2,000. This means that E-Games paid $2,000 more than the income tax expense recorded. As shown in Illustration 11–32, we add the decrease in income tax payable to income tax expense to calculate cash paid for income taxes.

ILLUSTRATION 11–32

Cash Paid for Income Taxes

Income tax expense	$ 16,000
+ Decrease in income tax payable	2,000
= Cash paid for income taxes	$18,000

Recording the payment of taxes during the year confirms this:

A = L + SE		Debit	Credit
−16,000 Exp	Income Tax Expense (from income statement)............................	16,000	
−2,000	Income Tax Payable (= $7,000 − $5,000)....................................	2,000	
−18,000	Cash (to balance)...		18,000
	(*Pay income taxes*)		

Illustration 11–33 shows the completed operating activities section using the direct method.

ILLUSTRATION 11–33

Operating Activities Using the Direct Method

E-GAMES, INC.
Statement of Cash Flows (partial)—Direct Method

Cash Flows from Operating Activities

Cash received from customers	$1,005,000
Cash paid to suppliers	(645,000)
Cash paid for operating expenses	(288,000)
Cash paid for interest	(4,000)
Cash paid for income taxes	(18,000)
Net cash flows from operating activities	$50,000

Note that the net cash flows from operating activities is $50,000—**the same amount we calculated earlier in Illustration 11–15 using the indirect method.** This will always be the case. The indirect method begins with net income, whereas the direct method considers each of the individual accounts that make up net income. Both methods take into consideration the *same changes* in current asset and current liability accounts.

KEY POINT

The indirect method and direct method differ only in the presentation of operating activities. In the indirect method, we start with net income and make adjustments to arrive at net cash flows from operating activities. In the direct method, we convert each individual line item in the income statement to its cash basis and directly list the cash inflows and cash outflows from operating activities. The net cash flows from operating activities are *the same under both methods.*

The income statement, balance sheet, and additional information from the accounting records of E-Phones, Inc., are provided below.

Let's Review

spiceland.mhhe.com/t22

E-PHONES, INC.
Income Statement
For the year ended December 31, 2012

Revenues		$2,200,000
Gain on sale of investment		5,000
Expenses:		
Cost of goods sold	$1,100,000	
Operating expenses	450,000	
Depreciation expense	25,000	
Income tax expense	217,000	
Total expenses		1,792,000
Net income		$ 413,000

E-PHONES, INC.
Balance Sheet
December 31, 2012 and 2011

	2012	2011	Increase (I) or Decrease (D)
Assets			
Current assets:			
Cash	$ 32,000	$ 48,000	$ 16,000 (D)
Accounts receivable	32,000	40,000	8,000 (D)
Inventory	100,000	70,000	30,000 (I)
Long-term assets:			
Investments	0	50,000	50,000 (D)
Land	280,000	180,000	100,000 (I)
Equipment	200,000	140,000	60,000 (I)
Accumulated depreciation	(53,000)	(28,000)	25,000 (I)
Total assets	$591,000	$500,000	
Liabilities and Stockholders' Equity			
Current liabilities:			
Accounts payable	$ 52,000	$ 62,000	$ 10,000 (D)
Income tax payable	55,000	12,000	43,000 (I)
Long-term liabilities:			
Bonds payable	0	200,000	200,000 (D)
Stockholders' equity:			
Common stock	200,000	100,000	100,000 (I)
Retained earnings	284,000	126,000	158,000 (I)
Total liabilities and stockholders' equity	$591,000	$500,000	

Additional Information for 2012:

1. Sold an investment in stock costing $50,000 for $55,000, resulting in a $5,000 gain on sale of investment.
2. Purchased $100,000 in land issuing $100,000 of common stock as payment. No cash was exchanged in the transaction.
3. Purchased equipment for $60,000 cash.
4. Retired the $200,000 balance in bonds payable at the beginning of the year.
5. Declared and paid a cash dividend of $255,000.

Required:

Prepare the statement of cash flows using the *direct method* for reporting operating activities. Disclose any noncash transactions in a note to the statement of cash flows.

Solution:

E-PHONES, INC.
Statement of Cash Flows—Direct Method
For the year ended December 31, 2012

Cash Flows from Operating Activities		
Cash received from customers	$2,208,000	
Cash paid to suppliers	(1,140,000)	
Cash paid for operating expenses	(450,000)	
Cash paid for income taxes	(174,000)	
Net cash flows from operating activities		$444,000
Cash Flows from Investing Activities		
Sale of investment	55,000	
Purchase of equipment	(60,000)	
Net cash flows from investing activities		(5,000)
Cash Flows from Financing Activities		
Retire bonds payable	(200,000)	
Payment of cash dividends	(255,000)	
Net cash flows from financing activities		(455,000)
Net increase (decrease) in cash		(16,000)
Cash at the beginning of the period		48,000
Cash at the end of the period		$ 32,000
Note: Noncash Activities		
Purchased land by issuing common stock		$100,000

Here are the supporting calculations for cash flows from operating activities under the direct method:

Revenues	$ 2,200,000
+ Decrease in accounts receivable	8,000
= Cash received from customers	$2,208,000
Cost of goods sold	$ 1,100,000
+ Increase in inventory	30,000
= Purchases	1,130,000
+ Decrease in accounts payable	10,000
= Cash paid to suppliers	$1,140,000
Cash paid for operating expenses	$ 450,000
Income tax expense	$ 217,000
− Increase in income tax payable	(43,000)
= Cash paid for income taxes	$ 174,000

Suggested Homework:
BE11-12, BE11-13;
E11-13, E11-14;
P11-6A&B; P11-7A&B

KEY POINTS BY LEARNING OBJECTIVE

LO1 Classify cash transactions as operating, investing, or financing activities.

Operating activities relate to income statement items. Investing activities primarily involve changes in long-term assets. Financing activities primarily involve changes in long-term liabilities and stockholders' equity.

Companies choose between the indirect method and direct method in reporting operating activities in the statement of cash flows. The indirect method is less costly to prepare, and most companies use it. The direct method more logically presents the cash inflows and outflows from operations. The investing and financing sections of the statement of cash flows are identical under both methods.

LO2 Prepare the operating activities section of the statement of cash flows using the indirect method.

Using the indirect method, we start with net income and adjust this number for (a) revenue and expense items that do not represent cash and (b) changes in current assets and current liabilities.

LO3 Prepare the investing activities section and the financing activities section of the statement of cash flows.

Most investing activities can be explained by changes in long-term asset accounts. Most

financing activities can be explained by changes in long-term liability and stockholders' equity accounts.

Analysis

LO4 Perform financial analysis using the statement of cash flows.

Cash return on assets indicates the amount of operating cash flow generated for each dollar invested in assets. We can separate cash return on assets to two components—cash flow to sales and asset turnover—to examine two important business strategies.

Appendix

LO5 Prepare the operating activities section of the statement of cash flows using the direct method.

The indirect method and direct method differ only in the presentation of operating activities. In the indirect method, we start with net income and make adjustments to arrive at net cash flows from operating activities. In the direct method, we convert each individual line item in the income statement to its cash basis and directly list the cash inflows and cash outflows from operating activities. The net cash flows from operating activities are *the same* under both methods.

GLOSSARY

Asset turnover: Sales revenue divided by average total assets; measures the sales revenue generated per dollar of assets. **p. 375**

Cash flow to sales: Net cash flows from operating activities divided by sales revenue; measures the operating cash flow generated per dollar of sales. **p. 375**

Cash return on assets: Net cash flows from operating activities divided by average total assets; measures the operating cash flow generated per dollar of assets. **p. 374**

Direct method: Adjusts the items on the income statement to directly show the cash inflows and outflows from operations, such as cash received from customers and cash paid for inventory, salaries, rent, interest, and taxes. **p. 360**

Financing activities: Includes cash transactions resulting from the external financing of a business. **p. 357**

Indirect method: Begins with net income and then lists adjustments to net income in order to arrive at operating cash flows. **p. 360**

Investing activities: Includes cash transactions involving the purchase and sale of long-term assets and current investments. **p. 356**

Noncash activities: Significant investing and financing activities that do not affect cash. **p. 359**

Operating activities: Includes cash receipts and cash payments for transactions relating to revenue and expense activities. **p. 356**

Statement of cash flows: A summary of cash inflows and cash outflows during the reporting period sorted by operating, investing, and financing activities. **p. 356**

SELF-STUDY QUESTIONS

■ LO1   1. The purchase of a long-term asset is classified in the statement of cash flows as a(n):
    a. Operating activity.
    b. Investing activity.
    c. Financing activity.
    d. Noncash activity.

■ LO1   2. The issuance of common stock is classified in the statement of cash flows as a(n):
    a. Operating activity.
    b. Investing activity.
    c. Financing activity.
    d. Noncash activity.

■ LO1   3. The payment of bonds payable is classified in the statement of cash flows as a(n):
    a. Operating activity.
    b. Investing activity.
    c. Financing activity.
    d. Noncash activity.

■ LO1   4. Which of the following is an example of a noncash activity?
    a. Sale of land for more than its cost.
    b. Purchase of land by issuing common stock.
    c. Sale of land for less than its cost.
    d. Purchase of land using cash proceeds from issuance of common stock.

■ LO2   5. We can identify operating activities from income statement information and changes in:
    a. Current asset and current liability accounts.
    b. Long-term asset accounts.
    c. Long-term liability accounts.
    d. Stockholders' equity accounts.

■ LO2   6. The indirect and direct methods:
    a. Are used by companies about equally in actual practice.
    b. Affect the presentations of operating, investing, and financing activities.
    c. Arrive at different amounts for net cash flows from operating activities.
    d. Are two allowable methods to present operating activities in the statement of cash flows.

■ LO3   7. Which of the following is an example of a cash inflow from an investing activity?
    a. Receipt of cash from the issuance of common stock.
    b. Receipt of cash from the sale of equipment.
    c. Receipt of cash from the issuance of a note payable.
    d. Receipt of cash from the sale of inventory.

■ LO3   8. Which of the following is an example of a cash outflow from a financing activity?
    a. Payment of interest.
    b. Purchase of an intangible asset.
    c. Payment of cash dividends.
    d. Purchase of land.

■ LO4   9. We can separate cash return on assets into:
    a. Cash flow to sales and return on assets.
    b. Profit margin and asset turnover.
    c. Cash flow to sales and profit margin.
    d. Cash flow to sales and asset turnover.

10. Which of the following items do we report in the statement of cash flows using the direct method? ■ LO5
    a. Depreciation expense.
    b. Gain on sale of an asset.
    c. Cash paid to suppliers.
    d. Loss on sale of an asset.

Answers to the Self-Study Questions
1. b   2. c   3. c   4. b   5. a   6. d   7. b   8. c   9. d   10. c

REVIEW QUESTIONS

1. Identify and briefly describe the three categories of cash flows reported in the statement of cash flows. ■ LO1

2. Changes in current assets and current liabilities are used in determining net cash flows from operating activities. Changes in which balance sheet accounts are used in determining net cash flows from investing activities? Changes in which balance sheet accounts are used in determining net cash flows from financing activities? ■ LO1

3. Explain what we mean by noncash activities and provide an example. ■ LO1

4. Why is it necessary to use an income statement, balance sheet, and additional information to prepare a statement of cash flows? ■ LO1

5. Describe the basic format used in preparing a statement of cash flows, including the heading, the three major categories, and what is included in the last three lines of the statement. ■ LO1

6. Briefly describe the four steps outlined in the text for preparing a statement of cash flows. ■ LO1

7. Distinguish between the indirect method and the direct method for reporting net cash flows from operating activities. Which method is more common in practice? Which method provides a more logical presentation of cash flows? ■ LO1

8. Describe the most common adjustments we use to convert net income to net cash flows from operations under the indirect method. ■ LO2

9. The executives at Peach, Inc., are confused. The company reports a net loss of $200,000, and yet its net cash flow from operating activities increased $300,000 during the same period. Is this possible? Explain. ■ LO2

10. Explain how we report depreciation expense in the statement of cash flows using the indirect method. Why do we report it this way? ■ LO2

11. Describe how we report a gain or loss on the sale of an asset in the statement of cash flows using the indirect method. Why do we report it this way? ■ LO2

12. Indicate whether we add or subtract each of the following items from net income in preparing the statement of cash flows using the indirect method: (a) an increase in current assets, (b) a decrease in current assets, (c) an increase in current liabilities, and (d) a decrease in current liabilities. ■ LO2

13. How does an increase in accounts receivable affect net income in relation to operating cash flows? Why? How does a decrease in accounts receivable affect net income in relation to operating cash flows? Why? ■ LO2

14. Bell Corporation purchases land by issuing its own common stock. How do we report this transaction, if at all? ■ LO3

■ LO2, 3

15. A $10,000 investment on the books of a company is sold for $9,000. Under the indirect method, how does this transaction affect operating, investing, and financing activities?

■ LO3

16. Provide three examples of financing activities reported in the statement of cash flows.

■ LO4

17. Explain the difference between the calculation of return on assets and cash return on assets. How can cash-based ratios supplement the analysis of ratios based on income statement and balance sheet information?

■ LO4

18. Describe the two primary strategies firms use to increase cash return on assets. Which strategy does Apple use, and which does Dell use?

■ LO5

19. What are the primary cash inflows and cash outflows under the direct method for determining net cash flows from operating activities?

■ LO5

20. Why do we exclude depreciation expense and the gain or loss on sale of an asset from the operating activities section of the statement of cash flows under the direct method?

For the following, please visit your instructor's *Connect* site.

BRIEF EXERCISES	1–15
EXERCISES	1–15
PROBLEMS: SET A	1–8
PROBLEMS: SET B	1–8
GREAT ADVENTURES	

Mc Graw Hill **connect** |ACCOUNTING

Note: Additional Perspectives assignments for Financial Analysis, Comparative Analysis, Internet Research, Written Communication, and Earnings Management are in Appendix F at the end of this book. For additional Exercises: Set B and for additional Problems: Set C, visit www.mhhe.com/spicelandMTC1e.

Financial Statement Analysis

AFTER STUDYING THIS CHAPTER, YOU SHOULD BE ABLE TO:

- **LO1** Perform vertical analysis.
- **LO2** Perform horizontal analysis.
- **LO3** Use ratios to analyze a company's risk.
- **LO4** Use ratios to analyze a company's profitability.
- **LO5** Distinguish persistent earnings from one-time items.
- **LO6** Explain quality of earnings and distinguish between conservative and aggressive accounting practices.

UNDER ARMOUR: **MAKING THE COMPETITION SWEAT**

It started with a simple plan to make a superior T-shirt—a shirt that provides compression and removes perspiration from your skin rather than absorbs it. Founded in 1996 by former University of Maryland football player Kevin Plank, **Under Armour** is now widely recognized for its performance apparel—clothing designed to keep athletes cool, dry, and light. With its introduction of football cleats, Under Armour has joined **Nike** and **Reebok** as one of only three authorized footwear suppliers for the National Football League. The company has expanded beyond football to supply athletic apparel for nearly every major sport. The Under Armour name is even stretching overseas with a strong market presence in the United Kingdom, Canada, Europe, Japan, Australia, New Zealand, and South Africa.

Under Armour sold over 12 million shares of stock to the general public in its initial public offering (IPO) in November 2005. The IPO, on the NASDAQ stock exchange, was a memorable one. The stock had one of the highest share price increases ever for the first day of trading, beginning at $13 and doubling to close the day at just over $26 per share. The stock has continued to do well. In December 2006, the company moved its listing to the New York Stock Exchange (under the ticker symbol UA).

Investors are very enthusiastic about Under Armour's growth potential. Some think the company is poised to become the next Nike. Why has Under Armour stock performed so well? Will it continue that success? What are the risks of investing in a company like Under Armour?

To find answers to questions like these, we use the tools described in this chapter to analyze financial statements—the same statements you've learned to prepare in the preceding chapters. The techniques we introduce here—such as vertical analysis, horizontal analysis, and ratio analysis—help analysts evaluate the riskiness and profitability of potential investments in companies such as Under Armour and compare them to industry leaders like Nike.

PART A

COMPARISON OF FINANCIAL ACCOUNTING INFORMATION

We use ratios to make comparisons every day. Consider major sports. Batting averages provide feedback in baseball about how well a player is hitting. Basketball and football use points per game to compare teams' offensive and defensive performance. In each case, the ratio is more meaningful than a single number by itself. For example, are 50 hits in baseball a good number? It depends on the number of at-bats. Similarly, 500 points are more informative about a team's performance when divided by the number of games played.

Likewise, we can use ratios to help evaluate a firm's performance and financial position. Is net income of $10 million a cause for shareholders to celebrate? Probably not, if shareholders' equity is $1 billion, because $10 million is then only a 1% return on equity. But if shareholders' equity is $20 million, net income of $10 million is a 50% return on equity and something for shareholders to celebrate. Ratios are most useful when compared to some standard. That standard of comparison may be the performance of a competing company, last year's performance by the same company, or an industry average. Illustration 12–1 provides a summary of these three different types of comparisons.

ILLUSTRATION 12–1

Three Types of Comparisons

Type of Comparison	Example

1. Comparisons between companies

Sales Growth   Sales Growth

Compare sales growth for **Under Armour** with sales growth for **Nike**.

2. Comparisons over time

2012   2011

Compare Under Armour's earnings this year with its earnings last year.

3. Comparisons to industry

Company Risk   Industry Risk

Compare Under Armour's level of risk with the average degree of risk for the sports apparel industry.*

*Industry averages can be obtained from websites such as Yahoo Finance or from financial ratings agencies such as Dun & Bradstreet, Moody's, and Standard & Poor's.

Vertical Analysis

■ LO1
Perform vertical analysis.

Common Terms Vertical analysis is also known as common-size analysis.

In performing vertical analysis, we express each item in a financial statement as a percentage of the same base amount. For instance, we can express each line item in an income statement as a percentage of sales. In a balance sheet, we can express each item as a percentage of total assets. Let's look at an example to see the benefits of vertical analysis.

VERTICAL ANALYSIS OF THE INCOME STATEMENT

Illustration 12–2 provides common-size income statements for **Under Armour** and **Nike**. Notice that the two companies end their fiscal years on different dates. Under

ILLUSTRATION 12–2
Common-Size Income Statements

	UNDER ARMOUR		NIKE	
For the year ended:	December 31, 2009		May 31, 2009	
	Amount	%	Amount	%
Net sales*	$856.4	100.0	$19,176.1	100.0
Cost of goods sold	443.4	51.8	10,571.7	55.1
Gross profit	413.0	48.2	8,604.4	44.9
Operating expenses	327.7	38.3	6,745.9	35.2
Operating income	85.3	9.9	1,858.5	9.7
Other income (expense)	(2.9)	(0.3)	98.0	0.5
Income before tax	82.4	9.6	1,956.5	10.2
Income tax expense	35.6	4.1	469.8	2.4
Net income	$ 46.8	5.5	$ 1,486.7	7.8

UNDER ARMOUR AND NIKE
Common-Size Income Statements
For the years ended December 31, 2009, and May 31, 2009
($ in millions)

*Net sales equal total sales revenue less sales returns, allowances, and discounts.

Common Terms Income tax expense is also called *provision for income taxes.*

Armour's year-end is December 31 while Nike's is May 31. Even though the year-ends do not exactly match, we can still make meaningful comparisons between the two companies.

What do we learn from this comparison? Nike reports net income of almost $1.5 billion while Under Armour reports only $46.8 million. Does this mean Nike's operations are over 30 times more profitable than Under Armour's? Not necessarily. Nike is a much larger company, reporting sales over $19 billion compared to $856.4 million for Under Armour. Because of its greater size, we expect Nike to report a greater *amount* of net income. To better compare the performance of the two companies, we can use vertical analysis to express each income statement item as a *percentage of sales.*

Under Armour's gross profit equals 48.2% of sales (= $413.0 ÷ $856.4) compared to Nike's 44.9%. This means that Under Armour earns a slightly higher gross profit for each item sold, consistent with its business strategy of focusing on high-quality performance apparel. However, Under Armour's higher gross profit is offset almost entirely by its proportionately higher operating expenses, 38.3% of sales compared to 35.2% for Nike. The net result is that operating income, as a percentage of sales, is quite similar for the two companies. Nike's net income, as a percentage of sales, exceeds Under Armour's, though. The reason: Nike reports $98 million in other income while Under Armour reports $2.9 million in other *expense*, and Nike has a lower portion of income reduced for income tax expense.

Decision Point

Question	Accounting information	Analysis
How do we compare income between companies of different size?	Common-size income statements	A vertical analysis using common-size income statements allows for the comparison of income statement items between companies of different size.

VERTICAL ANALYSIS OF THE BALANCE SHEET

Vertical analysis of the balance sheet is useful, too. For this, we divide each balance sheet item by total assets to get an idea of its relative significance. Illustration 12–3 provides common-size balance sheets for Under Armour and Nike.

ILLUSTRATION 12–3

Common-Size Balance Sheets

	UNDER ARMOUR		NIKE	
	December 31, 2009		May 31, 2009	
	Amount	%	Amount	%
Assets				
Current assets	$448.0	82.1	$ 9,734.0	73.4
Property and equipment	72.9	13.4	1,957.7	14.8
Intangible assets	5.7	1.0	660.9	5.0
Other assets	19.0	3.5	897.0	6.8
Total assets	$545.6	100.0	$13,249.6	100.0
Liabilities and Stockholders' Equity				
Current liabilities	$120.2	22.0	$ 3,277.0	24.7
Long-term liabilities	25.4	4.7	1,279.2	9.7
Common stock	197.8	36.3	3,242.0	24.5
Retained earnings	202.2	37.0	5,451.4	41.1
Total liabilities and stockholders' equity	$545.6	100.0	$13,249.6	100.0

UNDER ARMOUR AND NIKE
Common-Size Balance Sheets
December 31, 2009, and May 31, 2009
($ in millions)

What can we learn by analyzing the common-size balance sheets? Focusing on the asset portion of the balance sheet, we discover that Under Armour has a higher percentage of current assets than Nike and a slightly lower share of assets invested in property and equipment. Looking at liabilities and stockholders' equity, we see that the two companies maintain a similar proportion of current liabilities but differ in their proportion of long-term liabilities. Under Armour is financed more by equity than by debt; its long-term liabilities represent only 4.7% of total assets. In comparison, Nike reports a higher level of long-term liabilities at 9.7%.

Finally, it's interesting to note the relative contributions of common stock and retained earnings for the two companies. Under Armour reports a higher proportion of common stock and a lower proportion of retained earnings in comparison to Nike. Newer companies, like Under Armour, tend to have a greater portion of equity from investment in the company (common stock) than from earnings retained in the company (retained earnings). Just the opposite is true for many well-established companies, like Nike. Profitable operations over many years have created a retained earnings balance for Nike that exceeds the original investment in the company.

 KEY POINT

For vertical analysis, we express each item as a percentage of the same base amount, such as a percentage of sales in the income statement or as a percentage of total assets in the balance sheet.

spiceland.mhhe.com/c34

Horizontal Analysis

We use horizontal analysis to analyze trends in financial statement data for a single company over time. For example, are sales growing faster than cost of goods sold? Are operating expenses growing faster than sales? Are any specific expenses increasing at a greater rate than others? Questions such as these can help identify areas of concern or, perhaps, indications of better things to come.

■ **LO2**
Perform horizontal analysis.

Common Terms
Horizontal analysis is also known as *trend analysis* or *time-series analysis*.

HORIZONTAL ANALYSIS OF THE INCOME STATEMENT

Illustration 12–4 provides income statements over two years for Under Armour. The final two columns show the dollar amount and percentage changes.

ILLUSTRATION 12–4

Horizontal Analysis of Under Armour's Income Statement

UNDER ARMOUR Income Statement For the years ended December 31 ($ in millions)				
	Year		**Increase (Decrease)**	
	2009	**2008**	**Amount**	**%**
Net sales	$856.4	$725.2	$131.2	18.1
Cost of goods sold	443.4	370.3	73.1	19.7
Gross profit	413.0	354.9	58.1	16.4
Operating expenses	327.7	278.0	49.7	17.9
Operating income	85.3	76.9	8.4	10.9
Other expense	2.9	7.0	(4.1)	(58.6)
Income before tax	82.4	69.9	12.5	17.9
Income tax expense	35.6	31.7	3.9	12.3
Net income	$ 46.8	$ 38.2	$ 8.6	22.5

We calculate the *amount* of the increases or decreases by simply subtracting the 2008 balance from the 2009 balances. A positive difference indicates the amount increased in 2009. A negative amount represents a decrease, which we record in parentheses. We calculate the *percentage* increase or decrease based on the following formula:

$$\% \text{ Increase (Decrease)} = \frac{\text{Current-year amount} - \text{Prior-year amount}}{\text{Prior-year amount}}$$

In our example, the calculation would be:

$$\% \text{ Increase (Decrease)} = \frac{\text{2009 amount} - \text{2008 amount}}{\text{2008 amount}}$$

For example, the *amount* of sales increased $131.2 million—equal to sales of $856.4 million in 2009 minus sales of $725.2 million in 2008. We calculate the *percentage* increase of 18.1% by dividing the $131.2 million increase in sales by 2008 sales of $725.2 million. If the base-year amount (2008 in our example) is ever zero, we can't calculate a percentage. Also, if the base year is negative, a percentage change is not meaningful.

The horizontal analysis of Under Armour's income statement demonstrates steady growth in company operations. Gross profit increased 16.4% (= $58.1 ÷ $354.9), operating income increased 10.9% (= $8.4 ÷ $76.9), income before tax increased

17.9% (= $12.5 ÷ $69.9), and net income increased 22.5% (= $8.6 ÷ $38.2). The growth in these income measures definitely is a positive sign.

However, note that gross profit did not grow as quickly as sales. Under Armour did increase sales, but the cost of those sales (cost of goods sold) grew at an even greater rate. Another negative sign is that the company's operating expenses increased at a faster rate than its gross profit (17.9% vs. 16.4%). While sales are increasing, similar or even larger increases in the cost of goods sold and operating expenses raise some concerns.

HORIZONTAL ANALYSIS OF THE BALANCE SHEET

Illustration 12–5 provides balance sheet information for Under Armour for 2009 and 2008, with amount and percentage changes in the final two columns.

ILLUSTRATION 12–5

Horizontal Analysis of Under Armour's Balance Sheet

UNDER ARMOUR Balance Sheet December 31 ($ in millions)				
	Year		**Increase (Decrease)**	
	2009	**2008**	**Amount**	**%**
Assets				
Current assets	$ 448.0	$396.4	$ 51.6	13.0
Property and equipment	72.9	73.5	(0.6)	(0.8)
Intangible assets	5.7	5.5	0.2	3.6
Other assets	19.0	12.2	6.8	55.7
Total assets	$ 545.6	$487.6	$ 58.0	11.9
Liabilities and Stockholders' Equity				
Current liabilities	$ 120.2	$133.1	$(12.9)	(9.7)
Long-term liabilities	25.4	23.4	2.0	8.5
Common stock	197.8	175.1	22.7	13.0
Retained earnings	202.2	156.0	46.2	29.6
Total liabilities and stockholders' equity	$ 545.6	$487.6	$ 58.0	11.9

Using horizontal analysis, it's important to look at both the *amount* and the *percentage* changes. For example, if we focused solely on the percentage changes, "other assets" would receive the greatest attention due to the 55.7% increase in this account. However, in dollar amount, the increase in "other assets" is only $6.8 million, which is small compared to the company's total assets of $545.6 million.

The horizontal analysis of Under Armour's balance sheet further reflects its growth in operations during the year. Each of the asset categories increased, with the exception of a slight decrease in property and equipment. Under Armour had a stock offering again in 2009, as reflected in the $22.7 million increase in common stock. The company used some of the proceeds from the stock offering to reduce short-term debt. Retained earnings increased $46.2 million, or 29.6%, due primarily to net income of $46.8 million during the year.

KEY POINT

We use horizontal analysis to analyze trends in financial statement data, such as the amount of change and the percentage change, for one company over time.

The income statement for **Nike** for the years ending May 31, 2009 and 2008, is as follows:

Let's Review

spiceland.mhhe.com/t23

NIKE
Income Statement
For the years ended May 31
($ in millions)

			Increase (Decrease)	
	2009	2008	Amount	%
Net sales	$19,176.1	$18,627.0		
Cost of goods sold	10,571.7	10,239.6		
Gross profit	8,604.4	8,387.4		
Operating expenses	6,745.9	5,953.7		
Operating income	1,858.5	2,433.7		
Other income (expense)	98.0	69.2		
Income before tax	1,956.5	2,502.9		
Income tax expense	469.8	619.5		
Net income	$ 1,486.7	$ 1,883.4		

Required:

Complete the "Amount" and "%" columns in a horizontal analysis of Nike's income statement. Discuss the meaning of the major fluctuations during the year.

Solution:

NIKE
Income Statement
For the years ended May 31
($ in millions)

			Increase (Decrease)	
	2009	2008	Amount	%
Net sales	$19,176.1	$18,627.0	$549.1	2.9
Cost of goods sold	10,571.7	10,239.6	332.1	3.2
Gross profit	8,604.4	8,387.4	217.0	2.6
Operating expenses	6,745.9	5,953.7	792.2	13.3
Operating income	1,858.5	2,433.7	(575.2)	(23.6)
Other income (expense)	98.0	69.2	28.8	41.6
Income before tax	1,956.5	2,502.9	(546.4)	21.8
Income tax expense	469.8	619.5	(149.7)	(24.2)
Net income	$ 1,486.7	$ 1,883.4	(396.7)	(21.1)

Both Nike's sales and cost of goods sold increased slightly over the previous year. The largest fluctuation relates to operating expenses that increased $792.2 million, or 13.3%, over the prior year. While "other income" had the largest percentage change (41.6%), the overall amount of change is only $28.8 million. It is primarily the increase in operating expenses that caused the decrease in net income in comparison to the previous year.

Suggested Homework:
BE12-1, BE12-2;
E12-2, E12-3;
P12-2A&B, P12-3A&B

PART B

USING RATIOS TO ASSESS RISK AND PROFITABILITY

Beginning in Chapter 4, we provided an example of ratio analysis between two competing companies at the end of each chapter. Let's now apply what we learned in those separate ratio analyses in a detailed examination of **Under Armour**, comparing the results to the sports apparel industry leader—**Nike**. The income statement and balance sheet for Under Armour for the years ended December 31, 2009 and 2008, are presented in Illustration 12–6.

ILLUSTRATION 12–6

Under Armour's Financial Statements

UNDER ARMOUR
Income Statement
For the years ended December 31
($ in millions)

	2009	2008
Net sales	$856.4	$725.2
Cost of goods sold	443.4	370.3
Gross profit	413.0	354.9
Operating expenses	327.7	278.0
Operating income	85.3	76.9
Other income (expense)	2.9	7.0
Income before tax	82.4	69.9
Income tax expense	35.6	31.7
Net income	$ 46.8	$ 38.2

UNDER ARMOUR
Balance Sheet
December 31
($ in millions)

	2009	2008
Assets		
Current assets:		
Cash	$187.3	$102.0
Net receivables	92.2	94.1
Inventory	148.5	182.2
Other current assets	20.0	18.1
Total current assets	448.0	396.4
Property and equipment	72.9	73.5
Intangible assets	5.7	5.5
Other assets	19.0	12.2
Total assets	$545.6	$487.6
Liabilities and Stockholders' Equity		
Current liabilities	$120.1	$133.1
Long-term liabilities	25.4	23.4
Stockholders' equity	400.1	331.1
Total liabilities and stockholders' equity	$545.6	$487.6

We'll review 14 ratios classified into two categories: risk ratios and profitability ratios. When calculating ratios, remember how income statement accounts differ from balance sheet accounts: We measure income statement accounts over a *period* of time (like a video). We measure balance sheet accounts at a *point* in time (like a photograph). Therefore, ratios that compare an income statement account with a balance sheet account should express the balance sheet account as an *average* of the beginning and ending balances.

 COMMON MISTAKE

In comparing an income statement account with a balance sheet account, some students incorrectly use the balance sheet account's ending balance, rather than the *average* of its beginning and ending balances. Since income statement accounts are measured over a period of time, comparisons to related balance sheet accounts also need to be over time by taking the average of the beginning and ending balances.

Risk Analysis

Illustration 12–7 summarizes eight risk ratios, the chapters in which we discussed them, and how they're calculated. We divide the eight risk ratios into six liquidity ratios and two solvency ratios. **Liquidity** refers to a company's ability to pay its *current* liabilities. The accounts used to calculate liquidity ratios are located in the current assets and current liabilities sections of the balance sheet. **Solvency** refers to a company's ability to pay its *long-term* liabilities as well.

■ **LO3**
Use ratios to analyze a company's risk.

Risk Ratios	Chapter	Calculations
Liquidity		
Receivables turnover ratio	5	$\dfrac{\text{Net credit sales}}{\text{Average accounts receivable}}$
Average collection period	5	$\dfrac{365 \text{ days}}{\text{Receivables turnover ratio}}$
Inventory turnover ratio	6	$\dfrac{\text{Cost of goods sold}}{\text{Average inventory}}$
Average days in inventory	6	$\dfrac{365 \text{ days}}{\text{Inventory turnover ratio}}$
Current ratio	8	$\dfrac{\text{Current assets}}{\text{Current liabilities}}$
Acid-test ratio	8	$\dfrac{\text{Cash} + \text{Current investments} + \text{Accounts receivable}}{\text{Current liabilities}}$
Solvency		
Debt to equity ratio	9	$\dfrac{\text{Total liabilities}}{\text{Stockholders' equity}}$
Times interest earned ratio	9	$\dfrac{\text{Net income} + \text{Interest expense} + \text{Tax expense}}{\text{Interest expense}}$

ILLUSTRATION 12–7
Risk Ratios

CAREER CORNER

Let's calculate each of the eight risk ratios for Under Armour and then compare the results with Nike's. **We show the detailed calculations for Nike in a review problem at the end of this section.**

RECEIVABLES TURNOVER RATIO

The **receivables turnover ratio** measures how many times, on average, a company collects its receivables during the year. A low receivables turnover ratio may indicate that the company is having trouble collecting its accounts receivable. A high receivables turnover ratio is a positive sign that a company can quickly turn its receivables into cash. Illustration 12–8 shows the calculation of the receivables turnover ratio for Under Armour and compares it to Nike's.

ILLUSTRATION 12–8

Receivables Turnover Ratio

Receivables Turnover Ratio	Under Armour	Nike
$\dfrac{\text{Net credit sales}}{\text{Average accounts receivable}}$	$\dfrac{\$856.4}{(\$94.1 + \$92.2)/2} = 9.2$ times	6.2 times

In calculating the receivables turnover ratio, we have assumed that Under Armour's sales are all credit sales, typical of sporting goods stores such as **Academy Sports** or **Dick's Sporting Goods**. The bottom half of the fraction is the *average* accounts receivable during the year, calculated as beginning receivables plus ending receivables divided by two. Under Armour's receivables turnover ratio is 9.2, indicating that receivables turn over (are collected) 9.2 times per year. This is much higher than Nike's receivables turnover ratio of 6.2.

AVERAGE COLLECTION PERIOD

We often convert the receivables turnover ratio into days and call it the *average collection period*. The shorter the average collection period, the better. Illustration 12–9 displays the average collection period for Under Armour and Nike.

ILLUSTRATION 12–9

Average Collection Period

Average Collection Period	Under Armour	Nike
$\dfrac{365 \text{ days}}{\text{Receivables turnover ratio}}$	$\dfrac{365}{9.2} = 39.7$ days	58.9 days

---

[1] J. Mylonakis. 2003. "Functions and Responsibilities of Marketing Auditors in Measuring Organizational Performance." *International Journal of Technology Management 25*, no. 8, pp. 814–25.

Under Armour's average collection period of 39.7 days is 365 days divided by the receivables turnover ratio of 9.2. It takes Under Armour an average of over one month (39.7 days) to collect its accounts receivable. Nike's average collection period, at 58.9 days, is about 20 days longer.

INVENTORY TURNOVER RATIO

The inventory turnover ratio measures how many times, on average, a company sells its entire inventory during the year. A high inventory turnover ratio usually is a positive sign. It indicates that inventory is selling quickly, less cash is tied up in inventory, and the risk of outdated inventory is lower. However, an extremely high inventory turnover ratio might be a signal that the company is losing sales due to inventory shortages. Illustration 12–10 provides the inventory turnover ratios for Under Armour and Nike.

Inventory Turnover Ratio	Under Armour	Nike
$\dfrac{\text{Cost of goods sold}}{\text{Average inventory}}$	$\dfrac{\$443.4}{(\$182.2 + \$148.5)/2} = 2.7$ times	4.4 times

ILLUSTRATION 12–10

Inventory Turnover Ratio

Inventory at Under Armour turns over, on average, about 2.7 times per year compared to 4.4 times per year at Nike. The slower inventory turnover at Under Armour is a negative sign, indicating a greater risk of slow-moving inventory items.

AVERAGE DAYS IN INVENTORY

We can convert the inventory turnover ratio into days and call it the average days in inventory. As you can imagine, companies try to minimize the number of days they hold inventory. We calculate the average days in inventory in Illustration 12–11.

Average Days in Inventory	Under Armour	Nike
$\dfrac{365 \text{ days}}{\text{Inventory turnover ratio}}$	$\dfrac{365}{2.7} = 135.2$ days	83.0 days

ILLUSTRATION 12–11

Average Days in Inventory

Under Armour's average days in inventory is 135.2 days, calculated as 365 days divided by the inventory turnover ratio of 2.7. In comparison, Nike's average days in inventory is much lower at 83.0 days.

Inventory turnover ratios and the resulting average days in inventory vary significantly by industry. For example, compared with the sporting goods apparel industry, the dairy industry with its perishable products has a much higher inventory turnover, and car dealerships have a lower inventory turnover. Inventory turnover might even vary by product within the same industry. The inventory turnover for milk, for instance, is much higher than for aged cheddar cheese within the dairy industry. Similarly, the inventory turnover for Honda Civics is much higher than for the higher-priced Honda Crosstour.

ETHICAL DILEMMA

Michael Hechtner was recently hired as an assistant controller for Athletic Persuasions, a recognized leader in the promotion of athletic events. However, the past year has been a difficult one for the company's operations. In order to help with slowing sales, the company has extended credit to more customers and accepted payment over longer time periods, resulting in a significant increase in accounts receivable. Similarly, with slowing sales, its inventory of promotional supplies has increased dramatically.

One afternoon, Michael joined the controller, J.P. Sloan, for a visit with Citizens State Bank. Athletic Persuasions had used up its line of credit and was looking to borrow additional funds. In meeting with the loan officer at the bank, Michael was surprised at the positive spin J.P. Sloan put on the company operations. J.P. exclaimed, "Athletic Persuasions continues to prosper in a difficult environment. Our current assets have significantly increased in relation to current liabilities, resulting in a much improved current ratio over the prior year. It seems wherever I look, the company has been successful."

What do you think are Michael's ethical concerns in this situation? Is there anything truly unethical in the controller's statement to the banker? What should Michael do in this situation? Is it acceptable for Michael just to keep quiet?

CURRENT RATIO

The **current ratio** compares current assets to current liabilities. It's probably the most widely used of all liquidity ratios. A high current ratio indicates that a company has sufficient current assets to pay current liabilities as they become due. Illustration 12–12 presents the current ratios for Under Armour and Nike.

ILLUSTRATION 12–12

Current Ratio

Current Ratio	Under Armour	Nike
$\dfrac{\text{Current assets}}{\text{Current liabilities}}$	$\dfrac{\$448.0}{\$120.1} = 3.7 \text{ to } 1$	3.0 to 1

Under Armour's current ratio of 3.7 means the firm has $3.70 in current assets for each $1 in current liabilities. Under Armour's current ratio is higher than Nike's current ratio of 3.0. A company needs to maintain sufficient current assets to pay current liabilities as they become due. Thus, a higher current ratio usually indicates less risk.

However, a high current ratio is not always a good signal. A high current ratio might occur when a company has difficulty collecting receivables or carries too much inventory. Analysts become concerned if a company reports an increasing current ratio combined with either a lower receivables turnover ratio or a lower inventory turnover ratio.

ACID-TEST RATIO

The **acid-test ratio** is similar to the current ratio but is a more conservative measure of current assets available to pay current liabilities. Specifically, the top half of the fraction includes only cash, current investments, and accounts receivable. Because it eliminates current assets such as inventories and prepaid expenses that are less readily convertible into cash, the acid-test ratio may provide a better indication of a company's liquidity than does the current ratio. We calculate the acid-test ratio in Illustration 12–13.

Acid-Test Ratio	Under Armour	Nike
Cash + Current investments + Accounts receivable	$\dfrac{\$187.3 + 0 + \$92.2}{\$120.1} = 2.3$ to 1	2.0 to 1
Current liabilities		

ILLUSTRATION 12–13

Acid-Test Ratio

Under Armour's acid-test ratio is 2.3 to 1 and compares favorably with Nike's ratio of 2.0 to 1. Both companies appear to have more than enough liquid assets available to pay current liabilities as they become due.

DEBT TO EQUITY RATIO

Other things being equal, the higher the **debt to equity ratio**, the higher the risk of bankruptcy. The reason is that, unlike shareholders, debt holders have the ability to force a company into bankruptcy for failing to pay interest or repay the debt in a timely manner. Illustration 12–14 shows the calculation of the debt to equity ratio for Under Armour and Nike.

Debt to Equity Ratio	Under Armour	Nike
Total liabilities	$\dfrac{\$120.1 + \$25.4}{\$400.1} = 36.4\%$	52.4%
Stockholders' equity		

ILLUSTRATION 12–14

Debt to Equity Ratio

Under Armour has a debt to equity ratio of 36.4%, or $0.36 in liabilities for each $1 in stockholders' equity. Nike's debt to equity ratio is higher, at 52.4%.

Additional debt can be good for investors, as long as a company earns a return on borrowed funds in excess of interest costs. However, taking on additional debt can also be bad for investors, if a company earns less on borrowed funds than interest costs. This highlights the risk-return trade-off of debt. More debt increases the risk of bankruptcy, but it also increases the potential returns investors can enjoy.

TIMES INTEREST EARNED RATIO

We use the **times interest earned ratio** to compare interest payments with a company's income available to pay those charges. Interest payments are more often associated with long-term liabilities than with current liabilities such as wages, taxes, and utilities. That's why we classify this ratio as a solvency ratio rather than a liquidity ratio.

We calculate the times interest earned ratio by dividing net income *before* interest expense and income taxes by interest expense. To get to this amount, we just add interest expense and tax expense back to net income. We use net income before interest expense and income taxes as a reliable indicator of the amount available to pay the interest. Illustration 12–15 shows how the ratio is calculated.

ILLUSTRATION 12–15

Times Interest Earned Ratio

Times Interest Earned Ratio	Under Armour	Nike
$\dfrac{\text{Net income + Interest expense + Tax expense}}{\text{Interest expense}}$	$\dfrac{\$46.8 + \$2.4 + \$35.6}{\$2.4} = 35.3$	42.9

Under Armour's interest expense of $2.4 million is not listed separately on the income statement, but rather, is obtained from the notes to the financial statements. The times interest earned ratio for Under Armour is 35.3. That means Under Armour's net income before interest and taxes was 35.3 times the amount it needed for interest expense alone. In comparison, Nike has an even better times interest earned ratio of 42.9. Both Under Armour and Nike generate more than enough income to cover their interest payments.

spiceland.mhhe.com/c35

KEY POINT

We categorize risk ratios into liquidity ratios and solvency ratios. Liquidity ratios focus on the company's ability to pay *current* liabilities, whereas solvency ratios focus more on *long-term* liabilities.

Let's Review

spiceland.mhhe.com/t24

The income statement and balance sheet for **Nike** for the years ending May 31, 2009 and 2008, are shown below.

NIKE Income Statement For the years ended May 31 ($ in millions)		
	2009	**2008**
Net sales	$19,176.1	$18,627.0
Cost of goods sold	10,571.7	10,239.6
Gross profit	8,604.4	8,387.4
Operating expenses	6,745.9	5,953.7
Operating income	1,858.5	2,433.7
Other income (expense)	98.0*	69.2
Income before tax	1,956.5	2,502.9
Income tax expense	469.8	619.5
Net income	$ 1,486.7	$ 1,883.4

*Includes interest expense of $46.7

NIKE
Balance Sheet
May 31
($ in millions)

	2009	2008
Assets		
Current assets:		
Cash	$ 2,291.1	$ 2,133.9
Net receivables	3,156.3	3,022.5
Current investments	1,164.0	642.2
Inventory	2,357.0	2,438.4
Other current assets	765.6	602.3
Total current assets	$ 9,734.0	8,839.3
Property and equipment	1,957.7	1,891.1
Intangible assets	660.9	1,191.9
Other assets	897.0	520.4
Total assets	$13,249.6	$12,442.7
Liabilities and Stockholders' Equity		
Current liabilities	$ 3,277.0	$ 3,321.5
Long-term liabilities	1,279.2	1,295.6
Stockholders' equity	8,693.4	7,825.6
Total liabilities and stockholders' equity	$13,249.6	$12,442.7

Required:

Calculate the eight risk ratios we've discussed for Nike for the year ended May 31, 2009.

Solution:

Risk Ratios	Calculations	
Liquidity		
Receivables turnover ratio	$\dfrac{\$19,176.1}{(\$3,022.5 + \$3,156.3)/2}$	= 6.2 times
Average collection period	$\dfrac{365}{6.2}$	= 58.9 days
Inventory turnover ratio	$\dfrac{\$10,571.7}{(\$2,438.4 + \$2,357.0)/2}$	= 4.4 times
Average days in inventory	$\dfrac{365}{4.4}$	= 83.0 days
Current ratio	$\dfrac{\$9,734.0}{\$3,277.0}$	= 3.0 to 1
Acid-test ratio	$\dfrac{\$2,291.1 + \$1,164.0 + \$3,156.3}{\$3,277.0}$	= 2.0 to 1
Solvency		
Debt to equity ratio	$\dfrac{\$3,277.0 + \$1,279.2}{\$8,693.4}$	= 52.4%
Times interest earned ratio	$\dfrac{\$1,486.7 + \$46.7 + \$469.8}{\$46.7}$	= 42.9 times

Suggested Homework:
BE12-6, BE12-7;
E12-5, E12-7;
P12-4A&B, P12-6A&B

Profitability Analysis

■ LO4
Use ratios to analyze a company's profitability.

Our next six ratios focus on profitability, the primary measure of company success. Profitability ratios measure the earnings or operating effectiveness of a company. Not only is profitability necessary just to survive as a company, it's the primary indicator used by investors and creditors in making financial decisions. Illustration 12–16 summarizes the six profitability ratios we have examined, the chapters in which we discussed them, and how we calculate them.

ILLUSTRATION 12–16

Profitability Ratios

Profitability Ratios	Chapter	Calculations
Gross profit ratio	6	$\dfrac{\text{Gross profit}}{\text{Net sales}}$
Return on assets	7	$\dfrac{\text{Net income}}{\text{Average total assets}}$
Profit margin	7	$\dfrac{\text{Net income}}{\text{Net sales}}$
Asset turnover	7	$\dfrac{\text{Net sales}}{\text{Average total assets}}$
Return on equity	10	$\dfrac{\text{Net income}}{\text{Average stockholders' equity}}$
Price-earnings ratio	10	$\dfrac{\text{Stock price}}{\text{Earnings per share}}$

GROSS PROFIT RATIO

Common Terms Gross profit is also called *gross margin* or *gross profit margin*.

The gross profit ratio indicates the portion of each dollar of sales above its cost of goods sold. We calculate this ratio as gross profit (net sales minus cost of goods sold) divided by net sales. Gross profit ratios vary by industry. For example, consider the average gross profit ratio for the following major industries: retail grocery stores (27%), apparel stores (35%), and major drug manufacturers (68%). Illustration 12–17 presents the calculation of the gross profit ratio for Under Armour and a comparison with Nike. **We'll calculate Nike's profitability ratios in a review problem at the end of this section**.

ILLUSTRATION 12–17

Gross Profit Ratio

Gross Profit Ratio	Under Armour	Nike
$\dfrac{\text{Gross profit}}{\text{Net sales}}$	$\dfrac{\$413.0}{\$856.4} = 48.2\%$	44.9%

With a gross profit ratio of 48.2%, Under Armour sells its merchandise for about twice what it costs to produce. In comparison, Nike has a gross profit ratio of 44.9%. Nike's gross profit is still quite high, but not as high as Under Armour's.

Gross profit ratios normally decline as competition increases. For example, a patented drug can sell for many times its production cost. However, when the patent expires, competition from generic drug companies drives down selling prices, resulting in lower gross profit ratios.

How Warren Buffett Interprets Financial Statements

Decision Maker's Perspective

Warren Buffett is one of the world's wealthiest individuals, with investments in the billions. As founder and CEO of **Berkshire Hathaway**, an investment company located in Omaha, Nebraska, he is also highly regarded as one of the world's top investment advisors. So, what's the secret to his success? Warren Buffett is best known for his attention to details, carefully examining each line in the financial statements.

Warren Buffett seeks to invest in companies with a "durable competitive advantage." That means he is looking for profitable companies that can maintain their profitability over time. To find these companies, he carefully studies their income statements for evidence of above-average profits that can be sustained despite actions taken by competing companies. He also studies their balance sheets looking for financially healthy companies. Some of his major investments include **GEICO** insurance, **Burlington Northern** railroads, **Goldman Sachs**, **Pampered Chef**, **See's Candies**, and **Fruit of the Loom**. Warren Buffett uses nearly identical ratios to the ones covered in this chapter, but it's his unique ability to interpret those ratios in selecting the best possible investments that sets him apart. ●

RETURN ON ASSETS

Return on assets measures the income the company earns on each dollar invested in assets. We calculate it as net income divided by *average* (not *ending*) total assets. Average total assets are calculated as beginning total assets plus ending total assets divided by 2. Illustration 12–18 provides the calculation of return on assets for Under Armour and a comparison to Nike.

Common Terms Return on assets is referred to as *ROA*.

Return on Assets	Under Armour	Nike
$\dfrac{\text{Net income}}{\text{Average total assets}}$	$\dfrac{\$46.8}{(\$487.6 + \$545.6)/2} = 9.1\%$	11.6%

ILLUSTRATION 12–18

Return on Assets

Under Armour earned a return on assets of 9.1%, which is lower than Nike's return on assets of 11.6%. As we learned in Chapter 7, we can further separate return on assets into two ratios: profit margin and asset turnover. Illustration 12–19 shows the calculations.

Return on assets	=	Profit margin	×	Asset turnover
$\dfrac{\text{Net income}}{\text{Average total assets}}$	=	$\dfrac{\text{Net income}}{\text{Net sales}}$	×	$\dfrac{\text{Net sales}}{\text{Average total assets}}$

ILLUSTRATION 12–19

Components of Return on Assets

Some companies, like **Saks Fifth Avenue**, rely more on high profit margins, while other companies, like **Dollar General**, rely more on asset turnover. Investors are especially intrigued by companies that can obtain both—high profit margins and high asset turnover. For example, **Apple Inc.** introduced several extremely popular products such as the iPod and the iPhone that generated both high profit margin and high asset turnover for the company.

PROFIT MARGIN

Profit margin measures the income earned on each dollar of sales. We calculate it by dividing net income by net sales. Illustration 12–20 provides the calculation of profit margin for Under Armour and Nike.

	Profit Margin	Under Armour	Nike
ILLUSTRATION 12–20	Net income	$\dfrac{\$46.8}{\$856.4} = 5.5\%$	7.8%
Profit Margin	Net sales		

Under Armour has a profit margin of 5.5%, meaning that for every dollar of sales, 5.5 cents goes toward net income. Nike has a higher profit margin of 7.8%. Now let's look at asset turnover, the second factor influencing return on assets.

ASSET TURNOVER

Asset turnover measures sales volume in relation to the investment in assets. We calculate asset turnover as sales divided by *average* (not *ending*) total assets. Illustration 12–21 presents the calculation of asset turnover.

	Asset Turnover	Under Armour	Nike
ILLUSTRATION 12–21	Net sales	$\dfrac{\$856.4}{(\$487.6 + \$545.6)/2} = 1.7$ times	1.5 times
Asset Turnover	Average total assets		

Under Armour's asset turnover is 1.7. Under Armour generates $1.70 in sales for every dollar it invests in assets. Nike's asset turnover is just slightly lower at 1.5.

RETURN ON EQUITY

Common Terms Return on equity is referred to as *ROE*.

Return on equity measures the income earned for each dollar in stockholders' equity. Return on equity relates net income to the investment made by owners of the business. The ratio is calculated by dividing net income by *average* stockholders' equity. Average stockholders' equity is calculated as beginning stockholders' equity plus ending stockholders' equity divided by 2. Illustration 12–22 shows the calculation of return on equity.

	Return on Equity	Under Armour	Nike
ILLUSTRATION 12–22	Net income	$\dfrac{\$46.8}{(\$331.1 + \$400.1)/2} = 12.8\%$	18.0%
Return on Equity	Average stockholders' equity		

Under Armour has a return on equity of 12.8%. Its net income is 12.8 cents for every dollar invested in equity. Nike has an even higher return on equity of 18.0%.

Why is Nike's return on assets 2.5 percentage points higher than Under Armour's, while Nike's return on equity is over 5 percentage points higher than Under Armour's? The answer relates to *financial leverage*—the amount of debt each company carries. Recall that Nike has a higher debt to equity ratio. Remember, too, that debt can be good for the company as long as the return on investment exceeds the interest cost of borrowing. Both Under Armour and Nike enjoy returns well in excess of the interest cost on borrowed funds. By carrying greater debt, Nike is able to provide a higher return on equity in relationship to its return on assets, further benefiting the investors in the company.

PRICE-EARNINGS RATIO

The price-earnings (PE) ratio compares a company's share price with its earnings per share. The PE ratio is an indication of investors' expectations of future earnings for the company. Illustration 12–23 presents the PE ratios for Under Armour and Nike.

Price-Earnings Ratio	Under Armour	Nike
$\dfrac{\text{Stock price}}{\text{Earnings per share}}$	$\dfrac{\$27.27}{\$0.94} = 29.0$	18.6

ILLUSTRATION 12–23
Price-Earnings Ratio

At the end of 2009, Under Armour's closing stock price is $27.27, and the company reports earnings per share for 2009 of $0.94. This represents a PE ratio of 29.0. The stock price is trading at 29 times earnings. In contrast, the PE ratio for Nike is 18.6. Stocks commonly trade at a PE ratio somewhere between 15 and 20, similar to Nike's. At 29.0, Under Armour has a very high PE ratio. It appears that, at least at this point in time, investors are more optimistic about Under Armour's future earnings potential than Nike's, as shown by the price they are willing to pay for **Under Armour** stock.

As we discussed in Chapter 10, investors pursue two basic types of stock investments: growth stocks and value stocks. Growth stocks, like Under Armour, have high expectations of future earnings growth and therefore usually trade at higher PE ratios. Growth stocks are said to be *great* stocks at a *good* price. Value stocks have lower share prices in relationship to their fundamental ratios and therefore trade at lower (bargain) PE ratios. Value stocks are said to be *good* stocks at a *great* price. Some investors take the strategy of picking the stocks with the best future potential (growth stocks); other investors shop for the best bargains (value stocks); while most investors take a combined approach, searching for stocks based on both future potential and current stock price.

spiceland.mhhe.com/c36

 KEY POINT

Profitability ratios measure the earnings or operating effectiveness of a company over a period of time, such as a year. Investors view profitability as the number one measure of company success.

Let's Review

spiceland.mhhe.com/t25

The income statement and balance sheet for **Nike** for the years ending May 31, 2009 and 2008, follow. In addition, Nike reported earnings per share for the year ended May 31, 2009, of $3.07, and the closing stock price on May 31, 2009, was $57.05.

Required:

Calculate the six profitability ratios we've discussed for the year ended May 31, 2009.

NIKE Income Statement For the years ended May 31 ($ in millions)		
	2009	**2008**
Net sales	$19,176.1	$18,627.0
Cost of goods sold	10,571.7	10,239.6
Gross profit	8,604.4	8,387.4
Operating expenses	6,745.9	5,953.7
Operating income	1,858.5	2,433.7
Other income (expense)	98.0*	69.2
Income before tax	1,956.5	2,502.9
Income tax expense	469.8	619.5
Net income	$ 1,486.7	$ 1,883.4

NIKE Balance Sheet May 31 ($ in millions)		
	2009	**2008**
Assets		
Current assets:		
Cash	$ 2,291.1	$ 2,133.9
Net receivables	3,156.3	3,022.5
Current investments	1,164.0	642.2
Inventory	2,357.0	2,438.4
Other current assets	765.6	602.3
Total current assets	9,734.0	8,839.3
Property and equipment	1,957.7	1,891.1
Intangible assets	660.9	1,191.9
Other assets	897.0	520.4
Total assets	$13,249.6	$12,442.7
Liabilities and Stockholders' Equity		
Current liabilities	$ 3,277.0	$ 3,321.5
Long-term liabilities	1,279.2	1,295.6
Stockholders' equity	8,693.4	7,825.6
Total liabilities and stockholders' equity	$13,249.6	$12,442.7

Solution:

Profitability Ratios	Calculations	
Gross profit ratio	$\dfrac{\$8,604.4}{\$19,176.1}$	= 44.9%
Return on assets	$\dfrac{\$1,486.7}{(\$12,442.7 + \$13,249.6)/2}$	= 11.6%
Profit margin	$\dfrac{\$1,486.7}{\$19,176.1}$	= 7.8%
Asset turnover	$\dfrac{\$19,176.1}{(\$12,442.7 + \$13,249.6)/2}$	= 1.5 times
Return on equity	$\dfrac{\$1,486.7}{(\$7,825.6 + \$8,693.4)/2}$	= 18.0%
Price-earnings ratio	$\dfrac{\$57.05}{\$3.07}$	= 18.6

Suggested Homework:
**BE12-10, BE12-11;
E12-6, E12-8;
P12-5A&B, P12-6A&B**

EARNINGS PERSISTENCE AND EARNINGS QUALITY

PART C

As we just saw when analyzing the PE ratio, investors predict Under Armour's earnings will grow more than Nike's. That's why Under Armour's stock price is higher relative to its current earnings. If for some reason investors see Under Armour's growth in earnings begin to slow, the stock price will fall. Investors are interested in whether earnings will remain strong and in the quality of those earnings. We look at those topics in this section.

■ **LO5**
Distinguish persistent earnings from one-time items.

Earnings Persistence and One-Time Income Items

To make predictions of future earnings, investors look for the current earnings that will continue or *persist* into future years. Some items that are part of net income in the current year are not expected to persist. We refer to these as *one-time income items*. The prime examples are (1) discontinued operations and (2) extraordinary items.

DISCONTINUED OPERATIONS

A discontinued operation is the sale or disposal of a significant component of a company's operations. For example, **IBM** reported a $515 million loss on discontinued operations on the sale of its hard-disk drive business to **Hitachi**. Sometimes a company will dispose of one of its business activities by ending operations and selling the individual assets. **We report any profits or losses on discontinued operations in the current year, separately from profits and losses on the portion of the business that will continue.** This allows investors the opportunity to exclude discontinued operations in their estimate of income that will persist into future years.

For an example of accounting for discontinued operations, let's consider Federer Sports Apparel, which has two business activities: a very profitable line of tennis apparel and a less profitable line of tennis shoes. Let's say that during 2012, the company decides to sell the tennis shoe business to a competitor, and the loss from discontinued operations is $2.5 million. We report the $2.5 million loss "net of tax," which means the $2.5 million includes the effect of taxes. Illustration 12–24 shows the income statement presentation of discontinued operations for Federer Sports Apparel.

ILLUSTRATION 12–24

Presentation of a Discontinued Operation

FEDERER SPORTS APPAREL Income Statement For the year ended December 31, 2012	
Sales revenue	$15,500,000
Cost of goods sold	7,000,000
Gross profit	8,500,000
Operating expenses	1,200,000
Depreciation expense	1,000,000
Other revenues and expenses	300,000
Income before tax	6,000,000
Income tax expense	2,000,000
Income from continuing operations	4,000,000
Discontinued operation:	
Loss from disposal of tennis shoe segment, net of tax	2,500,000
Net income	$ 1,500,000

With discontinued operations reported separately in the income statement, investors can clearly see the reported net income *excluding* the effects of the discontinued tennis shoe segment, $4.0 million in this situation. Investors then can use the income excluding discontinued operations, $4.0 million, to estimate income that persists into future periods.

EXTRAORDINARY ITEMS

Sometimes, companies have gains or losses that do not reflect normal operations and that are not likely to happen again. Because of the one-time, unusual nature of these items, we don't want to combine their effects on net income with those of normal operations. These items are referred to as extraordinary items.

To be an extraordinary item, an event that produces a gain or loss must meet two conditions. It must be (1) *unusual* in nature and (2) *infrequent* in occurrence. Unusual in nature means that the event is not normal for that type of company. Infrequent in occurrence means the company does not expect the event to happen again in the near future.

A company must consider the definition of extraordinary in the context of the environment in which it operates. For example, uninsured losses from a natural disaster such as a flood, earthquake, or hurricane would normally be reported as an extraordinary loss in the income statement. However if, due to lower land prices, a grower planted in a flood zone with the expectation of periodic flood losses, the loss would be included as part of operating costs and not categorized separately as an extraordinary item.

We report extraordinary items separately, net of taxes, near the bottom of the income statement just below discontinued operations. To illustrate, let's assume Federer Sports Apparel suffers an uninsured loss to property and equipment from an earthquake. This event meets both criteria for an extraordinary item—it is unusual in nature and infrequent in occurrence. If the loss (net of taxes) is $600,000, we would report it separately as an extraordinary item in the income statement as shown in Illustration 12–25.

FEDERER SPORTS APPAREL
Income Statement
For the year ended December 31, 2012

Sales revenue	$15,500,000
Cost of goods sold	7,000,000
Gross profit	8,500,000
Operating expenses	1,200,000
Depreciation expense	1,000,000
Other revenues and expenses	300,000
Income before tax	6,000,000
Income tax expense	2,000,000
Income from continuing operations	4,000,000
Discontinued operation:	
Loss from disposal of tennis shoe segment, net of tax	2,500,000
Extraordinary item:	
Loss from earthquake damage, net of tax	600,000
Net income	$ 900,000

ILLUSTRATION 12–25

Presentation of an Extraordinary Item

As we do with discontinued operations, we report extraordinary items separately near the bottom of the income statement to allow investors to see that these are one-time items that should be excluded in estimating income that will persist into future periods.

Decision Point

Question ?	Accounting information 🗎	Analysis 🔍
Are any parts of the company's earnings not expected to persist into the future?	One-time items reported near the bottom of the income statement	Investors should normally exclude discontinued operations and extraordinary items in estimating future earnings performance

INTERNATIONAL FINANCIAL REPORTING STANDARDS (IFRS)

The FASB and the IASB work closely together in developing new standards. Discontinued operations are a good example. Rather than coming up with separate rules, the IASB reviewed the FASB's extensive work in the area and adopted nearly identical standards for the reporting of discontinued operations.

Unfortunately, the FASB and IASB do not always agree. Extraordinary items are a good example of that. The IASB does not allow the reporting of extraordinary items, due to the difficulty in determining across cultures what is unusual in nature and infrequent in occurrence. Hopefully, differences like this will be resolved as both standard setters continue their work toward global convergence of accounting standards.

For more discussion, see Appendix E.

OTHER REVENUES AND EXPENSES

The sale or disposal of a significant component of a company's operations is recorded as discontinued operations. However, the sale or disposal of most assets is reported, not as discontinued operations, but rather as other revenues and expenses. For example, **Marie Callender's** has both a restaurant business and a frozen-food business with its products sold in grocery stores. The sale of either the restaurant business or the frozen-food business would likely qualify as discontinued operations. On the other hand, the sale of a single restaurant or a single frozen-food product to another company would not be recorded as discontinued operations. Rather, the gain or loss on the sale of the asset would be included as "other revenues and expenses" (just below operating expenses) in the income statement.

Similarly, many items meet one, but not both, criteria for extraordinary item treatment. In that case, they are correctly excluded from extraordinary items. Common examples include losses due to the write-down of receivables, inventory, or long-term assets; gains or losses on the sale of long-term assets; losses due to an employee strike; or losses due to business restructuring. Each of these items is reported in the income statement as "other revenues and expenses" rather than as extraordinary items. Illustration 12–26 provides a summary.

ILLUSTRATION 12–26

Comparison of Extraordinary Items with Other Revenues and Expenses

Extraordinary Items	Other Revenues and Expenses
"Unusual in nature" *and* "Infrequent"	"Unusual in nature" *or* "Infrequent"
Examples	**Examples**
1. Uninsured losses from a natural disaster such as a flood, earthquake, or hurricane.	1. Losses due to the write-down of receivables, inventory, or long-term assets.
2. Takeover of property by a foreign government.	2. Gains or losses on the sale of long-term assets.
	3. Losses due to an employee strike.
	4. Losses due to business restructuring.

Decision Maker's Perspective

Does Location in the Income Statement Matter?

As manager of a company, would you prefer to show a loss as part of other expenses or as an extraordinary item in the income statement? Your first response might be that it really doesn't matter, since the choice affects only the location in the income statement and has no effect on the final net income number. This is true, yet many managers still prefer to show a loss near the bottom of the income statement as extraordinary, rather than placing it higher on the income statement as part of other expenses. Why?

One use of an income statement by investors is to estimate income that will persist into future years. Understandably, a manager might want to report a loss as extraordinary as a way to signal to investors that it is a one-time item and they should exclude it in estimating income for future years. Doing so would result in the appearance of a more profitable company, potentially boosting the company's stock price. So, at least in some situations, it's not just the final net income number that matters, but also the location of the item in the income statement that matters as well. ●

KEY POINT

When using a company's current earnings to estimate future earnings performance, investors normally should exclude discontinued operations and extraordinary items.

Quality of Earnings

Quality of earnings refers to the ability of reported earnings to reflect the company's true earnings, as well as the usefulness of reported earnings to predict future earnings. To illustrate the concept, we continue our example of Federer Sports Apparel.

FINANCIAL STATEMENTS BY MR. SAMPRAS

Let's move one year forward to 2013 for our example company, Federer Sports Apparel. Mr. Sampras, as chief financial officer (CFO), is responsible for all the accounting, finance, and MIS operations of the business. He has developed a reputation for his conservative, calm, laid-back management style. Illustration 12–27 presents the preliminary financial statements for 2013, prepared under the supervision of Mr. Sampras.

■ **LO6**
Explain quality of earnings and distinguish between conservative and aggressive accounting practices.

ILLUSTRATION 12–27
Financial Statements Prepared by Mr. Sampras

FEDERER SPORTS APPAREL
Income Statement
For the year ended December 31, 2013

Sales revenue	$ 18,800,000
Cost of goods sold	13,200,000
Gross profit	5,600,000
Operating expenses	1,600,000
Depreciation expense	1,000,000
Inventory write-down	200,000
Loss (litigation)	1,500,000
Income before tax	1,300,000
Income tax expense	450,000
Net income	$ 850,000

FEDERER SPORTS APPAREL
Balance Sheet
December 31

	2013	2012
Cash	$ 2,300,000	$ 800,000
Accounts receivable	1,500,000	1,200,000
Inventory	2,800,000	1,700,000
Buildings	11,000,000	11,000,000
Less: Accumulated depreciation	(2,000,000)	(1,000,000)
Total assets	$15,600,000	$13,700,000
Accounts payable	$ 1,450,000	$ 1,700,000
Contingent liability	1,500,000	0
Common stock	8,000,000	8,000,000
Retained earnings	4,650,000	4,000,000
Total liabilities and stockholders' equity	$15,600,000	$13,700,000

(continued)

ILLUSTRATION 12–27
(concluded)

FEDERER SPORTS APPAREL Statement of Cash Flows For the year ended December 31, 2013		
Cash Flows from Operating Activities		
Net income	$ 850,000	
Adjustments:		
Depreciation expense	1,000,000	
Increase in accounts receivable	(300,000)	
Increase in inventory	(1,100,000)	
Decrease in accounts payable	(250,000)	
Increase in contingent liability	1,500,000	
Net cash flows from operating activities		$1,700,000
Cash Flows from Investing Activities		
Net cash flows from investing activities		0
Cash Flows from Financing Activities		
Payment of cash dividends	(200,000)	
Net cash flows from financing activities		(200,000)
Net increase (decrease) in cash		1,500,000
Cash at the beginning of the period		800,000
Cash at the end of the period		$2,300,000

SAMPRAS RETIRES AND McENROE IS HIRED

After completing the preliminary financial statements for 2013, Mr. Sampras retires, and the company hires a new CFO, Mr. McEnroe. In contrast to Mr. Sampras, Mr. McEnroe has a more aggressive, in-your-face management style. Mr. McEnroe has made it clear that he is now in charge and some changes will need to be made. Illustration 12–28 outlines four accounting changes Mr. McEnroe proposed. They are based on accounting topics we discussed in Chapters 5, 6, 7, and 8.

ILLUSTRATION 12–28

Mr. McEnroe's
Proposed Changes

Mr. McEnroe's Proposed Changes

1. Estimate of bad debts. At the end of 2013, Mr. Sampras estimated that future bad debts will be 6% to 10% of current accounts receivable. He decided to play it safe and recorded an allowance equal to 10% of accounts receivable, or $150,000. Mr. McEnroe proposes changing the estimate to be 6% of accounts receivable, or $90,000. This change would increase net accounts receivable and decrease bad debt expense by $60,000.

2. Write-down of inventory. Mr. Sampras recorded a $200,000 write-down of inventory as follows:

December 31, 2013	Debit	Credit
Loss	200,000	
Inventory		200,000
(Write-down inventory)		

Mr. McEnroe insists the write-down was not necessary because the decline in inventory value was only temporary. Therefore, he proposes eliminating this entry, which would increase inventory and decrease loss on inventory write-down by $200,000.

3. Change in depreciation estimate. For the building purchased for $11 million at the beginning of 2012, Mr. Sampras recorded depreciation expense of $1 million in 2012 and 2013, using the straight-line method over 10 years with an estimated salvage value of $1 million. Beginning in 2013, Mr. McEnroe proposes calculating depreciation over 20 years instead of 10 and using an estimated salvage value of $500,000. That change decreases accumulated depreciation and depreciation expense in 2013 by $500,000.

(continued)

4. Loss contingency. At the end of 2013, the company's lawyer advised Mr. Sampras that there was a 70% chance of losing a litigation suit of $1,500,000 filed against the company. Mr. Sampras recorded the possible loss as follows:

ILLUSTRATION 12–28

(concluded)

December 31, 2013	Debit	Credit
Loss	**1,500,000**	
Contingent Liability		1,500,000
(Record litigation against the company)		

Mr. McEnroe argues that a 70% likelihood of losing the litigation is reasonably possible, but not probable. Therefore, he proposes removing the litigation entry from the accounting records. The change would remove the loss and decrease liabilities by $1,500,000.

FINANCIAL STATEMENTS BY MR. McENROE

How will the proposed accounting changes affect net income? Illustration 12–29 presents the preliminary income statement prepared by Mr. Sampras, the effect of the accounting changes, and the updated income statement prepared by Mr. McEnroe.

ILLUSTRATION 12–29

Income Statement
Revised by
Mr. McEnroe

FEDERER SPORTS APPAREL
Income Statement
For the year ended December 31, 2013

	Sampras	Changes	McEnroe
Sales revenue	$18,800,000		$18,800,000
Cost of goods sold	13,200,000		13,200,000
Gross profit	5,600,000		5,600,000
Operating expenses	1,600,000	$ (60,000)	1,540,000
Depreciation expense	1,000,000	(500,000)	500,000
Inventory write-down	200,000	(200,000)	0
Loss (litigation)	1,500,000	(1,500,000)	0
Income before tax	1,300,000	2,260,000	3,560,000
Income tax expense	450,000		450,000
Net income	$ 850,000	$2,260,000	$ 3,110,000

The four proposed accounting changes cause net income to more than triple, from $850,000 to $3,110,000. Notice that all four changes proposed by Mr. McEnroe increase net income: The change in the estimated allowance for uncollectible accounts increases net income $60,000; the elimination of the inventory write-down increases net income $200,000; the change in useful life to calculate depreciation method increases net income $500,000; and the elimination of the litigation liability increases net income $1,500,000. Note that income tax expense did not change because all of these changes affect financial income but not taxable income.

Look Out for Earnings Management at Year-End

Decision Maker's Perspective

Let's assume you're an auditor and all four of the final changes to the accounting records for the year increase income. Wouldn't you be just a little concerned? It may be that all four adjustments are perfectly legitimate, but it also may be an indication management is inflating earnings. Year-end adjustments, especially those with an increasing or decreasing pattern, should be investigated with greater skepticism. ●

How do positive changes to net income affect the balance sheet? Illustration 12–30 presents the balance sheet prepared by Mr. Sampras, the effect of the four accounting changes, and the updated balance sheet prepared by Mr. McEnroe.

ILLUSTRATION 12–30

Balance Sheet Revised by Mr. McEnroe

FEDERER SPORTS APPAREL
Balance Sheet
December 31

	Sampras	Changes	McEnroe
Assets			
Cash	$ 2,300,000		$ 2,300,000
Accounts receivable	1,500,000	$ 60,000	1,560,000
Inventory	2,800,000	200,000	3,000,000
Buildings	11,000,000		11,000,000
Less: Accumulated depreciation	(2,000,000)	500,000	(1,500,000)
Total assets	$15,600,000	760,000	$16,360,000
Liabilities and Stockholders' Equity			
Accounts payable	$ 1,450,000		$ 1,450,000
Contingent liability	1,500,000	(1,500,000)	0
Common stock	8,000,000		8,000,000
Retained earnings	4,650,000	2,260,000	6,910,000
Total liabilities and stockholders' equity	$15,600,000	$ 760,000	$16,360,000

The balance sheet also improves from the proposed adjustments. Total assets increase due to increases in receivables and inventory plus a decrease in accumulated depreciation. Total liabilities decrease due to the elimination of the $1.5 million litigation liability. Stockholders' equity also goes up, due to the increase in retained earnings caused by the increase in reported net income for the year.

What about the effects of the proposed adjustments on the statement of cash flows? Illustration 12–31 provides the statement of cash flows as revised by Mr. McEnroe.

ILLUSTRATION 12–31

Statement of Cash Flows Revised by Mr. McEnroe

FEDERER SPORTS APPAREL
Statement of Cash Flows
For the year ended December 31, 2013

	Sampras	Changes	McEnroe
Operating Activities			
Net income	$ 850,000	$2,260,000	$3,110,000
Adjustments:			
Depreciation expense	1,000,000	(500,000)	500,000
Increase in accounts receivable	(300,000)	(60,000)	(360,000)
Increase in inventory	(1,100,000)	(200,000)	(1,300,000)
Decrease in accounts payable	(250,000)		(250,000)
Increase in contingent liability	1,500,000	(1,500,000)	0
Net cash flows from operating activities	1,700,000	0	1,700,000
Investing Activities	0		0
Financing Activities			
Payment of cash dividends	(200,000)		(200,000)
Net cash flows from financing activities	(200,000)		(200,000)
Net increase (decrease) in cash	1,500,000		1,500,000
Cash at the beginning of the period	800,000		800,000
Cash at the end of the period	$2,300,000		$2,300,000

Interestingly, the proposed changes have **no effect at all on total operating cash flows or on the overall change in cash.** Net cash flows from operating activities remain at $1,700,000 after the four proposed transactions. The net increase in cash remains at $1,500,000. None of the proposed changes affects the underlying cash flows of the company. Rather, each improves the *appearance* of amounts reported in the income statement and the balance sheet.

SYMBOLISM REVEALED

By now you've probably guessed that Mr. Sampras and Mr. McEnroe are intended to symbolize an important accounting concept. Mr. Sampras represents **conservative accounting practices**. Conservative accounting practices are those that result in reporting lower income, lower assets, and higher liabilities. The larger estimation of the allowance for uncollectible accounts, the write-down of overvalued inventory, the use of a shorter useful life for depreciation, and the recording of a contingent litigation loss are all examples of conservative accounting.

In contrast, Mr. McEnroe represents **aggressive accounting practices**. Aggressive accounting practices result in reporting higher income, higher assets, and lower liabilities. Mr. McEnroe's lower estimation of the allowance for uncollectible accounts, waiting to report an inventory write-down, choosing a longer useful life for depreciation, and waiting to record a litigation loss all are examples of more aggressive accounting. Everyone involved in business, not just accountants, needs to recognize the difference between conservative and aggressive accounting practices.

 KEY POINT

Changes in accounting estimates and practices alter the appearance of amounts reported in the income statement and the balance sheet. Changes in accounting estimates and practices usually have no effect on a company's underlying cash flows.

Classify each of the following accounting practices as conservative or aggressive.

1. Increase the allowance for uncollectible accounts.
2. When costs are going up, change from LIFO to FIFO.
3. Increase the useful life for calculating depreciation.
4. Record a larger expense for warranties.
5. Wait to record revenue until the earnings process is complete.

Solution:

1. Conservative.
2. Aggressive.
3. Aggressive.
4. Conservative.
5. Conservative.

Let's Review

Suggested Homework:
BE12-14, BE12-15;
E12-14, E12-15

ETHICAL DILEMMA

Late one Friday afternoon, Dana Woo, the controller at Horrocks Storage & Transport (HST), is reviewing the financial statements she just prepared.

For over a year, the economy has been in a down cycle, and the transportation industry has been particularly hard hit. As a result, Dana expected HST's financial results would not be pleasant news to shareholders. However, what Dana saw in the preliminary statements made her sigh aloud. Results were much worse than she feared.

"Stew (the company president) already is in the doghouse with shareholders," Dana thinks to herself. "When they see these numbers, they'll hang him out to dry."

"I wonder if he's considered some strategic accounting changes," she says to herself, after reflecting on the situation. "The bad news could be softened quite a bit by changing inventory methods from LIFO to FIFO or reconsidering some of the estimates used in depreciation."

Would Dana violate ethical standards by proposing her ideas to the company president? When do aggressive accounting practices become unethical accounting practices?

KEY POINTS BY LEARNING OBJECTIVE

LO1 Perform vertical analysis.

For vertical analysis, we express each item as a percentage of the same base amount, such as a percentage of sales in the income statement or as a percentage of total assets in the balance sheet.

LO2 Perform horizontal analysis.

We use horizontal analysis to analyze trends in financial statement data, such as the amount of change and the percentage change, for one company over time.

LO3 Use ratios to analyze a company's risk.

We categorize risk ratios into liquidity ratios and solvency ratios. Liquidity ratios focus on the company's ability to pay *current* liabilities, whereas solvency ratios focus more on *long-term* liabilities.

LO4 Use ratios to analyze a company's profitability.

Profitability ratios measure the earnings or operating effectiveness of a company over a

period of time, such as a year. Investors view profitability as the number one measure of company success.

LO5 Distinguish persistent earnings from one-time items.

When using a company's current earnings to estimate future earnings performance, investors normally should exclude discontinued operations and extraordinary items.

LO6 Explain quality of earnings and distinguish between conservative and aggressive accounting practices.

Changes in accounting estimates and practices alter the appearance of amounts reported in the income statement and the balance sheet. Changes in accounting estimates and practices usually have no effect on a company's underlying cash flows.

GLOSSARY

Acid-test ratio: Cash, current investments, and accounts receivable divided by current liabilities; measures the availability of liquid current assets to pay current liabilities. **p. 403**

Aggressive accounting practices: Practices that result in reporting higher income, higher assets, and lower liabilities. **p. 419**

Asset turnover: Net sales divided by average total assets, which measures the sales per dollar of assets invested. **p. 408**

Average collection period: Approximate number of days the average accounts receivable balance is outstanding. It equals 365 divided by the receivables turnover ratio. **p. 400**

Average days in inventory: Approximate number of days the average inventory is held. It equals 365 days divided by the inventory turnover ratio. **p. 401**

Conservative accounting practices: Practices that result in reporting lower income, lower assets, and higher liabilities. **p. 419**

Current ratio: Current assets divided by current liabilities; measures the availability of current assets to pay current liabilities. **p. 402**

Debt to equity ratio: Total liabilities divided by stockholders' equity; measures a company's solvency risk. **p. 403**

Discontinued operation: The sale or disposal of a significant component of a company's operations. **p. 411**

Extraordinary item: An event that is (1) unusual in nature and (2) infrequent in occurrence. **p. 412**

Gross profit ratio: Gross profit divided by net sales; measures the amount by which the sale price of inventory exceeds its cost per dollar of sales. **p. 406**

Growth stocks: Stocks that have high expectations of future earnings growth and therefore usually trade at higher PE ratios. **p. 409**

Horizontal analysis: Analyzes trends in financial statement data for a single company over time. **p. 395**

Inventory turnover ratio: Cost of goods sold divided by average inventory; the number of times the firm sells its average inventory balance during a reporting period. **p. 401**

Liquidity: Refers to a company's ability to pay its current liabilities. **p. 399**

Price-earnings (PE) ratio: Compares a company's share price with its earnings per share. **p. 409**

Profit margin: Net income divided by net sales; indicates the earnings per dollar of sales. **p. 408**

Profitability ratios: Measure the earnings or operating effectiveness of a company. **p. 406**

Quality of earnings: Refers to the ability of reported earnings to reflect the company's true earnings, as well as the usefulness of reported earnings to predict future earnings. **p. 415**

Receivables turnover ratio: Net credit sales divided by average accounts receivable; the number of times during a year that the average accounts receivable balance is collected ("turns over"). **p. 400**

Return on assets: Net income divided by average total assets; measures the amount of net income generated for each dollar invested in assets. **p. 407**

Return on equity: Net income divided by average stockholders' equity; measures the income generated per dollar of equity. **p. 408**

Solvency: Refers to a company's ability to pay its long-term liabilities. **p. 399**

Times interest earned ratio: Ratio that compares interest expense with income available to pay those charges. **p. 403**

Value stocks: Stocks that have lower share prices in relationship to their fundamental ratios and therefore trade at lower (bargain) PE ratios. **p. 409**

Vertical analysis: Expresses each item in a financial statement as a percentage of the same base amount. **p. 392**

SELF-STUDY QUESTIONS

1. When using vertical analysis, we express income statement accounts as a percentage of: ■ **LO1**
   a. Net income.
   b. Sales.
   c. Gross profit.
   d. Total assets.

2. When using vertical analysis, we express balance sheet accounts as a percentage of: ■ **LO1**
   a. Total assets.
   b. Total liabilities.
   c. Total stockholders' equity.
   d. Sales.

3. Horizontal analysis examines trends in a company: ■ **LO2**
   a. Between income statement accounts in the same year.
   b. Between balance sheet accounts in the same year.
   c. Between income statement and balance sheet accounts in the same year.
   d. Over time.

■ LO2

4. Which of the following is an example of horizontal analysis?
   a. Comparing operating expenses with sales.
   b. Comparing the growth in sales with the growth in cost of goods sold.
   c. Comparing property, plant, and equipment with total assets.
   d. Comparing gross profit across companies.

■ LO3

5. Which of the following ratios is most useful in evaluating solvency?
   a. Receivables turnover ratio.
   b. Inventory turnover ratio.
   c. Debt to equity ratio.
   d. Current ratio.

■ LO3

6. Which of the following is a positive sign that a company can quickly turn its receivables into cash?
   a. A low receivables turnover ratio.
   b. A high receivables turnover ratio.
   c. A low average collection period.
   d. Both a high receivables turnover ratio and a low average collection period.

■ LO4

7. The Sports Shack reports net income of $120,000, sales of $1,200,000, and average assets of $960,000. The profit margin is:
   a. 10%.
   b. 12.5%.
   c. 80%.
   d. 125%.

■ LO4

8. The Sports Shack reports net income of $120,000, sales of $1,200,000, and average assets of $960,000. The asset turnover is:
   a. 0.10 times.
   b. 0.80 times.
   c. 8 times.
   d. 1.25 times.

■ LO5

9. An extraordinary item must meet which of the following criteria?
   a. Unusual in nature.
   b. Infrequent in occurrence.
   c. Unusual in nature *and* infrequent in occurrence.
   d. Unusual in nature *or* infrequent in occurrence.

■ LO6

10. Which of the following is an example of a conservative accounting practice?
    a. Adjust the allowance for uncollectible accounts to a larger amount.
    b. Record inventory at market rather than lower-of-cost-or-market.
    c. Change from double-declining-balance to straight-line depreciation.
    d. Record sales revenue before it is actually earned.

Answers to the Self-Study Questions
1. b   2. a   3. d   4. b   5. c   6. d   7. a   8. d   9. c   10. a

REVIEW QUESTIONS

■ LO1, 2

1. Identify the three types of comparisons commonly used in financial statement analysis.

■ LO1, 2

2. Explain the difference between vertical and horizontal analysis.

3. In performing vertical analysis, we express each item in a financial statement as a percentage of a base amount. What base amount is commonly used for income statement accounts? For balance sheet accounts?   ■ LO1

4. Two profitable companies in the same industry have similar total stockholders' equity. However, one company has most of its equity balance in common stock, while the other company has most of its equity balance in retained earnings. Neither company has ever paid a dividend. Which one is more likely to be an older and more established company? Why?   ■ LO1

5. Why, in performing horizontal analysis, is it important to look at both the amount and the percentage change?   ■ LO2

6. Explain why ratios that compare an income statement account with a balance sheet account should express the balance sheet account as an average of the beginning and ending balances.   ■ LO3

7. What is the difference between liquidity and solvency?   ■ LO3

8. Which risk ratios best answer each of the following financial questions?   ■ LO3
   a. How quickly is a company able to collect its receivables?
   b. How quickly is a company able to sell its inventory?
   c. Is the company able to make interest payments as they become due?

9. Determine whether each of the following changes in risk ratios is good news or bad news about a company.   ■ LO3
   a. Increase in receivables turnover.
   b. Decrease in inventory turnover.
   c. Increase in the current ratio.
   d. Increase in the debt to equity ratio.

10. Pro Leather, a supplier to sporting goods manufacturers, has a current ratio of 0.90, based on current assets of $450,000 and current liabilities of $500,000. How, if at all, will a $100,000 purchase of inventory on account affect the current ratio?   ■ LO3

11. Which profitability ratios best answer each of the following financial questions?   ■ LO4
    a. What is the income earned for each dollar invested in assets?
    b. What is the income earned for each dollar of sales?
    c. What is the amount of sales for each dollar invested in assets?

12. Determine whether each of the following changes in profitability ratios normally is good news or bad news about a company.   ■ LO4
    a. Increase in profit margin.
    b. Decrease in asset turnover.
    c. Decrease in return on equity.
    d. Increase in the price-earnings ratio.

13. Hash Mark, Inc., reports a return on assets of 8% and a return on equity of 12%. Why do the two rates differ?   ■ LO4

14. Define earnings persistence. How does earnings persistence relate to the reporting of discontinued operations and extraordinary items?   ■ LO5

15. Shifting Formations, Inc., reports earnings per share of $1.30. In the following year, it reports bottom-line earnings per share of $1.25 but earnings per share on income before extraordinary items of $1.50. Is this trend in earnings per share favorable or unfavorable? Explain why.   ■ LO5

16. Explain the difference between conservative and aggressive accounting practices.   ■ LO6

17. Provide an example of a conservative accounting practice. Why is this practice conservative?   ■ LO6

■ **LO6**   18. Provide an example of an aggressive accounting practice. Why is this practice aggressive?

■ **LO6**   19. Goal Line Products makes several year-end adjustments, including an increase in the allowance for uncollectible accounts, a write-down of inventory, a decrease in the estimated useful life for depreciation, and an increase in the liability reported for litigation. What, if anything, do all these adjustments have in common?

■ **LO6**   20. Provide an example of an adjustment that improves the income statement and the balance sheet, but has no effect on cash flows.

For the following, please visit your instructor's *Connect* site.

BRIEF EXERCISES	1-15
EXERCISES	1-15
PROBLEMS: SET A	1-6
PROBLEMS: SET B	1-6
GREAT ADVENTURES	

Note: Additional Perspectives assignments for Financial Analysis, Comparative Analysis, Internet Research, Written Communication, and Earnings Management are in Appendix F at the end of this book. For additional Exercises: Set B and for additional Problems: Set C, visit www.mhhe.com/spicelandMTC1e.

AMERICAN EAGLE
OUTFITTERS
ae.com

UNITED STATES SECURITIES AND EXCHANGE COMMISSION
Washington, D.C. 20549
Form 10-K

☑ **ANNUAL REPORT PURSUANT TO SECTION 13 OR 15(d) OF THE SECURITIES EXCHANGE ACT OF 1934**

For the Fiscal Year Ended January 30, 2010

OR

☐ **TRANSITION REPORT PURSUANT TO SECTION 13 OR 15(d) OF THE SECURITIES EXCHANGE ACT OF 1934**

Commission File Number: 1-33338

American Eagle Outfitters, Inc.
(Exact name of registrant as specified in its charter)

Delaware	**No. 13-2721761**
(State or other jurisdiction of incorporation or organization)	*(I.R.S. Employer Identification No.)*
77 Hot Metal Street, Pittsburgh, PA	**15203-2329**
(Address of principal executive offices)	*(Zip Code)*

Registrant's telephone number, including area code:
(412) 432-3300

Securities registered pursuant to Section 12(b) of the Act:

Common Shares, $0.01 par value	New York Stock Exchange
(Title of class)	*(Name of each exchange on which registered)*

Securities registered pursuant to Section 12(g) of the Act:
None

Indicate by check mark if the registrant is a well-known seasoned issuer, as defined in Rule 405 of the Securities Act.   YES ☑   NO ☐

Indicate by check mark if the registrant is not required to file reports pursuant to Section 13 or Sections 15(d) of the Act.   YES ☐   NO ☑

Indicate by check mark whether the registrant (1) has filed all reports required to be filed by Section 13 or 15(d) of the Securities Exchange Act of 1934 during the preceding 12 months (or for such shorter period that the registrant was required to submit and post such files), and (2) has been subject to the filing requirements for the past 90 days.   YES ☑   NO ☐

Indicate by check mark whether the registrant has submitted electronically and posted on its corporate Web site, if any, every Interactive Data File required to be submitted and posted pursuant to Rule 405 of Regulation S-T (§ 232.405 of this chapter) during the preceding 12 months (or for such shorter period that the registrant was required to submit and post such files).   YES ☐   NO ☐

Indicate by check mark if disclosure of delinquent filers pursuant to Item 405 of Regulation S-K (§ 229.405 of this chapter) is not contained herein, and will not be contained, to the best of registrant's knowledge, in definitive proxy or information statements incorporated by reference in Part III of this Form 10-K or any amendment to this Form 10-K.   ☐

Indicate by check mark whether the registrant is a large accelerated filer, an accelerated filer, a non-accelerated filer, or a smaller reporting company. See the definitions of "large accelerated filer," "accelerated filer" and "smaller reporting company" in Rule 12b-2 of the Exchange Act.

Large accelerated filer ☑   Accelerated filer ☐   Non-accelerated filer ☐   Smaller reporting company ☐
(Do not check if a smaller reporting company)

Indicate by check mark whether the registrant is a shell company (as defined in Rule 12b-2 of the Act).   YES ☐   NO ☑

The aggregate market value of voting and non-voting common equity held by non-affiliates of the registrant as of August 1, 2009 was $2,583,043,775.

Indicate the number of shares outstanding of each of the registrant's classes of common stock, as of the latest practicable date: 209,044,166 Common Shares were outstanding at March 19, 2010.

DOCUMENTS INCORPORATED BY REFERENCE
Part III — Proxy Statement for 2010 Annual Meeting of Stockholders, in part, as indicated.

Report of Independent Registered Public Accounting Firm

The Board of Directors and Stockholders of
American Eagle Outfitters, Inc.

We have audited the accompanying consolidated balance sheets of American Eagle Outfitters, Inc. (the Company) as of January 30, 2010 and January 31, 2009, and the related consolidated statements of operations, comprehensive income, stockholders' equity, and cash flows for each of the three years in the period ended January 30, 2010. These financial statements are the responsibility of the Company's management. Our responsibility is to express an opinion on these financial statements based on our audits.

We conducted our audits in accordance with the standards of the Public Company Accounting Oversight Board (United States). Those standards require that we plan and perform the audit to obtain reasonable assurance about whether the financial statements are free of material misstatement. An audit includes examining, on a test basis, evidence supporting the amounts and disclosures in the financial statements. An audit also includes assessing the accounting principles used and significant estimates made by management, as well as evaluating the overall financial statement presentation. We believe that our audits provide a reasonable basis for our opinion.

In our opinion, the financial statements referred to above present fairly, in all material respects, the consolidated financial position of American Eagle Outfitters, Inc. at January 30, 2010 and January 31, 2009, and the consolidated results of its operations and its cash flows for each of the three years in the period ended January 30, 2010, in conformity with U.S. generally accepted accounting principles.

As discussed in Note 13 to the consolidated financial statements, the Company changed its accounting for income tax uncertainties effective February 4, 2007.

We also have audited, in accordance with the standards of the Public Company Accounting Oversight Board (United States), American Eagle Outfitters, Inc.'s internal control over financial reporting as of January 30, 2010, based on criteria established in Internal Control — Integrated Framework issued by the Committee of Sponsoring Organizations of the Treadway Commission and our report dated March 26, 2010 expressed an unqualified opinion.

/s/ Ernst & Young LLP

Pittsburgh, Pennsylvania
March 26, 2010

AMERICAN EAGLE OUTFITTERS, INC.

CONSOLIDATED BALANCE SHEETS

	January 30, 2010	January 31, 2009
	(In thousands, except per share amounts)	

ASSETS

Current assets:		
Cash and cash equivalents	$ 693,960	$ 473,342
Short-term investments	4,675	10,511
Merchandise inventory	326,454	294,928
Accounts receivable	34,746	41,471
Prepaid expenses and other	47,039	59,660
Deferred income taxes	60,156	45,447
Total current assets	1,167,030	925,359
Property and equipment, at cost, net of accumulated depreciation and amortization	713,142	740,240
Goodwill	11,210	10,706
Long-term investments	197,773	251,007
Non-current deferred income taxes	27,305	15,001
Other assets, net	21,688	21,363
Total assets	$2,138,148	$1,963,676

LIABILITIES AND STOCKHOLDERS' EQUITY

Current liabilities:		
Accounts payable	$ 158,526	$ 152,068
Note payable	30,000	75,000
Accrued compensation and payroll taxes	55,144	29,417
Accrued rent	68,866	64,695
Accrued income and other taxes	20,585	6,259
Unredeemed gift cards and gift certificates	39,389	42,299
Current portion of deferred lease credits	17,388	13,726
Other liabilities and accrued expenses	19,057	18,299
Total current liabilities	408,955	401,763
Non-current liabilities:		
Deferred lease credits	89,591	88,314
Non-current accrued income taxes	38,618	39,898
Other non-current liabilities	22,467	24,670
Total non-current liabilities	150,676	152,882
Commitments and contingencies	—	—
Stockholders' equity:		
Preferred stock, $0.01 par value; 5,000 shares authorized; none issued and outstanding	—	—
Common stock, $0.01 par value; 600,000 shares authorized; 249,561 and 249,328 shares issued; 206,832 and 205,281 shares outstanding, respectively	2,486	2,485
Contributed capital	554,399	513,574
Accumulated other comprehensive income (loss)	16,838	(14,389)
Retained earnings	1,764,049	1,694,161
Treasury stock, 41,737 and 43,248 shares, respectively, at cost	(759,255)	(786,800)
Total stockholders' equity	1,578,517	1,409,031
Total liabilities and stockholders' equity	$2,138,148	$1,963,676

Refer to Notes to Consolidated Financial Statements

AMERICAN EAGLE OUTFITTERS, INC.

CONSOLIDATED STATEMENTS OF OPERATIONS

	For the Years Ended		
	January 30, 2010	January 31, 2009	February 2, 2008
	(In thousands, except per share amounts)		
Net sales	$2,990,520	$2,988,866	$3,055,419
Cost of sales, including certain buying, occupancy and warehousing expenses	1,832,471	1,814,765	1,632,281
Gross profit	1,158,049	1,174,101	1,423,138
Selling, general and administrative expenses	756,256	734,029	714,588
Loss on impairment of assets	17,992	6,713	592
Depreciation and amortization expense	145,408	131,219	109,203
Operating income	238,393	302,140	598,755
Other (expense) income, net	(5,062)	17,790	37,626
Total other-than-temporary impairment losses	(4,413)	(22,889)	—
Portion of loss recognized in other comprehensive income, before tax	3,473	—	—
Net impairment loss recognized in earnings	(940)	(22,889)	—
Income before income taxes	232,391	297,041	636,381
Provision for income taxes	63,369	117,980	236,362
Net income	$ 169,022	$ 179,061	$ 400,019
Basic income per common share	$ 0.82	$ 0.87	$ 1.85
Diluted income per common share	$ 0.81	$ 0.86	$ 1.82
Weighted average common shares outstanding — basic	206,171	205,169	216,119
Weighted average common shares outstanding — diluted	209,512	207,582	220,280

Refer to Notes to Consolidated Financial Statements

AMERICAN EAGLE OUTFITTERS, INC.

CONSOLIDATED STATEMENTS OF COMPREHENSIVE INCOME

	For the Years Ended		
	January 30, 2010	January 31, 2009	February 2, 2008
	(In thousands)		
Net income	$169,022	$179,061	$400,019
Other comprehensive income (loss):			
Temporary recovery (impairment) related to investment securities, net of tax	14,506	(22,795)	—
Reclassification adjustment for OTTI charges realized in net income related to ARS	940	751	—
Reclassification adjustment for losses realized in net income due to the sale of available-for-sale securities, net of tax	—	197	242
Unrealized (loss) gain on investments, net of tax	—	(378)	947
Foreign currency translation adjustment	15,781	(27,649)	12,582
Other comprehensive income (loss)	31,227	(49,874)	13,771
Comprehensive income	$200,249	$129,187	$413,790

Refer to Notes to Consolidated Financial Statements

AMERICAN EAGLE OUTFITTERS, INC.
CONSOLIDATED STATEMENTS OF STOCKHOLDERS' EQUITY

	Shares Outstanding (1)	Common Stock	Contributed Capital	Retained Earnings	Treasury Stock(2)	Accumulated Other Comprehensive Income (Loss)	Stockholders' Equity
			(In thousands, except per share amounts)				
Balance at February 3, 2007	221,284	2,461	453,418	1,302,345	(362,626)	21,714	1,417,312
Adoption of ASC 740 regarding accounting for unrecognized tax benefits	—	—	—	(13,304)	—	—	(13,304)
Balance at February 4, 2007	221,284	2,461	453,418	1,289,041	(362,626)	21,714	1,404,008
Stock awards	1,092	20	39,977	—	—	—	39,997
Repurchase of common stock as part of publicly announced programs	(18,750)	—	—	—	(438,291)	—	(438,291)
Repurchase of common stock from employees.	(415)	—	—	—	(12,310)	—	(12,310)
Reissuance of treasury stock	1,269	—	—	(6,480)	20,546	—	14,066
Net income	—	—	—	400,019	—	—	400,019
Other comprehensive income, net of tax	—	—	—	—	—	13,771	13,771
Cash dividends ($0.38 per share)	—	—	—	(80,796)	—	—	(80,796)
Balance at February 2, 2008	204,480	$2,481	$493,395	$1,601,784	$(792,681)	$ 35,485	$1,340,464
Stock awards	453	4	20,179	420	—	—	20,603
Repurchase of common stock from employees.	(164)	—	—	—	(3,432)	—	(3,432)
Reissuance of treasury stock	512	—	—	(4,710)	9,313	—	4,603
Net income	—	—	—	179,061	—	—	179,061
Other comprehensive loss, net of tax	—	—	—	—	—	(49,874)	(49,874)
Cash dividends ($0.40 per share)	—	—	—	(82,394)	—	—	(82,394)
Balance at January 31, 2009	205,281	$2,485	$513,574	$1,694,161	$(786,800)	$(14,389)	$1,409,031
Stock awards	41	1	40,825	—	—	—	40,826
Repurchase of common stock from employees.	(18)	—	—	—	(247)	—	(247)
Reissuance of treasury stock	1,528	—	—	(15,228)	27,792	—	12,564
Net income	—	—	—	169,022	—	—	169,022
Other comprehensive income, net of tax	—	—	—	—	—	31,227	31,227
Cash dividends and dividend equivalents ($0.40 per share)	—	—	—	(83,906)	—	—	(83,906)
Balance at January 30, 2010	206,832	$2,486	$554,399	$1,764,049	$(759,255)	$ 16,838	$1,578,517

(1) 600,000 authorized, 249,561 issued and 206,832 outstanding (excluding 992 shares of non-vested restricted stock), $0.01 par value common stock at January 30, 2010; 600,000 authorized, 249,328 issued and 205,281 outstanding (excluding 799 shares of non-vested restricted stock), $0.01 par value common stock at January 31, 2009; 600,000 authorized, 248,763 issued and 204,480 outstanding (excluding 687 shares of non-vested restricted stock), $0.01 par value common stock at February 2, 2008; The Company has 5,000 authorized, with none issued or outstanding, $0.01 par value preferred stock at January 30, 2010, January 31, 2009 and February 2, 2008.

(2) 41,737 shares, 43,248 shares and 43,596 shares at January 30, 2010, January 31, 2009 and February 2, 2008, respectively. During Fiscal 2009 Fiscal 2008 and Fiscal 2007, 1,528 shares, 512 shares and 1,269 shares, respectively, were reissued from treasury stock for the issuance of share-based payments.

Refer to Notes to Consolidated Financial Statements

AMERICAN EAGLE OUTFITTERS, INC.

CONSOLIDATED STATEMENTS OF CASH FLOWS

	For the Years Ended		
	January 30, 2010	January 31, 2009	February 2, 2008
	(In thousands)		
Operating activities:			
Net income	$ 169,022	$ 179,061	$ 400,019
Adjustments to reconcile net income to net cash provided by operating activities			
Depreciation and amortization	147,483	133,141	110,753
Share-based compensation	36,900	20,296	33,670
Provision for deferred income taxes	(36,027)	24,469	(8,147)
Tax benefit from share-based payments	7,995	1,121	7,260
Excess tax benefit from share-based payments	(2,812)	(693)	(6,156)
Foreign currency transaction loss (gain)	6,477	(1,141)	1,221
Loss on impairment of assets	17,992	6,713	592
Net impairment loss recognized in earnings	940	22,889	—
Realized loss on sale of investment securities	2,749	1,117	393
Changes in assets and liabilities:			
Merchandise inventory	(27,994)	(13,735)	(19,074)
Accounts receivable	7,052	(10,094)	(5,660)
Prepaid expenses and other	13,063	(24,781)	(1,334)
Other assets, net	1,146	390	(3,242)
Accounts payable	4,992	(3,053)	(15,559)
Unredeemed gift cards and gift certificates	(3,430)	(11,392)	(699)
Deferred lease credits	4,173	18,887	4,640
Accrued compensation and payroll taxes	25,528	(19,799)	(9,144)
Accrued income and other taxes	12,862	(20,697)	(31,416)
Accrued liabilities	(1,649)	611	6,546
Total adjustments	217,440	124,249	64,644
Net cash provided by operating activities	**386,462**	**303,310**	**464,663**
Investing activities:			
Capital expenditures	(127,419)	(265,335)	(250,407)
Purchase of available-for-sale securities	—	(48,655)	(1,772,653)
Sale of available-for-sale securities	80,353	393,559	2,126,891
Other investing activities	(2,003)	(2,297)	(1,563)
Net cash (used for) provided by investing activities	**(49,069)**	**77,272**	**102,268**
Financing activities:			
Payments on capital leases	(2,015)	(2,177)	(1,912)
Proceeds from issuance of note payable	—	75,000	—
Partial repayment of note payable	(45,000)	—	—
Repurchase of common stock as part of publicly announced programs	—	—	(438,291)
Repurchase of common stock from employees	(247)	(3,432)	(12,310)
Net proceeds from stock options exercised	7,630	3,799	13,183
Excess tax benefit from share-based payments	2,812	693	6,156
Cash dividends paid	(82,985)	(82,394)	(80,796)
Net cash used for financing activities	**(119,805)**	**(8,511)**	**(513,970)**
Effect of exchange rates on cash	3,030	(14,790)	3,363
Net increase in cash and cash equivalents	**220,618**	**357,281**	**56,324**
Cash and cash equivalents — beginning of period	473,342	116,061	59,737
Cash and cash equivalents — end of period	$ 693,960	$ 473,342	$ 116,061

Refer to Notes to Consolidated Financial Statements

AMERICAN EAGLE OUTFITTERS, INC.

NOTES TO CONSOLIDATED FINANCIAL STATEMENTS
FOR THE YEAR ENDED JANUARY 30, 2010

1. Business Operations

American Eagle Outfitters, Inc., a Delaware corporation, (the "Company"), operates under the American Eagle® ("AE"), aerie® by American Eagle, 77kids by american eagle® and MARTIN+OSA® brands.

Founded in 1977, American Eagle Outfitters is a leading apparel and accessories retailer that operates more than 1,000 retail stores in the U.S. and Canada, and online at ae.com®. Through its family of brands, AEO, Inc. offers high quality, on-trend clothing, accessories and personal care products at affordable prices. The Company's online business, AEO Direct, ships to 75 countries worldwide.

American Eagle Outfitters® boasts a passionate and loyal customer base ranging from college students to Hollywood celebrities. The Company focuses on delivering the right product at the right price, combined with a philosophy of operational excellence and discipline across the organization.

AE Brand

The American Eagle Outfitters® brand targets 15- to 25-year old girls and guys, achieving the perfect combination of American prep and current fashion. Denim is the cornerstone of the American Eagle® product assortment, which is completed by other key categories including sweaters, graphic t-shirts, fleece, outerwear and accessories. The American Eagle® attitude is honest, real, individual and fun. American Eagle® is priced to be worn by everyone, everyday, delivering value through quality and style.

aerie by American Eagle

In the fall of 2006, the Company launched aerie® by American Eagle ("aerie"), a collection of Dormwear®, intimates, and personal care products for the 15- to 25-year-old AE® girl. The collection is available in 137 standalone aerie stores throughout the country, online at aerie.com, and at select American Eagle® stores. aerie® features a complete fitness line called aerie f.i.t.™, as well as a personal care collection that includes fragrance, body care and cosmetics to complement the aerie lifestyle. Designed to be sexy, comfortable and cozy, aerie® offers AE® customers a new way to express their personal style everyday.

77kids by american eagle

Introduced in October of 2008 as an online-only brand, 77kids® by american eagle® ("77kids") offers on-trend, high-quality clothing and accessories for kids ages two to 10. The Company plans to open five 77kids® brick-and-mortar stores in Fiscal 2010. The brand draws from the strong heritage of American Eagle Outfitters®, with a point-of-view that's thoughtful, playful and real. Like American Eagle® clothing, 77kids focuses on great fit, value and style.

MARTIN+OSA

MARTIN+OSA® ("M+O") provides clothing and accessories for 28- to 40-year old men and women at its 28 stores and online at www.martinandosa.com.

Refer to Note 15 to the Consolidated Financial Statements for additional information regarding the planned closure of MARTIN+OSA.

AEO Direct

We sell merchandise via our e-commerce operations, ae.com, aerie.com, 77kids.com and martinandosa.com, which are extensions of the lifestyle that we convey in our stores. We currently ship to 75 countries.

AMERICAN EAGLE OUTFITTERS, INC.

NOTES TO CONSOLIDATED FINANCIAL STATEMENTS — (Continued)

Merchandise Mix

The following table sets forth the approximate consolidated percentage of net sales attributable to each merchandise group for each of the periods indicated:

	For the Years Ended		
	January 30, 2010	January 31, 2009	February 2, 2008
Men's apparel and accessories........................	40%	42%	38%
Women's apparel and accessories (excluding aerie)	51%	50%	55%
aerie	9%	8%	7%
Total	100%	100%	100%

2. Summary of Significant Accounting Policies

Principles of Consolidation

The Consolidated Financial Statements include the accounts of the Company and its wholly-owned subsidiaries. All intercompany transactions and balances have been eliminated in consolidation. At January 30, 2010, the Company operated in one reportable segment.

Fiscal Year

The Company's financial year is a 52/53 week year that ends on the Saturday nearest to January 31. As used herein, "Fiscal 2010" refers to the 52 week periods ending January 29, 2011. "Fiscal 2009","Fiscal 2008" and "Fiscal 2007" refer to the 52 week periods ended January 30, 2010, January 31, 2009 and February 2, 2008, respectively. "Fiscal 2006" refers to the 53 week period ended February 3, 2007. "Fiscal 2005" refers to the 52 week periods ended January 28, 2006.

Estimates

The preparation of financial statements in conformity with accounting principles generally accepted in the United States of America ("GAAP") requires the Company's management to make estimates and assumptions that affect the reported amounts of assets and liabilities and disclosure of contingent assets and liabilities at the date of the financial statements and the reported amounts of revenues and expenses during the reporting period. Actual results could differ from those estimates. On an ongoing basis, our management reviews its estimates based on currently available information. Changes in facts and circumstances may result in revised estimates.

Recent Accounting Pronouncements

In July 2009, the Financial Accounting Standards Board ("FASB") issued Statement of Financial Accounting Standards ("SFAS") 168, *The FASB Accounting Standards Codification and the Hierarchy of Generally Accepted Accounting Principles*, a replacement of FASB Statement No. 162 *The Hierarchy of Generally Accepted Accounting Principles*. SFAS 168 establishes the FASB Accounting Standard Codification ("ASC") as the single source of authoritative accounting principles recognized by the FASB to be applied by nongovernmental entities in the preparation of financial statements in conformity with GAAP. Effective July 2009, the FASB ASC is considered the single source of authoritative U.S. accounting and reporting standards, except for additional authoritative rules and interpretive releases issued by the Securities and Exchange Commission ("SEC"). The Company adopted SFAS 168, as codified in ASC 105, *Generally Accepted Accounting Principles,* as of October 31, 2009. All accounting references within this Annual Report on Form 10-K have been updated and, therefore, previous references to GAAP have been replaced with references to GAAP as codified in the ASC.

AMERICAN EAGLE OUTFITTERS, INC.

NOTES TO CONSOLIDATED FINANCIAL STATEMENTS — (Continued)

In September 2009, the FASB approved the consensus on Emerging Issues Task Force ("EITF") 08-1, *Revenue Arrangements with Multiple Deliverables,* primarily codified under ASC 605, *Revenue Recognition,* as Accounting Standards Update ("ASU") 2009-13, *Revenue Recognition (Topic 605): Multiple-Deliverable Revenue Arrangements* ("ASU 2009-13"). ASU 2009-13 requires entities to allocate revenue in an arrangement using estimated selling prices of the delivered goods and services based on a selling price hierarchy. The amendments eliminate the residual method of revenue allocation and require revenue to be allocated among the various deliverables in a multi-element transaction using the relative selling price method. This guidance is effective for revenue arrangements entered into or materially modified in fiscal years beginning after June 15, 2010. The Company is currently evaluating the impact that the adoption of ASU 2009-13 will have on its Consolidated Financial Statements.

In January 2010, the FASB issued ASU 2010-06, *Fair Value Measurements and Disclosures Topic 820: Improving Disclosures about Fair Value Measurements* ("ASU 2010-06"). ASU 2010-06 requires new disclosures regarding transfers in and out of the Level 1 and 2 and activity within Level 3 fair value measurements and clarifies existing disclosures of inputs and valuation techniques for Level 2 and 3 fair value measurements. The new disclosures and clarifications of existing disclosures are effective for interim and annual reporting periods beginning after December 15, 2009, except for the disclosure of activity within Level 3 fair value measurements, which is effective for fiscal years beginning after December 15, 2010, and for interim reporting periods within those years. The Company is currently evaluating the impact that the adoption of ASU 2010-06 will have on its Consolidated Financial Statements and disclosures.

Foreign Currency Translation

The Canadian dollar is the functional currency for the Canadian business. In accordance with ASC 830, *Foreign Currency Matters,* assets and liabilities denominated in foreign currencies were translated into U.S. dollars (the reporting currency) at the exchange rate prevailing at the balance sheet date. Revenues and expenses denominated in foreign currencies were translated into U.S. dollars at the monthly average exchange rate for the period. Gains or losses resulting from foreign currency transactions are included in the results of operations, whereas, related translation adjustments are reported as an element of other comprehensive income in accordance with ASC 220, *Comprehensive Income* (refer to Note 10 to the Consolidated Financial Statements).

Cash and Cash Equivalents, Short-term Investments and Long-term Investments

Cash includes cash equivalents. The Company considers all highly liquid investments purchased with a maturity of three months or less to be cash equivalents.

As of January 30, 2010, short-term investments included auction rate securities ("ARS") classified as available for sale that the Company expects to be redeemed at par within 12 months, based on notice from the issuer.

As of January 30, 2010, long-term investments included investments with remaining maturities of greater than 12 months and consisted of ARS classified as available-for-sale that have experienced failed auctions or have long-term auction resets. The remaining contractual maturities of our long-term investments are approximately 17 months to 38 years. The weighted average contractual maturity for our long-term investments is approximately 25 years.

Unrealized gains and losses on the Company's available-for-sale securities are excluded from earnings and are reported as a separate component of stockholders' equity, within accumulated other comprehensive income, until realized. The components of other-than-temporary impairment ("OTTI") losses related to credit losses, as defined by ASC 320 *Investments — Debt and Equity Securities* ("ASC 320"), are considered by the Company to be realized losses. When available-for-sale securities are sold, the cost of the securities is specifically identified and is used to determine any realized gain or loss.

Refer to Note 3 to the Consolidated Financial Statements for information regarding cash and cash equivalents, short-term investments and long-term investments.

AMERICAN EAGLE OUTFITTERS, INC.

NOTES TO CONSOLIDATED FINANCIAL STATEMENTS — (Continued)

Other-than-Temporary Impairment

The Company evaluates its investments for impairment in accordance with ASC 320. ASC 320 provides guidance for determining when an investment is considered impaired, whether impairment is other-than-temporary, and measurement of an impairment loss. An investment is considered impaired if the fair value of the investment is less than its cost. If, after consideration of all available evidence to evaluate the realizable value of its investment, impairment is determined to be other-than-temporary, then an impairment loss is recognized in the Consolidated Statement of Operations equal to the difference between the investment's cost and its fair value. As of May 3, 2009, the Company adopted ASC 320-10-65, *Transition Related to FSP FAS 115-2 and FAS 124-2, Recognition and Presentation of Other-Than-Temporary-Impairments* ("ASC 320-10-65"), which modifies the requirements for recognizing OTTI and changes the impairment model for debt securities. In addition, ASC 320-10-65 requires additional disclosures relating to debt and equity securities both in the interim and annual periods as well as requires the Company to present total OTTI in the Consolidated Statements of Operations, with an offsetting reduction for any non-credit loss impairment amount recognized in other comprehensive income ("OCI"). During Fiscal 2009, the Company recorded net impairment loss recognized in earnings related to credit losses on its investment securities of $0.9 million. During Fiscal 2008, the Company recorded net impairment loss recognized in earnings of $22.9 million in earnings related to certain investment securities.

Refer to Notes 3 and 4 to the Consolidated Financial Statements for additional information regarding net impairment loss recognized in earnings.

Merchandise Inventory

Merchandise inventory is valued at the lower of average cost or market, utilizing the retail method. Average cost includes merchandise design and sourcing costs and related expenses. The Company records merchandise receipts at the time merchandise is delivered to the foreign shipping port by the manufacturer (FOB port). This is the point at which title and risk of loss transfer to the Company.

The Company reviews its inventory levels to identify slow-moving merchandise and generally uses mark-downs to clear merchandise. Additionally, the Company estimates a markdown reserve for future planned permanent markdowns related to current inventory. Markdowns may occur when inventory exceeds customer demand for reasons of style, seasonal adaptation, changes in customer preference, lack of consumer acceptance of fashion items, competition, or if it is determined that the inventory in stock will not sell at its currently ticketed price. Such markdowns may have a material adverse impact on earnings, depending on the extent and amount of inventory affected. The Company also estimates a shrinkage reserve for the period between the last physical count and the balance sheet date. The estimate for the shrinkage reserve, based on historical results, can be affected by changes in merchandise mix and changes in actual shrinkage trends.

Property and Equipment

Property and equipment is recorded on the basis of cost with depreciation computed utilizing the straight-line method over the assets' estimated useful lives. The useful lives of our major classes of assets are as follows:

Buildings	25 years
Leasehold improvements	Lesser of 10 years or the term of the lease
Fixtures and equipment	5 years

In accordance with ASC 360, *Property, Plant, and Equipment*, the Company's management evaluates the value of leasehold improvements and store fixtures associated with retail stores, which have been open for a period of time sufficient to reach maturity. The Company evaluates long-lived assets for impairment at the individual store level, which is the lowest level at which individual cash flows can be identified. Impairment losses are recorded on long-lived assets used in operations when events and circumstances indicate that the assets might be impaired and the undiscounted cash flows estimated to be generated by those assets are less than the carrying amounts of the assets.

AMERICAN EAGLE OUTFITTERS, INC.

NOTES TO CONSOLIDATED FINANCIAL STATEMENTS — (Continued)

When events such as these occur, the impaired assets are adjusted to their estimated fair value and an impairment loss is recorded separately as a component of operating income under loss on impairment of assets.

During Fiscal 2009, the Company recorded asset impairment charges of $18.0 million related primarily to the impairment of 10 M+O stores. During Fiscal 2008 the Company recorded asset impairment charges of $6.7 million related primarily to the impairment of five M+O stores. Based on the Company's review of the operating performance and projections of future performance of these stores, the Company determined that these stores would not be able to generate sufficient cash flow over the life of the related leases to recover the Company's initial investment in them. During Fiscal 2007, the Company recognized impairment losses of $0.6 million related to AE stores.

When the Company closes, remodels or relocates a store prior to the end of its lease term, the remaining net book value of the assets related to the store is recorded as a write-off of assets. During Fiscal 2009, Fiscal 2008 and Fiscal 2007, the Company recorded $2.3 million, $4.9 million and $6.7 million related to asset write-offs within depreciation and amortization expense.

Refer to Note 15 to the Consolidated Financial Statements for additional information regarding the planned closure of MARTIN+OSA.

Goodwill

As of January 30, 2010, the Company had approximately $11.2 million of goodwill compared to $10.7 million as of January 31, 2009. The Company's goodwill is primarily related to the acquisition of its importing operations on January 31, 2000, as well as the acquisition of its Canadian business on November 29, 2000. The increase in goodwill is due to the fluctuation in the foreign exchange spot rate at which the Canadian goodwill is translated. In accordance with ASC 350, *Intangibles-Goodwill and Other,* the Company evaluates goodwill for possible impairment on at least an annual basis and last performed an annual impairment test as of January 30, 2010. Resulting from the Company's annual goodwill impairment test performed as of January 30, 2010, the Company concluded that its goodwill was not impaired.

Other Assets, Net

Other assets, net consist primarily of assets related to our deferred compensation plans and trademark costs, net of accumulated amortization. Trademark costs are amortized over five to 15 years.

Deferred Lease Credits

Deferred lease credits represent the unamortized portion of construction allowances received from landlords related to the Company's retail stores. Construction allowances are generally comprised of cash amounts received by the Company from its landlords as part of the negotiated lease terms. The Company records a receivable and a deferred lease credit liability at the lease commencement date (date of initial possession of the store). The deferred lease credit is amortized on a straight-line basis as a reduction of rent expense over the term of the original lease (including the pre-opening, build-out period) and any subsequent renewal terms. The receivable is reduced as amounts are received from the landlord.

Self-Insurance Liability

The Company is self-insured for certain losses related to employee medical benefits and worker's compensation. Costs for self-insurance claims filed and claims incurred but not reported are accrued based on known claims and historical experience. Management believes that it has adequately reserved for its self-insurance liability, which is capped through the use of stop loss contracts with insurance companies. However, any significant variation of future claims from historical trends could cause actual results to differ from the accrued liability.

AMERICAN EAGLE OUTFITTERS, INC.

NOTES TO CONSOLIDATED FINANCIAL STATEMENTS — (Continued)

Co-branded Credit Card and Customer Loyalty Program

The Company offers a co-branded credit card (the "AE Visa Card") and a private label credit card (the "AE Credit Card") under both the American Eagle and aerie brands. Both of these credit cards are issued by a third-party bank (the "Bank"), and the Company has no liability to the Bank for bad debt expense, provided that purchases are made in accordance with the Bank's procedures. Once a customer is approved to receive the AE Visa Card and the card is activated, the customer is eligible to participate in the Company's credit card rewards program. Under the rewards program that expired on December 31, 2009, points were earned on purchases made with the AE Visa Card at AE and aerie, and at other retailers where the card is accepted. Points earned under this credit card reward program resulted in the issuance of an AE gift card when a certain point threshold was reached. The AE gift card does not expire; however, points earned that have not been used towards the issuance of an AE gift card expire after 36 months of no purchase activity. On January 1, 2010, the Company modified the benefits on the AE Visa and AE Credit Card programs to make both credit cards a part of the rewards program. Customers who make purchases at AE, aerie and 77kids earn discounts in the form of savings certificates when certain purchase levels are reached. Also, AE Visa Card customers, who make purchases at other retailers where the card is accepted, earn additional discounts. Savings certificates are valid for 90 days from issuance.

Points earned under the credit card rewards program on purchases at AE and aerie are accounted for by analogy to ASC 605-25, *Revenue Recognition, Multiple Element Arrangements* ("ASC 605-25"). The Company believes that points earned under its point and loyalty programs represent deliverables in a multiple element arrangement rather than a rebate or refund of cash. Accordingly, the portion of the sales revenue attributed to the award points is deferred and recognized when the award is redeemed or when the points expire. Additionally, credit card reward points earned on non-AE or aerie purchases are accounted for in accordance with ASC 605-25. As the points are earned, a current liability is recorded for the estimated cost of the award, and the impact of adjustments is recorded in cost of sales.

Through December 31, 2009, the Company offered its customers the AE All-Access Pass, a customer loyalty program. On January 1, 2010, the Company replaced the Pass with the AEREWARD$^{sm} Loyalty Program (the "Program"). Under either loyalty program, customers accumulate points based on purchase activity and earn rewards by reaching certain point thresholds during three-month earning periods. Rewards earned during these periods are valid through the stated expiration date, which is approximately one month from the mailing date. These rewards can be redeemed for a discount on a purchase of merchandise. Rewards not redeemed during the one-month redemption period are forfeited. The Company determined that rewards earned using the Pass and the Program should be accounted for in accordance with ASC 605-25. Accordingly, the portion of the sales revenue attributed to the award credits is deferred and recognized when the awards are redeemed or expire.

Stock Repurchases

During Fiscal 2007, the Company's Board of Directors ("the Board") authorized a total of 60.0 million shares of its common stock for repurchase under its share repurchase program with expiration dates extending into Fiscal 2010. During Fiscal 2007, the Company repurchased 18.7 million shares as part of its publicly announced repurchase programs for approximately $438.3 million, at a weighted average price of $23.38 per share. The Company did not repurchase any common stock as part of its publicly announced repurchase program during Fiscal 2009 or Fiscal 2008. At January 30, 2010, the authorization to repurchase 11.3 million shares of the Company's common stock under its share repurchase program expired. As of March 26, 2010, the Company had 30.0 million shares remaining authorized for repurchase. These shares will be repurchased at the Company's discretion. The authorization relating to the remaining 30.0 million shares expires at the end of Fiscal 2010.

During Fiscal 2009 and Fiscal 2008, the Company repurchased approximately 18,000 and 0.2 million shares, respectively, from certain employees at market prices totaling $0.2 million and $3.4 million, respectively. These shares were repurchased for the payment of taxes in connection with the vesting of share-based payments, as permitted under the 2005 Stock Award and Incentive Plan, as amended (the "2005 Plan").

AMERICAN EAGLE OUTFITTERS, INC.

NOTES TO CONSOLIDATED FINANCIAL STATEMENTS — (Continued)

The aforementioned share repurchases have been recorded as treasury stock.

Income Taxes

The Company calculates income taxes in accordance with ASC 740, *Income Taxes* ("ASC 740"), which requires the use of the asset and liability method. Under this method, deferred tax assets and liabilities are recognized based on the difference between the Consolidated Financial Statement carrying amounts of existing assets and liabilities and their respective tax bases as computed pursuant to ASC 740. Deferred tax assets and liabilities are measured using the tax rates, based on certain judgments regarding enacted tax laws and published guidance, in effect in the years when those temporary differences are expected to reverse. A valuation allowance is established against the deferred tax assets when it is more likely than not that some portion or all of the deferred taxes may not be realized. Changes in the Company's level and composition of earnings, tax laws or the deferred tax valuation allowance, as well as the results of tax audits, may materially impact the Company's effective tax rate.

Effective February 4, 2007, the Company adopted the accounting pronouncement now codified in ASC 740 regarding accounting for unrecognized tax benefits. This pronouncement prescribes a comprehensive model for recognizing, measuring, presenting and disclosing in the financial statements tax positions taken or expected to be taken on a tax return, including a decision whether to file or not to file in a particular jurisdiction. Under ASC 740, a tax benefit from an uncertain position may be recognized only if it is "more likely than not" that the position is sustainable based on its technical merits.

The calculation of the deferred tax assets and liabilities, as well as the decision to recognize a tax benefit from an uncertain position and to establish a valuation allowance require management to make estimates and assumptions. The Company believes that its assumptions and estimates are reasonable, although actual results may have a positive or negative material impact on the balances of deferred tax assets and liabilities, valuation allowances or net income.

Revenue Recognition

Revenue is recorded for store sales upon the purchase of merchandise by customers. The Company's e-commerce operation records revenue upon the estimated customer receipt date of the merchandise. Shipping and handling revenues are included in net sales. Sales tax collected from customers is excluded from revenue and is included as part of accrued income and other taxes on the Company's Consolidated Balance Sheets.

Revenue is recorded net of estimated and actual sales returns and deductions for coupon redemptions and other promotions. The Company records the impact of adjustments to its sales return reserve quarterly within net sales and cost of sales. The sales return reserve reflects an estimate of sales returns based on projected merchandise returns determined through the use of historical average return percentages.

	For the Years Ended	
	January 30, 2010	January 31, 2009
	(In thousands)	
Beginning balance	$ 4,092	$ 4,683
Returns	(74,540)	(81,704)
Provisions	75,293	81,113
Ending balance	$ 4,845	$ 4,092

Revenue is not recorded on the purchase of gift cards. A current liability is recorded upon purchase, and revenue is recognized when the gift card is redeemed for merchandise. Additionally, the Company recognizes revenue on unredeemed gift cards based on an estimate of the amounts that will not be redeemed ("gift card breakage"), determined through historical redemption trends. Gift card breakage revenue is recognized in

AMERICAN EAGLE OUTFITTERS, INC.

NOTES TO CONSOLIDATED FINANCIAL STATEMENTS — (Continued)

proportion to actual gift card redemptions as a component of net sales. For further information on the Company's gift card program, refer to the Gift Cards caption below.

The Company sells off end-of-season, overstock, and irregular merchandise to a third-party. The proceeds from these sales are presented on a gross basis, with proceeds and cost of sell-offs recorded in net sales and cost of sales, respectively.

	For the Years Ended		
	January 30, 2010	January 31, 2009	February 2, 2008
	(In thousands)		
Proceeds from sell-offs.	$31,889	$38,240	$23,775
Marked-down cost of merchandise disposed of via sell-offs . .	$31,345	$38,012	$25,805

Cost of Sales, Including Certain Buying, Occupancy and Warehousing Expenses

Cost of sales consists of merchandise costs, including design, sourcing, importing and inbound freight costs, as well as markdowns, shrinkage and certain promotional costs (collectively "merchandise costs") and buying, occupancy and warehousing costs. Buying, occupancy and warehousing costs consist of compensation, employee benefit expenses and travel for our buyers and certain senior merchandising executives; rent and utilities related to our stores, corporate headquarters, distribution centers and other office space; freight from our distribution centers to the stores; compensation and supplies for our distribution centers, including purchasing, receiving and inspection costs; and shipping and handling costs related to our e-commerce operation. Merchandise margin is the difference between net sales and merchandise costs. Gross profit is the difference between net sales and cost of sales.

Selling, General and Administrative Expenses

Selling, general and administrative expenses consist of compensation and employee benefit expenses, including salaries, incentives and related benefits associated with our stores and corporate headquarters. Selling, general and administrative expenses also include advertising costs, supplies for our stores and home office, communication costs, travel and entertainment, leasing costs and services purchased. Selling, general and administrative expenses do not include compensation, employee benefit expenses and travel for our design, sourcing and importing teams, our buyers and our distribution centers as these amounts are recorded in cost of sales.

Advertising Costs

Certain advertising costs, including direct mail, in-store photographs and other promotional costs are expensed when the marketing campaign commences. As of January 30, 2010 and January 31, 2009, the Company had prepaid advertising expense of $5.4 million and $2.9 million, respectively. All other advertising costs are expensed as incurred. The Company recognized $68.9 million, $79.7 million and $74.9 million in advertising expense during Fiscal 2009, Fiscal 2008 and Fiscal 2007, respectively.

Design Costs

The Company has certain design costs, including compensation, rent, depreciation, travel, supplies and samples, which are included in cost of sales as the respective inventory is sold.

Store Pre-Opening Costs

Store pre-opening costs consist primarily of rent, advertising, supplies and payroll expenses. These costs are expensed as incurred.

AMERICAN EAGLE OUTFITTERS, INC.

NOTES TO CONSOLIDATED FINANCIAL STATEMENTS — (Continued)

Other (Expense) Income, Net

Other (expense) income, net consists primarily of a realized investment loss, interest income/expense and foreign currency transaction gain/loss.

Gift Cards

The value of a gift card is recorded as a current liability upon purchase and revenue is recognized when the gift card is redeemed for merchandise. Prior to July 8, 2007, if a gift card remained inactive for greater than 24 months, the Company assessed the recipient a one-dollar per month service fee, where allowed by law, which was automatically deducted from the remaining value of the card. For those jurisdictions where assessing a service fee was not allowable by law, the estimated breakage was recorded in a manner consistent with that described above, starting after 24 months of inactivity. Both gift card service fees and breakage estimates were recorded within other (expense) income, net.

On July 8, 2007, the Company discontinued assessing a service fee on active gift cards. As a result, the Company estimates gift card breakage and recognizes revenue in proportion to actual gift card redemptions as a component of net sales. The Company determines an estimated gift card breakage rate by continuously evaluating historical redemption data and the time when there is a remote likelihood that a gift card will be redeemed.

Legal Proceedings and Claims

The Company is subject to certain legal proceedings and claims arising out of the conduct of its business. In accordance with ASC 450, *Contingencies* ("ASC 450"), the Company records a reserve for estimated losses when the loss is probable and the amount can be reasonably estimated. If a range of possible loss exists and no anticipated loss within the range is more likely than any other anticipated loss, the Company records the accrual at the low end of the range, in accordance with ASC 450. As the Company believes that it has provided adequate reserves, it anticipates that the ultimate outcome of any matter currently pending against the Company will not materially affect the consolidated financial position, results of operations or consolidated cash flows of the Company.

Supplemental Disclosures of Cash Flow Information

The table below shows supplemental cash flow information for cash amounts paid during the respective periods:

	For the Years Ended		
	January 30, 2010	January 31, 2009	February 2, 2008
	(In thousands)		
Cash paid during the periods for:			
Income taxes	$61,869	$132,234	$260,615
Interest	$ 1,879	$ 1,947	$ —

Segment Information

In accordance with ASC 280, *Segment Reporting* ("ASC 280"), the Company has identified four operating segments (American Eagle Brand US and Canadian stores, aerie by American Eagle retail stores, MARTIN+OSA retail stores and AEO Direct) that reflect the basis used internally to review performance and allocate resources. All of the operating segments have been aggregated and are presented as one reportable segment, as permitted by ASC 280.

AMERICAN EAGLE OUTFITTERS, INC.

NOTES TO CONSOLIDATED FINANCIAL STATEMENTS — (Continued)

The following tables present summarized geographical information:

	For the Years Ended		
	January 30, 2010	January 31, 2009	February 2, 2008
	(In thousands)		
Net sales:			
United States	$2,715,583	$2,707,261	$2,770,119
Foreign(1)	274,937	281,605	285,300
Total net sales	$2,990,520	$2,988,866	$3,055,419

(1) Amounts represent sales from American Eagle and aerie Canadian retail stores, as well as AEO Direct sales, that are billed to and/or shipped to foreign countries.

	January 30, 2010	January 31, 2009
	(In thousands)	
Long-lived assets, net:		
United States	$678,385	$708,180
Foreign	45,967	42,766
Total long-lived assets, net	$724,352	$750,946

Reclassifications

Certain reclassifications have been made to the Consolidated Financial Statements for prior periods in order to conform to the current period presentation.

3. Cash and Cash Equivalents, Short-term Investments and Long-term Investments

The following table summarizes the fair market value of our cash and marketable securities, which are recorded as cash and cash equivalents on the Consolidated Balance Sheets, our short-term investments and our long-term investments:

	January 30, 2010		
	Balance	Unrealized Holding Gains	Unrealized Holding Losses
		(In thousands)	
Cash and cash equivalents:			
Cash	$144,391	$—	$ —
Commercial paper	25,420		
Treasury bills	119,988		
Money-market	404,161	—	—
Total cash and cash equivalents	$693,960	$—	$ —
Short-term investments:			
Student-loan backed ARS	$ 400	$—	$ —
State and local government ARS	4,275	—	—
Total short-term investments	$ 4,675	$—	$ —
Long-term investments:			
Student-loan backed ARS	$149,031	$—	$ (8,569)
State and local government ARS	35,969	—	(456)
Auction rate preferred securities	12,773	—	(1,287)
Total long-term investments	$197,773	$—	$(10,312)
Total	$896,408	$—	$(10,312)

AMERICAN EAGLE OUTFITTERS, INC.

NOTES TO CONSOLIDATED FINANCIAL STATEMENTS — (Continued)

| | January 31, 2009 | | |
	Balance	Unrealized Holding Gains	Unrealized Holding Losses
		(In thousands)	
Cash and cash equivalents:			
Cash	$ 61,355	$—	$ —
Money-market	411,987	—	—
Total cash and cash equivalents	$473,342	$—	$ —
Short-term investments:			
Preferred stock	$ 6,219	$—	$ —
Auction rate preferred securities	4,292	—	—
Total short-term investments	$ 10,511	$—	$ —
Long-term investments:			
Student-loan backed ARS	$169,254	$—	$(31,446)
State and local government ARS	69,970	—	(630)
Auction rate preferred securities	11,783	—	(3,217)
Total long-term investments	$251,007	$—	$(35,293)
Total	$734,860	$—	$(35,293)

Proceeds from the sale of available-for-sale securities were $80.4 million, $393.6 million and $2.127 billion for Fiscal 2009, Fiscal 2008 and Fiscal 2007, respectively. There were no purchases of investments during Fiscal 2009. The proceeds from the sale of available-for-sale securities for Fiscal 2008 and Fiscal 2007 are offset against purchases of $48.7 million and $1.773 billion, respectively. In addition to the net impairment loss recognized in earnings discussed below for Fiscal 2009 and Fiscal 2008, the Company recorded net realized losses related to the sale of available-for-sale securities of $2.7 million, $1.1 million and $0.4 million for Fiscal 2009, Fiscal 2008 and Fiscal 2007, respectively, in other (expense) income, net.

The following tables present the length of time available-for-sale securities were in continuous unrealized loss positions but were not deemed to be other-than-temporarily impaired:

	Less than 12 Months		Greater than or Equal to 12 Months	
	Gross Unrealized Holding Losses	Fair Value	Gross Unrealized Holding Losses	Fair Value
		(In thousands)		
January 30, 2010				
Student-loan backed ARS	$ (1,643)	$ 9,203	$(6,926)	$50,228
State and local government ARS	(273)	8,096	(183)	20,922
Auction rate preferred securities	—	—	(1,287)	12,773
Total(1)	$ (1,916)	$ 17,299	$(8,396)	$83,923
January 31, 2009				
Student-loan backed ARS	$(31,446)	$169,254	$ —	$ —
State and local government ARS	(630)	61,570	—	—
Auction rate preferred securities	(3,217)	11,783	—	—
Total(1)	$(35,293)	$242,607	$ —	$ —

AMERICAN EAGLE OUTFITTERS, INC.

NOTES TO CONSOLIDATED FINANCIAL STATEMENTS — (Continued)

(1) Fair value excludes $101.2 million as of January 30, 2010 and $8.4 million as of January 31, 2009 of investments whose fair value approximates par. Additionally, as of January 31, 2009, fair value excludes $10.5 million of securities on which net impairment loss recognized in earnings has been recorded.

As of January 30, 2010, we had a total of $896.4 million in cash and cash equivalents, short-term and long-term investments, which included $189.6 million of investments in ARS and $12.8 million of auction rate preferred securities ("ARPS"), net of $10.3 million ($6.4 million net of tax) of temporary impairment and $0.9 million in net impairment loss recognized in earnings. Our short-term and long-term investments consist of the following:

	No. of Issues	Par Value	Cumulative Unrealized Losses Recognized in OCI	Cumulative Losses Recognized in Earnings	Carrying Value as of January 30, 2010
			(In thousands, except no. of issues amount)		
Auction rate securities ("ARS"):					
Closed-end municipal fund ARS	5	$ 17,025	$ (9)	$ —	$ 17,016
Municipal Bond ARS	5	23,675	(447)	—	23,228
Auction rate preferred securities	2	15,000	(1,287)	(940)	12,773
Federally-insured student loan ARS	16	148,000	(6,012)	—	141,988
Private-insured student loan ARS	1	10,000	(2,557)	—	7,443
Total Auction rate securities	29	$213,700	$(10,312)	$(940)	$202,448

Lehman Brothers Holding, Inc. ("Lehman") acted as a broker and auction agent for all of the Company's ARPS. Lehman filed for Chapter 11 bankruptcy protection during September 2008, resulting in the dissolution of the investment trusts for most of the Company's ARPS. As a result, the Company received 760,000 preferred shares in Fiscal 2008 and an additional 576,000 preferred shares in Fiscal 2009. During the 13 weeks ended May 2, 2009, the Company liquidated all 1.3 million shares for $7.8 million and recorded an incremental loss of $2.7 million. The total realized loss on the sale of these securities was $25.6 million, of which $22.9 million was recorded as a net impairment loss recognized in earnings in Fiscal 2008.

The Company continues to monitor the market for ARS and ARPS and consider the impact, if any, on the fair value of its investments. If current market conditions deteriorate further, or the anticipated recovery in market values does not occur, we may be required to record additional impairment.

4. Fair Value Measurements

ASC 820, *Fair Value Measurement Disclosures* ("ASC 820"), defines fair value, establishes a framework for measuring fair value in accordance with GAAP, and expands disclosures about fair value measurements. Fair value is defined under ASC 820 as the exit price associated with the sale of an asset or transfer of a liability in an orderly transaction between market participants at the measurement date. The Company adopted the provisions of ASC 820 as of February 3, 2008, for items measured at fair value on a recurring basis, which consist of financial instruments including ARS and ARPS. The Company adopted the provisions of ASC 820-10-65 *Fair Value Measurements, Transition and Open Effective Date Information, Transition related to FASB Staff Position FAS 157-2, Effective Date of FASB Statement No. 157* as of February 1, 2009 for items measured at fair value on a nonrecurring basis, including goodwill and property and equipment. Additionally, the Company adopted the provisions of ASC 320-10-65 and ASC 820-10-65 *Fair Value Measurements, Transition and Open Effective Date Information, Transition related to FASB Staff Position 157-4, Determining Fair Value When the Volume and Level of Activity for the Asset or Liability*

AMERICAN EAGLE OUTFITTERS, INC.

NOTES TO CONSOLIDATED FINANCIAL STATEMENTS — (Continued)

Have Significantly Decreased and Identifying Transactions That Are Not Orderly as of May 3, 2009 for its financial instruments measured at fair value. The impact of adopting these was not significant on the Company's accompanying financial statements.

Financial Instruments

Valuation techniques used to measure fair value under ASC 820 must maximize the use of observable inputs and minimize the use of unobservable inputs. In addition, ASC 820 establishes this three-tier fair value hierarchy, which prioritizes the inputs used in measuring fair value. These tiers include:

- *Level 1* — Quoted prices in active markets for identical assets or liabilities.

- *Level 2* — Inputs other than Level 1 that are observable, either directly or indirectly, such as quoted prices for similar assets or liabilities; quoted prices in markets that are not active; or other inputs that are observable or can be corroborated by observable market data for substantially the full term of the assets or liabilities.

- *Level 3* — Unobservable inputs (i.e. projections, estimates, interpretations, etc.) that are supported by little or no market activity and that are significant to the fair value of the assets or liabilities.

As of January 30, 2010 and January 31, 2009, the Company held certain assets that are required to be measured at fair value on a recurring basis. These include cash equivalents and short and long-term investments, including ARS and ARPS.

In accordance with ASC 820, the following tables represent the fair value hierarchy for the Company's financial assets (cash equivalents and investments) measured at fair value on a recurring basis as of January 30, 2010 and January 31, 2009:

	Fair Value Measurements at January 30, 2010			
	Carrying Amount as of January 30, 2010	Quoted Market Prices in Active Markets for Identical Assets (Level 1)	Significant Other Observable Inputs (Level 2)	Significant Unobservable Inputs (Level 3)
		(In thousands)		
Cash and Cash Equivalents				
Cash..........................	$144,391	$144,391	$ —	$ —
Commercial paper..............	25,420	25,420	—	—
Treasury bills	119,988	119,988	—	—
Money-market	404,161	404,161	—	—
Total cash and cash equivalents......	$693,960	$693,960	$ —	$ —
Short-term Investments				
Student-loan backed ARS	$ 400	$ —	$ —	$ 400
State and local government ARS ...	4,275	—	—	4,275
Total Short-term Investments........	$ 4,675	$ —	$ —	$ 4,675
Long-term Investments				
Student-loan backed ARS	$149,031	$ —	$ —	$149,031
State and local government ARS ...	35,969	—	—	35,969
Auction rate preferred securities ...	12,773	—	—	12,773
Total Long-term Investments........	$197,773	$ —	$ —	$197,773
Total	$896,408	$693,960	$ —	$202,448
Percent to total.................	100.0%	77.4%	0.0%	22.6%

AMERICAN EAGLE OUTFITTERS, INC.

NOTES TO CONSOLIDATED FINANCIAL STATEMENTS — (Continued)

	Fair Value Measurements at January 31, 2009			
	Carrying Amount as of January 31, 2009	Quoted Market Prices in Active Markets for Identical Assets (Level 1)	Significant Other Observable Inputs (Level 2)	Significant Unobservable Inputs (Level 3)
		(In thousands)		
Cash and Cash Equivalents				
Cash	$ 61,355	$ 61,355	$ —	$ —
Money-market	411,987	411,987	—	—
Total cash and cash equivalents	$473,342	$473,342	$ —	$ —
Short-term Investments				
Preferred Stock	$ 6,219	$ 6,219	$ —	$ —
Auction rate preferred securities	4,292	—	4,292	
Total Short-term Investments	$ 10,511	$ 6,219	$4,292	$ —
Long-term Investments				
Student-loan backed ARS	$169,254	$ —	$ —	$169,254
State and local government ARS	69,970	—	—	69,970
Auction rate preferred securities	11,783	—	—	11,783
Total Long-term Investments	$251,007	$ —	$ —	$251,007
Total	$734,860	$479,561	$4,292	$251,007
Percent to total	100.0%	65.3%	0.6%	34.1%

The Company used a discounted cash flow ("DCF") model to value our Level 3 investments. For Fiscal 2009, the assumptions in the Company's model included different recovery periods, ranging from 0.5 year to 11 years, depending on the type of security and varying discount factors for yield, ranging from 0.3% to 6.6%, and illiquidity, ranging from 0.3% to 4.0%. For Fiscal 2008, the assumptions in the Company's model included different recovery periods, ranging from 1.1 years to 11 years, depending on the type of security and varying discount factors for yield, ranging from 1.7% to 18.8%, and illiquidity, ranging from 0.0% to 1.0%. These assumptions are subjective. They are based on the Company's current judgment and view of current market conditions. The use of different assumptions would result in a different valuation and related charge. As a result of the discounted cash flow analysis for Fiscal 2009, the Company recorded a net recovery of $25.0 million ($15.5 million, net of tax) which reduced the total cumulative impairment recognized in other comprehensive income ("OCI") as of January 30, 2010 to $10.3 million ($6.4 million, net of tax) from $35.3 million ($21.8 million, net of tax) at the end of Fiscal 2008. The reversal of temporary impairment was primarily driven by calls at par for the Company's private-insured student loan ARS. As a result of the calls, the securities which were previously impaired were revalued at par. These amounts were recorded in OCI and resulted in an increase in the investments' estimated fair values. The net increase in fair value was partially offset by $0.9 million of net impairment loss recognized in earnings during Fiscal 2009 as a result of credit rating downgrades.

AMERICAN EAGLE OUTFITTERS, INC.

NOTES TO CONSOLIDATED FINANCIAL STATEMENTS — (Continued)

The following table presents a rollforward of the amount of net impairment loss recognized in earnings related to credit losses:

	For the Year Ended January 30, 2010 (In thousands)
Beginning balance of credit losses previously recognized in earnings	$ —
Year-to-date OTTI credit losses recognized in earnings.	940
Ending balance of cumulative credit losses recognized in earnings	$940

The reconciliation of our assets measured at fair value on a recurring basis using unobservable inputs (Level 3) is as follows:

	Level 3 (Unobservable Inputs)			
	Total	Auction-Rate Municipal Securities	Student Loan-Backed Auction-Rate Securities	Auction-Rate Preferred Securities
Carrying value at February 2, 2008	$ —	$ —	$ —	$ —
Additions to Level 3 upon adoption of ASC 820(1)	340,475	84,575	212,000	43,900
Settlements.	(29,875)	(18,575)	(11,300)	—
Additions to Level 3(2).	4,600	4,600	—	—
Transfers out of Level 3(3)	(28,900)	—	—	(28,900)
Losses:				
Losses reported in OCI	(35,293)	(630)	(31,446)	(3,217)
Balance at January 31, 2009	$251,007	$ 69,970	$169,254	$ 11,783
Settlements.	(72,600)	(29,900)	(42,700)	—
Gains and (losses):				
Reported in earnings	(940)	—	—	(940)
Reported in OCI	24,981	174	22,877	1,930
Balance at January 30, 2010	$202,448	$ 40,244	$149,431	$ 12,773

(1) Represents amounts transferred upon the adoption of ASC 820 during the first quarter of Fiscal 2008.

(2) Additions to Level 3 include securities previously classified as Level 2, which were securities that had experienced partial calls prior to the fourth quarter of 2008 and were previously valued at par.

(3) Transfers out of Level 3 include preferred securities (into Level 1) and ARPS (into Level 2). The transfers to Level 1 occurred due to the Company acquiring exchange traded preferred shares as a result of the ARPS trusts liquidating. The transfers to Level 2 occurred as a result of the Company determining that it was more appropriate to value these investments using observable market prices of the underlying securities. The OTTI charge of $22.9 million that was reported in earnings was taken on Level 1 and Level 2 securities transferred from Level 3.

Non-Financial Assets

The Company's non-financial assets, which include goodwill and property and equipment, are not required to be measured at fair value on a recurring basis. However, if certain triggering events occur, or if an annual impairment test is required and the Company is required to evaluate the non-financial instrument for impairment, a resulting asset impairment would require that the non-financial asset be recorded at the estimated fair value.

AMERICAN EAGLE OUTFITTERS, INC.

NOTES TO CONSOLIDATED FINANCIAL STATEMENTS — (Continued)

Resulting from the Company's annual goodwill impairment test performed as of January 30, 2010, the Company concluded that its goodwill was not impaired.

Certain long-lived assets were measured at fair value on a nonrecurring basis using Level 3 inputs as defined in ASC 820. Based on the Company's review of the operating performance and projections of underperforming stores, the Company determined that certain underperforming stores would not be able to generate sufficient cash flow over the life of the related leases to recover the Company's initial investment in them. The fair value of those stores were determined by estimating the amount and timing of net future cash flows and discounting them using a risk-adjusted rate of interest. The Company estimates future cash flows based on its experience and knowledge of the market in which the store is located. During Fiscal 2009, certain long-lived assets with a carrying value of $18.0 million, primarily related to 10 M+O stores, were determined to be unable to recover their respective carrying values and, therefore, were written down to their fair value, resulting in a loss on impairment of assets of $18.0 million.

5. Earnings per Share

ASC 260-10-45, *Participating Securities and the Two-Class Method* ("ASC 260-10-45"), addresses whether awards granted in unvested share-based payment transactions that contain non-forfeitable rights to dividends or dividend equivalents (whether paid or unpaid) are participating securities and therefore are included in computing earnings per share under the two-class method, as described in ASC 260, *Earnings Per Share*. Participating securities are securities that may participate in dividends with common stock and the two-class method is an earnings allocation formula that treats a participating security as having rights to earnings that would otherwise have been available to common shareholders. Under the two-class method, earnings for the period are allocated between common shareholders and other shareholders, based on their respective rights to receive dividends. Restricted stock awards granted to certain employees under the Company's 2005 Plan are considered participating securities as these employees receive non-forfeitable dividends at the same rate as common stock. ASC 260-10-45 was adopted and retrospectively applied at the beginning of Fiscal 2009. For Fiscal 2009, Fiscal 2008 and Fiscal 2007, the application of ASC 260-10-45 resulted in no material change to basic EPS or diluted EPS.

The following is a reconciliation between basic and diluted weighted average shares outstanding:

	For the Years Ended		
	January 30, 2010	January 31, 2009	February 2, 2008
	(In thousands, except per share amounts)		
Weighted average common shares outstanding:			
Basic number of common shares outstanding	206,171	205,169	216,119
Dilutive effect of stock options and non-vested restricted stock	3,341	2,413	4,161
Dilutive number of common shares outstanding	209,512	207,582	220,280
Basic net income per common share			
Net income	$169,022	$179,061	$400,019
Less: Income allocated to participating securities	365	364	215
Net income available to common shareholders	$168,657	$178,697	$399,804
Basic net income per common share	$ 0.82	$ 0.87	$ 1.85
Dilutive net income per common share			
Net income	$169,022	$179,061	$400,019
Less: Income allocated to participating securities	360	360	210
Net income available to common shareholders	$168,662	$178,701	$399,809
Dilutive net income per common share	$ 0.81	$ 0.86	$ 1.82

AMERICAN EAGLE OUTFITTERS, INC.

NOTES TO CONSOLIDATED FINANCIAL STATEMENTS — (Continued)

Equity awards to purchase approximately 6.6 million, 7.6 million, and 2.5 million shares of common stock during the Fiscal 2009, Fiscal 2008 and Fiscal 2007, respectively, were outstanding, but were not included in the computation of weighted average diluted common share amounts as the effect of doing so would have been anti-dilutive.

Additionally, for Fiscal 2009 and Fiscal 2008, approximately 0.4 million and 0.8 million shares, respectively, of performance-based restricted stock were not included in the computation of weighted average diluted common share amounts because the number of shares ultimately issued is contingent on the Company's performance compared to pre-established annual performance goals.

6. Accounts Receivable

Accounts receivable are comprised of the following:

	January 30, 2010	January 31, 2009
	(In thousands)	
Construction allowances	$11,132	$11,139
Merchandise sell-offs	8,063	17,057
Interest income	217	1,355
Marketing cost reimbursements	2,556	2,363
Credit card receivable	7,832	5,175
Merchandise vendor receivables	375	2,899
Gift card receivable	1,413	115
Franchise receivable	1,419	—
Other	1,739	1,368
Total	$34,746	$41,471

7. Property and Equipment

Property and equipment consists of the following:

	January 30, 2010	January 31, 2009
	(In thousands)	
Land	$ 6,364	$ 6,364
Buildings	151,484	122,414
Leasehold improvements	645,794	605,299
Fixtures and equipment	590,610	536,009
Construction in progress	554	28,543
	$1,394,806	$1,298,629
Less: Accumulated depreciation and amortization	(681,664)	(558,389)
Net property and equipment	$ 713,142	$ 740,240

Depreciation expense is summarized as follows:

	For the Years Ended		
	January 30, 2010	January 31, 2009	February 2, 2008
	(In thousands)		
Depreciation expense	$144,883	$130,802	$108,919

AMERICAN EAGLE OUTFITTERS, INC.

NOTES TO CONSOLIDATED FINANCIAL STATEMENTS — (Continued)

8. Note Payable and Other Credit Arrangements

The Company has borrowing agreements with four separate financial institutions under which it may borrow an aggregate of $325.0 million United States dollars ("USD") and $25.0 million Canadian dollars ("CAD"). Of this amount, $200.0 million USD can be used for demand letter of credit facilities, $100.0 million USD and $25.0 million CAD can be used for demand line borrowings and the remaining $25.0 million USD can be used for either letters of credit or demand line borrowings at the Company's discretion. The $100.0 million USD of demand line credit is comprised of two facilities each with $50.0 million USD of borrowing capacity. The expiration dates of the two demand line facilities are April 21, 2010 and May 22, 2010. The $25.0 million CAD of demand line credit was established during Fiscal 2009, and is provided at the discretion of the lender.

During Fiscal 2009, the Company reduced the amount of credit available that could be used for either letters of credit or as a demand line from $100.0 million USD to $25.0 million USD. This request was made by the lender due to the Company's low utilization of this credit facility. The reduction was effective July 3, 2009 and had no material impact on the Company's Consolidated Financial Statements or on the Company's ability to fund its operations. Additionally, during Fiscal 2009, the Company increased its borrowing capacity for demand letters of credit from $150.0 million USD to $200.0 million USD.

As of January 30, 2010, the Company had outstanding trade and standby letters of credit of $51.5 million USD and demand line borrowings of $30.0 million USD, which reflects a $45.0 million USD reduction from January 31, 2009, as a result of a voluntary partial repayment made during Fiscal 2009. The outstanding amounts on the demand line borrowings can be called for repayment by the financial institutions at any time. Additionally, the availability of any remaining borrowings is subject to acceptance by the respective financial institutions. The average borrowing rate on the demand lines for Fiscal 2009 was 2.5% and the Company has incorporated the outstanding demand line borrowings into working capital.

9. Leases

The Company leases all store premises, some of its office space and certain information technology and office equipment. The store leases generally have initial terms of 10 years. Most of these store leases provide for base rentals and the payment of a percentage of sales as additional contingent rent when sales exceed specified levels. Additionally, most leases contain construction allowances and/or rent holidays. In recognizing landlord incentives and minimum rent expense, the Company amortizes the charges on a straight-line basis over the lease term (including the pre-opening build-out period). These leases are classified as operating leases.

A summary of fixed minimum and contingent rent expense for all operating leases follows:

	For the Years Ended		
	January 30, 2010	January 31, 2009	February 2, 2008
	(In thousands)		
Store rent:			
Fixed minimum	$229,428	$197,820	$167,051
Contingent	7,873	11,767	17,626
Total store rent, excluding common area maintenance charges, real estate taxes and certain other expenses	$237,301	$209,587	$184,677
Offices, distribution facilities, equipment and other	18,664	18,260	17,250
Total rent expense	$255,965	$227,847	$201,927

In addition, the Company is typically responsible under its store, office and distribution center leases for tenant occupancy costs, including maintenance costs, common area charges, real estate taxes and certain other expenses.

AMERICAN EAGLE OUTFITTERS, INC.

NOTES TO CONSOLIDATED FINANCIAL STATEMENTS — (Continued)

The table below summarizes future minimum lease obligations, consisting of fixed minimum rent, under operating leases in effect at January 30, 2010:

Fiscal years:	Future Minimum Lease Obligations
	(In thousands)
2010	$ 242,859
2011	226,699
2012	210,676
2013	194,613
2014	176,612
Thereafter	693,048
Total	$1,744,507

10.   Other Comprehensive Income (Loss)

The accumulated balances of other comprehensive income (loss) included as part of the Consolidated Statements of Stockholders' Equity follow:

	Before Tax Amount	Tax (Expense) Benefit	Accumulated Other Comprehensive Income (Loss)
		(In thousands)	
Balance at February 3, 2007	**$ 21,201**	**$ 513**	**$ 21,714**
Unrealized gain on investments	1,538	(591)	947
Reclassification adjustment for net losses realized in net income related to sale of available-for-sale securities	393	(151)	242
Foreign currency translation adjustment	12,582	—	12,582
Balance at February 2, 2008	**$ 35,714**	**$ (229)**	**$ 35,485**
Temporary impairment related to ARS	(36,825)	14,030	(22,795)
Reclassification adjustment for losses realized in net income related to sale of ARS	318	(121)	197
Reclassification adjustment for OTTI charges realized in net income related to ARS	1,214	(463)	751
Unrealized loss on investments	(607)	229	(378)
Foreign currency translation adjustment	(27,649)	—	(27,649)
Balance at January 31, 2009	**$(27,835)**	**$13,446**	**$(14,389)**
Temporary reversal of impairment related to ARS	24,041	(9,535)	14,506
Reclassification adjustment for OTTI charges realized in net income related to ARS	940	—	940
Foreign currency translation adjustment	15,781	—	15,781
Balance at January 30, 2010	**$ 12,927**	**$ 3,911**	**$ 16,838**

AMERICAN EAGLE OUTFITTERS, INC.

NOTES TO CONSOLIDATED FINANCIAL STATEMENTS — (Continued)

The components of accumulated other comprehensive income (loss) were as follows:

	For the Years Ended	
	January 30, 2010	January 31, 2009
	(In thousands)	
Net unrealized (loss) gain on available-for-sale securities, net of tax(1). . . .	$ (6,401)	$(21,847)
Foreign currency translation adjustment.	23,239	7,458
Accumulated other comprehensive (loss) income	$16,838	$(14,389)

(1) Amounts are shown net of tax of $3.9 million and $13.4 million for Fiscal 2009 and Fiscal 2008, respectively.

11. Share-Based Payments

At January 30, 2010, the Company had awards outstanding under three share-based compensation plans, which are described below.

The Company accounts for share-based compensation under the provisions of ASC 718, *Compensation — Stock Compensation* ("ASC 718"), which requires the Company to measure and recognize compensation expense for all share-based payments at fair value. Total share-based compensation expense included in the Consolidated Statements of Operations for Fiscal 2009, Fiscal 2008 and Fiscal 2007 was $36.9 million ($22.8 million, net of tax), $20.3 million ($12.5 million, net of tax) and $33.7 million ($20.7 million, net of tax), respectively.

ASC 718 requires recognition of compensation cost under a non-substantive vesting period approach. Accordingly, the Company recognizes compensation expense over the period from the grant date to the date retirement eligibility is achieved, if that is expected to occur during the nominal vesting period. Additionally, for awards granted to retirement eligible employees, the full compensation cost of an award must be recognized immediately upon grant.

Share-based compensation plans

1994 Stock Option Plan

On February 10, 1994, the Company's Board adopted the American Eagle Outfitters, Inc. 1994 Stock Option Plan (the "1994 Plan"). The 1994 Plan provided for the grant of 12.2 million incentive or non-qualified options to purchase common stock. The 1994 Plan was subsequently amended to increase the shares available for grant to 24.3 million shares. Additionally, the amendment provided that the maximum number of options that may be granted to any individual may not exceed 8.1 million shares. The options granted under the 1994 Plan were approved by the Compensation Committee of the Board, primarily vest over five years, and expire 10 years from the date of grant. The 1994 Plan terminated on January 2, 2004 with all rights of the optionees and all unexpired options continuing in force and operation after the termination.

1999 Stock Incentive Plan

The 1999 Stock Option Plan (the "1999 Plan") was approved by the stockholders on June 8, 1999. The 1999 Plan authorized 18.0 million shares for issuance in the form of stock options, stock appreciation rights ("SAR"), restricted stock awards, performance units or performance shares. The 1999 Plan was subsequently amended to increase the shares available for grant to 33.0 million. Additionally, the 1999 Plan provided that the maximum number of shares awarded to any individual may not exceed 9.0 million shares. The 1999 Plan allowed the Compensation Committee to determine which employees and consultants received awards and the terms and conditions of these awards. The 1999 Plan provided for a grant of 1,875 stock options quarterly (not to be adjusted for stock splits) to each director who is not an officer or employee of the Company starting in August 2003. The Company ceased making these quarterly stock option grants in June 2005. Under this plan, 33.2 million non-

AMERICAN EAGLE OUTFITTERS, INC.

NOTES TO CONSOLIDATED FINANCIAL STATEMENTS — (Continued)

qualified stock options and 6.7 million shares of restricted stock were granted to employees and certain non-employees (without considering cancellations to date of awards for 7.9 million shares). Approximately 33% of the options granted were to vest over eight years after the date of grant but were accelerated as the Company met annual performance goals. Approximately 34% of the options granted under the 1999 Plan vest over three years, 23% vest over five years and the remaining grants vest over one year. All options expire after 10 years. Performance-based restricted stock was earned if the Company met established performance goals. The 1999 Plan terminated on June 15, 2005 with all rights of the awardees and all unexpired awards continuing in force and operation after the termination.

2005 Stock Award and Incentive Plan

The 2005 Plan was approved by the stockholders on June 15, 2005. The 2005 Plan authorized 18.4 million shares for issuance, of which 6.4 million shares are available for full value awards in the form of restricted stock awards, restricted stock units or other full value stock awards and 12.0 million shares are available for stock options, SAR, dividend equivalents, performance awards or other non-full value stock awards. The 2005 Plan was subsequently amended and restated on June 16, 2009 to, among other things, increase the shares available for grant to 31.9 million effective as of January 31, 2009 without taking into consideration of 9.1 million non-qualified stock options, 2.9 million shares of restricted stock and 0.2 million shares of common stock that had been previously granted under the 2005 plan to employees and directors (without considering cancellations as of January 31, 2009 of awards for 2.9 million shares). The 2005 Plan provides that the maximum number of shares awarded to any individual may not exceed 6.0 million shares per year for options and SAR and no more than 4.0 million shares may be granted with respect to each of restricted shares of stock and restricted stock units plus any unused carryover limit from the previous year. The 2005 Plan allows the Compensation Committee of the Board to determine which employees receive awards and the terms and conditions of the awards that are mandatory under the 2005 Plan. The 2005 Plan provides for grants to directors who are not officers or employees of the Company, which are not to exceed 20,000 shares per year (not to be adjusted for stock splits). Through January 30, 2010, 12.6 million non-qualified stock options, 4.6 million shares of restricted stock and 0.2 million shares of common stock had been granted under the 2005 Plan to employees and directors (without considering cancellations to date of awards for 4.6 million shares). Approximately 99% of the options granted under the 2005 Plan vest over three years and 1% vest over five years. Options were granted for ten and seven year terms. Approximately 97% of the restricted stock awards are performance-based and are earned if the Company meets established performance goals. The remaining 3% of the restricted stock awards are time-based and vest over three years.

Stock Option Grants

The Company grants both time-based and performance-based stock options under the 2005 Plan. Time-based stock option awards vest over the requisite service period of the award or to an employee's eligible retirement date, if earlier. Performance-based stock option awards vest over three years and are earned if the Company meets pre-established performance goals during each year.

AMERICAN EAGLE OUTFITTERS, INC.

NOTES TO CONSOLIDATED FINANCIAL STATEMENTS — (Continued)

A summary of the Company's stock option activity under all plans for Fiscal 2009 follows:

	For the Year Ended January 30, 2010			
	Options	Weighted-Average Exercise Price	Weighted-Average Remaining Contractual Life (In Years)	Aggregate Intrinsic Value (In thousands)
Outstanding — January 31, 2009	14,496,734	$15.25		
Granted.............................	3,402,609	$11.34		
Exercised(1)	1,463,897	$ 7.08		
Cancelled	1,530,504	$16.70	—	—
Outstanding — January 30, 2010	14,904,942	$15.01	3.8	$60,091
Vested and expected to vest — January 30, 2010	14,546,241	$14.99	3.8	$58,809
Exercisable — January 30, 2010	5,031,264	$ 7.13	2.1	$44,063

(1) Options exercised during Fiscal 2009 ranged in price from $4.68 to $13.46.

The weighted-average grant date fair value of stock options granted during Fiscal 2009, Fiscal 2008 and Fiscal 2007 was $3.86, $7.16 and $10.64, respectively. The aggregate intrinsic value of options exercised during Fiscal 2009, Fiscal 2008 and Fiscal 2007 was $11.7 million, $3.9 million and $22.5 million, respectively. Cash received from the exercise of stock options and the actual tax benefit realized from stock option exercises were $7.6 million and $8.0 million, respectively, for Fiscal 2009. Cash received from the exercise of stock options and the actual tax benefit realized from stock option exercises were $3.8 million and $1.1 million, respectively, for Fiscal 2008. Cash received from the exercise of stock options and the actual tax benefit realized from stock option exercises were $13.2 million and $7.3 million, respectively, for Fiscal 2007.

The fair value of stock options was estimated at the date of grant using a Black-Scholes option pricing model with the following weighted-average assumptions:

	For the Years Ended		
Black-Scholes Option Valuation Assumptions	January 30, 2010	January 31, 2009	February 2, 2008
Risk-free interest rates(1)	1.7%	2.5%	4.5%
Dividend yield	3.4%	1.7%	0.9%
Volatility factors of the expected market price of the Company's common stock(2)	56.9%	44.4%	39.2%
Weighted-average expected term(3)...................	4.1 years	4.3 years	4.4 years

(1) Based on the U.S. Treasury yield curve in effect at the time of grant with a term consistent with the expected life of our stock options.

(2) Based on a combination of historical volatility of the Company's common stock and implied volatility.

(3) Represents the period of time options are expected to be outstanding. The weighted average expected option term for the years ended January 30, 2010 and January 31, 2009 were determined based on historical experience. The weighted average expected option terms for the year ended February 2, 2008 was determined using a combination of the "simplified method" for plain vanilla options as allowed by ASC 718, and past behavior. The "simplified method" calculates the expected term as the average of the vesting term and original contractual term of the options.

AMERICAN EAGLE OUTFITTERS, INC.

NOTES TO CONSOLIDATED FINANCIAL STATEMENTS — (Continued)

As of January 30, 2010, there was $8.5 million of unrecognized compensation expense related to nonvested stock option awards that is expected to be recognized over a weighted average period of 1.4 years.

Restricted Stock Grants

Time-based restricted stock awards include two types of awards; time-based restricted stock and time-based restricted stock units. Time-based restricted stock awards vest over three years and participate in nonforfeitable dividends. Time-based restricted stock units vest over three years, however, they may be accelerated to vest over one year if the Company meets pre-established performance goals in the year of grant. Time-based restricted stock units receive dividend equivalents in the form of additional time-based restricted stock units, which are subject to the same restrictions and forfeiture provisions as the original award.

Performance-based restricted stock awards include two types of awards; performance-based restricted stock and performance-based restricted stock units. Performance-based restricted stock awards vest over one year based upon the Company's achievement of pre-established goals and participate in nonforfeitable dividends. Performance-based restricted stock units cliff vest at the end of a three year period based upon the Company's achievement of pre-established goals. Performance-based restricted stock units receive dividend equivalents in the form of additional performance-based restricted stock units, which are subject to the same restrictions as the original award.

The grant date fair value of restricted stock awards is based on the closing market price of the Company's common stock on the date of grant. Historically, the Company has granted only restricted stock awards that entitled the holders to receive nonforfeitable dividends prior to vesting. Beginning with the Fiscal 2009 restricted stock awards, the Company began to also grant restricted stock unit awards to its employees. The restricted stock unit awards differ from the restricted stock awards in that they do not contain nonforfeitable rights to dividends and are therefore not considered participating securities in accordance with ASC 260-10-45.

A summary of the activity of the Company's restricted stock is presented in the following tables.

| | Time-Based Restricted Stock | | Performance-Based Restricted Stock | |
| | For the Year Ended January 30, 2010 | | For the Year Ended January 30, 2010 | |
	Shares	Weighted-Average Grant Date Fair Value	Shares	Weighted-Average Grant Date Fair Value
Nonvested — January 31, 2009	41,000	$19.97	757,812	$21.26
Granted	1,883	13.28	989,664	9.66
Vested	(41,000)	19.97	—	—
Cancelled	—	—	(757,812)	21.26
Nonvested — January 30, 2010	1,883	$13.28	989,664	$ 9.66

| | Time-Based Restricted Stock Units | | Performance-Based Restricted Stock Units | |
| | For the Year Ended January 30, 2010 | | For the Year Ended January 30, 2010 | |
	Shares	Weighted-Average Grant Date Fair Value	Shares	Weighted-Average Grant Date Fair Value
Nonvested — January 31, 2009	—	$ —	—	$ —
Granted	1,855,618	9.79	417,101	9.82
Vested	—	—	—	—
Cancelled	(187,526)	9.66	(10,870)	9.66
Nonvested — January 30, 2010	1,668,092	$9.79	406,231	$9.82

AMERICAN EAGLE OUTFITTERS, INC.

NOTES TO CONSOLIDATED FINANCIAL STATEMENTS — (Continued)

As of January 30, 2010, there was $2.1 million of unrecognized compensation expense related to nonvested restricted stock awards that is expected to be recognized over a weighted average period of one month. The total fair value of restricted stock awards vested during Fiscal 2009, Fiscal 2008 and Fiscal 2007 was $0.6 million, $9.6 million and $32.6 million, respectively.

As of January 30, 2010, the Company had 28.4 million shares available for all equity grants.

12. Retirement Plan and Employee Stock Purchase Plan

The Company maintains a profit sharing and 401(k) plan (the "Retirement Plan"). Under the provisions of the Retirement Plan, full-time employees and part-time employees are automatically enrolled to contribute 3% of their salary if they have attained 20½ years of age. In addition, full-time employee need to have completed 60 days of service and part-time employees must complete 1,000 hours worked to be eligible. Individuals can decline enrollment or can contribute up to 50% of their salary to the 401(k) plan on a pretax basis, subject to IRS limitations. After one year of service, the Company will match 100% of the first 3% of pay plus an additional 50% of the next 3% of pay that is contributed to the plan. Contributions to the profit sharing plan, as determined by the Board, are discretionary. The Company recognized $7.2 million, $6.3 million and $6.1 million in expense during Fiscal 2009, Fiscal 2008 and Fiscal 2007, respectively, in connection with the Retirement Plan.

The Employee Stock Purchase Plan is a non-qualified plan that covers all full-time employees and part-time employees who are at least 18 years old and have completed 60 days of service. Contributions are determined by the employee, with the Company matching 15% of the investment up to a maximum investment of $100 per pay period. These contributions are used to purchase shares of Company stock in the open market.

13. Income Taxes

The components of income before income taxes were:

	For the Years Ended		
	January 30, 2010	January 31, 2009	February 2, 2008
	(In thousands)		
U.S.	$197,948	$244,629	$568,519
Foreign	34,443	52,412	67,862
Total	$232,391	$297,041	$636,381

AMERICAN EAGLE OUTFITTERS, INC.

NOTES TO CONSOLIDATED FINANCIAL STATEMENTS — (Continued)

The significant components of the Company's deferred tax assets and liabilities were as follows:

	January 30, 2010	January 31, 2009
	(In thousands)	
Deferred tax assets:		
Deferred compensation	$ 36,018	$ 21,492
Tax credits	31,756	4,217
Rent	24,498	22,207
Inventories	11,422	14,828
Investment securities	10,677	8,721
Employee compensation and benefits	10,669	3,677
Foreign and state income taxes	7,484	12,984
Temporary impairment of investment securities	3,911	13,446
Other	8,384	10,158
Gross deferred tax assets	144,819	111,730
Valuation allowance	(15,688)	(12,933)
Total deferred tax assets	$129,131	$ 98,797
Deferred tax liabilities:		
Property and equipment	$ (37,896)	$ (36,641)
Prepaid expenses	(3,774)	(1,708)
Total deferred tax liabilities	$ (41,670)	$ (38,349)
Total deferred tax assets, net	$ 87,461	$ 60,448
Classification in the Consolidated Balance Sheet		
Current deferred tax assets	$ 60,156	$ 45,447
Noncurrent deferred tax assets	27,305	15,001
Total deferred tax assets	$ 87,461	$ 60,448

The net increase in deferred tax assets and liabilities was primarily due to an increase in the deferred tax asset for tax credit carryovers associated with the repatriation of earnings from Canada and an increase in the deferred tax asset for deferred compensation.

AMERICAN EAGLE OUTFITTERS, INC.

NOTES TO CONSOLIDATED FINANCIAL STATEMENTS — (Continued)

Significant components of the provision for income taxes were as follows:

	For the Years Ended		
	January 30, 2010	January 31, 2009	February 2, 2008
	(In thousands)		
Current:			
Federal	$ 73,095	$ 69,592	$172,604
Foreign taxes	14,526	16,341	24,030
State	11,948	7,578	27,987
Total current	99,569	93,511	224,621
Deferred:			
Federal	(38,810)	21,927	10,306
Foreign taxes	6,513	(340)	(2,077)
State	(3,903)	2,882	3,512
Total deferred	(36,200)	24,469	11,741
Provision for income taxes	$ 63,369	117,980	$236,362

As a result of additional tax deductions related to share-based payments, tax benefits have been recognized as contributed capital for Fiscal 2009, Fiscal 2008, and Fiscal 2007 in the amounts of $8.0 million, $1.1 million and $7.3 million, respectively.

During Fiscal 2009 the Company approved and repatriated $91.7 million from its Canadian subsidiaries. The proceeds from the repatriation were used for general corporate purposes. We plan to indefinitely reinvest accumulated earnings of our Canadian subsidiaries outside of the United States to the extent not repatriated in Fiscal 2009. Accordingly, no provision for U.S. income taxes has been provided thereon. Upon distribution of those earnings in the form of dividends or otherwise, we would be subject to income and withholding taxes offset by foreign tax credits. As of January 30, 2010, the unremitted earnings of our Canadian subsidiaries were $28.0 million.

As of January 30, 2010, the gross amount of unrecognized tax benefits was $31.6 million, of which $23.4 million would affect the effective income tax rate if recognized. The gross amount of unrecognized tax benefits as of January 31, 2009 was $41.1 million, of which $23.1 million would affect the effective income tax rate if recognized.

The following table summarizes the activity related to our unrecognized tax benefits:

	For the Years Ended		
	January 30, 2010	January 31, 2009	February 2, 2008
	(In thousands)		
Unrecognized tax benefits, beginning of the year balance	$ 41,080	$42,953	$39,311
Increases in tax positions of prior periods	1,679	205	2,562
Decreases in tax positions of prior periods	(13,471)	(1,705)	(5,026)
Increases in current period tax positions	14,842	4,221	8,057
Settlements	(6,204)	(4,529)	(1,764)
Lapse of statute of limitations	(6,291)	(30)	(187)
Translation adjustment	14	(35)	—
Unrecognized tax benefits, end of the year balance	$ 31,649	$41,080	$42,953

AMERICAN EAGLE OUTFITTERS, INC.

NOTES TO CONSOLIDATED FINANCIAL STATEMENTS — (Continued)

Unrecognized tax benefits decreased by $9.5 million and $1.9 million during Fiscal 2009 and 2008, respectively. The decreases were primarily due to federal and state income tax settlements and statute of limitation lapses. The Company does not anticipate any significant changes to the unrecognized tax benefits recorded at the balance sheet date over the next twelve months.

The Company records accrued interest and penalties related to unrecognized tax benefits in the provision for income taxes. Accrued interest and penalties related to unrecognized tax benefits included in the Consolidated Balance Sheet were $7.0 million and $11.4 million as of January 30, 2010 and January 31, 2009, respectively. During Fiscal 2009, the Company recognized a net benefit of $3.3 million in the provision for income taxes related to the reversal of accrued interest and penalties primarily due to federal and state income tax settlements. An immaterial amount of interest and penalties were recognized in the provision for income taxes during Fiscal 2008 and 2007.

The Company and its subsidiaries file income tax returns in the U.S. federal jurisdiction and various state and foreign jurisdictions. The Internal Revenue Service ("IRS") examination of the Company's U.S. federal income tax returns for the tax years ended July 2006 and July 2007 were completed in November of 2009. Additionally, the previously unagreed item for the tax years ended July 2003 to July 2005 was resolved through a review and agreement with IRS Appeals during Fiscal 2009. Accordingly, all years prior to July 2008 are no longer subject to U.S. federal income tax examinations by tax authorities. During Fiscal 2009, the Company changed its tax year end to a 52/53 week year that ends on the Saturday nearest January 31 from July 31 to conform to its financial statement year end. This change was effective for the tax year ended January 31, 2009. An IRS examination of the July 2008 and January 2009 federal income tax returns is scheduled to begin in the first quarter of Fiscal 2010. The Company does not anticipate that any adjustments will result in a material change to its financial position, results of operations or cash flow. With respect to state and local jurisdictions and countries outside of the United States, with limited exceptions, generally, the Company and its subsidiaries are no longer subject to income tax audits for tax years before 2003. Although the outcome of tax audits is always uncertain, the Company believes that adequate amounts of tax, interest and penalties have been provided for any adjustments that are expected to result from these years.

The Company has foreign tax credit carryovers associated with the repatriation of earnings from Canada in the amount of $26.8 million as of January 30, 2010. The foreign tax credit carryovers expire in Fiscal 2019 to the extent not utilized. No valuation allowance has been recorded on the foreign tax credit carryovers because we believe it is more likely than not the foreign tax credits will be utilized prior to expiration.

The Company has been certified to qualify for nonrefundable incentive tax credits in Kansas for additional expenditures related to the Ottawa, Kansas distribution center. As a result, the Company has a deferred tax asset related to Kansas tax credit carryforwards of $5.0 million (net of federal income taxes). These tax credits can be utilized to offset future Kansas income taxes and will generally expire in eight years. The use of these tax credits is dependent upon the level of income tax due to Kansas and the Company meeting certain requirements in future periods. Due to the contingencies related to the future use of these tax credits, we believe it is more likely than not that the full benefit of this asset will not be realized within the carryforward period. Thus, a valuation allowance of $5.0 million (net of federal income taxes) has been recorded as of January 30, 2010. The valuation allowance recorded as of January 31, 2009 was $3.8 million. The Company may earn additional tax credits or change its assessment of the valuation allowance if certain employment and training requirements are met.

During Fiscal 2009 and 2008, the Company recorded a valuation allowance against deferred tax assets arising from the other than temporary impairment or disposition of certain investment securities. The disposition of the investment securities results in a capital loss that can only be utilized to the extent of capital gains. These capital losses are subject to a three year carryback period and a five year carryforward period for tax purposes. The capital losses generally will expire in Fiscal 2014. Due to the contingencies related to the future use of these capital losses, we believe it is more likely than not that the full benefit of this asset will not be realized within the carryforward period. Thus, the Company has recorded a valuation allowance against the deferred tax assets arising from the other than temporary impairment or disposition of these investment securities. The valuation allowance related to these investment securities was $10.7 million and $9.1 million as of January 30, 2010 and January 31, 2009, respectively.

AMERICAN EAGLE OUTFITTERS, INC.

NOTES TO CONSOLIDATED FINANCIAL STATEMENTS — (Continued)

The Company has not recorded a valuation allowance on the temporary impairment of the investment securities recorded in other comprehensive income. The Company believes this treatment is consistent with the Company's intent and ability to hold the debt securities to recovery.

A reconciliation between the statutory federal income tax rate and the effective income tax rate from continuing operations follows:

	For the Years Ended		
	January 30, 2010	January 31, 2009	February 2, 2008
Federal income tax rate	35%	35%	35%
State income taxes, net of federal income tax effect	3	3	3
Canadian earnings repatriation	(7)	—	—
Tax settlements	(5)	—	—
Valuation allowance on ARS and ARPS impairment	1	3	
Tax impact of tax exempt interest	—	(1)	(1)
	27%	40%	37%

14. Quarterly Financial Information — Unaudited

The sum of the quarterly EPS amounts may not equal the full year amount as the computations of the weighted average shares outstanding for each quarter and the full year are calculated independently.

	Fiscal 2009 Quarters Ended			
	May 2, 2009	August 1, 2009	October 31, 2009	January 30, 2010
	(In thousands, except per share amounts)			
Net sales	$611,986	$657,596	$748,962	$971,976
Gross profit	220,925	248,833	300,128	388,163
Net income	21,967	28,572	59,159	59,324
Income per common share — basic	0.11	0.14	0.29	0.29
Income per common share — diluted	0.11	0.14	0.28	0.28

	Fiscal 2008 Quarters Ended			
	May 3, 2008	August 2, 2008	November 1, 2008	January 31, 2009
	(In thousands, except per share amounts)			
Net sales	$640,302	$688,815	$754,036	$905,713
Gross profit	263,667	289,384	309,412	311,638
Net income	43,895	59,831	42,604	32,731
Income per common share — basic	0.21	0.29	0.21	0.16
Income per common share — diluted	0.21	0.29	0.21	0.16

15. Subsequent Event

On March 5, 2010, the Company's Board approved management's recommendation to proceed with the closure of the M+O brand. The Company notified employees and issued a press release announcing this decision on March 9, 2010. The decision to take this action resulted from an extensive evaluation of the brand and review of

AMERICAN EAGLE OUTFITTERS, INC.

NOTES TO CONSOLIDATED FINANCIAL STATEMENTS — (Continued)

strategic alternatives, which revealed that it was not achieving performance levels that warranted further investment.

As a result of this decision, the Company plans to close all 28 stores and cease all online and corporate operations of M+O in Fiscal 2010. The timing of the store closures is dependent on a number of factors that include negotiating third-party agreements, adherence to notification requirements and local laws.

In conjunction with the closing of M+O, the Company expects the Fiscal 2010 cash outflow, net of associated tax benefits, to be approximately $10 million to $40 million. This is comprised of estimated pre-tax charges of approximately $32 million to $77 million, which includes lease-related items of approximately $18 million to $63 million, severance of approximately $10 million and other charges of approximately $4 million. Additionally, the Company estimates approximately $29 million of non-cash, pre-tax impairment charges and inventory write downs. These charges are expected to be recognized primarily over the first half of Fiscal 2010.

The above estimates are preliminary and based on a number of significant assumptions and could change materially.

Refer to Note 2 to the Consolidated Financial Statements for additional information regarding M+O store impairments previously recorded.

The Company has evaluated the existence of subsequent events through the filing date of this Annual Report on Form 10-K.

ITEM 9.   *CHANGES IN AND DISAGREEMENTS WITH ACCOUNTANTS ON ACCOUNTING AND FINANCIAL DISCLOSURE.*

None.

ITEM 9A.   *CONTROLS AND PROCEDURES.*

Disclosure Controls and Procedures

We maintain disclosure controls and procedures that are designed to provide reasonable assurance that information required to be disclosed in our reports under the Securities Exchange Act of 1934, as amended (the "Exchange Act"), is recorded, processed, summarized and reported within the time periods specified in the SEC's rules and forms, and that such information is accumulated and communicated to the management of American Eagle Outfitters, Inc. (the "Management"), including our Principal Executive Officer and our Principal Financial Officer, as appropriate, to allow timely decisions regarding required disclosure. In designing and evaluating the disclosure controls and procedures, Management recognized that any controls and procedures, no matter how well designed and operated, can provide only reasonable assurance of achieving the desired control objectives.

In connection with the preparation of this Annual Report on Form 10-K as of January 30, 2010, an evaluation was performed under the supervision and with the participation of our Management, including the Principal Executive Officer and Principal Financial Officer, of the effectiveness of the design and operation of the Company's disclosure controls and procedures (as defined in Rule 13a-15(e) under the Exchange Act). Based upon that evaluation, our Principal Executive Officer and our Principal Financial Officer have concluded that our disclosure controls and procedures were effective at the reasonable assurance level as of the end of the period covered by this Annual Report on Form 10-K.

Management's Annual Report on Internal Control Over Financial Reporting

Our Management is responsible for establishing and maintaining adequate internal control over financial reporting (as defined in Rule 13a-15(f) under the Exchange Act). Our internal control over financial reporting is designed to provide a reasonable assurance to our Management and our Board regarding the preparation and fair presentation of published financial statements.

All internal control systems, no matter how well designed have inherent limitations. Therefore, even those systems determined to be effective can provide only reasonable assurance with respect to financial statement preparation and presentation.

Our Management assessed the effectiveness of our internal control over financial reporting as of January 30, 2010. In making this assessment, our Management used the criteria set forth by the Committee of Sponsoring Organizations of the Treadway Commission (COSO) in Internal Control — Integrated Framework. Based on this assessment, our Management concluded that we maintained effective internal control over financial reporting as of January 30, 2010.

The Company's independent registered public accounting firm that audited the financial statements included in this Annual Report issued an attestation report on the Company's internal control over financial reporting.

Changes in Internal Control Over Financial Reporting

There were no changes in our internal control over financial reporting during the three months ended January 30, 2010 that have materially affected, or are reasonably likely to materially affect, our internal control over financial reporting.

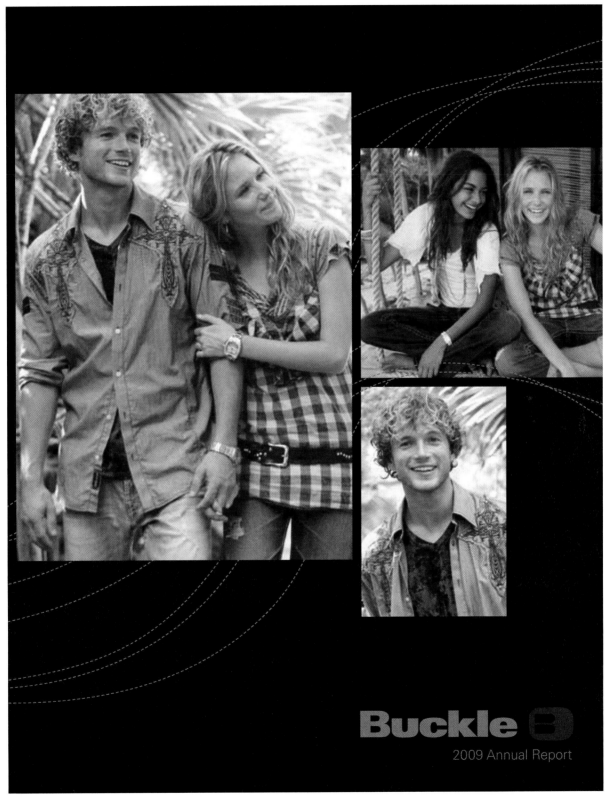

Buckle

2009 Annual Report

FINANCIAL HIGHLIGHTS

(Dollar Amounts In Thousands Except Per Share Amounts And Selected Operating Data)

	JANUARY 30, 2010	JANUARY 31, 2009	FEBRUARY 2, 2008
INCOME STATEMENT DATA			
Net sales	$ 898,287	$ 792,046	$ 619,888
Income before income taxes	$ 204,127	$ 164,868	$ 118,810
Provision for income taxes	$ 76,824	$ 60,459	$ 43,563
Net income	$ 127,303	$ 104,409	$ 75,247
Diluted earnings per share	$ 2.73	$ 2.24	$ 1.63
Net income as a percentage of net sales	14.2%	13.2%	12.1%
BALANCE SHEET DATA			
Working capital	$ 172,779	$ 197,539	$ 184,395
Long-term investments	$ 72,770	$ 56,213	$ 81,201
Total assets	$ 488,903	$ 465,340	$ 450,657
Long-term debt	$ –	$ –	$ –
Stockholders' equity	$ 354,259	$ 337,222	$ 338,320
SELECTED OPERATING DATA			
Number of stores open at year end	401	387	368
Average sales per square foot	$ 428	$ 401	$ 335
Average sales per store (000's)	$ 2,129	$ 1,995	$ 1,668
Comparable store sales change	7.8%	20.6%	13.2%

2009 BUCKLE HIGHLIGHTS

Opened 20 new stores and completed 22 substantial remodels; closed 1 store in April 2009, 1 store in October 2009, and 4 stores in January 2010 to end the fiscal year with 401 stores in 41 states.

Achieved average sales per store of $2.1 million, up from $2.0 million in fiscal 2008.

Average sales per square foot were $428, up from $401 in fiscal 2008.

Total denim sales increased for the tenth consecutive year, with the category representing approximately 43% of fiscal 2009 net sales.

Gross margin improved as a percentage of net sales for the seventh consecutive year, rising to 44.6% from 43.4% in fiscal 2008.

Average transaction value increased 6.4% to $93.85 and average price point increased 3.9% to $45.05.

NET SALES
(Amounts In Thousands)

2005	$ 501,101
2006 (a)	$ 530,074
2007	$ 619,888
2008	$ 792,046
2009	$ 898,287

DILUTED EARNINGS PER SHARE

2005	$ 1.13
2006 (a)	$ 1.24
2007	$ 1.63
2008	$ 2.24
2009	$ 2.73

(a) Consists of 53 weeks.

Fiscal 2009 marked another outstanding year for Buckle on a number of fronts. We achieved record sales of $898.3 million, a 13.4% increase over fiscal 2008. In addition, we reported record earnings of $127.3 million, or $2.73 per diluted share, a 21.9% increase over last year.

Reflecting our continued commitment to creating shareholder value, we returned more than $120.3 million to shareholders throughout the year. On top of our quarterly dividends of $0.20 per share, we paid a special cash dividend of $1.80 per share during the third quarter—marking our third special dividend in the last four fiscal years. This brings our total cash returned to shareholders over the past five years to $502.6 million, including $360.7 million in dividends and $141.9 million in share repurchases. As we look ahead, our balance sheet remains strong with $230.8 million in cash and investments, stockholders' equity of $354.3 million, and no long-term debt.

Our financial results are a function of our focused approach to creating the most enjoyable shopping experience possible for our guests. No matter what is happening in the marketplace, our commitment to delivering a wide selection of quality merchandise and outstanding service to our guests remains constant.

Store Performance – Through the end of 2009, Buckle achieved 13 consecutive quarters of positive comparable store sales. Driven by a 7.8% increase in comparable store sales, our average sales per store increased to $2.1 million from $2.0 million in 2008, and our average sales per square foot increased to $428 from $401. We also improved our gross margin to 44.6% from 43.4% and our operating margin to 22.2% from 20.5%.

Denim – Composing 43% of our total sales, denim continues to serve as the cornerstone of our business. Fiscal 2009 was no exception as we increased denim sales for the tenth year in a row—growing the category by 17.5% and selling a record-level 4.3 million pairs of jeans. Throughout the year, our skilled merchandising team expanded our selection of denim fits, brands, and styles—strengthening our reputation as a denim destination.

Merchandise – Our merchandising team, led by Pat Whisler and Bob Carlberg, did an exceptional job of providing newness by collaborating with an outstanding group of vendors to successfully anticipate trends, develop new styles, and update guests' favorites. Their talent and efforts enabled us to manage our inventory as we achieved record sales for the eighth consecutive year. For the fiscal year, the men's business grew 1.5% on top of growth of 25.5% and 20.5% in each of the past two years and the women's business grew 22.5% on top of growth of 29.5% and 14.0% in the past two years.

Shopping Experience – Led by Kari Smith and Michelle Hoffman, our sales team is driven by high expectations and is dedicated to meeting them. Our 20 district managers, each averaging 21 years with the company, have done a tremendous job of motivating their teams and finding new and innovative ways to educate our teammates—effectively raising the bar for service.

Real Estate – Expansion through carefully selected new store locations in regional malls and lifestyle shopping centers is also an important component of our overall growth. Led by Brett Milkie, our real estate team takes a practical approach to site selection driven by the economics of each individual location and the availability of an internal leader to successfully manage in a particular market. In 2009, we opened 20 new stores, including our first in New York and New Jersey, remodeled 22 stores, and closed 6, ending the year with 401 stores in 41 states. This year, we plan to open 20 new stores and remodel another 25 locations.

Building for the Future – Teammates in the home office and distribution center are essential to our success. Thanks to the efforts of our online team, we increased Buckle.com sales by 45% to $52.3 million. To support this growth, we invested $5.5 million during the year to expand our online fulfillment center. We also broke ground on a new distribution center that is estimated to cost $25-$27 million. Projected to be complete in July 2010, the new facility will be equipped to support more than 600 stores. Plans for 2010 also include the replacement of our point-of-sale software and hardware, allowing us to improve our customer loyalty program and better serve our guests.

As a specialty retailer, we are proud of what we've accomplished, but we're even more excited about where we are headed. Our progress is the collective result of 7,000+ teammates' efforts across all areas of the business. To each of you, I say thank you.

I would also like to take this opportunity to thank our loyal guests for choosing to shop with us. We never forget whom we are here to serve and will work hard to continue to earn your business.

Sincerely,

Dennis H. Nelson
President and Chief Executive Officer

Following a disciplined real estate strategy, we continue to increase our geographic presence by opening new retail locations in regional malls and lifestyle centers across the United States. In 2009, we opened 20 new stores. Plans for 2010 include 20 new stores—including additional stores in New Jersey and New York.

Buckle continues to enhance the in-store shopping experience. Over the past year, we rolled out new mannequins, tables, and fixtures and renovated 22 stores, bringing the total number of locations featuring our signature store design to 222 as of January 30, 2010. Plans for 2010 include 25 additional remodels.

401 STORES IN 41 STATES
(as of January 30, 2010)

★ Buckle Corporate Headquarters in Kearney, Nebraska

▤ 2010 New Store Openings

▤ 2010 Store Remodels & Relocations

Log on to buckle.com for a store locator.

2010 NEW STORE OPENINGS

Mall	Location	Mall	Location
Montgomery Mall	North Wales, PA	Governor's Square Mall	Clarksville, TN
The Domain II	Austin, TX	Arden Fair Mall	Sacramento, CA
The Village at Fairview	Fairview, TX	Kenwood Towne Center	Cincinnati, OH
Northgate Mall	San Rafael, CA	Eastview Mall	Victor, NY
Bellevue Square	Bellevue, WA	Dakota Square	Minot, ND
Cherry Hill Mall	Cherry Hill, NJ	Beachwood Place	Beachwood, OH
The Florida Mall	Orlando, FL	Jacksonville Mall	Jacksonville, NC
Deptford Mall	Deptford, NJ	Park City Center	Lancaster, PA
The Esplanade	Kenner, LA	Waterford Lakes Town Center	Orlando, FL
Crossgate Mall	Albany, NY	Summit Fair	Lee's Summit, MO

UNITED STATES
SECURITIES AND EXCHANGE COMMISSION
WASHINGTON, D.C. 20549

FORM 10-K

☒   **ANNUAL REPORT PURSUANT TO SECTION 13 OR 15(d) OF
THE SECURITIES EXCHANGE ACT OF 1934**

For the Fiscal Year Ended **January 30, 2010**

☐   **TRANSITION REPORT PURSUANT TO SECTION 13 OR 15(d) OF
THE SECURITIES EXCHANGE ACT OF 1934**

For the Transition Period from _____ to _____

Commission File Number: 001-12951

THE BUCKLE, INC.

(Exact name of Registrant as specified in its charter)

Nebraska   **47-0366193**

(State or other jurisdiction of incorporation or organization)   (I.R.S. Employer Identification No.)

2407 West 24th Street, Kearney, Nebraska   68845-4915

(Address of principal executive offices)   (Zip Code)

Registrant's telephone number, including area code: **(308) 236-8491**

Securities registered pursuant to Section 12(b) of the Act:

Title of class	Name of Each Exchange on Which Registered
Common Stock, $0.01 par value	New York Stock Exchange

Securities registered pursuant to Section 12(g) of the Act: None

Indicate by check mark if the registrant is a well-known seasoned issuer, as defined in Rule 405 of the Securities Act. Yes ☐   No ☒

Indicate by check mark if the registrant is not required to file reports pursuant to Section 13 or 15(d) of the Act. Yes ☐   No ☒

Indicate by check mark whether the registrant (1) has filed all reports required to be filed by Section 13 or 15(d) of the Securities Exchange Act of 1934 during the preceding 12 months (or for such shorter period that the Registrant was required to file such reports) and (2) has been subject to such filing requirements for the past 90 days. Yes ☒   No ☐

Indicate by check mark whether the registrant has submitted electronically and posted on its corporate Web site, if any, every Interactive Data File required to be submitted and posted pursuant to Rule 405 of Regulation S-T during the preceding 12 months (or for a shorter period that the registrant was required to submit and post such files). Yes ☐   No ☐

Indicate by check mark if disclosure of delinquent filers pursuant to Item 405 of Regulation S-K is not contained herein, and will not be contained, to the best of the Registrant's knowledge, in definitive proxy or information statements incorporated by reference in Part III of this Form 10-K or any amendment to this Form 10-K ☐.

Indicate by check mark whether the registrant is a large accelerated filer, accelerated filer, non-accelerated filer, or smaller reporting company. (See definition of "large accelerated filer," "accelerated filer," and "smaller reporting company" in Rule 12b-2 of the Exchange Act). Check one.

☑   Large accelerated filer; ☐ Accelerated filer; ☐ Non-accelerated filer; ☐ Smaller Reporting Company

Indicate by check mark whether the registrant is a shell company (as defined in Rule 12b-2 of the Act). Yes ☐No ☒

The aggregate market value (based on the closing price of the New York Stock Exchange) of the common stock of the registrant held by non-affiliates of the registrant was $785,519,774 on July 31, 2009. For purposes of this response, executive officers and directors are deemed to be the affiliates of the Registrant and the holdings by non-affiliates was computed as 25,388,487 shares.

The number of shares outstanding of the Registrant's Common Stock, as of March 26, 2010, was 46,659,195.

DOCUMENTS INCORPORATED BY REFERENCE

Portions of the definitive Proxy Statement for the registrant's 2010 Annual Meeting of Shareholders to be held June 4, 2010 are incorporated by reference in Part III.

ITEM 6 - SELECTED FINANCIAL DATA

SELECTED FINANCIAL DATA

(Amounts in Thousands Except Share, Per Share Amounts, and Selected Operating Data)

	Fiscal Years Ended				
	January 30, 2010	January 31, 2009	February 2, 2008	February 3, 2007 (d)	January 28, 2006
Income Statement Data					
Net sales	$898,287	$792,046	$619,888	$530,074	$501,101
Cost of sales (including buying, distribution, and occupancy costs)	497,668	448,558	365,350	322,760	307,063
Gross profit	400,619	343,488	254,538	207,314	194,038
Selling expenses	168,741	151,251	118,699	107,592	100,148
General and administrative expenses	32,416	30,041	26,212	20,701	17,568
Income from operations	199,462	162,196	109,627	79,021	76,322
Other income, net	3,674	7,829	9,183	9,032	6,123
Gain (loss) - impairment of securities	991	(5,157)	-	-	-
Income before income taxes	204,127	164,868	118,810	88,053	82,445
Provision for income taxes	76,824	60,459	43,563	32,327	30,539
Net income	$127,303	$104,409	$75,247	$55,726	$51,906
Basic earnings per share	$2.79	$2.30	$1.69	$1.29	$1.17
Diluted earnings per share	$2.73	$2.24	$1.63	$1.24	$1.13
Dividends declared per share (a)	$2.60	$2.73	$0.60	$1.71	$0.27
Selected Operating Data					
Stores open at end of period	401	387	368	350	338
Average sales per square foot	$428	$401	$335	$302	$298
Average sales per store (000's)	$2,129	$1,995	$1,668	$1,493	$1,474
Comparable store sales change (b)	7.8%	20.6%	13.2%	0.0%	1.4%
Balance Sheet Data (c)					
Working capital	$172,779	$197,539	$184,395	$189,017	$193,428
Long-term investments	$72,770	$56,213	$81,201	$31,958	$41,654
Total assets	$488,903	$465,340	$450,657	$368,198	$374,266
Long-term debt	-	-	-	-	-
Stockholders' equity	$354,259	$337,222	$338,320	$286,587	$299,793

(a) During fiscal 2005, cash dividends were $0.0533 per share in the first quarter, $0.0667 per share in the second quarter, and $0.0756 per share in the third and fourth quarters. During fiscal 2006, cash dividends were $0.0756 per share in the first and second quarters, $0.0889 per share in the third quarter, and $0.1333 per share in the fourth quarter. In addition, the Company paid a special one-time cash dividend of $1.3333 per share in the fourth quarter of fiscal 2006. During fiscal 2007, cash dividends were $0.1333 per share in the first and second quarters and $0.1667 per share in the third and fourth quarters. During fiscal 2008, cash dividends were $0.1667 per share in the first and second quarters and $0.20 per share in the third and fourth quarters. In addition, the Company paid a special one-time cash dividend of $2.00 per share in the third quarter of fiscal 2008. During fiscal 2009, cash dividends were $0.20 per share in each of the four quarters. The Company also paid a special one-time cash dividend of $1.80 per share in the third quarter of fiscal 2009. Dividend amounts prior to the Company's 3-for-2 stock split with distribution date of January 12, 2007 and 3-for-2 stock split with distribution date of October 30, 2008, have been adjusted to reflect the impact of these stock splits.

(b) Stores are deemed to be comparable stores if they were open in the prior year on the first day of the fiscal period presented. Stores which have been remodeled, expanded, and/or relocated, but would otherwise be included as comparable stores, are not excluded from the comparable store sales calculation. Online sales are excluded from comparable store sales.

(c) At the end of the period.

(d) Consists of 53 weeks.

ITEM 8 - FINANCIAL STATEMENTS AND SUPPLEMENTARY DATA

REPORT OF INDEPENDENT REGISTERED PUBLIC ACCOUNTING FIRM

To the Board of Directors and Stockholders of
The Buckle, Inc.
Kearney, Nebraska

We have audited the accompanying balance sheets of The Buckle, Inc. (the "Company") as of January 30, 2010 and January 31, 2009, and the related statements of income, stockholders' equity, and cash flows for each of the three fiscal years in the period ended January 30, 2010. Our audits also included the financial statement schedule listed in the Index at Item 15. These financial statements and financial statement schedule are the responsibility of the Company's management. Our responsibility is to express an opinion on the financial statements and financial statement schedule based on our audits.

We conducted our audits in accordance with the standards of the Public Company Accounting Oversight Board (United States). Those standards require that we plan and perform the audit to obtain reasonable assurance about whether the financial statements are free of material misstatement. An audit includes examining, on a test basis, evidence supporting the amounts and disclosures in the financial statements. An audit also includes assessing the accounting principles used and significant estimates made by management, as well as evaluating the overall financial statement presentation. We believe that our audits provide a reasonable basis for our opinion.

In our opinion, such financial statements present fairly, in all material respects, the financial position of The Buckle, Inc. as of January 30, 2010 and January 31, 2009, and the results of its operations and its cash flows for each of the three fiscal years in the period ended January 30, 2010, in conformity with accounting principles generally accepted in the United States of America. Also, in our opinion, such financial statement schedule, when considered in relation to the basic financial statements taken as a whole, presents fairly, in all material respects, the information set forth therein.

We have also audited, in accordance with the standards of the Public Company Accounting Oversight Board (United States), the Company's internal control over financial reporting as of January 30, 2010, based on the criteria established in *Internal Control — Integrated Framework* issued by the Committee of Sponsoring Organizations of the Treadway Commission and our report, dated March 31, 2010, expressed an unqualified opinion on the Company's internal control over financial reporting.

/s/ Deloitte & Touche LLP

DELOITTE & TOUCHE LLP
Omaha, Nebraska
March 31, 2010

THE BUCKLE, INC.

BALANCE SHEETS
(Dollar Amounts in Thousands Except Share and Per Share Amounts)

ASSETS	January 30, 2010	January 31, 2009
CURRENT ASSETS:		
Cash and cash equivalents	$ 135,340	$ 162,463
Short-term investments (Notes A, B, and C)	22,687	19,150
Accounts receivable, net of allowance of $35 and $46, respectively	6,911	3,734
Inventory	88,187	83,963
Prepaid expenses and other assets (Note F)	11,684	17,655
Total current assets	264,809	286,965
PROPERTY AND EQUIPMENT (Note D):	305,974	264,154
Less accumulated depreciation and amortization	(159,392)	(147,460)
	146,582	116,694
LONG-TERM INVESTMENTS (Notes A, B, and C)	72,770	56,213
OTHER ASSETS (Notes F and G)	4,742	5,468
	$ 488,903	$ 465,340

LIABILITIES AND STOCKHOLDERS' EQUITY

	January 30, 2010	January 31, 2009
CURRENT LIABILITIES:		
Accounts payable	$ 24,364	$ 22,472
Accrued employee compensation	41,463	40,460
Accrued store operating expenses	8,866	7,701
Gift certificates redeemable	13,507	10,144
Income taxes payable	3,830	8,649
Total current liabilities	92,030	89,426
DEFERRED COMPENSATION (Note I)	5,957	4,090
DEFERRED RENT LIABILITY	36,657	34,602
Total liabilities	134,644	128,118

COMMITMENTS (Notes E and H)

	January 30, 2010	January 31, 2009
STOCKHOLDERS' EQUITY (Note J):		
Common stock, authorized 100,000,000 shares of $.01 par value; 46,381,263 and 45,906,265 shares issued and outstanding at January 30, 2010 and January 31, 2009, respectively	464	459
Additional paid-in capital	78,837	68,894
Retained earnings	275,751	268,789
Accumulated other comprehensive loss	(793)	(920)
Total stockholders' equity	354,259	337,222
	$ 488,903	$ 465,340

See notes to financial statements.

THE BUCKLE, INC.

STATEMENTS OF INCOME
(Dollar Amounts in Thousands Except Per Share Amounts)

	Fiscal Years Ended		
	January 30, 2010	January 31, 2009	February 2, 2008
SALES, Net of returns and allowances of $73,596, $54,973, and $42,087, respectively	$898,287	$792,046	$619,888
COST OF SALES (Including buying, distribution, and occupancy costs)	497,668	448,558	365,350
Gross profit	400,619	343,488	254,538
OPERATING EXPENSES:			
Selling	168,741	151,251	118,699
General and administrative	32,416	30,041	26,212
	201,157	181,292	144,911
INCOME FROM OPERATIONS	199,462	162,196	109,627
OTHER INCOME, Net (Note A)	3,674	7,829	9,183
GAIN (LOSS) - IMPAIRMENT OF SECURITIES (Note B)	991	(5,157)	-
INCOME BEFORE INCOME TAXES	204,127	164,868	118,810
PROVISION FOR INCOME TAXES (Note F)	76,824	60,459	43,563
NET INCOME	$127,303	$104,409	$ 75,247
EARNINGS PER SHARE (Note K):			
Basic	$ 2.79	$ 2.30	$ 1.69
Diluted	$ 2.73	$ 2.24	$ 1.63

See notes to financial statements.

THE BUCKLE, INC.

STATEMENTS OF STOCKHOLDERS' EQUITY

(Dollar Amounts in Thousands Except Share and Per Share Amounts)

	Number of Shares	Common Stock	Additional Paid-in Capital	Retained Earnings	Accumulated Other Comprehensive Loss	Total
BALANCE, February 4, 2007	29,408,576	$ 294	$ 43,493	$ 242,800	$ -	$ 286,587
Net income	-	-	-	75,247	-	75,247
Dividends paid on common stock,						
($.1333 per share - 1st and 2nd quarters)	-	-	-	(12,014)	-	(12,014)
($.1667 per share - 3rd and 4th quarters)	-	-	-	(14,988)	-	(14,988)
Common stock issued on exercise						
of stock options	937,247	9	12,015	-	-	12,024
Issuance of non-vested stock, net of forfeitures	138,345	1	(1)	-	-	-
Amortization of non-vested stock grants,						
net of forfeitures	-	-	3,886	-	-	3,886
Stock option compensation expense	-	-	293	-	-	293
Common stock purchased and retired	(642,500)	(6)	(21,571)	-	-	(21,577)
Income tax benefit related to						
exercise of stock options	-	-	8,862	-	-	8,862
BALANCE, February 2, 2008	29,841,668	298	46,977	291,045	-	338,320
Net income	-	-	-	104,409	-	104,409
Dividends paid on common stock,						
($.1667 per share - 1st and 2nd quarters)	-	-	-	(15,269)	-	(15,269)
($.20 per share - 3rd and 4th quarters)	-	-	-	(18,474)	-	(18,474)
($2.00 per share - 3rd quarter)	-	-	-	(92,922)	-	(92,922)
Common stock issued on exercise						
of stock options	994,555	10	12,714	-	-	12,724
Issuance of non-vested stock, net of forfeitures	139,635	1	(1)	-	-	-
Amortization of non-vested stock grants,						
net of forfeitures	-	-	4,879	-	-	4,879
Stock option compensation expense	-	-	289	-	-	289
Common stock purchased and retired	(557,100)	(5)	(9,354)	-	-	(9,359)
Income tax benefit related to						
exercise of stock options	-	-	13,545	-	-	13,545
3-for-2 stock split	15,487,507	155	(155)	-	-	-
Unrealized loss on investments, net of tax	-	-	-	-	(920)	(920)
BALANCE, January 31, 2009	45,906,265	459	68,894	268,789	(920)	337,222
Net income	-	-	-	127,303	-	127,303
Dividends paid on common stock,						
($.20 per share - 1st, 2nd, 3rd, and 4th quarters)	-	-	-	(37,011)	-	(37,011)
($1.80 per share - 3rd quarter)	-	-	-	(83,330)	-	(83,330)
Common stock issued on exercise						
of stock options	278,430	3	1,823	-	-	1,826
Issuance of non-vested stock, net of forfeitures	196,568	2	(2)	-	-	-
Amortization of non-vested stock grants,						
net of forfeitures	-	-	4,988	-	-	4,988
Stock option compensation expense	-	-	175	-	-	175
Income tax benefit related to exercise						
of stock options	-	-	2,959	-	-	2,959
Unrealized loss on investments, net of tax	-	-	-	-	127	127
BALANCE, January 30, 2010	46,381,263	$ 464	$ 78,837	$ 275,751	$ (793)	$ 354,259

See notes to financial statements.

THE BUCKLE, INC.

STATEMENTS OF CASH FLOWS
(Dollar Amounts in Thousands)

	Fiscal Years Ended		
	January 30, 2010	January 31, 2009	February 2, 2008
CASH FLOWS FROM OPERATING ACTIVITIES:			
Net income	$ 127,303	$ 104,409	$ 75,247
Adjustments to reconcile net income to net cash flows from operating activities:			
Depreciation and amortization	25,135	21,779	20,384
Amortization of non-vested stock grants, net of forfeitures	4,988	4,879	3,886
Stock option compensation expense	175	289	293
Gain on involuntary conversion of aircraft to monetary asset	-	(2,963)	-
(Gain) loss - impairment of securities	(991)	5,157	-
Deferred income taxes	414	(595)	(1,509)
Other	38	574	146
Changes in operating assets and liabilities:			
Accounts receivable	(1,967)	(895)	1,246
Inventory	(4,224)	(6,324)	(7,333)
Prepaid expenses and other assets	6,282	(2,478)	(1,542)
Accounts payable	(2,916)	(844)	8,903
Accrued employee compensation	1,003	12,624	10,036
Accrued store operating expenses	1,165	1,997	1,236
Gift certificates redeemable	3,363	1,633	1,802
Income taxes payable	(5,731)	906	5,576
Long-term liabilities and deferred compensation	3,922	3,581	2,709
Net cash flows from operating activities	157,959	143,729	121,080
CASH FLOWS FROM INVESTING ACTIVITIES:			
Purchase of property and equipment	(50,561)	(47,448)	(27,484)
Proceeds from sale of property and equipment	308	11,819	21
Change in other assets	(74)	(29)	167
Purchases of investments	(52,604)	(46,687)	(153,511)
Proceeds from sales / maturities of investments	33,703	148,818	117,079
Net cash flows from investing activities	(69,228)	66,473	(63,728)
CASH FLOWS FROM FINANCING ACTIVITIES:			
Proceeds from the exercise of stock options	1,826	12,724	12,024
Excess tax benefit from stock option exercises	2,661	11,268	7,744
Purchases of common stock	-	(9,359)	(21,577)
Payment of dividends	(120,341)	(126,665)	(27,002)
Net cash flows from financing activities	(115,854)	(112,032)	(28,811)
NET INCREASE (DECREASE) IN CASH AND CASH EQUIVALENTS	(27,123)	98,170	28,541
CASH AND CASH EQUIVALENTS, Beginning of year	162,463	64,293	35,752
CASH AND CASH EQUIVALENTS, End of year	$ 135,340	$ 162,463	$ 64,293

See notes to financial statements.

THE BUCKLE, INC.
NOTES TO FINANCIAL STATEMENTS
(Dollar Amounts in Thousands Except Share and Per Share Amounts)

A. SUMMARY OF SIGNIFICANT ACCOUNTING POLICIES

Fiscal Year – The Buckle, Inc. (the "Company") has its fiscal year end on the Saturday nearest January 31. All references in these financial statements to fiscal years are to the calendar year in which the fiscal year begins. Fiscal 2009 represents the 52-week period ended January 30, 2010, fiscal 2008 represents the 52-week period ended January 31, 2009, and fiscal 2007 represents the 52-week period ended February 2, 2008.

Nature of Operations – The Company is a retailer of medium to better-priced casual apparel, footwear, and accessories for fashion conscious young men and women operating 401 stores located in 41 states throughout the continental United States as of January 30, 2010.

During fiscal 2009, the Company opened 20 new stores, substantially renovated 22 stores, and closed 6 stores. During fiscal 2008, the Company opened 21 new stores, substantially renovated 13 stores, and closed 2 stores. During fiscal 2007, the Company opened 20 new stores, substantially renovated 7 stores, and closed 2 stores.

Revenue Recognition – Retail store sales are recorded upon the purchase of merchandise by customers. Online sales are recorded when merchandise is delivered to the customer, with the time of delivery being based on estimated shipping time from the Company's distribution center to the customer. Shipping fees charged to customers are included in revenue and shipping costs are included in selling expenses. Shipping costs were $5,420, $3,813, and $1,882 during fiscal 2009, 2008, and 2007, respectively. Merchandise returns are estimated based upon the historical average sales return percentage and accrued at the end of the period. The reserve for merchandise returns was $647 and $526 as of January 30, 2010 and January 31, 2009, respectively. The Company accounts for layaway sales in accordance with FASB ASC 605, *Revenue Recognition*, recognizing revenue from sales made under its layaway program upon delivery of the merchandise to the customer. The Company has several sales incentives that it offers customers including a frequent shopper punch card, B-Rewards gift certificates, and occasional sweepstakes and gift with purchase offers. The frequent shopper punch card is recognized as a cost of goods sold at the time of redemption, using the actual amount tendered. The B-Rewards incentives, based upon $10 for each $300 in net purchases, are recorded as a liability and as a selling expense at the time the gift certificates are earned. Sweepstake prizes are recorded as cost of goods sold (if it is a merchandise giveaway) or as a selling expense at the time the prize is redeemed by the customer, using actual costs incurred, and gifts with purchase are recorded as a cost of goods sold at the time of the purchase and gift redemption, using the actual cost of the gifted item.

The Company records the sale of gift cards and gift certificates as a current liability and recognizes a sale when a customer redeems the gift card or gift certificate. The amount of the gift certificate liability is determined using the outstanding balances from the prior three years of issuance and the gift card liability is determined using the outstanding balances from the prior four years of issuance. The Company records breakage as other income when the probability of redemption, which is based on historical redemption patterns, is remote. Breakage reported for the fiscal years ended January 30, 2010, January 31, 2009, and February 2, 2008 was $434, $389, and $0, respectively. The Company recognizes a current liability for the down payment made when merchandise is placed on layaway and recognizes layaways as a sale at the time the customer makes final payment and picks up the merchandise.

Cash and Cash Equivalents – The Company considers all highly liquid debt instruments with an original maturity of three months or less when purchased to be cash equivalents.

Investments – The Company accounts for investments in accordance with FASB ASC 320, *Investments-Debt and Equity Securities.* Investments classified as short-term investments include securities with a maturity of greater than three months and less than one year, and a portion of the Company's investments in auction-rate securities ("ARS"), which are available-for-sale securities. Available-for-sale securities are reported at fair value, with unrealized gains and losses excluded from earnings and reported as a separate component of stockholders' equity (net of the effect of income taxes), using the specific identification method, until they are sold. The Company reviews impairments in accordance with FASB ASC 320 to determine the classification of potential impairments as either "temporary" or "other-than-temporary." A temporary impairment results in an unrealized loss being recorded in other comprehensive income. Impairments that are considered other-than-temporary are recognized as a loss in the statements of income. The Company considers various factors in reviewing impairments, including the length of time and extent to which the fair value has been less than the Company's cost basis, the financial condition and near-term prospects of the issuer, and the Company's intent and ability to hold the investments for a period of time sufficient to allow for any anticipated recovery in market value. Held-to-maturity securities are carried at amortized cost. The Company believes it has the ability and maintains its intent to hold these investments until recovery of market value occurs. Trading securities are reported at fair value, with unrealized gains and losses included in earnings, using the specific identification method.

Inventory – Inventory is stated at the lower of cost or market. Cost is determined using the average cost method. Management records a reserve for merchandise obsolescence and markdowns based on assumptions using calculations applied to current inventory levels by department within each of four different markdown levels. Management also reviews the levels of inventory in each markdown group, and the overall aging of inventory, versus the estimated future demand for such product and the current market conditions. The calculation for estimated markdowns and/or obsolescence reduced the Company's inventory valuation by $5,832 and $6,228 as of January 30, 2010 and January 31, 2009, respectively. The amount charged (credited) to cost of goods sold, resulting from changes in the markdown reserve balance, was $(396), $439, and $(581), for fiscal years 2009, 2008, and 2007, respectively.

Property and Equipment – Property and equipment are stated on the basis of historical cost. Depreciation is provided using a combination of accelerated and straight-line methods based upon the estimated useful lives of the assets. The majority of property and equipment have useful lives of five to ten years with the exception of buildings, which have estimated useful lives of 31.5 to 39 years. Leasehold improvements are stated on the basis of historical cost and are amortized over the shorter of the life of the lease or the estimated economic life of the assets. When circumstances indicate the carrying values of long-lived assets may be impaired, an evaluation is performed on current net book value amounts. Judgments made by the Company related to the expected useful lives of property and equipment and the ability to realize cash flows in excess of carrying amounts of such assets are affected by factors such as changes in economic conditions and changes in operating performance. As the Company assesses the expected cash flows and carrying amounts of long-lived assets, adjustments are made to such carrying values.

Pre-Opening Expenses – Costs related to opening new stores are expensed as incurred.

Advertising Costs – Advertising costs are expensed as incurred and were $8,521, $7,674, and $6,376 for fiscal years 2009, 2008, and 2007, respectively.

Health Care Costs - The Company is self-funded for health and dental claims up to $200 per individual per plan year. The Company's plan covers eligible employees, and management makes estimates at period end to record a reserve for unpaid claims based upon historical claims information. The accrued liability as a reserve for unpaid health care claims was $700 and $600 as of January 30, 2010 and January 31, 2009, respectively.

Operating Leases – The Company leases retail stores under operating leases. Most lease agreements contain tenant improvement allowances, rent holidays, rent escalation clauses, and/or contingent rent provisions. For purposes of recognizing lease incentives and minimum rental expenses on a straight-line basis over the terms of the leases, the Company uses the date of initial possession to begin expensing rent, which is generally when the Company enters the space and begins to make improvements in preparation of intended use.

For tenant improvement allowances and rent holidays, the Company records a deferred rent liability on the balance sheets and amortizes the deferred rent over the terms of the leases as reductions to rent expense on the statements of income.

For scheduled rent escalation clauses during the lease terms or for rental payments commencing at a date other than the date of initial occupancy, the Company records minimum rental expenses on a straight-line basis over the terms of the leases on the statements of income. Certain leases provide for contingent rents, which are determined as a percentage of gross sales in excess of specified levels. The Company records a contingent rent liability in "accrued store operating expenses" on the balance sheets and the corresponding rent expense when specified levels have been achieved or are reasonably probable to be achieved.

Other Income – The Company's other income is derived primarily from interest and dividends received on cash and investments, but also includes miscellaneous other sources of income.

Income Taxes – The Company records a deferred tax asset and liability for expected future tax consequences resulting from temporary differences between financial reporting and tax bases of assets and liabilities. The Company considers future taxable income and ongoing tax planning in assessing the value of its deferred tax assets. If the judgment of the Company's management determines that it is more than likely that these assets will not be realized, the Company would reduce the value of these assets to their expected realizable value, thereby decreasing net income. If the Company subsequently determined that the deferred tax assets, which had been written down, would be realized in the future, such value would be increased, thus increasing net income in the period such determination was made. The Company records tax benefits only for tax positions that are more than likely to be sustained upon examination by tax authorities. The amount recognized is measured as the largest amount of benefit that is greater than 50% likely to be realized upon ultimate settlement. Unrecognized tax benefits are tax benefits claimed in the Company's tax returns that do not meet these recognition and measurement standards.

Stock Splits – On September 15, 2008, the Company's Board of Directors approved a 3-for-2 stock split payable in the form of a stock dividend for shareholders of record as of October 15, 2008, with a distribution date of October 30, 2008. All share and per share data (except par value and historical stockholders' equity data) presented in the financial statements for all periods has been adjusted to reflect the impact of this stock split.

Financial Instruments and Credit Risk Concentrations – Financial instruments, which potentially subject the Company to concentrations of credit risk, are primarily cash, investments, and accounts receivable. The Company places its investments primarily in tax-free municipal bonds, auction-rate securities, or U.S. Treasury securities with short-term maturities and limits the amount of credit exposure to any one entity.

Of the Company's $230,797 in total cash and investments as of January 30, 2010, $22,792 was comprised of investments in auction-rate securities ("ARS"). ARS have a long-term stated maturity, but are reset through a "dutch auction" process that occurs every 7 to 49 days, depending on the terms of the individual security. Until February 2008, the ARS market was highly liquid. During February 2008, however, a significant number of auctions related to these securities failed, meaning that there was not enough demand to sell the entire issue at auction. The failed auctions have limited the current liquidity of certain of the Company's investments in ARS and the Company has reason to believe that certain of the underlying issuers of its ARS are currently at risk. The Company does not, however, anticipate that further auction failures will have a material impact on the Company's ability to fund its business.

Concentrations of credit risk with respect to accounts receivable are limited due to the nature of the Company's receivables, which include primarily employee receivables that can be offset against future compensation. The Company's financial instruments have a fair value approximating the carrying value.

Earnings Per Share – Basic earnings per share data are based on the weighted average outstanding common shares during the period. Diluted earnings per share data are based on the weighted average outstanding common shares and the effect of all dilutive potential common shares, including stock options. Basic and diluted earnings per share for fiscal 2007 have been adjusted to reflect the impact of the Company's 3-for-2 stock split paid in the form of a stock dividend on October 30, 2008.

Use of Estimates – The preparation of financial statements in conformity with accounting principles generally accepted in the United States of America requires management to make estimates and assumptions that affect the reported amounts of certain assets and liabilities, the disclosure of contingent assets and liabilities at the date of the financial statements, and the reported amounts of revenues and expenses during the reporting period. Actual results could differ from these estimates.

Comprehensive Income – Comprehensive income consists of net income and unrealized gains and losses on available-for-sale securities. Unrealized losses on the Company's investments in auction-rate securities have been included in accumulated other comprehensive loss and are separately included as a component of stockholders' equity, net of related income taxes.

	Fiscal Years Ended		
	January 30, 2010	January 31, 2009	February 2, 2008
Net income	$ 127,303	$ 104,409	$ 75,247
Changes in net unrealized losses on investments in auction-rate securities, net of taxes of $(75), $540, and $0, respectively	127	(920)	-
Comprehensive income	$ 127,430	$ 103,489	$ 75,247

Recently Issued Accounting Pronouncements – Effective February 3, 2008, the Company adopted the provisions of FASB ASC 820, *Fair Value Measurements and Disclosures*. FASB ASC 820 defines fair value, establishes a framework for measuring fair value, and expands disclosures about fair value measurements. The provisions of FASB ASC 820 apply to all financial instruments that are being measured and reported on a fair value basis. In addition, FASB ASC 820-10-15-1A delayed the effective date of FASB ASC 820 to fiscal years beginning after November 15, 2008, and interim periods within those fiscal years, for all non-financial assets and liabilities, except those that are recognized or disclosed at fair value in the financial statements on a recurring basis. The adoption of FASB ASC 820 during fiscal 2008 for all financial instruments and the adoption during fiscal 2009 for all non-financial assets and liabilities did not have any impact on the Company's financial position or results of operations.

Effective February 3, 2008, the Company adopted the provisions of FASB ASC 825, *Financial Instruments*. FASB ASC 825 provides an option for companies to report selected financial assets and liabilities at fair value. Although the Company adopted the provisions of FASB ASC 825 effective with the beginning of the Company's 2008 fiscal year, it did not elect the fair value option for any financial instruments or other items held by the Company. Therefore, the adoption of FASB ASC 825 did not have any impact on the Company's financial position or results of operations.

In May 2009, FASB issued FASB ASC 855, *Subsequent Events*. This guidance requires management to evaluate subsequent events through the date the financial statements are issued, or are available to be issued, and requires companies to disclose the date through which such subsequent events have been evaluated. FASB ASC 855 was effective for financial statements issued for interim or annual reporting periods ending after June 15, 2009. In February 2010, FASB issued Accounting Standards Update 2010-09 which removed the requirement for SEC filers to disclose the date through which subsequent events have been evaluated. The adoption of FASB ASC 855 did not have any impact on the Company's financial position or results of operations. The Company has determined that there were no subsequent events requiring recognition or disclosure in the financial statements presented herein.

In June 2009, FASB issued FASB ASC 105, *Generally Accepted Accounting Principles*, which establishes the FASB *Accounting Standards Codification* ("ASC") as the single source of GAAP recognized by FASB to be applied by nongovernmental entities. Rules and interpretive releases of the Securities and Exchange Commission ("SEC") under authority of federal securities laws are also sources of authoritative GAAP for SEC registrants. On the effective date of FASB ASC 105, the codification superseded all then-existing non-SEC accounting and reporting standards. All other non-grandfathered, non-SEC accounting literature not included in the codification became non-authoritative. FASB ASC 105 was effective for financial statements issued for interim or annual reporting periods ending after September 15, 2009. Therefore, the Company adopted the provisions of FASB ASC 105 on August 2, 2009. The adoption of FASB ASC 105 did not have any impact on the Company's financial position or results of operations.

Supplemental Cash Flow Information - The Company had non-cash investing activities during fiscal years 2009, 2008, and 2007 of $4,808, $1,839, and $1,582, respectively. The non-cash investing activity relates to unpaid purchases of property, plant, and equipment included in accounts payable as of the end of the year. Amounts reported as unpaid purchases are recorded as cash outflows from investing activities for purchases of property, plant, and equipment in the statement of cash flows in the period they are paid.

Additional cash flow information for the Company includes cash paid for income taxes during fiscal years 2009, 2008, and 2007 of $79,480, $48,879, and $31,730, respectively.

B.   INVESTMENTS

The following is a summary of investments as of January 30, 2010:

	Amortized Cost or Par Value	Gross Unrealized Gains	Gross Unrealized Losses	Other-than-Temporary Impairment	Estimated Fair Value
Available-for-Sale Securities:					
Auction-rate securities	$ 24,775	$ -	$ (1,258)	$ (725)	$ 22,792
Municipal bonds	8,116	14	(14)	-	8,116
Preferred stock	2,000	-	-	(1,974)	26
	$ 34,891	$ 14	$ (1,272)	$ (2,699)	$ 30,934
Held-to-Maturity Securities:					
State and municipal bonds	$ 47,036	$ 535	$ (10)	-	$ 47,561
Fixed maturities	8,890	92	-	-	8,982
Certificates of deposit	1,640	27	-	-	1,667
U.S. treasuries	1,000	1	-	-	1,001
	$ 58,566	$ 655	$ (10)	$ -	$ 59,211
Trading Securities:					
Mutual funds	$ 6,200	$ -	$ (243)	$ -	$ 5,957

The following is a summary of investments as of January 31, 2009:

	Amortized Cost or Par Value	Gross Unrealized Gains	Gross Unrealized Losses	Other-than-Temporary Impairment	Estimated Fair Value
Available-for-Sale Securities:					
Auction-rate securities	$ 35,495	$ -	$ (1,460)	$ (3,757)	$ 30,278
Preferred stock	2,000	-	-	(1,400)	600
	$ 37,495	$ -	$ (1,460)	$ (5,157)	$ 30,878
Held-to-Maturity Securities:					
State and municipal bonds	$ 31,965	$ 536	$ (90)	-	$ 32,411
Fixed maturities	2,500	37	(7)	-	2,530
Certificates of deposit	2,945	42	-	-	2,987
U.S. treasuries	2,985	19	(9)	-	2,995
	$ 40,395	$ 634	$ (106)	$ -	$ 40,923
Trading Securities:					
Mutual funds	$ 5,165	$ -	$ (1,075)	$ -	$ 4,090

The auction-rate securities and preferred stock were invested as follows as of January 30, 2010:

Nature	Underlying Collateral	Par Value
Municipal revenue bonds	92% insured by AAA/AA/A-rated bond insurers at January 30, 2010	$11,700
Municipal bond funds	Fixed income instruments within issuers' money market funds	9,325
Student loan bonds	Student loans guaranteed by state entities	3,750
Preferred stock	Underlying investments of closed-end funds	2,000
Total par value		$26,775

As of January 30, 2010, the Company's auction-rate securities portfolio was 57% AAA/Aaa-rated, 27% AA/Aa-rated, 9% A-rated, and 7% below A-rated.

The amortized cost and fair value of debt securities by contractual maturity as of January 30, 2010 is as follows:

	Amortized Cost	Fair Value
Available-for-sale securities		
Less than 1 year	$ 2,950	$ 2,950
1 - 5 years	1,452	1,454
5 - 10 years	1,206	1,209
Greater than 10 years	2,508	2,503
	$ 8,116	$ 8,116
Held-to-maturity securities		
Less than 1 year	$ 18,387	$ 18,520
1 - 5 years	35,802	36,234
5 - 10 years	1,926	1,978
Greater than 10 years	2,451	2,479
	$ 58,566	$ 59,211

At January 30, 2010 and January 31, 2009, $26,634 and $29,328 of available-for-sale securities and $40,179 and $22,795 of held-to-maturity investments are classified in long-term investments. Trading securities are held in a Rabbi Trust, intended to fund the Company's deferred compensation plan, and are classified in long-term investments.

The Company's investments in auction-rate securities ("ARS") are classified as available-for-sale and reported at fair market value. As of January 30, 2010, the reported investment amount is net of $1,258 of temporary impairment and $2,699 of other-than-temporary impairment ("OTTI") to account for the impairment of certain securities from their stated par value. The $1,258 temporary impairment is reported, net of tax, as an "accumulated other comprehensive loss" of $793 in stockholders' equity as of January 30, 2010. For the investments considered temporarily impaired, the Company believes that these ARS can be successfully redeemed or liquidated through future auctions at par value plus accrued interest. The Company believes it has the ability and maintains its intent to hold these investments until such recovery of market value occurs; therefore, the Company believes the current lack of liquidity has created the temporary impairment in valuation.

As of January 30, 2010, the Company had $24,775 invested in ARS and $2,000 invested in preferred securities, at par value, which are reported at their estimated fair value of $22,792 and $26, respectively. As of January 31, 2009, the Company had $35,495 invested in ARS and $2,000 invested in preferred securities, which were reported at their estimated fair value of $30,278 and $600, respectively. ARS have a long-term stated maturity, but are reset through a "dutch auction" process that occurs every 7 to 49 days, depending on the terms of the individual security. Until February 2008, the ARS market was highly liquid. During February 2008, however, a significant number of auctions related to these securities failed, meaning that there was not enough demand to sell the entire issue at auction. The failed auctions have limited the current liquidity of certain of the Company's investments in ARS and the Company has reason to believe that certain of the underlying issuers of its ARS are currently at risk. The Company does not, however, anticipate that further auction failures will have a material impact on the Company's ability to fund its business. During fiscal 2009, the Company was able to successfully liquidate $5,320 of its investments in ARS at par value. The Company also liquidated investments in preferred securities that were valued at $2,217 ($5,400 at par value) as of January 31, 2009 for $3,933, and recorded a gain of $1,716 in the statement of income for the fiscal year ended January 30, 2010. The Company reviews all investments for OTTI at least quarterly or as indicators of impairment exist and added $725 to OTTI during the fourth quarter of fiscal 2009. Indicators of impairment include the duration and severity of decline in market value. In addition, the Company considers qualitative factors including, but not limited to, the financial condition of the investee, the credit rating of the investee, and the current and expected market and industry conditions in which the investee operates.

As of January 30, 2010, $1,350 of the Company's investment in ARS and preferred securities was classified in short-term investments, due to known or anticipated subsequent redemptions, and $21,468 was classified in long-term investments. As of January 31, 2009, $1,550 of the Company's investment in ARS and preferred securities was classified in short-term investments and $29,328 was classified in long-term investments.

C.   FAIR VALUE MEASURMENTS

As defined by FASB ASC 820, *Fair Value Measurements and Disclosures*, fair value is the price that would be received to sell an asset or paid to transfer a liability in an orderly transaction between market participants at the measurement date. Financial assets and liabilities measured and reported at fair value are classified and disclosed in one of the following categories:

- Level 1 – Quoted market prices in active markets for identical assets or liabilities. Short-term and long-term investments with active markets or known redemption values are reported at fair value utilizing Level 1 inputs.
- Level 2 – Observable market-based inputs (either directly or indirectly) such as quoted prices for similar assets or liabilities, quoted prices in markets that are not active, or other inputs that are observable or inputs that are corroborated by market data.
- Level 3 – Unobservable inputs that are not corroborated by market data and are projections, estimates, or interpretations that are supported by little or no market activity and are significant to the fair value of the assets. The Company has concluded that certain of its ARS represent Level 3 valuation and should be valued using a discounted cash flow analysis. The assumptions used in preparing the discounted cash flow model include estimates for interest rates, timing and amount of cash flows, and expected holding periods of the ARS.

As of January 30, 2010 and January 31, 2009, the Company held certain assets that are required to be measured at fair value on a recurring basis including available-for-sale and trading securities. The Company's available-for-sale securities include its investments in ARS, as further described in Note B. The failed auctions, beginning in February 2008, related to certain of the Company's investments in ARS have limited the availability of quoted market prices. The Company has determined the fair value of its ARS using Level 1 inputs for known or anticipated subsequent redemptions at par value, Level 2 inputs using observable inputs, and Level 3 using unobservable inputs where the following criteria were considered in estimating fair value:

- Pricing was provided by the custodian of ARS;
- Pricing was provided by a third-party broker for ARS;
- Sales of similar securities;
- Quoted prices for similar securities in active markets;
- Quoted prices for publicly traded preferred securities;
- Quoted prices for similar assets in markets that are not active - including markets where there are few transactions for the asset, the prices are not current, or price quotations vary substantially either over time or among market makers, or in which little information is released publicly;
- Pricing was provided by a third-party valuation consultant (using Level 3 inputs).

In addition, the Company considers other factors including, but not limited to, the financial condition of the investee, the credit rating, insurance, guarantees, collateral, cash flows, and the current and expected market and industry conditions in which the investee operates. Management believes it has used information that was reasonably obtainable in order to complete its valuation process and determine if the Company's investments in ARS had incurred any temporary and/or other-than-temporary impairment as of January 30, 2010 and January 31, 2009.

Future fluctuations in fair value of ARS that the Company judges to be temporary, including any recoveries of previous write-downs, would be recorded as an adjustment to "accumulated other comprehensive loss." The value and liquidity of ARS held by the Company may be affected by continued auction-rate failures, the credit quality of each security, the amount and timing of interest payments, the amount and timing of future principal payments, and the probability of full repayment of the principal. Additional indicators of impairment include the duration and severity of the decline in market value. The interest rates on these investments will be determined by the terms of each individual ARS. The material risks associated with the ARS held by the Company include those stated above as well as the current economic environment, downgrading of credit ratings on investments held, and the volatility of the entities backing each of the issues.

The Company's financial assets measured at fair value on a recurring basis subject to the disclosure requirements of FASB ASC 820 were as follows:

| | Fair Value Measurements at Reporting Date Using | | | |
January 30, 2010	Quoted Prices in Active Markets for Identical Assets (Level 1)	Significant Observable Inputs (Level 2)	Significant Unobservable Inputs (Level 3)	Total
Available-for-sale securities				
Auction-rate securities	$ 1,261	$ 12,894	$ 8,637	$ 22,792
Municipal bonds	8,116	-	-	8,116
Preferred stock	26	-	-	26
Trading securities (including mutual funds)	5,957	-	-	5,957
Totals	$ 15,360	$ 12,894	$ 8,637	$ 36,891

| | Fair Value Measurements at Reporting Date Using | | | |
January 31, 2009	Quoted Prices in Active Markets for Identical Assets (Level 1)	Significant Observable Inputs (Level 2)	Significant Unobservable Inputs (Level 3)	Total
Available-for-sale securities				
Auction-rate securities	$ 1,550	$ 21,468	$ 7,260	$ 30,278
Preferred stock	600	-	-	600
Trading securities (including mutual funds)	4,090	-	-	4,090
Totals	$ 6,240	$ 21,468	$ 7,260	$ 34,968

ARS, municipal bonds, and preferred securities included in Level 1 represent securities which have a known or anticipated upcoming redemption as of January 30, 2010 and those that have publicly traded quoted prices. ARS included in Level 2 represent securities which have not experienced a successful auction subsequent to February 2, 2008. The fair market value for these securities was determined by applying a discount to par value based on auction prices for similar securities and by utilizing a discounted cash flow model, using market-based inputs, to determine fair value. The Company used a discounted cash flow model to value its Level 3 investments, using estimates regarding recovery periods, yield, and liquidity. The assumptions used are subjective based upon management's judgment and views on current market conditions, and resulted in $739 of the Company's recorded temporary impairment and $725 of the OTTI as of January 30, 2010. The use of different assumptions would result in a different valuation and related temporary impairment charge.

Changes in the fair value of the Company's financial assets measured at fair value on a recurring basis using significant unobservable inputs (Level 3), as defined in FASB ASC 820, are as follows:

	Fiscal Years Ended	
Available-for-Sale Auction-Rate Securities	January 30, 2010	January 31, 2009
Balance, beginning of year	$ 7,260	-
Total gains or losses (realized and unrealized):		
Included in net income	(725)	-
Included in other comprehensive income	(48)	(690)
Purchases, sales, issuances, and settlements (net)	(25)	-
Transfers in and/or out of Level 3	2,175	7,950
Balance, end of year	$ 8,637	$ 7,260

D.   PROPERTY AND EQUIPMENT

	January 30, 2010	January 31, 2009
Land	$ 1,959	$ 1,170
Building and improvements	14,678	13,447
Office equipment	6,105	6,043
Transportation equipment	19,005	18,997
Leasehold improvements	119,941	111,544
Furniture and fixtures	110,579	96,778
Shipping/receiving equipment	15,783	10,294
Screenprinting equipment	111	111
Construction-in-progress	17,813	5,770
	$ 305,974	$ 264,154

E.   FINANCING ARRANGEMENTS

The Company has available an unsecured line of credit of $17,500 of which $10,000 is available for letters of credit. During fiscal 2009, this line of credit was extended through July 31, 2012. Borrowings under the line of credit and letter of credit provide for interest to be paid at a rate equal to the prime rate as set by the Wells Fargo Bank, N.A. index on the date of the borrowings. There were no bank borrowings at January 30, 2010 and January 31, 2009. There were no bank borrowings during fiscal 2009, 2008, and 2007. The Company had outstanding letters of credit totaling $618 and $1,059 at January 30, 2010 and January 31, 2009, respectively.

F.   INCOME TAXES

The provision for income taxes consists of:

	Fiscal Years Ended		
	January 30, 2010	January 31, 2009	February 2, 2008
Current income tax expense (benefit):			
Federal	$ 66,059	$ 52,905	$ 38,224
State	10,351	8,149	6,849
Deferred income tax expense (benefit):	414	(595)	(1,509)
Total	$ 76,824	$ 60,459	$ 43,564

Total income tax expense for the year varies from the amount which would be provided by applying the statutory income tax rate to earnings before income taxes. The primary reasons for this difference (expressed as a percent of pre-tax income) are as follows:

	Fiscal Years Ended		
	January 30, 2010	January 31, 2009	February 2, 2008
Statutory rate	35.0 %	35.0 %	35.0 %
State income tax effect	3.4	3.6	4.0
Tax exempt interest income	(0.3)	(1.0)	(2.0)
Other	(0.5)	(0.9)	(0.3)
Effective tax rate	37.6 %	36.7 %	36.7 %

Deferred income tax assets and liabilities are comprised of the following:

	January 30, 2010	January 31, 2009
Deferred income tax assets (liabilities):		
Inventory	$ 3,641	$ 3,681
Stock-based compensation	3,337	3,112
Accrued compensation	3,373	2,547
Accrued store operating costs	390	262
Unrealized loss on securities	2,021	2,847
Gift certificates redeemable	550	495
Allowance for doubtful accounts	13	17
Deferred rent liability	13,563	12,803
Property and equipment	(15,841)	(14,228)
Net deferred income tax asset	$ 11,047	$ 11,536

At January 30, 2010 and January 31, 2009, respectively, the net current deferred income tax assets of $7,396 and $7,085 are classified in "prepaid expenses and other assets." The net non-current deferred income tax assets of $3,651 and $4,451 are classified in "other assets" at January 30, 2010 and January 31, 2009, respectively. There are no unrecognized tax benefits to be recorded in the Company's financial statements at January 30, 2010 or January 31, 2009. The Company has no open examinations with the Internal Revenue Service and fiscal years 2006, 2007, 2008, and 2009 remain subject to examination by the Internal Revenue Service as well as state taxing authorities.

G. RELATED PARTY TRANSACTIONS

Included in other assets is a note receivable of $1,035 at January 30, 2010 and $1,005 at January 31, 2009, respectively, from a life insurance trust fund controlled by the Company's Chairman. The note was created over three years, beginning in July 1994, when the Company paid life insurance premiums of $200 each year for the Chairman on a personal policy. The note accrues interest at 5% of the principal balance per year and is to be paid from the life insurance proceeds. The note is secured by a life insurance policy on the Chairman.

H. COMMITMENTS

Leases - The Company conducts its operations in leased facilities under numerous non-cancelable operating leases expiring at various dates through fiscal 2021. Most of the Company's stores have lease terms of approximately ten years and generally do not contain renewal options. Most lease agreements contain tenant improvement allowances, rent holidays, rent escalation clauses, and/or contingent rent provisions. For purposes of recognizing lease incentives and minimum rental expenses on a straight-line basis over the terms of the leases, the Company uses the date of initial possession to begin amortization, which is generally when the Company enters the space and begins to make improvements in preparation of intended use. For tenant improvement allowances and rent holidays, the Company records a deferred rent liability on the balance sheets and amortizes the deferred rent over the terms of the leases as reductions to rent expense on the statements of income. For scheduled rent escalation clauses during the lease terms or for rental payments commencing at a date other than the date of initial occupancy, the Company records minimum rental expenses on a straight-line basis over the terms of the leases on the statements of income. Certain leases provide for contingent rents, which are determined as a percentage of gross sales in excess of specified levels. The Company records a contingent rent liability on the balance sheets and the corresponding rent expense when specified levels have been achieved or are reasonably probable to be achieved. Operating lease base rental expense for fiscal 2009, 2008, and 2007 was $45,805, $41,687, and $38,298, respectively. Most of the rental payments are based on a minimum annual rental plus a percentage of sales in excess of a specified amount. Percentage rents for fiscal 2009, 2008, and 2007 were $4,153, $3,202, and $1,159, respectively.

Total future minimum rental commitments under these operating leases with remaining lease terms in excess of one year as of January 30, 2010 are as follows:

Fiscal Year	Minimum Rental Commitments
2010	$ 49,006
2011	43,806
2012	39,313
2013	35,644
2014	31,592
Thereafter	104,595
Total minimum rental commitments	$ 303,956

Litigation - From time to time, the Company is involved in litigation relating to claims arising out of its operations in the normal course of business. As of the date of these financial statements, the Company was not engaged in any legal proceedings that are expected, individually or in the aggregate, to have a material effect on the Company.

I.   EMPLOYEE BENEFITS

The Company has a 401(k) profit sharing plan covering all eligible employees who elect to participate. Contributions to the plan are based upon the amount of the employees' deferrals and the employer's discretionary matching formula. The Company may contribute to the plan at its discretion. The total expense under the profit sharing plan was $1,130, $1,022, and $887 for fiscal years 2009, 2008, and 2007, respectively.

The Buckle, Inc. Deferred Compensation Plan covers the Company's executive officers. The plan is funded by participant contributions and a specified annual Company matching contribution not to exceed 6% of the participant's compensation. The Company's contributions were $428, $341, and $390 for fiscal years 2009, 2008, and 2007, respectively.

J.   STOCK-BASED COMPENSATION

The Company has several stock option plans which allow for granting of stock options to employees, executives, and directors. The options are in the form of non-qualified stock options and are granted with an exercise price equal to the market value of the Company's common stock on the date of grant. The options generally expire ten years from the date of grant. The Company also has a restricted stock plan that allows for the granting of non-vested shares of common stock to employees and executives and a restricted stock plan that allows for the granting of non-vested shares of common stock to non-employee directors.

As of January 30, 2010, 641,748 shares were available for grant under the various stock option plans, of which 452,111 were available for grant to executive officers. Also as of January 30, 2010, 208,372 shares were available for grant under the various restricted stock plans, of which 129,248 were available for grant to executive officers.

The Company accounts for stock-based compensation in accordance with FASB ASC 718, *Compensation-Stock Compensation*. Compensation expense was recognized fiscal 2009, 2008, and 2007 for new awards, based on the grant date fair value, as well as for the portion of awards granted in fiscal years prior to FASB ASC 718 adoption that was not vested as of the beginning of fiscal 2006. The fair value of stock options is determined using the Black-Scholes option pricing model, while the fair value of grants of non-vested common stock awards is the stock price on the date of grant.

Information regarding the impact of stock-based compensation expense is as follows:

	Fiscal Years Ended		
	January 30, 2010	January 31, 2009	February 2, 2008
Stock-based compensation expense, before tax:			
Stock options	$ 175	$ 289	$ 293
Non-vested shares of common stock	4,988	4,879	3,886
Total stock-based compensation expense, before tax	$ 5,163	$ 5,168	$ 4,179
Total stock-based compensation expense, after tax	$ 3,253	$ 3,256	$ 2,633

FASB ASC 718 requires the benefits of tax deductions in excess of the compensation cost recognized for stock options exercised during the period to be classified as financing cash inflows. This amount is shown as "excess tax benefit from stock option exercises" on the statements of cash flows. For fiscal 2009, 2008, and 2007, the excess tax benefit realized from exercised stock options was $2,661, $11,268, and $7,744, respectively.

No stock options were granted during fiscal 2009. Stock options granted during fiscal 2008 and 2007 were granted under the Company's 1993 Director Stock Option Plan. Grants were made with an exercise price equal to the market value of the Company's common stock on the date of grant and a contractual term of ten years. Options granted under the 1993 Director Stock Option Plan typically vest over a period of three years.

The weighted average grant date fair value of options granted during the fiscal year was $8.41 and $8.54 per option for fiscal 2008 and 2007, respectively. The fair value of options granted was estimated at the date of grant using the Black-Scholes option pricing model with the following assumptions:

	Fiscal Years Ended	
	January 31, 2009	February 2, 2008
Risk-free interest rate *(1)*	3.10 %	4.80 %
Dividend yield *(2)*	2.40 %	2.40 %
Expected volatility *(3)*	33.00 %	39.00 %
Expected lives - years *(4)*	7.0	7.0

(1) Based on the U.S. Treasury yield curve in effect at the time of grant with a term consistent with the expected lives of stock options.

(2) Based on expected dividend yield as of the date of grant.

(3) Based on historical volatility of the Company's common stock over a period consistent with the expected lives of stock options.

(4) Based on historical and expected exercise behavior.

On September 15, 2008, the Board of Directors authorized a $3.00 per share ($2.00 per share after 3-for-2 stock split) special one-time cash dividend to be paid on October 27, 2008 to shareholders of record at the close of business on October 15, 2008. Additionally, on September 21, 2009, the Board of Directors authorized a $1.80 per share special one-time cash dividend to be paid on October 27, 2009 to shareholders of record at the close of business on October 15, 2009. To preserve the intrinsic value for option holders, the Board also approved on each occasion, pursuant to the terms of the Company's various stock option plans, a proportional adjustment to both the exercise price and the number of shares covered by each award for all outstanding stock options. This adjustment did not result in any incremental compensation expense.

A summary of the Company's stock-based compensation activity related to stock options for the fiscal year ended January 30, 2010 is as follows:

	Shares	Weighted Average Exercise Price	Weighted Average Remaining Contractual Life		Aggregate Intrinsic Value
Outstanding - beginning of year	1,635,163	$ 6.91			
Granted	-	-			
Other (1)	447	5.83			
Expired/forfeited	(5,069)	24.21			
Exercised	(278,430)	6.56			
Outstanding - end of year	1,352,111	$ 5.02	3.29	years	$ 34,237
Exercisable - end of year	1,331,816	$ 4.75	3.22	years	$ 34,076

(1) An adjustment was made to the exercise price and number of options outstanding for the special cash dividend paid during October 2009. "Other" represents additional options issued as a result of this adjustment in the third quarter of fiscal 2009.

The total intrinsic value of options exercised during fiscal 2009, 2008, and 2007, respectively, was $7,477, $35,447, and $23,135. As of January 30, 2010, there was $64 of unrecognized compensation expense related to non-vested stock options. It is expected that this expense will be recognized over a weighted average period of approximately 1.0 year.

Non-vested shares of common stock granted during fiscal 2007 and 2008 were granted pursuant to the Company's 2005 Restricted Stock Plan. Non-vested shares granted during fiscal 2009 were granted pursuant to the Company's 2005 Restricted Stock Plan and the Company's 2008 Director Restricted Stock Plan. Shares granted under the 2005 Plan typically vest over a period of four years, only upon certification by the Compensation Committee of the Board of Directors that the Company has achieved its pre-established performance targets for the fiscal year. Shares granted under the 2008 Director Plan vest 25% on the date of grant and then in equal portions on each of the first three anniversaries of the date of grant.

A summary of the Company's stock-based compensation activity related to grants of non-vested shares of common stock for the fiscal year ended January 30, 2010 is as follows:

	Shares		Weighted Average Grant Date Fair Value
Non-Vested - beginning of year	423,171	$	23.84
Granted	243,800		21.20
Forfeited	(47,232)		22.66
Vested	(214,394)		22.14
Non-Vested - end of year	405,345	$	23.29

As of January 30, 2010, there was $4,066 of unrecognized compensation expense related to grants of non-vested shares. It is expected that this expense will be recognized over a weighted average period of approximately 1.9 years. The total fair value of shares vested during fiscal 2009, 2008, and 2007 was $6,517, $5,128, and $4,398, respectively.

K.   EARNINGS PER SHARE

The following table provides reconciliation between basic and diluted earnings per share:

	Fiscal Years Ended								
	January 30, 2010			January 31, 2009			February 2, 2008		
	Income	Weighted Average Shares	Per Share Amount	Income	Weighted Average Shares	Per Share Amount	Income	Weighted Average Shares	Per Share Amount
Basic EPS									
Net income	$ 127,303	45,699	$ 2.79	$ 104,409	45,367	$ 2.30	$ 75,247	44,551	$ 1.69
Effect of Dilutive Securities									
Stock options and non-vested shares	-	993	(0.06)	-	1,207	(0.06)	-	1,703	(0.06)
Diluted EPS	$ 127,303	46,692	$ 2.73	$ 104,409	46,574	$ 2.24	$ 75,247	46,254	$ 1.63

Stock options to purchase 72,637 shares of common stock were not included in the computation of diluted earnings per share for fiscal 2008 because the options would be considered anti-dilutive. No stock options were deemed anti-dilutive and excluded from the computation of diluted earnings per share for either fiscal 2009 or 2007.

L.   SEGMENT INFORMATION

The Company is a retailer of medium to better-priced casual apparel, footwear, and accessories. The Company operated 401 stores located in 41 states throughout the continental United States as of January 30, 2010. The Company operates its business as one segment.

The following is information regarding the Company's major product lines and is stated as a percentage of the Company's net sales:

	Fiscal Years Ended		
	January 30, 2010	January 31, 2009	February 2, 2008
Denims	42.9 %	41.4 %	43.2 %
Tops (including sweaters)	36.7	39.0	36.1
Accessories	7.7	7.7	7.7
Sportswear/fashions	5.0	4.6	4.3
Footwear	4.7	4.6	5.6
Outerwear	2.5	2.0	2.0
Casual bottoms	0.4	0.6	1.0
Other	0.1	0.1	0.1
	100.0 %	100.0 %	100.0 %

M.   SELECTED QUARTERLY FINANCIAL DATA (UNAUDITED)

Selected unaudited quarterly financial information for fiscal 2009 and 2008 are as follows:

Fiscal 2009	Quarter			
	First	Second	Third	Fourth
Net sales	$ 199,697	$ 192,906	$ 231,238	$ 274,446
Gross profit	$ 86,703	$ 82,278	$ 102,117	$ 129,521
Net income	$ 26,862	$ 24,994	$ 33,305	$ 42,142
Basic earnings per share	$ 0.59	$ 0.55	$ 0.73	$ 0.92
Diluted earnings per share	$ 0.58	$ 0.54	$ 0.71	$ 0.90

Fiscal 2008	Quarter			
	First	Second	Third	Fourth
Net sales	$ 160,300	$ 169,765	$ 210,567	$ 251,414
Gross profit	$ 65,622	$ 70,268	$ 91,805	$ 115,793
Net income	$ 18,717	$ 22,276	$ 29,076	$ 34,340
Basic earnings per share	$ 0.42	$ 0.49	$ 0.64	$ 0.75
Diluted earnings per share	$ 0.41	$ 0.48	$ 0.62	$ 0.74

Basic and diluted shares outstanding are computed independently for each of the quarters presented and, therefore, may not sum to the totals for the year.

ITEM 9 - CHANGES IN AND DISAGREEMENTS WITH ACCOUNTANTS ON ACCOUNTING AND FINANCIAL DISCLOSURE

None.

ITEM 9A - CONTROLS AND PROCEDURES

The Company maintains a system of disclosure controls and procedures that are designed to provide reasonable assurance that material information, which is required to be timely disclosed, is accumulated and communicated to management in a timely manner. An evaluation of the effectiveness of the design and operation of our disclosure controls and procedures (as defined in Rules 13a-15(e) of the Securities Exchange Act of 1934 (the "Exchange Act")) was performed as of the end of the period covered by this report. This evaluation was performed under the supervision and with the participation of the Company's Chief Executive Officer and Chief Financial Officer. Based upon that evaluation, the Chief Executive Officer and Chief Financial Officer concluded that, as of the end of the period covered by this report, the Company's disclosure controls and procedures are effective to provide reasonable assurance that information required to be disclosed by the Company in the Company's reports that it files or submits under the Exchange Act is accumulated and communicated to management, including its Chief Executive Officer and Chief Financial Officer, as appropriate, to allow timely decisions regarding required disclosure and are effective to provide reasonable assurance that such information is recorded, processed, summarized, and reported within the time periods specified by the SEC's rules and forms.

Change in Internal Control Over Financial Reporting – There were no changes in the Company's internal control over financial reporting that occurred during the Company's last fiscal quarter that have materially affected, or are reasonable likely to materially affect, the Company's internal control over financial reporting.

Management's Report on Internal Control Over Financial Reporting – Management of the Company is responsible for establishing and maintaining adequate internal control over financial reporting as defined in Rules 13a-15(f) and 15d-15(f) under the Securities Exchange Act of 1934. The Company's internal control over financial reporting is designed to provide reasonable assurance regarding the reliability of financial reporting and the preparation of financial statements for external purposes in accordance with accounting principles generally accepted in the United State of America ("GAAP").

All internal control systems, no matter how well designed, have inherent limitations. Therefore, even those systems determined to be effective can provide only reasonable assurance with respect to financial statement preparation and presentation. Because of its inherent limitations, internal control over financial reporting may not prevent or detect misstatements.

Management has assessed the effectiveness of the Company's internal control over financial reporting as of January 30, 2010, based on the criteria set forth by the Committee of Sponsoring Organizations ("COSO") of the Treadway Commission in their *Internal Control–Integrated Framework*. In making its assessment of internal control over financial reporting, management has concluded that the Company's internal control over financial reporting was effective as of January 30, 2010.

The Company's independent registered public accounting firm, Deloitte & Touche LLP, has audited the effectiveness of the Company's internal control over financial reporting. Their report appears herein.

REPORT OF INDEPENDENT REGISTERED PUBLIC ACCOUNTING FIRM

To the Board of Directors and Stockholders of
The Buckle, Inc.
Kearney, Nebraska

We have audited the internal control over financial reporting of The Buckle, Inc. (the "Company") as of January 30, 2010, based on criteria established in *Internal Control — Integrated Framework* issued by the Committee of Sponsoring Organizations of the Treadway Commission. The Company's management is responsible for maintaining effective internal control over financial reporting and for its assessment of the effectiveness of internal control over financial reporting, included in the accompanying *Management's Report on Internal Control Over Financial Reporting*. Our responsibility is to express an opinion on the Company's internal control over financial reporting based on our audit.

We conducted our audit in accordance with the standards of the Public Company Accounting Oversight Board (United States). Those standards require that we plan and perform the audit to obtain reasonable assurance about whether effective internal control over financial reporting was maintained in all material respects. Our audit included obtaining an understanding of internal control over financial reporting, assessing the risk that a material weakness exists, testing and evaluating the design and operating effectiveness of internal control based on the assessed risk, and performing such other procedures as we considered necessary in the circumstances. We believe that our audit provides a reasonable basis for our opinion.

A company's internal control over financial reporting is a process designed by, or under the supervision of, the company's principal executive and principal financial officers, or persons performing similar functions, and effected by the company's board of directors, management, and other personnel to provide reasonable assurance regarding the reliability of financial reporting and the preparation of financial statements for external purposes in accordance with generally accepted accounting principles. A company's internal control over financial reporting includes those policies and procedures that (1) pertain to the maintenance of records that, in reasonable detail, accurately and fairly reflect the transactions and dispositions of the assets of the company; (2) provide reasonable assurance that transactions are recorded as necessary to permit preparation of financial statements in accordance with generally accepted accounting principles, and that receipts and expenditures of the company are being made only in accordance with authorizations of management and directors of the company; and (3) provide reasonable assurance regarding prevention or timely detection of unauthorized acquisition, use or disposition of the company's assets that could have a material effect on the financial statements.

Because of the inherent limitations of internal control over financial reporting, including the possibility of collusion or improper management override of controls, material misstatements due to error or fraud may not be prevented or detected on a timely basis. Also, projections of any evaluation of the effectiveness of the internal control over financial reporting to future periods are subject to the risk that the controls may become inadequate because of changes in conditions, or that the degree of compliance with the policies or procedures may deteriorate.

In our opinion, the Company maintained, in all material respects, effective internal control over financial reporting as of January 30, 2010, based on the criteria established in *Internal Control — Integrated Framework* issued by the Committee of Sponsoring Organizations of the Treadway Commission.

We have also audited, in accordance with the standards of the Public Company Accounting Oversight Board (United States), the financial statements and financial statement schedule as of and for the fiscal year ended January 30, 2010, of the Company and our report dated March 31, 2010 expressed an unqualified opinion on those financial statements and financial statement schedule.

/s/ Deloitte & Touche LLP

DELOITTE & TOUCHE LLP
Omaha, Nebraska
March 31, 2010

ITEM 9B – OTHER INFORMATION

As required by Section 303A of the New York Stock Exchange's Corporate Governance Standards, the Company's Chief Executive Officer submitted a certification to the New York Stock Exchange in fiscal 2009 that he was not aware of any violation by the Company of the New York Stock Exchange's Corporate Governance Standards as of the date of the certification, June 29, 2009.

PART III

ITEM 10 – DIRECTORS, EXECUTIVE OFFICERS, AND CORPORATE GOVERNANCE

The information required by this item appears under the captions "Executive Officers of the Company" appearing on pages 10 and 11 of this report and "Election of Directors" in the Company's Proxy Statement for its 2010 Annual Shareholders' Meeting and is incorporated by reference.

ITEM 11- EXECUTIVE COMPENSATION

Information required by this item appears under the following captions in the Company's Proxy Statement for its 2010 Annual Shareholders' Meeting and is incorporated by reference: "Executive Compensation," "Director Compensation" (included under the "Election of Directors" section), and "Report of the Audit Committee."

ITEM 12 - SECURITY OWNERSHIP OF CERTAIN BENEFICIAL OWNERS AND MANAGEMENT AND RELATED STOCKHOLDER MATTERS

The information required by this item appears under the captions "Beneficial Ownership of Common Stock" and "Election of Directors" in the Company's Proxy Statement for its 2010 Annual Shareholders' Meeting and in the Notes to Financial Statements under Footnote J on pages 46 to 48 of this report and is incorporated by reference.

ITEM 13 - CERTAIN RELATIONSHIPS AND RELATED TRANSACTIONS AND DIRECTOR INDEPENDENCE

The information required by this item appears under the captions "Independence" and "Related Party Transactions" (included under the "Election of Directors" section) in the Company's Proxy for its 2010 Annual Shareholders' Meeting and is incorporated by reference.

ITEM 14 – PRINCIPAL ACCOUNTANT FEES AND SERVICES

Information regarding the fees billed by our independent registered public accounting firm and the nature of services comprising the fees for each of the two most recent fiscal years is set forth under the caption "Ratification of Independent Registered Public Accounting Firm" in the Company's Proxy Statement for its 2010 Annual Shareholders' Meeting and is incorporated by reference.

PART IV

ITEM 15 – EXHIBITS AND FINANCIAL STATEMENT SCHEDULE

(a) Financial Statement Schedule
Valuation and Qualifying Account. This schedule is on page 54.
All other schedules are omitted because they are not applicable or the required information is presented in the financial statements or notes thereto.

(b) Exhibits
See index to exhibits on pages 55 and 56.

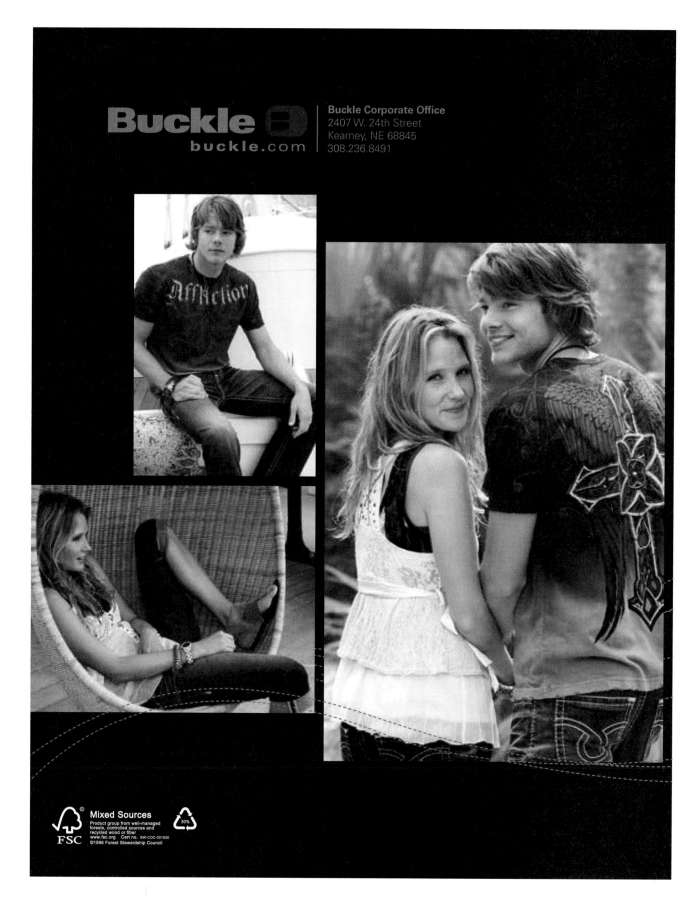

Time Value of Money

Learning Objectives

AFTER STUDYING THIS APPENDIX, YOU SHOULD BE ABLE TO:

■ **LO1** Contrast simple and compound interest.

■ **LO2** Calculate the future value and present value of a single amount.

■ **LO3** Calculate the future value and present value of an annuity.

Congratulations! While at a local convenience store, you bought a lottery ticket and won $1,000. The ticket gives you the option of receiving (a) $1,000 today or (b) $1,000 one year from now. Which do you choose?

Probably, all of us would choose $1,000 today. Choosing to take the money today instead of one year from now just makes common sense. It also makes good economic sense. You could take your $1,000 winnings today, put it in a savings account, earn interest on it for one year, and have an amount greater than $1,000 a year from now. So, $1,000 today is not equal to $1,000 a year from now. This simple example demonstrates the time value of money, which means that interest causes the value of money received today to be greater than the value of that same amount of money received in the future.

Time value of money concepts are useful—in fact, essential—in solving many business decisions. These decisions include valuing assets and liabilities, making investment decisions, paying off debts, and establishing a retirement plan, to name just a few. We'll discuss some of these next.

Simple versus Compound Interest

Interest is the cost of borrowing money. If you borrow $1,000 today and agree to pay 10% interest, you will pay back $1,100 a year from now. It is this interest that gives money its time value.

■ LO1
Contrast simple and compound interest.

Simple interest is interest you earn on the initial investment only. Calculate it as the initial investment times the applicable interest rate times the period of the investment or loan:

Simple interest = Initial investment × Interest rate × Time

For example, suppose you put $1,000 into a savings account that pays simple interest of 10% and then withdraw the money at the end of three years. Illustration C–1 demonstrates that the amount of simple interest you earned on your $1,000 in each of the three years is $100 (= $1,000 × 10%).

With simple interest at 10% annually, the $1,000 initial investment generates $100 of interest each year and grows to **$1,300** by the end of the third year.

Time	Simple Interest (= Initial investment × Interest rate)	Outstanding Balance
Initial investment		$1,000
End of year 1	$1,000 × 10% = $100	$1,100
End of year 2	$1,000 × 10% = $100	$1,200
End of year 3	$1,000 × 10% = $100	$1,300

ILLUSTRATION C–1

Calculation of Simple Interest

Compound interest works differently. Compound interest is interest you earn on the initial investment *and on previous interest.* Because you are earning "interest on interest" each period, compound interest yields increasingly larger amounts of interest earnings for each period of the investment (unlike simple interest, which yielded the same $100 in each year of our example above). Illustration C–2 shows calculations of compound interest for a $1,000, three-year investment that earns 10%.

ILLUSTRATION C–2

Calculation of Compound Interest

Time	Compound Interest (= Outstanding balance × Interest rate)	Outstanding Balance
Initial investment		$1,000
End of year 1	$1,000 × 10% = $100	$1,100
End of year 2	$1,100 × 10% = $110	$1,210
End of year 3	$1,210 × 10% = $121	$1,331

With compound interest at 10% annually, the $1,000 initial investment grows to **$1,331** at the end of three years. This compares to only **$1,300** for simple interest. The extra $31 represents *compounding,* or interest earned on interest. Nearly all business applications use compound interest, and compound interest is what we use in calculating the time value of money.

KEY POINT

Simple interest is interest we earn on the initial investment only. Compound interest is the interest we earn on the initial investment plus previous interest. We use compound interest in calculating the time value of money.

Time Value of a Single Amount

LO2
Calculate the future value and present value of a single amount.

To better understand how compound interest affects the time value of money, we'll examine this topic from two perspectives. First, we'll calculate how much an amount today will grow to be at some point in the future (*future value*), and then we'll take the opposite perspective and examine how much an amount in the future is worth today (*present value*).

FUTURE VALUE

In the example above, in which we invested $1,000 for three years at 10% compounded annually, we call $1,331 the future value. Future value is how much an amount today will grow to be in the future. The timeline in Illustration C–3 provides a useful way to visualize future values. Time $n = 0$ indicates today, the date of the initial investment.

ILLUSTRATION C–3

Future Value of a Single Amount

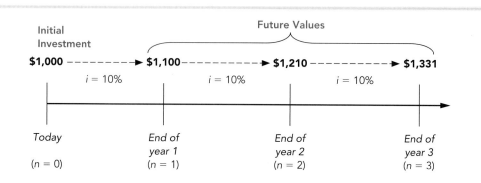

Notice that at the end of each year, the investment grows by 10%. The future value at the end of the first year is **$1,100** (= $1,000 × 1.10). After three years, the investment has a future value of **$1,331** (= $1,000 × 1.10 × 1.10 × 1.10), representing 10% growth of a growing base amount each year.

To calculate future value, we can use a mathematical formula, time value of money tables, a calculator, or a computer spreadsheet. We show all four methods below.

Formula.   We can determine the future value of any amount with a formula, as follows:

$$FV = I (1 + i)^n$$

where: FV = future value of the invested amount

I = initial investment

i = interest rate

n = number of compounding periods

Table 1.   Instead of using a formula, we can also determine future value by using time value of money tables. Table 1, Future Value of $1, located at the end of this book, contains the future value of $1 invested for various periods of time, n, and various interest rates, i. With this table, it's easy to determine the future value of any invested amount. To do so, simply multiply the invested amount by the table value you find at the intersection of the *column* for the desired interest rate and the *row* for the number of periods. Illustration C–4 contains an excerpt from Table 1.

Periods (n)	\<Interest Rates (i)\>						ILLUSTRATION C–4
	7%	8%	9%	10%	11%	12%	Future Value of $1
1	1.07000	1.08000	1.09000	1.10000	1.11000	1.12000	(excerpt from Table 1)
2	1.14490	1.16640	1.18810	1.21000	1.23210	1.25440	
3	1.22504	1.25971	1.29503	1.33100	1.36763	1.40493	
4	1.31080	1.36049	1.41158	1.46410	1.51807	1.57352	
5	1.40255	1.46933	1.53862	1.61051	1.68506	1.76234	
6	1.50073	1.58687	1.67710	1.77156	1.87041	1.97382	
7	1.60578	1.71382	1.82804	1.94872	2.07616	2.21068	
8	1.71819	1.85093	1.99256	2.14359	2.30454	2.47596	

The table shows various values of $(1 + i)^n$ for different combinations of i and n. From the table you can find the future value factor for three periods (n = 3) at 10% interest to be 1.33100. This means that $1 invested at 10% compounded annually will grow to $1.331 (= $1 × 1.331) in three years. The table uses $1 as the initial investment, whereas our example used $1,000. Therefore, we need to multiply the future value factor by $1,000.

$$FV = I \times FV \text{ factor}$$
$$FV = \$1,000 \times 1.33100^* = \$1,331$$
*Future value of $1; n = 3, i = 10%

Calculator.   Of course, you can do the same future value calculations by using a calculator. Future values are automatically stored in the memory of financial calculators. To compute a future value, you input three amounts: (1) initial investment, (2) interest rate per period, and (3) number of periods. Illustration C–5 shows the inputs and output using a financial calculator.

ILLUSTRATION C-5

Calculate the Future
Value of a Single
Amount Using a
Financial Calculator

CALCULATOR INPUTS

Inputs	Key	Amount
1. Present value (initial investment)	PV	$1,000
2. Interest rate per period	i	10%
3. Number of periods	n	3

CALCULATOR OUTPUT

Future value	FV	$1,331

The key symbols used
to input the interest rate
and number of periods
differ across calculators,
so be sure to check
which key is appropriate
for your calculator.

Excel.   Another option is to use an Excel spreadsheet, which has automatically stored the time value factors. To see how this is performed, see Illustration C–6.

ILLUSTRATION C-6

Calculate the Future
Value of a Single
Amount Using Excel

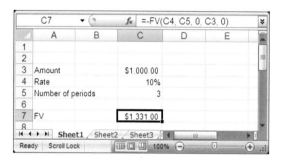

Interest compounding more than annually.   In our example, interest was compounded annually (once per year). Remember that the n in the future value formula refers to the number of compounding *periods*—which is not necessarily the number of years. For example, suppose the three-year, $1,000 investment earns 10% compounded *semiannually*, or twice per year. The number of periods over three years is now six (= 3 years × 2 semiannual periods per year). The interest rate per period is 5% (= 10% annual rate ÷ 2).[1] The future value of the three-year, $1,000 investment that earns 10% compounded semiannually is calculated below.

$$\textbf{FV} = \textbf{I} \times \textbf{FV factor}$$
$$FV = \$1,000 \times 1.34010^* = \$1,340$$
$$\text{*Future value of \$1; } n = 6, i = 5\%$$

Notice that the future amount is slightly higher for semiannual compounding ($1,340) compared to annual compounding ($1,331). **The more frequent the rate of compounding, the more interest we earn on previous interest, resulting in a higher future value.**

To confirm your understanding, let's look at a couple of examples of how to calculate the future value of a single amount.

Example 1.   Suppose a company's top executive, Shirley McDaniel, currently owns stock in the company worth $800,000. Shirley is ready to retire but will not do so until her stock is worth at least $1,000,000. Over the next three years, the company's stock is expected to grow 8% annually. Will Shirley be ready to retire in three years?

---

[1]The rate of compounding can be broken into any number of periods. For example, if we instead assume *quarterly* compounding (four times per year), the number of periods over three years would be 12 (= 3 years × 4 quarters) and the interest rate per period would be 2.5% (= 10% ÷ 4 quarters).

The future value of $800,000 in three years with an annual interest rate of 8% equals $1,007,768 (= $800,000 × 1.25971, time value factor from Table 1, Future Value of $1, with $n = 3$ and $i = 8\%$). With 8% growth, Shirley *will* be ready to retire in three years.

Example 2.   Now suppose you are 20 years old and would like to retire by age 60. A goal of yours has always been to retire as a millionaire. You don't have any money to invest, but you do have a pretty nice car. If you sold your car for $28,000, bought a six-year-old car for $5,000, and invested the difference of $23,000 earning a 10% annual return, how much would you have at retirement?

The future value of $23,000 in 40 years (your proposed retirement age minus your present age) with an annual interest rate of 10% equals $1,040,963 (= $23,000 × 45.25926, time value factor from Table 1, Future Value of $1, with $n = 40$ and $i = 10\%$). With a 10% annual return, just $23,000 today will grow to over 1 million dollars in 40 years. If you swap your expensive wheels, you'll have that million-dollar nest egg.

PRESENT VALUE

Present value is precisely the opposite of future value. Instead of telling us how much some amount today will grow to be in the future, present value tells us the value today of receiving some larger amount in the future. What is it worth today to receive $1,331 in three years? To answer this, we need to determine the discount rate. The discount rate is the rate at which we would be willing to give up current dollars for future dollars. If you would be willing to give up $100 today to receive $108 in one year, then your discount rate, or time value of money, equals 8%.

Continuing with our example, let's assume that your discount rate is 10%. In this case, the present value of receiving $1,331 in three years is $1,000. We could have figured this from Illustration C–3 by working backwards from the future value. The timeline in Illustration C–7 depicts this relationship between present value and future value.

To calculate present value, we can use a formula, time value of money tables, a calculator, or a computer spreadsheet. We show all four methods below.

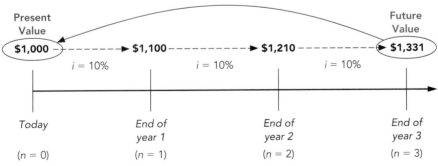

ILLUSTRATION C–7

Present Value of a Single Amount

Formula.   We can calculate present values with the following formula:

$$PV = \frac{FV}{(1 + i)^n}$$

Table 2.   Alternatively, we can use Table 2, Present Value of $1, located at the end of this book. Illustration C–8 shows an excerpt of Table 2.

ILLUSTRATION C–8

Present Value of $1
(excerpt from Table 2)

			Interest Rates (i)			
Periods (n)	7%	8%	9%	10%	11%	12%
1	.93458	.92593	.91743	.90909	.90090	.89286
2	.87344	.85734	.84168	.82645	.81162	.79719
3	.81630	.79383	.77218	.75131	.73119	.71178
4	.76290	.73503	.70843	.68301	.65873	.63552
5	.71299	.68058	.64993	.62092	.59345	.56743
6	.66634	.63017	.59627	.56447	.53464	.50663
7	.62275	.58349	.54703	.51316	.48166	.45235
8	.58201	.54027	.50187	.46651	.43393	.40388

From the table you can find the present value factor for three periods ($n = 3$) at 10% is 0.75131. This means that $1 received in three years where there is interest of 10% compounded annually is worth about $0.75 today. So, the present value of $1,331 is approximately $1,000.

$$\textbf{PV} = \textbf{FV} \times \textbf{PV factor}$$
$$\text{PV} = \$1,331 \times 0.75131 = \$1,000^*$$
*Rounded to the nearest whole dollar

Calculator.   Illustration C–9 shows the same example worked out with a financial calculator.

ILLUSTRATION C–9

Calculate the Present
Value of a Single
Amount Using a
Financial Calculator

CALCULATOR INPUTS

Inputs	Key	Amount
1. Future value	FV	$1,331
2. Interest rate per period	i	10%
3. Number of periods	n	3

CALCULATOR OUTPUT

Present value	PV	$1,000

Excel.   In Illustration C–10, we see the same example worked out using an Excel spreadsheet.

ILLUSTRATION C–10

Calculate the Present
Value of a Single
Amount Using Excel

To confirm your understanding, let's look at a couple of examples of how to calculate the present value of a single amount.

Example 1.   Suppose Fisher Realtors lists for sale a 2,500-square-foot business building for $500,000. Someone offers to purchase the building, taking occupancy today, and then pay $575,000 in two years. If Fisher's discount rate is 7% compounded annually, should it accept the customer's offer?

The present value of receiving $575,000 in two years with an annual interest rate of 7% equals $502,228 (= $575,000 × 0.87344, time value factor from Table 2, Present Value of $1, with $n = 2$ and $i = 7\%$). The present value of the future $575,000 payment is $502,228, which is greater than the $500,000 listed selling price, so Fisher should accept the offer.

Example 2. Let's assume you would like to be a millionaire in 40 years. Investing aggressively in higher-risk securities, you are pretty confident you can earn an average return of 12% a year. How much do you need to invest today to have $1,000,000 in 40 years?

The present value of $1,000,000 in 40 years with an annual interest rate of 12% equals $10,750 (= $1,000,000 × 0.01075, time value factor from Table 2, Present Value of $1, with $n = 40$ and $i = 12\%$). An investment of only $10,750 today would grow to $1,000,000 in 40 years, assuming a 12% annual interest rate.

If you could earn only 6% annually rather than 12%, you would have to invest quite a bit more. The present value of $1,000,000 in 40 years with an interest rate of 6% equals $97,220 (= $1,000,000 × 0.09722, time value factor from Table 2, Present Value of $1, with $n = 40$ and $i = 6\%$). Over longer periods, the investment return you can achieve really makes a difference in the wealth you can accumulate.

KEY POINT

The *future value* of a single amount is how much that amount today will grow to be in the future. The *present value* of a single amount is the value today of receiving that amount in the future.

Let's Review

Below are four scenarios related to the future value and present value of a single amount.

1. Manuel is saving for a new car. He puts $10,000 into an investment account today. He expects the account to earn 12% annually. How much will Manuel have in five years?

2. Ingrid would like to take her family to Disney World in three years. She expects the trip to cost $4,500 at that time. If she can earn 9% annually, how much should she set aside today so that she can pay for the trip in three years?

3. John puts $6,000 in a savings account today that earns 8% interest compounded semiannually. How much will John have in six years?

4. Anna purchases a ring with a selling price of $4,000 today but doesn't have to pay cash until one year from the purchase date. Assuming a discount rate of 16% compounded quarterly, what is Anna's actual cost of the ring today?

Required:
Calculate the time value of money for each scenario.

Solution:
(Rounded to the nearest whole dollar)

1. $10,000 × 1.76234 (FV of $1, $n = 5$, $i = 12\%$) = $17,623
2. $4,500 × 0.77218 (PV of $1, $n = 3$, $i = 9\%$) = $3,475
3. $6,000 × 1.60103 (FV of $1, $n = 12$, $i = 4\%$) = $9,606
4. $4,000 × 0.85480 (PV of $1, $n = 4$, $i = 4\%$) = $3,419

Suggested Homework:
BEC-2, BEC-4;
EC-1, EC-3;
PC-1A&B

Time Value of an Annuity

Up to now, we've focused on calculating the future value and present value of a *single* amount. However, many business transactions are structured as a series of receipts and payments of cash rather than a single amount. If we are to receive or pay the same amount each period, we refer to the cash flows as an annuity. Familiar examples of annuities are monthly payments for a car loan, house loan, or apartment rent. Of course, payments need not be monthly. They could be quarterly, semiannually, annually, or any interval. **As long as the cash payments are of equal amounts over equal time intervals, we refer to the cash payments as an annuity.**

As with single amounts, we can calculate both the future value and the present value of an annuity.

FUTURE VALUE

Let's suppose that you decide to invest $1,000 at the end of *each year* for the next three years, earning 10% compounded annually. What will the value of these three $1,000 payments be at the end of the third year? The timeline in Illustration C–11 demonstrates how to calculate the future value of this annuity.

ILLUSTRATION C–11

Future Value of an Annuity

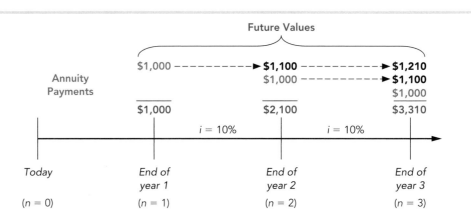

By the end of year 1, the investment's future value equals the $1,000 annuity payment. No interest has been earned because you invest the $1,000 at the *end* of the year. By the end of year 2, though, the first annuity payment has grown by 10% ($1,100 = $1,000 × 1.10), and you make the second $1,000 annuity payment. Adding these together, your total investment has grown to **$2,100**. By the end of the third year, the first annuity payment has grown by another 10% ($1,210 = $1,100 × 1.10), the second annuity payment has grown by 10% ($1,100 = $1,000 × 1.10), and you make the final $1,000 annuity payment. Add these together to find that the total investment has grown to **$3,310**. This is the future value of a $1,000 annuity for three years at 10% interest compounded annually.

Table 3. Since annuities consist of multiple payments, calculating the future value of an annuity can be time-consuming, especially as the length of the annuity increases. To make this task more efficient, we can calculate the future value of an annuity using the time value of money tables located at the end of this book, a financial calculator, or a computer spreadsheet.[2]

---

[2]The mathematical formula for calculating the future value of an annuity is a bit more complicated than are these other methods, so we'll focus on those.

Illustration C–12 shows an excerpt of Table 3, Future Value of an Annuity of $1.

Periods (n)	Interest Rates (i)					
	7%	8%	9%	10%	11%	12%
1	1.0000	1.0000	1.0000	1.0000	1.0000	1.0000
2	2.0700	2.0800	2.0900	2.1000	2.1100	2.1200
3	3.2149	3.2464	3.2781	3.3100	3.3421	3.3744
4	4.4399	4.5061	4.5731	4.6410	4.7097	4.7793
5	5.7507	5.8666	5.9847	6.1051	6.2278	6.3528
6	7.1533	7.3359	7.5233	7.7156	7.9129	8.1152
7	8.6540	8.9228	9.2004	9.4872	9.7833	10.0890
8	10.2598	10.6366	11.0285	11.4359	11.8594	12.2997

ILLUSTRATION C–12

Future Value of an Annuity of $1 (excerpt from Table 3)

We calculate the future value of an annuity (FVA) by multiplying the annuity payment by the factor corresponding to three periods and 10% interest:

$$FVA = \$1,000 \times 3.3100 = \$3,310$$

Calculator. You can also calculate the future value of an annuity using a financial calculator. To compute the future value of an annuity, you simply input three amounts: (1) payment amount, (2) interest rate per period, and (3) number of periods. Make sure the present value (PV) is set equal to zero. Illustration C–13 presents the inputs and output using a financial calculator.

CALCULATOR INPUTS

Inputs	Key	Amount
1. Payment amount	PMT	$1,000
2. Interest rate per period	i	10%
3. Number of periods	n	3

CALCULATOR OUTPUT

Future value	FV	$3,310

ILLUSTRATION C–13

Calculate the Future Value of an Annuity Using a Financial Calculator

Excel. Illustration C–14 shows the Excel method for calculating the future value of an annuity.

ILLUSTRATION C–14

Calculate the Future Value of an Annuity Using Excel

Again, let's look at two examples.

Example 1.   Suppose **Pixar Productions** borrows $100 million to produce a sequel to *Toy Story 3* and is required to pay back this amount in five years. If, at the end of each of the next five years, Pixar puts $16 million in an account that is expected to earn 12% interest compounded annually, will the company have enough cash set aside to pay its debt?

The future value of a $16 million annuity over five years that earns 12% annually equals $101,644,800 (= $16,000,000 × 6.3528, time value factor from Table 3, Future Value of an Annuity of $1, with $n = 5$ and $i = 12\%$). Pixar will have enough cash to pay its $100 million debt.

Example 2.   You still have aspirations of being a millionaire in 40 years, but you do not have much money to invest right now. If you set aside just $2,500 at the end of each year with an average annual return of 10%, how much will you have at the end of 40 years?

The future value of a $2,500 annuity over 40 years that earns 10% annually equals $1,106,482 (= $2,500 × 442.5926, time value factor from Table 3, Future Value of an Annuity of $1, with $n = 40$ and $i = 10\%$). You will have quite a bit less assuming an average annual return of 8% ($647,641) and quite a bit more if you can achieve an average annual return of 12% ($1,917,729). Interest rates matter!

PRESENT VALUE

One application of the present value of an annuity relates back to Chapter 9. There, you learned that we report certain liabilities in financial statements at their present values. Most of these liabilities specify that the borrower must pay the lender periodic interest payments (or an annuity) over the life of the loan. As a result, we use the present value of an annuity to determine what portion of these future interest payments the borrower must report as a liability today.

To understand the idea behind the present value of an annuity, you need to realize that each annuity payment represents a single future amount. We calculate the present value of *each* of these future amounts and then add them together to determine the present value of an annuity. This idea is depicted in the timeline in Illustration C–15.

ILLUSTRATION C–15

Present Value of an Annuity

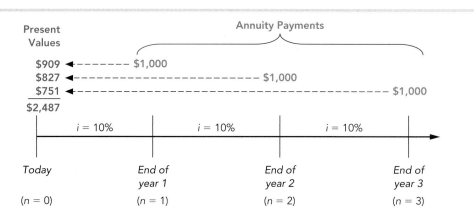

The present value of three $1,000 annual payments discounted at 10% equals the present value of the first payment (**$909**), plus the present value of the second payment (**$827**), plus the present value of the third payment (**$751**). You can verify these amounts by looking at the present value factors in Table 2, Present Value of $1, with $n = 1, 2,$ and 3 and $i = 10\%$. The total present value of the annuity is **$2,487**.

Table 4. Instead of calculating the present value of each annuity payment, a more efficient method is to use time value of money tables. An excerpt of Table 4, Present Value of an Annuity of $1, located at the end of this book, is shown in Illustration C-16.

Periods (n)	7%	8%	9%	10%	11%	12%
			Interest Rates (i)			
1	0.93458	0.92593	0.91743	0.90909	0.90090	0.89286
2	1.80802	1.78326	1.75911	1.73554	1.71252	1.69005
3	2.62432	2.57710	2.53129	2.48685	2.44371	2.40183
4	3.38721	3.31213	3.23972	3.16987	3.10245	3.03735
5	4.10020	3.99271	3.88965	3.79079	3.69590	3.60478
6	4.76654	4.62288	4.48592	4.35526	4.23054	4.11141
7	5.38929	5.20637	5.03295	4.86842	4.71220	4.56376
8	5.97130	5.74664	5.53482	5.33493	5.14612	4.96764

ILLUSTRATION C-16

Present Value of an Annuity of $1 (excerpt from Table 4)

We calculate the present value of an annuity (PVA) by multiplying the annuity payment by the factor corresponding to three periods and 10% interest:

$$PVA = \$1,000 \times 2.48685 = \$2,487$$

Calculator. Illustration C-17 shows the calculator solution.

CALCULATOR INPUTS

Inputs	Key	Amount
1. Payment amount	PMT	$1,000
2. Interest rate per period	i	10%
3. Number of periods	n	3

CALCULATOR OUTPUT

Present value	PV	$2,487

ILLUSTRATION C-17

Calculate the Present Value of an Annuity Using a Financial Calculator

Excel. Illustration C-18 shows the Excel solution.

ILLUSTRATION C-18

Calculate the Present Value of an Annuity Using Excel

Again, let's look at some examples.

Example 1. A movie theatre considers upgrading its concessions area at a cost of $10,000. The upgrades are expected to produce additional cash flows from concession sales of $2,000 per year over the next six years. Should the movie theatre upgrade its concessions area if its discount rate is 8% annually?

The present value of a $2,000 annuity over six years at 8% interest is $9,245.76 (= $2,000 × 4.62288, time value factor from Table 4, Present Value of an Annuity of $1, with $n = 6$ and $i = 8\%$). The $10,000 cost of the upgrade is greater than the present value of the future cash flows of $9,245.76 generated. The theatre will be better off *not* making the investment.

Example 2.   Each year you play the Monopoly game at **McDonald's**. This is your year: As you peel back the sticker, you realize you have both Park Place and Boardwalk. You have just won a million dollars payable in $50,000 installments over the next 20 years. Assuming a discount rate of 10%, how much did you really win?

The present value of a $50,000 annuity over 20 periods at 10% is $425,678 (= $50,000 × 8.51356, time value factor from Table 4, Present Value of an Annuity of $1, with $n = 20$ and $i = 10\%$). The value today of $50,000 per year for the next 20 years is actually less than half a million dollars, though you'd probably not be too disappointed with these winnings.

KEY POINT

Cash payments of equal amounts over equal time intervals are called an annuity. The *future* value of an annuity is the sum of the future values of a series of cash payments. Similarly, the *present* value of an annuity is the sum of the present values of a series of cash payments.

Let's Review

Below are four scenarios related to the future value and present value of an annuity.

1. Manuel is saving for a new car. He puts $2,000 into an investment account at the end of each year for the next five years. He expects the account to earn 12% annually. How much will Manuel have in five years?

2. Ingrid would like to take her family to Disney World in three years. She decides to purchase a vacation package that requires her to make three annual payments of $1,500 at the end of each year for the next three years. If she can earn 9% annually, how much should she set aside today so that the three annual payments can be made?

3. John puts $500 in a savings account at the end of each six months for the next six years that earns 8% interest compounded semiannually. How much will John have in six years?

4. Anna purchases a ring with a selling price of $4,000 and will make four payments of $1,000 at the end of each quarter for the next four quarters. Assuming a discount rate of 16% compounded quarterly, what is Anna's actual cost of the ring today?

Required:

Calculate the time value of money for each scenario.

Solution:

(Rounded to the nearest whole dollar)

1. $2,000 × 6.3528 (FV of Annuity of $1, $n = 5$, $i = 12\%$) = $12,706

2. $1,500 × 2.53129 (PV of Annuity of $1, $n = 3$, $i = 9\%$) = $3,797

3. $500 × 15.0258 (FV of Annuity, $n = 12$, $i = 4\%$) = $7,513

4. $1,000 × 3.62990 (PV of Annuity, $n = 4$, $i = 4\%$) = $3,630

Suggested Homework:
BEC-6, BEC-8;
EC-6, EC-8;
PC-3A&B

KEY POINTS BY LEARNING OBJECTIVE

LO1 Contrast simple and compound interest.

Simple interest is interest we earn on the initial investment only. Compound interest is the interest we earn on the initial investment plus previous interest. We use compound interest in calculating the time value of money.

LO2 Calculate the future value and present value of a single amount.

The *future value* of a single amount is how much that amount today will grow to be in the future. The *present value* of a single amount is the value today of receiving that amount in the future.

LO3 Calculate the future value and present value of an annuity.

Cash payments of equal amounts over equal time intervals are called an annuity. The *future* value of an annuity is the sum of the future values of a series of cash payments. Similarly, the *present* value of an annuity is the sum of the present values of a series of cash payments.

GLOSSARY

Annuity: Cash payments of equal amounts over equal time intervals. **p. C–8**

Compound interest: Interest earned on the initial investment and on previous interest. **p. C–2**

Discount rate: The rate at which someone would be willing to give up current dollars for future dollars. **p. C–5**

Future value: How much an amount today will grow to be in the future. **p. C–2**

Present value: The value today of receiving some amount in the future. **p. C–5**

Simple interest: Interest earned on the initial investment only. **p. C–1**

Time value of money: The value of money today is greater than the value of that same amount of money in the future. **p. C–1**

SELF-STUDY QUESTIONS

1. How does simple interest differ from compound interest?   ■ LO1
   a. Simple interest includes interest earned on the initial investment plus interest earned on previous interest.
   b. Simple interest includes interest earned on the initial investment only.
   c. Simple interest is for a shorter time interval.
   d. Simple interest is for a longer time interval.

2. What is the future value of $100 invested in an account for eight years that earns 10% annual interest, compounded semiannually (rounded to the nearest whole dollar)?   ■ LO2
   a. $214.
   b. $216.
   c. $218.
   d. $220.

3. Present value represents: ■ LO2
   a. The value today of receiving money in the future.
   b. The amount that an investment today will grow to be in the future.
   c. The difference between the initial investment and the growth of that investment over time.
   d. A series of equal payments.

4. Cooper wants to save for college. Assuming he puts $5,000 into an account at the end of each year for five years and earns 12% compounded annually, how much   ■ LO3

will he have saved by the end of the fifth year (rounded to the nearest whole dollar)?

a. $25,000.

b. $31,764.

c. $18,024.

d. $14,096.

Answers to the Self-Study Questions

1. b   2. c   3. a   4. b

REVIEW QUESTIONS

■ **LO1**   1. Define interest. Explain the difference between simple interest and compound interest.

■ **LO2**   2. Identify the three items of information necessary to calculate the future value of a single amount.

■ **LO2**   3. Define the present value of a single amount. What is the discount rate?

■ **LO3**   4. What is an annuity?

■ **LO3**   5. What is the relationship between the present value of a single amount and the present value of an annuity?

For the following, please visit your instructor's *Connect* site.

BRIEF EXERCISES	1-13
EXERCISES	1-8
PROBLEMS: SET A	1-3
PROBLEMS: SET B	1-3

connect
|ACCOUNTING

Learning Objectives

AFTER STUDYING THIS APPENDIX, YOU SHOULD BE ABLE TO:

- ■ **LO1** Explain why companies invest in other companies.
- ■ **LO2** Account for investments in equity securities when the investor has *insignificant* influence.
- ■ **LO3** Account for investments in equity securities when the investor has *significant* influence.
- ■ **LO4** Account for investments in equity securities when the investor has *controlling* influence.
- ■ **LO5** Account for investments in debt securities.

Why Companies Invest in Other Companies

To finance growing operations, a company raises additional funds either by issuing *equity securities,* such as the common and preferred stock we discussed in Chapter 10, or by issuing *debt securities,* such as the bonds we discussed in Chapter 9. These equity and debt securities are purchased by individual investors, by mutual funds, and also by other companies. In this appendix, we focus on investments by companies in equity and debt securities issued by other companies. Companies invest in other companies for a variety of reasons, primarily those indicated in Illustration D–1.

■ **LO1**
Explain why companies invest in other companies.

ILLUSTRATION D–1
Why Companies Invest in Other Companies

1. To receive dividends, earn interest, and gain from the increase in the value of their investment.

2. To temporarily invest excess cash created by operating in seasonal industries.

3. To build strategic alliances, increase market share, or enter new industries.

Companies purchase *equity securities* for dividend income and for appreciation in the value of the stock. Many companies pay a stable dividend stream to their investors. Historically, **General Electric** has been one of the most reliable, highest-dividend-paying stocks on the New York Stock Exchange. However, even GE cut its quarterly dividend payout in 2009, for the first time since 1938, to help free up cash during a severe down cycle in the economy. In contrast, some companies pay little or no dividends. Companies with large expansion plans, called *growth companies,* prefer to reinvest earnings in the growth of the company rather than distribute earnings to investors in the form of cash dividends. For example, **Starbucks**, founded in 1987, did not pay a cash dividend until March 2010. Even without receiving dividends, investors still benefit when companies reinvest earnings, leading to even more profits in the future and eventually higher stock prices.

Companies purchase *debt securities* primarily for the interest revenue they provide, although investment returns also are affected when the values of debt securities change over time. As we discussed in Chapter 9, the value of a debt security with fixed interest payments changes in the opposite direction of interest rates. For example, when general market interest rates decrease, the market value of a bond with fixed interest payments goes up because the fixed interest payments are now more attractive to investors.

The seasonal nature of some companies' operations also influences their investment balances. *Seasonal* refers to the revenue activities of a company varying based on the time (or season) of the year. For instance, agricultural and construction companies enjoy more revenues in the summer, and ski resorts earn most of their revenues in the winter. Most retail companies see their sales revenues increase dramatically during the holiday season. As a result of having seasonal operations, companies save excess cash generated during the busy part of the year to maintain operations during the slower time of the year. With this excess cash, companies tend to purchase low-risk investments such as money market funds (savings accounts), government bonds, or highly rated corporate bonds. These low-risk investments enable companies to earn some interest, while ensuring the funds will be available when needed during the slow season. Investing excess cash in stocks is more risky because the value of stocks varies more than the value of bonds. Stocks typically have greater upside potential, providing a higher average return to their investors than do bonds over the long run. However, stocks can lose value in the short run, making them a better choice for investments that are more long-term in nature.

Companies also can make sizeable long-run stock investments in other companies for strategic purposes. For instance, **AT&T** acquired **Cingular Wireless** to gain a stronger presence in the market for cell phones. **Coca-Cola** acquired **Minute Maid**, and **PepsiCo** purchased **Tropicana**, in order to diversify beyond soft drinks. Sometimes, a company will remove competition and increase market share by purchasing a controlling interest (more than 50% of its voting stock) in a competing company. Companies also might purchase a controlling interest in an established company in a *different* industry to expand into that industry and avoid many of the start-up costs associated with beginning a new business from scratch.

KEY POINT

Companies invest in other companies primarily to receive dividends, earn interest, and gain from the increase in the value of their investment. Companies in seasonal industries often invest excess funds generated during the busy season and draw on these funds in the slow season. Many companies also make investments for strategic purposes to develop closer business ties, increase market share, or expand into new industries.

PART A   EQUITY INVESTMENTS

Equity investments are the "flip side" of issuing stock. One company issues stock, and another company invests by purchasing that stock. We discussed the issuance of stock in Chapter 10. Here, we discuss how companies that purchase stock account for their investment.

The way we account for equity investments is determined by the *degree of influence* an investor has over the company in which it invests. **A guideline for determining the degree of influence is the percentage of stock held by the investor.** Illustration D–2 summarizes the reporting methods for equity investments.

ILLUSTRATION D–2   Accounting for Equity Investments

When one company (investor) purchases more than 50% of the voting stock of another company (investee), the investor has *controlling influence;* by voting those shares, the investor actually can *control* the investee's operations. Companies account for their controlling investments using the consolidation method. Under this method, both companies continue to operate as separate legal entities, but the investing company uses *consolidated* financial statements to report operations, as if the two companies were operating as a single combined company. We'll discuss consolidated statements in more detail later in this appendix.

When ownership is below 50% of the voting shares, the investor still might be able to exercise *significant influence* over the investee. This would be the case if the investor owns a large percentage of the outstanding shares *relative to other shareholders.* By voting all those shares with a single intent, the purchasing company can sway decisions in the direction it desires. When significant influence exists, we account for the investment using the equity method. In the absence of evidence to the contrary, an investor exercises significant influence when it owns between 20% and 50% of the voting shares.

In the most common investment scenario, a corporate investor has *insignificant* influence, often indicated by ownership of less than 20% of the voting shares. In this case, we use the *fair value method.* Fair value is the amount an investment could be bought or sold for in a current transaction between willing parties. For example, when you purchased your car, you and the car dealership (or whomever you bought the car from) came to an agreement on the purchase price, or fair value, of the car. What could you sell that car for today? That's the car's current fair value. When an investor has insignificant influence, we report the investment at fair value. We discuss accounting for equity securities with insignificant influence in more detail next.

Equity Investments with Insignificant Influence

As mentioned above, when the purchasing company has insignificant influence, we use the fair value method. Under the fair value method, equity investments are classified as either trading securities or available-for-sale securities. Trading securities are securities that the investor expects to sell (trade) in the near future. Available-for-sale securities are securities held for reasons other than attempting to profit from trading in the near future.

We first discuss some basic investment transactions, including the purchase of an investment, the receipt of cash dividends, and the sale of an investment. We then address how companies actually adjust their investments to fair value; that adjustment will depend on whether the investment is classified as trading securities or available-for-sale securities.

■ **LO2**
Account for investments in equity securities when the investor has *insignificant* influence.

PURCHASE EQUITY INVESTMENTS

To see how a company accounts for the purchase of an equity investment, let's assume Nathan's Sportswear purchases 100 shares of Canadian Falcon common stock for $30 per share on December 6, 2012. Nathan's Sportswear records the investment as follows:

A	=	L	+	SE	December 6, 2012	Debit	Credit
+3,000					Investments	3,000	
−3,000					Cash		3,000
					(Purchase common stock)		
					($3,000 = 100 shares × $30)		

RECEIVE CASH DIVIDENDS

If Canadian Falcon pays cash dividends of $0.50 per share on December 15, 2012, Nathan's Sportswear records the cash receipt on its 100 shares of stock as follows:

A	=	L	+	SE	December 15, 2012	Debit	Credit
+50					Cash	50	
				+50 Rev↑	Dividend Revenue		50
					(Receive cash dividends)		
					($50 = 100 shares × $0.50)		

SELL EQUITY INVESTMENTS

Now let's assume that Nathan's Sportswear wants to sell its shares of Canadian Falcon. We record the sale of equity investments similar to the sale of many other assets, such as land (discussed in Chapter 7). If the investment sells for *more* than its recorded amount, we record a *gain* on the sale of investments. If the investment sells for *less* than its recorded amount, we record a *loss* on the sale of investments. Gains and losses on the sale of investments are reported in the income statement, with gains being reported as part of other revenues and losses as part of other expenses.

If Nathan's Sportswear sells 10 shares for $36 per share on December 18, 2012, we record the following:

A	=	L	+	SE	December 18, 2012	Debit	Credit
+360					Cash (10 shares × $36)	360	
−300					Investments (10 shares × $30)		300
				+60 Rev↑	Gain (difference)		60
					(Sell investments above recorded amount)		

The difference between the selling price of $36 per share and the currently recorded amount of $30 per share represents a $6 gain on each of the 10 shares. If Nathan's Sportswear then decides on December 26, 2012, to sell another 10 shares for only $28 per share, we record the following:

A	=	L	+	SE	December 26, 2012	Debit	Credit
+280					Cash (10 shares × $28)	280	
				−20 Exp↑	Loss (difference)...	20	
−300					Investments (10 shares × $30)		300
					(Sell investments below recorded amount)		

ADJUST TO FAIR VALUE: TRADING SECURITIES

At the end of each period, we adjust equity investments to fair value. For example, after selling 20 shares, Nathan's Sportswear still owns 80 shares of Canadian Falcon, originally purchased for $30 per share. If Canadian Falcon's stock at the end of 2012 has a current price of $32, then Nathan's Sportswear needs to adjust the recorded amount of the investment ($30) to its current fair value ($32). This requires a $2 upward adjustment to the Investments account.[1]

December 31, 2012	Debit	Credit		A	=	L	+	SE	
Investments	160			+160					
Unrealized Holding Gain—Net Income		160						+160 Rev↑	
(Increase investments to fair value)									
($160 = 80 shares × $2)									

Recording the adjustment to fair value involves an account we've not yet discussed, called *Unrealized Holding Gain—Net Income*. The term *unrealized* means the gain has not been realized (has not been obtained) in the form of actual cash (or the right to receive cash). The gain is *realized* when the investment has been sold and the gain is "locked in." **Because Nathan's Sportswear classifies this investment as a trading security, it reports the unrealized holding gain in the current year's income statement when calculating net income.** Even though the gain is unrealized, reporting it as part of current net income is appropriate because trading securities are actively managed for the purpose of profiting from short-term market price changes. Thus, gains and losses that result from holding trading securities represent measures of success or lack of success in managing investments, and these gains and losses are properly included as part of net income.

ADJUST TO FAIR VALUE: AVAILABLE-FOR-SALE SECURITIES

Unlike trading securities, available-for-sale securities are *not* acquired for the purpose of profiting from short-term price changes. Thus, unrealized gains and losses from holding available-for-sale securities are not considered current measures of performance to be included in net income. Instead, unrealized gains and losses from changes in the fair value of available-for-sale securities are reported as *other comprehensive income*, which we discuss below.

Referring to our previous example, if Nathan's Sportswear accounts for its investment in Canadian Falcon as available-for-sale securities, it will report the $2 increase in fair value at the end of the year as part of other comprehensive income rather than as part of net income:

December 31, 2012	Debit	Credit		A	=	L	+	SE	
Investments	160			+160					
Unrealized Holding Gain—Other Comprehensive Income		160						+160 Rev↑	
(Increase investments to fair value)									
($160 = 80 shares × $2)									

Most revenues, expenses, gains, and losses are included in net income that is reported in the typical income statement. **Comprehensive income** is a broader measure of income in which we report all changes in stockholders' equity other than investment by stockholders and payment of dividends. Comprehensive

---

[1]Many companies increase the investment *indirectly* with a debit to a Fair Value Adjustment allowance rather than to the Investments account itself. We record the fair value adjustment directly to the Investments account, as this is simpler and reinforces the concept that the adjustment to fair value directly affects the Investments account.

income includes all of the typical income statement items plus other comprehensive income items, such as unrealized holding gains and losses on available-for-sale securities:

Comprehensive income = Net income + Other comprehensive income

Illustration D–3 shows an example of the statement of comprehensive income for Nathan's Sportswear for 2012. The statement includes:

- revenues earned from receiving dividends on December 15.
- realized gain on the sale of 10 shares of stock on December 18.
- realized loss on the sale of 10 shares on December 26.
- and unrealized holding gain resulting from the upward fair value adjustment on December 31, the end of the year.

To complete the statement of comprehensive income, we assume sales revenue totals $2,000 and operating expenses are $1,500.

ILLUSTRATION D–3

Statement of Comprehensive Income

NATHAN'S SPORTSWEAR
Statement of Comprehensive Income (condensed)
For the year ended 2012

Sales revenue	$2,000
Operating expenses	1,500
Operating income	500
Dividend revenue	50
Gain on sale of investments	60
Loss on sale of investments	(20)
Net income	590
Unrealized holding gain	160
Comprehensive income	$ 750

Income Statement

Statement of Comprehensive Income

KEY POINT

We report investments at fair value when a company has an insignificant influence over another company in which it invests, often indicated by an ownership interest of less than 20%. For investments classified as trading securities, unrealized holding gains and losses are included in net income. For investments classified as available-for-sale securities, unrealized holding gains and losses are included as other comprehensive income.

Let's Review

Flip Side

This problem is the flip side of a Let's Review problem presented in Chapter 10, on page 474. Sheer Designs, a custom clothing designer, has heard great things about Slacks 5th Avenue and has decided to make a small investment (insignificant influence) in the corporation's common stock. Sheer Designs has the following transactions relating to its investment in Slacks 5th Avenue.

January	1	Purchase 500 shares of common stock for $20 per share.
June	30	Receive a cash dividend of $1 per share.
October	1	Sell 100 shares of common stock for $25 per share.
December 31		The fair value of Slacks 5th Avenue's stock equals $23 per share.

Required:

1. Record each of these transactions, including the fair value adjustment on December 31. Assume the investment is classified as available-for-sale securities.
2. Calculate the balance in the Investments account on December 31.

Solution:

1. Record transactions:

January 1	Debit	Credit
Investments	10,000	
Cash		10,000
(Purchase common stock)		
($10,000 = 500 shares × $20)		
June 30		
Cash	500	
Dividend Revenue		500
(Receive cash dividends)		
($500 = 500 shares × $1)		
October 1		
Cash *(100 shares × $25)*..	2,500	
Investments *(100 shares × $20)*		2,000
Gain *(difference)*		500
(Sell investments above recorded amount)		
December 31		
Investments	1,200	
Unrealized Holding Gain—Other Comprehensive Income		1,200
(Adjust investments to fair value)		
($1,200 = 400 shares × $3)		

2. The balance in the Investments account on December 31 is $9,200, which equals the 400 remaining shares times $23 per share fair value. The balance in the Investments account can be verified by posting all transactions to a T-account, as follows.

Investments

10,000	
	2,000
1,200	
Bal. 9,200	

Suggested Homework:
**BED-3, BED-4;
ED-2, ED-3;
PD-1A&B**

 INTERNATIONAL FINANCIAL REPORTING STANDARDS (IFRS)

International accounting standards differ from U.S. accounting standards in the classification of investments. Under IFRS, the default classification for investments in equity securities is called FVTPL (Fair Value through Profit and Loss). Accounting for FVTPL is similar to that for trading securities under U.S. GAAP. Investments in equity securities classified as FVTOCI (Fair Value through Other Comprehensive Income) are treated similar to available-for-sale securities under U.S. GAAP. Investments in the FVTOCI category have *unrealized* gains and losses included in other comprehensive income.

Equity Investments with Significant Influence

■ LO3
Account for investments in equity securities when the investor has *significant* influence.

When a company owns between 20% and 50% of the common stock in another company, it is presumed that the investing company exercises significant influence over the investee. Share ownership provides voting rights, and by voting these shares, the investing company can sway decisions in the direction it desires, such as the selection of members of the board of directors. This significant influence changes the accounting for the investment. When a company has significant influence over an investee, the company is required to use the equity method. Under this method, the investor records the investment as if the investee is a part of the company. Let's discuss some specific transactions using the equity method.

PURCHASE EQUITY INVESTMENTS

Assume that, on December 6, 2012, Nathan's Sportswear purchases 25% of Canadian Falcon's common stock for $25,000. By holding 25% of the stock, Nathan's Sportswear can now exert significant influence over the operations of Canadian Falcon. Nathan's Sportswear records this equity investment as:

A = L + SE	December 6, 2012	Debit	Credit
+25,000	Investments	25,000	
−25,000	Cash		25,000
	(Purchase common stock)		

RECOGNIZE EQUITY INCOME

Under the equity method, the investor (Nathan's Sportswear) includes in net income its portion of the investee's (Canadian Falcon's) net income. Assume that on December 31, 2012, Canadian Falcon reports net income of $30,000 for the year. Nathan's Sportswear records $7,500 of equity income, which represents its 25% share of Canadian Falcon's net income of $30,000.

A = L + SE	December 31, 2012	Debit	Credit
+7,500	Investments	7,500	
+7,500 Rev↑	Equity Income		7,500
	(Earn equity income)		
	($7,500 = $30,000 × 25%)		

Equity Income is a revenue account included in the "other revenue" portion of the income statement. The reason Nathan's Sportswear can record a portion of Canadian Falcon's net income as its own is that significant ownership essentially eliminates the independent operations of the two companies. Nathan's Sportswear can significantly influence the operations of Canadian Falcon. **Therefore, the success (or failure) of Canadian Falcon's operations should partially be assigned to Nathan's Sportswear and recognized as income (or loss) in its income statement, based on its portion of ownership.**

RECEIVE CASH DIVIDENDS

Because we record equity income when the investee reports net income (as in the transaction above), it would be inappropriate to record equity income again when the investee distributes that same net income as dividends to the investor. To do so would be to double-count equity income. Instead, the investor records dividend payments received from the investee as a *reduction* in the Investments account. Assuming Canadian Falcon pays total dividends of $500 to all shareholders,

Nathan's Sportswear receives its share of $125 (= $500 × 25%) and records the following:

	Debit	Credit	A	=	L	+	SE
Cash	125		+125				
Investments		125	−125				
(Receive cash dividends)							
($125 = $500 × 25%)							

The rationale for this accounting is that the investee is distributing cash in the form of dividends. This distribution of assets by the investee reduces company value. Therefore, the value of the investment goes down based on its portion of ownership. The investor records this decrease in investment value by decreasing the Investments account.

We can see the balances in the Investments and Equity Income accounts for Nathan's Sportswear after posting the three transactions above.

Investments

Initial investment	25,000		
25% of net income	7,500	125	25% of dividends
	Bal. 32,375		

Equity Income

	7,500	25% of net income
	Bal. 7,500	

The Investments account increases by the initial investment and the investor's share of the investee's net income, and it decreases by the investor's share of the investee's dividends. The Equity Income account reflects the investor's share of net income rather than its share of dividends.

 KEY POINT

We initially record equity investments at cost. Under the equity method, the balance of the Investments account increases for the investor's share of the investee's net income and decreases for the investor's share of the investee's cash dividends. Equity Income reflects the investor's share of the investee's net income.

The equity method can differ significantly from recording investments under the fair value method. Under the fair value method, the investment by Nathan's Sportswear would be recorded at the purchase price of $25,000 and then be adjusted to fair value at the end of each period. Under the equity method, no adjustment is made to fair value.[2] In addition, Nathan's Sportswear would record only $125 of dividend revenue under the fair value method, rather than the $7,500 of equity income recorded using the equity method.

Let's Review

Sheer Designs, a custom clothing designer, has heard great things about Slacks 5th Avenue and has decided to make a 40% investment (significant influence) in the corporation's common stock. Sheer Designs has the following transactions relating to its investment in Slacks 5th Avenue.

[2]Adjustment to fair value is an allowable alternative under the equity method but is not common in practice.

January	1	Purchases 500 shares of common stock for $20 per share.
June	30	Receives a cash dividend of $500 (or $1 per share), representing its 40% share of Slacks 5th Avenue's total dividend distribution of $1,250.
December 31		Slacks 5th Avenue reports total net income of $5,000 for the year.
December 31		The fair value of Slacks 5th Avenue's stock equals $23 per share.

Required:

1. Record each of these transactions.
2. Calculate the balance of the Investments account on December 31.

Solution:

1. Record transactions:

January 1	Debit	Credit
Investments	10,000	
Cash		10,000
(*Purchase common stock*)		
June 30		
Cash	500	
Investments		500
(*Receive cash dividends*)		
(*$500 = 500 shares × $1*)		
December 31		
Investments	2,000	
Equity Income		2,000
(*Earn equity income*)		
(*$2,000 = $5,000 × 40%*)		
December 31		
No adjustments are recorded for fair value changes when using the equity method.		

2. The balance of the Investments account on December 31 is $11,500. The balance of the Investments account can be verified by posting all transactions to a T-account.

Investments	
10,000	
	500
2,000	
Bal. 11,500	

Suggested Homework:
BED-7, BED-8;
ED-6, ED-7;
PD-2A&B

INTERNATIONAL FINANCIAL REPORTING STANDARDS

Like U.S. GAAP, international accounting standards require the equity method when the investor exerts significant influence over investees (which they call "associates"). A difference, though, is that IFRS requires that the accounting policies of investees be adjusted to correspond to those of the investor when applying the equity method. U.S. GAAP has no such requirement.

Equity Investments with Controlling Influence

If a company purchases more than 50% of the voting stock of another company, it's said to have a *controlling influence*. By voting these shares, the investor actually can control the acquired company. The investor is referred to as the *parent;* the investee is the *subsidiary*. Investments involving the purchase of more than 50% of the voting stock are accounted for by the parent using the **consolidation method**.

Under the consolidation method, the parent company prepares **consolidated financial statements**. These statements combine the parent's and subsidiary's operating activities as if the two companies were a *single* reporting company, even though both companies continue to operate as separate legal entities. Illustration D–4 demonstrates the concept of consolidation.

■ LO4
Account for investments in equity securities when the investor has *controlling* influence.

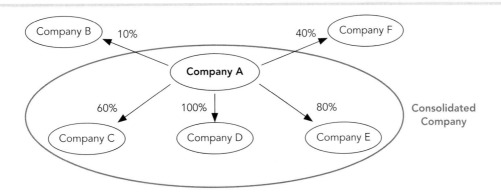

ILLUSTRATION D–4

Consolidation Method

Suppose Company A owns at least part of the common stock of five other companies. When preparing financial statements, Company A combines its financial statement results with those of all companies in which it has greater than 50% ownership (in this instance, Companies C, D, and E). For example, if Company A has $10 million cash and Companies C, D, and E have $2 million, $4 million, and $6 million, respectively, the consolidated balance sheet would report cash of $22 million.[3] The cash balances for Companies B and F are not included in the consolidated financial statements of Company A. The 10% ownership (insignificant influence) in Company B is accounted for using the fair value method, while the 40% ownership (significant influence) in Company E is accounted for using the equity method.

 KEY POINT

We account for investments involving the purchase of more than 50% of the voting stock of another company using the consolidation method. Under the consolidation method, the parent company prepares consolidated financial statements, in which the companies are combined as if they were a single company.

---

[3]Any transactions between Companies A, C, D, and E are eliminated from consolidated reporting because these transactions are not with external parties. This avoids "double-counting" those amounts in the consolidated statements. For example, we report amounts owed by Company C to Company D as accounts payable in Company C's balance sheet and as accounts receivable in Company D's balance sheet. However, these amounts are not included in the consolidated balance sheet because a company can't owe money to itself, and the consolidated company is treated as a single company for financial reporting purposes.

■ **LO5**
Account for
investments in debt
securities.

Flip Side

DEBT INVESTMENTS

Debt investments are the "flip side" of long-term debt: One party *borrows* by issuing a debt instrument, while another party *lends* by investing in the debt instrument. In Chapter 9, we discussed how to record the issuance of bonds (a specific type of debt instrument). Here, we discuss how to record an investment in bonds.

PURCHASE DEBT INVESTMENTS

Assume that on January 1, 2012, Nathan's Sportswear purchases $100,000 of 7%, 10-year bonds issued by RC Enterprises, with interest receivable semiannually on June 30 and December 31 each year. If the market rate of interest is 8%, Nathan's Sportswear will purchase the bonds at a discount, paying only $93,205 for the bonds.[4] Because the bonds pay only 7% compared to the prevailing market rate of 8%, we know that Nathan's Sportswear will buy them at less than the face amount of $100,000. Nathan's Sportswear records this bond investment as:

A = L + SE	January 1, 2012	Debit	Credit
+93,205	**Investments**	**93,205**	
−93,205	Cash		**93,205**
	(Purchase bonds)		

Nathan's Sportswear initially records the investment at $93,205. The carrying value will increase from $93,205 (purchase price) to $100,000 (face value) over the 10-year life of the bonds. Let's see why.

EARN INTEREST REVENUE

Interest revenue is the carrying value ($93,205 to start) times the market rate (8% annually, or 4% semiannually). The cash received is the face value ($100,000) times the stated rate (7% annually, or 3.5% semiannually). On June 30, 2012, six months after the initial bond investment, Nathan's Sportswear records interest revenue and cash received as follows:

A = L + SE	June 30, 2012	Debit	Credit
+3,500	**Cash** (= $100,000 × 7% × ½)......................................	**3,500**	
+228	**Investments** (difference)...	**228**	
+3,728 Rev↑	Interest Revenue (= $93,205 × 8% × ½)		**3,728**
	(Receive semiannual interest revenue)		

The investment earned interest revenue of $3,728, but the investor received cash of only $3,500. Therefore, Nathan's Sportswear is entitled to receive the remaining $228 when the bond matures. That's why the investment's carrying value increases by that amount. Because the carrying value of bonds increases over time, interest revenue will also increase each semiannual interest period because it's calculated as a constant rate (8% × ½ in this example) times that increasing carrying value. On December 31, 2012, Nathan's Sportswear records cash received and interest revenue for the second six-month period as:

A = L + SE	December 31, 2012	Debit	Credit
+3,500	**Cash** (= $100,000 × 7% × ½)......................................	**3,500**	
+237	**Investments** (difference)...	**237**	
+3,737 Rev↑	Interest Revenue (= [$93,205 + 228] × 8% × ½)		**3,737**
	(Receive semiannual interest revenue)		

[4]The bond price of $93,205 is calculated in Illustration 9–5.

The amortization schedule in Illustration D–5 demonstrates how the carrying amount of the bond investment would increase until it reaches maturity. Notice that the amounts in the amortization schedule are identical to those in the schedule we used for *bonds payable* in Chapter 9, Illustration 9–13.

Flip Side

(1) Date	(2) Cash Received	(3) Interest Revenue	(4) Increase in Carrying Value	(5) Carrying Value
	Face Amount × Stated Rate	Carrying Value × Market Rate	(3) − (2)	Prior Carrying Value + (4)
1/1/12				$ 93,205
6/30/12	$3,500	$3,728	$228	93,433
12/31/12	3,500	3,737	237	93,670
*	*	*	*	*
*	*	*	*	99,057
6/30/21	3,500	3,962	462	99,519
12/31/21	3,500	3,981	481	$100,000

ILLUSTRATION D–5

Amortization Schedule for Bonds Issued at a Discount

SELL DEBT INVESTMENTS

Let's assume that market interest rates have dropped from 8% to 6% during 2012. Nathan's Sportswear decides to sell the bonds on December 31, 2012, when their carrying value is $93,670 (see amortization schedule in Illustration D–5). When interest rates go down, the investment value of bonds goes up. If the market rate drops to 6%, the value of the bonds will increase to $106,877.[5] The bonds have a carrying value on December 31, 2012, of only $93,670, but Nathan's Sportswear sells them for $106,877 and records a gain for the difference.

December 31, 2012	Debit	Credit
Cash	106,877	
Investments		93,670
Gain (difference)		13,207
(Sell bonds before maturity)		

A = L + SE
+106,877
−93,670
+13,207 Rev↑

The gain on the sale of bonds is reported in the income statement as an increase to net income. Of course, if the bond was sold for a loss, net income would decrease.

ADJUST TO FAIR VALUE

We classify debt investments as either (1) held-to-maturity securities, (2) trading securities, or (3) available-for-sale securities. Held-to-maturity securities are debt securities that the company expects to hold until they *mature*, which means until they become payable.[6] Since we do not expect to sell these securities until they mature, companies are not required to adjust held-to-maturity securities to fair value.[7]

The accounting for debt investments classified as trading securities or available-for-sale securities is nearly identical to that already discussed for equity securities. Recall that *trading securities* are securities that the investor expects to sell (trade)

[5]The $106,877 is based on the following inputs: future value, $100,000; interest payment each semiannual period, $3,500; market interest rate each semiannual period, 3% (6% ÷ 2 semiannual periods); and periods to maturity, 18 (9 years left × 2 semiannual periods each year).
[6]Equity securities do not have a held-to-maturity classification because equity securities do not have a maturity date.
[7]However, U.S. GAAP does allow companies to elect a fair value option. Under this option, companies may report held-to-maturity securities at fair value, with unrealized gains and losses recognized in income in the period in which they occur—the same approach we use to account for trading securities.

in the near future. These investments are adjusted to fair value with the unrealized gain or loss included in net income. *Available-for-sale securities* are investments that do not fit the other two categories; they are not expected to be sold in the near future, yet they are not expected to be held to maturity either. These investments are adjusted to fair value with the unrealized gain or loss included in comprehensive income.

 KEY POINT

Bond investments are the "flip side" of bonds payable. Bond investments are long-term assets that earn interest revenue, while bonds payable are long-term liabilities that incur interest expense.

Let's Review

Assume that on January 1, 2012, Wally World issues $200,000 of 9% bonds, due in 10 years, with interest payable semiannually on June 30 and December 31 each year. American Life Insurance Company (ALICO) purchases all of the bonds.

Required:

1. If the market rate is 9%, the bonds will sell for $200,000. Record the investment in bonds by ALICO on January 1, 2012, and receipt of the first semiannual interest payment on June 30, 2012.

2. If the market rate is 10%, the bonds will sell for $187,538. Record the investment in bonds by ALICO on January 1, 2012, and receipt of the first semiannual interest payment on June 30, 2012.

3. If the market rate is 8%, the bonds will sell at $213,590. Record the investment in bonds by ALICO on January 1, 2012, and receipt of the first semiannual interest payment on June 30, 2012.

Solution:

1. Market rate of 9%:

January 1, 2012	Debit	Credit
Investments	200,000	
Cash		200,000
(Purchase bonds)		

June 30, 2012		
Cash	9,000	
Interest Revenue		9,000
(Receive semiannual interest revenue)		
(= $9,000 = $200,000 × 9% × ½)		

2. Market rate of 10%:

January 1, 2012	Debit	Credit
Investments	187,538	
Cash		187,538
(Purchase bonds)		

June 30, 2012		
Cash *(= $200,000 × 9% × ½)*	9,000	
Investments *(difference)*	377	
Interest Revenue *(= $187,538 × 10% × ½)*		9,377
(Receive semiannual interest revenue)		

3. Market rate of 8%:

January 1, 2012	Debit	Credit
Investments	213,590	
Cash		213,590
(Purchase bonds)		
June 30, 2012		
Cash (= $200,000 \times 9\% \times \frac{1}{2}$)...	9,000	
Investments (difference)		456
Interest Revenue (= $213,590 \times 8\% \times \frac{1}{2}$)		8,544
(Receive semiannual interest revenue)		

Suggested Homework:
**BED-11, BED-12;
ED-10, ED-11;
PD-4A&B**

KEY POINTS BY LEARNING OBJECTIVE

LO1 Explain why companies invest in other companies.

Companies invest in other companies primarily to receive dividends, earn interest, and gain from the increase in the value of their investment. Companies in seasonal industries often invest excess funds generated during the busy season and draw on these funds in the slow season. Many companies also make investments for strategic purposes to develop closer business ties, increase market share, or expand into new industries.

LO2 Account for investments in equity securities when the investor has *insignificant* influence.

We report investments at fair value when a corporation has an insignificant influence over another company in which it invests, often indicated by an ownership interest of less than 20%. For investments classified as trading securities, unrealized holding gains and losses are included in net income. For investments classified as available-for-sale securities, unrealized holding gains and losses are included as other comprehensive income.

LO3 Account for investments in equity securities when the investor has *significant* influence.

We initially record equity investments at cost. Under the equity method, the balance of the Investments account increases for the investor's share of the investee's net income and decreases for the investor's share of the investee's dividend payment. Equity income reflects the investor's share of the investee's net income.

LO4 Account for investments in equity securities when the investor has *controlling* influence.

We account for investments involving the purchase of more than 50% of the voting stock of another company using the consolidation method. Under the consolidation method, the parent company prepares consolidated financial statements, in which the companies are combined as if they were a single company.

LO5 Account for investments in debt securities.

Bond investments are the "flip side" of bonds payable. Bond investments are long-term assets that earn interest revenue, while bonds payable are long-term liabilities that incur interest expense.

GLOSSARY

Available-for-sale securities: Securities held for reasons other than attempting to profit from trading in the near future. **p. D–3**

Comprehensive income: A broad measure of income that reports all changes in stockholders' equity other than investment by stockholders and payment of dividends. **p. D–5**

Consolidated financial statements: Combination of the separate financial statements of the parent (purchasing company) and the subsidiary (acquired company) into a single set of financial statements. **p. D–11**

Consolidation method: Method of recording equity investments when one company owns more than 50% of the voting stock of another company. Under this method, the investing company uses *consolidated* financial statements to report operations, as if the two companies were operating as a single combined company. **pp. D–3, D–11**

Debt investments: Investments made in the debt issued by another party. **p. D–12**

Equity investments: Investments made in the equity (or stock) issued by another party. **p. D–2**

Equity method: Method of recording equity investments when an investor has significant influence over, yet does not control, the operations of the investee, often indicated by ownership of between 20% and 50% of the voting shares. Under this method, the investor company records the investment as if the investee is a part of the company. **pp. D–3, D–8**

Fair value: The amount for which the investment could be bought or sold in a current transaction between willing parties. **p. D–3**

Fair value method: Method of recording equity investments when an investor has insignificant influence, often indicated by ownership of less than 20% of the voting shares. Under this method, we classify equity investments as either trading securities or available-for-sale securities and report investments at their fair value. **p. D–3**

Held-to-maturity securities: Debt securities that are expected to be held until they *mature,* which means until they become payable. **p. D–13**

Trading securities: Securities that the investor expects to sell in the near future. **p. D–3**

SELF-STUDY QUESTIONS

■ LO1

1. One of the primary reasons for investing in equity securities includes:
   a. Receiving dividend payments.
   b. Acquiring debt of competing companies.
   c. Earning interest revenue.
   d. Deducting dividend payments for tax purposes.

■ LO1

2. One of the primary reasons for investing in debt securities includes:
   a. Deducting interest payments for tax purposes.
   b. Receiving dividend payments.
   c. Earning interest revenue.
   d. Acquiring ownership control in other companies.

■ LO2

3. On November 17, 2012, Tasty Foods purchased 1,000 shares (10%) of Eco-Safe Packaging's voting stock for $12 per share. Because Tasty Foods' intent in making the investment is to make a quick profit by trading in the near term, the investment is classified as a trading security. By the end of 2012, Eco-Safe Packaging's stock price has dropped to $10 per share. How would the drop in stock price affect Tasty Foods' net income in 2012?
   a. Decrease net income by $12,000.
   b. Decrease net income by $10,000.
   c. Decrease net income by $2,000.
   d. No effect.

■ LO2

4. On November 17, 2012, Tasty Foods purchased 1,000 shares (10%) of Eco-Safe Packaging's voting stock for $12 per share. Because Tasty Foods has no immediate plans to sell the stock, the investment is classified as an available-for-sale security. By the end of 2012, Eco-Safe Packaging's stock price has dropped to $10 per share. How would the drop in stock price affect Tasty Foods' net income in 2012?
   a. Decrease net income by $12,000.
   b. Decrease net income by $10,000.
   c. Decrease net income by $2,000.
   d. No effect.

■ LO3

5. On January 1, 2012, Tasty Foods purchased 3,000 shares (30%) of Eco-Safe Packaging's voting stock for $12 per share. On December 31, 2012, Eco-Safe Packaging reports net income $10,000 and a total dividend payment of $2,000, and the stock price has dropped to $10 per share. For how much would Tasty Foods report its investment in Eco-Safe Packaging at the end of 2012?

a. $30,000.
b. $38,400.
c. $36,000.
d. $39,000.

6. On January 1, 2012, Tasty Foods purchased 10,000 shares (100%) of Eco-Safe Packaging's ■ LO4
voting stock for $12 per share. Throughout the year, both companies continue to operate
as separate legal entities. By December 31, 2012, Eco-Safe Packaging's cash balance
is $2,000, and Tasty Foods' cash balance is $5,000. In preparing its year-end financial
statements, for how much would Tasty Foods report its cash balance?
a. $7,000.
b. $5,000.
c. $3,000.
d. $2,000.

7. On January 1, 2012, Eco-Safe Packaging issues $100,000 of 8%, 5-year bonds with ■ LO5
interest payable semiannually on June 30 and December 31. The market interest
rate for bonds of similar risk and maturity is 6%. Tasty Foods purchases all of the
bonds for $108,530. Which of the following would correctly record Tasty Foods'
investment in bonds on January 1?

a. Cash	108,530	
Investments		108,530
b. Investments	108,530	
Cash		108,530
c. Cash	100,000	
Investments		100,000
d. Investments	100,000	
Cash		100,000

8. Refer to question 7. How much interest revenue would Tasty Foods record at the ■ LO5
time it receives the first semiannual payment on June 30?
a. $4,341.
b. $8,000.
c. $6,512.
d. $3,256.

Answers to the Self-Study Questions
1. a   2. c   3. c   4. d   5. b   6. a   7. b   8. d

REVIEW QUESTIONS

1. Explain why a company might invest in another company. ■ LO1
2. How can an investor benefit from an equity investment that does not pay dividends? ■ LO1
3. How might the investing activity for a company that operates a ski resort vary ■ LO1
throughout the year?
4. Provide an example of an equity investment in another company undertaken for ■ LO1
strategic purposes.
5. What is the "flip side" of an investment in equity securities? ■ LO1
6. How does a company determine whether to account for an equity investment using ■ LO1
the fair value method, equity method, or consolidation method?
7. Investments in *equity* securities for which the investor has insignificant influence ■ LO2
over the investee are classified for reporting purposes under the fair value method
in one of two categories. What are these two categories?

■ LO2   8. Explain how we report dividends received from an investment under the fair value method.

■ LO2   9. Discuss the difference between an unrealized holding gain and a realized gain.

■ LO2   10. When using the fair value method, we adjust the reported amount of the investment for changes in fair value after its acquisition. If the security is classified as trading, how do we report unrealized holding gains and losses?

■ LO2   11. When using the fair value method, we adjust the reported amount of the investment for changes in fair value after its acquisition. If the security is classified as available-for-sale, how do we report unrealized holding gains and losses?

■ LO3   12. Under what circumstances do we use the equity method to account for an investment in stock?

■ LO3   13. Explain how we report dividends received from an investment under the equity method.

■ LO4   14. Discuss the meaning of consolidated financial statements.

■ LO4   15. When is it appropriate to consolidate financial statements of two companies? Discuss your answer in terms of the relation between the parent and the subsidiary.

■ LO5   16. What is the "flip side" of an investment in debt securities?

■ LO5   17. If bonds are purchased at a *discount*, what will happen to the carrying value of the investment in bonds and the amount recorded for interest revenue over time?

■ LO5   18. If bonds are purchased at a *premium*, what will happen to the carrying value of the investment in bonds and the amount recorded for interest revenue over time?

■ LO5   19. When interest rates go down, what happens to the value of an investment in bonds that pay a fixed interest rate?

■ LO5   20. Investments in *debt* securities are classified for reporting purposes in one of three categories. Explain each of these three categories.

For the following, please visit your instructor's *Connect* site.

BRIEF EXERCISES	1-12
EXERCISES	1-11
PROBLEMS: SET A	1-4
PROBLEMS: SET B	1-4

International Financial Reporting Standards

Learning Objectives

AFTER STUDYING THIS APPENDIX, YOU SHOULD BE ABLE TO:

- ■ **LO1** Explain the reasons for differences in accounting practices across countries and the need for convergence.
- ■ **LO2** Understand the role of the International Accounting Standards Board (IASB) in the development of International Financial Reporting Standards (IFRS).
- ■ **LO3** Recognize the major differences between U.S. GAAP and IFRS.

The Globalization of Accounting Standards

On November 15, 2007, the U.S. Securities and Exchange Commission voted unanimously to accept from "foreign private issuers" financial statements that are prepared using International Financial Reporting Standards (IFRS) without reconciliation to U.S. generally accepted accounting principles. There is no doubt that the United States, followed by most of the rest of the world, is moving toward converging U.S. GAAP with IFRS. Convergence refers to the process by which U.S. GAAP and IFRS will eventually merge to become a single set of accounting standards.

But convergence of standards hasn't happened yet, and much misunderstanding exists about the status and timing of the convergence process. Why are these changes taking place? Who are the key players? What critical differences between U.S. and international GAAP exist currently? How can you keep up-to-date with this changing landscape of converging accounting standards? This appendix is designed to answer these questions.

We first explore the reasons for differences in accounting practices across countries. These differences created the need for convergence to a single set of international financial reporting standards. Then, we discuss a brief history and background regarding the development of international financial reporting standards. Finally, we review key differences between U.S. GAAP and IFRS for each chapter of the text. Given the fast pace of change in this area, this appendix will be updated periodically on our website to make sure you are up-to-date with the convergence process.

Differences in Accounting Practices

Most countries have organizations responsible for determining accounting and reporting standards. In some countries, the United Kingdom for instance, the organization responsible for standard setting is a private standard setter similar to the FASB in the United States. In other countries, like France, the organization responsible for standard setting is part of the government.

Financial accounting standards and practices differ from country to country for many reasons, including different legal systems, the influence of tax laws, sources of financing, inflation, culture, political influence of other countries, and the level of economic development. Illustration E–1 (next page) provides a summary and further explanation of the reasons why accounting practices differ across countries.

■ **LO1**
Explain the reasons for differences in accounting practices across countries and the need for convergence.

ILLUSTRATION E–1

Reasons Why
Accounting Practices
Differ across Countries

Reason	Further Explanation
1. Legal system	Common-law countries (the United States, the United Kingdom, and Canada) place greater emphasis on public information, while code-law countries (Germany and France) rely more heavily on private information.
2. Tax laws	For countries whose tax standards are closely tied to financial reporting standards (continental Europe and Japan), accounting earnings tend to be lower so companies can minimize tax payments.
3. Sources of financing	In countries where debt financing is more common (Germany and Japan) than equity financing, there is greater emphasis on reporting the ability of the company to repay debt than on its ability to earn profits for its investors.
4. Inflation	Historically high inflation in some countries (Argentina and Brazil) has created a need to account for the effect of inflation on assets and liabilities.
5. Culture	Some countries (Brazil and Switzerland) are more secretive, leading to fewer financial disclosures.
6. Political and economic ties	Countries that share strong political and/or economic ties (British colonies) often have similar accounting practices.
7. Economic development	More economically developed economies (the United States and the United Kingdom) have a need for more complex accounting standards.

Note that overlap exists in the reasons described. Accounting research has extensively focused on the legal system (common law vs. code law) as a way to describe overall differences in accounting practices between countries. *Common law* derives from English case law, in which rules are established over time primarily through private-sector professional organizations. *Code law* derives from Roman law, in which rules are an all-embracing set of requirements and procedures. Common-law countries such as the United States, the United Kingdom, Australia, and Canada share many similarities. For instance, these countries have separate rules for financial accounting and tax accounting, rely more on equity financing, and have political and economic ties with Britain. Code-law countries such as those in Central Europe and Japan also are influenced by the same factors, but in contrasting ways. Code-law countries have similar rules for financial accounting and tax accounting and rely more on debt financing. Many code-law countries have political and economic ties that began with Germany in World War II.

 KEY POINT

Differences in legal systems, tax laws, sources of financing, inflation, culture, political and economic ties, and economic development influence accounting practices across countries.

As you might imagine, differences in accounting practices can cause problems for investors who must struggle to compare companies whose financial statements are prepared under different methods. Investors unfamiliar with the accounting practices of a particular country are less likely to invest in firms from that country because of this uncertainty. Many believe that convergence of accounting practices among countries will increase the flow of resources across borders, making it easier for companies to raise international capital.

Divergent accounting rules also can cause problems for multinational corporations. A company doing business in more than one country may find it difficult and costly to comply with more than one set of accounting standards.

 KEY POINT

Differences in accounting practices make it more difficult for investors to compare companies from different countries. Variations in accounting standards also make it more difficult for multinational corporations to comply with multiple accounting standards. Convergence of accounting practices is expected to increase the flow of investment across borders.

International Financial Reporting Standards

INTERNATIONAL ACCOUNTING STANDARDS BOARD

In response to differences in accounting standards and practices across countries, the **International Accounting Standards Committee (IASC)** was formed in 1973 to develop a single set of global accounting standards. The IASC reorganized itself in 2001 and created a new standard-setting body called the International Accounting Standards Board (IASB). The IASB has two objectives: (1) to develop a single set of high-quality, understandable, and enforceable global accounting standards that lead to transparent and comparable information in general purpose financial statements, and (2) to cooperate with national accounting standard-setters to achieve convergence in accounting standards around the world.

The IASC issued 41 International Accounting Standards (IAS), which the IASB endorsed at its formation. Since then, the IASB has revised many of the previous standards and has issued standards of its own, called International Financial Reporting Standards (IFRS), sometimes pronounced "eye-furs." Compliance with these standards is voluntary, since the IASB has no enforcement authority. However, many countries now base their national accounting standards on international accounting standards. The International Organization of Securities Commissions (IOSCO) approved a resolution permitting its members to use these standards to prepare their financial statements for cross-border offerings and listings. Over 100 jurisdictions, including China, Australia, and all of the countries in the European Union (EU), either require or permit the use of IFRS or a local variant of IFRS.[1]

■ **LO2**
Understand the role of the International Accounting Standards Board (IASB) in the development of International Financial Reporting Standards (IFRS).

PRINCIPLES- VS. RULES-BASED STANDARDS

Many Europeans, in comparing IFRS with U.S. GAAP, claim that IFRS is more principles-based and U.S. GAAP is more rules-based. *Principles-based accounting standards* emphasize broad principles of accounting with relatively less emphasis on detailed implementation rules. In comparison, *rules-based accounting standards* provide additional detailed guidance to help users implement the standards. An advantage of principles-based standards is that they are more concise, allowing preparers and users of accounting information to exercise judgment in focusing on the key issues. An advantage of rules-based standards is that they are more precise, providing additional guidance to preparers and users on an issue.

In reality, both U.S. GAAP and IFRS have standards that are more principles-based and standards that are more rules-based. However, both standard setters (the FASB and IASB) recognize that in order to achieve convergence and reduce the

[1]See *http://www.iasplus.com/useias.htm*.

volume of accounting rules internationally, future international accounting standards will need to be more principles-based.

NORWALK AGREEMENT

The FASB and IASB signed the *Norwalk Agreement* in 2002, formalizing their commitment to the convergence of U.S. GAAP and IFRS. Under this agreement, the two boards pledged to remove existing differences between their standards and to coordinate their future standard-setting agendas so that major issues are worked on together. Robert Herz, chairman of the FASB, testified before Congress: "We believe now is the appropriate time to develop a plan for moving all U.S. public companies to an improved version of IFRS and to consider any actions needed to strengthen the IASB as the global accounting standard setter." In fact, in that testimony he advocated working to develop a blueprint for moving U.S. public companies from U.S. standards to an improved version of IFRS. Herz emphasized that this move would need to be accompanied by consistent, high-quality enforcement, auditing, and education of participants in the capital markets.

Arguments against convergence to IFRS.   Not everyone agrees, though, with the idea of convergence set forth in the Norwalk Agreement. Although many argue that a single set of global standards will improve comparability of financial reporting and facilitate access to capital, others argue that U.S. standards should remain customized to fit the stringent legal and regulatory requirements of the U.S. business environment. There also is concern that differences in implementation and enforcement from country to country will make accounting appear more uniform than actually is the case. Another argument for maintaining the two sets of standards is that competition between alternative standard-setting regimes is healthy and can lead to improved standards.

Where convergence currently stands.   The Norwalk Agreement did not specify a timetable for convergence, but active efforts have been ongoing since 2002. U.S. standards and IFRS have not fully converged, but beginning in 2007 the SEC eliminated the costly requirements for foreign companies that issue stock in the United States to include in their financial statements a reconciliation of IFRS to U.S. GAAP. There also is serious discussion of allowing U.S. companies to choose whether to prepare their financial statements according to U.S. GAAP or IFRS.

 KEY POINT

The IASB seeks (1) to develop a single set of high-quality, understandable, and enforceable global accounting standards that lead to transparent and comparable information in general purpose financial statements, and (2) to cooperate with national accounting standard setters to achieve convergence in accounting standards around the world.

Differences between U.S. GAAP and IFRS

■ LO3
Recognize the major differences between U.S. GAAP and IFRS.

In this section, we provide chapter-by-chapter descriptions of the important differences that remain between U.S. GAAP and IFRS. Many of these differences are highlighted in IFRS boxes throughout the text.

Conceptual framework

Chapter 1: Accounting Information and Decision Making   In the United States, the FASB's conceptual framework serves primarily to guide standard setters, while internationally the IASB's conceptual framework also serves to indicate GAAP when more specific standards are not available. The FASB and the IASB are working together to develop a common conceptual framework that would underlie a uniform set of standards internationally. This framework will build upon the existing IASB and FASB frameworks and will consider developments since the original frameworks were issued.

Chapter 2: The Accounting Information System

U.S. GAAP and IFRS provide similar general guidance concerning the timing and measurement of revenue recognition. However, U.S. GAAP includes many additional rules and other guidance promulgated by the FASB, the SEC, and others. Some of those rules are designed to specify appropriate accounting for particular industries; others are designed to discourage aggressive revenue recognition.

It is unclear currently how the additional rules that are included in U.S. GAAP will be handled in the convergence process. Also, the FASB and IASB have undertaken a major project that is reconsidering the definition of revenue and when it should be recognized. Depending on the outcome of that project, revenue recognition practices could change dramatically.

Chapter 3: The Financial Reporting Process

The FASB and IASB are working on a project to establish a common standard for presenting information in financial statements, including the classification and display of line items and the aggregation of line items into subtotals and totals. This standard will have a dramatic impact on the presentation of financial statements.

An important part of the current proposal involves organizing all of the basic financial statements using a common format—operating, investing, and financing activities. These three classifications would be used in the income statement, statement of stockholders' equity, balance sheet, and statement of cash flows.

Chapter 4: Cash and Internal Controls

Accounting for cash under both U.S. GAAP and IFRS is essentially the same. No major convergence efforts are anticipated.

In the United States, *Section 404* of the Sarbanes-Oxley Act (SOX) requires management to document and assess the effectiveness of all internal control processes that could affect financial reporting. Many U.S. corporate executives complain about the high cost of compliance with Section 404. In other countries, the burden of documenting effective internal controls is much less, or even nonexistent. In fact, many feel that the increased burden of compliance with Section 404 has caused many foreign companies to be reluctant to list their shares on U.S. stock exchanges. Bob Greifeld, president and CEO of the NASDAQ stock exchange, stated: "In my travels to countries like China, India, and Israel, I meet with the new generation of international entrepreneurs who are building businesses and dreaming of the day they can take their companies public. . . . 90% of international small companies intending to go public are choosing to list abroad because of SOX costs and concerns."

Chapter 5: Receivables and Sales

Accounting for receivables, including the allowance for uncollectible accounts, is essentially the same under both U.S. GAAP and IFRS. No major convergence efforts are anticipated.

Revenue recognition

Common format for financial statements

Cash

Assessing internal control

Receivables

Chapter 6: Inventory and Cost of Goods Sold

LIFO

Inventory cost flow assumptions.   The LIFO inventory method is not allowed under IFRS, which likely will be a major convergence challenge. The *LIFO conformity rule,* which requires U.S. companies that use LIFO for tax purposes to also use LIFO for financial reporting, means that the elimination of LIFO for financial reporting also would require the elimination of its use for tax purposes. As discussed in Chapter 6, an advantage of using LIFO when inventory costs are rising is that it results in a lower tax burden. Resolving this issue would require agreement not only by the FASB and IASB, but also by the U.S. Congress, as it is responsible for setting tax laws in the United States.

Because of the LIFO restriction, many U.S. multinational companies use LIFO only for their domestic inventories and use FIFO or average cost for their foreign subsidiaries. **General Mills** provides an example (see Illustration E–2) with a disclosure note included in a recent annual report.

ILLUSTRATION E–2

Disclosure Note about Inventories

> **GENERAL MILLS**
> **Notes to the Financial Statements (excerpt)**
>
> **Inventories**
>
> All inventories in the United States other than grain are valued at the lower of cost, using the last-in, first-out (LIFO) method, or market. Inventories outside of the United States are valued at the lower of cost, using the first-in, first-out (FIFO) method, or market.

Market value in lower-of-cost-or-market

Lower-of-cost-or-market.   Under both U.S. GAAP and IFRS, inventory is reported at the lower-of-cost-or-market. In the United States, market value is defined as *replacement cost,* which is the cost to replace the item in its identical form. However, the designated market value according to IFRS is *net realizable value,* which is the selling price of inventory less any selling costs.

Cadbury Schweppes plc, a U.K. company, prepares its financial statements according to IFRS. The disclosure note in Illustration E–3 shows the designation of market as net realizable value.

ILLUSTRATION E–3

Disclosure Note about Net Realizable Value

> **CADBURY SCHWEPPES plc**
> **Notes to the Financial Statements (excerpt)**
>
> **Inventories**
>
> Inventories are recorded at the lower of average cost and estimated net realizable value.

Reversal of inventory write-downs

When market value falls below cost, companies are required to write down inventory from cost to market value, causing total assets to decrease and total expenses to increase. If in a future period the market value of this inventory increases, reversal of the inventory write-down is *required* for most types of inventory under IFRS, but *not allowed* under U.S. GAAP. This means that U.S. GAAP is more conservative by not allowing the asset reduction and expense recognition to be reversed when circumstances indicate that they should.

Chapter 7: Long-Term Assets

Valuation of property, plant, and equipment.   Under U.S. GAAP, companies are not allowed to revalue property, plant, and equipment (PP&E) to fair value for financial reporting purposes. IFRS allows, but does not require, revaluation of PP&E to fair value. *IAS No. 16* allows a company to value PP&E subsequent to initial valuation at (1) cost less accumulated depreciation or (2) fair value (revaluation). If revaluation is chosen, all assets within a class of PP&E must be revalued on a regular basis.

Fair values for PP&E

British Airways plc, a U.K. company, prepares its financial statements according to IFRS. The disclosure note in Illustration E–4 describes the company's choice to value PP&E at cost.

BRITISH AIRWAYS plc
Notes to the Financial Statements (excerpt)

Property, plant, and equipment

Property, plant, and equipment is held at cost. The Group has a policy of not revaluing tangible fixed assets.

ILLUSTRATION E–4

Disclosure Note about Valuation of Property, Plant, and Equipment

---

Valuation of intangible assets.   U.S. GAAP also prohibits revaluation of intangible assets to fair value. *IAS No. 38* allows a company to value an intangible asset subsequent to initial valuation at (1) cost less accumulated amortization or (2) fair value if fair value can be determined by reference to an active market. If revaluation is chosen, all assets within that class of intangibles must be revalued on a regular basis.

Fair values for intangibles

 COMMON MISTAKE

Many students have been taught that financial statements are based on historical cost. This is no longer the case. The only historical cost amounts in financial statements are those for cash and land in the domestic currency. All other amounts reflect changes in time, events, or circumstances since the transaction date. For instance, companies record an allowance on accounts receivable, write down inventory for impairment, depreciate or amortize long-term assets and write them down to fair value when impaired, recognize most investments at fair value, and amortize the discount or premium on long-term debt.

Research and development expenditures.   U.S. GAAP requires all research and development expenditures to be expensed in the period incurred. IFRS, though, draws a distinction between research activities and development activities. Research expenditures are expensed in the period incurred. However, development expenditures that meet specified criteria are capitalized as an intangible asset.

R&D expensed vs. capitalized

Heineken, a company based in Amsterdam, prepares its financial statements according to IFRS. The disclosure note in Illustration E–5 (next page) describes the criteria used for capitalizing development expenditures.

Chapter 8: Current Liabilities

Definition of liabilities.   As we discussed earlier, the FASB and the IASB presently are working together to develop a common conceptual framework that might eventually underlie a uniform set of standards internationally. One aspect of the project is examining the definition of liabilities, a change which could affect the way some current liabilities are reported.

Liabilities definition

ILLUSTRATION E–5

Disclosure Note about Capitalization of Development Expenditures

HEINEKEN
Notes to the Financial Statements (excerpt)

Software, research and development, and other intangible assets

Expenditures on research activities, undertaken with the prospect of gaining new technical knowledge and understanding, are recognized in the income statement when incurred. Development activities involve a plan or design for the production of new or substantially improved products and processes. Development expenditures are capitalized only if development costs can be measured reliably, the product or process is technically and commercially feasible, future economic benefits are probable, and Heineken intends to and has sufficient resources to complete development and to use or sell the asset.

Threshold for contingent liabilities

Contingencies. Accounting for contingencies is part of a broader international standard, *IAS No. 37,* "Provisions, Contingent Liabilities, and Contingent Assets." U.S. GAAP has no equivalent general standards on "provisions," but does provide specific guidance on contingencies. A difference in accounting relates to determining the existence of a contingent liability. We accrue a contingent liability under U.S. GAAP if it's both probable and can be reasonably estimated. IFRS rules are similar, but the threshold is "more likely than not," representing a lower threshold than "probable."

Valuation of long-term contingencies

Another difference is whether to report a long-term contingency at its face amount or its present value. Under IFRS, the present value of the estimated cash flows is reported when the effect of *time value of money is material.* According to U.S. GAAP, though, discounting of cash flows is allowed when the *timing of cash flows is certain.* Illustration E–6 shows a portion of a footnote from the financial statements of **Electrolux**, which reports under IFRS.

ILLUSTRATION E–6

Disclosure Note about Recognition of Contingencies

ELECTROLUX
Notes to the Financial Statements (excerpt)

Note 29: U.S. GAAP information

Discounted provisions
Under IFRS and U.S. GAAP, provisions are recognized when the Group has a present obligation as a result of a past event, and it is probable that an outflow of resources will be required to settle the obligation, and a reliable estimate can be made of the amount of the obligation. Under IFRS, where the effect of time value of money is material, the amount recognized is the present value of the estimated expenditures. *IAS 37* states that long-term provisions shall be discounted if the time value is material. According to U.S. GAAP, discounting of provisions is allowed when the timing of cash flow is certain.

Chapter 9: Long-Term Liabilities The joint project of the FASB and the IASB to develop a common conceptual framework includes examining the definition of liabilities, potentially affecting the way we account for long-term liabilities. More specifically, the two boards are collaborating on projects related to "hybrid" securities that likely will eliminate differences in how we account for convertible debt. Longer term, the two boards are cooperating on a project that addresses the distinction between liabilities and equity, which likely will eliminate many existing differences.

Distinction between liabilities and equity

Treatment of convertible debt

Convertible bonds. Under IFRS, convertible debt is divided into its liability (bonds) and equity (conversion option) elements. Under U.S. GAAP, the entire issue price is recorded as a liability.

Chapter 10: Stockholders' Equity   The joint "financial statement presentation" project, referred to earlier under the heading for Chapter 3, will dramatically change the format and display of all financial statements, including the balance sheet—referred to in the project as the *statement of financial position*. The proposed organization of all of the basic financial statements using the same format—operating, investing, and financing activities—will significantly affect the presentation of stockholders' equity items. Current differences between U.S. GAAP and IFRS include the following:

Use of the term "reserves."   Stockholders' equity is classified under IFRS into two categories: common stock and "reserves." The term *reserves* is considered misleading and thus is discouraged under U.S. GAAP.

Stockholders' equity "reserves"

Distinction between debt and equity for preferred stock.   Under IFRS, most preferred stock ("preference shares") is reported as debt, with the dividends reported in the income statement as interest expense. Under U.S. GAAP, most preferred stock is included in stockholders' equity, with the dividends reported as a reduction in retained earnings. Under U.S. GAAP, only "mandatorily redeemable" preferred stock is reported as debt. **Unilever** describes such a difference in a disclosure note, shown in Illustration E–7.

Classification of preferred stock

UNILEVER
Notes to the Financial Statements (excerpt)

Additional information for U.S. investors

Preference shares
Under *IAS 32,* Unilever recognizes preference shares that provide a fixed preference dividend as borrowings with preference dividends recognized in the income statement. Under U.S. GAAP such preference shares are classified in shareholders' equity with dividends treated as a deduction to shareholders' equity.

ILLUSTRATION E–7
Disclosure Note about Preferred Stock

Reacquired shares.   IFRS does not permit the "retirement" of shares. All buybacks are treated as treasury stock.

Retirement of shares

Chapter 11: Statement of Cash Flows   Like U.S. GAAP, international standards also require a statement of cash flows. Consistent with U.S. GAAP, cash flows are classified as operating, investing, or financing. However, U.S. GAAP designates cash outflows for interest payments and cash inflows from interest and dividends received as operating cash flows. IFRS allows companies to report cash outflows from interest payments as either operating *or* financing cash flows and cash inflows from interest and dividends as either operating *or* investing cash flows. U.S. GAAP classifies dividends paid to shareholders as financing cash flows. The international standard allows companies to report dividends paid as either financing *or* operating cash flows.

Classification of cash flows

In the proposed organization of the basic financial statements, the classification currently used in the statement of cash flows—operating, investing, and financing activities—will remain. The FASB is leaning toward requiring the direct method of reporting operating activities; the IASB is leaning toward permitting *either* the direct or indirect method.

Direct or indirect method

U.S. GAAP requires that significant noncash activities be reported either on the face of the statement of cash flows or in a disclosure note. IFRS requires reporting in a disclosure note, disallowing presentation on the face of the statement.

Disclosure of noncash activities

Chapter 12: Financial Statement Analysis

Definition of
discontinued operations

Discontinued operations.   U.S. GAAP considers a discontinued operation to be a component of an entity whose operations and cash flows can be clearly distinguished from the rest of the entity that has either been disposed of or classified as held for sale. IFRS also defines a discontinued operation as a component of an entity that has been disposed of or is classified as held for sale. What constitutes a component of an entity, however, differs considerably between U.S. GAAP and IFRS. IFRS considers a component to be primarily either a major line of business or geographical area of operations. The U.S. definition is much broader than its international counterpart.

To better understand the effects of the different definitions on financial reporting, consider the case of **Gottschalks, Inc.**, a department and specialty store chain operating in the western United States. During the fiscal year ended February 3, 2007, the company reported a discontinued operation in its income statement and disclosed the following in a note, shown in Illustration E–8.

ILLUSTRATION E–8

Disclosure Note
about Discontinued
Operations

GOTTSCHALKS, INC.
Notes to the Financial Statements (excerpt)

Discontinued operations

The Company closed one underperforming store in the Seattle metro-area during the third quarter of fiscal 2006 and one underperforming store in the Seattle/Tacoma market during the first quarter of fiscal 2006. During fiscal 2005, the Company closed two underperforming stores in the Seattle/Tacoma market. These stores . . . are considered discontinued operations.

Because these closures qualified as discontinued operations under U.S. GAAP, Gottschalks reported the discontinued operations as a separate item in the income statement. However, because Gottschalks continued to operate eight stores in the state of Washington, the company's closing of a few stores does not constitute the discontinuance of either a major line of business or geographical area, so this would not be treated as a discontinued operation under IFRS. Instead, the income effects of operating the stores during the year and their sale would have been reported in various locations throughout the income statement.

Definition of
extraordinary items

Extraordinary items.   U.S. GAAP provides for the separate reporting, as an extraordinary item, of a material gain or loss that is unusual in nature and infrequent in occurrence. In 2003, the IASB revised *IAS No. 1,* "Presentation of Financial Statements." The revision states that neither the income statement nor any notes may contain any items called "extraordinary."

 KEY POINT

U.S. GAAP and IFRS are converging, but many differences still exist.

KEY POINTS BY LEARNING OBJECTIVE

LO1 Explain the reasons for differences in accounting practices across countries and the need for convergence.

Differences in legal systems, tax laws, sources of financing, inflation, culture, political and economic ties, and economic development influence accounting practices across countries.

Differences in accounting practices make it more difficult for investors to compare companies from different countries. Variations in accounting standards also make it more difficult for multinational corporations to comply with multiple accounting standards. Convergence of accounting practices is expected to increase the flow of investment across borders.

LO2 Understand the role of the International Accounting Standards Board (IASB) in the development of International Financial Reporting Standards (IFRS).

The IASB seeks (1) to develop a single set of high-quality, understandable, and enforceable global accounting standards that lead to transparent and comparable information in general purpose financial statements,

and (2) to cooperate with national accounting standard setters to achieve convergence in accounting standards around the world.

LO3 Recognize the major differences between U.S. GAAP and IFRS.

U.S. GAAP and IFRS are converging, but many differences still exist.

GLOSSARY

Convergence: The process by which U.S. GAAP and IFRS will eventually merge to become a single set of accounting standards. **p. E–1**

International Accounting Standards Board (IASB): The body primarily responsible for creating a single set of global accounting standards. **p. E–3**

International Financial Reporting Standards (IFRS): Pronounced "eye-furs," these are the accounting rules previously set by the International Accounting Standards Committee (IASC) and currently set by the International Accounting Standards Board (IASB). **p. E–3**

SELF-STUDY QUESTIONS

1. Which of the following reason(s) help explain why accounting practices may differ across countries?   ■ **LO1**
   a. Legal system.
   b. Culture.
   c. Political and economic ties.
   d. All of the above.

2. The body primarily responsible for creating a single set of global accounting standards is the: ■ **LO2**
   a. International Federation of Accountants.
   b. International Accounting Standards Board.
   c. Financial Accounting Standards Board.
   d. International Organization of Securities Commissions.

3. For which of the following topics is accounting under both U.S. GAAP and IFRS essentially the same?   ■ **LO3**
   a. Receivables.
   b. Long-term assets.
   c. Stockholders' equity.
   d. Statement of cash flows.

4. Which inventory cost flow assumption does IFRS not allow?   ■ **LO3**
   a. Specific identification.
   b. FIFO.
   c. LIFO.
   d. Average cost.

5. Which of the following statements is true regarding revaluation of property, plant, and equipment to fair value?   ■ **LO3**
   a. Both U.S. GAAP and IFRS allow revaluation of property, plant, and equipment to fair value.
   b. Neither U.S. GAAP nor IFRS allows revaluation of property, plant, and equipment to fair value.

    c. U.S. GAAP allows, but IFRS does not allow, revaluation of property, plant, and equipment to fair value.

    d. U.S. GAAP does not allow, but IFRS allows, revaluation of property, plant, and equipment to fair value.

Answers to the Self-Study Questions
1. d   2. b   3. a   4. c   5. d

REVIEW QUESTIONS

■ LO1   1. How is the organization responsible for standard setting in the United Kingdom different from that in France? Which is closer to the organization responsible for standard setting in the United States (the FASB)?

■ LO1   2. Describe at least five reasons why accounting practices differ across countries.

■ LO1   3. Which factor explaining why accounting practices differ across countries do you think is most important? Explain why.

■ LO1   4. What difficulties do differences in accounting standards create for investors?

■ LO1   5. What difficulties do differences in accounting standards create for multinational corporations in preparing their financial statements?

■ LO2   6. What are the two primary objectives of the International Accounting Standards Board (the IASB)?

■ LO2   7. Provide at least one argument against the trend toward convergence between U.S. GAAP and IFRS.

■ LO2   8. Describe the Norwalk Agreement. What is the significance of this agreement?

■ LO3   9. What is meant by a conceptual framework in accounting? Why is it important that the FASB and the IASB develop a common conceptual framework?

■ LO3   10. Explain how an income statement might be organized along the same categories currently used in the statement of cash flows—operating, investing, and financing activities.

■ LO3   11. Which inventory cost flow assumption is allowed under U.S. GAAP but not under IFRS? Explain why some U.S. companies will lobby strongly to keep this method as an allowable alternative.

■ LO3   12. When using the lower-of-cost-or-market inventory method, how is market value defined under U.S. GAAP and under IFRS?

■ LO3   13. What effect does writing down inventory have on total assets and net income in that reporting period? The reversal of an inventory write-down in a future period, which is required under IFRS but not allowed under U.S. GAAP, has what effect on total assets and net income?

■ LO3   14. What does it mean to revalue a long-term asset? How do U.S. GAAP and IFRS differ regarding revaluation of long-term assets?

■ LO3   15. How do IFRS rules differ in the reporting of research and development costs? Which is more conservative in the reporting of research and development costs, U.S. GAAP or IFRS?

■ LO3   16. Would a company be more likely to report a contingent liability under U.S. GAAP or IFRS? Which is more conservative in the reporting of loss contingencies, U.S. GAAP or IFRS?

■ LO3   17. How is preferred stock reported differently under U.S. GAAP and IFRS? Do you think preferred stock is a liability or an equity item? Why?

■ LO3   18. How does the reporting of extraordinary items differ under U.S. GAAP and IFRS?

For the following, please visit your instructor's *Connect* site.

EXERCISES   1-8

Additional Perspectives

Great Adventures

(The Great Adventures problem continues in each chapter.)

Continuing Problem

AP1–1 Tony Matheson plans to graduate from college in May 2012 after spending four years earning a degree in sports and recreation management. Since beginning T-ball at age five, he's been actively involved in sports and enjoys the outdoors. Each summer growing up, he and his father would spend two weeks at a father/son outdoor camp. These fond memories are part of the reason he chose his major. He wants to remain involved in these outdoor activities and provide others with the same adventures he was able to share with his dad. He decides to start an outdoor adventure company. However, he's not sure he has the business background necessary to do this.

This is where Suzie Ramos can help. Suzie also plans to graduate in May 2012 with a major in business. Suzie and Tony first met their sophomore year and have been friends ever since as they share a strong interest in sports and outdoor activities.

They decide to name their company Great Adventures. They will provide clinics for a variety of outdoor activities such as kayaking, mountain biking, rock climbing, wilderness survival techniques, orienteering, backpacking, and other adventure sports.

Required:
1. What are the three primary forms of business organizations Tony and Suzie might choose for Great Adventures? Explain the advantages and disadvantages of each. Which form do you recommend for Great Adventures?
2. Discuss some of the typical financing, investing, and operating activities that a company like Great Adventures is likely to have.
3. What specific account names for assets, liabilities, stockholders' equity, revenues, and expenses would the company likely use to record its business transactions?
4. To report company performance, Suzie plans to prepare the four primary financial statements. Explain the type of information provided by each statement.

American Eagle Outfitters, Inc.

Financial Analysis

AP1–2 Financial information for **American Eagle** is presented in Appendix A at the end of the book.

Required:
1. Determine the amounts American Eagle reports for total assets, total liabilities, and total stockholders' equity in the balance sheet for the most recent year. Verify that the basic accounting equation balances.
2. American Eagle refers to its income statement using another name. What is it?
3. Determine the amounts American Eagle reports for net sales and net income in its income statement for the most recent year.
4. For investing activities, what are the largest inflows and largest outflows for the most recent year reported in the statement of cash flows? For financing activities, what are the largest inflows and largest outflows?

5. Who is the company's auditor? (See the Report of Independent Registered Public Accounting Firm.) What does the report indicate about the amounts reported in the company's financial statements?

Financial Analysis

The Buckle, Inc.

AP1–3 Financial information for **The Buckle** is presented in Appendix B at the end of the book.

Required:

1. Determine the amounts The Buckle reports for total assets, total liabilities, and total stockholders' equity in the balance sheet for the most recent year. Verify that the basic accounting equation balances.
2. The Buckle refers to its income statement using another name. What is it?
3. Determine the amounts The Buckle reports for net sales and net income in its income statement for the most recent year.
4. For investing activities, what are the largest inflows and largest outflows for the most recent year reported in the statement of cash flows? For financing activities, what are the largest inflows and largest outflows?
5. Who is the company's auditor? (See the Report of Independent Registered Public Accounting Firm.) What does the report indicate about the amounts reported in the company's financial statements?

Comparative Analysis

American Eagle Outfitters, Inc. vs. The Buckle, Inc.

AP1–4 Financial information for **American Eagle** is presented in Appendix A at the end of the book, and financial information for **The Buckle** is presented in Appendix B at the end of the book.

Required:

1. Which company reports higher total assets?
2. Which company reports higher total liabilities? Does this always mean this company has a higher chance of not being able to repay its debt and declare bankruptcy? Explain.
3. What relevant information do total assets and total liabilities provide to creditors deciding whether to lend money to American Eagle versus The Buckle?
4. Which company reports higher net income? Does this always mean this company's operations are more profitable? Explain.
5. What relevant information does net income provide to investors who are deciding whether to invest in American Eagle versus The Buckle?

Ethics

AP1–5 Management has the responsibility of accurately preparing financial statements when communicating with investors and creditors. Another group, auditors, serves an independent role by helping to ensure that management has in fact appropriately applied GAAP in preparing the company's financial statements. Auditors examine (audit) financial statements to express a professional, independent opinion. The opinion reflects the auditors' assessment of the statements' fairness, which is determined by the extent to which they are prepared in compliance with GAAP.

Suppose an auditor is being paid $1,000,000 by the company to perform the audit. In addition, the company plans to pay the auditor $500,000 over the next year for business consulting advice and another $200,000 for preparing its tax returns. The auditor and management of the company have always shared a friendly relationship, which partly explains the company's willingness to give the auditor additional work for $700,000.

Required:
How might an auditor's ethics be challenged while performing an audit?

Internet Research

AP1–6 The purpose of this research case is to introduce you to the Internet home pages of the Securities and Exchange Commission (SEC) and the Financial Accounting Standards Board (FASB).

Required:
1. Access the SEC home page on the Internet (*www.sec.gov*). Under "About the SEC," choose "What We Do." What is the mission of the SEC? Why was the SEC created? What are the two objectives of the 1933 Securities Act? The 1934 Securities Exchange Act established the SEC. What does the 1934 Act empower the SEC to require?
2. Access *www.sec.gov/investor/pubs/begfinstmtguide.htm*. What are the four main financial statements discussed by the SEC? What does each report? What information is disclosed in the notes and management discussion and analysis (MD&A)?
3. Access the FASB home page on the Internet (*www.fasb.org*). Select "Facts About FASB." Describe the mission of the FASB. What is the relation between the SEC and the FASB?
4. Obtain a copy of the annual report of **ConocoPhillips** for the most recent year. You can find the annual report at the company's website (*www.conocophillips.com*) in the investor information section or at the SEC's website (*www.sec.gov*) using EDGAR (Electronic Data Gathering, Analysis, and Retrieval). The SEC requires that Form 10-K, which includes the annual report, be filed on EDGAR. Answer the following questions:
   (a) Did ConocoPhillips prepare the four financial statements discussed by the SEC?
   (b) In the MD&A section, how does the company describe its business environment?
   (c) Find the note disclosures to the financial statements. What does the disclosure on segment information discuss?

Written Communication

AP1–7 Maria comes to you for investment advice. She asks, "Which company's stock should I buy? There are so many companies to choose from and I don't know anything about any of them."

Required:
Respond to Maria by explaining the two functions of financial accounting. Specifically address the four financial statements reported by companies and the information contained in each. Also explain the role of the auditor in the preparation of financial statements. What advice can you give her about finding a company's stock to buy?

Chapter 2

Continuing Problem

Great Adventures

(This is a continuation of the Great Adventures problem from Chapter 1.)

AP2–1 Tony and Suzie graduate from college in May 2012 and begin developing their new business. They begin by offering clinics for basic outdoor activities such as mountain biking or kayaking. Upon developing a customer base, they'll hold their first adventure races. These races will involve four-person teams that race from one checkpoint to the next using a combination of kayaking, mountain biking, orienteering, and trail running. In the long run, they plan to sell outdoor gear and develop a ropes course for outdoor enthusiasts.

On July 1, 2012, Tony and Suzie organize their new company as a corporation, Great Adventures Inc. The articles of incorporation state that the corporation will sell 20,000 shares of common stock for $1 each. Each share of stock represents a unit of ownership. Tony and Suzie will act as co-presidents of the company. The following business activities occur during July.

July 1	Suzie purchases $10,000 of Great Adventures' common stock using cash she saved during college.
1	Tony purchases $10,000 of Great Adventures' common stock by borrowing from a local bank using his personal vehicle as collateral.
1	Suzie purchases a one-year insurance policy for $4,800 ($400 per month) to cover injuries to participants during outdoor clinics.
2	The company pays legal fees of $1,500 associated with incorporation.
4	Suzie purchases office supplies of $1,800 on account.
7	Suzie pays advertising of $300 to a local newspaper for an upcoming mountain biking clinic to be held on July 15. Attendees will be charged $50 the day of the clinic.
8	Tony purchases 10 mountain bikes, paying $12,000 cash.
15	On the day of the clinic, Great Adventures receives cash of $2,000 from 40 bikers. Tony conducts the mountain biking clinic.
22	Because of the success of the first mountain biking clinic, Tony holds another mountain biking clinic and the company receives $2,300.
24	Suzie pays advertising of $700 to a local radio station for a kayaking clinic to be held on August 10. Attendees can pay $100 in advance or $150 on the day of the clinic.
30	Great Adventures receives cash of $4,000 in advance from 40 kayakers for the upcoming kayak clinic.

Required:
1. Record each transaction in July.
2. Post each transaction to T-accounts.
3. Prepare a trial balance.

Financial Analysis

American Eagle Outfitters, Inc.

AP2–2 Financial information for **American Eagle** is presented in Appendix A at the end of the book.

Required:
1. Is American Eagle's company size increasing? To answer, calculate the percentage change in total assets and percentage change in net sales for the most recent year.
2. Is American Eagle's total profitability increasing? Determine your answer by calculating the percentage change in net income for the most recent year.

3. Did American Eagle issue any common stock in the most recent year?
4. Do you see the term *debit* or *credit* listed in the balance sheet? Which account types in the balance sheet increase with a debit and which ones increase with a credit?
5. Do you see the term *debit* or *credit* listed in the income statement? Which account types in the income statement increase with a debit? Which increase with a credit?

The Buckle, Inc.

Financial Analysis

AP2–3 Financial information for **The Buckle** is presented in Appendix B at the end of the book.

Required:

1. Is The Buckle's company size increasing? Determine your answer by calculating the percentage change in total assets and percentage change in net sales for the most recent year.
2. Is The Buckle's total profitability increasing? Determine your answer by calculating the percentage change in net income for the most recent year.
3. Did The Buckle issue any common stock in the most recent year?
4. Do you see the term *debit* or *credit* listed in the balance sheet? Which account types in the balance sheet increase with a debit and which ones increase with a credit?
5. Do you see the term *debit* or *credit* listed in the income statement? Which account types in the income statement increase with a debit? Which increase with a credit?

American Eagle Outfitters, Inc., vs. The Buckle, Inc.

Comparative Analysis

AP2–4 Financial information for **American Eagle** is presented in Appendix A at the end of the book, and financial information for **The Buckle** is presented in Appendix B at the end of the book.

Required:

Determine which company's growth rate in total assets, net sales, and net income is greater. Why do you think this might be the case?

Ethics

AP2–5 Larry has been the chief financial officer (CFO) of Maxima Auto Service for the past 10 years. The company has reported profits each year it's been in business. However, this year has been a tough one. Increased competition and the rising costs of labor have reduced the company's profits. On December 30, Larry informs Robert, the company's president and Larry's closest friend for the past 10 years, that it looks like the company will report a net loss (total expenses will be greater than total revenues) of about $50,000 this year.

The next day, December 31, while Larry is preparing the year-end reports, Robert stops by Larry's office to tell him that an additional $75,000 of revenues needs to be reported and that the company can now report a profit. When Larry asks about the source of the $75,000, Robert tells him, "Earlier in the month some customers paid for auto services with cash, and with this cash I bought additional assets for the company. That's why the $75,000 never showed up in the bank statement. I just forgot to tell you about this earlier." When Larry asks for more specifics about these transactions, Robert mumbles, "I can't recall where I placed the customer sales invoices or the purchase receipts for the assets, but don't worry; I know they're here. We've been friends for a lot of years and you can trust me. Now, let's hurry and finish those reports and I'll treat you to dinner tonight at the restaurant of your choice."

Required:

Discuss the ethical dilemma Larry faces.

Internet Research

AP2–6 Obtain a copy of the annual report of **Apple Inc.** for the most recent year. You can find the annual report at the company's website (*www.apple.com*) in the investor information section or at the Securities and Exchange Commission's website (*www.sec .gov*) using EDGAR (Electronic Data Gathering, Analysis, and Retrieval). Form 10-K, which includes the annual report, is required to be filed on EDGAR. Search or scroll within the annual report to find the financial statements.

Required:
Determine the following from the company's financial statements:
1. What amount does the company report for accounts receivable? What does this amount represent?
2. What amount does the company report for accounts payable? What does this amount represent?
3. The company reports a single amount for accrued expenses in the liability section of the balance sheet. What are some possible liabilities included in this amount?
4. What amount does the company report for common stock? What does this amount represent?
5. Determine whether the company's total assets equal total liabilities plus total stockholders' (or shareholders') equity.
6. Apple refers to its income statement as the statement of operations. What amount does the company report for net sales? This amount represents sales of the company's products over what period of time?
7. What are some of the expenses listed in the income statement?
8. Do the company's total revenues exceed total expenses? By how much?

Written Communication

AP2–7 Barth Interior provides decorating advice to its clients. Three recent transactions of the company include:
a. Providing decorating services of $500 on account to one of its clients.
b. Paying $1,200 for an employee's salary in the current period.
c. Purchasing office equipment for $2,700.

Required:
Write a memo to your instructor describing each step of the six-step measurement process presented in Illustration 2–1 for each of the three transactions.

Chapter 3

Continuing Problem

Great Adventures

(This is a continuation of the Great Adventures problem from earlier chapters. To complete the requirements for this problem, be sure to account for the July transactions presented in AP2-1 on p. F–4.)

AP3–1 The following transactions occur over the remainder of the year.

Aug. 1   Suzie applies for and obtains a $30,000 low-interest loan for the company from the city council, which has recently passed an initiative encouraging business development related to outdoor activities. The loan is due in three years, and 6% annual interest is due each year on July 31.

Aug. 4   The company purchases 14 kayaks, costing $28,000.

Aug. 10   Twenty additional kayakers pay $3,000 ($150 each), in addition to the $4,000 that was paid in advance on July 30, on the day of the clinic. Tony conducts the first kayak clinic.

Aug. 17   Tony conducts a second kayak clinic and receives $10,500 cash.

Aug. 24   Office supplies of $1,800 purchased on July 4 are paid in full.

Sep. 1   To provide better storage of mountain bikes and kayaks when not in use, the company rents a storage shed, purchasing a one-year rental policy for $2,400 ($200 per month).

Sep. 21   Tony conducts a rock-climbing clinic. The company receives $13,200 cash.

Oct. 17   Tony conducts an orienteering clinic. Participants practice how to understand a topographical map, read an altimeter, use a compass, and orient through heavily wooded areas. Clinic fees total $17,900.

Dec. 1   Tony decides to hold the company's first adventure race on December 15. Four-person teams will race from checkpoint to checkpoint using a combination of mountain biking, kayaking, orienteering, trail running, and rock-climbing skills. The first team in each category to complete all checkpoints in order wins. The entry fee for each team is $500.

Dec. 5   To help organize and promote the race, Tony hires his college roommate, Victor. Victor will be paid $50 in salary for each team that competes in the race. His salary will be paid after the race.

Dec. 8   The company pays $1,200 to purchase a permit from a state park where the race will be held. The amount is recorded as a miscellaneous expense.

Dec. 12   The company purchases racing supplies for $2,800 on account due in 30 days. Supplies include trophies for the top-finishing teams in each category, promotional shirts, snack foods and drinks for participants, and field markers to prepare the racecourse.

Dec. 15   Forty teams pay a total of $20,000 to race. The race is held.

Dec. 16   The company pays Victor's salary of $2,000.

Dec. 31   The company pays a dividend of $4,000 ($2,000 to Tony and $2,000 to Suzie).

Dec. 31   Using his personal money, Tony purchases a diamond ring for $4,500. Tony surprises Suzie by proposing that they get married. Suzie accepts!

The following information relates to year-end adjusting entries as of December 31, 2012.

a. Depreciation of the mountain bikes purchased on July 8 and kayaks purchased on August 4 totals $8,000.

b. Six months' worth of insurance has expired.

c. Four months' worth of rent has expired.

d. Of the $1,800 of office supplies purchased on July 4, $300 remains.

e. Interest expense on the $30,000 loan obtained from the city council on August 1 should be recorded.

f. Of the $2,800 of racing supplies purchased on December 12, $200 remains.

g. Suzie calculates that the company owes $14,000 in income taxes.

Required:

1. Record transactions from August 1 through December 31.
2. Record adjusting entries as of December 31, 2012.
3. Post transactions from August 1 through December 31 and adjusting entries on December 31 to T-accounts.
4. Prepare an adjusted trial balance as of December 31, 2012.
5. For the period July 1 to December 31, 2012, prepare an income statement and statement of stockholders' equity. Prepare a classified balance sheet as of December 31, 2012.
6. Record closing entries as of December 31, 2012.
7. Post closing entries to T-accounts.
8. Prepare a post-closing trial balance as of December 31, 2012.

Financial Analysis

American Eagle Outfitters, Inc.

AP3–2 Financial information for **American Eagle** is presented in Appendix A at the end of the book.

Required:

1. For the most recent year, what amount does American Eagle report for current assets? What assets are listed as current assets? What is the ratio of current assets to total assets?
2. For the most recent year, what amount does American Eagle report for current liabilities? What liabilities are listed as current liabilities? What is the ratio of current liabilities to total liabilities?
3. List any current assets or current liabilities that likely relate to adjusting entries.
4. What is the change in retained earnings reported in the balance sheet?
5. For the most recent year, what is the amount of net income reported in the income statement?
6. Using your answers in 4 and 5, calculate the amount of dividends paid during the year. Verify your answer by looking at the retained earnings column in the statement of stockholders' equity.

Financial Analysis

The Buckle, Inc.

AP3–3 Financial information for **The Buckle** is presented in Appendix B at the end of the book.

Required:

1. For the most recent year, what amount does The Buckle, Inc., report for current assets? What assets are listed as current assets? What is the ratio of current assets to total assets?
2. For the most recent year, what amount does The Buckle, Inc., report for current liabilities? What liabilities are listed as current liabilities? What is the ratio of current liabilities to total liabilities?
3. List any current assets or current liabilities that likely relate to adjusting entries.
4. For the most recent year, what is the change in retained earnings reported in the balance sheet?
5. For the most recent year, what is the amount of net income reported in the income statement?
6. Using your answers in parts 4 and 5 above, calculate the amount of dividends paid during the year. Verify your answer by looking at the retained earnings column in the statement of stockholders' equity.

Comparative Analysis

American Eagle Outfitters, Inc. vs. The Buckle, Inc.

AP3–4 Financial information for **American Eagle** is presented in Appendix A at the end of the book, and financial information for **The Buckle** is presented in Appendix B at the end of the book.

Required:

1. Determine which company maintains a higher ratio of current assets to total assets. How might this be an advantage for the company?
2. Determine which company maintains a higher ratio of current liabilities to total liabilities. How might this be a disadvantage for the company?
3. The dividend payout ratio equals dividends paid during the year divided by net income. Determine which company has a higher dividend payout ratio. Why might this be the case?

Ethics

AP3–5 You have recently been hired as the assistant controller for Stanton Temperton Corporation, which rents building space in major metropolitan areas. Customers are required to pay six months of rent in advance. At the end of 2012, the company's president, Jim Temperton, notices that net income has fallen compared to last year. In 2011, the company reported before-tax profit of $330,000, but in 2012 the before-tax profit is only $280,000. This concerns Jim for two reasons. First, his year-end bonus is tied directly to before-tax profits. Second, shareholders may see a decline in profitability as a weakness in the company and begin to sell their stock. With the sell-off of stock, Jim's personal investment in the company's stock, as well as his company-operated retirement plan, will be in jeopardy of severe losses.

After close inspection of the financial statements, Jim notices that the balance of the Unearned Revenue account is $120,000. This amount represents payments in advance from long-term customers ($80,000) and from relatively new customers ($40,000). Jim comes to you, the company's accountant, and suggests that the firm should recognize as revenue in 2012 the $80,000 received in advance from long-term customers. He offers the following explanation: "First, we have received these customers' cash by the end of 2012, so there is no question about their ability to pay. Second, we have a long-term history of fulfilling our obligation to these customers. We have always stood by our commitments to our customers and we always will. We earned that money when we got them to sign the six-month contract."

Required:
Discuss the ethical dilemma you face.

Internet Research

AP3–6 Obtain a copy of the annual report of **McDonald's Corporation** for the most recent year. You can find the annual report at the company's website (*www.mcdonalds.com*) in the investor information section or at the Securities and Exchange Commission's website (*www.sec.gov*) using EDGAR (Electronic Data Gathering, Analysis, and Retrieval). Form 10-K, which includes the annual report, is required to be filed on EDGAR. Search or scroll within the annual report to find the financial statements.

Required:
Determine the following from the company's financial statements:

1. Do the company's revenues exceed expenses? What is the amount of net income?
2. Did net income increase in the most recent year compared to the previous year?
3. Which assets are listed as current assets? Why are other assets not listed as current assets?
4. Which liabilities are listed as current liabilities? Why are other liabilities not listed as current liabilities?
5. By how much did retained earnings increase/decrease in the most recent year compared to the previous year?
6. What is the amount of dividends paid to common stockholders? This information can be found in the statement of shareholders' equity or the statement of cash flows.
7. Explain the relationship between the change in retained earnings, net income, and dividends.

Written Communication

AP3–7 You are a tutor for introductory financial accounting. You tell the students, "Recording adjusting entries is a critical step in the accounting cycle, and the two major classifications of adjusting entries are prepayments and accruals." Chris, one of the students in the class, says, "I don't understand."

Required:

Respond to Chris.

1. When do prepayments occur? When do accruals occur?
2. Describe the appropriate adjusting entry for prepaid expenses and for unearned revenues. What is the effect on net income, assets, liabilities, and stockholders' equity of not recording a required adjusting entry for prepayments?
3. Describe the required adjusting entry for accrued expenses and for accrued revenues. What is the effect on net income, assets, liabilities, and shareholders' equity of not recording a required adjusting entry for accruals?

Chapter 4

Continuing Problem

QB

Great Adventures

(This is a continuation of the Great Adventures problem from earlier chapters.)

AP4–1 An examination of the cash activities during the year shows the following.

GREAT ADVENTURES
Cash Account Records
July 1, 2012, to December 31, 2012

Deposits			Checks/Debit Cards			
Date	Desc.	Amount	Date	No.	Desc.	Amount
7/1	Stock sale	$ 20,000	7/1	101	Insurance	$ 4,800
7/15	Clinic receipts	2,000	7/2	102	Legal fees	1,500
7/22	Clinic receipts	2,300	7/7	DC	Advertising	300
7/30	Clinic receipts	4,000	7/8	103	Bikes	12,000
8/1	Borrowing	30,000	7/24	DC	Advertising	700
8/10	Clinic receipts	3,000	8/4	104	Kayaks	28,000

Deposits			Checks/Debit Cards			
Date	Desc.	Amount	Date	No.	Desc.	Amount
8/17	Clinic receipts	10,500	8/24	DC	Office supplies	1,800
9/21	Clinic receipts	13,200	9/1	105	Rent	2,400
10/17	Clinic receipts	17,900	12/8	106	Race permit	1,200
12/15	Race receipts	20,000	12/16	107	Salary	2,000
			12/31	108	Dividend	2,000
			12/31	109	Dividend	2,000
		$122,900				$58,700

SUMMARY OF TRANSACTIONS

Beginning Cash Balance July 1, 2012	+	Deposits	–	Checks	=	Ending Cash Balance December 31, 2012
$0		$122,900		$58,700		$64,200

Suzie has not reconciled the company's cash balance with that of the bank since the company was started. She asks Summit Bank to provide her with a six-month bank statement. To save time, Suzie makes deposits at the bank only on the first day of each month.

Summit Bank
Leading You to the Top

Member FDIC

Account Holder: Great Adventures, Inc.

Account Number:	1124537774
Statement Date:	Dec. 31, 2012

Account Summary

Beginning Balance July 1, 2012	Deposits and Credits		Withdrawals and Debits		Ending Balance December 31, 2012
	No.	Total	No.	Total	
$0	8	$103,400	11	$52,900	$50,500

Account Details

Deposits and Credits			Withdrawals and Debits				Daily Balance	
Date	Amount	Desc.	Date	No.	Amount	Desc.	Date	Amount
7/1	$ 20,000	DEP	7/1	101	$ 4,800	CHK	7/1	$15,200
8/1	8,300	DEP	7/7	102	1,500	CHK	7/7	13,400
8/1	30,000	DEP	7/7		300	DC	7/14	1,400
9/1	13,500	DEP	7/14	103	12,000	CHK	7/24	700
9/30	200	INT	7/24		700	DC	8/1	39,000
10/1	13,200	DEP	8/9	104	28,000	CHK	8/9	11,000
11/1	17,900	DEP	8/24		1,800	DC	8/24	9,200
12/31	300	INT	9/2	105	2,400	CHK	9/1	22,700
			9/30		100	SF	9/2	20,300
			12/10	106	1,200	CHK	9/30	20,400
			12/31		100	SF	10/1	33,600
							11/1	51,500
							12/10	50,300
	$103,400				$52,900		12/31	$50,500

Desc.	**DEP** Customer deposit	**INT** Interest earned	**SF** Service fees
	CHK Customer check	**DC** Debit card	

After comparing the two balances, Suzie has some concern because the bank's balance of $50,500 is substantially less than the company's balance of $64,200.

Required:

1. Discuss any problems you see with Great Adventures' internal control procedures related to cash.
2. Prepare Great Adventures' bank reconciliation for the six-month period ended December 31, 2012, and any necessary entries to adjust cash.
3. How did failure to reconcile the bank statement affect the reported amounts for assets, liabilities, stockholders' equity, revenues, and expenses?

American Eagle Outfitters, Inc.

Financial Analysis

AP4–2 Financial information for **American Eagle** is presented in Appendix A at the end of the book.

Required:

1. What does the Report of Independent Registered Public Accounting Firm indicate about American Eagle's internal controls?

2. In the summary of significant accounting policies, how does American Eagle define cash equivalents?

3. What is the amount of cash reported in the two most recent years? By how much has cash increased/decreased?

4. Determine the amounts American Eagle reports for net cash flows from operating activities, investing activities, and financing activities in its statement of cash flows for the most recent year. What are total cash flows for the year?

5. Compare your answers in question 4 to the increase/decrease you calculated in question 3. (Note: Include any effect of exchange rates on cash as an additional cash flow in question 4.)

6. What does American Eagle's trend in net income versus free cash flows over the three most recent years suggest about the company's earnings quality?

Financial Analysis

The Buckle, Inc.

AP4–3 Financial information for **The Buckle** is presented in Appendix B at the end of the book.

Required:

1. What does the Report of Independent Registered Public Accounting Firm indicate about The Buckle's internal controls?

2. In the summary of significant accounting policies, how does The Buckle define cash equivalents?

3. What is the amount of cash reported in the two most recent years? By how much has cash increased/decreased?

4. Determine the amounts The Buckle reports for net cash flows from operating activities, investing activities, and financing activities in its statement of cash flows for the most recent year. What are total cash flows for the year?

5. Compare your answers in question 4 to the increase/decrease you calculated in question 3. (Note: Include any effect of exchange rates on cash as an additional cash flow in question 4.)

6. What does The Buckle's trend in net income versus free cash flows over the three most recent years suggest about the company's earnings quality?

Comparative Analysis

American Eagle Outfitters, Inc., vs. The Buckle, Inc.

AP4–4 Financial information for **American Eagle** is presented in Appendix A at the end of the book, and financial information for **The Buckle** is presented in Appendix B at the end of the book.

Required:

1. Which company has a greater amount of cash relative to total assets? What might this mean about the two companies' potential growth opportunities?

2. Based on the trend in net income versus free cash flows over the three most recent years, which company would you predict to have a greater percentage increase in net income in the following year? Why?

Ethics

AP4–5 Between his freshman and sophomore years of college, Jack takes a job as ticket collector at a local movie theatre. Moviegoers purchase a ticket from a separate employee outside the theatre and then enter through a single set of doors. Jack takes half their ticket, and they proceed to the movie of their choice.

Besides trying to earn enough money for college the next year, Jack loves to watch movies. One of the perks of working for the movie theatre is that all employees are allowed to watch one free movie per day. However, in the employee handbook it states that friends and family of employees are not allowed to watch free movies. In addition, employees must pay full price for all concession items.

Soon after starting work at the theatre, Jack notices that most other employees regularly bring their friends and family to the movie without purchasing a ticket. When Jack stops them at the door to ask for their ticket, they say, "Jack, no one really follows that policy. Just be cool and let us in. You can do the same." Jack even notices that upper management does not follow the policy of no family and friends watching free movies. Furthermore, employees commonly bring their own cups to get free soft drinks and their own containers to eat free popcorn.

Jack considers whether he should also start bringing friends and family and enjoying the free popcorn and beverages. He reasons, "Why should I be the only one following the rules? If everyone else is doing it, including upper management, what harm would it be for me to do it too? After all, when you watch a movie you aren't really stealing anything, and popcorn and drinks cost hardly anything. Plus, I really need to save for college."

Required:
Discuss the ethical dilemma Jack faces.

Internet Research

AP4–6 Financial accounting information can often be found at financial websites. These websites are useful for collecting information about a company's stock price, analysts' forecasts, dividend history, historical financial accounting information, and much more. One such site is Yahoo! Finance (*finance.yahoo.com*).

Required:

1. Visit Yahoo! Finance and get a stock quote for **Google**. To do this, type "GOOG" in the "Get Quotes" box. Under "Financials" click on the "Cash Flow" link. Calculate Google's free cash flows for the three most recent years.
2. Calculate **IBM**'s free cash flows in the same way by typing "IBM" in the "Get Quotes" box.
3. Compare the trends in free cash flows between the companies. What would explain differences between these two companies' free cash flows?
4. Click on "Historical Prices" and compare the trend in these companies' stock prices over the same three-year period used to calculate free cash flows.

Written Communication

AP4–7 Consider the following independent situations:

1. John Smith is the petty-cash custodian. John approves all requests for payment out of the $200 fund, which is replenished at the end of each month. At the end of each month, John submits a list of all accounts and amounts to be charged, and a check is written to him for the total amount. John is the only person ever to tally the fund.
2. All of the company's cash disbursements are made by check. Each check must be supported by an approved voucher, which is in turn supported by the appropriate invoice and, for purchases, a receiving document. The vouchers are approved by Dean Leiser, the chief accountant, after reviewing the supporting documentation. Betty Hanson prepares the checks for Leiser's signature. Leiser also maintains the company's check register (the cash disbursements journal) and reconciles the bank account at the end of each month.
3. Fran Jones opens the company's mail and lists all checks and cash received from customers. A copy of the list is sent to Jerry McDonald who maintains the general ledger accounts. Fran prepares and makes the daily deposit at the bank. Fran also maintains the subsidiary ledger for accounts receivable, which is used to generate monthly statements to customers.

Required:

Write a memo to your instructor indicating the apparent internal control weaknesses and suggest alternative procedures to eliminate the weaknesses.

Chapter 5

Continuing Problem

Great Adventures

(This is a continuation of the Great Adventures problem from earlier chapters.)

AP5–1 Tony and Suzie are ready to expand Great Adventures even further in 2013. Tony believes that many groups in the community (for example, Boy Scouts, church groups, civic groups, and local businesses) would like to hold one-day outings for their members. Groups would engage in outdoor activities such as rock climbing, fishing, capture the flag, paintball, treasure hunts, scavenger hunts, nature hikes, and so on. The purpose of these one-day events would be for each member of the group to learn the importance of TEAM (Together Everyone Achieves More).

Tony knows that most people are not familiar with these types of activities, so to encourage business he allows groups to participate in the event before paying. He offers a 5% quick-payment discount to those that pay within 10 days after the event. He also guarantees that at least eight hours of outdoor activities will be provided or the customer will receive a 20% discount. For the first six months of the year, the following activities occur for TEAM operations.

Jan.	24	Great Adventures purchases outdoor gear such as ropes, helmets, harnesses, compasses, and other miscellaneous equipment for $5,000 cash.
Feb.	25	Mr. Kendall's Boy Scout troop participates in a one-day TEAM adventure. Normally, Tony would charge a group of this size $3,500, but he wants to encourage kids to exercise more and enjoy the outdoors so he charges the group only $3,000.
Feb.	28	The Boy Scout troop pays the full amount owed, less the 5% quick-payment discount.
Mar.	19	Reynold's Management has its employees participate in a one-day TEAM adventure. Great Adventures charges $4,000, and Reynold's agrees to pay within 30 days.
Mar.	27	Reynold's pays the full amount owed, less the 5% quick-payment discount.
Apr.	7	Several men from the Elks Lodge decide to participate in a TEAM adventure. They pay $7,500, and the event is scheduled for the following week.
Apr.	14	The TEAM adventure is held for members of the Elks Lodge.
May	9	Myers Manufacturing participates in a TEAM adventure. Great Adventures charges $6,000, and Myers agrees to pay within 30 days.
Jun. 1–30		Several MBA groups participate in TEAM adventures during June. Great Adventures charges $24,000 to these groups, with payment due in July.
Jun.	30	Myers Manufacturing fails to pay the amount owed within the specified period and agrees to sign a three-month, 8% note receivable to replace the existing account receivable.

Required:

1. Record TEAM adventure transactions occurring during the first six months of 2013.
2. As of June 30, 2013, Great Adventures finishes its first 12 months of operations. If Suzie wants to prepare financial statements, part of the process would involve allowing for uncollectible accounts receivable.

a. Suppose Suzie estimates uncollectible accounts to be 10% of accounts receivable (which does not include the $6,000 note receivable from Myers Manufacturing). Record the adjustment for uncollectible accounts on June 30, 2013.

b. Prepare a partial balance sheet showing the net accounts receivable section.

American Eagle Outfitters, Inc.

AP5–2 Financial information for **American Eagle** is presented in Appendix A at the end of the book.

Required:

1. Determine whether the trend in net sales has been increasing or decreasing for the past three years.
2. Where is accounts receivable reported? Explain why using net sales to calculate the receivables turnover ratio might not be a good indicator of a company's ability to efficiently manage receivables for a retail company like American Eagle, which typically sells clothing for cash.
3. Does American Eagle report an allowance for uncollectible accounts in the balance sheet? If so, how much is reported for the most recent year?

The Buckle, Inc.

AP5–3 Financial information for **The Buckle** is presented in Appendix B at the end of the book.

Required:

1. Determine whether the trend in net sales has been increasing or decreasing for the past three years.
2. Where is accounts receivable reported? Explain why using net sales to calculate the receivables turnover ratio might not be a good indicator of a company's ability to efficiently manage receivables for a retail company like The Buckle, which typically sells clothing for cash.
3. Does The Buckle report an allowance for uncollectible accounts in the balance sheet? If so, how much is reported for the most recent year?

American Eagle Outfitters, Inc., vs. The Buckle, Inc.

AP5–4 Financial information for **American Eagle** is presented in Appendix A at the end of the book, and financial information for **The Buckle** is presented in Appendix B at the end of the book.

Required:

Try to estimate each company's ratio of total current receivables to total current assets. Do you see problems with either company's management of receivables?

Ethics

AP5–5 You have recently been hired as the assistant controller for Stanton Industries. Your immediate superior is the controller who, in turn, reports to the vice president of finance.

The controller has assigned you the task of preparing the year-end adjustments. For receivables, you have prepared an aging of accounts receivable and have applied historical percentages to the balances of each of the age categories. The analysis indicates that an appropriate balance for Allowance for Uncollectible Accounts is $180,000. The existing balance in the allowance account prior to any adjustment is a $20,000 credit balance.

After showing your analysis to the controller, he tells you to change the aging category of a large account from over 120 days to current status and to prepare a new invoice to the customer with a revised date that agrees with the new aging category. This will change the required allowance for uncollectible accounts from $180,000 to $135,000. Tactfully, you ask the controller for an explanation for the change and he tells you, "We need the extra income; the bottom line is too low."

Required:

1. What is the effect on income before taxes of the change requested by the controller?
2. Discuss the ethical dilemma you face. Consider your options and responsibilities along with the possible consequences of any action you might take.

Internet Research

AP5–6 Obtain a copy of the annual report of **Avon Products, Inc.**, for the most recent year. You can find the annual report at the company's website (*www.avon.com*) in the investor information section or at the Securities and Exchange Commission's website (*www.sec.gov*) using EDGAR (Electronic Data Gathering, Analysis, and Retrieval). Form 10-K, which includes the annual report, is required to be filed on EDGAR. Search or scroll within the annual report to find the financial statements.

Required:

Answer the following questions related to the company's accounts receivable and bad debts:

1. What is the amount of net accounts receivable at the end of the year? What is the amount of total accounts receivable?
2. What is the amount of bad debt expense for the year? (*Hint:* Check the statement of cash flows.)
3. Determine the amount of actual bad debt write-offs made during the year. Assume that all bad debts relate only to trade accounts receivable. Did the company underestimate or overestimate bad debts?
4. Calculate the receivables turnover ratio and average collection period for the most recent year. Assuming the industry averages for the receivables turnover ratio and average collection period are 10.5 times and 34.8 days, respectively, what do you conclude about the receivables of Avon?

Written Communication

AP5–7 You have been hired as a consultant by a parts manufacturing firm to provide advice as to the proper accounting methods the company should use in some key areas. In the area of receivables, the company president does not understand your recommendation to use the allowance method for uncollectible accounts. She stated, "Financial statements should be based on objective data rather than the guesswork required for the allowance method. Besides, since my uncollectibles are fairly constant from period to period, with significant variations occurring infrequently, the direct write-off method is just as good as the allowance method."

Required:

Draft a one-page response in the form of a memo to the president in support of your recommendation for the company to use the allowance method.

Earnings Management

AP5–8 Ernie Upshaw is the supervising manager of Sleep Tight Bedding. At the end of the year, the company's accounting manager provides Ernie with the following information, before any adjustment.

Accounts receivable	$500,000
Estimated percent uncollectible	9%
Allowance for uncollectible accounts	$20,000 (*debit*)
Operating income	$320,000

In the previous year, Sleep Tight Bedding reported operating income (after adjustment) of $275,000. Ernie knows that it's important to report an upward trend in earnings. This is important not only for Ernie's compensation and employment, but also for the company's stock price. If investors see a decline in earnings, the stock price could drop significantly, and Ernie owns a large amount of the company's stock. This has caused Ernie many sleepless nights.

Required:
1. Record the adjustment for uncollectible accounts using the accounting manager's estimate of 9% of accounts receivable.
2. After the adjustment is recorded in *Requirement* 1, what is the revised amount of operating income? Does operating income increase or decrease compared to the previous year?
3. Ernie instructs the accounting manager to record the adjustment for uncollectible accounts using 4% rather than 9% of accounts receivable. After this adjustment, does operating income increase or decrease compared to the previous year?
4. By how much would total assets and expenses be misstated using the 4% amount?

Chapter 6

Great Adventures

(This is a continuation of the Great Adventures problem from earlier chapters.)

Continuing Problem

AP6–1 Now that operations for outdoor clinics and TEAM events are running smoothly, Suzie thinks of another area for business expansion. She notices that a few clinic participants wear multiuse (MU) watches. Beyond the normal timekeeping features of most watches, MU watches are able to report temperature, altitude, and barometric pressure. MU watches are waterproof, so moisture from kayaking, rain, fishing, or even diving up to 100 feet won't damage them. Suzie decides to have MU watches available for sale at the start of each clinic. The following transactions relate to purchases and sales of watches during the second half of 2013. All watches are sold for $300 each.

Jul. 17   Purchased 50 watches for $7,500 ($150 per watch) on account.
Jul. 31   Sold 40 watches for $12,000 cash.
Aug. 12   Purchased 40 watches for $6,400 ($160 per watch) cash.
Aug. 22   Sold 30 watches for $9,000 on account.
Sep. 19   Paid for watches ordered on July 17.
Sep. 27   Received full payment for watches sold on account on August 22.
Oct. 27   Purchased 80 watches for $13,600 ($170 per watch) cash.
Nov. 20   Sold 90 watches for $27,000 cash.
Dec. 4   Purchased 100 watches for $18,000 ($180 per watch) cash.
Dec. 8   Sold 40 watches for $12,000 on account.

Required:
1. (a) Calculate sales revenue, cost of goods sold, and ending inventory as of December 31, 2013, assuming Suzie uses FIFO to account for inventory.
   (b) Prepare the gross profit section of a partial income statement for transactions related to MU watches.
2. Late in December, the next generation of multiuse (MU II) watches is released. In addition to all of the features of the MU watch, the MU II watches are equipped with a

global positioning system (GPS) and have the ability to download and play songs and videos off the Internet. The demand for the original MU watches is greatly reduced. As of December 31, the estimated market value of MU watches is only $100 per watch.

(a) Record any necessary adjustment on December 31, 2013, related to this information.

(b) For what amount would MU inventory be reported in the December 31, 2013, balance sheet?

(c) Prepare an updated gross profit section of a partial income statement accounting for this additional information. Compare your answer to *Requirement* 1(b).

Financial Analysis

American Eagle Outfitters, Inc.

AP6–2 Financial information for **American Eagle** is presented in Appendix A at the end of the book.

Required:

1. In the summary of significant accounting policies, what is American Eagle's procedure in accounting for inventory?
2. For the most recent year, what is the amount of inventory in the balance sheet? What does this amount represent?
3. American Eagle refers to its cost of goods sold using a different name. What is it?
4. For the most recent year, what is the amount of cost of goods sold in the income statement? What does this amount represent?
5. Calculate American Eagle's inventory turnover ratio and average days in inventory for the most recent year.
6. Calculate American Eagle's gross profit ratio for each of the three years. Do you notice any trend?
7. For the most recent year, calculate American Eagle's ratio of operating expenses to net sales.

Financial Analysis

The Buckle, Inc.

AP6–3 Financial information for **The Buckle** is presented in Appendix B at the end of the book.

Required:

1. In the summary of significant accounting policies, what is The Buckle's procedure in accounting for inventory?
2. For the most recent year, what is the amount of inventory in the balance sheet? What does this amount represent?
3. The Buckle refers to its cost of goods sold using a different name. What is it?
4. For the most recent year, what is the amount of cost of goods sold in the income statement? What does this amount represent?
5. Calculate The Buckle's inventory turnover ratio and average days in inventory for the most recent year.
6. Calculate The Buckle's gross profit ratio for each of the three years. Do you notice any trend?
7. For the most recent year, calculate The Buckle's ratio of operating expenses to net sales.

Comparative Analysis

American Eagle, Inc., vs. The Buckle, Inc.

AP6–4 Financial information for **American Eagle** is presented in Appendix A at the end of the book, and financial information for **The Buckle** is presented in Appendix B at the end of the book.

Required:

1. Which company carries a greater inventory balance as a percentage of total assets?
2. Analyze each company's inventory using the inventory turnover ratio and average days in inventory.

3. Determine which company's operations are more profitable using the gross profit ratio.

4. Considering the companies' ratio of operating expenses to net sales, does your answer to *Requirement* 3 change? Explain.

Ethics

AP6–5 Horizon Corporation manufactures personal computers. The company began operations in 2003 and reported profits for the years 2003 through 2010. Due primarily to increased competition and price slashing in the industry, 2011's income statement reported a loss of $20 million. Just before the end of the 2012 fiscal year, a memo from the company's chief financial officer to Jim Fielding, the company controller, included the following comments:

> If we don't do something about the large amount of unsold computers already manufactured, our auditors will require us to record a write down. The resulting loss for 2012 will cause a violation of our debt covenants and force the company into bankruptcy. I suggest that you ship half of our inventory to J.B. Sales, Inc., in Oklahoma City. I know the company's president, and he will accept the inventory and acknowledge the shipment as a purchase. We can record the sale in 2012 which will boost our loss to a profit. Then J.B. Sales will simply return the inventory in 2013 after the financial statements have been issued.

Required:
Discuss the ethical dilemma faced by Jim Fielding.

Internet Research

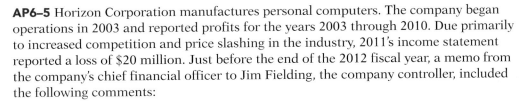

AP6–6 Obtain copies of the annual reports of **The Coca-Cola Company** and **PepsiCo Corporation** for the most recent year. You can find the annual reports at the companies' websites (*www.coca-cola.com* and *www.pepsico.com*) in the investor information section or at the Securities and Exchange Commission's website (*www.sec.gov*) using EDGAR (Electronic Data Gathering, Analysis, and Retrieval). The SEC requires Form 10-K, which includes the annual report, to be filed on EDGAR. Search or scroll within the annual reports to find the financial statements.

Required:
1. For each company, calculate the gross profit ratio, inventory turnover ratio, and average days in inventory.
2. Compare the management of each company's investment in inventory.

Written Communication

AP6–7 You have just been hired as a consultant to Gilbert Industries, a newly formed company. The company president, Mindy Grayson, is seeking your advice as to the appropriate inventory method Gilbert should use to value its inventory and cost of goods sold. Ms. Grayson has narrowed the choice to LIFO and FIFO. She has heard that LIFO might be better for tax purposes, but FIFO has certain advantages for financial reporting to investors and creditors. You have been told that the company will be profitable in its first year and for the foreseeable future.

Required:
Prepare a report for the president describing the factors that should be considered by Gilbert in choosing between LIFO and FIFO.

Earnings Management

AP6–8 Eddie's Galleria sells billiard tables. The company has the following purchases and sales for 2012.

Date	Transactions	Units	Cost per Unit	Total Cost
January 1	Beginning inventory	150	$540	$ 81,000
March 8	Purchase	120	570	68,400
August 22	Purchase	100	600	60,000
October 29	Purchase	80	640	51,200
		450		$260,600
Jan. 1–Dec. 31	Sales ($700 each)	400		

Eddie is worried about the company's financial performance. He has noticed an increase in the purchase cost of billiard tables, but at the same time, competition from other billiard table stores and other entertainment choices have prevented him from increasing the sales price. Eddie is worried that if the company's profitability is too low, stockholders will demand he be replaced. Eddie does not want to lose his job. Since 60 of the 400 billiard tables sold have not yet been picked up by the customers as of December 31, 2012, Eddie decides incorrectly to include these tables in ending inventory. He appropriately includes the sale of these 60 tables as part of total revenues in 2012.

Required:

1. What amount will Eddie calculate for ending inventory and cost of goods sold using FIFO, assuming he erroneously reports that 110 tables remain in ending inventory?
2. What amount would Eddie calculate for cost of goods sold using FIFO if he correctly reports that only 50 tables remain in ending inventory?
3. What effect will the inventory error have on reported amounts for (a) ending inventory, (b) retained earnings, (c) cost of goods sold, and (d) net income (ignoring tax effects) in 2012?
4. Assuming that ending inventory is correctly counted at the end of 2013, what effect will the inventory error in 2012 have on reported amounts for (a) ending inventory, (b) retained earnings, (c) cost of goods sold, and (d) net income (ignoring tax effects) in 2013?

Chapter 7

Continuing Problem

Great Adventures

(This is a continuation of the Great Adventures problem from earlier chapters.)

AP7–1 Tony and Suzie see the need for a rugged all-terrain vehicle to transport participants and supplies. They would love to buy a Hummer, but it is just too expensive and too small for their needs, so they settle on a used Suburban. The cost of the Suburban is $12,000. The vehicle is purchased in late June and will be put into use on July 1, 2013. Annual insurance from **GEICO** runs $1,800 per year. The paint is starting to fade, so they spend an extra $3,000 to repaint the vehicle, placing the Great Adventures logo on the front hood, back, and both sides. An additional $2,000 is spent on a deluxe roof rack and a trailer hitch. They expect to use the Suburban for five years and then sell the vehicle for $4,500.

Required:

1. Determine the amount that should be recorded for the new vehicle.
2. Indicate where any amounts not included in the Equipment account should be recorded.

3. Prepare a depreciation schedule using the straight-line method. Follow the example in Illustration 7–11, except the first and last years will have a half-year of depreciation to reflect the beginning of its service life on July 1, 2013.
4. Record the sale of the vehicle two years later on July 1, 2015, for $10,000.

American Eagle Outfitters, Inc.

Financial Analysis

AP7–2 Financial information for **American Eagle** is presented in Appendix A at the end of the book.

Required:

1. The summary of significant accounting polices is located in footnote 2 to the financial statements. Locate the section on property and equipment. What depreciation method does American Eagle use? What are the estimated useful lives for buildings, leasehold improvements, and fixtures and equipment?
2. Find footnote 7 entitled Property and Equipment. What are the cost and the book value of property and equipment? What is the trend in depreciation expense for the past three years?
3. Find footnote 9 entitled Leases. Retail stores, like American Eagle, tend to lease rather than buy their stores. What is the most common term for the store leases? What are the future minimum lease obligations under operating leases at January 30, 2010?

The Buckle, Inc.

Financial Analysis

AP7–3 Financial information for **The Buckle** is presented in Appendix B at the end of the book.

Required:

1. The summary of significant accounting polices is located in footnote A to the financial statements. Locate the section on property and equipment. What depreciation method does The Buckle use? What are the estimated useful lives for buildings, leasehold improvements, and property and equipment?
2. Find footnote D entitled Property and Equipment. What is the cost of property and equipment? What is the trend in property and equipment for the past two years?
3. Find footnote H entitled Commitments. Retail stores, like The Buckle, tend to lease rather than buy their stores. What is the most common term for the leases? What are the future minimum rental commitments under operating leases at February 6, 2010?

American Eagle Outfitters, Inc., vs. The Buckle, Inc.

Comparative Analysis

AP7–4 Financial information for **American Eagle** is presented in Appendix A at the end of the book, and financial information for **The Buckle** is presented in Appendix B at the end of the book.

Required:

1. Calculate American Eagle's return on assets, profit margin, and asset turnover ratio.
2. Calculate The Buckle's return on assets, profit margin, and asset turnover ratio.
3. Which company is doing better based on return on assets? Which company has the higher profit margin? Which company has the higher asset turnover?

Ethics

AP7–5 Companies often are under pressure to meet or beat Wall Street earnings projections in order to increase stock prices and also to increase the value of stock options. Some resort to earnings management practices to artificially create desired results.

Required:

1. How can a company increase earnings by changing its depreciation method?
2. How can a company increase earnings by changing the estimated service lives of depreciable assets?
3. How can a company increase earnings by changing the estimated residual value of depreciable assets?

Internet Research

AP7–6 Companies are increasingly making their accounting information, especially their annual reports, available through their websites. Select a well-known publicly traded company and go to its website. Look for the investment section, and then click on annual reports. Select the most recent annual report. If you have difficulty, try another company. Answer the following questions based on the company's most recent annual report.

Required:

1. What is the official name of the company?
2. What is its fiscal year-end?
3. At the end of the year, what is the net balance in property, plant, and equipment? (*Hint: Requirements* 3 and 4 are reported in the balance sheet.)
4. Does the company have any intangible assets? If so, how much is reported for intangible assets?
5. What is the balance in accumulated depreciation? (*Hint:* This is either in the balance sheet or in a note about property, plant, and equipment.)
6. Which method of depreciation is used? (*Hint:* It's usually disclosed in the notes under summary of accounting policies.)

Written Communication

AP7–7 At a recent luncheon, you were seated next to Mr. Fogle, the president of a local company that manufactures food processors. He heard that you were in a financial accounting class and asked:

> Why is it that I'm forced to record depreciation expense on my property when I could sell it for more than I originally paid? I thought that the purpose of the balance sheet is to reflect the value of my business and that the purpose of the income statement is to report the net change in value or wealth of a company. It just doesn't make sense to penalize my profits when the building hasn't lost any value.

At the conclusion of the luncheon, you promised to send him a short explanation of the rationale for current depreciation practices.

Required:

Prepare a memo to Mr. Fogle. Explain the accounting concept of depreciation and contrast this with the dictionary definition of depreciation.

Earnings Management

AP7–8 Edward L. Vincent is CFO of Energy Resources, Inc. The company specializes in the exploration and development of natural gas. It's near year-end, and Edward is feeling terrific. Natural gas prices have risen throughout the year, and Energy Resources is set to report record-breaking performance that will greatly exceed analysts' expectations. However, during an executive meeting this morning, management agreed to "tone down" profits due to concerns that reporting excess profits could encourage additional government regulations in the industry, hindering future profitability.

Edward decides to adjust the estimated service life of development equipment from 10 years to six years. He also plans to adjust estimated residual values on development equipment to zero as it is nearly impossible to accurately estimate residual values on equipment like this anyway.

Required:

1. Explain how the adjustment of estimated service life from 10 years to six years will affect depreciation expense and net income.
2. Explain how the adjustment of estimated residual values to zero will affect depreciation expense and net income.
3. In addition to heading off additional government regulations, why might Energy Resources have an incentive to report lower profits in the current period?

Chapter 8

Great Adventures

(This is a continuation of the Great Adventures problem from earlier chapters.)

AP8–1 Great Adventures is a defendant in litigation involving a biking accident during one of its adventure races. The front tire on one of the bikes came off during the race, resulting in serious injury to the rider. However, Great Adventures can document that each bike was carefully inspected prior to the race. It may have been that the rider loosened the wheel during the race and then forgot to tighten the quick-release mechanism.

Continuing Problem

Required:

For each of the following scenarios, determine the appropriate way to report the situation. Explain your reasoning and record any necessary entry.

1. The likelihood of a payment occurring is probable, and the estimated amount is $120,000.
2. The likelihood of a payment occurring is probable, and the amount is estimated to be in the range of $100,000 to $150,000.
3. The likelihood of a payment occurring is reasonably possible, and the estimated amount is $120,000.
4. The likelihood of a payment occurring is remote, while the estimated potential amount is $120,000.

American Eagle Outfitters, Inc.

AP8–2 Financial information for **American Eagle** is presented in Appendix A at the end of the book.

Financial Analysis

Required:

1. Calculate the current ratio for the past two years. Did the current ratio improve or weaken in the more recent year?
2. Calculate the acid-test (quick) ratio for the past two years. Did the acid-test ratio improve or weaken in the more recent year?
3. If American Eagle used $100 million in current investments to pay $100 million in accounts payable, how would its current ratio and acid-test ratio change? Show your calculations.

Financial Analysis

The Buckle, Inc.

AP8–3 Financial information for **The Buckle** is presented in Appendix B at the end of the book.

Required:

1. Calculate the current ratio for the past two years. Did the current ratio improve or weaken in the more recent year?
2. Calculate the acid-test (quick) ratio for the past two years. Did the acid-test ratio improve or weaken in the more recent year?
3. If The Buckle purchased $50 million of inventory by debiting Inventory and crediting Accounts Payable, how would its current ratio and acid-test ratio change? Show your calculations.

Comparative Analysis

American Eagle Outfitters, Inc., vs. The Buckle, Inc.

AP8–4 Financial information for **American Eagle** is presented in Appendix A at the end of the book, and financial information for **The Buckle** is presented in Appendix B at the end of the book.

Required:

1. Calculate the current ratio for both companies for the year ended January 30, 2010. Which company has the better ratio? Compare your calculations with those for **United Airlines** and **Southwest Airlines** reported in the chapter text. Which industry maintains a higher current ratio?
2. Calculate the acid-test (quick) ratio for both companies for the year ended January 30, 2010. Which company has the better ratio? Compare your calculations with those for United Airlines and Southwest Airlines reported in the chapter text. Which industry maintains a higher acid-test ratio?
3. How would the purchase of additional inventory with accounts payable affect the current ratio for these two companies? Why is the answer for American Eagle and The Buckle opposite that for United Airlines?

Ethics

AP8–5 Eugene Wright is CFO of Caribbean Cruise Lines. The company designs and manufactures luxury boats. It's near year-end, and Eugene is feeling kind of queasy. The economy is in a recession, and demand for luxury boats is way down. Eugene did some preliminary liquidity analysis and noted the company's current ratio is slightly below the 1.2 minimum stated in its debt covenant with First Federal Bank. Eugene realizes that if the company reports a current ratio below 1.2 at year-end, the company runs the risk that First Federal will call its $10 million loan. He just cannot let that happen.

Caribbean Cruise Lines has current assets of $12 million and current liabilities of $10.1 million. Eugene decides to delay the delivery of $1 million in inventory purchased on account from the originally scheduled date of December 26 to a new arrival date of January 3. This maneuver will decrease inventory and accounts payable by $1 million at December year-end. Eugene believes the company can somehow get by without the added inventory, as manufacturing slows down some during the holiday season.

Required:

1. How will the delay in the delivery of $1 million in inventory purchased on account affect the company's current ratio on December 31? Provide supporting calculations of the current ratio before and after this proposed delivery delay.
2. Is this practice ethical? Provide arguments both for and against.

Internet Research

AP8–6 A very helpful site to learn about individual publicly traded companies is *finance.yahoo.com*. Go to this website and look up a well-known publicly traded company. Once you find the company page, perform the following tasks.

Required:
1. Click on "Basic Chart." How has the stock price changed over the past year?
2. Click on "Profile." In what industry does the company operate?
3. Click on "Key Statistics." What is the current ratio for the company?
4. Click on "SEC Filings." When was the most recent 10-K, also called the annual report, submitted?
5. Click on "Competitors." Who are the company's primary competitors?

Written Communication

AP8–7 Western Manufacturing is involved with several potential contingent liabilities. Your assignment is to draft the appropriate accounting treatment for each situation described below. Western's fiscal year-end is December 31, 2012, and the financial statements will be issued in early February 2013.
   a. During 2012, Western experienced labor disputes at three of its plants. Management hopes an agreement will soon be reached. However, negotiations between the company and the unions have not produced an acceptable settlement, and employee strikes are currently under way. It is virtually certain that material costs will be incurred, but the amount of possible costs cannot be reasonably estimated.
   b. Western warrants most products it sells against defects in materials and workmanship for a period of a year. Based on its experience with previous product introductions, warranty costs are expected to approximate 2% of sales. A new product introduced in 2012 had sales of $2 million, and actual warranty expenditures incurred so far on the product are $25,000. The only entry made so far relating to warranties on this new product was to debit Warranty Expense $25,000 and credit Cash $25,000.
   c. Western is involved in a suit filed in January 2013 by Crump Holdings seeking $88 million, as an adjustment to the purchase price in connection with the company's sale of its textile business in 2012. The suit alleges that Western misstated the assets and liabilities used to calculate the purchase price for the textile division. Legal counsel advises that it is reasonably possible that Western could lose up to $88 million.

Required:
In a memo, describe the appropriate means of reporting each situation and explain your reasoning.

Earnings Management

AP8–8 Quattro Technologies, a hydraulic manufacturer in the aeronautics industry, has reported steadily increasing earnings over the past few years. The company reported net income of $120 million in 2010 and $140 million in 2011. The stock is receiving increasing analyst attention because many investors expect the steady earnings growth to continue well into the future.

One of the factors increasing sales is the superior warranty Quattro offers. Based on experience, warranty expense in 2012 should be around $40 million. However, in a recent executive meeting it was suggested that the CFO report a larger, more conservative, estimate of warranty expense. Income before warranty expense in 2012 is $210 million. By recording a warranty expense of $50 million this year, Quattro could maintain its steady earnings growth and be in a better position to maintain earnings growth again next year.

Required:

1. Can Quattro use warranty expense to manage its earnings? How?
2. Assume income before warranty expense is $210 million in 2012 and 2013, and total warranty expense over the two years is $80 million. What is the impact of the executive meeting suggestion on income in 2012? In 2013?
3. Is the executive meeting suggestion ethical? What would you do if you were the CFO?

Chapter 9

Continuing Problem

Great Adventures

(This is a continuation of the Great Adventures problem from earlier chapters.)

AP9–1 Tony's favorite memories of his childhood were the times he spent with his dad at camp. Tony was daydreaming of those days a bit as he and Suzie jogged along a nature trail and came across a wonderful piece of property for sale. He turned to Suzie and said, "I've always wanted to start a camp where families could get away and spend some quality time together. If we just had the money, I know this would be the perfect place." They called several banks and on January 1, 2014, Great Adventures obtained a $500,000, 6%, 10-year installment loan from Summit Bank. Monthly payments of $5,551 are required at the end of each month over the life of the 10-year loan. Each monthly payment of $5,551 includes both interest expense and principal payments (i.e., reduction of the loan amount.)

Late that night Tony exclaimed, "$500,000 for our new camp, this has to be the best news ever." Suzie snuggled close and said, "There's something else I need to tell you, Tony, I'm expecting!" They decided right then, if it was a boy, they would name him Venture.

Required:

1. Complete the first three rows of an amortization table.
2. Record the note payable on January 1, 2014, and the first two payments on January 31, 2014, and February 28, 2014.

Financial Analysis

American Eagle Outfitters, Inc.

AP9–2 Financial information for **American Eagle** is presented in Appendix A at the end of the book.

Required:

1. Calculate the debt to equity ratio for the past two years. Did the ratio improve or weaken in the more recent year?
2. Calculate the return on equity. Would investors obtain a higher return on equity if American Eagle borrowed more money?
3. *Review the balance sheet and note 8 to the financial statements.* Based on this information, how would you rate the bankruptcy risk of American Eagle?

Financial Analysis

The Buckle, Inc.

AP9–3 Financial information for **The Buckle** is presented in Appendix B at the end of the book.

Required:

1. Calculate the debt to equity ratio for the past two years. Did the ratio improve or weaken in the more recent year?

2. Calculate the return on equity. Would investors obtain a higher return on equity if The Buckle borrowed more money?
3. *Review the balance sheet and note E to the financial statements.* Based on this information, how would you rate the bankruptcy risk of The Buckle?

American Eagle Outfitters, Inc., vs. The Buckle, Inc.

Comparative Analysis

AP9–4 Financial information for **American Eagle** is presented in Appendix A at the end of the book, and financial information for **The Buckle** is presented in Appendix B at the end of the book.

Required:

1. Calculate the debt to equity ratio for American Eagle and The Buckle for the most recent year. Which company has the better ratio? Compare your calculations with those for **Coca-Cola** and **PepsiCo** reported earlier in the chapter. Which industry maintains a higher debt to equity ratio?
2. Calculate the return on assets and the return on equity for American Eagle and The Buckle for the most recent year. Which company has the better profitability ratios?

Ethics

AP9–5 The Tony Hawk Skate Park was built in early 2010. The construction was financed by $10 million of 5% bonds issued at face value, due in 10 years, with interest payable on June 30 and December 31 each year. The park did well initially, reporting net income in both 2010 and 2011. However, the discussion at the executive board meeting in late 2012 focused on falling skate-park revenues and increasing maintenance expenses. While several ideas were proposed, Jim Trost, the VP of finance, had an intriguing short-term solution. Jim stated, "Interest rates have steadily climbed the past three years. At the current market interest rate of 9%, we could repurchase our bonds for just under $8 million, recording a gain of over $2 million on the repurchase. We could then reissue new bonds at the current 9% rate."

Required:

1. Calculate the actual repurchase price on December 31, 2012, assuming the 10-year, 5% bonds paying interest semiannually were initially issued at a face value of $10 million three years earlier on January 1, 2010. (*Hint:* The periods to maturity (n) will now be 14, calculated as 7 years remaining times 2 periods each year.)
2. Record the bond retirement on December 31, 2012.
3. Is it ethical to time the repurchase of bonds in 2012 in order to include a $2 million gain on repurchase in a bad year? What if the transaction is fully disclosed?
4. From a business standpoint, is the retirement of 5% bonds and the reissue of 9% bonds a good idea? Explain why or why not.

Internet Research

AP9–6 Standard & Poor's is a global leader in credit ratings and credit risk analysis. Go to its website at *standardandpoors.com*. Select "U.S." Click on "Products and Services."

Required:

1. Begin on the homepage. Click on "About S&P" listed at the top right of the page. About how much debt is covered by Standard & Poor's credit ratings?
2. Go back to the homepage. Click on "Ratings." Click on "Learn About Corporate Ratings." Click on "Corporates: News & Commentary" at the bottom of the page. Briefly summarize an item in the news today.

3. Go back to the homepage. Click on "Indices." Click on "S&P 500." When did the S&P 500 begin?
4. Go back to the homepage. Click on "Products and Services." Briefly summarize one of the products listed.

Written Communication

AP9–7 Western Entertainment is considering issuing bonds to finance its business expansion. The company contacts you, a business consultant charging $200 an hour, to answer the following questions.
1. What are the advantages of issuing bonds over borrowing funds from a bank?
2. What are the advantages of issuing bonds over issuing common stock?
3. How is a bond price determined?

Required:
Write a memo providing answers worthy of your billing rate.

Earnings Management

AP9–8 Adrenaline Entertainment is struggling financially and its CFO, David Plesko, is starting to feel the heat. Back on January 1, 2010, Adrenaline Entertainment issued $100 million of 6% bonds, due in 15 years, with interest payable semiannually on June 30 and December 31 each year. The market interest rate on the date of issue was 5%.

It is now the end of 2014, and David has a plan to increase reported net income in 2014. The market interest rate has risen to 9% by the end of 2014. David wants to retire the $100 million, 6% bonds and reissue new 9% bonds instead.

Required:
1. Show that the bonds originally were issued on January 1, 2010, for $110,465,146.
2. Calculate the carrying value of the bonds five years later on December 31, 2014. (*Hint:* Use a market rate of 2.5% (5% ÷ 2), and the number of periods is now 20 semiannual periods.)
3. Calculate the market value of the bonds five years later on December 31, 2014. (*Hint:* The market rate is now 4.5% (9% ÷ 2) rather than 2.5% (5% ÷ 2), and the number of periods is now 20 semiannual periods.)
4. Record the early retirement of the bonds on December 31, 2014. Does the transaction increase net income? By how much (ignoring any tax effect)?
5. Is David Plesko's plan ethical? Do you think investors would agree with David Plesko that the retirement of the 6% bonds and the reissue of 9% bonds is a good idea? Explain why or why not.

Chapter 10

Continuing Problem

Great Adventures

(This is a continuation of the Great Adventures problem from earlier chapters.)

AP10–1 Tony and Suzie purchased land costing $500,000 for a new camp in January 2014. Now they need money to build the cabins, dining facility, a ropes course, and an outdoor swimming pool. Tony and Suzie first checked with Summit Bank to see if they could borrow another million dollars, but unfortunately the bank turned them down as too risky. Undeterred, they promoted their idea to close friends they had made through the outdoor clinics and TEAM events. They decided to go ahead and sell shares of stock in the company to raise the additional funds for the camp. Great Adventures has two classes of stock authorized: 8%, $10 par preferred, and $1 par value common.

When the company began on July 1, 2012, Tony and Suzie each purchased 10,000 shares of $1 par value common stock at $1 per share. The following transactions affect stockholders' equity during 2014, its third year of operations:

Jul.	2	Issue an additional 100,000 shares of common stock for $12 per share.
Sep.	10	Repurchase 10,000 shares of its own common stock (i.e., treasury stock) for $15 per share.
Nov.	15	Reissue 5,000 shares of treasury stock at $16 per share.
Dec.	1	Declare a cash dividend on its common stock of $115,000 ($1 per share) to all stockholders of record on December 15. The dividend is payable on December 31.

Required:
1. Record each of these transactions.
2. Great Adventures has net income of $150,000 in 2014. Retained earnings at the beginning of 2014 was $140,000. Prepare the stockholders' equity section of the balance sheet for Great Adventures as of December 31, 2014.

American Eagle Outfitters, Inc.

Financial Analysis

AP10–2 Financial information for the year ended January 31, 2009, is presented in the text of the chapter. Financial information for **American Eagle** for the year ended January 31, 2010, is presented in Appendix A at the end of the book. Using the financial information presented in Appendix A, answer the following.

Required:
1. What is the par value per share for the common stock?
2. How many common shares were issued at the end of the most recent year?
3. Did the company have any treasury stock? How many shares?
4. How much did the company pay in cash dividends in the most recent year?

The Buckle, Inc.

Financial Analysis

AP10–3 Financial information for **The Buckle** is presented in Appendix B at the end of the book.

Required:
1. What is the par value per share for the common stock?
2. How many common shares were issued at the end of the most recent year?
3. Did the company have any treasury stock? How many shares?
4. How much did the company pay in cash dividends in the most recent year?
5. Has the company ever issued a stock dividend or stock split? If so, describe.

American Eagle Outfitters, Inc., vs. The Buckle, Inc.

Comparative Analysis

AP10–4 Financial information for **American Eagle** is presented in Appendix A at the end of the book, and financial information for **The Buckle** is presented in Appendix B at the end of the book. The stock prices as of January 30, 2010, for American Eagle and The Buckle were $15.89 and $30.34, respectively.

Required:
1. Calculate the return on equity for American Eagle and The Buckle in 2010. Which company has a higher return on equity?
2. Calculate the return on the market value of equity for American Eagle and The Buckle in 2010. Which company has a higher return on the market value of equity?
3. Why is the return on the market value of equity for American Eagle and The Buckle so much lower than the return on equity?
4. Calculate the price-earnings ratio for American Eagle and The Buckle. Which is trading at a lower price per dollar of earnings?

Ethics

AP10–5 Put yourself in the shoes of a company president: The extremely successful launch of a new product has resulted in an additional $5 million in unexpected operating cash flows. You can think of several ways to use the extra $5 million.

One alternative is to pay out a special dividend to the shareholders. As president, you are accountable to the board of directors, which is elected by the shareholders. Rather than pay a dividend, you could repurchase shares of the company's own stock. The stock seems currently to be underpriced, and by purchasing treasury shares you are distributing surplus cash to shareholders without giving them taxable dividend income.

You could also pay a special year-end bonus to your employees. With 500 employees, that would average $10,000 per employee, quite a nice holiday bonus. After all, it was the employees' hard work and dedication that earned the money in the first place.

Or you could use the money to reinvest in the company. By reinvesting the money, it might be easier to continue the upward earnings trend in the future.

Finally, you could approach the board of directors for a compensation adjustment of your own. It's been a great year, and you are the president of the company. Shouldn't you at least share in the success?

Required:

Determine how you would allocate the additional $5 million. Are there other areas in which to spend the money not mentioned in the above case? Is it ethical for the president to be directly compensated based on the company's performance each year?

Internet Research

AP10–6 EDGAR, the Electronic Data Gathering, Analysis, and Retrieval system, is a giant database of documents the U.S. Securities and Exchange Commission (SEC) requires that companies submit. All publicly traded domestic companies use EDGAR to make the majority of their filings. (Filings by foreign companies are not required to be filed on EDGAR, but many of these companies do so voluntarily.) Form 10-K, which includes the annual report, is an important document required to be filed on EDGAR. The SEC makes this information available, free to the public, on the Internet.

Required:

1. Access EDGAR on the Internet. The web address is *www.sec.gov*.
2. Search for a public company with which you are familiar. Access its most recent 10-K filing, and search or scroll to find the statement of stockholders' equity.
3. Determine from the statement the transactions that affected common stock during the past year.
4. Determine from the statement the transactions that affected retained earnings during the past year.
5. Explain how the totals on the statement of stockholders' equity agree with the amounts reported in the stockholders' equity section in the balance sheet.

Written Communication

AP10–7 Preferred stock has characteristics of both liabilities and stockholders' equity. Convertible bonds are another example of a financing arrangement that blurs the line between liabilities and stockholders' equity. Items like these have led some to conclude that the present distinction between liabilities and equity should be eliminated. Under this approach, liabilities and equity would be combined into one category that includes both creditor and owner claims to resources.

Required:

1. Define liabilities and stockholders' equity.
2. Provide arguments in support of maintaining the distinction between liabilities and stockholders' equity in the balance sheet.

3. Provide arguments in support of eliminating the distinction between liabilities and stockholders' equity in the balance sheet.
4. Which do you recommend? Why?

Earnings Management

AP10–8 Renegade Clothing is struggling to meet analysts' forecasts. It's early December 2012, and the year-end projections are in. Listed below are the projections for the year ended 2012 and the comparable actual amounts for 2011.

	Projected 2012	Actual 2011
Sales	$14,000,000	$16,023,000
Net income	878,000	1,113,000
Total assets	$ 6,500,000	$ 6,821,000
Total liabilities	$ 2,500,000	$ 2,396,000
Stockholders' equity	4,000,000	4,425,000
Total liabilities and stockholders' equity	$ 6,500,000	$ 6,821,000
Shares outstanding	950,000	950,000

Analysts forecast earnings per share for 2012 to be $0.95 per share. It looks like earnings per share will fall short of expectations in 2012.

Ronald Outlaw, the director of marketing, has a creative idea to improve earnings per share and the return on equity for 2012. He proposes the company borrow additional funds and use the proceeds to repurchase some of its own stock—treasury shares. Is this a good idea?

Required:
1. Calculate the projected earnings per share and return on equity for 2012 before any repurchase of stock.

Now assume Renegade Clothing purchases 100,000 shares of its own stock at $10 per share. The projections for 2012 will change as follows:

	2012	2011
Sales	$14,000,000	$16,023,000
Net income	878,000	1,113,000
Total assets	$ 6,500,000	$ 6,821,000
Total liabilities	$ 3,500,000	$ 2,396,000
Stockholders' equity	3,000,000	4,425,000
Total liabilities and stockholders' equity	$ 6,500,000	$ 6,821,000
Shares outstanding	850,000	950,000

2. Calculate the new projected earnings per share and return on equity for 2012, assuming the company goes through with the treasury stock repurchase. (*Hint:* In computing earnings per share, average shares outstanding is now 900,000 = (850,000 + 950,000) ÷ 2.)
3. Explain how the repurchase of treasury stock near year-end improves earnings per share and the return on equity ratio.

Chapter 11

**Continuing
Problem**

Great Adventures

(This is a continuation of the Great Adventures problem from earlier chapters.)

AP11–1 The income statement, balance sheet, and additional information for Great Adventures, Inc., are provided below.

GREAT ADVENTURES, INC.
Income Statement
For the year ended December 31, 2014

Revenues:		
Service revenue (clinic, racing, TEAM)	$543,000	
Sales revenue (MU watches)	118,000	
Total revenues		$661,000
Expenses:		
Cost of goods sold (watches)	70,000	
Operating expenses	304,276	
Depreciation expense	50,000	
Interest expense	29,724	
Income tax expense	57,000	
Total expenses		511,000
Net income		$150,000

GREAT ADVENTURES, INC.
Balance Sheet
December 31, 2014 and 2013

	2014	2013	Increase (I) or Decrease (D)
Assets			
Current assets:			
Cash	$ 322,362	$138,000	$ 184,362 (I)
Accounts receivable	45,000	35,000	10,000 (I)
Inventory	17,000	14,000	3,000 (I)
Other current assets	13,000	11,000	2,000 (I)
Long-term assets:			
Land	$ 500,000	$ 0	$ 500,000 (I)
Buildings	1,000,000	0	1,000,000 (I)
Equipment	65,000	65,000	
Accumulated depreciation	(75,250)	(25,250)	50,000 (I)
Total assets	$1,887,112	$237,750	
Liabilities and Stockholders' Equity			
Current liabilities:			
Accounts payable	$ 12,000	$ 9,000	$ 3,000 (I)
Interest payable	750	750	
Income tax payable	57,000	38,000	19,000 (I)
Long-term liabilities:			
Notes payable	492,362	30,000	462,362 (I)
Stockholders' equity:			
Common stock	120,000	20,000	100,000 (I)
Paid-in capital	1,105,000	0	1,105,000 (I)
Retained earnings	175,000	140,000	35,000 (I)
Treasury stock	(75,000)	0	(75,000) (I)
Total liabilities and stockholders' equity	$1,887,112	$237,750	

Additional Information for 2014:
1. Borrowed $500,000 in January 2014. Made 12 monthly payments during the year, reducing the balance of the loan by $37,638.
2. Issued common stock for $1.2 million.
3. Purchased 10,000 shares of treasury stock for $15 per share.
4. Reissued 5,000 shares of treasury stock at $16 per share.
5. Declared and paid a cash dividend of $115,000.

Required:

Prepare the statement of cash flows for the year ended December 31, 2014, using the *indirect* method.

American Eagle Outfitters, Inc.

Financial Analysis

AP11–2 Financial information for **American Eagle** is presented in Appendix A at the end of the book.

Required:
1. What was the amount of increase or decrease in cash and cash equivalents for the most recent year?
2. What was net cash from operating activities for the most recent year? Is net cash from operating activities increasing each year? What is the largest reconciling item between net income and net operating cash flows during the most recent year?
3. What was net cash from investing activities for the most recent year? Is it positive or negative? What is the largest investing activity during the most recent year?
4. What was net cash from financing activities for the most recent year? Is negative financing activities a good sign or a bad sign? What is the largest financing activity during the most recent year?

The Buckle, Inc.

Financial Analysis

Buckle ⊟

AP11–3 Financial information for **The Buckle** is presented in Appendix B at the end of the book.

Required:
1. What was the amount of increase or decrease in cash and cash equivalents for the most recent year?
2. What was net cash from operating activities for the most recent year? Is net cash from operating activities increasing each year? What is the largest reconciling item between net income and net operating cash flows during the most recent year?
3. What was net cash from investing activities for the most recent year? Is it positive or negative? What is the largest investing activity during the most recent year?
4. What was net cash from financing activities for the most recent year? Is negative financing activities a good sign or a bad sign? What is the largest financing activity during the most recent year?

American Eagle Outfitters, Inc., vs. The Buckle, Inc.

Comparative Analysis

Buckle ⊟

AP11–4 Financial information for **American Eagle** is presented in Appendix A at the end of the book, and financial information for **The Buckle** is presented in Appendix B at the end of the book.

Required:
1. Calculate American Eagle's cash return on assets, cash flow to sales, and asset turnover ratio.

2. Calculate The Buckle's cash return on assets, cash flow to sales, and asset turnover ratio.
3. Which company is doing better based on cash return on assets? Which company has the higher cash flow to sales? Which company has the higher asset turnover?

Ethics

AP11–5 Aggressive Corporation approaches Matt Taylor, a loan officer for Oklahoma State Bank, seeking to increase the company's borrowings with the bank from $100,000 to $150,000. Matt has an uneasy feeling as he examines the loan application from Aggressive Corporation, which just completed its first year of operations. The application included the following financial statements.

AGGRESSIVE CORPORATION		
Income Statement		
For the year ended December 31, 2012		
Revenues		$200,000
Expenses:		
Cost of goods sold	$110,000	
Operating expenses	50,000	
Depreciation expense	10,000	
Total expenses		170,000
Net income		$ 30,000

AGGRESSIVE CORPORATION		
Balance Sheet		
December 31		
	2012	**2011**
Assets		
Current assets:		
Cash	$ 10,000	$0
Accounts receivable	60,000	0
Inventory	40,000	0
Long-term assets:		
Equipment	100,000	0
Accumulated depreciation	(10,000)	0
Total assets	$200,000	$0
Liabilities and Stockholders' Equity		
Current liabilities:		
Accounts payable	$ 20,000	$0
Interest payable	10,000	0
Long-term liabilities:		
Note payable	100,000	0
Stockholders' equity:		
Common stock	40,000	0
Retained earnings	30,000	0
Total liabilities and stockholders' equity	$200,000	$0

The income statement submitted with the application shows net income of $30,000 in the first year of operations. Referring to the balance sheet, this net income represents a more-than-acceptable 15% rate of return on assets of $200,000.

Matt's concern stems from his recollection that the $100,000 note payable reported on the balance sheet is a three-year loan from his bank, approved earlier this year. He recalls another promising new company that, just recently, defaulted on its loan due to its inability to generate sufficient cash flows to meet its loan obligations.

Seeing Matt's hesitation, Larry Bling, the CEO of Aggressive Corporation, closes the door to the conference room and shares with Matt that he owns several other businesses. He says he will be looking for a new CFO in another year to run Aggressive Corporation along with his other businesses and Matt is just the kind of guy he is looking for. Larry mentions that as CFO, Matt would receive a significant salary. Matt is flattered and says he will look over the loan application and get back to Larry concerning the $50,000 loan increase by the end of the week.

Required:

1. Prepare a statement of cash flows for Aggressive Corporation.
2. Explain how Aggressive Corporation can have positive net income but negative operating cash flows. How does the finding of negative operating cash flows affect your confidence in the reliability of the net income amount?
3. Why do you think Larry mentioned the potential employment position? Should the potential employment position with Aggressive Corporation have any influence on the loan decision?

Internet Research

AP11–6 EDGAR, the Electronic Data Gathering, Analysis, and Retrieval system, is a giant database of documents required to be submitted to the U.S. Securities and Exchange Commission (SEC). All publicly traded domestic companies use EDGAR to make the majority of their filings. (Filings by foreign companies are not required to be filed on EDGAR, but many of these companies do so voluntarily.) Form 10-K, which includes the annual report, is an important document required to be filed on EDGAR. The SEC makes this information available, free to the public, on the Internet.

Required:

1. Access EDGAR on the Internet. The web address is *www.sec.gov*.
2. Search for a public company with which you are familiar. Access its most recent 10-K filing. Search or scroll to find the statement of cash flows.
3. Is the direct or indirect method used to report operating activities? What is the largest adjustment to net income in reconciling net income and cash flows from operations in the most recent year?
4. What has been the most significant investing activity for the company in the most recent three years?
5. What has been the most significant financing activity for the company in the most recent three years?

Written Communication

AP11–7 "Why can't we pay our shareholders a dividend?" shouts your new boss at Polar Opposites. "This income statement you prepared for me says we earned $5 million in our first year!" You recently prepared the financial statements below.

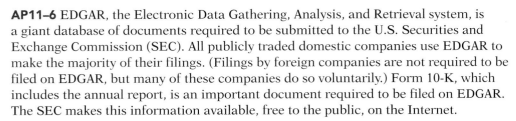

POLAR OPPOSITES	
Income Statement	
For the year ended December 31, 2012	
	($ in millions)
Sales revenue	$65
Cost of goods sold	(35)
Depreciation expense	(4)
Operating expenses	(21)
Net income	$ 5

POLAR OPPOSITES
Balance Sheet
December 31, 2012

	($ in millions)
Cash	$ 1
Accounts receivable (net)	16
Merchandise inventory	14
Machinery (net)	44
Total	$75
Accounts payable	$ 7
Accrued expenses payable	9
Notes payable	29
Common stock	25
Retained earnings	5
Total	$75

Although net income was $5 million, cash flow from operating activities was a negative $5 million. This just didn't make any sense to your boss.

Required:

Prepare a memo explaining how net income could be positive and operating cash flows negative. Include in your report a determination of operating cash flows of negative $5 million using the *indirect* method.

Earnings Management

AP11–8 Bryan Eubank began his accounting career as an auditor for a Big 4 CPA firm. He focused on clients in the high-technology sector, becoming an expert on topics such as inventory write-downs, stock options, and business acquisitions. Impressed with his technical skills and experience, General Electronics, a large consumer electronics chain, hired Bryan as the company controller responsible for all of the accounting functions within the corporation. Bryan was excited about his new position—for about a week, until he took the first careful look at General Electronics' financial statements.

The cause of Bryan's change in attitude is the set of financial statements he's been staring at for the past few hours. For some time prior to his recruitment, he had been aware that his new employer had experienced a long trend of moderate profitability. The reports on his desk confirm the slight but steady improvements in net income in recent years. The disturbing trend Bryan is now noticing, though, is a decline in cash flows from operations. Bryan has sketched out the following comparison ($ in millions):

	2012	2011	2010	2009
Operating income	$1,400	$1,320	$1,275	$1,270
Net income	385	350	345	295
Cash flows from operations	16	110	120	155

Profits? Yes. Increasing profits? Yes. So what is the cause of his distress? The trend in cash flows from operations, which is going in the opposite direction of net income. Upon closer review, Bryan noticed a couple events that, unfortunately, seem related:
a. The company's credit policy has been loosened, credit terms relaxed, and payment periods lengthened. This has resulted in a large increase in accounts receivable.
b. Several of the company's salary arrangements, including that of the CEO and CFO, are based on reported net income.

Required:
1. What is likely causing the increase in accounts receivable? How does an increase in accounts receivable affect net income differently than operating cash flows?
2. Explain why salary arrangements for officers, such as the CEO and CFO, might increase the risk of earnings management.
3. Why is the trend in cash flows from operations, combined with the additional events, such a concern for Bryan?
4. What course of action, if any, should Bryan take?

Chapter 12

Great Adventures

(This is the conclusion of the Great Adventures problem from earlier chapters.)

AP12–1 Income statement and balance sheet data for Great Adventures, Inc., are provided below.

Continuing Problem

GREAT ADVENTURES, INC.
Income Statement
For the year ended December 31, 2014

Revenues:		
Service revenue (clinic, racing, TEAM)	$543,000	
Sales revenue (MU watches)	118,000	
Total revenues		$661,000
Expenses:		
Cost of goods sold (MU watches)	70,000	
Operating expenses	304,276	
Depreciation expense	50,000	
Interest expense	29,724	
Income tax expense	57,000	
Total expenses		511,000
Net income		$150,000

GREAT ADVENTURES, INC.
Balance Sheet
December 31, 2014 and 2013

	2014	2013	Increase (I) or Decrease (D)
Assets			
Current assets:			
Cash	$ 322,362	$138,000	$ 184,362 (I)
Accounts receivable	45,000	35,000	10,000 (I)
Inventory	17,000	14,000	3,000 (I)
Other current assets	13,000	11,000	2,000 (I)
Long-term assets:			
Land	500,000	0	500,000 (I)
Buildings	1,000,000	0	1,000,000 (I)
Equipment	65,000	65,000	
Less: Accumulated depreciation	(75,250)	(25,250)	50,000 (I)
Total assets	$1,887,112	$237,750	

(continued)

(concluded)

GREAT ADVENTURES, INC.			
Balance Sheet			
December 31, 2014 and 2013			
	2014	**2013**	**Increase (I) or Decrease (D)**
Liabilities and Stockholders' Equity			
Current liabilities:			
Accounts payable	$ 12,000	$ 9,000	$ 3,000 (I)
Interest payable	750	750	
Income tax payable	57,000	38,000	19,000 (I)
Long-term liabilities:			
Notes payable	492,362	30,000	462,362 (I)
Stockholders' equity:			
Common stock	120,000	20,000	100,000 (I)
Paid-in capital	1,105,000	0	1,105,000 (I)
Retained earnings	175,000	140,000	35,000 (I)
Treasury stock	(75,000)	0	(75,000) (I)
Total liabilities and stockholders' equity	$1,887,112	$237,750	

As you can tell from the financial statements, 2014 was an especially busy year. Tony and Suzie were able to use the $1.2 million received from the issuance of 100,000 shares of stock and hire a construction company for $1 million to build the cabins, dining facilities, ropes course, and the outdoor swimming pool. They even put in a baby pool to celebrate the birth of their firstborn son, little Venture Matheson.

Required:

1. Calculate the following risk ratios for 2014.

   a. Receivables turnover ratio.   e. Current ratio.
   b. Average collection period.   f. Acid-test ratio.
   c. Inventory turnover ratio.   g. Debt to equity ratio.
   d. Average days in inventory.   h. Times interest earned ratio.

2. Calculate the following profitability ratios for 2014.

   a. Gross profit ratio (on the MU watches).   d. Asset turnover.
   b. Return on assets.   e. Return on equity.
   c. Profit margin.

3. Briefly comment on Great Adventures' risk and profitability in 2014.

Financial Analysis

American Eagle Outfitters, Inc.

AP12–2 Financial information for **American Eagle** is presented in Appendix A at the end of the book.

Required:

1. Complete the "Amount" and "%" columns to be used in a horizontal analysis of American Eagle's income statement for the year ended January 30, 2010. Discuss the major fluctuations during the year.

2. Calculate the following risk ratios for the year ended January 30, 2010:

   a. Receivables turnover ratio.   e. Current ratio.
   b. Average collection period.   f. Acid-test ratio.
   c. Inventory turnover ratio.   g. Debt to equity ratio.
   d. Average days in inventory.

3. Calculate the following profitability ratios for the year ended January 30, 2010:
   a. Gross profit ratio.
   b. Return on assets.
   c. Profit margin.
   d. Asset turnover.
   e. Return on equity.

The Buckle. Inc.

AP12–3 Financial information for **The Buckle** is presented in Appendix B at the end of the book.

Required:
1. Complete the "Amount" and "%" columns to be used in a horizontal analysis of The Buckle's income statement for the year ended January 30, 2010. Discuss the major fluctuations during the year.
2. Calculate the following risk ratios for the year ended January 30, 2010:
   a. Receivables turnover ratio.
   b. Average collection period.
   c. Inventory turnover ratio.
   d. Average days in inventory.
   e. Current ratio.
   f. Acid-test ratio.
   g. Debt to equity ratio.
3. Calculate the following profitability ratios for the year ended January 30, 2010:
   a. Gross profit ratio.
   b. Return on assets.
   c. Profit margin.
   d. Asset turnover.
   e. Return on equity.

American Eagle Outfitters, Inc., vs. The Buckle. Inc.

AP12–4 Financial information for **American Eagle** is presented in Appendix A at the end of the book, and financial information for **The Buckle** is presented in Appendix B at the end of the book.

Required:
1. Calculate the following risk ratios for both companies for the year ended January 30, 2010. Based on these calculations, which company appears to be more risky?
   a. Receivables turnover ratio.
   b. Average collection period.
   c. Inventory turnover ratio.
   d. Average days in inventory.
   e. Current ratio.
   f. Acid-test ratio.
   g. Debt to equity ratio.
2. Calculate the following profitability ratios for both companies for the year ended January 30, 2010. Based on these calculations, which company appears to be more profitable?
   a. Gross profit ratio.
   b. Return on assets.
   c. Profit margin.
   d. Asset turnover.
   e. Return on equity.

Ethics

AP12–5 After years of steady growth in net income, The Performance Drug Company sustained a loss of $1.6 million in 2012. The loss was primarily due to $5 million in expenses related to a product recall. The company designs and produces health supplements and had to recall a product in 2012 because of potential health risks.

The company controller, Joe Mammoth, suggests the loss be included in the 2012 income statement as an extraordinary item. "If we report it as an extraordinary item, our income from continuing operations will actually show an increase from the prior year. Investors will appreciate the continued growth in ongoing profitability and will discount the one-time loss." Joe further notes that executive bonuses are tied to income from continuing operations, not net income.

The CEO asks Joe to justify this treatment. "I know we have had product recalls before and, of course, they do occur in our industry," Joe replies, "but we have never had a recall of this magnitude, and have upgraded our quality control procedures so this should never happen again."

Required:
Discuss the ethical dilemma faced by Joe Mammoth and the CEO. Who are the stakeholders and how are they affected?

Internet Research

AP12–6 Companies like Reuters provide updated ratio analysis on publicly traded companies free of charge. Go to *www.investor.reuters.com*. Choose stocks in the left-hand margin. Look up a company's ticker symbol. For example, Pepsi's ticker symbol is PBG. Type in the ticker symbol and click on "Ratios."

Required:
1. Evaluate the company's risk (both liquidity and solvency) in relation to the industry and sector averages.
2. Evaluate the company's profitability in relation to the industry and sector averages.

Written Communication

AP12–7 Roseburg Corporation manufactures cardboard containers. In 2008, the company purchased several large tracts of timber for $20 million with the intention of harvesting its own timber rather than buying timber from outside suppliers. However, in 2012, Roseburg abandoned the idea, and sold all of the timber tracts for $30 million. Net income for 2012, before considering this event, was $12 million.

Required:
Write a memo providing your recommended income statement presentation of the gain on the sale of the timber tracts. Be sure to include a discussion of the alternatives that might be considered.

Earnings Management

AP12–8 Major League Products was founded in 1992 to provide high-quality merchandise carrying the logos of each fan's favorite major league team. In recent years, the company has struggled to compete against new Internet-based companies selling products at much lower prices. Andrew Ransom, in his second year out of college, was assigned to audit the financial statements of Major League Products. One of the steps in the auditing process is to examine the nature of year-end adjustments. Andrew's investigation reveals that the company has made several year-end adjustments, including (a) a decrease in the allowance for uncollectible accounts, (b) a reversal in the previous write-down of inventory, (c) an increase in the estimated useful life used to calculate depreciation expense, and (d) a decrease in the liability reported for litigation.

Required:
1. Classify each adjustment as conservative or aggressive.
2. What, if anything, do all these adjustments have in common?
3. How do these adjustments affect the company's cash balance?
4. Why might these year-end adjustments, taken together, raise concerns about earnings management?

Photo Credits

Subject Index

Note: Page numbers followed by *n* indicate material in footnotes.

Company Index

Present and Future Value Tables

This table shows the future value of $1 at various interest rates (i) and time periods (n). It is used to calculate the future value of any single amount.

TABLE 1 Future Value of $1

$$FV = \$1\,(1 + i)^n$$

n/i	1.0%	1.5%	2.0%	2.5%	3.0%	3.5%	4.0%	4.5%	5.0%	5.5%	6.0%	7.0%	8.0%	9.0%	10.0%	11.0%	12.0%	20.0%
1	1.01000	1.01500	1.02000	1.02500	1.03000	1.03500	1.04000	1.04500	1.05000	1.05500	1.06000	1.07000	1.08000	1.09000	1.10000	1.11000	1.12000	1.20000
2	1.02010	1.03022	1.04040	1.05063	1.06090	1.07123	1.08160	1.09203	1.10250	1.11303	1.12360	1.14490	1.16640	1.18810	1.21000	1.23210	1.25440	1.44000
3	1.03030	1.04568	1.06121	1.07689	1.09273	1.10872	1.12486	1.14117	1.15763	1.17424	1.19102	1.22504	1.25971	1.29503	1.33100	1.36763	1.40493	1.72800
4	1.04060	1.06136	1.08243	1.10381	1.12551	1.14752	1.16986	1.19252	1.21551	1.23882	1.26248	1.31080	1.36049	1.41158	1.46410	1.51807	1.57352	2.07360
5	1.05101	1.07728	1.10408	1.13141	1.15927	1.18769	1.21665	1.24618	1.27628	1.30696	1.33823	1.40255	1.46933	1.53862	1.61051	1.68506	1.76234	2.48832
6	1.06152	1.09344	1.12616	1.15969	1.19405	1.22926	1.26532	1.30226	1.34010	1.37884	1.41852	1.50073	1.58687	1.67710	1.77156	1.87041	1.97382	2.98598
7	1.07214	1.10984	1.14869	1.18869	1.22987	1.27228	1.31593	1.36086	1.40710	1.45468	1.50363	1.60578	1.71382	1.82804	1.94872	2.07616	2.21068	3.58318
8	1.08286	1.12649	1.17166	1.21840	1.26677	1.31681	1.36857	1.42210	1.47746	1.53469	1.59385	1.71819	1.85093	1.99256	2.14359	2.30454	2.47596	4.29982
9	1.09369	1.14339	1.19509	1.24886	1.30477	1.36290	1.42331	1.48610	1.55133	1.61909	1.68948	1.83846	1.99900	2.17189	2.35795	2.55804	2.77308	5.15978
10	1.10462	1.16054	1.21899	1.28008	1.34392	1.41060	1.48024	1.55297	1.62889	1.70814	1.79085	1.96715	2.15892	2.36736	2.59374	2.83942	3.10585	6.19174
11	1.11567	1.17795	1.24337	1.31209	1.38423	1.45997	1.53945	1.62285	1.71034	1.80209	1.89830	2.10485	2.33164	2.58043	2.85312	3.15176	3.47855	7.43008
12	1.12683	1.19562	1.26824	1.34489	1.42576	1.51107	1.60103	1.69588	1.79586	1.90121	2.01220	2.25219	2.51817	2.81266	3.13843	3.49845	3.89598	8.91610
13	1.13809	1.21355	1.29361	1.37851	1.46853	1.56396	1.66507	1.77220	1.88565	2.00577	2.13293	2.40985	2.71962	3.06580	3.45227	3.88328	4.36349	10.69932
14	1.14947	1.23176	1.31948	1.41297	1.51259	1.61869	1.73168	1.85194	1.97993	2.11609	2.26090	2.57853	2.93719	3.34173	3.79750	4.31044	4.88711	12.83918
15	1.16097	1.25023	1.34587	1.44830	1.55797	1.67535	1.80094	1.93528	2.07893	2.23248	2.39656	2.75903	3.17217	3.64248	4.17725	4.78459	5.47357	15.40702
16	1.17258	1.26899	1.37279	1.48451	1.60471	1.73399	1.87298	2.02237	2.18287	2.35526	2.54035	2.95216	3.42594	3.97031	4.59497	5.31089	6.13039	18.48843
17	1.18430	1.28802	1.40024	1.52162	1.65285	1.79468	1.94790	2.11338	2.29202	2.48480	2.69277	3.15882	3.70002	4.32763	5.05447	5.89509	6.86604	22.18611
18	1.19615	1.30734	1.42825	1.55966	1.70243	1.85749	2.02582	2.20848	2.40662	2.62147	2.85434	3.37993	3.99602	4.71712	5.55992	6.54355	7.68997	26.62333
19	1.20811	1.32695	1.45681	1.59865	1.75351	1.92250	2.10685	2.30786	2.52695	2.76565	3.02560	3.61653	4.31570	5.14166	6.11591	7.26334	8.61276	31.94800
20	1.22019	1.34686	1.48595	1.63862	1.80611	1.98979	2.19112	2.41171	2.65330	2.91776	3.20714	3.86968	4.66096	5.60441	6.72750	8.06231	9.64629	38.33760
21	1.23239	1.36706	1.51567	1.67958	1.86029	2.05943	2.27877	2.52024	2.78596	3.07823	3.39956	4.14056	5.03383	6.10881	7.40025	8.94917	10.80385	46.00512
25	1.28243	1.45095	1.64061	1.85394	2.09378	2.36324	2.66584	3.00543	3.38635	3.81339	4.29187	5.42743	6.84848	8.62308	10.83471	13.58546	17.00006	95.39622
30	1.34785	1.56308	1.81136	2.09757	2.42726	2.80679	3.24340	3.74532	4.32194	4.98395	5.74349	7.61226	10.06266	13.26768	17.44940	22.89230	29.95992	237.37631
40	1.48886	1.81402	2.20804	2.68506	3.26204	3.95926	4.80102	5.81636	7.03999	8.51331	10.28572	14.97446	21.72452	31.40942	45.25926	65.00087	93.05097	1469.77160

This table shows the present value of $1 at various interest rates (i) and time periods (n). It is used to calculate the present value of any single amount.

TABLE 2 Present Value of $1

$$PV = \frac{\$1}{(1+i)^n}$$

n/i	1.0%	1.5%	2.0%	2.5%	3.0%	3.5%	4.0%	4.5%	5.0%	5.5%	6.0%	7.0%	8.0%	9.0%	10.0%	11.0%	12.0%	20.0%
1	0.99010	0.98522	0.98039	0.97561	0.97087	0.96618	0.96154	0.95694	0.95238	0.94787	0.94340	0.93458	0.92593	0.91743	0.90909	0.90090	0.89286	0.83333
2	0.98030	0.97066	0.96117	0.95181	0.94260	0.93351	0.92456	0.91573	0.90703	0.89845	0.89000	0.87344	0.85734	0.84168	0.82645	0.81162	0.79719	0.69444
3	0.97059	0.95632	0.94232	0.92860	0.91514	0.90194	0.88900	0.87630	0.86384	0.85161	0.83962	0.81630	0.79383	0.77218	0.75131	0.73119	0.71178	0.57870
4	0.96098	0.94218	0.92385	0.90595	0.88849	0.87144	0.85480	0.83856	0.82270	0.80722	0.79209	0.76290	0.73503	0.70843	0.68301	0.65873	0.63552	0.48225
5	0.95147	0.92826	0.90573	0.88385	0.86261	0.84197	0.82193	0.80245	0.78353	0.76513	0.74726	0.71299	0.68058	0.64993	0.62092	0.59345	0.56743	0.40188
6	0.94205	0.91454	0.88797	0.86230	0.83748	0.81350	0.79031	0.76790	0.74622	0.72525	0.70496	0.66634	0.63017	0.59627	0.56447	0.53464	0.50663	0.33490
7	0.93272	0.90103	0.87056	0.84127	0.81309	0.78599	0.75992	0.73483	0.71068	0.68744	0.66506	0.62275	0.58349	0.54703	0.51316	0.48166	0.45235	0.27908
8	0.92348	0.88771	0.85349	0.82075	0.78941	0.75941	0.73069	0.70319	0.67684	0.65160	0.62741	0.58201	0.54027	0.50187	0.46651	0.43393	0.40388	0.23257
9	0.91434	0.87459	0.83676	0.80073	0.76642	0.73373	0.70259	0.67290	0.64461	0.61763	0.59190	0.54393	0.50025	0.46043	0.42410	0.39092	0.36061	0.19381
10	0.90529	0.86167	0.82035	0.78120	0.74409	0.70892	0.67556	0.64393	0.61391	0.58543	0.55839	0.50835	0.46319	0.42241	0.38554	0.35218	0.32197	0.16151
11	0.89632	0.84893	0.80426	0.76214	0.72242	0.68495	0.64958	0.61620	0.58468	0.55491	0.52679	0.47509	0.42888	0.38753	0.35049	0.31728	0.28748	0.13459
12	0.88745	0.83639	0.78849	0.74356	0.70138	0.66178	0.62460	0.58966	0.55684	0.52598	0.49697	0.44401	0.39711	0.35553	0.31863	0.28584	0.25668	0.11216
13	0.87866	0.82403	0.77303	0.72542	0.68095	0.63940	0.60057	0.56427	0.53032	0.49856	0.46884	0.41496	0.36770	0.32618	0.28966	0.25751	0.22917	0.09346
14	0.86996	0.81185	0.75788	0.70773	0.66112	0.61778	0.57748	0.53997	0.50507	0.47257	0.44230	0.38782	0.34046	0.29925	0.26333	0.23199	0.20462	0.07789
15	0.86135	0.79985	0.74301	0.69047	0.64186	0.59689	0.55526	0.51672	0.48102	0.44793	0.41727	0.36245	0.31524	0.27454	0.23939	0.20900	0.18270	0.06491
16	0.85282	0.78803	0.72845	0.67362	0.62317	0.57671	0.53391	0.49447	0.45811	0.42458	0.39365	0.33873	0.29189	0.25187	0.21763	0.18829	0.16312	0.05409
17	0.84438	0.77639	0.71416	0.65720	0.60502	0.55720	0.51337	0.47318	0.43630	0.40245	0.37136	0.31657	0.27027	0.23107	0.19784	0.16963	0.14564	0.04507
18	0.83602	0.76491	0.70016	0.64117	0.58739	0.53836	0.49363	0.45280	0.41552	0.38147	0.35034	0.29586	0.25025	0.21199	0.17986	0.15282	0.13004	0.03756
19	0.82774	0.75361	0.68643	0.62553	0.57029	0.52016	0.47464	0.43330	0.39573	0.36158	0.33051	0.27651	0.23171	0.19449	0.16351	0.13768	0.11611	0.03130
20	0.81954	0.74247	0.67297	0.61027	0.55368	0.50257	0.45639	0.41464	0.37689	0.34273	0.31180	0.25842	0.21455	0.17843	0.14864	0.12403	0.10367	0.02608
21	0.81143	0.73150	0.65978	0.59539	0.53755	0.48557	0.43883	0.39679	0.35894	0.32486	0.29416	0.24151	0.19866	0.16370	0.13513	0.11174	0.09256	0.02174
24	0.78757	0.69954	0.62172	0.55288	0.49193	0.43796	0.39012	0.34770	0.31007	0.27666	0.24698	0.19715	0.15770	0.12640	0.10153	0.08170	0.06588	0.01258
25	0.77977	0.68921	0.60953	0.53939	0.47761	0.42315	0.37512	0.33273	0.29530	0.26223	0.23300	0.18425	0.14602	0.11597	0.09230	0.07361	0.05882	0.01048
28	0.75684	0.65910	0.57437	0.50088	0.43708	0.38165	0.33348	0.29157	0.25509	0.22332	0.19563	0.15040	0.11591	0.08955	0.06934	0.05382	0.04187	0.00607
29	0.74934	0.64936	0.56311	0.48866	0.42435	0.36875	0.32065	0.27902	0.24295	0.21168	0.18456	0.14056	0.10733	0.08215	0.06304	0.04849	0.03738	0.00506
30	0.74192	0.63976	0.55207	0.47674	0.41199	0.35628	0.30832	0.26700	0.23138	0.20064	0.17411	0.13137	0.09938	0.07537	0.05731	0.04368	0.03338	0.00421
31	0.73458	0.63031	0.54125	0.46511	0.39999	0.34423	0.29646	0.25550	0.22036	0.19018	0.16425	0.12277	0.09202	0.06915	0.05210	0.03935	0.02980	0.00351
40	0.67165	0.55126	0.45289	0.37243	0.30656	0.25257	0.20829	0.17193	0.14205	0.11746	0.09722	0.06678	0.04603	0.03184	0.02209	0.01538	0.01075	0.00068

This table shows the future value of an ordinary annuity of $1 at various interest rates (i) and time periods (n). It is used to calculate the future value of any series of equal payments made at the end of each compounding period.

TABLE 3 Future Value of an Ordinary Annuity of $1

$$FVA = \frac{(1+i)^n - 1}{i}$$

n/i	1.0%	1.5%	2.0%	2.5%	3.0%	3.5%	4.0%	4.5%	5.0%	5.5%	6.0%	7.0%	8.0%	9.0%	10.0%	11.0%	12.0%	20.0%
1	1.0000	1.0000	1.0000	1.0000	1.0000	1.0000	1.0000	1.0000	1.0000	1.0000	1.0000	1.0000	1.0000	1.0000	1.0000	1.0000	1.0000	1.0000
2	2.0100	2.0150	2.0200	2.0250	2.0300	2.0350	2.0400	2.0450	2.0500	2.0550	2.0600	2.0700	2.0800	2.0900	2.1000	2.1100	2.1200	2.2000
3	3.0301	3.0452	3.0604	3.0756	3.0909	3.1062	3.1216	3.1370	3.1525	3.1680	3.1836	3.2149	3.2464	3.2781	3.3100	3.3421	3.3744	3.6400
4	4.0604	4.0909	4.1216	4.1525	4.1836	4.2149	4.2465	4.2782	4.3101	4.3423	4.3746	4.4399	4.5061	4.5731	4.6410	4.7097	4.7793	5.3680
5	5.1010	5.1523	5.2040	5.2563	5.3091	5.3625	5.4163	5.4707	5.5256	5.5811	5.6371	5.7507	5.8666	5.9847	6.1051	6.2278	6.3528	7.4416
6	6.1520	6.2296	6.3081	6.3877	6.4684	6.5502	6.6330	6.7169	6.8019	6.8881	6.9753	7.1533	7.3359	7.5233	7.7156	7.9129	8.1152	9.9299
7	7.2135	7.3230	7.4343	7.5474	7.6625	7.7794	7.8983	8.0192	8.1420	8.2669	8.3938	8.6540	8.9228	9.2004	9.4872	9.7833	10.0890	12.9159
8	8.2857	8.4328	8.5830	8.7361	8.8923	9.0517	9.2142	9.3800	9.5491	9.7216	9.8975	10.2598	10.6366	11.0285	11.4359	11.8594	12.2997	16.4991
9	9.3685	9.5593	9.7546	9.9545	10.1591	10.3685	10.5828	10.8021	11.0266	11.2563	11.4913	11.9780	12.4876	13.0210	13.5795	14.1640	14.7757	20.7989
10	10.4622	10.7027	10.9497	11.2034	11.4639	11.7314	12.0061	12.2882	12.5779	12.8754	13.1808	13.8164	14.4866	15.1929	15.9374	16.7220	17.5487	25.9587
11	11.5668	11.8633	12.1687	12.4835	12.8078	13.1420	13.4864	13.8412	14.2068	14.5835	14.9716	15.7836	16.6455	17.5603	18.5312	19.5614	20.6546	32.1504
12	12.6825	13.0412	13.4121	13.7956	14.1920	14.6020	15.0258	15.4640	15.9171	16.3856	16.8699	17.8885	18.9771	20.1407	21.3843	22.7132	24.1331	39.5805
13	13.8093	14.2368	14.6803	15.1404	15.6178	16.1130	16.6268	17.1599	17.7130	18.2868	18.8821	20.1406	21.4953	22.9534	24.5227	26.2116	28.0291	48.4966
14	14.9474	15.4504	15.9739	16.5190	17.0863	17.6770	18.2919	18.9321	19.5986	20.2926	21.0151	22.5505	24.2149	26.0192	27.9750	30.0949	32.3926	59.1959
15	16.0969	16.6821	17.2934	17.9319	18.5989	19.2957	20.0236	20.7841	21.5786	22.4087	23.2760	25.1290	27.1521	29.3609	31.7725	34.4054	37.2797	72.0351
16	17.2579	17.9324	18.6393	19.3802	20.1569	20.9710	21.8245	22.7193	23.6575	24.6411	25.6725	27.8881	30.3243	33.0034	35.9497	39.1899	42.7533	87.4421
17	18.4304	19.2014	20.0121	20.8647	21.7616	22.7050	23.6975	24.7417	25.8404	26.9964	28.2129	30.8402	33.7502	36.9737	40.5447	44.5008	48.8837	105.9306
18	19.6147	20.4894	21.4123	22.3863	23.4144	24.4997	25.6454	26.8551	28.1324	29.4812	30.9057	33.9990	37.4502	41.3013	45.5992	50.3959	55.7497	128.1167
19	20.8109	21.7967	22.8406	23.9460	25.1169	26.3572	27.6712	29.0636	30.5390	32.1027	33.7600	37.3790	41.4463	46.0185	51.1591	56.9395	63.4397	154.7400
20	22.0190	23.1237	24.2974	25.5447	26.8704	28.2797	29.7781	31.3714	33.0660	34.8683	36.7856	40.9955	45.7620	51.1601	57.2750	64.2028	72.0524	186.6880
21	23.2392	24.4705	25.7833	27.1833	28.6765	30.2695	31.9692	33.7831	35.7193	37.7861	39.9927	44.8652	50.4229	56.7645	64.0025	72.2651	81.6987	225.0256
30	34.7849	37.5387	40.5681	43.9027	47.5754	51.6227	56.0849	61.0071	66.4388	72.4355	79.0582	94.4608	113.2832	136.3075	164.4940	199.0209	241.3327	1181.8816
40	48.8864	54.2679	60.4020	67.4026	75.4013	84.5503	95.0255	107.0303	120.7998	136.6056	154.7620	199.6351	259.0565	337.8824	442.5926	581.8261	767.0914	7343.8578

This table shows the present value of an ordinary annuity of $1 at various interest rates (i) and time periods (n). It is used to calculate the present value of any series of equal payments made at the *end* of each compounding period.

TABLE 4 Present Value of an Ordinary Annuity of $1

$$PVA = \frac{1 - \frac{1}{(1+i)^n}}{i}$$

n/i	1.0%	1.5%	2.0%	2.5%	3.0%	3.5%	4.0%	4.5%	5.0%	5.5%	6.0%	7.0%	8.0%	9.0%	10.0%	11.0%	12.0%	20.0%
1	0.99010	0.98522	0.98039	0.97561	0.97087	0.96618	0.96154	0.95694	0.95238	0.94787	0.94340	0.93458	0.92593	0.91743	0.90909	0.90090	0.89286	0.83333
2	1.97040	1.95588	1.94156	1.92742	1.91347	1.89969	1.88609	1.87267	1.85941	1.84632	1.83339	1.80802	1.78326	1.75911	1.73554	1.71252	1.69005	1.52778
3	2.94099	2.91220	2.88388	2.85602	2.82861	2.80164	2.77509	2.74896	2.72325	2.69793	2.67301	2.62432	2.57710	2.53129	2.48685	2.44371	2.40183	2.10648
4	3.90197	3.85438	3.80773	3.76197	3.71710	3.67308	3.62990	3.58753	3.54595	3.50515	3.46511	3.38721	3.31213	3.23972	3.16987	3.10245	3.03735	2.58873
5	4.85343	4.78264	4.71346	4.64583	4.57971	4.51505	4.45182	4.38998	4.32948	4.27028	4.21236	4.10020	3.99271	3.88965	3.79079	3.69590	3.60478	2.99061
6	5.79548	5.69719	5.60143	5.50813	5.41719	5.32855	5.24214	5.15787	5.07569	4.99553	4.91732	4.76654	4.62288	4.48592	4.35526	4.23054	4.11141	3.32551
7	6.72819	6.59821	6.47199	6.34939	6.23028	6.11454	6.00205	5.89270	5.78637	5.68297	5.58238	5.38929	5.20637	5.03295	4.86842	4.71220	4.56376	3.60459
8	7.65168	7.48593	7.32548	7.17014	7.01969	6.87396	6.73274	6.59589	6.46321	6.33457	6.20979	5.97130	5.74664	5.53482	5.33493	5.14612	4.96764	3.83716
9	8.56602	8.36052	8.16224	7.97087	7.78611	7.60769	7.43533	7.26879	7.10782	6.95200	6.80169	6.51523	6.24689	5.99525	5.75902	5.53705	5.32825	4.03097
10	9.47130	9.22218	8.98259	8.75206	8.53020	8.31661	8.11090	7.91272	7.72173	7.53763	7.36009	7.02358	6.71008	6.41766	6.14457	5.88923	5.65022	4.19247
11	10.36763	10.07112	9.78685	9.51421	9.25262	9.00155	8.76048	8.52892	8.30641	8.09254	7.88687	7.49867	7.13896	6.80519	6.49506	6.20652	5.93770	4.32706
12	11.25508	10.90751	10.57534	10.25776	9.95400	9.66333	9.38507	9.11858	8.86325	8.61852	8.38384	7.94269	7.53608	7.16073	6.81369	6.49236	6.19437	4.43922
13	12.13374	11.73153	11.34837	10.98319	10.63496	10.30274	9.98565	9.68285	9.39357	9.11708	8.85268	8.35765	7.90378	7.48690	7.10336	6.74987	6.42355	4.53268
14	13.00370	12.54338	12.10625	11.69091	11.29607	10.92052	10.56312	10.22283	9.89864	9.58965	9.29498	8.74547	8.24424	7.78615	7.36669	6.98187	6.62817	4.61057
15	13.86505	13.34323	12.84926	12.38138	11.93794	11.51741	11.11839	10.73955	10.37966	10.03758	9.71225	9.10791	8.55948	8.06069	7.60608	7.19087	6.81086	4.67547
16	14.71787	14.13126	13.57771	13.05500	12.56110	12.09412	11.65230	11.23402	10.83777	10.46216	10.10590	9.44665	8.85137	8.31256	7.82371	7.37916	6.97399	4.72956
17	15.56225	14.90765	14.29187	13.71220	13.16612	12.65132	12.16567	11.70719	11.27407	10.86461	10.47726	9.76322	9.12164	8.54363	8.02155	7.54879	7.11963	4.77463
18	16.39827	15.67256	14.99203	14.35336	13.75351	13.18968	12.65930	12.15999	11.68959	11.24607	10.82760	10.05909	9.37189	8.75563	8.20141	7.70162	7.24967	4.81219
19	17.22601	16.42617	15.67846	14.97889	14.32380	13.70984	13.13394	12.59329	12.08532	11.60765	11.15812	10.33560	9.60360	8.95011	8.36492	7.83929	7.36578	4.84350
20	18.04555	17.16864	16.35143	15.58916	14.87747	14.21240	13.59033	13.00794	12.46221	11.95038	11.46992	10.59401	9.81815	9.12855	8.51356	7.96333	7.46944	4.86958
21	18.85698	17.90014	17.01121	16.18455	15.41502	14.69797	14.02916	13.40472	12.82115	12.27524	11.76408	10.83553	10.01680	9.29224	8.64869	8.07507	7.56200	4.89132
25	22.02316	20.71961	19.52346	18.42438	17.41315	16.48151	15.62208	14.82821	14.09394	13.41393	12.78336	11.65358	10.67478	9.82258	9.07704	8.42174	7.84314	4.94759
30	25.80771	24.01584	22.39646	20.93029	19.60044	18.39205	17.29203	16.28889	15.37245	14.53375	13.76483	12.40904	11.25778	10.27365	9.42691	8.69379	8.05518	4.97894
40	32.83469	29.91585	27.35548	25.10278	23.11477	21.35507	19.79277	18.40158	17.15909	16.04612	15.04630	13.33171	11.92461	10.75736	9.77905	8.95105	8.24378	4.99660

Summary of Ratios Used in This Book

	Chapter	Calculations
RISK RATIOS		
Liquidity		
Receivables turnover ratio	5	$\dfrac{\text{Net credit sales}}{\text{Average accounts receivables}}$
Average collection period	5	$\dfrac{365 \text{ days}}{\text{Receivables turnover ratio}}$
Inventory turnover ratio	6	$\dfrac{\text{Cost of goods sold}}{\text{Average inventory}}$
Average days in inventory	6	$\dfrac{365 \text{ days}}{\text{Inventory turnover ratio}}$
Current ratio	8	$\dfrac{\text{Current assets}}{\text{Current liabilities}}$
Acid-test ratio	8	$\dfrac{\text{Cash} + \text{Current investments} + \text{Accounts receivable}}{\text{Current liabilities}}$
Solvency		
Debt to equity ratio	9	$\dfrac{\text{Total liabilities}}{\text{Stockholders' equity}}$
Times interest earned ratio	9	$\dfrac{\text{Net income} + \text{Interest expense} + \text{Tax expense}}{\text{Interest expense}}$
PROFITABILITY RATIOS		
Gross profit ratio	6	$\dfrac{\text{Gross profit}}{\text{Net sales}}$
Return on assets	7	$\dfrac{\text{Net income}}{\text{Average total assets}}$
Profit margin	7	$\dfrac{\text{Net income}}{\text{Net sales}}$
Asset turnover	7	$\dfrac{\text{Net sales}}{\text{Average total assets}}$
Return on equity	10	$\dfrac{\text{Net income}}{\text{Average stockholders' equity}}$
Return on the market value of equity	10	$\dfrac{\text{Net income}}{\text{Stock price} \times \text{Number of shares outstanding}}$
Earnings per share	10	$\dfrac{\text{Net income} - \text{Preferred stock dividends}}{\text{Average shares of common stock outstanding}}$
Price-earnings ratio	10	$\dfrac{\text{Stock price}}{\text{Earnings per share}}$

Framework for Financial Accounting

Two primary functions of financial accounting are to *measure* activities of a company and *communicate* those measurements to investors and other people for making decisions. The measurement process involves recording transactions into accounts. The balances of these accounts are used to communicate information in the four primary financial statements, which are linked. For more detailed illustrations of financial statements, see the corresponding page in parentheses. A comprehensive list of accounts used to measure activities in this textbook is provided on the next page.

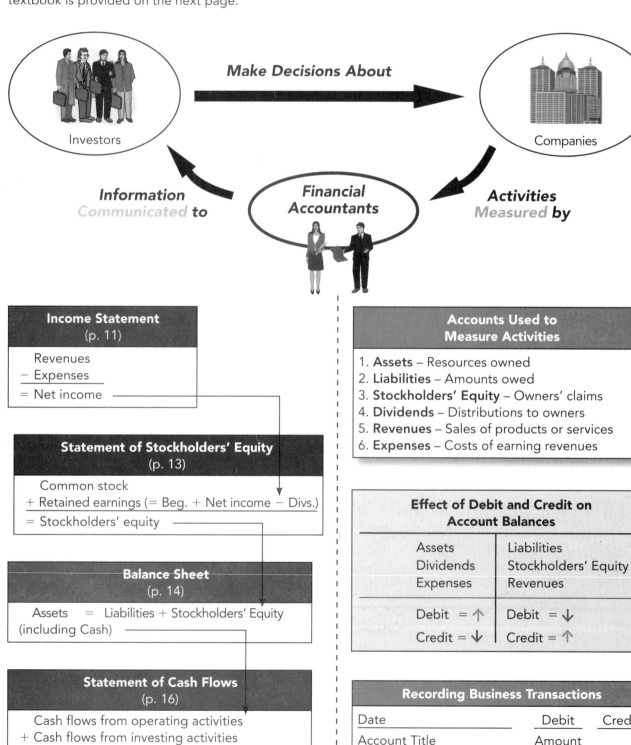

Make Decisions About

Investors

Companies

Information
Communicated **to**

Financial Accountants

Activities
Measured **by**

Income Statement
(p. 11)

Revenues
− Expenses
= Net income

Statement of Stockholders' Equity
(p. 13)

Common stock
+ Retained earnings (= Beg. + Net income − Divs.)
= Stockholders' equity

Balance Sheet
(p. 14)

Assets = Liabilities + Stockholders' Equity
(including Cash)

Statement of Cash Flows
(p. 16)

Cash flows from operating activities
+ Cash flows from investing activities
+ Cash flows from financing activities
= Change in cash

Accounts Used to Measure Activities

1. **Assets** – Resources owned
2. **Liabilities** – Amounts owed
3. **Stockholders' Equity** – Owners' claims
4. **Dividends** – Distributions to owners
5. **Revenues** – Sales of products or services
6. **Expenses** – Costs of earning revenues

Effect of Debit and Credit on Account Balances

Assets Dividends Expenses	Liabilities Stockholders' Equity Revenues
Debit = ↑	Debit = ↓
Credit = ↓	Credit = ↑

Recording Business Transactions

Date	Debit	Credit
Account Title	Amount	
Account Title		Amount
(Description of transaction)		